P9-DHS-722

To DeAnna, who actually volunteered for this crazy mission.

"La mejor salsa del mundo
es la hambre."

"Hunger is the best sauce
in the world."

//////////////////////////////////

CERVANTES

GOOD

EATS

THE EARLY YEARS

ALTON BROWN

STEWART, TABORI & CHANG

NEW YORK

CONTENTS

SEASON 4

SEASON 5

SEASON 6

INTERVIEW

Alton Brown Interviews Alton Brown on the Making of *Good Eats*

ALTON BROWN: So, how did this phenomenal success come into being?

ALTON BROWN: Well, one day in 1991 I was sitting in my office staring at a pad of paper. Back then I directed TV commercials for a living, and I was supposed to be crafting a presentation that would hopefully convince some advertising exec somewhere that I was the director to take his precious snowflake of an idea and kindle it into high art. Diapers, tires, insurance—don't remember what it was for, but I knew didn't want to do it. I was thinking instead about cooking and specifically about cooking shows, most of which I thought were pretty dull, and uninformative and . . . did I mention dull? I wanted someone to make a show for my generation. I jotted down three names: Julia Child, Mr. Wizard, and Monty Python.

AB: Amazing. You do know, of course, that Monty Python isn't actually a person.

AB: I said I jotted down three *names*, not three names of *people*.

AB: Good point. I am sorry. Go on.

AB: Well, now I don't remember what I was talking about.

AB: *Good Eats*.

AB: Ah, yes. I thought if I could combine all these styles into one show, viewers could actually learn something about cooking, what makes food tick, rather than simply being hit over the head with recipes. And they would hopefully be so entertained in the process they'd never know they were being educated. If my high school years taught me anything it's that people don't like to be educated to.

AB: What about a host?

AB: Well, the show would have to have a smart host with lots of knowledge, a slightly snarky attitude, and dead-on comedic timing. I was thinking we would probably get someone out of the Actor's Studio or maybe the Royal Academy.

AB: So did you keep the idea to yourself?

AB: No, I dropped by the office of the production manager at this commercial house who was a friend of mine and told her my idea.

AB: What did she say?

AB: I don't remember, but two years later we were married and living in Vermont, where I was a student at New England Culinary Institute.

AB: So you guys just dropped everything and left Atlanta for Vermont?

AB: No, we took everything with us, except for the pool furniture.

AB: Did people think you were crazy to take such a huge risk?

AB: Actually, anyone who's known me for any length of time quickly comes to expect erratic behavior. Anyway, over the next few years, things happened very slowly. I graduated, worked in restaurants . . .

AB: Excuse me, but how did you like that . . . restaurant work?

AB: I learned a lot of things, like how to catch a falling steak on top of my shoe so that it wouldn't hit the floor. Because if it hits the floor you have to wash it off.

AB: But not if it lands on your shoe?

(At this point the interview subject takes a sip of water and looks out the window).

AB: Finally, one day my wife turns to me in our run-down little rental and says: "Don't you think you should write those shows now?" So I wrote a couple of pilot scripts, and my wife reads them and says: "Hey, let's call it *Good Eats*."

AB: It really is a good name.

AB: I wanted to name it *Chef Alton's Flying Food Circus*, but I think there was a copyright problem.

AB: When did you become the host?

AB: That was a money thing. We raised enough money to make two pilot episodes, but it was only going to be enough money if we paid the host absolutely nothing and nothing's tough to sell to most actors.

AB: So you just fell into the job.

AB: And through it and around it and over it. I'm still the weak link. I think one of the reasons people keep watching is to see if I ever improve. I will say I get some joy out of the fact that my family always told me the only thing a theater degree would get me is a job in a restaurant. But I think they might have meant waiting tables.

AB: What happened after you made the pilots?

AB: Nothing. You have to remember we knew how to shoot stuff, but we knew absolutely nothing about the television business. We thought if we sent people tapes that they'd watch them. But they don't. What they do is set beverages on them.

AB: Is it true that early VHS versions of the pilots recently sold on Ebay for five thousand dollars apiece?

AB: That's so wrong. Those tapes belong in a museum. Anyway, in 1998 Food Network called—finally—and in a couple of months we had a deal. We went to work on Season One, thirteen shows at the time, and on July 7, 1999, at 9 pm Eastern Time, *Good Eats* made its national debut.

AB: And now it's July 7, 2009.

AB: Ten years and two hundred and thirty-something episodes are history. Most of my crew is still with me. My wife (amazingly) is still with me and she runs our production company, which continues to crank out what I feel certain are precious half-hour snowflakes we carefully kindle into high art.

AB: It is just a cooking show, you know.

AB: (*long pause*) Sure, it's just a cooking show, but we like to think it's the best darned cooking show ever.

AB: *Good Eats* recently won a coveted Peabody award. The only other food personality to ever win one is . . .

AB: . . . Julia Child. Yeah, that's pretty cool. Totally makes up for being shunned by the Emmys . . . every year for, you know . . . the last ten years.

AB: So, why the book? Why now? And what can fans expect?

AB: Actually this first book is just Volume One of a three-volume set. So it's, you know, like, "the trilogy."

AB: You mean . . . like *Lord of the Rings*.

AB: Sure, only without the funny names and invisibility rings and dragons and stuff. It's an epic, only with cool pictures and graphs and stuff. And it's heavy, so you know it's important.

AB: Heavy?

AB: We add depleted uranium to the ink for added heft.

AB: So what can readers expect from *Good Eats: The Early Years*? Besides of course, weight.

AB: Each of the first eighty episodes has its own mini chapter, containing the basic knowledge of the show—we call that the Knowledge Concentrate—and remastered applications.

AB: What's an application?

AB: We don't have recipes, we have applications. We call them that because we like to think that they are applied knowledge. We'd call them "proofs," you know, like mathematic proofs, but math kind of scares me. Anyway, we've reworked most of them and just adjusted others.

AB: Which leads one to wonder what was wrong with them in the first place.

AB: No. No, it's . . . Let me ask you something. Is there anything wrong with *Astral Weeks*?

AB: You mean the 1968 Van Morrison album?

AB: That's the one. Is there anything wrong with it?

AB: Well no. It's generally considered to be a masterpiece.

AB: Darned tootin' it is. And yet just this year ol' Van re-recorded the whole thing, tune for tune, live. Does that mean that there was something wrong with it in the first place?

AB: No. But as musical artists mature they often return to their early work in order to inject it with new . . .

(At this point Brown simply stares at the interviewer and raises his eyebrows.)

AB: Exactly. We've enhanced some dishes, added new flavors, and, yes, we've made a few small repairs based upon input from fans. We've also converted most of the baking applications to weights because weights are more precise and that's what baking is all about. There are also brand new applications, for dishes we would have included in the shows if we'd been given an hour slot instead of just thirty minutes. There are hundreds of images from the shows and lots of anecdotes, you know, for the fans. But it's not a fan book, per se.

AB: Why not?

AB: I'm saving that stuff for my autobiography. I've got a ghost writer working on it now.

AB: And it even looks like your daughter got involved. These are her illustrations, I assume.

AB: No. Those are . . . mine.

AB: (Long pause) Ah, well . . . so this *Good Eats* book is like a retrospective double album in a sense.

AB: Actually it's more like four hundred pages of liner notes, but really *good* liner notes.

AB: Will *Good Eats* fans have to wait long for Volume Two?

AB: Oh no. "The Middle Years" is already in the works.

AB: Often times sequels are something of a disappointment. Does that concern you?

AB: We're talking *Star Wars* here, not *Indiana Jones*. Two will be even better than one.

AB: And what about Volume Three?

AB: Well, that's when we'll be like *Indiana Jones* instead of *Star Wars*.

AB: Ah, so no recipes for Ewok then?

AB: Applications.

AB: Sorry.

THE EPISODES

GOOD EATS | THE EARLY YEARS

Yumion

STEAK YOUR CLAIM

EPISODE 1 | SEASON 1 | GOOD EATS

I chose steak for our first episode for two simple reasons. First, it's the uncontested quintessential American meal—an honest, straightforward, plain-talking promise of plenty. Steak is an edible Copland symphony, and to eat one is to commune with the ghost of John Wayne. And yet most Americans can't get a decent one on the plate to save their lives. I hoped to fix that.

I also chose steak because I wanted *Good Eats* to be a show about the actual processes of cooking. From that standpoint, steak is perfect. Sure, there's plenty to know about the meat itself, but aside from a few drops of oil and some salt and pepper it's all technique. In fact, good technique (not to mention the right pan) can salvage a mediocre steak, and bad technique can ruin a great one.

TRIVIA | NECI stands for New England Culinary Institute, my cooking alma mater.

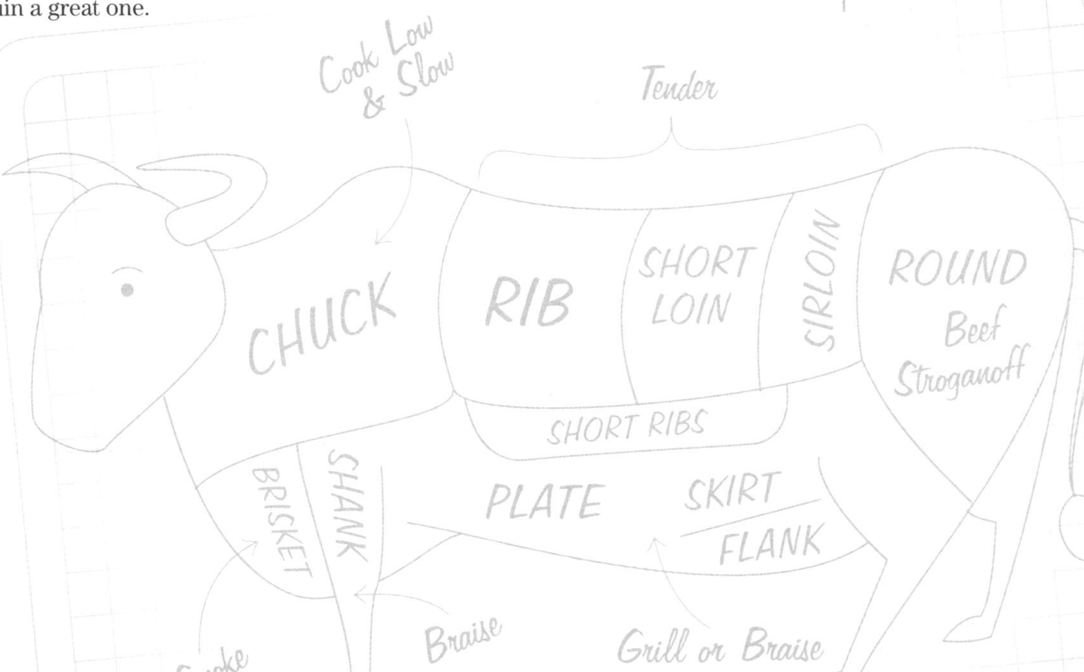

KNOWLEDGE CONCENTRATE

- A steak is any cross-cut slab of meat (especially beef), usually between 1 and 2 inches thick, that is meant to be cooked quickly with relatively high heat.

- Steaks are cut from large hunks of meat called sub-primals. Each steer has two of the following sub-primal sections: chuck, rib, short loin, sirloin, round, flank, plate, brisket, and shank.

- In meat, as in real estate, what matters most is location, location, location. Although a lot of factors contribute to the texture of a piece of meat, the most decisive is from whence on the critter the cut doth come. Typically, the further the cut is from the hoof or horn, the more tender it will be. This is because muscles near the legs, rump, and shoulder do most of the work and therefore develop high concentrations of tough connective tissue. Cuts from the back, specifically the rib and short loin area, are the most tender—and the most expensive.

- Most American beef comes from cattle raised in feedlots where they're fed a lot of corn, a situation designed to yield tender but not necessarily more interesting or more flavorful meat. Some growers, however, still make their cows walk around and eat grass, which cultivates considerable flavor but a fair amount of chewiness. Take the source of your meat into consideration when deciding how to cook it.

- A grade of Select, Choice, or Prime (the latter being the most desirable) is bestowed on meat based on its color, weight, fat-to-body ratio, age, and other physical considerations. Non-graded meat (or "no-roll" meat, a reference to the rolling ink stamp used to affix the grade information) is not necessarily inferior to graded meat; in some cases the producer has simply opted to save money by skipping the grading process, which, unlike USDA inspection, is voluntary.

- "Marbling," a common marker of a good steak, refers to the small bits of fat running through the meat in swirls, flecks, or streaks. When the meat is cooked, this fat melts, essentially lubricating the muscle strands. That's why marbled meat feels so tender in the mouth. (Also: Fat tastes good.) The rib-eye is one of the best steaks for beginner cooks because it contains plenty of intramuscular fat and so feels juicy even if a little too much actual moisture is lost via overcooking.

Tenderloin | Porterhouse

Filet (Mignon)

Bacon Wrap

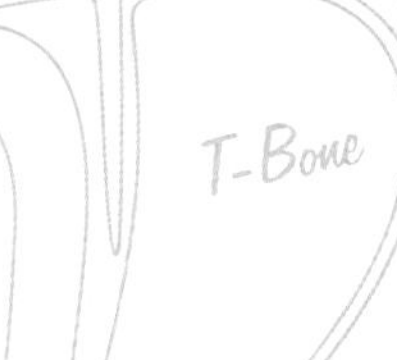

New York Strip or Kansas City Strip depending on where you live

Bone in Rib-Eye also called Cowboy Steak

What we're cooking

Rib-Eye or Eye Steak

TRIVIA The hardware-store scene was the first *Good Eats* scene shot, and was filmed on August 20, 1997.

APPLICATION

PAN-SEARED RIB-EYE STEAK

2 STEAKS, TO SERVE 2 TO 4

As far as I'm concerned, a perfect steak is one with a darkly seared exterior and an interior cooked not one degree past 130°F. Although this can certainly be accomplished on a grill or broiler, it's a tricky proposition at best—especially with a cut like the rib-eye, whose melting lipids tend to cause nasty, soot-producing flare-ups in open-flame environments. Your best bet is pan roasting, in which a hot, heavy, dense cast-iron skillet does the branding on the stovetop and the relatively gentle heat of the oven finishes the interior.

It can't be said enough: Remember to let your meat—especially that of the red variety—rest for about 5 minutes after it's removed from the heat. Heat is akin to pressure, and cutting into a steak before it's had a chance to cool a bit is like opening a spigot. Cover the meat loosely with aluminum foil or a metal bowl as it rests, and it'll stay plenty hot.

// SOFTWARE

2	1½-inch-thick	boneless rib-eye steaks	about 15 ounces each
1	teaspoon	canola oil	to coat
1	teaspoon	kosher salt	
½	teaspoon	black pepper	freshly ground

// PROCEDURE

1. Allow steaks to come to room temperature for 1 hour.
2. Position rack in center of oven. Crank to 500°F and slide in a **12-inch cast iron skillet**.
3. When oven hits temperature, carefully move skillet to cook top over high heat for 5 minutes.
4. Lightly coat steaks with canola oil then liberally sprinkle with the salt and pepper, place carefully in pan, and don't touch for 30 seconds. (You should use a kitchen timer.)
5. Flip the steaks with **tongs** and cook for another 30 seconds.
6. Move skillet back to the oven for 2 minutes. Flip the steaks and cook for another 2 minutes.

TIP | To clean the skillet, return it to medium heat and add 1 tablespoon canola oil and 1 tablespoon kosher salt. Grab a wad of paper towels with your tongs and use them to scrub the salt around the skillet until the salt and the towels are black and the pan is slick as a mambo band. Kill the heat. Dump the salt. Let the pan cool. Wipe with clean paper towels, and store. If your skillet has a good cure, odds are you'll never have to use water on it.

7 Remove skillet to a heat-safe surface. For medium-rare, the temperature of the steaks should be between 130–140°F.

8 Rest in **resting rig**[1] (see sketch at right) for 5 minutes. Rest and serve.

NOTE: There's going to be smoke. Turn on your hood (if you have one) and open a window. I even take the battery out of the smoke detector.

Temping from the side gives a reliable reading through thick part of meat.

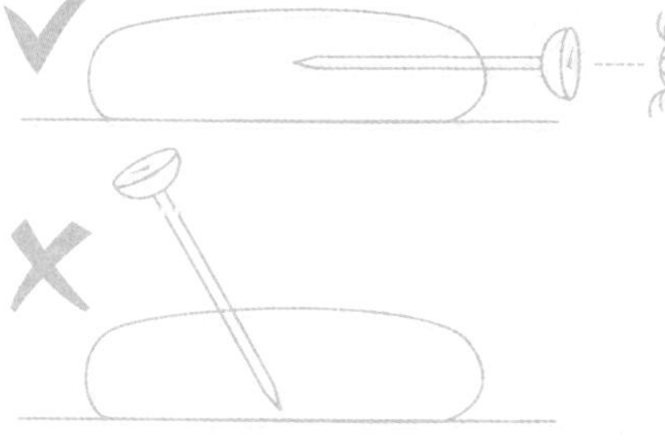

Temping from top through shallow part gives unreliable data.

10 MINUTES MORE

COGNAC PAN SAUCE

⅓ CUP; ENOUGH FOR 2 PAN-SEARED RIB-EYE STEAKS

This application had to be cut from the original show because I spent so much time (21 minutes, 30 seconds) on the steaks.

// SOFTWARE

¼	cup	Cognac	(plus 1 ounce for yourself)
1	ounce	soft, blue-veined cheese such as blue or Gorgonzola	crumbled, at room temperature
2	tablespoons	unsalted butter	chilled, cut in half

// PROCEDURE

1 Cool skillet for 1 minute. Pour in the Cognac and **whisk** to dissolve all the good bits stuck to the skillet.[2]

2 Reduce Cognac for about 30 seconds (the residual heat of the skillet will do the job, no need to return it to stovetop).

3 Add the cheese and whisk 30 seconds.

4 Whisk the butter pieces in one at a time and continue whisking until the sauce thickens slightly.

5 Serve in **ramekins** alongside steak for dipping.

1 - Pot lid
2 - Colander
3 - Steaks
4 - Metal bowl
5 - Drippings (liquid gold)

I used to use a wire rack—this is better because it's easier to capture juices.

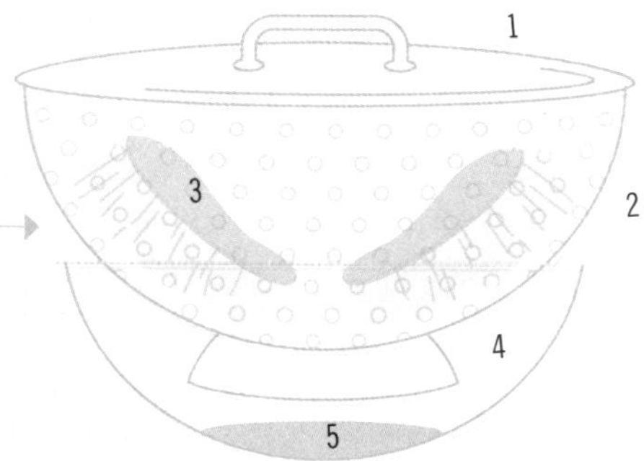

For a fast sauce simply move bowl to cooktop over high heat & whisk in a little butter.

[1] Even better, put the steaks on top of thick slices of toast (preferably sourdough), which will absorb any escaping juices and make for a nice side bite in themselves.

[2] This is called "deglazing," and is a basic procedure we'll call for time and again over the next thousand pages or so.

THIS SPUD'S FOR YOU

EPISODE 2 | SEASON 1 | GOOD EATS

If you're making two pilots for a new food show and the first is about steak, you really don't have to think too hard about what the next subject should be: potatoes. Besides being perennial plate-mates, in the case of both steak and spud successful cooking begins with the selection of an appropriate specimen. Just as you can't pan-sear a hunk of chuck and hope to call it "steak," if you try to bake, say, a Great Northern or a Pontiac Red, doom will be your destination. This is compounded by the fact that there are hundreds of potato varieties, and many of them can't be told apart, even by skilled producemen.

Starch is one of the basic building blocks of food that we deal with on *Good Eats*, and through the years we have dug deep into the mysteries of its character. The goal of this show, however, was simply to introduce people to the fact that in every potato small, hard granules containing many coiled starches await. By heating the water inside the potato, these granules can be made to swell, resulting in a fluffy texture. However, these "balloons" can also burst, resulting in a gluey, globby texture that is in no way good eats.

TRIVIA | My wife's grandfather Bob.

TRIVIA | In its original version the show included a scene featuring me and my dog floating potatoes in a washtub of water out on the deck. The point was to show that you can determine the starch content of a spud by whether it sinks or floats. All we ended up proving is that the float test is completely bogus. The scene was cut.

2 COMMON STARCHES

Amylopectin Amylose

STARCHES ARE JUST LONG CHAINS OF GLUCOSE MOLECULES

battery battery battery battery

STORING ENERGY LIKE D-BATTERIES

KNOWLEDGE CONCENTRATE

Potatoes are essentially fuel tanks containing starch molecules, which are little more than long chains made up of a simple sugar called glucose.[1] In potatoes, starches are folded up and stored in tiny granules that swell when the moisture inside the potato is heated.

A potato's cooking characteristics depend greatly on its starch content. There are three basic categories of potato:

HIGH-STARCH, or *mealy*, potatoes, such as Idaho Russet "baking" potatoes, and purple-skinned Caribe potatoes, are ideal for baking because they fluff—and yes, that's a technical term. They're also good for French fries, but because they fall apart they're lousy for roasting or boiling for potato salad.[2]

MEDIUM-STARCH potatoes, like Yukon gold and Yellow Finn, will hold their shape when cooked but just barely—which makes them perfect for layered applications like gratins.

LOW-STARCH, or *waxy*, potatoes, which include round white and round red (boiling) potatoes, as well as most fingerlings, do not fluff and hold their shape when cooked. Hash, potato salad, and pot roast are good applications.

GREAT MOMENTS IN POTATO HISTORY

Archaeological digs in Chile and Peru have produced evidence that potatoes have been a staple since about 500 B.C. Spanish conquistadors stumbled over them in the 1530s while hunting for gold, and supposedly, a Spanish explorer, Gonzalo Jimenez de Quesada, brought the spud back to Spain.

As is true of several New World foods that have become globally ubiquitous, spuds faced considerable contempt and suspicion in Europe. After all, they are members of the nightshade family, which includes several plants so poisonous that several notable noble families were known to use them to off each other.

In the end, a French botanist named Parmentier, who had survived being a prisoner of war by consuming potatoes, convinced Louis XVI to endorse the untrusted tuber. To this day, many classic French potato recipes include *Parmentier* in the name.

The Irish famine that drove so many citizens from that island to America was caused by an airborne fungus (*Phytophthora Infestans*) that probably blew onto the island from ships traveling from the New World to England.

American horticulturist Luther Burbank (1849–1926) developed his famed russet potato while trying to come up with a fungus-resistant plant that would give Ireland new hope. As of this writing every McDonald's French fry is cut from a Burbank.

APPLICATION

MASHERS

8 SERVINGS

The goal here is to use the starch profile of two different potato varieties to produce rustic and chunky mashed spuds possessing contrasting and complementary textures.

SOFTWARE

2	pounds	russet potatoes	rinsed, peeled, and cut into ½-inch chunks
2	pounds	red "boiling" potatoes	rinsed, unpeeled, cut into ½-inch chunks
2	teaspoons	kosher salt	divided
¾	cup	low-fat buttermilk	
¼	cup	heavy cream	
6	cloves	garlic	peeled and smashed

PROCEDURE

1. Place all spud hunks in a **4-quart saucepan** and add just enough cold tap **water** to cover.[3] (You can put the potatoes in the water and refrigerate them for up to 8 hours before cooking.) Add 1 teaspoon of the salt to the pot, **cover**, and bring to a boil over high heat. (This will take about 15 minutes).
2. Meanwhile, combine the buttermilk, cream, and garlic in a **2-quart saucepan** and bring to a bare simmer over low heat, watching to make sure the mixture doesn't boil over. Keep the mixture barely bubbling until the potatoes are done.
3. When the spud water boils, ditch the lid, drop the heat to a simmer, and cook until the spuds are easily crushed with **tongs**, 15 to 20 minutes. Drain the potatoes, then return them to the pan and the heat. Toss and shake gently for 30 seconds or so to knock off any excess surface moisture. (The drier the spuds the better.)
4. Move the pan to a **trivet, hot pad, or towel** on the countertop and sprinkle with the remaining 1 teaspoon salt. Pour on about a quarter of the buttermilk mixture and start **mashing**.
5. As the spuds break down, add more of the buttermilk mixture until you're happy with the results.[4] Remember, these are mashed potatoes, not whipped potatoes. If you over-mash in an attempt to smooth every piece you will inevitably rupture starch granules, which can and most likely will result in gummy potatoes.

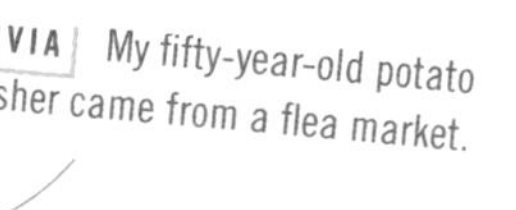

TRIVIA My fifty-year-old potato masher came from a flea market.

10 MINUTES MORE

MASHER CAKES

6 CAKES

Although I confess I have never encountered "leftover" mashed potatoes in the home environment (which may explain at least some portion of my current state of heft), I'm told that documented cases of their appearance have been reported. Had we had a little more time we might have dealt with this issue in the following manner.

// SOFTWARE

10	ounces	leftover Mashers (opposite page)	about 2 servings
1	tablespoon	chopped fresh parsley, thyme, or green onion	
1	large	egg	
½	cup	Japanese-style breadcrumbs	a.k.a. panko
		olive oil (not extra-virgin)	for frying

// PROCEDURE

1. Use a **large spoon or spatula** to combine the mashers, herbs, and egg in a **mixing bowl**. Divide the mixture into 6 equal balls. Flatten these gently into rounds approximately 3 inches in diameter. Set aside on **parchment paper**.
2. Scatter the breadcrumbs in a **pie pan or other shallow dish** and coat the cakes one at a time (I find that shaking the pan helps, as you don't want to handle the cakes any more than necessary). Return each coated cake to the **parchment**. (At this point the cakes can be refrigerated for several hours.)
3. Pour enough oil into a **12-inch sauté pan** to cover the bottom completely. Place the pan over medium heat until the oil shimmers and shimmies but doesn't quite smoke.
4. Gently place the cakes in the pan and cook for 2 to 3 minutes per side, turning with a **large slotted spoon or a flat spatula**, until GBD.[5]
5. Remove to **draining rig** and let cool for 2 to 3 minutes before serving.

[1] Glucose is a simple sugar, which is why a bite of baked potato will taste sweet if you chew on it long enough for the enzymes in your saliva to break down the chains.

[2] See episode 68 for more on high-starch potatoes.

[3] In the show we used hot water, which is what I'd always done in the past. However, a couple of plumbers got in touch with me and pointed out that hot water is a more efficient solvent than cold water and if there are any soldered joints in the pipes, some lead from that solder could leach into hot water. Although the chances that the potential contamination could reach levels that are even remotely harmful are very small, we've decided to stay clear of hot tap water in general.

[4] Although you may actually need all the mixture, don't give the mashers more than they need lest they become soupy. Any leftover garlic-dairy mixture can be saved for soups, sauces, breakfast cereal . . .

[5] Golden, brown, and delicious—and yes, that's a technical term.

TIP | Technically speaking, a "new" potato is any potato picked before maturity. You can tell a real "new" potato from others by the skin, which is always thin and almost always somewhat flakey. Whenever I come across true new potatoes I usually mash them skin and all.

TIDBIT | Potato cake goes on a plate. A little dab of sour cream goes on top of the cake, followed by a few slices of smoked salmon (nova, lox, that sort of thing, see page 204). This in turn is topped with a bit of microgreen salad tossed with your favorite vinaigrette (such as the one on page 27). Why, look, you have a positively delightful luncheon plate. How clever!

1 - Baker's cooling rack
2 - Newspaper
3 - Half sheet pan

Note - once oil has dripped onto newspaper it makes an excellent charcoal starter.

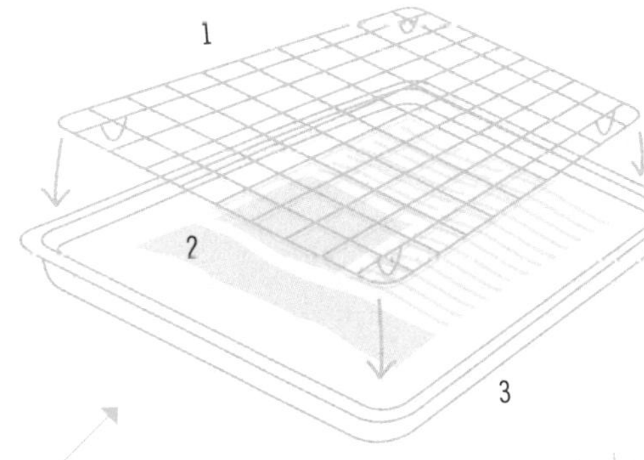

This rig is also good for all fried foods: chicken, fries, twinkies, you name it.

TIDBIT | Interested in more potato possibilities? Don't worry, "This Spud's For You Too" is coming up in a couple hundred pages.

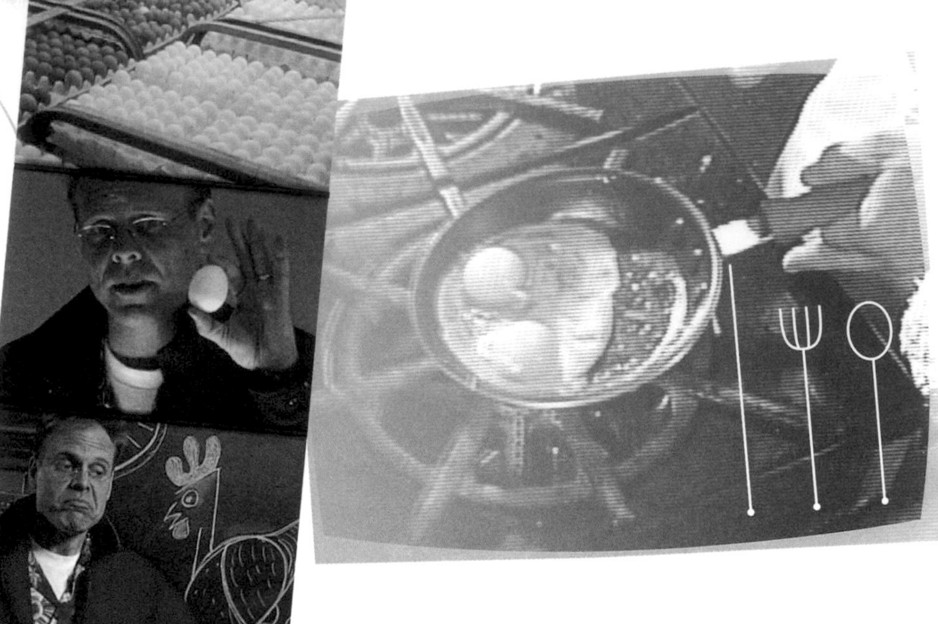

THE EGG-FILES I

EPISODE 3 | SEASON 1 | GOOD EATS

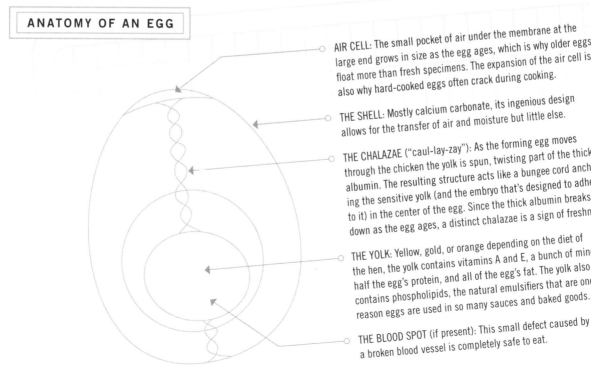

Egg cookery is the basis of all cuisine. When people tell me they want to start learning to cook, I say, "Eggs." And when I grow weary of cooking, which does sometimes happen, I reach for the unfertilized ovum of *Gallus domesticus* to get my groove back.

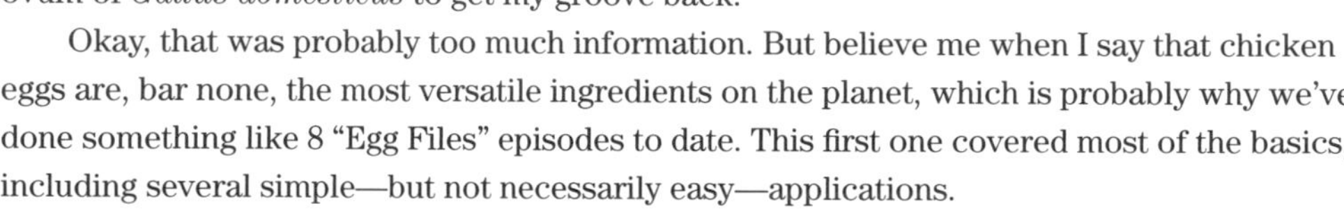

Okay, that was probably too much information. But believe me when I say that chicken eggs are, bar none, the most versatile ingredients on the planet, which is probably why we've done something like 8 "Egg Files" episodes to date. This first one covered most of the basics, including several simple—but not necessarily easy—applications.

ANATOMY OF AN EGG

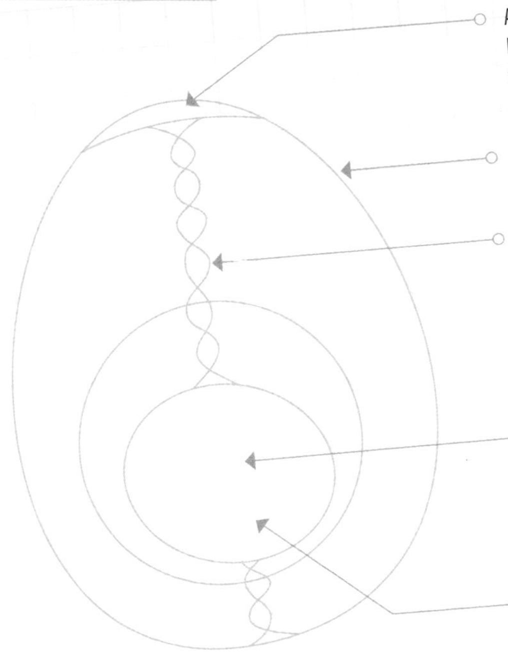

AIR CELL: The small pocket of air under the membrane at the large end grows in size as the egg ages, which is why older eggs float more than fresh specimens. The expansion of the air cell is also why hard-cooked eggs often crack during cooking.

THE SHELL: Mostly calcium carbonate, its ingenious design allows for the transfer of air and moisture but little else.

THE CHALAZAE ("caul-lay-zay"): As the forming egg moves through the chicken the yolk is spun, twisting part of the thick albumin. The resulting structure acts like a bungee cord anchoring the sensitive yolk (and the embryo that's designed to adhere to it) in the center of the egg. Since the thick albumin breaks down as the egg ages, a distinct chalazae is a sign of freshness.

THE YOLK: Yellow, gold, or orange depending on the diet of the hen, the yolk contains vitamins A and E, a bunch of minerals, half the egg's protein, and all of the egg's fat. The yolk also contains phospholipids, the natural emulsifiers that are one reason eggs are used in so many sauces and baked goods.

THE BLOOD SPOT (if present): This small defect caused by a broken blood vessel is completely safe to eat.

KNOWLEDGE CONCENTRATE

- The average laying hen produces an egg about every twenty-five hours for 1 to 2 years.
- The egg is considered to be the worldwide gold standard for protein (nutritionally speaking).
- If you want to know how old a carton of eggs is, look for a "day of year" number on the end of the box. (In the show I mistakenly refer to it as a Julian date, but in fact it's closer to a Gregorian date.) Other dates, such as expiration dates, may be required by state law. To tell the truth, I don't pay any attention to these numbers. Most eggs in the United States sell quickly, and I've never seen an expired one. I have, however, seen some improperly refrigerated.
- An unrefrigerated egg ages in a day as much as a refrigerated egg ages in a week. Due to the amazing germ-stopping powers of the shell and outer membranes, most eggs will actually dry out inside before they spoil.
- Never wash store-bought shell eggs. You'll remove the mineral oil coating, which is applied at the processing plant to keep the eggs fresher longer. If, however, your eggs come from your own chickens or your neighbor's, wash away.
- At processing plants, freshness is sometimes determined by a "breakout test." A fresh egg (grade A or AA) will look like this in the shell:

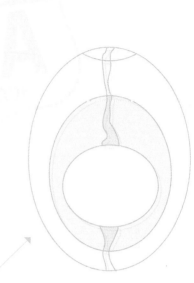

. . . while a not-so-fresh egg (grade B) might look like this:

That's because not only has the thick albumin broken down but the membrane surrounding the yolk has weakened as well. And so we see that not only is grade an expression of quality, but quality is, in no small part, a factor of age.

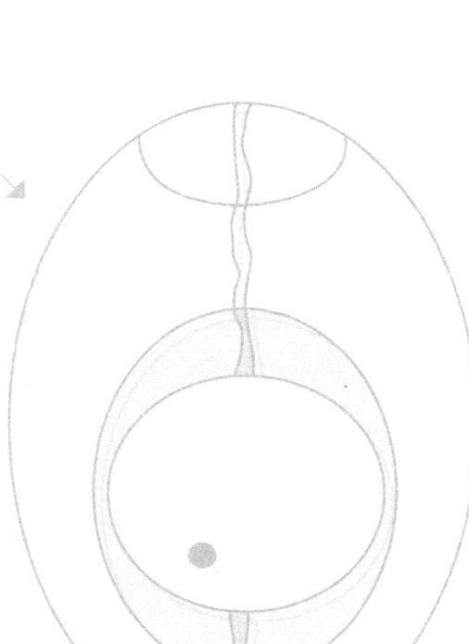

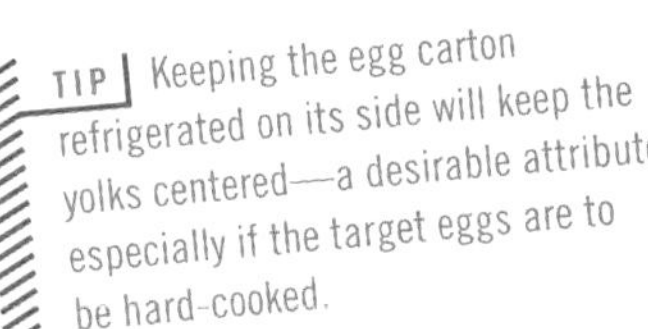

TIP | Keeping the egg carton refrigerated on its side will keep the yolks centered—a desirable attribute, especially if the target eggs are to be hard-cooked.

APPLICATION

EGGS OVER EASY

1 OR 2 SERVINGS

Odds are you're going to be eating these on a plate. If so, I strongly suggest you park an oven-safe one in a low oven or in hot water while you're cooking. Cold plates suck heat right out of food, and few things are worse in the morning than cold eggs. In fact, I try to never put hot food on a cold plate.

SOFTWARE

1	tablespoon	unsalted butter	(and don't you dare skimp)
2	large	eggs	the fresher, the better
1	pinch	kosher salt	
1	grind	black pepper	freshly ground

PROCEDURE

1. Place an **8-inch nonstick skillet** over low heat and add the butter.
2. When the butter stops foaming, crack the eggs into the pan, then quickly lift the handle just enough for the eggs to pool slightly on the far side. This will prevent the thin albumin from running out all over the pan.
3. After 10 to 15 seconds, smoothly lower the handle. Wait another 10 seconds, then lightly jiggle the pan just to make sure that nothing is sticking. Season with the salt and pepper and cook, still over low heat, for 1 to 1½ minutes. Jiggle again and examine the white for opaqueness; when it is fully set but not hard, it's time to flip.
4. Here comes the hard part: Flip the egg by pushing the pan away from you and snapping the far edge upward. As the egg turns, try to bring the pan up to meet it, thus preventing a hard—and potentially yolk-busting—landing.
5. Return the pan to the heat and slowly count to 10. Reflip the egg to its original side. (This time it won't be so difficult.) Slide onto a warmed plate and serve immediately with toast for wiping up all the goodness.

WHY EGGS STICK

Eggs are notorious for sticking to pans because they are protein-laden liquids, which is another way of describing good old-fashioned glue. Once proteins denature, they're like sticky snakes, which will wiggle their way into any crack or crevice they find on your pan's surface. The best way to stop them: fat. Since fats, like butter and oil, are hydrophobic, they repel the proteins and their watery home.

TIP Getting the yolk away from the albumin without breaking it is an operation best attempted with cold, fresh eggs. Although many cooks break the egg open and then pour the yolk back and forth between the two shell halves, allowing the white to run into a waiting vessel below, this opens up the possibility of contaminating the egg with whatever is on the shell. I suggest you do it the messy way: Wash your hands very well and crack the egg onto the fingers of your upturned hand. Allow the white to run through your fingers into a waiting vessel. The yolk, free of the white, will rest lightly in your hand. What power you now possess.

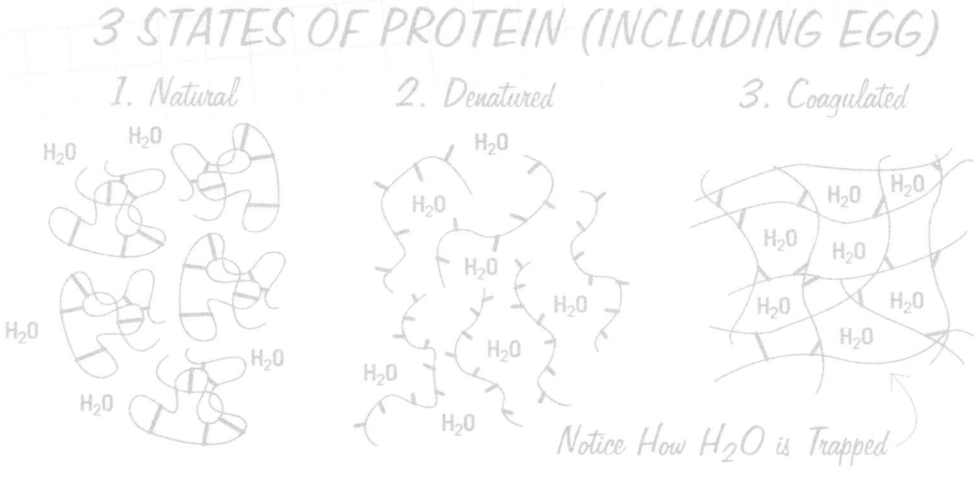

3 STATES OF PROTEIN (INCLUDING EGG)

SHELL EGGS AND SALMONELLA

People used to eat raw egg applications all the time: eggs sunny side up, Caesar salad, hollandaise sauce, chocolate chip cookie dough. But about twenty years ago the government, via the USDA and CDC, started telling us that shell eggs can be infected by *Salmonella Enteritidis* (SE), which can make healthy people mighty sick and sick people dead. The fact that this happened rather suddenly is some evidence that this is not an egg problem or even a chicken problem as much as it is a production problem that stems exclusively from the fact that we've decided to treat the chicken like machine parts that just so happen to have pulses. Instead of forcing agribusiness to clean up its collective act, the USDA (which was formed, by the way, to promote the agriculture industry, not protect us from things like salmonella) tells us that in order to safely consume eggs we must cook them to 160°F, which pretty much ruins them as far as I'm concerned.

Well, you know what I say? I say I'm not going to marginalize the world's best ingredient just so the poultry industry can play it loose and we can have eggs that are cheaper than they ought to be. Find a local farmer who keeps a few chickens roaming around the yard and buy his eggs. Oh, sure, they'll be all shapes and sizes and colors and they'll cost twice or even three times as much as grocery-store eggs, but guess what: They'll taste great and you won't have to worry. Better yet, get your own chickens. Most municipalities in this country allow the average homeowner to keep a few cluckers around the yard. And heck, when one stops laying: stew!

Although they weren't widely available when we shot this episode, eggs that have been pasteurized in their shells are now easily found at your local megamart. They've been gently heat-treated to kill any tagalong pathogens. The whites of pasteurized eggs are slightly foggy due to the process, but they work just like their unpasteurized kin.

RIGHT
Flat blow cracks egg cleanly.

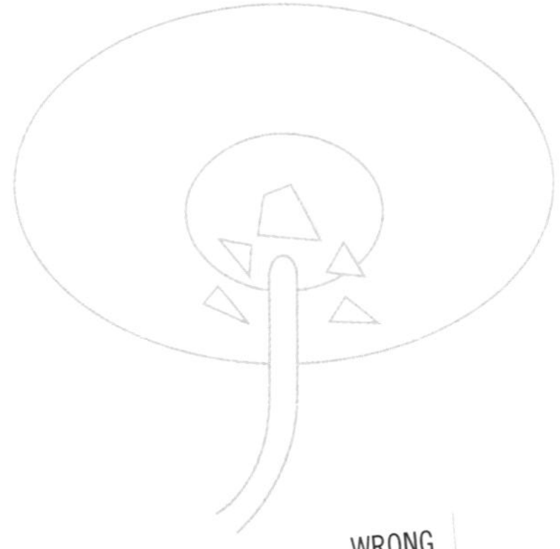

WRONG
Edge of bowl drives shell fragments and any outside germs deep into egg.

TIP | Although your mama may have taught you to crack eggs on the edges of pans and bowls, I respectfully suggest that this only serves to drive small shards of shell up into the part you want to eat. By cracking on a flat surface like a counter or plate, you avoid such inconvenience. The trick is to hold the egg in your hand in such a way as to prevent cracking from advancing to smashing.

APPLICATION — SCRAMBLED EGGS

2 SERVINGS

If there's a rocky reef threatening to ground your happy little egg boat it is the specter of overcooking. This danger stems from the nature of proteins. A perfectly cooked scrambled egg is like Jell-O.

Jell-O is a mesh of coagulated proteins (gelatin rendered from collagen) gently holding molecules of flavored water. A properly scrambled egg is essentially the same thing.

If we leave the eggs in contact with heat too long, the proteins will coagulate so tightly that they'll squeeze out all the liquid. If you've ever been served a plate of scrambled eggs and noticed that they seem to be sitting in a small puddle of water, that's what happened: that water was supposed to be in the eggs, not under them. But don't worry, this doesn't have to happen to you or to your eggs.

The main thing to remember is that if your eggs are cooked in the pan, they'll be overcooked on the plate. Also, I've found over the years that beating some bubbles into the eggs helps to keep the march of heat into the eggs slow and steady, as air acts as an insulator.

TIDBIT | If you enjoyed this episode why not go ahead and turn to page 150 for "Egg-Files 2: Man with a Flan."

SOFTWARE

3	large	eggs	
1	pinch	kosher salt	
1	grind	black pepper	freshly ground
3	tablespoons	whole milk[1]	
1	tablespoon	unsalted butter	

PROCEDURE

1. Warm a **platter** as suggested in the preceding application.
2. **Whisk** the eggs, salt, pepper, and milk together until light and foamy. Add the butter to a **10- to 12-inch nonstick skillet** and put it over high heat.
3. When the butter bubbles (after about a minute), pour the eggs straight into the middle of the pan, which will force the butter to the edges, where it's needed. Stir slowly with a **rubber or silicone spatula**.
4. As soon as curds (big soft lumps) of eggs begin to form, drop the heat to low and shift from stirring to folding the curds over on themselves while gently shaking the pan with the other hand.
5. As soon as no more liquidous egg is running around the pan, kill the heat and gently transfer the scramble to the warmed platter.
6. Let the eggs rest for 1 minute to finish cooking before serving.

[1] Why add milk? Because the proteins in eggs can "set" more liquid than they have with them. Adding milk will render your scrambled eggs softer, creamier, and richer.

SALAD DAZE

EPISODE 4 | SEASON 1 | GOOD EATS

TRIVIA | This title comes from Shakespeare's, *Antony and Cleopatra*, Act 1, Scene V, and refers to days of youthful exuberance and innocence.

If any culinary form suffered during the '80s and '90s it was the salad. During those decades of unnecessary excess, we dressed it up, drenched it down, and denied it the simplicity that made it great. And as for lettuce, well, what we did to that poor leaf was a crime against nature.

This episode was all about getting back to basics, which isn't the easiest thing when the basics have been all but forgotten.

TIDBIT | Although they're all the rage these days, microgreens often deliver far less flavor than their adult counterparts.

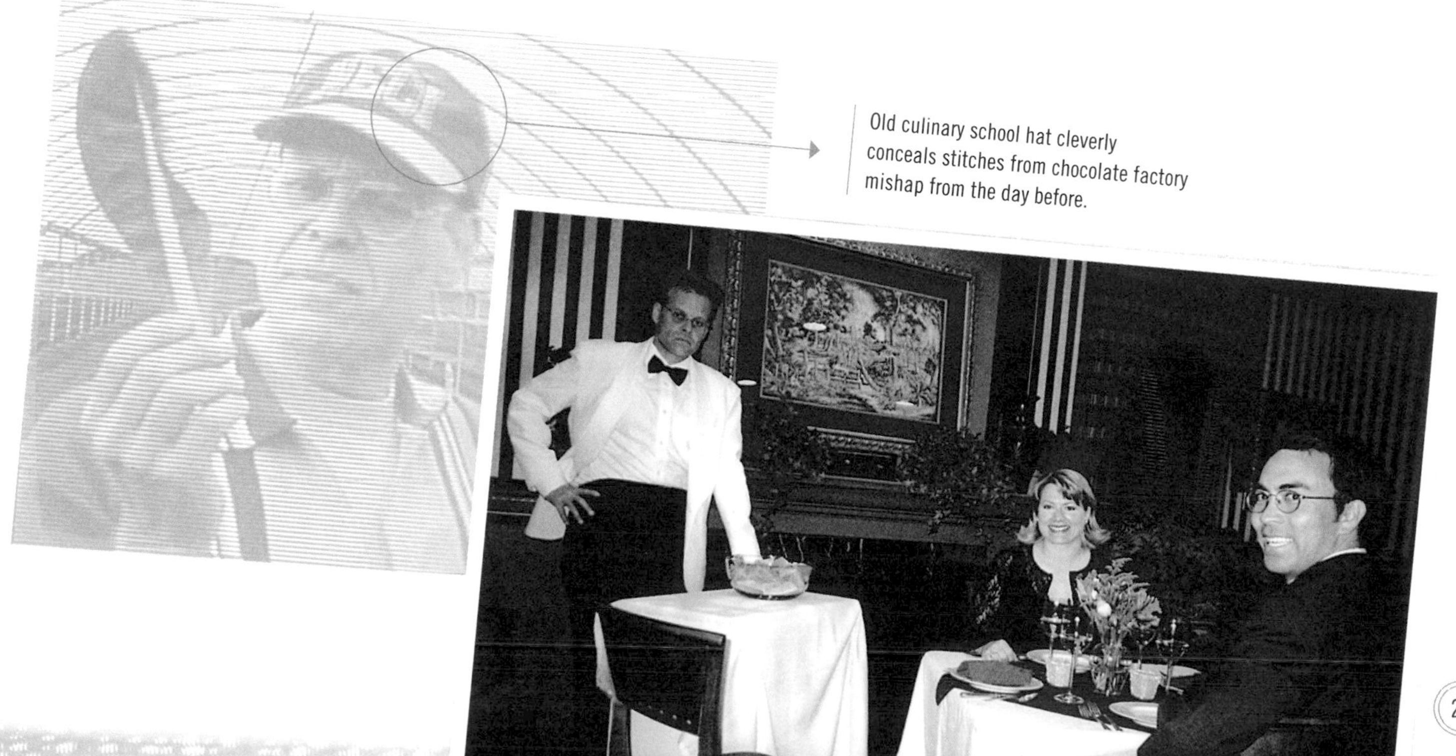

Old culinary school hat cleverly conceals stitches from chocolate factory mishap from the day before.

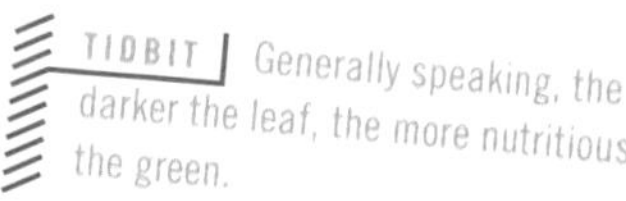

TIDBIT Generally speaking, the darker the leaf, the more nutritious the green.

KNOWLEDGE CONCENTRATE

Remember, above all, that lettuce hates violence. Be gentle with it even as you're tearing it to bits.

The word *salad* comes from the Roman word *sal*, which in turn is from the Latin *sel*, or "salt." What's salt got to do with a bowl of leaves? Some say that salt was the Romans' favorite dressing, and that they liked to salt fresh greens heavily enough so that they wilted before they ate them. Yum?

There are two main categories of greens: mild, sweet greens (romaine, bibb, and butter) and mean greens (chicory, watercress, escarole, radicchio, endive, arugula). The art in constructing a salad is to strike the right mix of sweet and mean, thus creating the proper balance of flavor and texture. It's simple, but not always easy.

Mesclun is a blend of about a dozen young greens originally engineered by French monks during the Middle Ages. Today, mesclun can contain just about anything as long as the leaves are young.

When shopping for lettuce, look for blemish-free heads with bright colors and crisp leaves. No slimy spots. Heavily ribbed heads such as romaine and loose-head radicchios should stand up straight without any signs of cracks along the ribs.

After harvest, lettuces, like most greens, go on about their business: metabolizing nutrients and respiring. As cooks, we want to limit these activities by suspending the leaves' animation, so to speak. Thoroughly clean leaves in a sink full of cold water, allowing dirt and debris to settle to the bottom. Use a salad spinner to dry the greens, then wrap them in paper towels and stash them in a zip-top bag. And here's the clincher: suck (yes . . . suck) as much air out of the bag as possible. Less air means less respiration, and that translates to longer fridge life.

Here's how you dress a salad for four:

- Get a big bowl, about twice the size you'd think you need.
- Put about 2 tablespoons dressing in the bottom of said bowl or, better yet, whisk together some oil and vinegar, a little dry mustard, and some salt and pepper.
- Place two large, loose handfuls of mixed lettuces on top. Open your fingers, cup your hands, and gently fold the lettuces to coat them with dressing. I cannot overstress the importance of gentleness here; salad simply will not stand for being manhandled. If you have room you can even toss, which of course would give you a "tossed salad."
- Serve immediately. Not in 5 minutes or 3 or 2 . . . now! Once the oil is on the leaves, the clock is ticking.[1]

TRIVIA I really like the bubble wrap scene, where we compare the structure of bubble wrap to a leaf of lettuce. When I asked the rigging guys to suspend the roll over my head so that I could just pull it down into the frame, they thought I was crazy.

APPLICATION

VENI VEDI VINAIGRETTE[2]

1 CUP

The classic salad dressing is a vinaigrette composed of three parts oil to one part vinegar. The problem is that oil and vinegar don't get along. It's a surface tension thing. Oil wants to spread out and coat everything in the place, while vinegar wants to bead up and roll away. Physical agitation can force them together temporarily by breaking the vinegar into tiny droplets so they become suspended in the oil, resulting in a creamy, smooth mixture. But then those vinegar beads will slowly draw back together and eventually separate from the oil and sink to the bottom (because water is denser than oil).

Keeping a vinaigrette together requires the deployment of an emulsifying agent of some sort such as mustard powder, finely ground garlic, or egg yolk. Vinaigrettes can also be emulsified with pureed vegetables or even peas such as lentils.

I'm still using a cocktail shaker for my vinaigrettes, as I did on the show, but recently I've added a twist inspired by a can of spray paint (see Tip).

SOFTWARE

¼	cup	red wine vinegar	
2	teaspoons	Dijon mustard[3]	
2	cloves	garlic	smashed
1	heavy pinch	kosher salt	
1	pinch	black pepper	freshly ground
¾	cup	extra-virgin olive oil	

PROCEDURE

1. Put the vinegar, mustard, garlic, salt, and pepper in a **1-pint canning jar or cocktail shaker** and shake to combine.
2. Add the oil and shake vigorously until the dressing emulsifies and thickens to a creamlike consistency.
3. Leave the dressing alone for 1 hour at room temperature to let the flavors mellow, then strain out the garlic and shake again to re-emulsify. (If you're using a shaker with a strainer you can use the built-in strainer.) The dressing can be refrigerated almost indefinitely but should always be brought to room temperature and shaken before serving.

TIP | Not too long ago I got a hold of a couple of ½-inch stainless-steel ball bearings. I put them in with the dressing before I shake it, and they act like that bearing that clatters around when you shake a can of spray paint. I imagine small, smooth pebbles would work just as well, but since there aren't any "food-grade small pebbles" on the market I cannot recommend their use, for fear of spending more time with lawyers.[4]

TIDBIT | An old kitchen proverb states that it takes three cooks to make a vinaigrette: a miser for the vinegar, a spendthrift for the oil, and a wise man for the salt.

APPLICATION

HAIL CAESAR SALAD

8 SERVINGS

Shortly after its invention, Caesar's Salad was hailed by the International Society of Epicures as America's greatest dish in fifty years.[5] I strongly suggest that you prepare this dish at tableside while wearing either a tuxedo or a smoking jacket. This is an elegant dish, and you should dress appropriately.

Note: THIS DISH CALLS FOR RAW EGGS! CONSUME AT YOUR OWN RISK. Of course, I eat it and haven't had a problem. But I use farm-fresh eggs. If you can't land the same, and you don't trust your megamart's supply, then by all means buy yourself some pasteurized shell eggs (see page 23).

SOFTWARE

8	ounces	day-old Italian bread	approximately half a standard loaf
3	cloves	garlic	mashed (but not smashed to smithereens)
½	teaspoon, plus a pinch	kosher salt	
8	tablespoons	extra-virgin olive oil	divided
2	large	eggs	at room temperature
2	heads (1 pound total)	romaine lettuce hearts	that is . . . inner leaves only
7	grinds	black pepper	freshly ground
½	small	lemon	juiced
½	teaspoon	Worcestershire sauce	
4	ounces	Parmesan cheese	freshly grated

PROCEDURE

1. Crank the oven to 350°F.
2. Cut the bread into ¾-inch cubes and spread on a **half sheet pan.** Bake until thoroughly dry but not brown, 10 to 12 minutes. Set aside. (Congratulations, you just made croutons.)
3. Bring 2 cups water to a boil in a **2-quart saucepan**.
4. Meanwhile, place the garlic and ½ teaspoon of the salt in a **mortar** and mash with the **pestle** to make a paste.[6] Add 4 tablespoons of the oil to the paste and mash to combine. Pour the oil through a **fine-mesh sieve** into a **12-inch sauté pan**. Place the pan over medium heat. Add the croutons and sauté, tossing constantly until all of the oil is absorbed by the bread and the croutons turn gold, approximately 5 minutes. Set aside.

TRIVIA This is the first episode in which we attempted to rework an established "historical" dish—here the Caesar Salad.

5 Add the eggs to the boiling water and cook for 1 minute. Immediately transfer to an **ice-water bath** to stop the cooking. Set aside.

6 Everything from here on should be done at the table, with great flair and flourish. In a **very large bowl**, tear the lettuce and toss, using **tongs**, with 2 tablespoons of the oil.

7 Sprinkle with the remaining pinch of salt and the pepper. Add the remaining 2 tablespoons olive oil. Toss well.

8 Add the lemon juice and Worcestershire sauce, and break in the eggs. Toss until a creamy dressing forms. Toss in the Parmesan cheese and serve topped with croutons.

[1] I have never encountered a salad dressing that preserves lettuce.

[2] As you can tell, with this episode I started trying to get cute with the nomenclature.

[3] "Dijon" refers to a wide variety of strong prepared mustards made famous in the city of Dijon in eastern France. Although many whole-grain mustards are prepared in the region, a smooth specimen would be best for this application.

[4] In fact, the whole thing about stainless-steel bearings is nonsense. I really do use the small pebbles but I can't tell you to because . . . well, you know. That said, I have checked, and stainless-steel ball bearings are readily available. Just not as available as small, smooth pebbles.

[5] The fact that it's Mexican didn't seem to bother any of the society members.

[6] I've tried to do this with just about every device imaginable and there's just no replacing a good mortar and pestle.

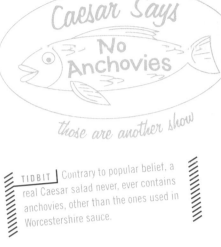

Caesar Says
No Anchovies
those are another show

TIDBIT | Contrary to popular belief, a real Caesar salad never, ever contains anchovies, other than the ones used in Worcestershire sauce.

A LENGTHY DISCOURSE CONCERNING THE NATURE OF WORCESTERSHIRE SAUCE WHEREIN THE AUTHOR CALLS INTO QUESTION SEVERAL POINTS OF MARKETING MYTHOLOGY

Although a popular myth suggests that English chemists Lea and Perrins concocted Worcestershire sauce by following a recipe for a sauce brought back from India by a Lord Sandys, "ex governor of Bengal," another version of the story is somewhat different. Apparently a Lady Sandy was given a recipe for curry powder by a writer named Ms. Grey, whose uncle had come across the list of ingredients and proportions while serving as a judge in India. The recipe in question was given to the aforementioned chemists, who (although they couldn't procure the entire list of spices and powders exactly) did manage to fill the order. Someone at their shop suggested that a solution made from this powder might make a good sauce, but the results were inedible. Instead of throwing the stuff out someone stashed it in a barrel in the basement. A couple of years later the barrel was opened and the contents tested. Miraculously, the noxious fluid had been transmuted by time and wood into the delectable elixir we all know and love.

I don't buy this story one bit for two simple reasons: (1) Curry powder is not Indian, it's British. So although I don't doubt there are curry powder recipes in England, the idea of one being brought back from India is very suspect indeed. (2) Take a look at the ingredients on the bottle. See anything common to curry powders? Nope, me either. Sure, tamarind grows in India, but anchovies? Molasses? No way.

So check out this theory: We know that the Romans occupied much of England (up to Hadrian's wall) between A.D. 40 and 410, and it's doubtful that they made the trip without the ubiquitous Roman fermented fish sauce called *garum*, which was like their ketchup, only with rotten fish guts. During the centuries of occupation, it's easy to imagine that someone attempted to make *garum* on English soil. The only ingredient that might have been added later is tamarind, which is not uncommon in East Asian fermented fish sauces. But India?

A BIRD IN THE PAN

EPISODE 5 | SEASON 1 | GOOD EATS

Producing a properly roasted *Gallus domesticus* is not easy. In fact, it's one of the toughest culinary tasks there is. I blame the bird, because it possesses an awkward shape, two different types of meat, and an unhelpful surface-to-mass ratio. We set out here to fix all that.

TRIVIA | The opening scene was our first "oven-cam" shot. Since we were shooting in a real kitchen we had to bring another oven in, cut out the back, and redress the rest of the room to get the perspective right. It was a pain.

KNOWLEDGE CONCENTRATE

- Rock Cornish game hens are very young, small broiler/fryer chickens and weigh between one and two pounds.
- Broiler/fryers are the most popular eating birds in the United States. They average in weight from two and a half to four and a half pounds, which means the target chicken is somewhere around seven weeks old when shown the axe. Such birds are very tender because they haven't done much in the way of heavy lifting in their short lives. Broiler/fryers are best suited to fast cooking methods such as . . . you get it.
- Roasters are the next most common chickens, at five to seven pounds and three to five months old. Although they can be broiled, slower roasting is usually the best approach because there's more connective tissue to be broken down.
- At ten months to one and a half years, stewing chickens are the oldest of the common market types. Since they're older, they possess more chickeny flavor than broiler/fryers, but they're also much tougher. When stewed, the connective tissue is broken down by time and moisture, which is why stewing chickens are great for chicken and dumplings, not to mention chicken pot pie. But that's another show.

Although you don't see them often in the United States, a capon is a castrated male of the species, between sixteen weeks and eight months old and weighing between four and seven pounds. Some folks say that clipping once upon a rooster leads to more flavorful and tender meat. Well, I've had capon and I don't agree.

A cock or rooster is a mature, uncastrated male between five to seven pounds.

Why does a chicken have light and dark meat? In their natural state, chickens spend a lot of time walking around, an activity involving constant, slow movement. The muscles that have evolved to make this possible are called "slow-twitch" muscles, which are aerobic, meaning that they burn a fair amount of oxygen. The resulting muscle color is brownish red. Chickens do not fly very often, but when they do there is a great deal of fast fluttering. This type of motion requires "fast-twitch" muscles, which do not rely on much oxygen and so are light pink when raw and white when cooked.

A few fun facts about chicken labeling:

Any chicken not containing synthetic ingredients or chemical preservatives can be called "natural." Since the aforementioned substances aren't usually present in chicken I would not pay more for a "natural" chicken any more than I would pay for "natural" water.

"HORMONE FREE" is a label you see on a lot of food these days. However, to be effective growth hormones have to be frequently injected—which is not very practical with poultry anyway. So again, this doesn't really mean a thing.

"FREE-RANGE" birds often cost more despite the fact that all it really means is that the chickens' cages are opened from time to time.

"ORGANIC" chickens can be superior in quality to conventional birds but laws concerning use of the term have become so convoluted and third-party certification so complex that it's hardly worth bothering to buy "organic" anymore.

All that being said, look for a bird that is appropriately sized for the application and that is not packed in water or a saline solution.

TRIVIA The scene with the big dinosaur was filmed at the Fernbank Science Center in Atlanta. Technically it's an *Allosaurus* not a *T. Rex*, which of course would have two fingers on its scrawny little arms instead of three. The similarity in skeletal structure between birds and dinosaurs is shocking.

I've got one word for you: Floss

APPLICATION

B&B CHICKEN[1]

4 SERVINGS

By massaging gremolata, a zest-and-herb mixture which serves as both seasoning and garnish, under the chicken's skin, we end up with a finished bird that has crisp skin, seasoned meat, and a flavorful jus. I've cooked this dish about six hundred times in the last decade and have simplified it over time. Gremolata is also the classic topping for osso bucco.

SOFTWARE

1½	teaspoons	black peppercorns	
3	medium cloves	garlic	coarsely chopped
1	teaspoon	kosher salt	divided
1	large	lemon	zested
1	teaspoon	fresh parsley	chopped
4	tablespoons	olive oil	divided
1		onion	quartered
4	large	carrots	cut into 3-inch chunks
3	ribs	celery	cut into 3-inch chunks
1	3- to 4-pound	broiler/fryer chicken	
1	cup	red wine	
1	cup	chicken broth	

PROCEDURE

1. Position top rack 8 inches under broiler and crank broiler to high.
2. Make the gremolata: Coarsely grind peppercorns in **mortar and pestle**. Work in the garlic and ½ teaspoon of the salt. Follow with the lemon zest, then the parsley, and finally 2 tablespoons of the oil. Work into a rough paste.
3. Arrange vegetables in a **heavy roasting pan**, creating a bed for the bird.
4. Butterfly chicken (see sidebar, opposite page).
5. Loosen the skin over the breast and thigh and distribute all but 1 tablespoon of the gremolata evenly underneath. Massage skin with the remaining oil.
6. Place bird skin down on veggie bed. Move to oven and broil 25 minutes.
7. Carefully flip bird, season skin with ½ teaspoon of salt, and return to oven for another 25 minutes, or until the deepest meat of the thigh and breast reach 160°F.

8 Remove bird from pan and set in **draining rig** (see episode 1).

9 Position **roasting pan** on cook top so that it straddles 2 burners—both cranked to high. Add the wine and the broth. Push the vegetables around to loosen any stuck-on bits of goodness.

10 Discard the veggies—they've given their all. Continue cooking the liquid for 2 minutes or boil until reduced to 1 cup.

11 Drain liquid into **gravy separator**. Carve the bird while the fat floats to the top. What's left in the bottom is jus[2] (see illustration).

12 Sauce the chicken with the jus and garnish with reserved gremolata.

NOTE 1: There may be smoke . . . actually there will be![3]

NOTE 2: Carryover will complete the cooking

Fat floats to top.

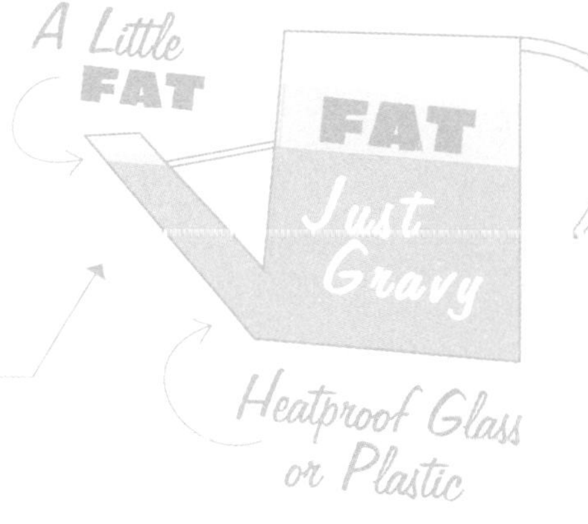

[1] As in "butterflied and broiled."

[2] Jus ("zhoo") is simply concentrated cooking juices. If you thicken a jus you have a gravy.

[3] Don't worry: Odds are nothing will catch on fire.

[4] Since they contain a fair amount of connective tissue, I freeze the backs and save up a dozen, then I make stock. But that's another book.

BUTTERFLYING A BIRD

The first step to butterflying a bird is to cut out the backbone.[4] I realize this is not an everyday maneuver for most cooks, so let's take a little time and space to examine the procedure in some detail. There are two ways to go:

WITH A REALLY BIG KNIFE: Place the chicken on a cutting board breast up. Open up the back end of the chicken and find the backbone. It's the long bunch of little bones that runs right up to where the head used to be. Slide the knife in along the spine all the way up to the neck hole. Now, hold the handle firmly but don't press down with it. Do that by pressing down on the chicken breast with your other hand. Once you're through, move the knife to the other side of the backbone and repeat.

WITH A BIG PAIR OF SHEARS: This is how I do it at home. It takes a little more hand strength but is a lot easier to control. Turn the bird over so that the back is up and the breast is down, with the bottom opening facing you. Take a heavy pair of shears (culinary or otherwise) and cut down one side of the back. Repeat on the other side.

Next, open the chicken book-style with the legs facing you. In the center you'll see a clear membrane covering the flat section of the keel bone that separates the two sides of the breast. Take a paring knife and slice through this membrane. Then work your index and middle finger underneath the keel bone and gently lever it up and out. On young birds, the keel tends to break at the calcification line where the thinner part of the keel turns from bone to cartilage. Now the bird will lie flat. Hold the main part of the body and pull the legs toward you. You now have a butterflied chicken.

CROSS CONTAMINATION

Raw chicken can indeed carry salmonella. But unlike eggs, undercooked chicken isn't exactly tasty, so the odds of getting sick from the bird itself (in the home environment, at least) isn't very high. The problem is cross contamination.

Cross contamination happens when a toxin or pathogen or some other consumable baddie jumps ship. One of the most common cross-contamination scenarios is one that befell a good friend of mine a while back. He was having a get-together at his house and grilled up a bunch of chicken, which he carried to the grill on a large platter. In all the excitement (and beer), he forgot to wash the tray before putting the cooked chicken on it. Three people ended up sick, my friend from salmonella and two others from *Campylobacter Jejuni*, which is more common than salmonella and requires fewer actual pathogens to make you sick. In this case the problem wasn't undercooking the chicken; it was putting the perfectly prepared chicken right back in the nasty juice from which it came. The nastiness could have just as easily hopped to salad or dessert.

Avoiding cross contamination is all about isolation and annihilation. You isolate the pathogens from the moment you spot the chicken at the market, where you tie it up in a plastic bag and sequester it away from other foods during transport to the domestic site of your choice. In the refrigerator, solitary confinement is essential and best accomplished in the very bottom of the box in a drip-proof container of some sort.

I have a cutting board that I use only for cutting raw poultry. It's red, so I never confuse it with any of my other cutting boards. I also quarantine my poultry butchery in a specific part of my kitchen counter so it's easy to isolate when it's time to clean up. Packaging and trimmings go straight into a plastic bag, which is tied off and transported by robotic drone to an incinerator where they're turned to microdust by plasma burst . . . Okay, that's a lie. But I really am careful.

As for the annihilation, soap and warm water will take care of your hands. Surfaces like counters can be sanitized with a solution of ¼ teaspoon bleach to 1 cup water (or 1 tablespoon to a gallon), or even plain vinegar, which has the advantage of not losing its efficiency after a few hours.

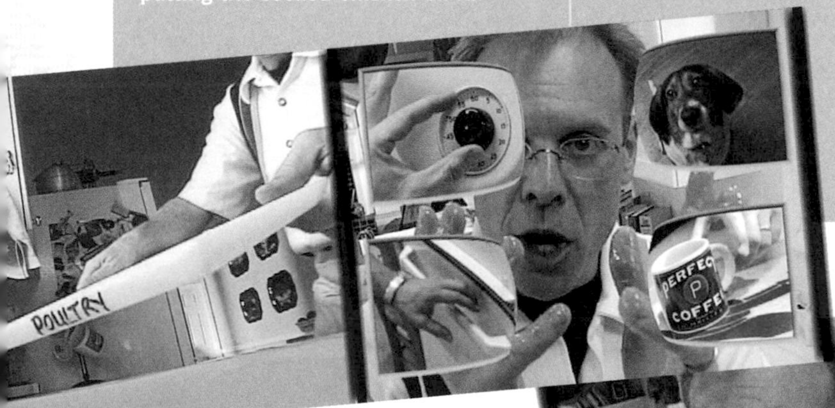

WASH THOSE CHICKENY HANDS!

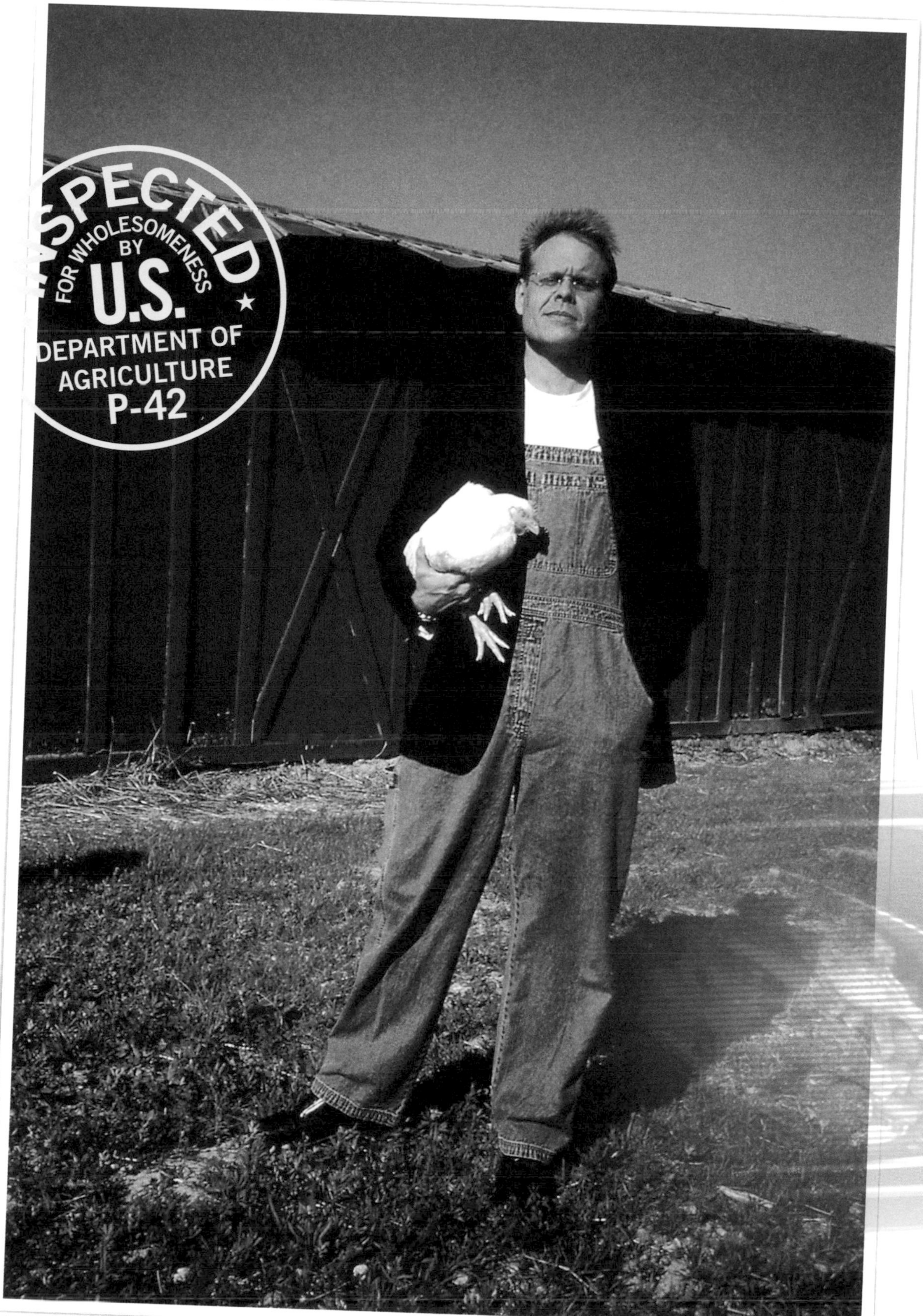

INSPECTED
FOR WHOLESOMENESS
BY
U.S.
DEPARTMENT OF
AGRICULTURE
P-42

I predict that one day all the fashionistas will be sporting chickens.

CHURN, BABY, CHURN

EPISODE 6 | SEASON 1 | GOOD EATS

Ice cream has always fascinated me, ever since the days of cranking and cranking and cranking that churn out behind my grandparents' house. I still contend that homemade ice cream is the only way to go, and that the hand churn is still vastly superior to electric machines. That's because as the mixture begins to freeze the dasher speed should increase to push more air into the mix. No mechanized churn that I know of can sense this critical point. Of course, most eight-year-old boys won't bother to sense it either.

TRIVIA | The ice cream parlor in the opening scene is part of a revered Atlanta greasy spoon called the Silver Skillet. Several scenes of other Season 1 shows were shot there as well. It's one of the only restaurants I've actually wanted to own.

TIP | Ice cream can be melted and rechurned over and over. If your kid wants chocolate chip and all you've got is vanilla, melt the stuff down and rechurn it while drizzling in melted chocolate. You're a hero.

KNOWLEDGE CONCENTRATE

- Sucrose is one of the "key molecules" that *Good Eats* deals with, and you will see its name often in these pages. Understanding sucrose is essential if the cook wishes to conquer the confectionary arts, which include ice cream making. If you've never thought of ice cream as candy, consider this: All candy making is about controlling sugar crystals. Ice cream ups the ante by adding ice crystals to the mix. Sucrose molecules prevent large ice crystals from forming by physically getting in the way of water, and that helps to create a smooth texture and creamy mouthfeel.

- If ice cream didn't contain air it would be too hard to eat. In manufactured ice creams, air is called "overrun," and legally an ice cream can contain up to 100 percent overrun, meaning that half of its volume is in fact air. Such ice creams feel light and melt fast, and, if you ask me, they're a rip-off. Top-quality ice creams usually contain 10 to 25 percent overrun, which is about what I shoot for in homemade.

- Since hand-cranked and electric countertop machines churn at a relatively slow speed, the ice creams they produce contain relatively little overrun. After a few hours in the freezer, they can become so hard that they'll need to sit at room temperature before they're soft enough to serve.

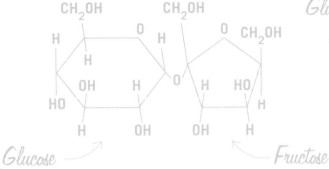

Glucose + Fructose = SUCROSE

$C_{12}H_{22}O_{11}$

Glucose

Fructose

Table sugar or "sucrose" is a disaccharide or "double" sugar composed of one glucose and one fructose molecule.

TRIVIA The little boy sitting on the wall is my brother in-law, Cody. I didn't pay him a dime.

There are two kinds of countertop ice cream makers: expensive machines that freeze by way of compressors and refrigeration units and cheaper machines that have a gel core, made up of water, salt, and a polysaccharide, that have to be frozen for up to eighteen hours in advance in order to be cold enough to make one or maybe two small batches. Although I prefer hand-cranked machines to either of these, for many folks having a small electric countertop model is the difference between making ice cream or not. Cuisinart makes a fine frozen core model for about fifty bucks.

The ability of salt and ice to combine to form a liquid brine that's colder than the ice was in the first place is a result of an amazingly complex phenomenon called *endothermic reaction*.

A few definitions:

ICE CREAM: flavored cream (usually lighter creams or cream and milk).

SHERBET: flavored milk (usually fruit flavored).

GELATO: flavored heavy cream (you got a problem with that?).

SORBET: flavored water.

"LIGHT" ICE CREAM: flavored air.

Traditionally, ice creams containing eggs were called French or custard style, while those without eggs were referred to as Philadelphia or New York style.

As an ice cream or sorbet freezes, ice crystals form. Since only water has to leave whatever it's carrying behind when it joins other ice crystals, as the process continues more and more dissolved solids like sugar and substances like fats and salts and proteins are cramped into less and less water. Eventually, this solution becomes so concentrated that it won't freeze, at least not at consumer freezer temperatures. Thus, ice creams and sorbets are always a solid and a liquid. Balancing these so that flavor and texture will be optimized is the primary challenge faced by the frozen dessert designer.

Ice creams should be stored as air tight as possible to prevent freezer burn—that is, the drying of the surface. Pack your hard work into vessel with a tight lid, and press a layer of plastic wrap right down on the surface of the ice cream.

TIDBIT During Prohibition, many bars converted to ice cream parlors. Many were so profitable they never changed back after the repeal.

APPLICATION

SERIOUS VANILLA ICE CREAM

1 QUART

When I first developed this recipe, more than a few folks thought the peach preserves were a crazy addition. But consider this: Jams and preserves contain pectins, which are gigantic molecules that have considerable gelling power. Including just a wee bit not only smoothes out the texture and elevates the subtler flavor of the vanilla; it can also actually retard melting a bit.

And as we'll learn in a few dozen episodes, salt, in small amounts, can turn up the volume on almost any flavor. I include a pinch in most dessert applications.

SOFTWARE

2	cups	half-and-half	
1	cup	heavy cream[1]	
5½	ounces	sugar	
2	ounces	peach preserves or jam	(not jelly)
1		vanilla bean	split and scraped[2]
1	pinch	kosher salt	

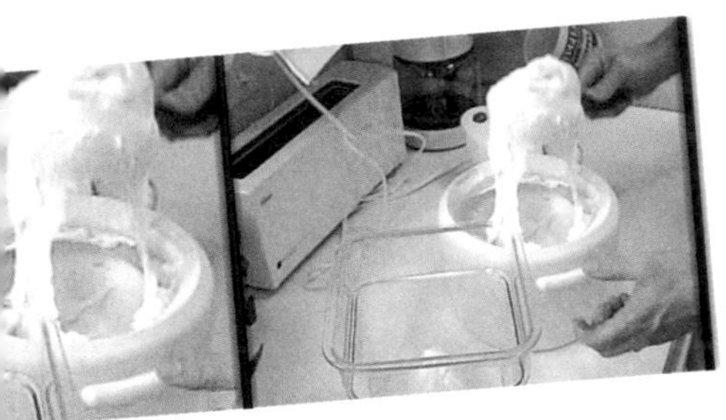

TIDBIT The crank ice cream machine was invented by a New Jersey housewife named Nancy Johnson in 1843. She sold her patent rights for $200.

PROCEDURE

1. Combine the half-and-half and heavy cream in a **medium saucepan** and place over medium heat. Attach a **candy or deep-fry thermometer** and bring the mixture to 175°F[3], stirring occasionally. Remove from heat.
2. Add the sugar, preserves, vanilla bean, and salt and keep stirring until the sugar is completely dissolved, then cover and steep 20 minutes.
3. Fish out the vanilla pod and transfer the mixture to an **airtight container** and refrigerate for at least 6 hours or up to overnight.[4]
4. Assemble your **ice cream churn** according to the manufacturer's instructions. If you're using an electric machine, turn it on, then pour in the ice cream mixture. (This will prevent seizing.)
5. Churn the ice cream until it reaches soft-serve consistency and almost doubles in volume.
6. Move to an **airtight container** and harden in the freezer for at least 2 hours before serving.

APPLICATION

KEY LIME SORBET

1½ QUARTS

If you replace the dairy mixture in ice cream with flavored water like juice or puree, you'll churn up a sorbet, which is actually trickier to make than ice cream because you don't have the benefit of milk fat to soften the texture. And so we have to rely on sugar and, oddly enough, alcohol, a natural antifreeze that can go a long way toward controlling crystallization. Alcohol also serves an important flavor function. Cold dulls the taste buds, so mixtures destined for the churn should have their flavor knobs turned to 11.5, if not 12.

A lot of sorbet recipes call for alcohol to act as an ice crystal minimizer. Although it works, the pectin from jam and preserves works even better.

SOFTWARE

7	ounces	sugar	
10	ounces	key lime preserves	
1	quart	lime-flavored club soda or seltzer	
1	medium	lemon	zested and juiced
1	medium	lime	zested and juiced
1	pinch	kosher salt	

PROCEDURE

1. Combine the sugar, preserves, and 1 cup of the soda in a **small saucepan** and **stir** over medium-low heat until everything gritty and gooshy dissolves into smoothness.
2. Remove from the heat and add the zests, juices, salt, and remaining soda and move to an **airtight container**. (Chill until the mixture is below 40°F, 2 to 3 hours.)
3. Assemble your **ice cream churn** according to the manufacturer's instructions. If you're using an electric machine, turn it on, then pour in the flavorful solution. (This will prevent seizing.) Churn until the mixture is a firm slush.
4. Transfer said slush back to the **airtight container** and put in the freezer to harden for 2 hours before serving.

[1] Heavy cream is often labeled "heavy whipping cream" or "whipping cream" and has a fat content of 36 to 40 percent.

[2] Bean splitting can be a tough job. I use a strange little device called a bean Frencher to do the job. Though it's designed for green beans, it handles vanilla pods easily and can save you a lot of mess and frustration with a knife.

[3] Why the heat? Well, for one thing we need to dissolve the sugar, but just as important, we need to shut down certain chemical structures in the dairy that could be an impediment to the smoothness we so desire.

[4] If you're going to freeze the stuff, why bother chilling it first? Texture again, my friend. Chilling to 38°F (which is what I hope your refrigerator is) means that the thermal trip to the frozen state is relatively short. The shorter the trip, the finer the ice crystals will be—and that will deliver a much smoother texture than if you just go straight to the churn. But, hey, it's your food.

TRIVIA | There's a scene at a dairy stable (at UGA) where the camera and I are walking together and I keep magically lifting different containers of dairy up into the frame. I'm often asked how we pulled off this bit of slight-of-hand, and the answer is pretty simple. We rigged a little shelf with a six-foot handle on it that my longtime key grip, Marshall Millard, carried while walking behind the cameraman. The loaded shelf floated just under the camera frame.

THE DOUGH ALSO RISES

EPISODE 7 | SEASON 1 | GOOD EATS

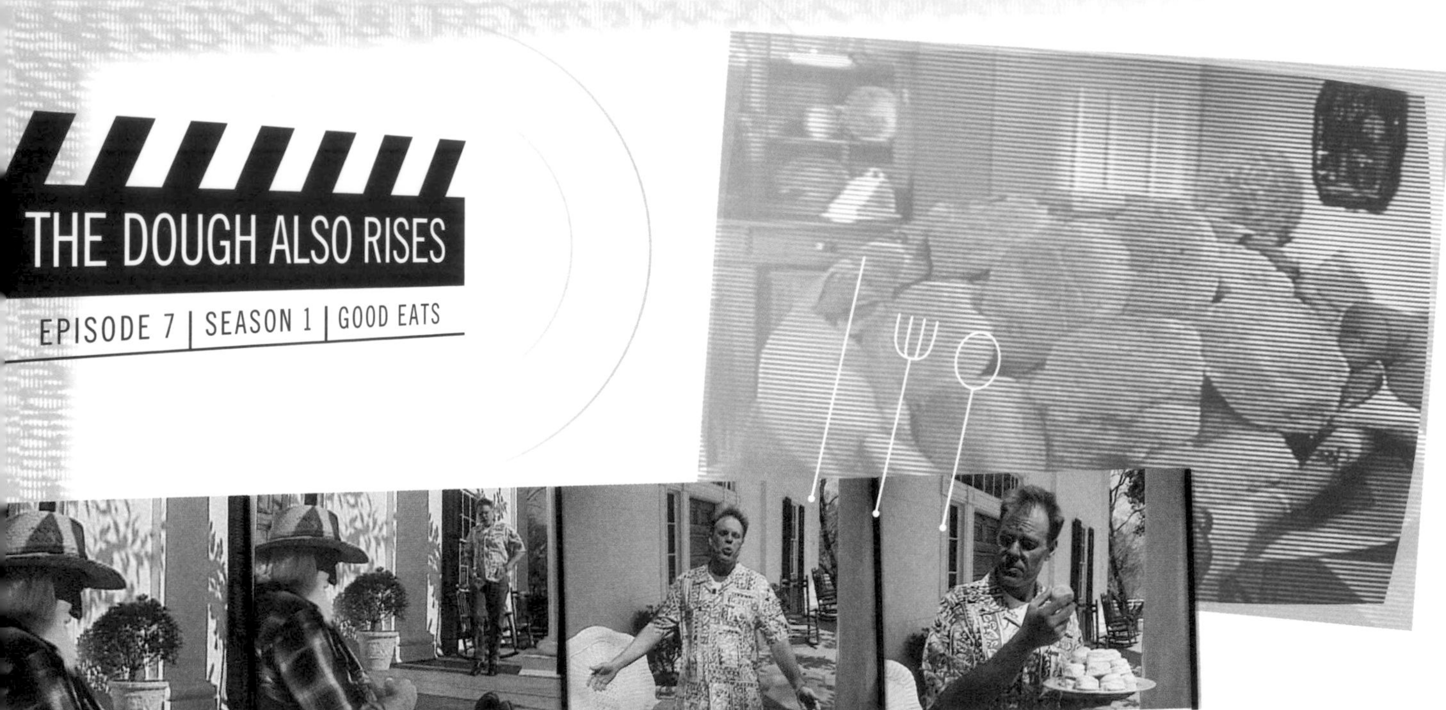

Through the years I've often been asked to name my favorite *Good Eats* episode, and I have to say that no show rises above this one. The reason: My grandmother, Ma Mae, appeared in nearly every scene with me. I loved the old girl—and her amazingly light biscuits—dearly and am thankful to have had the opportunity to make this show before she passed away only three years later. Now, my daughter can watch the rerun and see the kind of character her great-grandmother was. But enough sentimentality, let's get to the biscuits.

This was our first baking show, and I wanted to stress the fact that baking isn't like regular cooking. It's a science. Baking recipes are balanced equations, and if you mess with one part of the equation there will be ramifications in another. This doesn't mean you can't add nuts, or flavorants, but if you mess around in the engine room—that is, the fat-flour-eggs-sugar-moisture end of things—you'd better know what you're doing. And that goes double for the beguilingly simple biscuit.

TRIVIA | If you don't get the episode title I suggest you put this book down and head for the classics—American classics, that is.

TIDBIT | Most . . . no, *all* good southern biscuits contain buttermilk, which provides moisture, body, and a distinctive twang. Once upon a time buttermilk was the byproduct of butter making, which was naturally inoculated by lactic bacteria. Commercial buttermilk is typically pasteurized and homogenized lowfat milk to which acids and bacteria are added. The result is considerably more viscous than the original.

TIDBIT | Tartaric acid is a crystalline acid that's found in many plants including grapes. It's often harvested from the inside of barrels where red wine has aged.

KNOWLEDGE CONCENTRATE

- The key to a good, light, Southern-style biscuit is "soft" flour—a flour that contains less protein than bread flour or even all-purpose flour. Some popular Southern flours are also milled to a finer grain consistency, which aids in fast mixing, another contributor to lightness. If you don't have access to soft Southern flour you can approximate it by mixing three parts all-purpose flour with one part cake flour.
- Solid fats such as shortening, butter, and lard provide lubrication, which tenderizes or "shortens" the protein structures (gluten) that can form in kneaded wheat flour doughs. Working solid fats into the dough creates open pockets in the final baked good, which also contributes to tenderness. Although I've always been a lard fan (lard melts between 86° and 104°F), my grandmother swore by good ol' vegetable shortening (117° to 119°F), which with its higher melting point can handle higher oven temperatures to produce a very different rise. There's no right or wrong fat of the two, as long as you don't try to switch them out in a recipe. Since butter melts in the 90s it's a better substitute for lard than shortening, but the only thing that can replace shortening might be (gulp) margarine.
- Shortening is produced by hydrogenizing vegetable oil. That means that hydrogen atoms are added to its molecules in order to make it act like a saturated fat, which of course is solid at room temperature. Up until a few years ago, such fats were called "trans" fats. Now that we know that trans fats are as bad if not worse for us than saturated fats, manufacturers have changed their formulas. Still, it might be good to keep in mind that shortening isn't exactly a natural ingredient. Lard and butter both are.
- As for the moisture chord, I just don't think anything can touch the tangy twang of buttermilk. That said, since it's an acidic ingredient and reacts with bases like baking soda to create CO_2, you can't just trade it for milk or cream.

Vinegar
Baking Soda

Remember the old vinegar/baking soda rockets? That's leavening.

ON CHEMICAL LEAVENERS

When alkaline (or "base") ingredients and acidic ingredients come together in the presence of liquid, carbon dioxide is given off. This gas can be captured to provide a lift to breads, which ordinarily would have to catch a rise on the burps of yeasts.

The acid can come from a variety of goods, from sour milk to yogurt to lemon juice to cream of tartar.

The base is usually sodium bicarbonate (baking soda), which besides egg whites and amonia is just about the only base in the kitchen. Baking powder contains a base and one or two acids and only requires moisture to release CO_2. Most modern baking powders are "double-acting"—they release a burst of CO_2 when they first come into contact with water and then another when they hit oven temperatures. A single-acting baking powder can be manufactured in the home kitchen by mixing two parts cream of tartar with one part baking soda and one part cornstarch.[1]

Something to keep in mind about chemical leavening is that only a balanced acid-base equation produces maximum lift. Since so many ingredients—chocolate, buttermilk, fruit juices—can throw off this balance, most leavened baked goods contain both baking powder and baking soda.

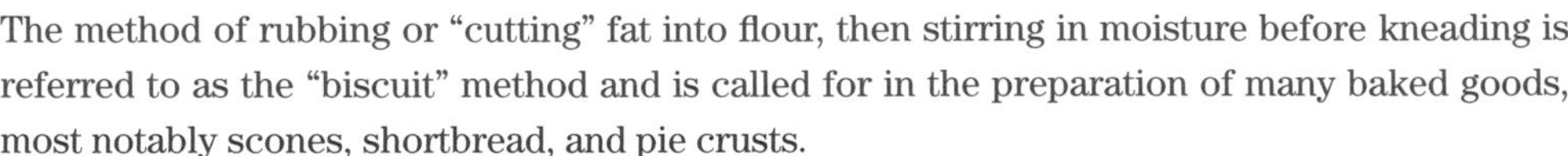

APPLICATION

SOUTHERN BISCUITS[2]

1 DOZEN

The method of rubbing or "cutting" fat into flour, then stirring in moisture before kneading is referred to as the "biscuit" method and is called for in the preparation of many baked goods, most notably scones, shortbread, and pie crusts.

I never really thought I could beat my grandmother's biscuits. Since she passed away, though, I've come close if for no other reason than that I realized that her arthritis was actually an ingredient. Her fingers hurt so much she couldn't really bend them when she kneaded the dough. When I started imitating her movements, my biscuits got better. While we're on the subject of family cooking, let me say that the most important recipes you can collect are family recipes. When a couple gets married, the best gift they can receive is a handmade book of recipes from both sides of the family.

SOFTWARE

12	ounces	all-purpose flour	plus an additional ½ cup for dusting
4	teaspoons	baking powder	
¼	teaspoon	baking soda	
¾	teaspoon	kosher salt	
1	ounce	unsalted butter	chilled[3]
2	ounces	shortening	chilled
1	cup	low-fat buttermilk	chilled

PROCEDURE

1. Heat the oven to 400°F.
2. **Whisk** together all the dry, powdery stuff (except the flour for dusting, of course) in a **large mixing bowl**.
3. Using your fingertips, rub the butter and shortening into the dry goods until the mixture resembles coarse crumbs.
4. Make a well in the middle of this mixture and pour in the buttermilk. Stir with a **large spoon** until the dough just comes together. Then knead in the bowl until all the flour has been taken up.

5 Turn the dough out onto a lightly floured surface, then start folding the dough over on itself, gently kneading for 30 seconds, or until the dough is soft and smooth.

6 Press the dough into a 1-inch-thick round. Using a **3-inch round cutter**, cut out biscuits, being sure to push the cutter all the way through the dough to the work surface before twisting to "punch" out the biscuit. Make your cuts as close together as possible to limit waste.

7 Place the biscuits on a **half sheet pan** (preferably aluminum, which is highly conductive) so that they just barely touch. Reroll scraps and punch out as many biscuits as possible.

8 Use your thumb to create a shallow dimple in the top center of each biscuit,[4] and bake until the biscuits are tall and light gold on top, 15 to 20 minutes. Turn the biscuits out into a **kitchen towel–lined basket** and let cool for several minutes before buttering and devouring.

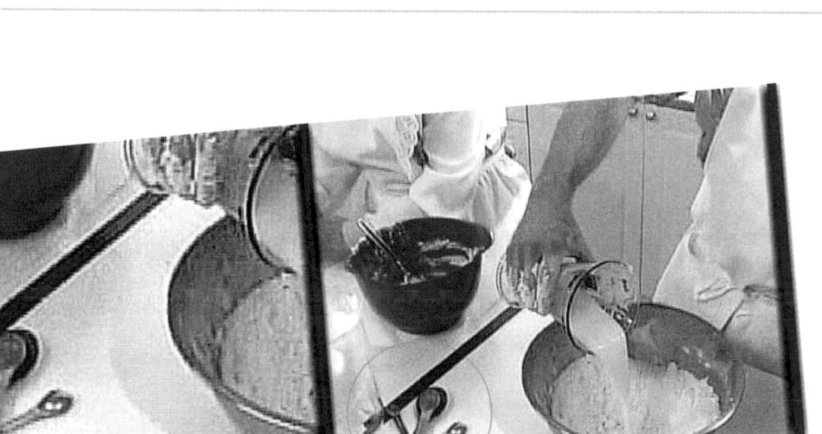

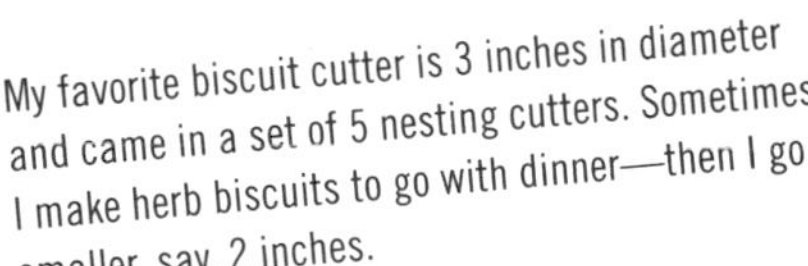

My favorite biscuit cutter is 3 inches in diameter and came in a set of 5 nesting cutters. Sometimes I make herb biscuits to go with dinner—then I go smaller, say, 2 inches.

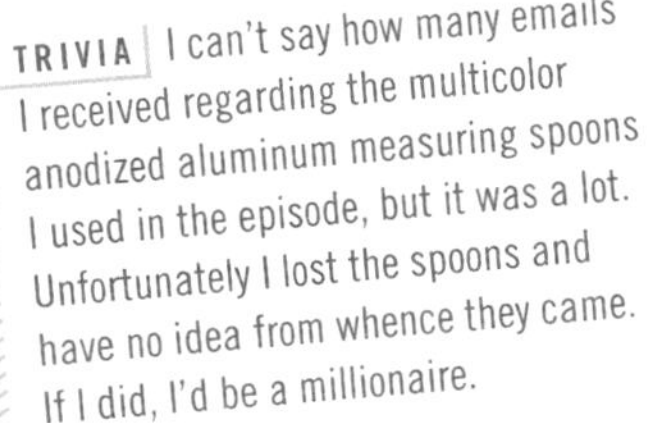

TRIVIA I can't say how many emails I received regarding the multicolor anodized aluminum measuring spoons I used in the episode, but it was a lot. Unfortunately I lost the spoons and have no idea from whence they came. If I did, I'd be a millionaire.

APPLICATION

SHORTCAKE

8 SHORTCAKES

Although there are many variations on the biscuit theme, the following is by far my favorite. Notice that the buttermilk has been replaced with half-and-half, which changes the acid-base equation. Also, the addition of sugar will further tenderize these extraordinary devices.

SOFTWARE

12	ounces	all-purpose flour	
4	teaspoons	baking powder	
¼	teaspoon	baking soda	
2	ounces	sugar	plus additional for sprinkling
¾	teaspoon	kosher salt	
1	ounce	unsalted butter	chilled, plus 1 tablespoon melted butter for brushing
2	ounces	shortening	chilled
¾	cup	half-and-half	chilled
		Macerated Strawberries	(page 328)
		whipped cream[5]	

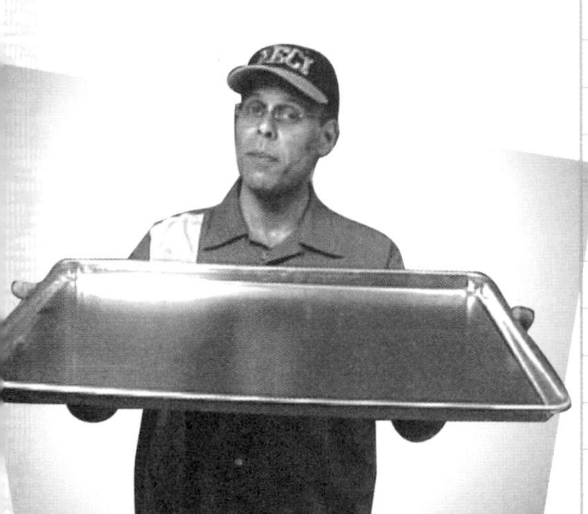

PROCEDURE

1. Heat the oven to 450°F.
2. **Whisk** all the dry, powdery stuff (except the sugar for sprinkling, of course) in a **large mixing bowl**.
3. Using your fingertips, rub the chilled butter and shortening into the dry goods until the mixture resembles coarse crumbs.
4. Mix in the half-and-half and stir until a sticky batter forms.
5. Use a **big spoon** to drop 8 large blobs of batter onto an **aluminum half sheet pan**. **Brush** with melted butter and sprinkle with sugar.
7. Bake for 15 minutes, or until GBD.[6]
8. Turn out into a **kitchen towel-lined basket** and cool 10 minutes before making strawberry shortcake (see page 328).

[1] The same mixture can be used to create various devices that are rather mischievous in nature. But that's another book.

[2] As opposed to harder, Northern "beaten" biscuits, which are, well . . . not these.

[3] If you're "hot handed" you definitely want to chill the fats in the freezer before attempting to cut them in.

[4] This helps to ensure flat tops on the finished biscuit.

[5] And ice cream if you want to go all the way.

[6] Golden, brown, and delicious. It's a technical term.

Any excuse to fly

GRAVY CONFIDENTIAL

EPISODE 8 | SEASON 1 | GOOD EATS

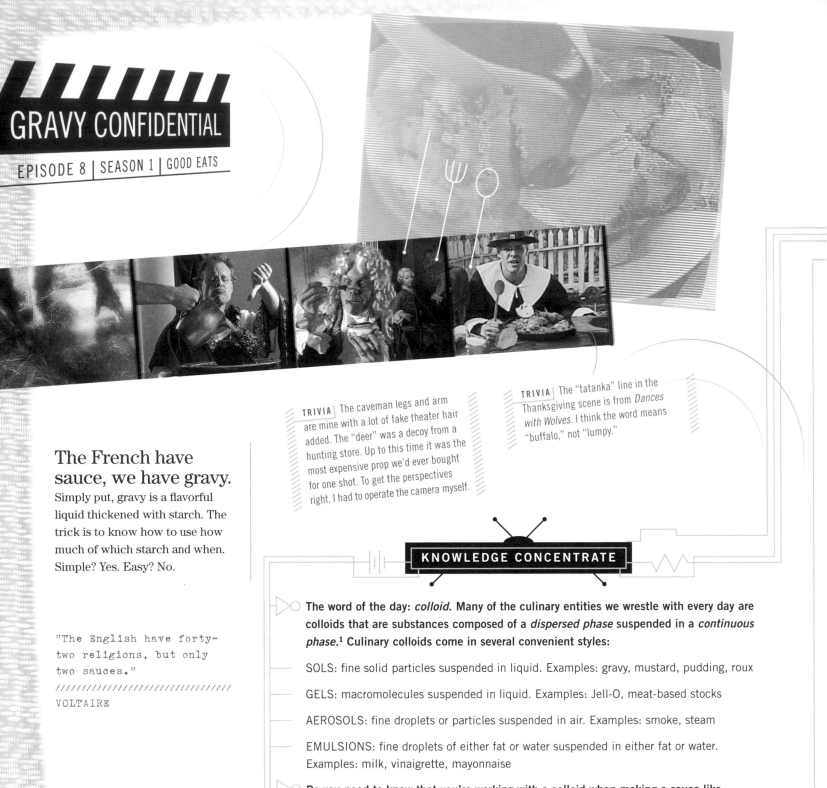

TRIVIA | The caveman legs and arm are mine with a lot of fake theater hair added. The "deer" was a decoy from a hunting store. Up to this time it was the most expensive prop we'd ever bought for one shot. To get the perspectives right, I had to operate the camera myself.

TRIVIA | The "tatanka" line in the Thanksgiving scene is from *Dances with Wolves*. I think the word means "buffalo," not "lumpy."

The French have sauce, we have gravy.

Simply put, gravy is a flavorful liquid thickened with starch. The trick is to know how to use how much of which starch and when. Simple? Yes. Easy? No.

"The English have forty-two religions, but only two sauces."

VOLTAIRE

KNOWLEDGE CONCENTRATE

The word of the day: *colloid*. Many of the culinary entities we wrestle with every day are colloids that are substances composed of a *dispersed phase* suspended in a *continuous phase*.[1] Culinary colloids come in several convenient styles:

- SOLS: fine solid particles suspended in liquid. Examples: gravy, mustard, pudding, roux
- GELS: macromolecules suspended in liquid. Examples: Jell-O, meat-based stocks
- AEROSOLS: fine droplets or particles suspended in air. Examples: smoke, steam
- EMULSIONS: fine droplets of either fat or water suspended in either fat or water. Examples: milk, vinaigrette, mayonnaise

Do you need to know that you're working with a colloid when making a sauce like gravy? I think so, because managing a colloid is not about "making a thing" but about "managing a relationship." When you start making gravy—or any sauce, for that matter—keep in mind that you're managing the characteristics of substances that might not automatically get along with each other.

SPECIAL COLLOIDAL MANAGEMENT HARDWARE

This pan is called a SAUCIER, and I find it to be one of the two tools absolutely necessary to colloid management. What makes the saucier so special is the bowl-like shape, which makes for easy access by the other required colloidal management tool, the . . .

WHISK. Colloids depend on suspension, and suspensions don't just happen. In fact, a good, stable suspension generally has to be beaten, whipped, and otherwise coerced into being. Although this can—and in some cases should—be done in a blender, food processor, or other power tool, many times those instruments simply deliver too much energy too quickly. Nope, the whisk is the tool for me, and I like a balloon whisk over the more traditional French whisk

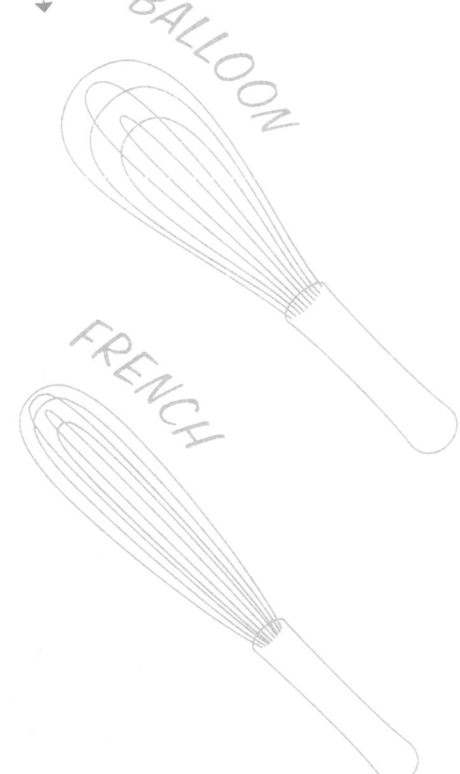

The *dispersed phase* in gravy is starch. As we saw in the potato episode (page 16), starches are big molecules that reside in granules that swell and eventually burst in hot, water-based liquids. When this happens they tangle up, capturing liquid and thus thickening it. Many starches can be employed to this purpose, including cornstarch, arrowroot, and tapioca, and we'll get to those in the pages to come. But flour is the most common kitchen starch, so we'll stick to it for now.

Depending on the type of flour, the actual starch content may range from 6 percent in cake flour to as high as 14.5 percent in high-gluten flours.

Gravies thickened with flour will continue to gel as they cool. This is why I usually bring gravy to the table not in a gravy boat but a Thermos, and I typically make them a little looser than I want them because they will thicken a bit no matter how you store them.

Flour clumps. This is one of the inconvenient truths of colloidal engineering. Dry starches don't want to be dumped into liquids, and that goes double for hot liquids. To get around this, we use what I call a "delivery suspension" to get the starch in clean and unclumped. Here are a few common delivery suspensions:

SLURRY: Shake up the flour with a cold liquid (wine, broth, water), then whisk this colloid into the hot liquid to be thickened. Slurries are especially effective with cornstarch. But that's another show.

BEURRE MANIÉ: Equal parts softened butter and flour are kneaded together into a paste. Bits of this mixture can be whisked directly into the hot liquid. After a couple of minutes at a simmer, the liquid will thicken. Unfortunately, the finished dish will always have a faint flour taste.

ROUX: Equal parts by weight of fat and flour are cooked together to various states of doneness. Usually the target liquid is then added to the roux rather than the other way around. Two ounces of a lightly cooked or "white" roux can thicken 16 ounces of liquid with little if any change in flavor. However, if the roux is cooked to successive stages of doneness—white, blond, brown, brick, black—it delivers more flavor but much less thickening power. A brick roux (which is usually cooked in the oven to prevent burning) adds considerable flavor to, say, a Cajun-style stew like gumbo but it possesses a mere quarter of the thickening power of a similar amount of white roux. That's because as a roux cooks, the very high heat destroys many of the starch granules.

APPLICATION

WHITE ROUX

ENOUGH ROUX TO THICKEN 16 OUNCES LIQUID

This simple procedure produces a magical paste that can thicken any water-type liquid, including but not limited to: wine, broth, stock, juice, milk, and of course water—though I can't imagine why you'd want to do that.

SOFTWARE

2	ounces	unsalted butter	(or pan drippings from roast beast or chicken[2])
2	ounces	all-purpose flour	

PROCEDURE

1. Melt the butter in **3-quart saucier** over medium-high heat.
2. When the bubbles begin to subside (a sure sign that most of the water has cooked out of the butter), add the flour all at once. **Whisk** vigorously. At first the mixture will thin out and bubble. Reduce the heat to low and slow down on the whisking.
3. Stir occasionally until you smell a toasty aroma, then cook for another 2 minutes.
4. Remove from heat, cool 1 minute before using. Refrigerate for up to 2 weeks.

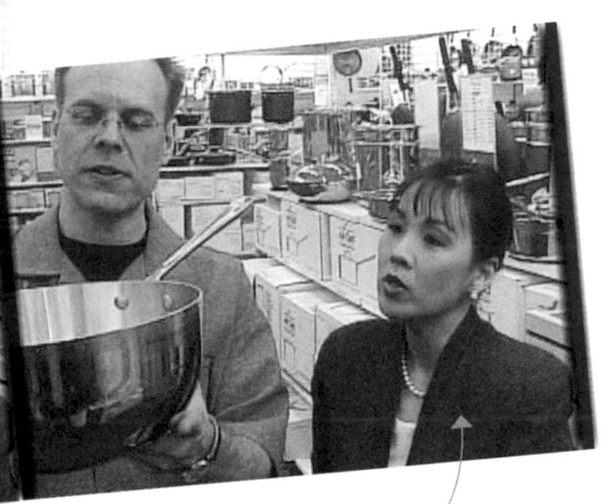

TRIVIA | W, who has appeared in countless *Good Eats* episodes, is of course a take-off on Q from the James Bond films. An actress named Vickie Eng, who also happens to be a pretty good chiropractor, plays her. Although several actresses read for the part, Vickie was the only one who seemed to take an immediate dislike to me. It seemed to work. To this day people stop her in the street to ask for advice about cooking implements because they think she's really W. It's called *acting*.

THE WHOLE "HOT LIQUID, COLD ROUX" DEBATE

Posters on culinary websites love to argue about this one. The longstanding wisdom about integrating roux into liquids has been that you should combine hot roux with cold liquids and hot liquids with cold roux. No one, to my mind, has successfully explained why. My own experiments have only gone so far as to convince me of the following:

1. No liquid should be added to a scorching hot roux because of the inevitable splattering that takes place when water hits something that's a good hundred degrees above its boiling point. The splattering of the roux does seem to reduce its effectiveness. My theory is that in this instance the fat and water move away from each other with such violence and speed that the flour actually gets abandoned and is once again alone to fend for itself in the liquid, and that can produce clumping. But this is just a hunch.

2. A super-cold liquid shouldn't be added to a roux because it can harden the fat, and then you'll have to wait around until it melts, which, given the specific heat of water, could be quite a while.

APPLICATION

SAWMILL GRAVY

4 SERVINGS

If you added 10 ounces of milk to 1 ounce of roux you'd be well on your way to producing one of the most versatile of the five French "mother" sauces of yore: béchamel. In the South, however, we make it another way.

SOFTWARE

1	pound	breakfast sausage	(bulk style, not links)
1¼	ounces	all-purpose flour	
2	cups	whole milk	
	to taste	kosher salt	
	to taste (lots)	black pepper	freshly ground

TRIVIA The shot at the beginning with all the Easter eggs was meant to be an homage to a shot from *Apocalypse Now*. If you know the movie, you know the one I mean. The shot was harder to do than you might think. We shot in the winter, and the only outdoor location we could find was a hot tub that was about 150°F. I had to submerge and wait for the eggs to settle, which took about 30 seconds. I nearly poached.

PROCEDURE

1. Crumble the sausage in a **10- to 12-inch cast-iron skillet**. Brown over medium heat. Remove the cooked sausage and pour off all but 2 tablespoons of the fat, making sure you leave the stuck-on bits behind.[3]
2. **Whisk** the flour into the fat in the skillet and cook over medium heat for 3 minutes.
3. Kill the heat and whisk in the milk 2 ounces at a time.
4. Return to medium-high heat and whisk occasionally while the gravy comes to a simmer and thickens, 2 to 3 minutes.
5. Crumble the cooked sausage into the gravy, season with salt, add an insane amount of pepper, and serve hot over toast or biscuits (see page 40).

NOTE: If you fry up some country ham instead of sausage and pour in black coffee rather than milk, you will have made yourself some red-eye gravy, which is an acquired taste if ever there was one.[4]

[1] I know that right now, across America, some 4,271 (conservative estimate) of these books just quietly closed, never to be opened again. Ah, the price of science.

[2] In fact, chicken fat, or schmaltz, makes a great roux.

[3] *Fond* is French for "stuck-on bits."

[4] It's called "red-eye" because of the way the reddish fat spreads out across the gravy (see also page 222).

A BOWL OF ONION

EPISODE 9 | SEASON 1 | GOOD EATS

As far as I'm concerned, French onion soup is the ultimate expression of *Allium cepa*. Thanks to the efforts of Julia Child, this humble soup rode onto the American table along with other French classics in the '60s but by the mid-'70s was considered passé. I suspect this had nothing to do with the onion per se but rather the nasty, salty, canned beef "bouillon" we poured onto it. It doesn't matter how great the onions are, if the broth isn't any good, the soup will fall flat. At the time we produced this show I was convinced that proper process could overcome bad broth, but in the years since I've started to doubt it. If you really want to do this right, use the Beefy Broth recipe from "Pressure" on page 208. It's easy to make and can be frozen for a thousand years. I'm not telling you not to use a packaged product, but the extra effort will not go wasted.

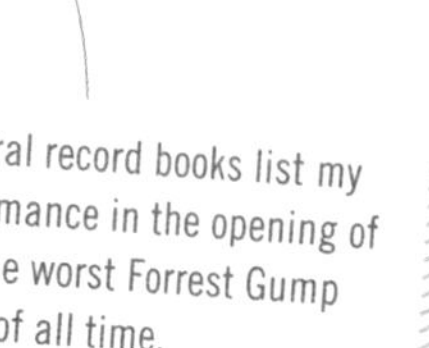

TRIVIA | Several record books list my opening performance in the opening of this show as the worst Forrest Gump impersonation of all time.

TRIVIA | My favorite scene:

KEN DOLL: Hey, Barbie.

BARBIE DOLL: Yes, Ken.

KD: I brought you flowers. (Ken offers up a bouquet garni, a tied bundle of fresh herbs including thyme and rosemary)

BD: Uh, they're ugly. *(storms off)*

KD: Jezebel.

KNOWLEDGE CONCENTRATE

Onions, along with garlic, leeks, chives, and shallots, are a member of the lily family, grown from bulbs rather than seeds. The onion's layers are actually concentric leaves called "scales."

The word *onion* stems from the Old French *oignon*, from the Latin *unionem*, which in colloquial use meant "unity." This was probably inspired by the fact that the many layers of an onion work together to form a unified whole.

There are two major divisions of globe onions: storage and fresh (also referred to as "sweet").

STORAGE onions contain a relatively small amount of water and a high concentration of the potent sulfur compounds we associate with the flavor of onion. They store well and are available all year long. Since they're so "hot" in flavor, they are usually cooked before consumption. Storage onions are typically marketed by color: red, yellow, white. Dark red varieties are typically sweeter than white.

FRESH onions have a much higher water content than storage onions and in some cases a higher sugar content. Popular varieties include Walla Wallas from Washington State, Texas Sweet 1015s from Texas, and, of course, the legendary Vidalia from Georgia. Even when refrigerated Vidalias won't keep very long.

Onions should be stored in a dry, cool, dark location like a root cellar. Ideally they should not touch one another. Some serious Vidalia fans tie individual onions in panty-hose (I'm told L'eggs® are best) and store them strung over beams and pipes in the basement.

ABOUT VIDALIAS

In 1931, farmer Mose Coleman made an interesting discovery. He noticed that some of his onion crop tasted sweet rather than hot. He harvested the onions and passed them on to family and friends, and they started planting them and replanting them until over the years a new onion known as the F1 Granix Hybrid emerged. The soil all around Vidalia contains oddly low amounts of sulfur and therefore the onions don't develop the heat of other varieties.

A federal marketing order enacted in 1989 makes it legal for onions from thirteen Georgia counties (and parts of seven others) to market their onions as "Vidalia."

TIDBIT | During the American Civil War, slices of onion were often placed on open wounds in order to keep them "sterile." Cabbage leaves have been used to the same end, though that may just be because they give good coverage.

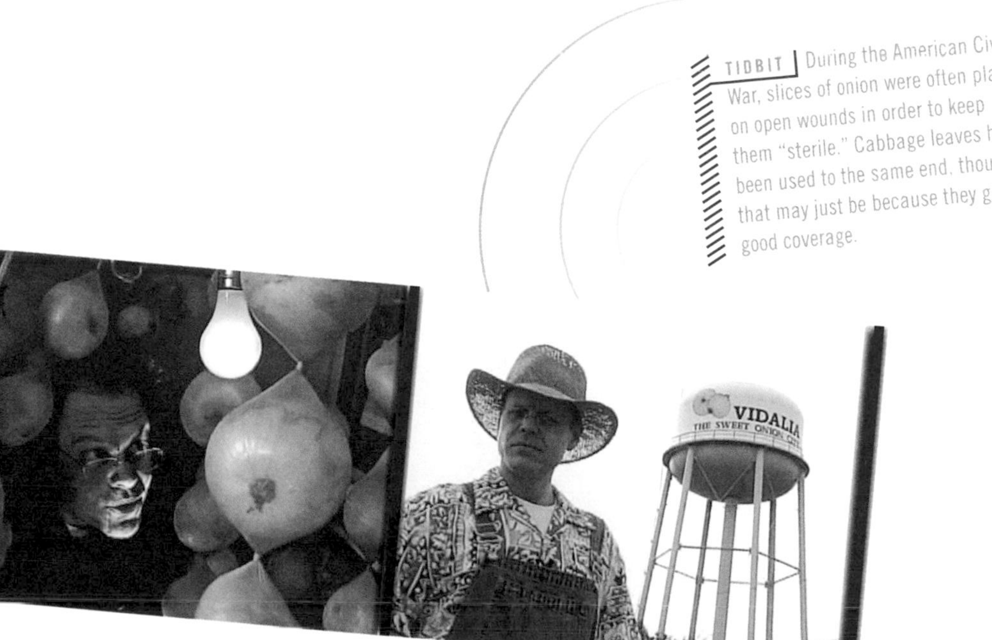

APPLICATION

FRENCH ONION SOUP

8 SERVINGS

"Frenching an Onion"

1

2

3
Use front of knuckles to guide knife

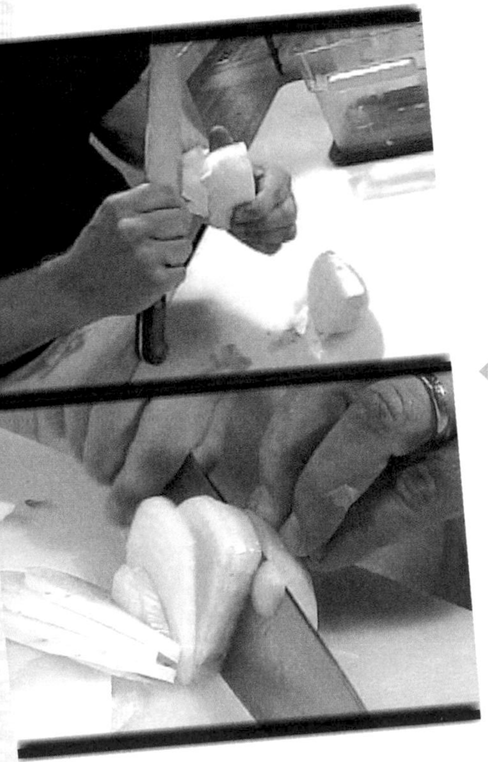

Adding a few red onions to the mix will result in a darker soup, which I happen to like.

SOFTWARE

5	pounds	sweet onions such as Vidalia	or a combination of sweet and red onions
3	tablespoons	unsalted butter	
3	teaspoons	kosher salt	divided
2	cups	white wine	such as Pinot Grigio or Sauvignon Blanc (you may need less)
3	cups	canned beef consommé (clarified beef broth) or good-quality beef broth[1]	
2	cups	chicken broth	
1		bouquet garni	2 sprigs each of thyme and parsley, and 2 bay leaves
1	loaf	country-style bread	
	to taste	black pepper	freshly ground
1	splash	Cognac	(optional, but highly recommended)
4	ounces	melting cheese such as fontina or Gruyère	grated

PROCEDURE

1. Set a **12-inch electric skillet**[2] to 250°F (or set a 4-quart sauce pan over low heat).
2. Peel the onions. Halve the onions end to end, then slice into thin half-moons.
3. Melt the butter in the skillet. Add the onions to the skillet in 3 layers, adding about 1 teaspoon of salt to the top of each addition.
4. Sweat the onions (cook them over low heat) for 15 to 20 minutes without stirring; do not let the onions sizzle or brown. Continue to cook, stirring occasionally, until the onions are dark mahogany and reduced to approximately 2 cups, 45 minutes to 1 hour.
5. Add just enough wine to cover the onions, then turn the heat to 375° (or high). Cook until the wine is reduced to a syrupy consistency, 5 to 10 minutes. Add the beef consommé, the chicken broth, and the bouquet garni. Reduce the heat and simmer for 15 to 20 more minutes.

6 Meanwhile, set an oven rack in the top third of the oven and set the broiler to high. Cut the bread into rounds that will fit into the tops of the **crocks**. (You can do this with the crocks by inverting them over the bread and pressing down, like a cookie cutter.)

7 Place the bread rounds on a **half sheet pan** and broil for about 1 minute, or until they just start to brown.

8 Season the soup with pepper and Cognac, if using. Place **8 oven-safe crocks** on a **half sheet pan** and **ladle** in the soup, leaving about 1 inch of space at the top.[3] Place the toast rounds, toasted side down, on top of the soup and top with the cheese.

9 Broil until the cheese is bubbly and golden, 1 to 2 minutes.

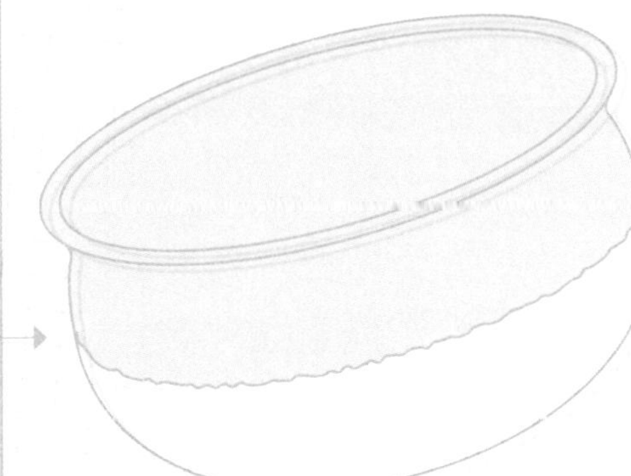

The standard two-tone brown oven-safe crocks are easy to find at restaurant supply stores.

[1] Make your own if you know what's good for you. See "Pressure," page 208.

[2] Do you absolutely have to use this tool? No. But volumetrically it's the biggest pan I have so it makes some sense.

[3] I'm kinda clumsy, so I do this by setting the pan on the open door of the oven.

[4] Here's what bugs me about Yumion: Everyone knows that once onions sprout (check out the Don King headgear) they're no good for eating.

TRIVIA | If you visit Vidalia, GA, or any of the other counties allowed by law to call their onions "Vidalias," you may catch a glimpse of "Yumion," the allium's official mascot.[4] One of our crewmen, John Crow, donned the suit this particular day.

HOOK, LINE & DINNER

EPISODE 10 | SEASON 1 | GOOD EATS

Fish flummoxes home cooks more than any other ingredient. This show set out to lay down the basics and to provide two versatile methods for dealing with almost anything with fins.

TRIVIA | The dive scene at the top of the show was filmed in the Gulf of Mexico tank at the Tennessee Aquarium in Chattanooga. I feel certain that at the time, it was the only underwater dialogue scene ever shot for a cooking show. The necklace on the sand is of course a goof on the "heart of the ocean" from *Titanic*, which was a pretty big movie back then.

KNOWLEDGE CONCENTRATE

John Huston once said that 90 percent of directing is casting. I would argue that 75 percent of fish cookery is accomplished at the fish counter. Another 20 percent goes to post-purchase handling (proper chilling cannot be overemphasized), and the final 5 percent to actual cooking. In short, if you can land quality finned goods, and keep them cold till cooking, all you have to do is not overcook them.

Keys to purchasing fish:

GET TO KNOW A FISHMONGER[1]: This is not always an easy task at the modern American megamart, where sometimes the guy behind the counter knows less than you will six pages hence. Still, if you see someone doing some skilled cutting back there, ask questions, strike up a conversation. (If you don't see fish cutting happening on the premises, then you have to ask yourself, Where is it happening? How far away from here is that, and how is the fish being handled in transit? You don't want your food moving around more than it has to.) Truly knowledgeable mongers love to talk about their product, and they take pride in it. So ask questions; in particular, ask what they would buy.

USE YOUR NOSE: That business about fresh fish having bright fish eyes and gills is only true with certain makes and models. So ask for a smell. Fresh fish will never smell "fishy." In fact, fresh king salmon smells like cucumbers to me.

BUY ON ICE: Fresh fish, whether whole or cut, must be kept on well-drained ice. If it's not directly on the ice, the metal tray it sits on must be. Without ice in the cabinet there is no fresh fish. End of story. The ice should look clean and there should be no slush. Ice: Remember that. Also ask for your purchase to be sealed in a plastic bag and then sealed in another bag containing ice.

BRING A COOLER: Think of fresh fish as a time bomb, and if that bomb gets above about 36°F . . . boom. Disaster usually strikes in the market or during transit. So bring a cooler. That way you'll also have a place to stash all your frozen foods and other chilled items (always being mindful of cross contamination, of course).

STORE IT RIGHT: Once you've got it home, cook your fish immediately and eat it on the spot. Okay, if that doesn't really work for you, refrigeration is an option but only if you bring _________ to the party. What word do you think might go in that blank? If you said "ice," then proceed with this section. If you said anything other than "ice," go back to the beginning and try again. If you really want to maximize your investment, I suggest you wrap your cuts tightly in plastic wrap and stash them in a rig like this:

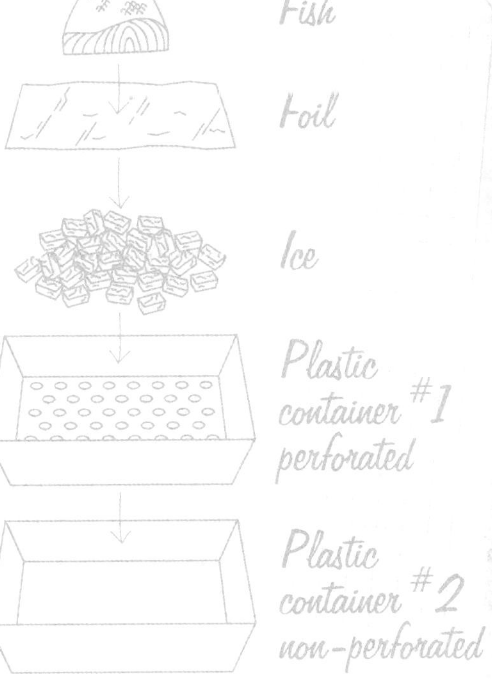

This should buy you twenty-four hours, tops. Remember what Benjamin Franklin used to say: "Fish and visitors stink in three days." Believe me, the "tastes bad" phase sets in long before the "smells bad" phase.

Different cooking methods work with different types and cuts of fish. In general:

Fish from the bass family are well suited to cooking whole because their skeletal structure is relatively straightforward and their flesh contains moderate levels of fat to help guard against overcooking and falling apart. My favorite whole fish method is the salt dome, which may also be applied to snappers, small salmon, groupers, and rockfish. (Actually I really don't like red snapper, which almost always looks better than it tastes. And man . . . those spines.)

Small, whole fillets from fresh- or saltwater fish such as brim, hake, catfish, flounder, and trout are perfect for pan-frying. A fillet is a lateral cut taken from along the longitudinal axis. It looks like this:

Steaks are usually cut from medium-size, meaty fish such as salmon and smaller halibut. Tuna steaks are usually cut from just one of the four large tubes or "loins" of meat that runs the length of the body.

Steaks, cross sections of fish cut perpendicular to the spine, are especially well suited for grilling because as with a beef steak the ends of the meat fibers face the fire (and the metal of the grill). This means that steaks tend not to stick or fall apart the way fillets so often do.

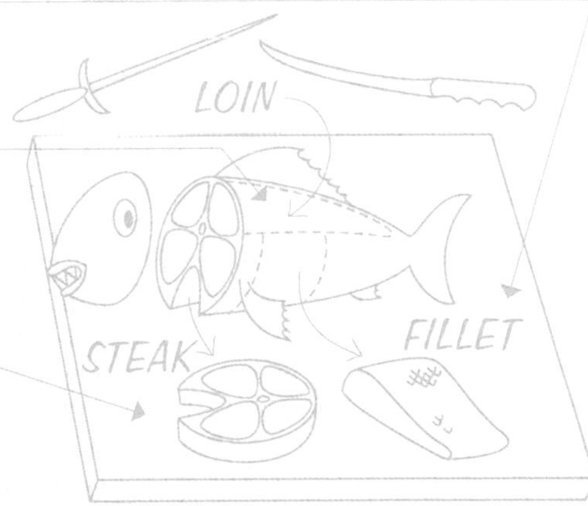

Here are some of the ways fish are sold at the market:

ROUND: Whole fish straight from the water are considered to be "in the round." Since they tend to decompose quickly, fish rarely if ever make it to market in this form.

DRAWN: Fish has had entrails, gills, and scales removed.

BONED/BONELESS: Fish has been processed to remove backbone and rib bones.

DRESSED: Fish is drawn, and the fins have also been removed (usually; there are no absolutes when it comes to fish).

APPLICATION — FISH MEUNIÈRE

1 SERVING[2]

Meunière means "in the style of the miller's wife," and in French cuisine refers to almost any fish that's dredged in flour and pan-fried. The application is for one 8- to 10-ounce trout fillet. But these ingredients would also handle two 6-ounce pieces that get crispy on the outside, moist inside, in just one take.

// SOFTWARE

1	large (about 8 ounces)	skin-on fish fillet	rainbow trout, small sockeye salmon, or brown trout
		kosher salt	
		black pepper	freshly ground
½	cup	all-purpose flour	for dredging
1	tablespoon	canola or refined (but not extra-virgin) olive oil	
2	tablespoons	unsalted butter	divided
1	tablespoon	capers	drained but not rinsed
½	medium	lemon	juiced
2	tablespoons	finely chopped parsley	(optional)

// PROCEDURE

1. Park a **12-inch skillet** or **frying pan** over medium-high heat (avoid non-stick).
2. Season flesh side of fish with salt and pepper.
3. **Dredge** fish with all-purpose flour. Tip: I add ½ cup flour per fish fillet to a **rectangular, lidded container** (plastic, glass—doesn't matter). The fish goes in one piece at a time. I add the lid and gently shake. Remove the lid, lift the fish, shake off the excess, and proceed.
4. Add oil and 1 tablespoon of butter to hot pan. The butter will melt, then foam, then turn light brown.

TIDBIT | Capers, which come in several sizes, are the unopened buds of an evergreen bush native to the Mediterranean (*capparis spinosa L*). These buds can be pickled in a liquid brine or cured in a dry salt mixture. The fruit of the caper tree, caper berries, are also pickled but are nowhere near as sharp in flavor as capers and may be eaten out of hand. Once opened, jars of either capers or the berries may be refrigerated almost until the end of time.

5 Add fish to pan, flesh side down.[3] Gently jiggle the pan to make sure there's no sticking.[4]

6 Cook until a golden crust forms on the fish (about 2 minutes). If the fat in the pan starts smoking around the edges, drop the heat a bit.

7 Using a **slotted spatula** or **fish turner**, flip the fish away from you and jiggle a little harder than before and cook another 2 minutes (or until the meat facing up starts to flake or separate).

8 Remove fish to a **plate**. Add the remaining butter to the pan and when it melts, add the capers. Fry them for 30 seconds, then kill the heat and squeeze in the lemon juice. Swirl until sauce thickens slightly (from the flour).[5]

9 Pour the sauce over the fish and garnish with parsley.

TRIVIA | The tent-bound trout meunière scene was one long single take, but what you can't see is that it's on a hill. I nearly slid out of the tent and into the pan.

This style of fish turner is also referred to as a "paltec." Although wood and metal models are common, my favorite is an all-nylon model made by Mafter.

APPLICATION

A DOME FULL OF BASS

8 SERVINGS

Make sure that the fish you plan on cooking isn't longer than the diagonal length of your biggest sheet pan. If it is, you may need to cut off the head, and that would be a shame.

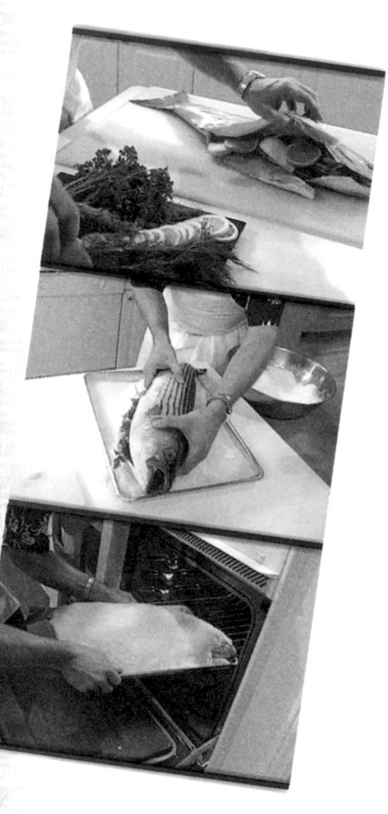

SOFTWARE

1	5- to 6-pound	striped bass	dressed (cleaned, gills removed, fins trimmed)
1	handful	fresh parsley	
1	large	fennel bulb	with partial stems, quartered
1	bunch	fresh thyme	
1	medium	lemon	thinly sliced
½	large	orange	thinly sliced
6	pounds	kosher salt	(two 3-pound boxes)
4	large	egg whites	
½	cup	H_2O	cold
		extra-virgin olive oil	for serving
		sea salt	for serving

PROCEDURE

1. Heat the oven to 450°F. Cover a **half sheet pan** with **parchment paper**.
2. Rinse the fish inside and out with cold water. Drain and pat dry. Stuff the body cavity with as much of the parsley, fennel, thyme, and citrus as it can comfortably hold.[6]
3. Combine the kosher salt, egg whites, and water in a **large mixing bowl** and work it into a paste with your hands.
4. Lay down a ½-inch-thick bed of the salt paste for the fish that's big enough to stick out an inch in every direction once the fish is laid down.

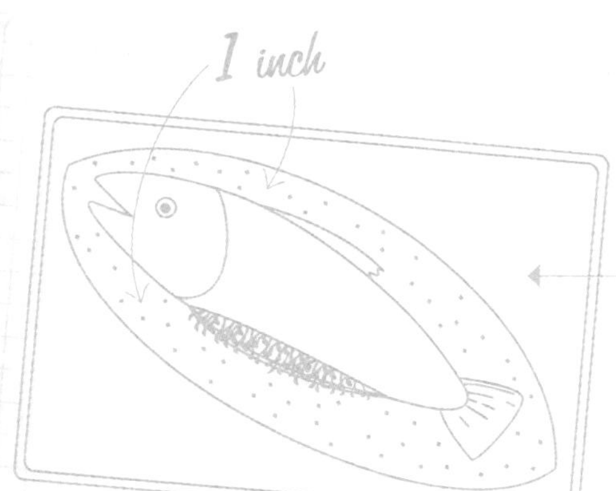

5. Lay on the fish and pile on the remaining salt paste, smoothing and mounding it to form a sealed dome approximately ½ inch thick all around. You may not use all the paste.
6. Cook for 35 minutes, or until the internal temperature reads 130°F on an **instant-read thermometer** stuck through the salt into the thickest part of the fish. Let the fish rest for 10 minutes.
7. Either transfer to a **platter** (by sliding the parchment onto the platter) or simply bring the pan to table.

8 Tap the top of the dome several times with a **small hammer,** lifting off any slabs you can get hold of. Once the fish is fully revealed (this is like archaeology, isn't it?), use a **basting brush** to sweep away any remaining salt.

9 Carefully remove the dorsal (back) fin, which should easily pull free. Use a **fish knife or serrated pie server** to make an incision all the way down the back of the fish and around the gill plate. Lift the skin off, working from the head to the tail. Remove the fillet, in pieces if necessary, from the top side of the fish. Once the top fillet is gone, grip the tail and gently pull up and forward. The skeleton should come away in one piece, revealing the fillet below. Serve the bottom fillet, leaving the skin behind.

10 Let everyone eat as you serve them, simply dipping the pieces of fish in a bit of oil and sprinkling with sea salt if needed.

[1] In this case *monger,* stemming from the old English *mangere,* or "agent." And just so you know, a costermonger is a seller of produce.

[2] Which is kind of sad, but *Good Eats* is for lonely guys. If you want to make it for two, go with slightly higher heat and double all the ingredients. If you have smaller fish—say, 5 to 6 ounces—you can cook two or even three in the 12-inch skillet.

[3] Whichever side you want up on the plate should go down first in the pan.

[4] Because the only thing that sticks worse than fish is eggs—and they stick pretty badly.

[5] There will be a fair amount of hissing and popping, which will of course distribute tiny droplets of fat all over the surfaces surrounding the cooking area. This is one of the reasons I prefer to perform this application in the out-of-doors.

[6] Truth be told, these aromatics do but subtle magic on the flavor of the meat. But upon the cracking of the dome their perfume permeates the room, and that more than justifies their presence.

TRIVIA Some of the best fish I've ever cooked and eaten was frozen at sea and kept frozen until I thawed it. What you want to avoid is double- or twice-frozen fish, which is frozen at sea, thawed at a processing plant, then frozen again. Nasty. Avoid heavily packaged frozen fish—that's a big sign the fish has been twice frozen.

NOTE: OBVIOUSLY YOU SHOULD SERVE THIS AT THE TABLE.
IT'S A PERFORMANCE!

I regret the use of such a prissy implement. Use a real hammer or mallet.

PANTRY RAID I: USE YOUR NOODLE

EPISODE 11 | SEASON 1 | GOOD EATS

When it comes to preparing pasta dishes, most Americans invest 99 percent of their budget, time, and attention to the preparation of the sauce, which makes about as much sense as putting thousand-count Egyptian cotton sheets on a bale of hay. In any pasta application, the pasta—the noodles—are the actual food. Everything else is frosting . . . metaphorically, of course. The point is, with proper care and handling, your noodles can and will provide a delicious return on very little investment if you're willing to show them a little care and respect.

"Life is a combination of magic and pasta."
////////////////////////////////////
FEDERICO FELLINI

STRINGS: vermicelli, spaghetti, capellini, fedelini

RIBBONS: linguine, fettucine, tagliatelle[1], bavette

TUBES: penne rigate, tubetti, ziti, rigatoni, tortiglioni, mostaccioli, elbows of course. (These shapes are best for heavy sauces. Penne make great mac and cheese.)

SHAPES: dischetti, fusilli, farfalle (bow ties), orecchiette (little ears), radiatore (little radiators. . .yes, radiators)

KNOWLEDGE CONCENTRATE

- There are two types of pasta, dry and fresh. This episode deals with the former. Later shows deal with the latter.

- The flours that go into pastas are usually milled from a very high protein (or "hard") wheat called durum, which can be milled into the relatively coarse semolina flour or into the much finer durum flour. It should be noted that these flours are absolutely necessary for dry pasta but not necessarily for fresh.

- If you want to get technical, the world of dry pasta breaks down into two divisions: "macaroni," which is made from semolina and water, and dry "noodles," which are made from the finer durum flour and eggs. In fact, in the United States, the term *noodle* almost always implies the presence of eggs.

- Tradition holds that adding a little oil (olive, of course) to pasta water will prevent sticking. It doesn't. But I am convinced that a little oil in the water can help to prevent boil-over. It does this by altering the surface tension in the bubbles that form on the top of the boiling water as starch is flushed off the noodles. That said, your best protection against both boil-over and sticking is to cook pasta in plenty of water—at least a gallon—in a large pot.

- On salting pasta water: Salting pasta water, while it doesn't make the water boil faster, is absolutely necessary for flavor. I use 4 teaspoons salt to 1 gallon water, a ratio that tastes about like seawater.

- On overcooking: Americans do this . . . a lot—and I'm not sure why. My suggestion is that you taste your pasta often while it cooks and be prepared to drain at a moment's notice.

- On draining: Personally, I never drain my noodles all the way, because dry noodles stick and once they're exposed to air they get gummy fast. So I always leave them a little wet, even if I'm going to dress them in nothing but oil.

- On the application of oil: When I dress noodles in olive oil, I use enough to coat them thoroughly but not so much that it pools in the bottom of the bowl. Since that's not always an easy amount to judge, I toss all the noodles I'm serving and the oil in a mixing bowl, let it just sit there for ten seconds, then dose it out. Whatever is in the bottom of the mixing bowl stays there.

- On dressing pasta: I always try to cook my sauce in a pan large enough to accommodate the noodles. I pull the noodles out of the water a little early and allow them to finish cooking in the sauce. And I always save a cup or so of the starchy pasta water just in case I need to loosen up the sauce a bit.

A FEW FUN FACTS CONCERNING BOILING WATER

- The boiling point of water is 212°F at sea level. This means that once water absorbs this much heat at this atmospheric pressure, the water molecules begin to escape the liquid phase into the vapor phase. Now, if you go below or above sea level that temperature will change, and we'll get into that a little on down the line.

- Water has a high specific heat, which means that it can absorb and give off a considerable amount of energy without actually undergoing a change in temperature.[2] After pouring energy into water (whether from flame, coil, induction, or other heat source) to get it to boil, you can actually back way off on the heat and maintain that boil. So there's no need to waste energy by continuing to pile on the coals.

- Some folks say that water boils faster if it has salt in it. It doesn't.

- Although you'll be tempted, I have to warn you against using hot tap water for cooking (see footnote 3, page 19).

TIDBIT There are approximately 360 different shapes of pasta, give or take a dozen.

APPLICATION

PLAIN OL' PASTA

4 SERVINGS

This is how to cook dried pasta, and the method can be applied to pasta cooked for just about any dish. However, when I cook pasta for a secondary application in which it will be cooked a second time (such as Mac & Cheese, page 309) I typically undercook it just a tad with the understanding that it will soak up a bit more of whatever sauce it's in.

This cooked pasta is also good in pasta salad (I'm a big fan), but contrary to most recipes, I prefer to dress the pasta while it's hot and still a bit porous, then add the bits and pieces after it cools.

TRIVIA Although he's best remembered for his work in the pickle episode, this was actually my brother BA's first *Good Eats* appearance.

SOFTWARE

1	gallon	H_2O[3]	
4	teaspoons	kosher salt	
1	pound	dried pasta	
3	tablespoons	extra-virgin olive oil[4]	
1	teaspoon	garlic	finely minced (optional)

TRIVIA My mom's in the Tupperware party scene.

SECONDARY SOFTWARE

Fresh herbs
Capers
Sun-dried tomatoes (cut into strips)
Red bell pepper
Bacon
Olives
Sautéed greens (radicchio and broccoli rabe are my favorites)
Walnuts
Hard cheeses such as Asiago or Parmesan
Soft or veined cheeses such as chèvre or Gorgonzola
Bacon
Marinated artichoke hearts
Smoked oysters
Coarsely ground black pepper
Heavy cream
Did I mention bacon?
Truffles
Anchovies
Coarse-grain mustard
Crumbled saltines
Hunger[5]
And of course . . . butter—good butter

PROCEDURE

1. Water into a **5-quart pot**. Pot on the stove. Salt in the pot. **Lid** on the pot. Bring to a boil over high heat.
2. Add the pasta. If you're using long noodles, fan them out and after 30 seconds or so use **tongs** or a **wooden spoon** to gently bend them down into the water. Don't break them to make them fit.
3. Cover, reduce the heat to medium-high, and return to a rolling boil. Remove lid and stir once a minute. Five minutes later, start tasting. Properly cooked pasta should always give some resistance to the tooth.

4 Scoop out a cup of the cooking water (just in case you need it to finish your sauce). Quickly drain in a **large colander** but don't rinse.

5 Place the oil and garlic (if using) in the bottom of a **large serving bowl**.[6] Add the pasta and toss using **tongs** to coat. Serve with any of the suggested bits and pieces.

TRIVIA This episode included footage from our first big road trip, which took us to San Francisco. The pasta shop where we shot the extrusion process is Florence Gourmet, Inc., on Stockton Street. Unfortunately, after some owner changes the shop closed in 2003.

10 MINUTES MORE — CRACKER-NOODLE-DO

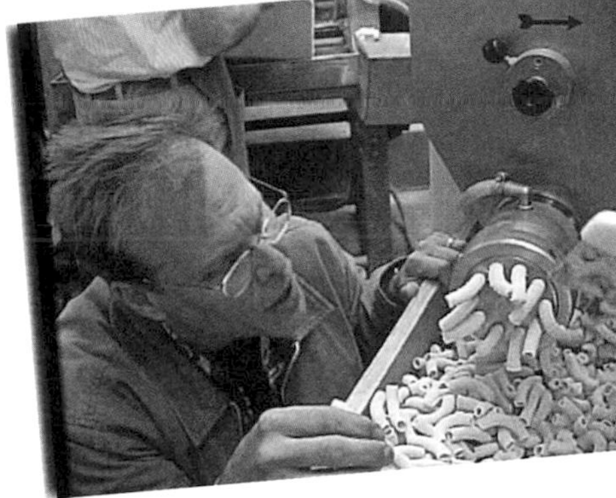

If I'd had a little more time on the show I'd have done something like this:

SOFTWARE

1	pound	dried pasta	
3	tablespoons	unsalted butter	
¼	cup	saltines	crumbled
	to taste	salt	
	to taste	black pepper	freshly ground
	handful	fresh parsley	chopped

PROCEDURE

1. Cook pasta as left (say, fettucine).
2. Heat up a **10-inch sauté pan**.
3. Add the butter.
4. Crumble in a handful of saltines.
5. Sauté until crackers brown, 3 to 4 minutes.
6. Add pasta, salt, black pepper, and chopped parsley.
7. Devour. The contrast between the crunch of the pan-fried cracker bits, the pepper, and the soft, buttery goodness of the noodles . . . Dang!

TRIVIA The outdoor "Italian" street scene with the scooter was shot just off the town square of Marietta, Georgia. At this point in my life I had yet to acquire any motorcycle skills and had never been on a scooter. As a result I lost control and almost ran into a $10,000 scenic backdrop, which I avoided by colliding with one of the giant stands that held it. Although the scooter sustained minimal damage, my right leg was black and blue for a month.

[1] Not that it matters, but handmade tagliatelle are my favorite pasta . . . just in case you were wondering.

[2] This phenomenon explains why the wind at the beach usually blows inland during the day and out to sea at night. But that's another show . . . entirely.

[3] If your tap water tastes good, go for it. If it's a little on the swimming pool side (chlorine-y), boil it for a few minutes before adding the pasta. Filtered water is fine too.

[4] Extra-virgin olive oils, which result from the first pressing of the fruit with no chemicals or heat added, can deliver an amazingly wide variety of flavors, colors, and even textures. Nowhere can these be better displayed than on pasta.

[5] As Cervantes said, "Hunger is the best sauce."

[6] Once upon a time, Americans brought salads to the table in large, wooden bowls called "salad bowls." I like them for this application.

POWER TO THE PILAF

EPISODE 12 | SEASON 1 | GOOD EATS

I've always been a huge rice fan, but like many Americans most of the grains I wolfed down during the '60s, '70s, and '80s were boil-in-the-bag converted-instant-flavorless Pablum. I think most home cooks are still unclear on rice varieties and what they can offer. As for cooking methodologies, we know the standard boil-simmer-cover maneuver and to some degree the risotto method, which we'll get to in a later episode. But the most powerful and versatile rice procedure on earth has got to be the one that results in pilaf.

TRIVIA | Back before 9/11, airlines didn't mind if you shot a scene or two on a plane as long as you didn't bother anybody. Nowadays it makes them very grumpy indeed.

TIDBIT | About half of the people on the planet fuel up on rice every day. Antarctica is the only continent where rice isn't grown.

TIDBIT | After harvest many American rice paddies convert into crawfish farms.

A GRAIN OF HISTORY

Rice cultivation began in the Kohrat region of northern Thailand around 5000 B.C. The Chinese were cultivating the sativa species by 2800 B.C. By the fourth century B.C., India was shipping rice to Greece.

Legend has it that in 1625 a storm-beaten galleon bound for Madagascar limped into Charleston harbor. A local planter lent considerable assistance to ship and crew and was rewarded by the captain with a small bag of golden seeds.[1] The soft, muddy Carolina lowlands turned out to be the perfect place to grow rice, and by the mid-1800s fifty thousand tons of Carolina Gold rice was shipping out of Charleston every year, each grain planted and harvested by slaves. After abolition, planters attempted to replace their labor force with beast and then machine, but both sank into the soil. And thus ended the era of big rice in the Carolinas.[2]

Today most U.S. rice is grown in Texas, Arkansas, and Louisiana.

KNOWLEDGE CONCENTRATE

All of the ten thousand or so varieties of rice fall into three commercial classes:

SHORT-GRAIN RICE is grown mostly in Asia (and California). When cooked, short-grain rices are sticky enough to be formed into shapes (as in sushi) or to be easily picked up with chopsticks. Short-grain rice is often called "sweet" or "glutinous" rice despite the fact that it doesn't taste sweet and contains no gluten whatsoever. What it does contain is a considerable amount of amylopectin starch, which is typically sticky stuff.

The starch coats worn by MEDIUM-GRAIN RICE, such as the famed arborio of Italy, can be coaxed right off the grain to produce the creamy sauces that make risotto and rice pudding so gosh-darned irresistible. Since the starches in medium-grain rices don't recrystallize the way they do in long-grain rices, these are the best varieties for cold applications such as rice salads.

LONG-GRAIN RICE grains are four to six times longer than they are wide, and they don't release their starch the way medium- or even short-grain rices do, which is why they can cook up so nice and fluffy. (Americans just love that.) Many long-grain varieties such as basmati and jasmine are highly aromatic, often smelling of popcorn or even fresh-baked bread.[3]

Grains of rice (which are actually the seed of the plant) are dried, then threshed from the stalk. At this point the product is called "rough" rice. A rice huller removes the chaff (or husk). Now you have brown rice, which since it still has its bran coat, takes significantly longer to cook than white rice. But that's another show. Milling removes the bran and the protein-rich germ, leaving "white" rice. At this point the grains can be enriched or parboiled for instant rice. It may also be polished with glucose or talc (though talc was banned as a rice additive in the United States in the 1980s), which whitens the grains.

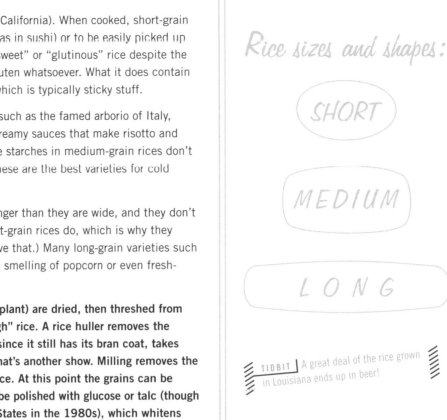

Rice sizes and shapes:

SHORT

MEDIUM

LONG

TIDBIT | A great deal of the rice grown in Louisiana ends up in beer!

TRIVIA | We shot at the International Rice Festival in Crowley, Louisiana. It's a hoot, and the food is great. If you want more info to plan your own trip, go to www.ricefestival.com. I have to say, besides rice the festival also served up the best pork cracklin's I've ever had, and there was a swell ferris wheel.

APPLICATION — RICE PILAF

6 SERVINGS

This application rescues pilaf from the bag or box with, believe it or not, a kitchen towel. The word *pilaf* comes from the Persian *pilaw*, which basically means "rice dish." Any rice dish that begins with cooking the rice in fat before adding the liquid is technically a pilaf. The power and versatility of the technique comes from the fact that it heightens the flavor of the rice and that a lot of other flavors can be brought to the party.

SOFTWARE

1	tablespoon	unsalted butter	
½	medium	onion	finely chopped
½	medium	red bell pepper	finely chopped
1½	teaspoons	kosher salt	plus 2 pinches
2	cups	long-grain white rice[4]	
1	pinch	saffron	steeped in ¼ cup hot but not boiling H_2O
2½	cups	chicken broth	
1	1-by-2-inch strip	orange zest	
2		bay leaves	
½	cup	peas	fresh or frozen
¼	cup	golden raisins	
¼	cup	pistachios	chopped

TIDBIT | The spice saffron is the threadlike stigma (female reproductive structure) of the fall-flowering crocus flour. Picked by hand, saffron has a market value of about $1,000 a pound, making it one of the most expensive foods on the planet (beluga caviar and truffles can run much higher). Luckily, a little goes a very long way. Any recipe calling for more than a pinch should be regarded with considerable suspicion. Saffron dries out easily, so I'd suggest buying it in very small batches and keeping it tightly sealed and away from bright light.

TIDBIT | Rice bran oil is becoming increasingly popular in cooking because of its neutral flavor and tolerance to high heat.

// **PROCEDURE**

1. Heat the oven to 350°F.
2. Melt the butter in a **3-quart saucier** over medium heat.
3. Stir in the onion, bell pepper, and two pinches of salt.
4. Decrease the heat to low and sweat until the onion is translucent and aromatic but not browned, 3 to 4 minutes. Then increase the heat to medium and add the rice. Cook, stirring frequently, until you smell nuts, another 3 to 4 minutes.
5. Add the saffron and its water, the broth, orange zest, bay leaves, and the remaining salt. Increase the heat and bring to a boil.
6. Okay, now the weird part: Thoroughly wet a **clean towel**, kill the heat, scatter the peas on top of the rice, then place the towel across the top of the saucier. Top with the lid, then fold the towel corners up over the lid.[5]
7. Transfer the saucier (towel and all) to the oven and bake for 15 minutes.
8. Remove and rest at room temperature for 15 minutes more without removing the lid.
9. Fish out the orange zest and bay leaves. Turn the pilaf out onto a **platter**, fluff with a **large fork**, and garnish with the raisins and pistachios and serve family-style, right in the middle of the table.

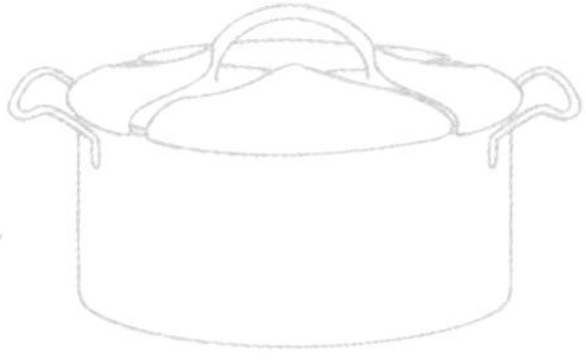

Fold towel over lid

Soak the towel with water so you don't have to worry about it catching on fire!

[1] Yes, I know this sounds a little too Jack and the Bean Stalk to be true. But I have yet to find a source that disproves the tale, so I'm going with it.

[2] Until now. Armed with new hybrid varieties, a few growers have brought rice production back to South Carolina. It's tough to find, as yields are relatively low, but it's well worth snapping up.

[3] Acetyl proline is the compound responsible for these aromas.

[4] Rice is an agricultural product, and some package instructions may call for rinsing the rice before cooking. Unless the rice looks really dusty, I'd skip it for this application.

[5] So why the towel? Two reasons: First, it helps to create a tight seal, which creates a wee bit of pressure inside the saucier, which is good, because it accelerates cooking. It also changes the dynamic of "back-drip"—that is, the way moisture circulates in the pan.

TIP | If the rice is done but still watery, drain in a colander, spread on a sheet pan, and put in a 350°F oven for 5 minutes to dry. Underdone but dry: add ½ cup hot water to the pan, replace the lid, and wait 5 minutes. If the pan is still hot, the steam produced should finish the rice. Gooey/gummy: Consider making rice pudding, or feed it to the dog.

TRIVIA | The roll-out hardware box we used to display rice varieties is not—I repeat: not—a practical rice storage vessel.

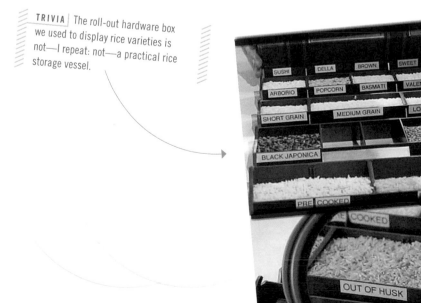

THE ART OF DARKNESS I

EPISODE 13 | SEASON 1 | GOOD EATS

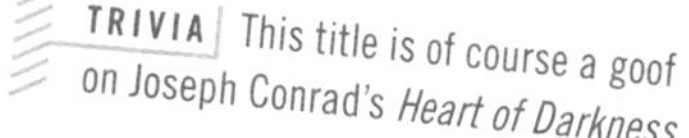

TRIVIA | This title is of course a goof on Joseph Conrad's *Heart of Darkness.*

Americans love chocolate, but we don't generally know much about it, like where it comes from, how it's made, what forms it takes, and how to handle it in the kitchen. Of course, the best thing you can do with chocolate is simply eat it, and we've got that down.

TIDBIT | Chocolate contains caffeine, theobromine, phenylethylamine, dopamines, and anandamide. And it tastes good to boot.

KNOWLEDGE CONCENTRATE

There are three types of cacao:

CRIOLLO: Soft-skinned pods, light in color, pleasant aroma. Resulting chocolate is the least bitter of chocolates. Used for 5 to 10 percent of world production.

FORASTERO: More plentiful than criollo, and easier to cultivate. The pod is thick, and the beans are quite strong in flavor. Used for 80 percent of world production.

TRINITARIO: Hybrid of criollo and forastero. Aromatic, easy to cultivate, acidic. Used for 15 percent of world production.

Making chocolate is so simple I don't know why everyone doesn't do it for themselves. Here's all you have to do:

1. Find some cacao trees (cinch). As long as the tree is happy and under canopy, it will continuously grow pods, straight out of its trunk, from the age of five years to around thirty. Each pod takes five to six months to fully ripen.

2. Harvest ripe pods. Since a tree usually bears pods in various stages of maturity, this can't be done by machine. Of course, you'll need tools such as a hook-blade knife on a long pole, which you'll use to get even the highest pods without nicking the pod or the bark of the tree. After you have a few hundred pods, hack them open with a machete and remove the pulp-covered seeds.

3. Scoop the seeds into heaps and cover them with banana leaves so that they can ferment in the tropical sun. When the seeds turn dark brown you're done . . . with this step. Then dry the seeds thoroughly, pack them into 125- to 200-pound burlap sacks, and ship them to a chocolate manufacturer halfway around the world, being sure to take a few bags home so you can continue the chocolate-making process yourself.

4. Roast the beans. As is true of coffee, you can make chocolate out of unroasted beans, but it wouldn't be worth eating. Of course, over-roasting is just as bad if not worse. Getting the temperature just right is critical.

5. Place the roasted beans in a winnowing machine, which cracks open the shells. Fans blow away the chaff. The remaining inner part of the bean is called the "nib".

6. Grind the nibs, which are composed of around 53 percent fat (cocoa butter) and 47 percent solid matter. You need to separate them, and that means crushing with heavy steel or stone disks. The resulting paste is called cocoa liquor.

7. Some of the liquor (zero booze content) goes into a twenty-five-ton hydraulic press, which squeezes the cocoa butter out.[1] Some of the cocoa butter will go back into the chocolate, but a great deal will be sold to the cosmetics industry. The remaining solids will be broken into a fine powder called cocoa powder.[2]

8. To make eating chocolate, mix some unpressed liquor with condensed milk, some sugar, various spices (vanilla, cinnamon, even cayenne pepper), and extra cocoa butter. Once it's all mixed up this mixture will be called "crumb."

9. Now you've got some more mashing to do. Sending the crumb through a series of steel rollers will break down the particles into something smoother.

10. Are you done? Are you kidding? Next this paste goes into another vat, where a massive roller sloshes, blends, and kneads the molten chocolate, driving away volatile flavor compounds, smashing any remaining particles, and blending the whole into a creamy ambrosia. This process, called "conching", can last up to a week. In fact, one of the most costly ingredients in chocolate making is the time it takes to conch. But it also explains the high quality of German and Swiss chocolates, which are typically conched far longer than American chocolates, though that is changing at boutique chocolate processors like Scharffen Berger.

11. Now the next step is the complex "tempering." You see, cocoa butter is what's called a polymorphic fat, which means that the fatty acids that make up the cocoa butter don't all melt at exactly the same point. Through careful repeated heating and cooling, the melting (and crystallization) points of these fats can be aligned so that when the chocolate cools it sets into the shiny, snappy confection we all know and love.[3]

12. Now with the chocolate in temper, you may mold your deep brown goodness into whatever shape you like, be it bar or bunny.[4] Once cooled, your chocolate is good to go. Wasn't that easy?

Chocolate is classified by the percentage of chocolate liquor it contains. Here are some terms to keep in mind when shopping:

BAKING CHOCOLATE: cocoa liquor with no sugar, milk, or flavorings

BITTER CHOCOLATE: (hard to find) 90 percent liquor

BITTERSWEET: at least 35 percent liquor

SEMISWEET: 15 to 30 percent liquor

MILK CHOCOLATE: at least 10 percent liquor and 12 percent whole milk

WHITE CHOCOLATE: no chocolate liquor and so not legally chocolate in the United States. White chocolate does contain cocoa butter, so it still comes from cacao.

TIP | A serrated knife is the perfect tool for chopping chocolate off large blocks.

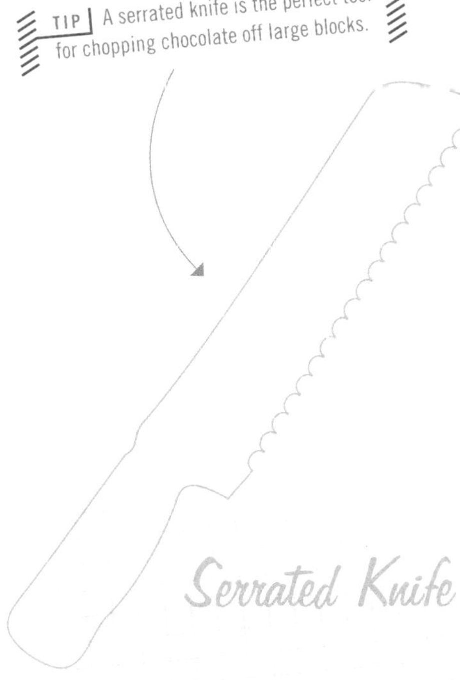

TIDBIT | Chocolate is the world's third largest export crop after sugar and coffee. Seventy percent of the world's cacao comes from Africa.

TIDBIT | The average Brit eats thirty pounds of chocolate a year. That's three times more than the average American.

APPLICATION

CHOCOLATE LAVA MUFFINS[5]

12 MUFFINS

When we made these on the show in 1999 the notion of a little cake with a molten center was still a novelty. They may be more common now, but they're still a favorite in my house: deep chocolate flavor, molten center, perfectly cakey exterior.. And yes, they really are just artfully undercooked muffins. In the show we used a hand mixer but that was an old mixer with a very strong motor. These days hand mixers are too wimpy so the stand mixer it is.

TRIVIA | This is my wife's favorite *Good Eats* recipe of all time.

SOFTWARE

8	ounces	bittersweet chocolate[6]	finely chopped
4	ounces	unsalted butter	plus 1 tablespoon for the pan
1	teaspoon	vanilla extract	
1½	ounces	all-purpose flour	
4	ounces	sugar	
2	tablespoons	natural cocoa powder	divided (not Dutch-process, see page 296)
¼	teaspoon	kosher salt	
4	large	eggs	

FOR THE SAUCE

1	cup	vanilla ice cream	
1	teaspoon	instant espresso powder	

PROCEDURE

1. Heat the oven to 375°F. Add enough **water** to the bottom of a **large saucepan** to come 1 inch up the side. Bring to a simmer.
2. Place the chocolate and 4 ounces butter in the **bowl of your stand mixer** and set over the water. It should sit about 2 inches above the water. Stir frequently with a **rubber or silicone spatula**, wiping around the sides until melted.
3. Add the vanilla and stir to combine. Remove from the heat and mount on the **mixer fitted with a paddle**. Meanwhile, set a **sifter** over a **paper plate** and add the flour, sugar, 1 tablespoon of the cocoa powder, and the salt. Sift onto the paper plate and set aside.
4. Crank the mixer to medium speed and add the eggs one at a time to the chocolate-butter mixture. Don't add the next egg until the previous one is completely absorbed. Drop the speed to low.

5 Bend the paper plate so that you can slowly add the dry mixture to the mixer. Scrape down the work bowl if necessary. When the dry goods are worked in, boost the mixer to high and beat until the batter is creamy and lightens in color, about 5 minutes.

6 Chill the batter for 30 minutes.[7]

7 Coat the bottom and sides of each cup of a standard **12-cup muffin tin** with the remaining 1 tablespoon butter. Dust with the remaining 1 tablespoon cocoa powder. Shake out the excess. Spoon the mixture into the cups using a **4-ounce disher**.[8]

8 Bake for 10 to 11 minutes. When the muffins are done, they won't be. That is, the outer crust will be firm, but a toothpick pushed into the middle will come out gooey as all getout.

9 Meanwhile, melt the ice cream in a **small saucepan**. Stir in the espresso powder.

10 Use a **small offset spatula** to carefully remove the cakes. Serve topped with the warm sauce.

11 Try not to eat them all.

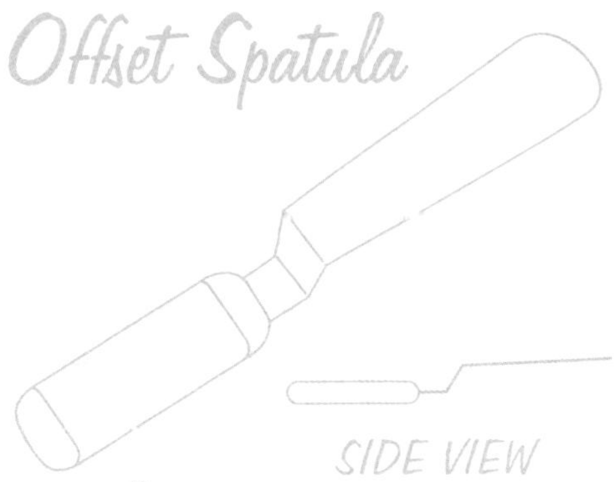

Offset Spatula

SIDE VIEW

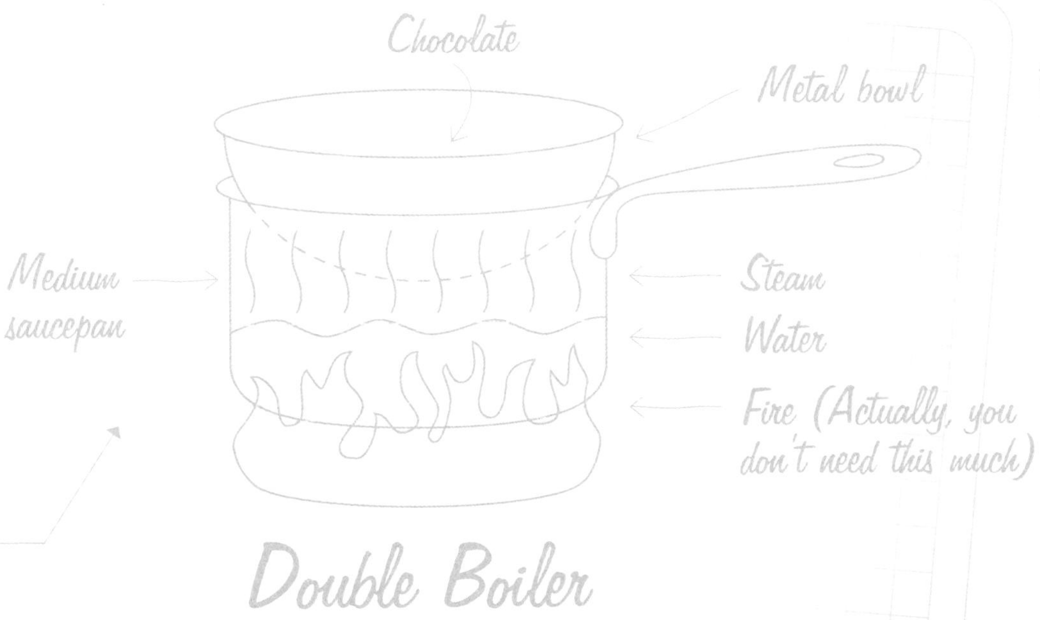

Chocolate

Metal bowl

Medium saucepan

Steam

Water

Fire (Actually, you don't need this much)

Double Boiler

TRIVIA There's a peculiar scene where I'm interviewing chocolate maker Robert Steinberg at his Scharffen Berger plant in South San Francisco. The interview's odd because the whole time we're talking I'm turned in profile to the camera, and my interviewee's eyes keep darting down and up. He was watching blood run down the left side of my face. A few minutes before, I'd been moving lights around and ran right into a cargo door that was raised to a height of about 5-foot-9, opening up a pretty nasty gash. We didn't have a first aid kit on hand, so we tried closing it up with duct tape. It didn't work too well.

Ouch

Blood!

APPLICATION — CHOCOLATE MOUSSE

8 SERVINGS

Take a handful of ingredients and two techniques, which are the basic knots of the dessert world—whipping cream and melting chocolate—put them together and you get something that is light, airy, and melts in your mouth.

TIDBIT | Me on chocolate and health: Nothing that tastes this good, this rich, and creamy and complex and dark, and mysterious and sensual, and naughty and completely and utterly satisfying can be good for you. It's a shame that modern Americans need "a mounting body of evidence . . . blah blah blah antioxidant . . . blah blah blah flavanoids . . ." to justify enjoying something. But that's just my opinion.

// SOFTWARE

12	ounces	semisweet or bittersweet chocolate	finely chopped
1	pinch	kosher salt	
3	ounces	brewed espresso or strong coffee	
1	tablespoon	dark rum	(not spiced)
2	ounces	unsalted butter	
1½	cups	heavy cream	cold, divided
1	teaspoon	unflavored gelatin	

// PROCEDURE

1. Add enough **water** to a **large saucepan** to come up the side 1 inch. Bring to a simmer over medium heat.
2. Place the chocolate, salt, coffee, rum, and butter in a **large mixing bowl** and set over the simmering water.
3. Stir occasionally until almost completely melted (pull while a couple of small pieces are still floating around in there).
4. Cool until just a bit warmer than body temperature (just touch the bowl).
5. Pour 2 ounces of the cream into a **metal 1-cup measure** and sprinkle in the gelatin. Let soak or "bloom" for 10 minutes.
6. Add the remaining cream to the **bowl of a stand mixer with whisk attachment** and beat to medium peaks.
7. Carefully heat the bloomed gelatin by swirling the measuring cup over a low gas flame. Don't boil it or the world will end.[9]

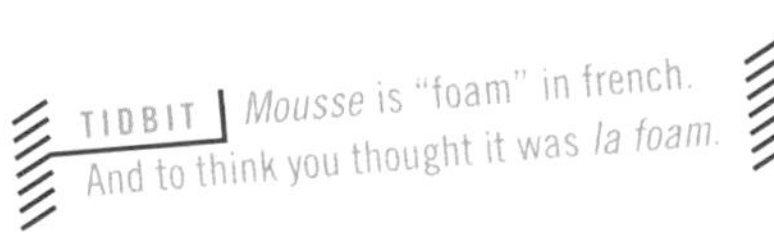

TIDBIT | *Mousse* is "foam" in french.
And to think you thought it was *la foam*.

8 Stir the cream-gelatin mixture into the cooled chocolate.

9 Stir one quarter of the whipped cream into the chocolate mixture to lighten it.

10 Fold in the rest of the whipped cream in two doses. There may be streaks of whipped cream still visible in the chocolate, and that's okay. Whatever you do, *don't over-mix the mousse*.

11 Spoon into **bowls or mugs or martini glasses** and chill for at least 1 hour. Garnish with . . . you know what? Don't garnish. Just eat. If you want to keep them refrigerated overnight, cover tightly with plastic wrap.

NOTE: Don't get water in melting chocolate or it'll seize up.

TIDBIT | The Maya started grinding cacao and frothing it with water to make a beverage somewhere between A.D. 250 and 900. The Aztecs picked up the habit around 1400, and by the time the Spanish showed up rumor has it that Montezuma II was drinking fifty goblets of chocolate a day. Maybe they were small goblets.

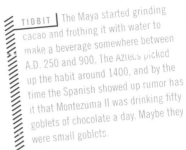

[1] In the nineteenth century Conrad Von Houten (Dutch) developed the process of pressing cacao, making powder and fat, and re-incorporating them to create a bar.

[2] More on that in Art of Darkness II, page 296.

[3] For a great example of temper, buy a Lindt chocolate Easter bunny and break off the head. Dang, is that snappy!

[4] I collect antique Easter-bunny molds that look like little rabbit iron maidens (maniacal laughter).

[5] Please note that this batter contains eggs, and when finished the interior of the muffins may not reach a temperature considered by the U.S. government to be sufficient to kill salmonella. If you're concerned, consider using pasteurized shell eggs.

[6] This application originally called for plain old chocolate chips, because at the time good-quality dark chocolate wasn't easy to find in the average megamart.

[7] The key to the molten interior.

[8] The very same spring-loaded scoop wielded so effectively by lunch ladies all over America.

[9] Okay, that's not true. But the gelatin could be damaged, and that would be bad.

TRIVIA | We learned of two cacao trees within driving distance of us. The one at the Atlanta Botanical Gardens had pods on it, but it was runty and sad. The specimen at the Georgia Botanical Gardens in Athens was tall and full and proud. But it had no pods. So we got someone to ship some pods in from Costa Rica and used florist wire to connect them to the tree. I'm not exactly sure how we got raw agricultural product from a foreign country into this one, and I don't want to know. But I am thankful that we didn't have to fall back to plan B, which called for the deployment of craftily modified Nerf footballs.

MEDIUM PEAKS

Twin Beater

STIFF PEAKS

Single Beater

ROMANCING THE BIRD

EPISODE 14 | SEASON 2 | GOOD EATS

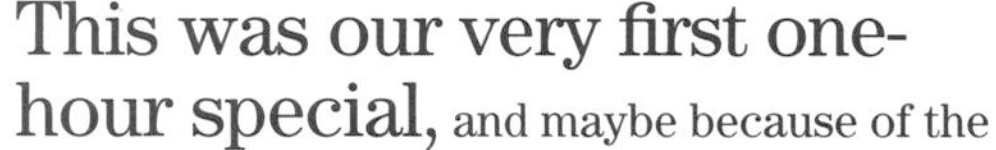

This was our very first one-hour special, and maybe because of the fact that it's full of strangeness (turkey trucks, transvestites, science-fiction rip-offs) it's become something of a cult classic. I had two goals here: I really wanted to set the record straight on Thanksgiving history while also getting to what I think of as the perfect turkey. That is, a turkey that tastes like what we all think turkey tastes like although it rarely does. Our answer was to go with a brine, which back in '99 was considered an obscure procedure. This episode also brought quite a few characters to the party.

As for real people, Deb Duchon returned to play herself in a history scene, which was blatantly ripped from *The Matrix*. Shirley Corriher dropped by to give us a science lesson on brining in which we employed our newest slapped-together prop, the Mystery Food Science Theater 3000, a thinly veiled homage to the *Mystery Science Theater* series. The rest of the dialogue was inspired by *Seinfeld* and *Monty Python*.

Note: I'm pretty sure this episode was the first program in Food Network history to feature a man in drag.

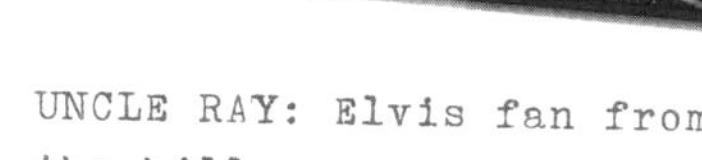

UNCLE RAY: Elvis fan from the hills

AUNT VERA: Uncle Ray in drag

UNCLE MORTIE: Stratalounger owner/operator

SISTER MARSHA[1]: Martha Stewart wannabe

CHUCK: Neighbor and turkey enthusiast

THE STRANGER: Historic figure of tragedy[2]

TURKEY FACTS TO KNOW AND TELL

All poultry is inspected for wholesomeness, but grading is voluntary.

GRADE A
The highest quality and, generally speaking, the only birds you'll see at the ol' megamart. This is the Norman Rockwell turkey.

GRADES B AND C
Most end up in "processed" foods. You can occasionally find them in "warehouse" markets, but when you get them unwrapped they usually look like they've been hit by a truck. That said, if you're making sausage, this might be the bird for you.

HERITAGE
Turkey varieties that were common before the broad-breasted white took over the world. The Bourbon Red and the Narragansett are good examples. Heritage birds are shaped like natural birds rather than engineered breast bombs.

FREE RANGE OR FREE ROAMING
Birds must be given access to outdoors.

YOUNG
Turkeys less than eight months old. Although they're not quite as flavorful as more senior birds, they are considerably more tender.

TOM
Larger then hens, but they taste the same.

"SELF-BASTING"
Birds that have been injected with a cocktail of fat, broth, water, spices, etc. Technically these birds can be considered prebrined, but with what, I ask you. And since they're significantly heavier than noninjected birds, you are paying more to have someone else do what you can do better yourself.

KNOWLEDGE CONCENTRATE

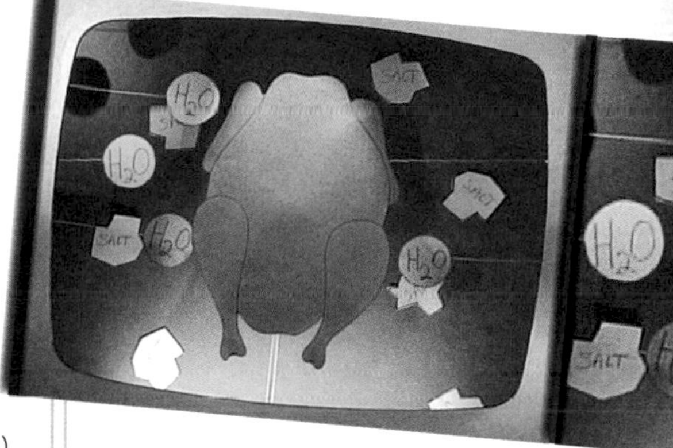

So what's with this brining business? Growing up, I came to treat a big slice of Thanksgiving turkey as a trencher, a plate on which other stuff that I actually wanted to eat was placed. Cranberry sauce, congealed salad, green bean casserole, and mashed potatoes with gravy all sat upon the turkey slice, which I ate only if I was really hungry. Around 1996 I started playing with the concept of brining—that is, soaking meats in salt solutions in order to render them more tender and tastier. This is made possible by the fact that nature likes systems that balance.

When you sink your bird in a brine you, dear cook, have created an imbalance. Inside the flesh of the bird is water and a variety of dissolved solids. Outside the bird, there's even more water and a much higher concentration of dissolved solids. In the eyes of nature this just won't do. The water moves from the area of higher concentration (the brine) to the area of lower concentration (the turkey) via a process called osmosis. The dissolved solids move from the brine to the turkey via diffusion. Given time, the turkey will absorb a considerable amount of moisture and dissolved salt and sugar. And that's a big deal because when salt and water mingle up with proteins in the meat, some of those tight, wound-up protein structures unwind, or denature. When this happens they trap much of the extra liquid that's been loaded into the cells. When the meat cooks, moisture and flavor are trapped inside. This doesn't mean my mother-in-law can roast her birds for twelve hours without turning them into cinders, but it does give the cook a bit of leeway.

When it comes to turkey, Stuffing Is Evil. That's because stuffing goes into the middle of the bird and is extremely porous. That means that as the turkey around it cooks, juices that may contain salmonella bacteria soak into the stuffing, which then must be cooked to a minimum of 165°F in order to be safe. Getting the stuffing to this temperature usually means overcooking the turkey. The way I see it, cooking stuffing inside a turkey turns the turkey into a rather costly seal-a-meal bag. If you're a stuffing fan, I suggest cooking it separately (in which case it's "dressing," not stuffing) and inserting it into the bird while it rests. Odds are no one will notice the difference.

Oh, and while we're on the subject of evil, let's talk basting. Some folks say it makes meat moister. Think about that a second. What's skin meant to do? Keep what's out, out. I don't care how much oil/butter/drippings you paint on, it's like showering in a raincoat. Sure, you'll have a tasty, mahogany coating on that bird, but at a terrible cost. You see, every time you open that door to paint your bird, you let heat out. And that does nothing but increase the cooking time, which does nothing but dry the bird out. So, stuffing may be evil, but basting is über evil.

CARVER

SLICER

TIP In the episode we featured a $15 electric knife from a hardware store, which I still hold to be the finest turkey-carving tool around. However, if you wish to carve old school, do try an actual carving knife rather than a slicer. A slicer looks like this:

while a carver looks like this:

The curved tip of the carver makes for smooth, clean slices. And I arm the other hand with spring-loaded tongs rather than a carving fork.

TRIVIA This episode was shot during the unbearably hot summer of 1999. I had a nasty gash on my head from running head-first into a porch light, and the makeup kept sliding off in the 100-degree heat.

TIDBIT Turkey was the first meal eaten on the moon.

APPLICATION

GOOD EATS ROAST TURKEY[3]

AT LEAST 10 TO 12 SERVINGS

If you really want a flavorful turkey with juicy white and dark meats it's going to take a little time . . . but it's worth it.

SOFTWARE

FOR BRINING

1	14- to 16-pound	frozen[4] natural, young turkey	
1	gallon	vegetable broth	homemade or canned
1	cup	kosher salt	
½	cup	brown sugar	packed, light or dark
1	tablespoon	black peppercorns	
1½	teaspoons	allspice berries	
1½	tablespoons	candied ginger	chopped
1	gallon	H_2O	iced

FOR ROASTING

1		red apple	quartered
½		onion	quartered
1	stick	cinnamon	
1	cup	H_2O	
4	sprigs	rosemary	
6	leaves	sage	
		canola oil	

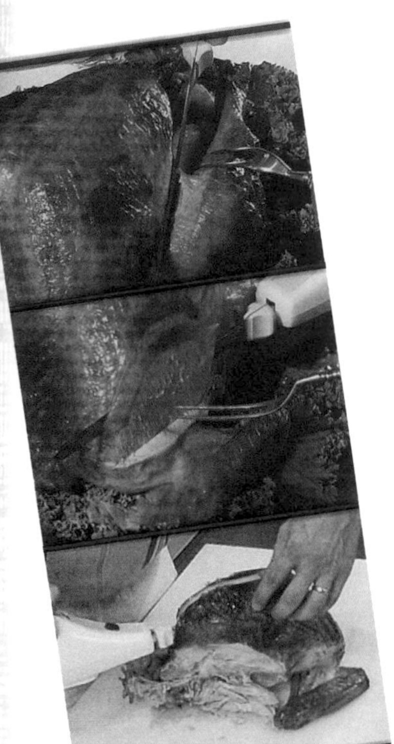

TIP Although the romantic vision is of breast slices coming off the turkey right at the table, I would argue that slices cut against the grain of the meat have shorter fibers and are therefore more tender. Producing such cuts requires that the breast lobe (all the breast meat to one side of the keel bone) be removed in one hunk then moved to the board for slicing.

PROCEDURE

1. Two to three days before roasting, thaw the turkey in the refrigerator or in a **cooler** kept at 38°F, tops.
2. Combine the broth, salt, sugar, peppercorns, allspice, and ginger in a **large stockpot** and bring to a boil over medium-high heat. Stir until the salt and sugar dissolve. Remove from the heat. Cool to room temperature, then refrigerate the brine.
3. The eve before roasting, combine the brine and iced water in a **cooler**. Place the thawed turkey (guts, neck, and whatnot removed) breast side down in the brine. Seal up the cooler and use it as an ottoman. Target brine time: 12 hours; flip the bird once about halfway through.
4. Roasting day: Heat the oven to 500°F.
5. Remove the bird from the brine and rinse inside and out. Discard brine.

6 Place the bird on a **roasting rack** and place inside a **roasting pan**. Pat the bird dry (inside and out) with **paper towels**.

7 Combine the apple, onion, cinnamon, and water in a **microwave-safe bowl**. Microwave on high for 5 minutes. Add to the turkey's cavity, along with the rosemary and sage. Truss, if you like.

8 Lightly coat the bird with canola oil. Roast the bird on the lowest rack of the oven for 30 minutes.

9 Insert a **probe thermometer** into the thickest part of the breast and reduce the oven temperature to 350°F.

10 Roast until the thermometer registers 155°F, about 2½ hours.

11 Remove from the oven, cover loosely with **aluminum foil**, and let rest for at least 15 minutes before carving.

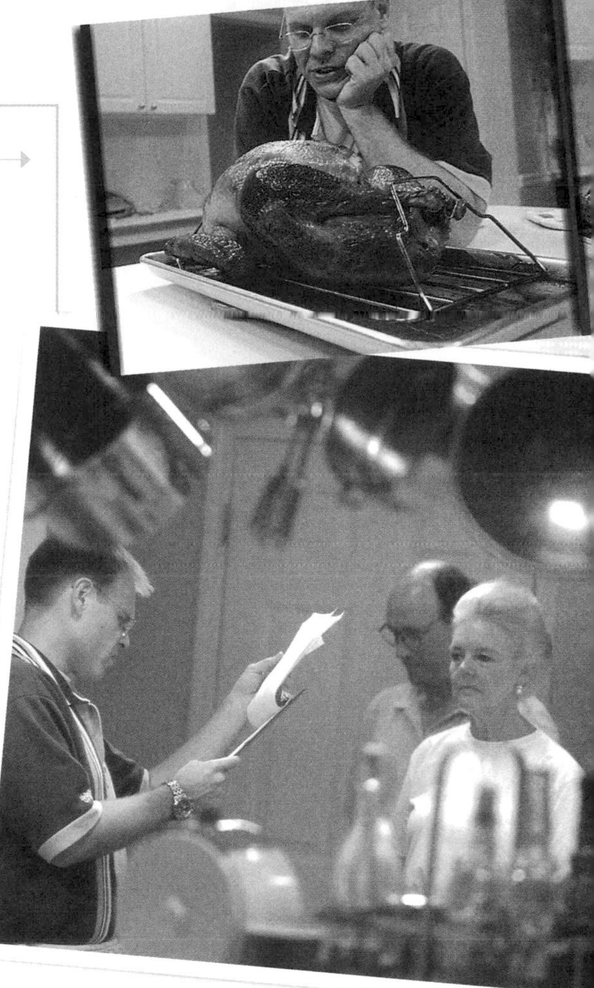

[1] Just to set the record straight, I don't have a sister. But if I did, well, this would be the worse-case scenario.

[2] To the best of my knowledge I've only died twice on *Good Eats*, once as "the Stranger" who chokes to death, then again as myself, by heart attack, in "The Other Red Meat." Although I've not researched it, I feel quite certain that these are the only instances in food television history in which characters have died on screen.

[3] Nobel Prize pending.

[4] The way I figure it, frozen birds take shipping and handling better than fresh birds.

[5] To English tastes, cranberries were far too bitter to consume without sugar, and by all accounts the settlers' sugar was long gone.

A FEW FUN THANKSGIVING FACTS

The historical event most of us think of as the "first" Thanksgiving took place sometime between late September and early October 1621, near Plymouth, Massachusetts. Only two firsthand accounts of the three-day event survive, and mention is made of many fowl (including turkeys) and five deer. However, there is no mention of sweet potatoes with marshmallows, no whipped potatoes, no congealed salad, and no cranberry sauce.[5] To make matters worse, there were no pies. Ninety percent of American households have turkey on Thanksgiving, but if you're interested in preparing an "authentic" Thanksgiving, consider serving one or more of the following as well:

Goose
Swan
Venison
Lobster
Oysters
Cod
Bass
Eels
Pumpkin
Purslane
Dried gooseberries
Chestnuts

If you're a Thanksgiving fan, you have not a president or congressman but a Philadelphia magazine editor named Sarah Hale to thank. Unsettled by the anonymous mechanizations of the Industrial Revolution, Mrs. Hale got it in her head that what Americans needed was a day that focused on hearth, home, and family values. Hale started a letter-writing campaign that lasted some forty years. President Lincoln himself received so much "Hale Mail" that he finally broke down and proclaimed the last Thursday in November as Thanksgiving.

In 1939, hoping to boost the depressed economy by extending the Christmas shopping season, Franklin D. Roosevelt proclaimed a day of "thanksgiving" for the second-to-last Thursday in November. Some states went along and some didn't. Some, like Texas, took both days. Finally, in 1941 Congress took action and passed a bill that legally placed Thanksgiving on the fourth Thursday in November, which means that sometimes it's the last and sometimes the next-to-last Thursday in the month.

I used to smoke cigars. I gave it up.

TIDBIT | Once upon a time in America, fruitcakes were cooked in fruitcake ovens. These large metal (usually tin) cabinets had water reservoirs on the bottom and multiple racks for cakes. When positioned on top of a wood burning oven or other heat element, the water simmered, creating steam, which slowly cooked the cakes with moist heat. There was even a refill tube that allowed water to be added without opening the door. If we all had one of these, fruitcake would still be king.

Everyone thought I was crazy. Good eats: fruitcake? Isn't that a contradiction in terms? How can the most dreaded of comestible regifts be rendered not only edible but enjoyable? I admit that up to this point in time I had never, ever tasted a fruitcake that I liked . . . or could stand, and I never would have thought such a thing existed. But then I read Truman Capote's excellent *Christmas Memory*, a memoir of poor rural life in the South centered around the production of fruitcakes, which turns out to be a considerable undertaking. I finished the tale and dove into research that revealed there was indeed a time when fruitcakes were not dense, stinky bricks full of fruit of unnatural origin but rather cherished and quite desirable acts of cookery love. I set out to re-create that which had been sullied.

KNOWLEDGE CONCENTRATE

- To qualify as a fruitcake there must be: cake, nuts, dried fruits, and spices.
- Few things can upgrade the flavor of a fruitcake like quality spices. Problem is the FDA doesn't require shelf life information to be printed on megamart ground spices. More times than not, they taste like dust, which is why I buy whole spices from reputable Internet sources.
- Most dried fruits, especially those with yellow or orange flesh, are usually treated with sulfides, which stabilize the color and stave off microbial attack. Some people suffer allergic responses to sulfides. If you want to avoid them, check the ingredient list.

TIDBIT | Pecans are members of the hickory family. They are not nuts but "drupes"—that is, a fleshy fruit containing a shell-encased seed or cotyledon. Other drupes include mangoes, peaches, cherries, and walnuts. Unshelled nuts and drupes can be sealed in zip-top bags and frozen for up to twelve months. Shelled nuts packaged in the same manner will keep for four months.

A FEW FUN FRUITCAKE FACTS TO KNOW AND TELL

- In ancient Egypt, fruit-laden breads were often buried with the dead.[1]
- The Romans packed pomegranates, raisins, and pine nuts into a light golden cake known today as pan forte.
- American fruitcake descends from the Old English plum pudding, which was a boiled or steamed cake cooked with fruit—*plum* being pretty much synonymous with *fruit* at the time.
- Traditionally, fruitcakes are wrapped in alcohol-soaked cloth and stored for months to "ripen."
- Today Panettone is the Italian version of "crusade cake."
- In the Middle Ages, knights destined for the crusades were often sent off with small cakes, dense with fruit (energy) and soaked with liquor (preservative). One could think of fruitcakes as medieval power bars.
- A group of Trappist monks in Arkansas earn their living making fruitcakes. They used to make concrete blocks.
- An Italian legend holds that once upon a time a nun was cooking a cake and just to be mean the devil appeared in the form of a black cat and knocked a shelf of expensive spices into the batter. Instead of throwing the cake with its expensive payload out, the nun baked it.

This orchard is in Vienna, GA.

TIDBIT | Marinate: to soak meat in a flavorful liquid. Macerate: to soak fruit in a flavorful liquid.

APPLICATION

FREE-RANGE FRUITCAKE[2]

1 CAKE; 10 TO 12 SLICES

The goal here is to free fruitcake from its reputation as a Holiday Horror. Notice, please, that there is no "candied" fruit in this recipe. Please be careful to keep it that way. The acquisition of quality ingredients is half the battle. Make that four-fifths of the battle. A fruitcake is only as good as its ingredients.

TIDBIT Golden raisins are made from Thompson seedless grapes like regular raisins, but they're not left to darken on the vine. And here's a nasty nomenclatural conflict: Unlike true currants, which are kin to the gooseberry, the currants used here are actually dried tiny Zante grapes.

SOFTWARE

4½	ounces	golden raisins	dark raisins will not taste the same
4	ounces	currants	
2½	ounces	dried cranberries	
2½	ounces	dried blueberries	
2½	ounces	dried cherries	
4	ounces	dried apricots	chopped, try to find whole without sulfates
1		lemon	zest only, chopped
1		orange	zest only, chopped
1½	ounces	candied ginger[3]	chopped
1	cup	gold rum[4]	dark works too
4		cloves	
6		allspice berries	they look like peppercorns only bigger and smoother
½		cinnamon stick	
8	ounces	sugar	
5	ounces	unsalted butter	
1	cup	unfiltered apple juice	in some parts of the country this is called cider
1	teaspoon	ground ginger	dry not fresh
9	ounces	all-purpose flour	
1½	teaspoons	kosher salt	
1	teaspoon	baking soda	
1	teaspoon	baking powder	
2	large	eggs	
3	ounces	pecans	toasted and roughly chopped
¼	cup	brandy	the cheap stuff, put in a **spritz bottle**

// **PROCEDURE**

1. Combine the first 10 ingredients in a **plastic storage container**.
2. Cover and macerate overnight at room temperature.
3. The next day, load up a **coffee grinder** or **spice mill** with the cloves, allspice, and cinnamon and grind to a fine powder.
4. Put the spices, along with the macerated fruit (and liquid), in a **large saucepan**. Add the sugar, butter, apple juice, and ginger.
5. Bring to a boil, stirring often, then reduce the heat and simmer for 10 minutes.
6. Remove from the heat and cool for at least 15 minutes. (At this point you can either complete the batter or cover and refrigerate for up to 2 days, which is what I usually do.)
7. Place oven racks in the center and bottom of the oven. Place a **roasting pan** on the bottom rack and fill halfway with warm water. Crank the oven to 325°F.
8. Put the flour, salt, baking soda, and baking powder in a **sifter** and sift onto the fruit mixture in the saucepan, bringing the batter together as quickly as possible with a **large wooden spoon**.
9. One at a time, stir in the eggs. Finally, fold in the pecans.
10. Spoon the resulting goo into a **10-inch nonstick loaf pan** and bake for 1 hour, or until the interior hits 200°F on an **instant-read thermometer**.
11. Remove to a **cooling rack or trivet**. Spritz the top with brandy[5] and cool completely.
12. Wrap the cake in a few layers of **cheesecloth**, spritz with more brandy, and stash in a **tin** or any other airtight, food safe containment vessel.
13. Every 2 to 3 days, feel the cake and, if dry, hit with more brandy. The cake's flavor and texture will continue to improve over the next 2 weeks.[6]
14. Devour or gift to a very lucky recipient indeed.

TIP | When facing an application with a lot of dosing of ingredients, it really helps to have a digital scale with a tare or "zero" function. Start by turning on the scale and making sure it's set to ounces (unless you want to do the math and work in metric). Place the container on the scale and zero it out. Start weighing ingredients into the container, zeroing out each addition all the way through the rum. As long as you remember to hit that tare button, this method will be fast and dead-on accurate.

[1] I realize this could simply be a method of stealthy disposal, but perhaps they really were valued.

[2] Yes, all the ingredients were given access to the outdoors.

[3] You may find this labeled "crystallized" ginger—same thing. Most of it comes from Australia.

[4] Good rum is basically light rum that has been aged in wood.

[5] I assume we all keep small spritz bottles, the pump trigger type, loaded with either brandy or bourbon at all time, right?

[6] Truth be told, I think it improves over the next 2 months.

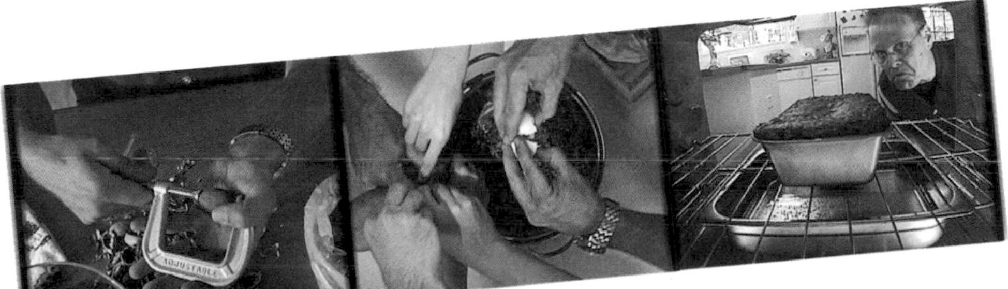

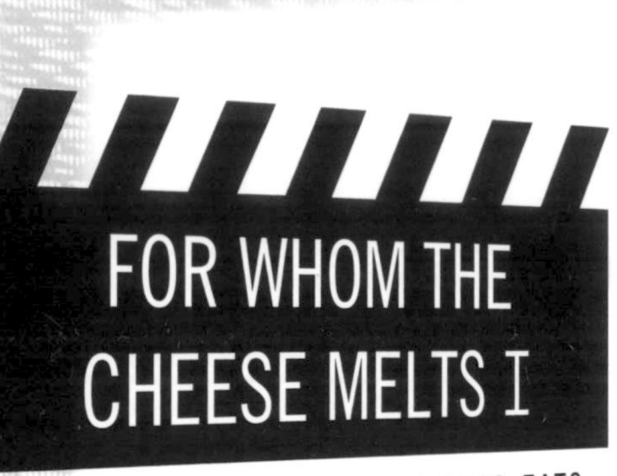

FOR WHOM THE CHEESE MELTS I

EPISODE 16 | SEASON 2 | GOOD EATS

TRIVIA This title is as close to Hemingway as I'm ever likely to get.

"Never commit yourself to a cheese without having examined it first."
//////////////////////////////////
T. S. ELIOT

Our first cheese episode focused on the basics of cheese making. Although one of my favorite *Good Eats* applications of all time, the Big Cheese Squeeze, is included, the show really was less about cooking and more about appreciation.

TRIVIA In case you're wondering: 237 mousetraps.

My favorite rotary cheese grater.

My favorite micrograter.

KNOWLEDGE CONCENTRATE

Although variations abound, most cheese making involves seven steps:

1. COAGULATION: There are two types of protein in milk: casein and whey. The casein is packaged inside little capsules. The first step of cheese making is making these capsules stick together, which is tough because the capsules have a kind of hairy coat on them that keeps them apart. And they're repelled by an electrical charge. The coat can be removed with the addition of rennet, an enzyme taken from the fourth (abomasum) stomach of ruminant animals. Also, the addition of certain bacteria creates lactic acid, which changes the electrical charge. Depending on the style of cheese and the milk being used, rennet and bacterial cultures can be used independently or in tandem to coagulate the milk into a semisolid gel.

2. CUTTING: The curd is cut into small pieces to help expel the whey-laden water. Dry cheeses have more whey removed; moist cheeses, less. Cheddar cheese, for example, starts out with a moisture content of around 87 percent but is reduced down to 37 percent.

3. COOKING: The curds are heated and stirred, which expels more whey. The harder the cheese, the higher the temperature and more extensive the stirring.

4. DRAINING/KNITTING: The curds are left to drain for a specific amount of time. During this process the caseins begin to "knit" together, creating a solid mass.

5. PRESSING: Weight is applied to the young cheese. Often this is done in a mold that gives the cheese its final shape. The amount of weight and length of time depends on the kind of cheese that's desired.

6. SALTING: Salt can be introduced by sprinkling or rubbing it on the cheese or by submerging the cheese in a brine. Not only does this flavor the cheese, it aids in preservation and of course pulls out even more moisture.[1]

7. AGING: Cheese may be aged for hours or years. Sometimes molds and other bacteria are added. Some cheeses, such as Roquefort, are defined by their aging in special caves where naturally occurring molds go to work on the cheese.

Choosing a cheese grater depends on the type of cheese. Rotary or crank graters and micro-graters are well suited to hard cheeses like Parmesan, while traditional box graters are better suited to softer cheeses like provolone or fontina. When it comes to a box grater, weight and stability should be the main concerns—and of course blade sharpness. Unfortunately, the perfect box grater has yet to hit the market.

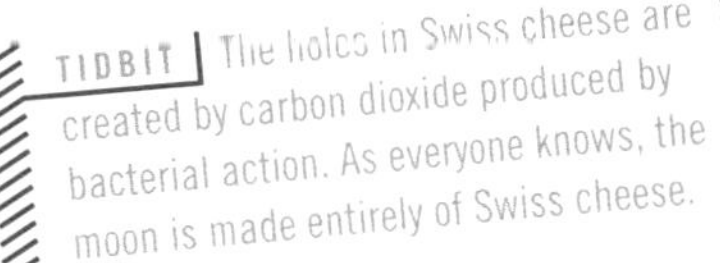

TIDBIT | The holes in Swiss cheese are created by carbon dioxide produced by bacterial action. As everyone knows, the moon is made entirely of Swiss cheese.

TIDBIT | The United States leads global cheese production, at 6.8 billion pounds a year, all of which the French find inedible.

A FEW MORSELS OF CHEESY HISTORY

- The word *cheese* comes from the Latin *caseus*, from which we also get *casein* and *queso*.
- It's believed that cheese making began shortly after the domestication of sheep around 8000 B.C. It was no doubt an accidental discovery that came about when milk was stored in "skins" made from the stomachs of young animals. (We're talking pre-pre-Tupperware here.)
- By Roman times cheese making was an established craft, with hundreds of regional styles being manufactured.
- The first commercial cheese factory opened in Switzerland in 1851. Up until then, cheese was a cottage industry.

APPLICATION

BIG CHEESE SQUEEZE

1 SIMPLE, PERFECT SANDWICH

There are times when our appetites should be free to comfort us without having to bow to the censorship of our culinary consciousness. What could possibly get us through the winters of our discontent better than the warm embrace of melted cheese nestled between perfectly crisped bread. That's right: Nothing.

I like to use a mixture of semihard and semisoft cheeses here. My favorite duo is equal portions of smoked Gouda and Gruyère. Fontina and Asiago are good too. Could you use one by itself? Sure, but working with combinations will give you the best marriage of flavor and texture. But hey, at 3 A.M., sharp cheddar will do just fine.

TRIVIA | The sandwich scene takes place in the middle of the night, and it is an honest reenactment of my first foray into the two-skillet method of replicating a panini press, which I didn't own at the time. Now that I do have a panini press, I still use the two skillets because I swear it makes a better sandwich. I suspect this is because unlike the press, the pans start very hot but cool while the sandwich is inside.

SOFTWARE

2	slices	hearty country bread[2]	whole wheat or white
1	teaspoon	smooth Dijon mustard	
3	ounces	cheese	grated
	to taste	black pepper	freshly ground
1	ounce	unsalted butter	clarified[3]

PROCEDURE

1. Place **two 10-inch cast-iron skillets** over high heat for 5 minutes.
2. Meanwhile, spread the mustard on one slice of bread. Distribute the cheese evenly over the mustard, season with pepper, and top with the second slice of bread.[4]
3. Brush the bread surface that's looking up at you with the clarified butter. Go for even coverage, but don't soak the bread or it won't brown.
4. When the pans are hot, kill the heat and place the sandwich, top side down, in the middle of skillet #1. **Brush** the newly exposed bread face with butter and lay the bottom of skillet #2 right down on top of the sandwich.
5. Wait. In 3 to 5 minutes you will hear the sizzle of melted cheese oozing out into the pan. (If you don't, you went skimpy with the cheese.)
6. Gently remove the top skillet and use a **flat metal spatula** to remove the sandwich to a waiting **cutting board** and wait 60 seconds. You will be hungry, so at this time you may want to examine skillet number 1 for toasty little bits of cheese, which you can hungrily devour. When 60 seconds is up you may wish to cut the sandwich in half with a **serrated knife**. It won't make the sandwich taste any better, but there's something about biting into that cut side that's very satisfying.

APPLICATION

PIMENTO CHEESE

1 PINT

I love pimento and cheese sandwiches, cold, hot, in a box with a fox with a goat in a . . . well, you get the point. The problem is, there is something about jarred, processed pimentos that does not agree with my stomach a bit. I get around this digestive peccadillo by roasting red bell peppers, which actually bring even more flavor to the party.

Roasting a whole bell pepper is actually easier done right on a gas burner because you can turn it more readily; if you don't have a gas stove, use the broiler method below.

My cheese cutter made from two 3" diameter key migs (janitor issue) and a guitar B string. Also works for discreet mob hits.

SOFTWARE

1	medium	red pepper	
4	ounces	cream cheese	at room temperature
2	tablespoons	mayonnaise	homemade shines here, but Duke's makes a fine substitute
¼	teaspoon	red pepper flakes	
	to taste	black pepper	freshly ground
	pinch	kosher salt	
8	ounces	sharp cheddar cheese	grated

TIDBIT The best melting cheeses contain at least 40 percent fat. Keep in mind, though, that fat in cheese is calculated as a percentage of dry solids. Since such cheeses are usually half water, you're really talking 20 to 25 percent fat.

TIP "Real" cheese has a considerable amount of life left in it. Even as you slice it on your board, bacteria continue to munch, enzymes are catalyzing, mold is growing. This is why cheese that isn't allowed to breathe, even during storage, gets nasty and funky fast. Cheese should be consumed as soon as possible after purchase, and it should never be wrapped in plastic.

PROCEDURE

1. Set the broiler to high. Slice both ends from the red pepper; discard the seeds from the stem end. Open the pepper by slicing from top to bottom and remove the white rib. Lay the pepper (ends too) on a **half sheet pan** and place 6 inches under the **broiler**, until blackened, approximately 5 minutes. Remove to a **metal mixing bowl**, cover with a **spare pot lid** (one that fits just inside the bowl but above the pepper) and cool for 5 minutes. Remove the blackened skin from the pepper by rubbing with a **clean kitchen towel**. Finely chop and set aside.

2. Combine the cream cheese, mayo, red pepper flakes, black pepper, and salt in a **food processor**, pulsing 10 times. Add the cheddar cheese and chopped pepper and pulse 5 times to combine. The mixture should not be smooth and maintain large bits of both peppers and cheese. Store in an **airtight container** in the fridge for up to a week.

[1] You may have noticed that most hard cheeses are pretty darned salty.

[2] If you ask me, plain old commercial loaf bread is too flimsy to be of any use here.

[3] Clarified butter has had its easy-to-burn proteins and solids removed. See page 97 for details, and, yes, it's really worth it.

[4] I'm not going to tell you that a smear of Duke's mayonnaise on that second piece is absolutely perfect because that might sound like a product endorsement. Duke's is a southern thing, so it may not be available where you live, but that's why we have the Internet.

TRIVIA The '70s outfit I wore in the Bed, Bath & Beyond scene was burned immediately following the shoot.

APPLE FAMILY VALUES

EPISODE 17 | SEASON 2 | GOOD EATS

Wearing a Kangol backward was a big mistake.

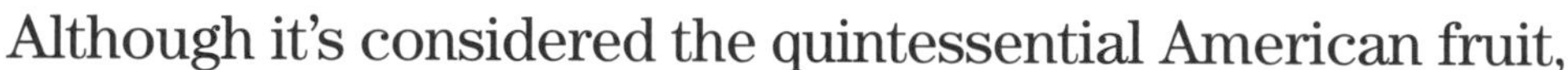

Although it's considered the quintessential American fruit, most of us don't know beans about apples. Once upon a time, hundreds of varieties were cultivated around the country, some of which were grown specifically for eating out of hand while others were for baking and still others for the production of cider, which was once the most popular beverage in the nation (the hard kind, that is). After reaching something of a nadir in the 1970s when only three or four varieties (including the packing material known as the Red Delicious) dominated the megamart scene, we're now witnessing an apple upswing. In Georgia now we're seeing Pink Ladies when they're in season along with Winesaps, Rome Beauties, Arkansas Blacks, and many more. It would be a shame to not know enough to take advantage of this resurgence.

The applications used in this show were developed to showcase two specific attributes of different apple varieties: raw, cooked but intact, and cooked and dissolved to mush.

TRIVIA | The apple orchard in the show is Mercier Orchards, in Blue Ridge, Georgia. I don't remember whose arm played Eve, but I remember it was tough to shoot.

TIDBIT | The United States leads the world in apple production and grows more than three thousand varieties.

TRIVIA | Our Steadicam operator Ramon made his first appearance as a doctor, a role he has reprised a dozen times over the years.[1]

KNOWLEDGE CONCENTRATE

- Because they reproduce sexually, every wild apple tree is a new variety. The only way varieties can be commercially replicated is by splicing pieces of an existing tree (called a scion) onto rootstock. The scion determines the type of apple that will grow, while the rootstock determines how heavily it will produce, how hardy it will be, and how long it will live.
- Apple varieties such as Braeburn, Baldwin, Jonagold, Northern Spy, Rome, Granny Smith, Fuji, and Cortland are considered good baking apples because their structure softens but doesn't collapse when cooked.
- Apples are available year round due to the use of atmosphere-controlled refrigerated storage, which makes it possible for apples picked in October to ripen in your refrigerator in February. Nitrogen is used in such chambers as a replacement for the O_2 in air that acts as a catalyst for apple respiration and ripening. Once upon a time, apples in New England were sealed in barrels and sunk in rivers and ponds for the winter. When extracted in spring, they were fresh as the day they were picked.
- Apples release a gas called ethylene that hastens ripening of many fruits, which is why it's not a good idea to close up apples with bananas, whose skin will darken much quicker with apples around. This doesn't mean that the bananas will actually ripen quicker. They won't. But they'll *look* riper, which is unfortunately all that matters to many American shoppers.

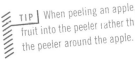

A FEW FUN APPLE-HISTORY FACTS TO KNOW AND TELL

- The apple, a member of the rose family believed to have originated in the mountains of Kazakhstan, is one of the most widely cultivated fruit trees in the world.
- English settlers brought apples to the United States in the 1600s.
- Until the seventeenth century, almost any mysterious or unknown fruit was referred to as an "apple."
- John Chapman, a.k.a. Johnny Appleseed, was a real person who was responsible for planting many apple nurseries (not orchards) in the Midwest, especially in Ohio, Illinois, and Indiana. And yes, he often wore a pot on his head.
- Washington's apple industry became the giant that it is mostly through irrigation projects set in motion in the early twentieth century.

TIP | When peeling an apple, feed the fruit into the peeler rather than moving the peeler around the apple.

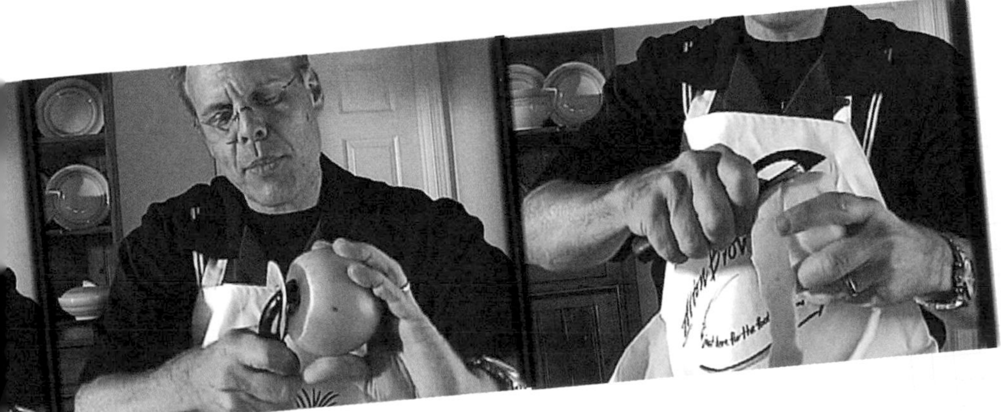

APPLICATION

THE WALDORF HYSTERIA

4 TO 6 SERVINGS

Legend has it the Waldorf Salad was concocted in 1893 by Oscar Tschirky, the legendary maître d' of New York's Waldorf Astoria hotel. This compound salad[2] shows how well certain apple varieties work and play with other raw ingredients.

SOFTWARE

2		Ginger Gold apples	Gala, Golden Delicious, Jonagold, or Fuji would do well here
1		Red Delicious apple	
3	tablespoons	cider vinegar[3]	
½	teaspoon	kosher salt	
1	pinch	black pepper	freshly ground
2½	ounces	walnuts	toasted and chopped
5½	ounces	golden raisins	
2	teaspoons	curry powder	
2	ribs	celery	thinly sliced on the bias
10	leaves	mint	chiffonade[4]
½	small	onion	frenched[5]
1	cup	mayonnaise[6]	
1	head	romaine lettuce	heart only

TRIVIA The game-show Waldorf Salad scene was of course inspired by *Who Wants to Be a Millionaire*, which was pretty darned big back in '99.

PROCEDURE

1. **Cut** the apples in half (don't peel them) and use a **melon baller** to scrape out the core; dice the apples, tossing them in a **large mixing bowl** with the vinegar as you work.
2. Add the salt and pepper and all the bits and pieces (except the lettuce), then fold in the mayonnaise.
3. Although you can serve this straightway, I'd cover and refrigerate for at least 1 hour to allow the flavors to mingle. When serving, arrange a couple of romaine leaves on the plate and pile the good stuff on top.

APPLICATION

10-MINUTE APPLESAUCE

1 QUART

This is one of my most favorite *Good Eats* recipes of all time. I love applesauce, and I often serve this with pork chops and, of course, Roesti (page 318). I also like this application because it's such a perfect use of the microwave oven, which really is a handy tool despite what "gourmets" say about it.

By choosing the right apples, you can make an utterly delicious applesauce in minutes. I love the combination of Golden Delicious and Fuji, but Rome, Gala, Crispin, McIntosh, or Idared would do nicely in this applesauce as well.

SOFTWARE

3		Golden Delicious apples	peeled, cored, and quartered
3		Fuji apples	ditto
1	cup	unfiltered apple juice	
2	tablespoons	Cognac or brandy	
2	tablespoons	unsalted butter	
3	tablespoons	light honey	(such as clover, orange blossom, or "wildflower")
½	teaspoon	ground cinnamon	

PROCEDURE

1. Place all of the ingredients in a **4-quart microwave-safe container**. Close the lid, leaving one corner open to allow steam to escape.
2. Cook in the microwave oven on high for 10 minutes. If your microwave doesn't have a carousel, carefully give the container a quarter turn every 2 minutes.
3. Remove carefully and use an **immersion/stick blender** to blend to desired consistency and serve.[7]

CHIFFONADE

French for "little ribbons"

Roll Into

A Tight Little Cigar

Then Slice

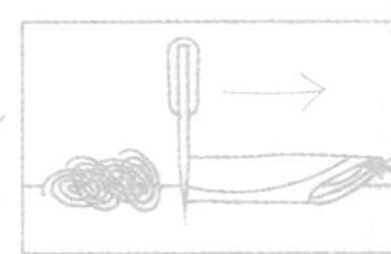

[1] The rule on *Good Eats* is that if you're going to work on the show you have to be willing to be *in* the show, and just about everyone on the crew has appeared on screen . . . sometimes over and over again.

[2] A salad that's all mixed up and bound with a sauce can be called "compound." If most of the ingredients are leaves of some sort, the salad is "tossed," and if they're layered or carefully constructed the salad is "composed."

[3] Besides enhancing flavor, the acetic acid in the vinegar will prevent the enzyme polyphenoloxidase from turning the apple pieces brown. (Just so you know, if a chemical name ends in "-ase," it's an enzyme.)

[4] See illustration:

[5] It's like a julienne, only different. See illustration on page 52.

[6] As you might suspect, I'm a fan of *Good Eats* Homemade Mayonnaise (page 242), but you may use whatever you like as long as the container doesn't include the phrase "salad dressing."

[7] Although it's mighty fine hot, chilling allows the pectin in the apples to firm a bit, and I find that more texturally satisfying.

CRUSTACEAN NATION I

EPISODE 18 | SEASON 2 | GOOD EATS

TRIVIA Of course, when this episode was produced it was simply "Crustacean Nation," because we had no way of knowing there would be more to follow. At this point I was still expecting to be canceled any day.

Here my goal was to set the record straight on one of the more maligned of Neptune's nibbles and find a way to produce a shrimp cocktail that could recapture that dish's once glamorous reputation. I think we nailed it.

TRIVIA It doesn't take a very observant observer to see that the shrimp boat we're on isn't moving. Sure, the camera rocks, and I rock, but the shadows don't move and that's just not right. Truth is, there were only four of us on the crew, including the producer, who was great with child. So great that we were a bit trepidatious about heading out to sea.[1] Besides, there wasn't really any room for us out there. So the entire sequence took place at dock in Ft. Meyers, FL.

TRIVIA This is the only cooking show in history in which Beethoven has appeared. As you can see by the eraser, he's *decomposing*.

KNOWLEDGE CONCENTRATE

- The shrimp is a decapod from the subphylum Crustacia. There are more than three hundred varieties; the most common belong to the genus *Farfantepenaeus*.
- *Jumbo, medium, large*: These are all just words that can be interpreted in too many ways to be of real use. Many packers and processors use a numeric system in which the number represents the count per pound. Some common ranges include:
  - 60–70s: tiny (sea monkeys, in other words)
  - 26–30s: medium (good for working into pasta sauces and the like)
  - 21–25s: large
  - 16–20s: jumbo in my world
  - U-16s: fewer than sixteen shrimp to a pound
  - U-10s: usually referred to as giant prawns, even though shrimp aren't technically prawns
- Frozen shrimp come in two forms: block frozen and IQF or "individual quick frozen." Although IQF are easier to dish out, block shrimp tend to suffer less freezer burn because they're encased in ice. To get a few off, just float the block in water until the right number thaw off. Either way, you want them in the shell (unpeeled) because that shell protects them against moisture loss.
- Although the tool that removes them is called a deveiner (my favorite "deveiner" is a small pair of barber scissors), that isn't a vein running along the back just under the skin. It's the digestive tract. When thoroughly cooked, it's perfectly okay to eat it, though in larger specimens it can be gritty. But again: digestive tract. I'll leave decisions concerning appropriate actions to you.
- Brining—that is, soaking in a salt-and-sugar solution—loads the shrimp with extra water and seasoning, which makes them crisp, plump, and more flavorful. Just don't soak them too long, as they have a very high surface-to-mass ratio.
- In the years since this episode first aired, I've become very concerned about the state of the oceans and the food we take from them. Some 85 percent of the shrimp sold in the United States comes from China, Vietnam, India, Taiwan, Ecuador, and other countries where shrimp farming is big business . . . big, dirty, planet-choking, shipped-from-the-other-side-of-the-globe, flavorless-shrimp producing business. I'm not a protectionist, but I strongly urge you to buy only shrimp harvested or farmed in the U.S. and Canada. The waters of the Florida gulf give forth some two hundred million pounds of pink, brown, and white shrimp a year. Oh, and steer clear of black tiger shrimp at all costs.

TIDBIT | Shrimp often change gender from male to female.

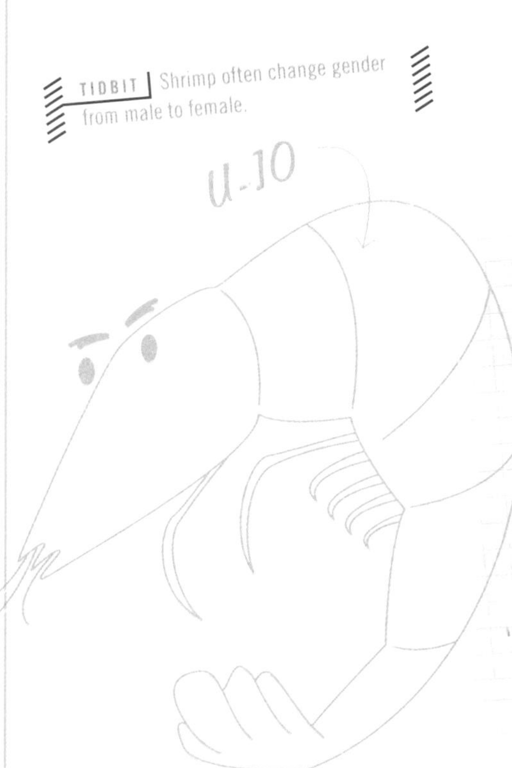

APPLICATION — SHRIMP COCKTAIL

4 SERVINGS

Just look at what we've done to the shrimp cocktail, relegated it to cut-rate motel buffets and low-class cafeterias. The proud, flavorful shrimp of my youth have been reduced to rubbery sauce shovels sadly sharing sherbet cups with week-old lemon wedges. It's just not right.

The shrimp "cocktail" as we know it originated in the late nineteenth or early twentieth century. A ketchup-based sauce is used, and the shrimp are served along the edge of a metal cup or glass stemware. The most famous purveyor of shrimp cocktails is no doubt the Golden Gate Casino and Hotel in Las Vegas, which started offering a fifty-cent serving of shrimp and spicy sauce in a glass back in the '50s. Here, we put the king of appetizers back on its throne.

SOFTWARE

2	ounces	kosher salt	
2	ounces	sugar	
1	cup	H_2O	at room temperature
8	ounces	ice cubes	
32		head-on shrimp (21–25 count)	
FOR THE COCKTAIL SAUCE			
1	14-ounce can	diced tomatoes	drained
½	cup	prepared chili sauce	
¼	cup	prepared horseradish	(not sauce)
1	teaspoon	sugar	
1	pinch	black pepper	freshly ground
½	teaspoon	kosher salt	
1	tablespoon	olive oil	
1	pinch	Old Bay seasoning[2]	

PROCEDURE

1. Combine the salt, sugar, and water in a **mixing bowl**, stirring to dissolve. Add the ice and set aside while prepping the shrimp.
2. Use a **pair of scissors** to remove the veins from the shrimp without removing the shell.
3. Put the shrimp in the brine and refrigerate for 20 to 25 minutes.

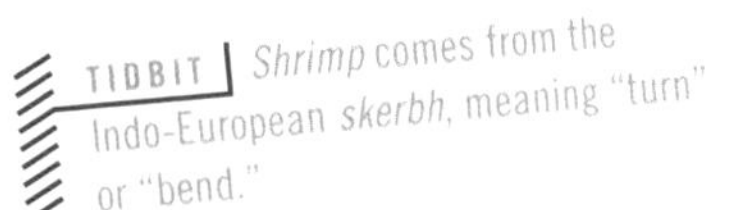

TIDBIT | *Shrimp* comes from the Indo-European *skerbh*, meaning "turn" or "bend."

4 Meanwhile, to make the cocktail sauce, take the tomatoes, chili sauce, horseradish, sugar, pepper, and salt for a spin in a **food processor** until almost smooth. Refrigerate.

5 Place a **half sheet pan or foil-lined broiler pan** about 8 inches under the broiler and heat for 5 minutes.

6 Remove the shrimp from the brine and rinse under cold water. Dry thoroughly on **paper towels**. In the same bowl (discard the brine), toss the shrimp with the oil and sprinkle with the Old Bay.

7 Arrange the shrimp on the sizzling-hot sheet pan and slide back under the broiler. Set your timer for 2 minutes.

8 Clean out the **bowl** and stick it in the freezer.

9 Flip the shrimp quickly with **tongs** and return to the broiler for 1 minute.

10 Transfer the shrimp to the **chilled bowl** and toss a few times to knock down the heat. Place in the freezer, tossing every few minutes until the shrimp are thoroughly cooled (shouldn't take more than 15 minutes).

11 Peel the shrimp and serve alongside the sauce.

[1] The fact that the producer in question was and is my wife did little to quell said trepidation.

[2] This blend of over a dozen herbs and spices was created by a German gentleman named Gustav Brunn who came to America, spice grinder in hand, in 1939 and worked up this mix in Baltimore. If your megamart doesn't carry this special and highly secretive blend, you can easily find satisfaction on the Internet.

[3] Ever heard the Joe Jackson song "Big World"? There's a line that goes: "Looking over Hong Kong Harbour. Throw a shrimp in yellow wine. Eat it when it ceases moving. Just before is fine too."

GOOD EATS TIPS FOR HAPPY SHRIMP CONSUMPTION

1. Avoid thawed or precooked shrimp. Unless you're within a couple hours' drive of a beach, buy frozen and thaw yourself. It's best to buy shrimp with the heads on. Shrimp decompose faster with the heads on, and so they have to be processed or get to market faster than headless shrimp.

2. When buying fresh shrimp, all specimens should be on ice. Avoid any with dark spots, pitted shells, or off aromas.

3. Ponder the best size for your dish. U-10s may be sweet on the grill but not so great in pasta sauces.

4. Cook shrimp in the shell whenever possible. There's flavor in there.

5. Brine is always in fashion.

6. Although boiling and poaching are the norm, remember that dry, hot cooking methods concentrate natural flavors.[3]

7. Deveining: It's your choice.

8. Remember, shrimp are darned nutritious with lots of good clean protein and very little fat. Consume often.

The offending vein we all know is really a poop tube!

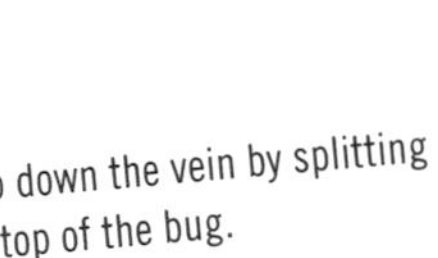
Snip down the vein by splitting
the top of the bug.

THE FUNGAL GOURMET

EPISODE 19 | SEASON 2 | GOOD EATS

TRIVIA This title is a goof, of course, on *The Frugal Gourmet*, my all-time favorite cooking show. Say what you will about Jeff Smith, he was a hell of a teacher. His original *Frugal Gourmet* book is a dog-eared, stained, and much-loved standard in my kitchen.

It was my goal here to lay out a basis for responsible mushroom cookery, whether the fungi in question are wild or cultivated. Note, however, that unless you have trained long and hard under an experienced (and hopefully old) master forager or possess advanced degrees in mycology, never pick wild mushrooms yourself. Although a relatively small percentage are poisonous, most of your deadlier models (such as the aptly named "destroying angel") look a lot like edible specimens. I won't go into the medical details of what some of these nasty fungi can do to your innards other than to say that unless you're already at the front of the line for liver and kidney transplants, I wouldn't take any chances here.

TRIVIA The mushroom farm location was in Avondale, PA. There are a lot of mushroom farms in Pennsylvania because there are a lot of horses in Pennsylvania. In fact, most of what happens on a big mushroom operation isn't growing mushrooms, it's making growth medium—that is, pasteurized horse manure compost.

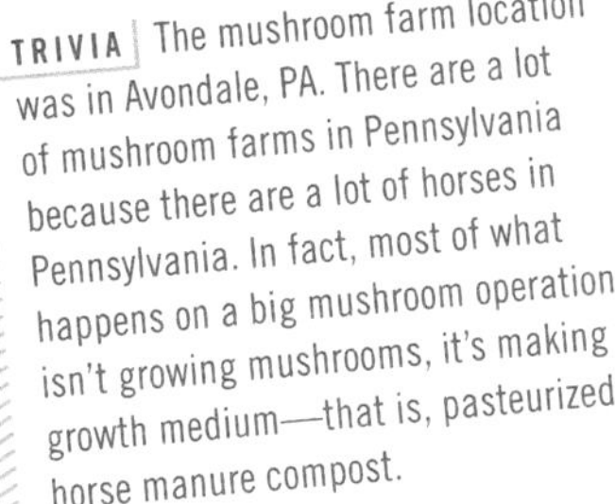

TIDBIT Scientifically speaking, there is no such thing as a portobello mushroom. It's a marketing name for overgrown cremini. I guess "portobello" sounds better than "overgrown."

TRIVIA This was the first time Death ever appeared on a cooking show.

KNOWLEDGE CONCENTRATE

- Mushrooms, which are 80 to 90 percent water, not only contain more protein than most vegetables but also impart a meaty, earthy, and satisfying flavor the Japanese call "umami" to dishes. When it comes to cooking, I find that most mushrooms like to be treated like meat and respond best to fast cooking at high temperatures.

- Loose or "bulk" mushrooms are not always fresher or of higher quality than packaged mushrooms. But if the package in question shows a fair amount of condensation, I pass. As for presliced mushrooms, let me say this: Quality and convenience are rarely seen holding hands.[1]

- Most mushrooms keep well if they're refrigerated in a paper bag, which holds on to some moisture while allowing air to pass through. Plastic and mushrooms don't get along.[2]

- Most "gourmets" will tell you not to wash mushrooms in water because they'll become waterlogged. Instead, you're supposed to use a brush to remove any clinging pasteurized horse poop compost. Have you ever tried brushing a mushroom? I have, and I can tell you right now that I wash my mushrooms. The key is to not soak them. Place them in a colander and give them a cleansing squirt from the ol' water-pistol thingy on the long hose that never goes back in right. Once clean, move them to paper towels to drain. When it comes to slicing white button or cremini mushrooms, the handiest tool you can own is an egg slicer.

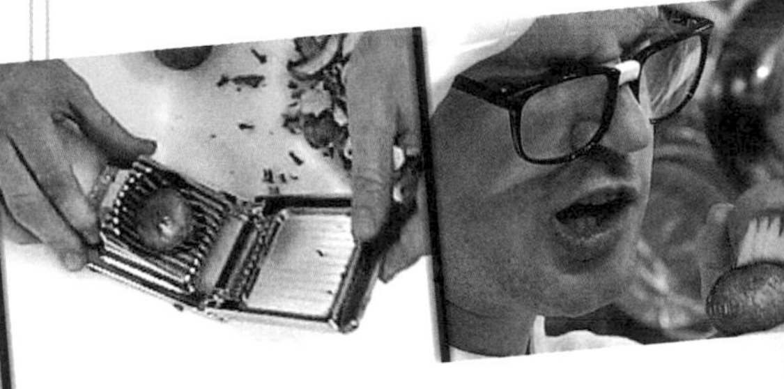

TIDBIT The mushroom is not a plant but a fungus. Since they're not plants they take no energy from the sun. They take everything from the growth medium, be it a tree, a pile of horse manure, or a dead gopher.

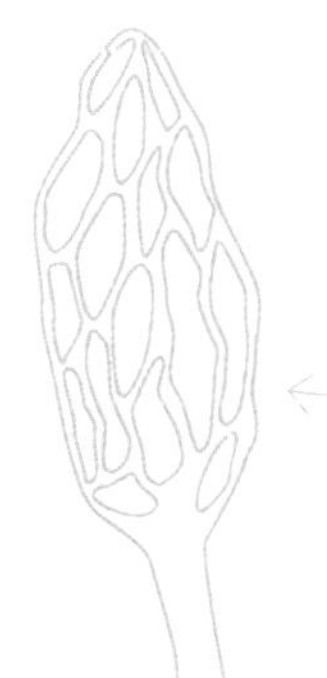

APPLICATION — THAT OL' CAP MAGIC

4 SERVINGS

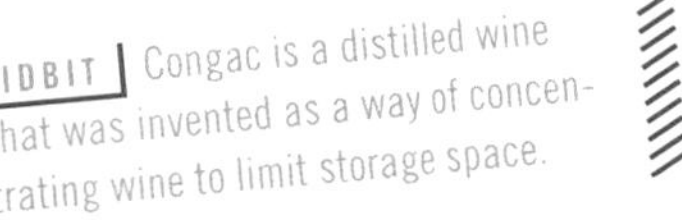

I feel certain that the Good Lord would not have made mushroom caps bowl-shaped if He hadn't meant for us to fill them with something. Although this fern-bar standby is somewhat notorious, I hope this particular application provides some redemption.

Actually, this is three applications in one, as the caps can be served with some other filling and the filling can, if prepared halfway, be served as a side dish or as a component to another dish altogether.

TIDBIT | Congac is a distilled wine that was invented as a way of concentrating wine to limit storage space.

SOFTWARE

FOR THE CAPS

20		white mushroom caps	stems removed
	just enough	olive oil	
1	teaspoon	fresh rosemary	chopped
1	teaspoon	fresh thyme	chopped
1	clove	garlic	crushed and chopped fine

FOR THE FILLING

2	tablespoons	unsalted butter	clarified, see sidebar
2	pounds	cremini or shiitake mushrooms	thinly sliced
1	tablespoon	shallot	minced
1½	fluid ounces	Cognac	(that's a jigger)
2	teaspoons	chives	chopped
⅓	cup	heavy cream	
1	ounce	Parmesan cheese	grated
1	teaspoon	dried tarragon	
	to taste	black pepper	freshly ground
2	tablespoons	breadcrumbs	preferably homemade, divided

PROCEDURE

1. Heat oven to 350°F and position rack in middle.
2. Toss the mushrooms with the oil, followed by the herbs and garlic.
3. Position caps, concave side down, on a **cooling rack** set on a **half sheet pan** and roast until the tip of a **paring knife** slips easily in, 10 to 15 minutes.[3]

4 Meanwhile, make the filling. Heat the clarified butter in a **12-inch skillet** over high heat. When the fat shimmers, add the sliced 'shrooms and sauté until brown and fragrant, roughly 12 to 15 minutes, stirring constantly. (If moisture builds up in pan, you either need higher heat or a bigger pan.)

5 Toss in shallot and cook until just fragrant. Kill the heat, if you're cooking with gas, to prevent a fire ball, and deglaze with the Cognac.

6 Return heat to medium and invite the chives, heavy cream, Parmesan, tarragon, and pepper to the party. Combine well and simmer for 1 minute. Kill the heat, stir in 1 tablespoon of the breadcrumbs, and cool 10 minutes.[4]

7 Position oven rack 8 inches from broiler and crank broiler to high. (And remember, gas is hotter than electric.)

8 Turn the baked mushroom caps concave side up on the rack and mound each with 1 tablespoon of filling (I use a small disher) and sprinkle with the remaining breadcrumbs.

9 Broil 3 to 4 minutes or until the top of the filling browns.

10 Cool slightly and serve.

TIDBIT | Russians are mad for mushrooms and actually have a word for "mushroom crazy:" *raszh*. It is said that Lenin had a serious *raszh*, which I find seriously amusing.

TIDBIT | Like apples, mushrooms are fruiting bodies that send out spores instead of seeds. The mushroom "tree," called "mycelium", is underground or inside the tree stump or other growth medium. Mushroom mycelium can live for hundreds of years and cover up to an acre of land. In fact, mushrooms are some of the largest organisms on Earth.

[1] Do the math: If a mushroom is 90 percent water, wouldn't you want to minimize its surface area as much as possible for as long as possible?

[2] Yes, I know, most megamart mushrooms are packaged under plastic. That's so you can see them. Very few produce items actually like being under plastic. In fact, I can't think of a one.

[3] These roasted mushroom caps can be served as a side dish as they are, or you can fill them with something uncooked—pimento cheese, for instance, or blue cheese.

[4] The filling can be assembled to this point and refrigerated for up to 48 hours, or served as a side dish.

CLARIFIED BUTTER

By removing the milk solids and most of the proteins, the smoke point of the butter is significantly raised. It's a great sauté fat and it keeps for a very long time. I always keep some on hand. In this episode, to emphasize its simplicity I gave the entire recipe in one breath. Here it is word for word:

(deep breath) "Melt a pound of butter in a heavy saucepan over low heat and slowly cook until the bubbling ceases and the liquid turns clear, 30 to 40 minutes depending on the water content. Strain and cool, being sure to leave any solids in the bottom of the pan. Or, once the butter is clear, remove the pan from the heat and quickly add 2 inches of hot tap water. Since it is less dense than water, the now clarified butter will float to the top, and in a few hours in the refrigerator will solidify it into a big yellow Frisbee that you can lift out and use. Use it immediately or wrap in wax paper and refrigerate or add foil and freeze it for 2 months."

CRUST NEVER SLEEPS

EPISODE 20 | SEASON 2 | GOOD EATS

Consider the opening "teaser" from the show: I'm sitting in a diner booth (really the café at Whole Foods) contemplating pie.

> ME: Pi . . . Mathematicians have pondered the depths of its nature for centuries, only to find more questions. For many cooks, "pie" is no less enigmatic. Of course when we say "pie," we mean fruit pie and therefore crust. And therein lies the contradiction. Ask any American to describe the perfect crust, and you're going to get the same cockamamie answer: tender and flaky.

At this point in the action two strange puppets appear over my shoulders, one with a "T" on its chest and another with an "F." One looks a lot like Queen Elizabeth, while the other bears a striking resemblance to Jerry Garcia. They wear boxing gloves, with which they begin to pummel me. The crew giggles, though you can't hear it on TV.

> ME: How the oxymoron torments me. Why can't anyone see that they're opposites? Flaky is crisp, structural—like puff pastry. Tender is soft, pliant—like a biscuit. Put them together, you've got a biscuit that will snap. No matter what we do, tender and flaky will forever remain polar extremes on the pie-crust continuum. Of course, opposites do attract. If we apply the right science, cunning technique, the right ingredients, we could, we should, we will create a pie crust that's truly good eats, without being "good grief."

Well, it was a swell show teaser, but ultimately it made a promise that went unkept. I did not crack the tender/flaky code in this show (though I think we came closer in later pie-oriented episodes—lemon meringue, apple). But the show wasn't a failure, because it led me to a rustic crust application that I hold near and dear to my culinary heart (that is, my stomach). This crust tastes great, delivers a very satisfying crumbly crunch, and is extremely user friendly.

TRIVIA | Crew members fought over who would get to operate these pugilistic puppets. Everyone wanted to spend some time slugging me, so whenever Tender and Flaky were called into action we held a lottery to see who would get to be in the driver's seat.

TIDBIT | Pies, or fillings wrapped in crust, have been with us since the Middle Ages. Back then the dough was often treated as a temporary pot, which was discarded after the cooking was done. When I first started making pies, my crusts were very much in this tradition.

KNOWLEDGE CONCENTRATE

There are only three essential ingredients to pie crust: flour, fat, moisture. Success is based on choosing wisely from these categories and then handling them properly (that is, lightly).

THE FLOUR: Go with straightforward all-purpose flour, which has a middle-of-the-road protein content. I prefer unbleached AP because it browns better and has a slightly higher nutritional value.

THE FAT: Although I often use shortening because it has a melting point well above body heat and is therefore easier to work with especially in summer, in this case I went with butter for one simple reason: flavor. Just remember: It melts at body temperature, so work cool and work quick.

THE MOISTURE: I never use straight water. Why would you when subtle flavors can be added to the party? Also, acidic liquids such as vinegar and lemon juice can produce a more tender crust by interrupting gluten formation. Sweetened liquids such as apple juice can tenderize (because of sugar) and promote browning.

Proportions and mixing: Many bakers work with a 3:2:1 ratio, meaning three parts flour to two parts fat to one part water, which I tend to find a little on the tough side. I usually push the envelope by going with more fat and less moisture, but this can be risky if your methodology's not sound.

ON HARDWARE

FOOD PROCESSOR

To my mind there is no better way to bring dough together than with a food processor. The trick is in knowing when to stop. When it's done right, the dough doesn't look finished, so don't stand there watching it spin, getting tougher by the moment.

SPRITZ BOTTLE

When it comes to adding the moisture, you want to be able to apply as little as possible as evenly as possible. The spritz bottle is the best tool I've tried; indispensable, in fact.

ROLLING PIN

If you've never given thought to your rolling pin, now is the time. I recommend a 14-inch-long rock-solid maple number, between 1½ and 2 pounds. It's got the heft and smooth texture to roll any dough you could bring together. I put wide rubber bands on the ends to help ensure I get the thickness I want.

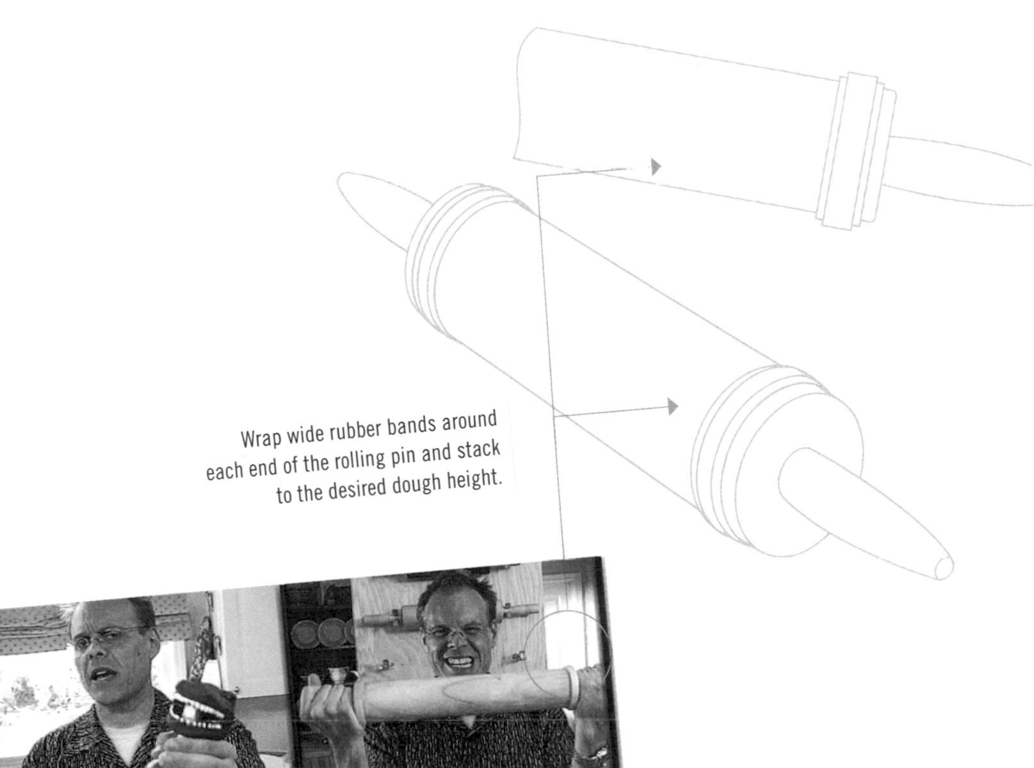

Wrap wide rubber bands around each end of the rolling pin and stack to the desired dough height.

APPLICATION

NO-PAN PEAR PIE

1 FREEFORM PIE; 6 TO 8 SERVINGS

One of the things that gets in the way of attaining a flaky/tender equalibrium is the pan itself — so let's get rid of it. This is actually a galette—a freeform tart. In France, a galette can be either sweet or savory.

TIDBIT | You'll notice that the butter in the dough takes two forms, room temperature and soft. Why? Because the fat has two very specific jobs in the dough:

A small amount of butter will be fully homogenized into the flour. By coating the flour particles, the fat will limit the development of gluten,[1] thus creating a relatively tender (ouch) crust. When rolled, the cold pieces will turn into very thin flakes of fat, which will melt during baking. As this butter melts, striations will form in the dough, creating flakiness (stop that) in the final product.

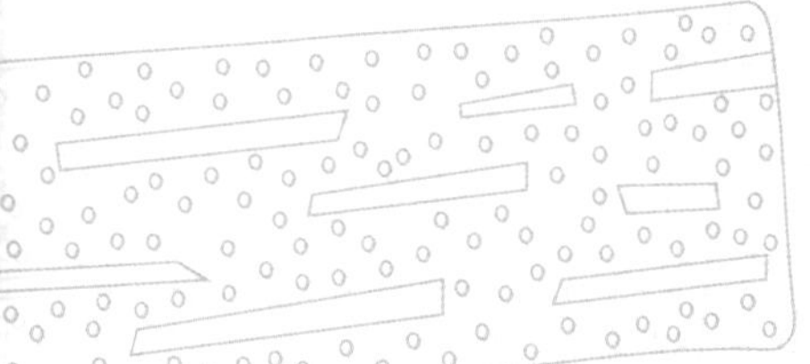

Cold + Warm Butter
Flaky + Tender Crust

SOFTWARE

FOR THE DOUGH

12	ounces	all-purpose flour	plus additional for dusting
2¼	ounces	stone-ground cornmeal[2]	
1½	ounces	sugar	
1	teaspoon	kosher salt	
2	ounces	unsalted butter	diced, at room temperature
6	ounces	unsalted butter	diced, chilled, divided
½	cup	iced apple juice[3]	in spritz bottle

FOR THE FILLING

2		Anjou pears	peeled, cored, and thinly sliced
3	tablespoons	balsamic vinegar	
2	ounces	sugar	
1	pinch	nutmeg[4]	freshly grated
¼	teaspoon	ground cinnamon	
1	ounce	unsalted butter	
5	ounces	fresh blueberries	(frozen will work in a pinch)
1	teaspoon	all-purpose flour	

FOR THE PIE CONSTRUCTION

4	ounces	pound cake	cubed
1	ounce	unsalted butter	cubed
1	large	egg	beaten with 1 tablespoon H_2O
½	teaspoon	sugar	

// PROCEDURE

MAKE THE DOUGH:

1. Pulse the flour, cornmeal, sugar, and salt in a **food processor** to combine. Add the room-temperature butter and pulse until the fat completely disappears into the dry ingredients.

2. Add half of the chilled butter and pulse 18 times, or until the flour mixture resembles peasized crumbs. Add the rest of the chilled butter and pulse 3 or 4 times.

3. Transfer this mixture to a **medium-size mixing bowl**. **Spritz** with just enough juice to moisten the surface of the proto-dough. Mix with a **spatula**. Continue spritzing and mixing until a handful of dough, when squeezed, remains compressed. (You may not use all.) When you've got good adhesion, gather the dough into a round disk, cover with **plastic wrap**, and refrigerate for 20 minutes so that the flour can absorb the moisture.

MAKE THE FILLING:

4. Heat a **12-inch nonstick pan** over medium heat. Add the pears and toss for 2 minutes. Add the vinegar and continue tossing for another 30 seconds. Sprinkle with the sugar and cook until the pears have softened, about 2 minutes. Kill the heat and add the nutmeg, cinnamon, and butter. When the butter has melted, fold in the blueberries. Sprinkle in the 1 teaspoon flour, and stir to combine. Cool to room temperature.

CONSTRUCT AND BAKE THE PIE:

5. Crank the hot box to 400°F. Place the dough on a floured **piece of parchment** and roll it out to a ¼-inch-thick disk, rolling the pin from the center out, turning the dough on the paper every few seconds to maintain evenness.

6. Use a **pizza cutter** to cut the dough into a circle with a uniform edge, then transfer (on the parchment) to an **inverted half sheet pan**.

7. Place the pound cake in the middle of the dough, leaving about a 3-inch margin all the way around. **Spoon** the pear filling over the cake cubes and top with the cubed butter. Lift the edges of the dough circle and fold over toward the middle, working clockwise. **Brush** the tart with the egg wash and sprinkle the crust with sugar.

8. Bake for 30 to 35 minutes, until the filling bubbles and the crust is golden brown and delicious. Remove from the oven, slide off sheet pan (carefully of course) and cool completely before serving.

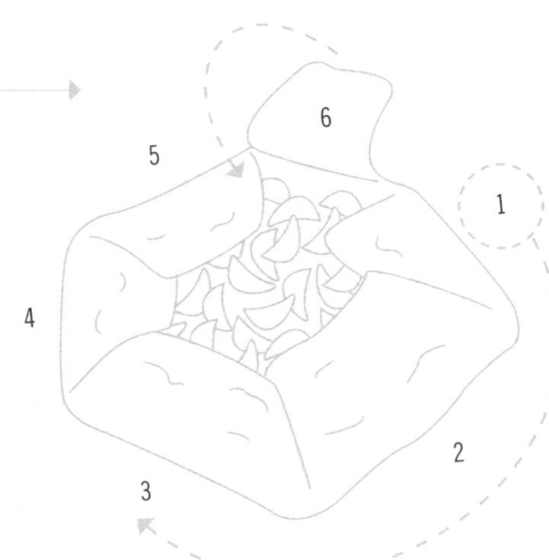

[1] The tough, springy protein structure that results when wheat flour and water are agitated together.

[2] "Stone-ground" means that the kernels were cracked and ground on stone rather than steel wheels. This means that the grinding was accomplished at relatively low temperatures, thus preserving more of the corny goodness of the grain.

[3] Just put the juice and a couple of ice cubes in a spritzer.

[4] Ground nutmeg should never, ever be found in your kitchen. Whole nutmeg is readily available, keeps forever (literally), and is easily grated as you use it.

TRUE BREW I

EPISODE 21 | SEASON 2 | GOOD EATS

This episode wasn't so much about making a cup of coffee as it was learning what goes into a cup of coffee. Remember, this was '99, and the coffee bar revolution was just getting under way. I figured if people were willing to pay $4 for a latte they might be willing to learn a little more than open can/dump into filter/turn on machine.

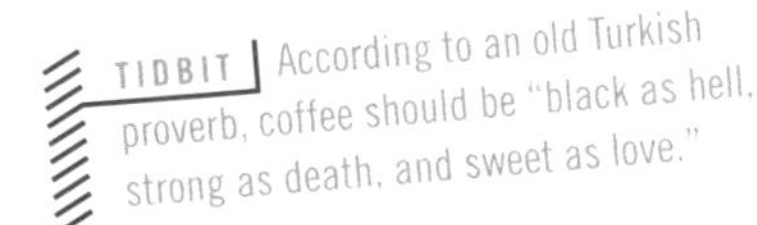

TIDBIT | According to an old Turkish proverb, coffee should be "black as hell, strong as death, and sweet as love."

THE BREW AND YOU

- Buy whole beans and keep them properly stored in an airtight canister. Only freeze beans as a method of long-term storage, as each time they are removed from the freezer condensation will take its toll.
- Grind fresh right before brewing. Think of coffee as you would nutmeg or black pepper. It's a spice, and the less time between grinding and use the better. Different methods of brewing require different grind sizes, and consistency is crucial, which is why I use a burr grinder. French presses require a relatively coarse grind, drips medium, espresso fine.
- Use enough coffee. The golden ratio for drip or press coffee brewing: 2 heaping tablespoons ground coffee for each 6 ounces fresh water. It's a popular misconception that brewing with less coffee will give you a "lighter" brew. This is not so. Brewing with less coffee most often results in overextraction of the bean, and that's what leads to bitterness. If you like weak coffee, brew full strength, then cut it in the cup with hot water.[1]
- Use fresh or filtered water. Your coffee will never be better than your water. I suggest you use filtered water or at least boil it for a couple of minutes to help drive away excess chlorine. Also, water that sits around for a long time loses its power as a solvent. So if you really love your brew, consider skipping the overnight timer function on your drip machine; eight hours is a long time to have water just hanging around.
- Water can extract the best the bean has to offer if it's between 195° and 205°F—that is, just off the boil.
- Heat kills. The longer the pot sits on that heat element the faster the subtle flavor compounds in your brew go belly up. Better to brew into an insulated carafe or Thermos. If you really have to have a hotplate-style machine, go with one that has a variable hold temperature and keep it dialed down as low as it'll go.

KNOWLEDGE CONCENTRATE

There are two varieties of coffee bean used to make the drink we know and love: Robusta and Arabica.

COFFEA ROBUSTA or CANEFORA trees are hardy and high-yielding but produce a very unidimensional brew with little character and a lot of caffeine.

COFFEA ARABICA trees are shy, finicky, and produce only a couple of pounds of beans a year. As one might expect, this is the good stuff with flavor, balanced acidity, body, and aroma. Many canned coffees use a mixture of Arabica and Robusta.

So, if there are only two varieties, why are there so many different bags of beans at the megamart? The answer lies in the roast.

LIGHT, A.K.A. CITY ROAST: Beans are taken to 375°F in about 7 minutes of roast time. The beans swell and pop. The finished bean is dry looking and brews up with a light body, bright acidity, and full flavor in the cup.

MEDIUM, A.K.A. AMERICAN, A.K.A. FULL CITY ROAST: Achieved in 9 to 11 minutes of roasting. Dry bean surface, brews up bright and flavorful but with a deeper richness of body than the light roast. This is the most popular roast level on the planet.

DARK, A.K.A. FRENCH, VIENNA, OR CONTINENTAL ROAST: Beans are roasted for 12 to 13 minutes; the surface of the bean becomes slightly shiny as oils come to the surface. Brews from such roasts are less aromatic but sweeter than lesser roasts. The flavor of the roast itself begins to emerge.

DARKEST, A.K.A. ITALIAN, A.K.A. ESPRESSO ROAST: Beans are roasted for 14 minutes, with a final temperature in the neighborhood of 425°F. At this point there are very few actual coffee flavors left: It's all roast. The beans are very oily. This oiliness helps produce the heavy body of fast-brew methods like espresso (but that's another book).

FUN COFFEE FACTS TO KNOW AND TELL

- Coffee plants, of the genus *Coffea*, which includes more than ninety flowering shrubs, grows best in tropical and subtropical climes. The word *coffee* probably began as *ahwat al-būnn*, Arabic for "wine of the bean."
- The coffee bean is the pit of a cherrylike fruit (drupe) that grows on two varieties of coffee tree. The berries are picked from the tree, the pulp is removed, and the beans are dried.
- Coffee trees usually fruit after three to five years of growth and produce for some fifty to sixty years thereafter.
- Legend has it that coffee was "discovered" around 800 B.C. by Ethiopian goatherds who noticed that their charges became excited after consuming berries from a mysterious shrub. Arab tribesmen were roasting and brewing beans by A.D. 1000. By the thirteenth century, they were drinking coffee regularly and selling the beans to the world. But fertile beans weren't allowed outside of Africa and Arabia until the 1600s. The Dutch got hold of a coffee plant in 1696. Most Latin American coffee descends from a plant stolen from the garden of Louis XIV by a French naval officer named Gabriel Mathieu de Clieu.

TIDBIT The American Civil War was the first major caffeinated conflict. Many soldiers ranked the importance of coffee well above food.

TIDBIT Caffeine levels drop as the roast level darkens.

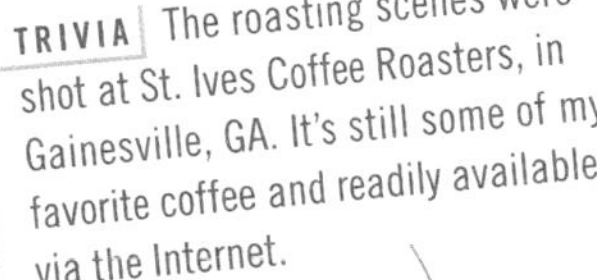

TRIVIA The roasting scenes were shot at St. Ives Coffee Roasters, in Gainesville, GA. It's still some of my favorite coffee and readily available via the Internet.

APPLICATION

GOOD EATS TRUE BREW

4 SERVINGS

Although the ratio below might require adjustment for an auto-drip machine, I think it's just right for a manual.

// SOFTWARE

28	fluid ounces	fresh, filtered H_2O	
8	tablespoons	whole beans	freshly ground

// PROCEDURE

1. Bring water to a boil. (Use an electric kettle, pictured left.)
2. Meanwhile, set up device: Place **manual drip filter holder**[2] atop **32-ounce thermos** and place either appropriately sized **gold mesh** or **paper filter** into **holder**.
3. Grind coffee and place in **filter**.
4. Slowly pour water into filter, pausing when it fills. It will take 3 minutes to get it all through. (If it takes more than 4 minutes, your grind is too fine.)
5. Remove filter and enjoy . . . you might want to pour it into a **mug** of course.
6. Tightly seal thermos to preserve heat.

NOTE: GETTING THE GRIND RIGHT

Using a burr grinder with an indexed grind setting greatly simplifies this because the best drip setting on a scale of 1 to 10 is usually between 6 and 7. If you're using a blade grinder, you'll have to eyeball it. Since I don't trust my eyeballs first thing in the morning when using a blade machine, I rely on a weight/volume conversion. When properly ground, 1½ ounces (32 grams) of beans should equal 8 tablespoons of ground coffee. (Less than that means too fine; more means too coarse.) After a few runs you'll figure out how many seconds of grind time gives you the desired grind. Heck, even I can count in the morning . . . as long as the numbers are small.

This manual-drip method is designed to give you the most control over the temperature of the water, the size of the grind, the proportion of coffee to water, and the overall brew time—the most important factors contributing to a perfect brew.

TRIVIA This show brought my neighbor "Chuck" into action. Keeping a straight face during the kitchen-cleaning scene was . . . difficult.

10 MINUTES MORE

I realize that most of you are not going to seek out a manual drip coffee filter cone. Nor are you going to stand there for 3 to 4 minutes slowly pouring boiling water into a relatively small target, no matter how good the coffee is. To be completely honest, as the years have passed, I've gone over to a French press, which looks like this:

French press

The steps are the same but pressure is used as the filter pushes the grounds to the bottom. This requires a coarser grind (1 oz of beans ground to 6 tablespoons). The coffee goes in, 24 ounces of boiling water go on. Set timer for 4 minutes, then slowly plunge. Immediately pour off the brew to a thermos. The really cool thing is that the French press emulsifies the oils of the beans into the extraction, resulting in a fuller-bodied cup. This is strong, potent stuff that I usually cut with a little condensed milk. (Note that Beethoven believed in a 60:1 bean-to-cup ratio. That's hard-core.) Paper filters tend to remove the oils. A French press can also be used for tea.

As for beans, I'm not loyal to a particular region but I will say that I prefer a medium or "full city" roast, which allows for more of the flavor and acidity of the bean to come through.

[1] When I want a regular coffee at my local espresso bar I have an Americano, which is espresso watered down with hot water. Same concept.

[2] These aren't that hard to find. Mine is made by Nissan and is matched to fit several of their insulated mugs. You can also find them at camping or outdoor stores. On the Internet, try searching "one cup brewer" and see what you come up with.

TIP If you don't have a coffee grinder or don't want to mess with grinding, buy small batches of beans from a neighborhood roaster or shop, have them do the grinding right then and there, and use the coffee within the week. When purchasing beans, beware open bins, where light and air can degrade quality.

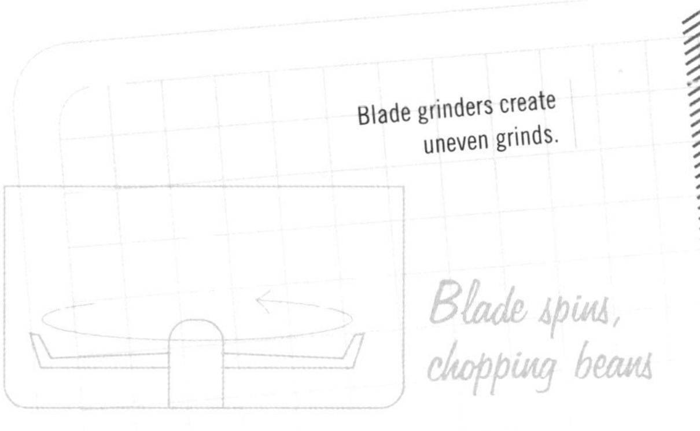
Blade grinders create uneven grinds.
Blade spins, chopping beans

BLADE GRINDER

Large studded wheel turns
Large studded collar stationary
Burr grinders create even and equal pieces.

BURR GRINDER

SALT AND COFFEE

It has long been held by cowboys, pilgrims, and others who brew mostly over fire that a pinch of salt added to the grounds can reduce the bitterness suffered by many a brew. The practice may have originated on commercial fishing vessels where potable water is stored for long periods of time. Not only does the salt cut the bitterness of the coffee, but it also smooths out the "stale" taste of tank-stored water. I've taken to adding a quarter teaspoon of kosher salt to every 6 tablespoons of grounds. That isn't really enough to taste but it'll do the trick. And by the way, recent research has proven that salt is actually better at neutralizing bitterness than sugar.

A GRIND IS A TERRIBLE THING TO WASTE

EPISODE 22 | SEASON 2 | GOOD EATS

If America has an official dish it's the hamburger. To any who would argue, I say 29 billion hamburger portions of beef per year cannot be wrong. Now whether that qualifies as a cuisine or not—that's another question. Anthropologist Sidney Mintz[1] in fact argues that it's not enough for a food to be eaten a lot or even cooked a lot. It must be debated. It must be discussed often by those who produce it. Now by that standard, well, the hamburger may have been cuisine at one point but not now. I mean, we've handed all of our burger making over to drive-thru drones, and the only discussions we have on the issue are when we're yelling orders at three-inch speakers.

I don't know if Mintz is right. But I do know if we take burgers into our own hands, treat them like food again instead of *Soylent Green*, then we just might get our cuisine back. Then who knows what might happen? Flavorful meatloaf, succulent meatballs . . . the sky's the limit, really.

"Sacred cows make the best hamburger."

MARK TWAIN

TIDBIT | Although no one can say for sure who invented the hamburger-as-sandwich concept, we do know that the hamburger bun was concocted by Walt Anderson, a Kansas cook who later founded White Castle.

The Hamburger Cuts

CHUCK

SIRLOIN

ROUND

Ground round and sirloin come (surprise) from the round and sirloin primals, respectively. These are flavorful but lean cuts that dry out and crumble badly if overcooked.

KNOWLEDGE CONCENTRATE

Most American hamburgers (especially fast-food burgers) are ground from the chuck primal, which is generally around 30 percent fat but not as flavorful as the back-end cuts. The best hamburger meat contains meat from both the chuck and the sirloin or round. Butcher shops and some megamarts with full-service meat counters still grind their own hamburger meat from cut scraps. If a store sells a lot of, say, tenderloin, and they cut it themselves, odds are good there will be a high percentage of tenderloin in the ground meat. So always ask your butcher what's going into the grinder that day.

I only buy ground meat that I know for certain was ground on premises by butchers working with meat they cut right there on the spot. If no such product is available, I grind or chop my own. I will not purchase factory-ground meat. Why? Safety. When you bite down on a hamburger cooked from factory-ground beef, you may be consuming dozens of animals. The chances of encountering a nasty bacterial agent picked up along the way are considerably higher than if only one or two animals are involved.

I'm sorry, but the only hamburger worth eating (in my opinion) is a medium-rare burger, and medium-rare means a maximum temperature of no more than 135°F, which is not—I repeat: not—hot enough to kill the dreaded . . . *Escherichia Coli.*

***E. coli* is a very diverse group of bacteria, most of which are harmless. Some *E. coli* produce a toxin called Shiga, which can make you very sick indeed.[2] A particular strain of *E. coli,* 0157, is particularly nasty and just so happens to call the insides of ruminant animals home sweet home. Although this bacteria should only be found in fecal matter (try saying that on television) in massive slaughterhouses and meatpacking facilities, it's easy for a little of this material to enter the food chain. To the best of my knowledge, every single meat-related outbreak of *E. coli* recorded in recent years has involved factory-ground meat.**

Why? Since steaks and larger cuts are not ground, any gut bacteria present is only on the surface of the meat, and the surface is, in most cases at least, exposed to much higher temperatures than the 160°F required to kill *E. coli.* If your ground meat came from a factory, you've got to cook it to an internal temperature of 160°F in order to be safe. But although 160°F is fine for meatloaf and spaghetti sauce and sloppy joes it is not okay for hamburgers. If you really want that medium-rare burger you have three choices:

1. Trust your butcher to use quality meat, grind it responsibly, and hold it at proper temperatures. Convenient but potentially risky.

2. Buy whole cuts and request that they be ground on the spot. Less risky but still sorta risky because you can't be sure of the cleanliness of the equipment. You get the added benefit of seeing and knowing exactly what is going into your ground meat.

3. Buy whole cuts and grind them yourself at home. By far the safest way to go, but, yes, it does require more labor on your part. You're either going to have to set up the grinder or go with the chopped method recommended in this episode.

TIDBIT | Ground beef as we know it may have been born under the saddles of Tartar tribesmen, who placed tough cuts of beef between horse and leather in order to tenderize them. Legend has it that this meal was usually consumed raw. Thus: *steak tartare.* Cooks in Hamburg, Germany, applied heat to steak tartare. Thus: *hamburger.* A giant culinary leap for all concerned, I'd say.

TIDBIT | A roasted hamburger patty with gravy is known as Salisbury steak. It was invented by a British doctor (John Salisbury) as a health food for invalids.

TIDBIT | Right now 60 percent of American refrigerators contain ground beef.

APPLICATION

BURGER OF THE GODS

4 BURGERS

This may seem like a lot of work for a burger, but if you really love them you won't mind.

TIP | Before doing any weighing of meat, wrap the top of your scale in plastic wrap.

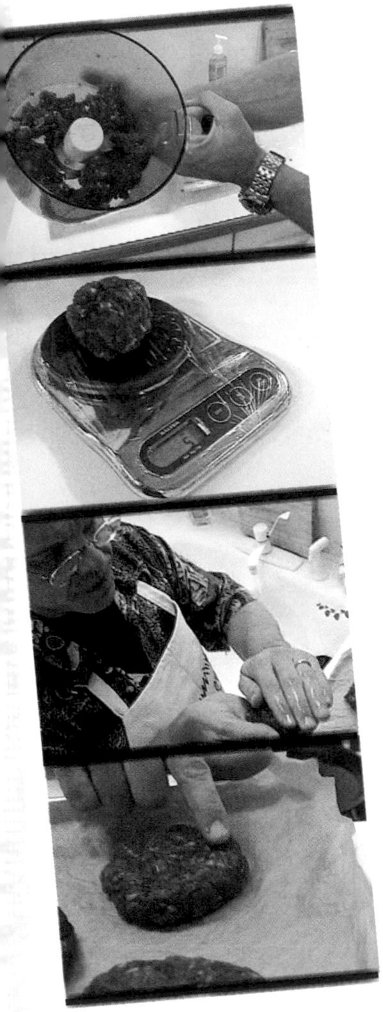

SOFTWARE

10	ounces	beef sirloin	trimmed and cut into 1½-inch cubes, chilled
10	ounces	beef chuck	ditto, chilled
½	teaspoon	kosher salt	

PROCEDURE

1. Put the sirloin in a **food processor** and pulse—that is, turn the motor on for 1 second, then turn it off for 1 second—10 times. Remove the sirloin to a **medium mixing bowl**.
2. Introduce the chuck to the **food processor** and pulse 10 times.
3. Mix the chuck into the sirloin, along with the salt. Knead gently together with your fingers.[3]
4. Weigh out 5-ounce portions of meat with your **scale** and roughly shape them into patties about ¾ inch thick and 4 inches in diameter. When shaping, keep in mind that as they cook they will tend to swell in the middle. Since no squeezing or squishing will be allowed once they hit the griddle, you may want to dimple them a bit in the center.
5. Heat a **griddle**: If your cook-top has a built-in griddle, heat it to medium-high. Alternatively, heat a properly cured **cast-iron griddle** over medium-high heat for 2 to 3 minutes.
6. Place the patties on the griddle, and make sure you don't crowd the cooking surface. (Each burger needs about 2 inches of personal space on all sides.)
7. *Resist the urge to smash the patties down with a **spatula**.*
8. Cook for 4 minutes on each side for medium-rare, or 5 minutes for medium. Let rest for 2 minutes, then serve.

Perfect patty!

But! I'd rather have a misshapen burger than a perfect-looking, overworked burger.

3/4 inch

4 inches X Round

APPLICATION

FLAME-BROILED BURGER

4 BURGERS

Special equipment: Chimney starter, all-natural lump charcoal, and kettle grill.

SOFTWARE

8	ounces	sirloin steak meat	trimmed and cut into 1-inch cubes
8	ounces	chuck steak meat	trimmed and cut into 1-inch cubes
8	ounces	lamb shoulder	trimmed and cut into 1-inch cubes
1	teaspoon	kosher salt	
4	ounces	cheddar cheese	grated, smoked if preferred
4		hamburger buns	
		mayonnaise	see page 242

PROCEDURE

1. Pass the meat through the **coarsest die** of a **food grinder**. Place the ground meat into a **bowl** and mix together to evenly distribute the different types of meat. Place in the refrigerator, uncovered, for 2 hours.
2. After 2 hours, fill one **large chimney starter** with charcoal and light. Once the coals are ashy white, transfer to a **kettle grill** and spread evenly. Set **grate** over coals.
3. While the coals are heating, shape the meat into 4 patties that are 6 ounces in weight and ¾-inch thick. Sprinkle each patty on both sides with the salt. Place on the grill and do not move for 2 minutes. Flip the burgers every 2 minutes until they reach an internal temperature of 135°F. Watch for hot spots and move the burgers if flare-ups occur. *Resist the urge to smash down on the patties.* Remove the burgers from the heat and prepare the buns by placing them on the grill, cut side down, for 1 to 2 minutes. Remove and place them cut side up on a **platter**. Divide the cheese evenly between the top buns, set the meat patty on top of the cheese, coat the cut side of each bottom bun with a little mayo, and set atop the meat. Allow each burger to sit upside down for a minute before flipping and consuming.

A QUICK NOTE ON BUNS

I have to admit an affinity for sesame seed buns. Not because they adorn the top of Big Macs and Whoppers nationwide, but because I like sesame seeds, which came to the United States from Africa. When toasted, their flavor is distinct and their crunch can upgrade many breads and crackers. By the way—a proper Big Mac has 180 of them.

TIP | Since mayonnaise is mostly fat and therefore hydrophobic, spreading a thin layer of it on the bottom bun will prevent the bread from being soaked by burger juice. And it tastes good to boot.

Mayo protects bun from meat juices

"Flame grilled" is good for advertising—but because it deposits soot on food, not good for "eats."

APPLICATION

MEATLOAF AGAIN[4]

6 TO 8 SERVINGS

When I was a kid, meatloaf was a necessary budget-stretcher and while it's still a smart money play today, this one I eat for the flavor.

SOFTWARE

6	ounces	homemade croutons (see page 28)	
½	teaspoon	black pepper	freshly ground
½	teaspoon	cayenne pepper	
1	teaspoon	chili powder	
1	teaspoon	dried thyme	
½		onion	peeled and quartered
1		carrot	cleaned and broken into chunks
3	cloves	garlic	peeled but left whole
½		red bell pepper	roughly chopped
18	ounces	sirloin	trimmed and cut into 1½-inch cubes, chilled
18	ounces	chuck	same as above, chilled
1½	teaspoons	kosher salt	
1	large	egg	lightly beaten
½	cup	ketchup	catsup, whatever
1	teaspoon	ground cumin	
1	dash	Worcestershire sauce	
1	dash	hot pepper sauce	
1	tablespoon	honey	

TIDBIT | Recipes for ground meat dishes "stretched" with other ingredients such as bread and vegetables started showing up in American cookbooks in the nineteenth century.

// PROCEDURE

1. Heat the oven to 325°F.
2. Combine the croutons, black pepper, cayenne, chili powder, and thyme in a **food processor** and pulse until the mixture is like sand. Transfer to a **large bowl**.
3. Combine the onion, carrot, garlic, and red bell pepper in the **food processor** and pulse until finely chopped but not pureed. Dump into breadcrumb mixture.
4. Load the sirloin into the **food processor** and pulse 10 times. Dump the sirloin into the **mixing bowl** and repeat with the chuck.
5. Add the salt, then the egg to the **mixing bowl**, and using your clean hands, combine thoroughly (avoiding the squishy squeeze we discussed in the hamburger application).
6. Line a **half sheet pan** with parchment paper. Plop the meatloaf mixture into the middle of the pan and shape it into a loaf.
7. Insert the probe of a **remote probe thermometer** so that the tip is in the middle of the loaf. Set the thermometer alarm to go off at 155°F.
8. Bake in the middle of the oven for 10 minutes.
9. Meanwhile, combine the ketchup, cumin, Worcestershire sauce, hot pepper sauce, and honey in a **small bowl**.
10. After 10 minutes,[5] **brush** the glaze onto the meatloaf and continue to cook for 25 minutes, or until the loaf hits 155°F.
11. Cool for 10 minutes before slicing and serving.

I like the crusty exterior that forms all over this loaf. You don't get that in a pan. Besides, going with this method means less to wash.

[1] Mintz is best known for his work on Caribbean cuisine.

[2] Small children, the elderly, and those with compromised immune systems can, and do, die from such infections.

[3] I usually wear vinyl gloves when doing this kind of thing. Otherwise, you're left with two contaminated hands. How will you turn the water on to wash them? By wearing gloves, all you have to do is take one off: instant clean hand. Oh, and by the way, notice I say "fingers." Try not to mash the meat into a paste.

[4] If you've ever been to a midnight movie, this requires no explanation. In any case, none shall be given.

[5] Seems like an odd step, I know, but 10 minutes will harden the outside of the loaf enough to prevent exiting juices from pushing off the glaze. Also, if the glaze went on at the start it would probably burn—and burnt ketchup is never good eats.

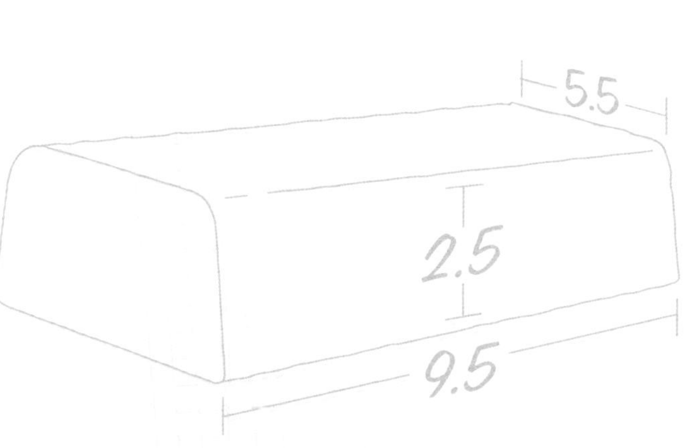

Ideal Loaf Shape

FRY HARD I

EPISODE 23 | SEASON 2 | GOOD EATS

Besides water and air, fat is the only ingredient that moonlights as a cooking environment. In fact, when it comes to the efficient use of energy, enhanced flavor, and enhanced texture, it's tough to beat frying. So why don't we use it more often? Well, possibly because we have the entire restaurant industry to do it for us. But I think it's high time we take frying into our own hands. This episode set out to show how it can be done.

OIL, FIRE, AND YOU

Although it's actually really difficult to heat oil to the flash-point, the temperature at which oil spontaneously burns, if you were to, say, accidentally drop water (an ice cube) into really hot oil, some of the oil could aerosolize, like fuel in a piston cylinder. If those tiny droplets come into contact with an open flame, an impressive pyrotechnic display could occur. If this were to happen, your best bet is to apply a lid or even a sheet pan or pizza pan. Shut off the air, shut off the fire. Once that's out, shut off the flame—carefully. If the fire spreads to other flammables, then reach for the fire extinguisher. Above all—never walk away from a hot pot of oil.

TRIVIA | I thought Merrilyn Crouch outdid herself as my sister.

KNOWLEDGE CONCENTRATE

Fats and oils are efficient cooking mediums because they can heat food to temperatures well above the boiling point of water. And they heat up much quicker than water, so cooking with fat is also potentially a better use of cooking fuel.

A lot of writers (especially those on the Internet) claim that fry oil should be used once and then discarded. Reasons cited usually involve the lowering of the oil's "smoke point." The implication is that as a fat degrades, the temperature at which that oil begins to give off smoke and rapidly degrade goes down. Apparently just beyond the smoke point is something called the "flash point," and the way these writers tell it, if you move beyond the flash point, several city blocks could be taken out by the primary explosion.

Well, I've tried on several occasions (highly controlled occasions) to make oil catch on fire all by itself, and it's actually pretty difficult. You need a lot of heat—oil temperatures in the 500°F-plus range—and an ignition point. This could be accomplished by, say, dropping a frozen turkey in the oil. As the vaporizing liquid tries to exit the pot as quickly as possible, zillions of tiny, hot droplets are aerosolized. As soon as they come in contact with the gas flame or electric calrod: ignition.[1]

That said, you are not going to incinerate your town because you make fries with the same oil twice. And I would go further to suggest that food writers who warn against oil reuse are simply hedging their bets against being sued by some numbskull who puts a pot of oil on high heat, drenches the drapes with lighter fluid, and goes to the movies.

Tossing your oil after a single fry session is a tragic waste of a perfectly good natural resource. Besides, it's just getting good and broken in. As we'll see in later episodes, as oil is used, chemical compounds are created that make it more efficient and aid in browning. This is why skilled fry cooks always mix old oil with new when they're changing out their vats. My M.O. is to use fry oil at least five times before replacing half. Here's what I do:

1. After use, cool the oil to room temperature (this can take a couple of hours).

2. Line a sieve or fine mesh strainer with big paper coffee filters.[2]

3. Strain the oil into an airtight, food-grade container. The vessel I use is cylindrical, and each time I filter a batch of oil I put a rubber band around it so I know how many batches are in there. When I get to five, I pour out half of it in a corner of the yard[3] and replace it with new.

4. Store in the freezer for up to forever. Recycled oil like this should never be pushed beyond 350°F. Push it to 400°F just once, and its useful life will effectively be over.

Done properly, frying contributes relatively little fat to food. Shirley O. Corriher was a guest on this show, and she nicely summed up the entire frying process thusly:

"When fries go into hot fat there's a shhhshshhsssss. And that's the water, the moisture in the fry turning into steam in the high temperature and pushing out. Now as long as the steam is pushing out, there is no way for the fat to go in. But the split second you run out of moisture in the food or in the batter, guess what. The fat literally gets sucked in."

And that, my friends, is the long and short of it.

TIDBIT The word *fry* comes from the Old French *frire*, which comes from the Latin *frigere*, from the Greek *phygein* ("to roast" or "bake").

APPLICATION

CHIPS[4] AND FISH

4 SERVINGS

Although flavorings and batters have their place, good fish and chips is really about technique, specifically temperature control. Oh, and don't forget about the malt vinegar.

SOFTWARE

FOR THE FISH

1½	pounds	firm-fleshed white fish	cut into 1-ounce strips (Tradition would dictate cod here, but pollock, haddock, and especially halibut would all work nicely. Avoid tilapia unless you just hate fish.)
1	cup	all-purpose flour	
1½	teaspoons	baking powder	
1	teaspoon	kosher salt	
¼	teaspoon	cayenne pepper	
1	dash	Old Bay seasoning	
1	cup	brown beer[5]	cold
3	quarts	safflower oil	
	enough	cornstarch	for dredging

FOR THE CHIPS

2	large (12 ounce)	russet potatoes	scrubbed and rinsed
		kosher salt	whizzed in a food processor or fine popcorn salt
		malt vinegar	for serving

TIDBIT Malt vinegar is made by malting barley, which causes the starch in the grain to turn to maltose. An ale is then brewed from the maltose and allowed to turn into vinegar.

PROCEDURE

1. Heat the oven to 200°F.
2. Run the potatoes through a **mandolin or V-slicer** with a thick julienne or fry blade.[6] As you cut, move the fries to a **large container** and submerge in cold water.[7]
3. **Whisk** together the flour, baking powder, salt, cayenne, and Old Bay in a **medium mixing bowl**. Slowly whisk in the beer, whisking until the batter is completely smooth. Refrigerate for 15 minutes to give the flour time to hydrate, thus creating a "stickier" batter. This can be done up to 1 hour ahead, but after that the batter goes downhill fast.
4. Heat the safflower oil in a **5-quart Dutch oven** over high heat. Attach a **fry thermometer** to the side of the pot and make sure you know how to read it.

Metal Mesh

Wood or Bamboo

I don't like models with metal handles because they conduct heat.

Spider

5 Drain the potatoes in the **colander insert of a salad spinner**, then spin to remove as much water as possible.[8]

6 When the oil reaches 320°F, cook the fries in 4 batches for 2 to 3 minutes, or until they are pale and floppy.

7 Remove from the oil with a **spider** and transfer to a **draining rig** (see page 19).

8 Increase the oil temperature to 350°F.

9 While the oil is heating, dredge the fish in the cornstarch (a **pie pan** would be an ideal vessel for this). Tap off as much excess cornstarch as you can.[9]

10 When the oil hits 350°F, dip the fish into the batter and ease it into the oil. Don't crowd the pan. When the batter is set on one side, turn the fish over and cook until golden brown and delicious. Move the fish to the oven to keep warm.

11 Boost the oil temperature to 375°F.

12 Working in small batches, refry the potatoes until they too are GBD. Drain on the same **draining rig** you rested them on after the first fry.

13 Season fish and fries with salt and sprinkle with vinegar. Consume.

[1] In essence, this is how an internal combustion engine works.

[2] I keep really big industrial paper coffee filters around for straining all sorts of things, such as stock, big batches of tea, and so on. You can get them at office supply and restaurant supply stores. If you really don't want to go that way you can use cheesecloth, but that's a waste, if you ask me.

[3] Greenpeace will not circle your home with Zodiacs. Cooking oil (unlike motor oil) is completely biodegradable.

[4] The OED notes that the earliest usage (in print) of the word *chip* as a descriptor for what we know as French fries is in Dickens's *A Tale of Two Cities*, published in 1859.

[5] Cold beer holds its CO_2 better than warm, and that will make for a lighter batter.

[6] I like French fries—a lot. Which is why I have a wall-mount, restaurant-grade manual fry cutter, which looks like this:

[7] Cold water is crucial because it will rinse off excess surface starch, which could gum up the steam release critical to fry cookery. Why cold? Because cold speeds the conversion of starch to simple sugars, and simple sugars are very good at browning. Many restaurants cut the potatoes a day ahead, place them in 5-gallon buckets of water, and stash them in the walk-in overnight.

[8] If you don't have a spinner, drain and dry on a towel. And then buy a spinner.

[9] You want this primer coat to be as thin as possible so that it can grab the batter and the fish at the same time. If there's too much starch, the batter will simply fall off.

A FEW FAT FACTS TO KNOW AND TELL

▸ All fat molecules are triglycerides; that is, they are composed of one unit of glycerol (modified slightly) and three fatty acids (hence *tri-glyceride*).

▸ Each fatty acid is essentially a long chain of carbon atoms with hydrogen attached. If all the carbon-bonding positions have hydrogen on them, the fatty acid is "saturated." If one spot is empty it's "monounsaturated," and if there are multiple empties it's "polyunsaturated." Where the empties fall also matters. For instance, in omega-3 fatty acids, there is an empty bond (which becomes a double carbon bond) three positions (seats, if you will) back from the methyl end of the fatty acid.

▸ In any given fat, all three of these molecules can be present. In fact, they can all exist in the same triglyceride.

▸ When we say that a certain fat—say, olive oil—is high in monounsaturated fatty acids, we only mean that those fatty acids are in the majority.

▸ Where hydrogen molecules are missing, double bonds form between carbons. These junctions kink. The more of these crooked fatty acids there are, the longer the oil will remain liquidous as the temperature drops.

▸ Saturated fats tend to be solid at room temperature, while poly and mono remain liquid. Put more simply: Fats are solid, while oils are liquid. Most edible oils solidify to some degree at refrigerator temperatures. Two exceptions are safflower oil, which remains completely liquid (this is probably why it's often used in salad dressings), and palm oil, which is highly saturated. Since palm oil can provide baked goods with a moist mouthfeel and long shelf life (since all their molecular bonding points are occupied, saturated fatty acids don't go rancid as quickly as other fats), manufacturers traditionally love it.

▸ Hydrogenated shortenings are vegetable oils (unsaturated) that have been artificially saturated with hydrogen so that they will be solid at room temperature. For most of the twentieth century, these "shortenings" were thought to be more healthful (or at least less unhealthful) than saturated fats. Then we found out that their particular shape, called "trans" fat, was even worse. Ah, science!

▸ The more unsaturated a fatty acid is, the more vulnerable it is to rancidity, as unwelcome elements hook up with the molecule.

TRIVIA Although it's a gross oversimplification of science, the "fat train" is probably my favorite *Good Eats* prop.

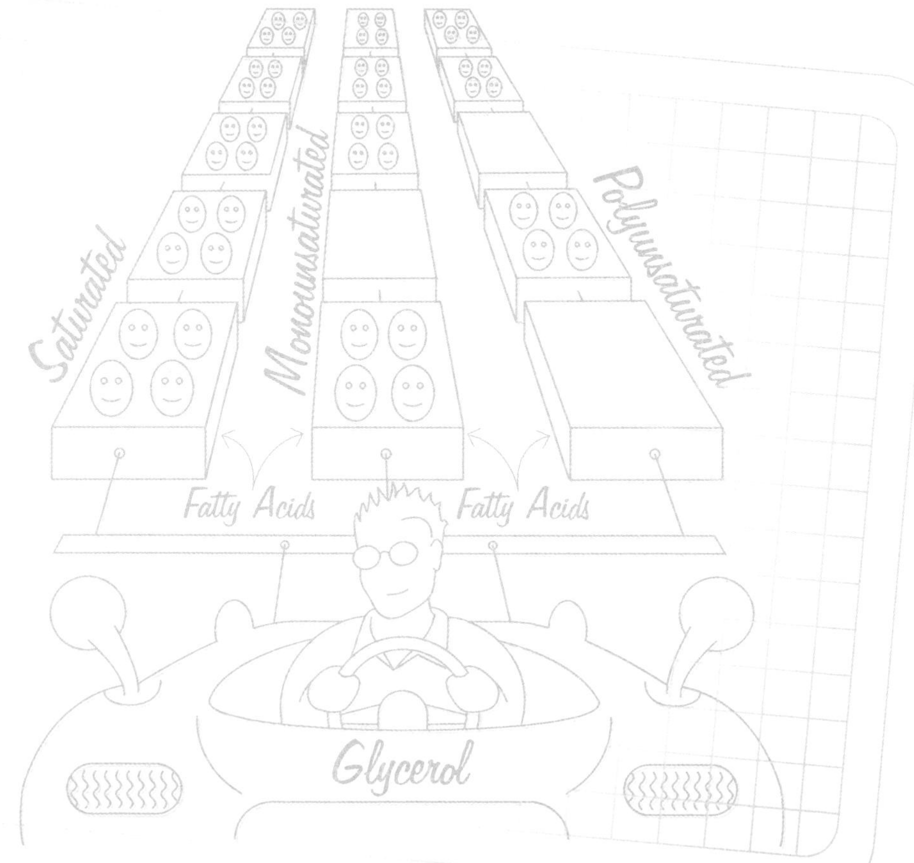

A triglyceride is an acid composed of two fatty acids and a glycerol that holds them all together. The fatty acids can be saturated, monounsaturated, or polyunsaturated. These terms refer to how many bonding positions on the fatty acid chains are vacant.

URBAN PRESERVATION I: JAM SESSION

EPISODE 24 | SEASON 2 | GOOD EATS

Preserves taste great, they're easy to make, and are a great way to utilize large amounts of locally grown fruits. I know, it seems a little too Aunt Bea for most modern folk and yes, it takes some time . . . and effort . . . and special equipment. Is it worth it? Trust me: The stuff's like gold. This particular application is perfect on toast or cake and melted on ice cream; I've actually melted it in cream and made ice cream out of it (see page 38). With a little added oil, it's a flank steak marinade or sauce, and it's the best floor wax you'll ever hope to buy.

Community Canning Center
Dawsonville, GA.

TRIVIA The Wheel of Sanitation prop featured in the scene with Dr. Brooks of the CDC was inspired by a similar scene in *Mad Max: Beyond Thunderdome*. That wheel featured things like Death, Auntie's Choice, and Gulag.

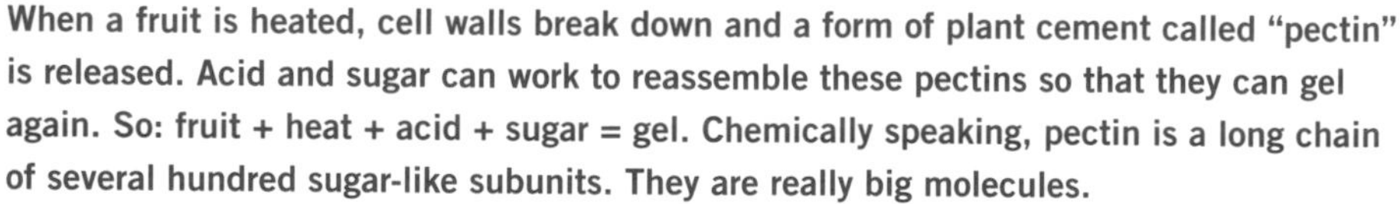

KNOWLEDGE CONCENTRATE

When a fruit is heated, cell walls break down and a form of plant cement called "pectin" is released. Acid and sugar can work to reassemble these pectins so that they can gel again. So: fruit + heat + acid + sugar = gel. Chemically speaking, pectin is a long chain of several hundred sugar-like subunits. They are really big molecules.

Some fruits, such as apples, blackberries, cranberries, and grapefruit, contain enough pectin and acid to set into gels with nothing but sugar added. Others, such as blueberries, cherries, and sweet oranges, have the pectin but need help with more acid. Apricots and pineapples have plenty of acid but not enough pectin to gel. Mangoes, bananas, peaches, and raspberries possess neither sufficient pectin nor enough acid to set into a gel, which is why we have to add both.

Acidic foods like fruits (and pickles) are easier to preserve than low-acid foods such as meat and vegetables because bacteria generally aren't comfortable in low-PH environments.

SPECIAL JAMMIN' HARDWARE

- Six 8-ounce mason-style preserving jars with lids and rings: the jars and rings are reusable; the lids are not. When kettle-processing canned goods, size of vessel matters, so always stick to the recipe. You don't want to play around with food safety.
- Wide-mouth canning funnel
- Canning tongs (a.k.a. a jar lifter): you can get by with spring-loaded tongs with rubber bands wrapped around the ends—if you're careful.
- Large (8-ounce) ladle
- 12-quart stockpot or canning kettle: the hardware store is the place to look for these.
- Measuring spoons and cups
- Digital scale
- 4-quart nonreactive (stainless-steel, enameled, or anodized aluminum) saucepan
- Wooden spoon
- Hand masher
- Candy thermometer
- Jar rack to keep jars off the bottom of the kettle: most canning kettles come with a rack. If you don't have a jar rack, use a round cake cooling rack. If you don't have that, just fold up a kitchen towel and place it in the bottom of the kettle.
- Paper towels
- Magnetized "lid wand" or magnet tool from the hardware store: optional, but how else you gonna get those lids out of the hot water?

ABOUT BOILING WATER AT ALTITUDE

All you need to remember is that the higher you go, the less sky there is pushing down on the top of the pot. And so the boiling point goes down. The lower you go (say, Death Valley), the more sky there is, and the more energy is needed for water to break out into a vapor. So the boiling point goes up. The boiling point changes 1 degree for every 500 feet of change in elevation.

> PHYSICIST: On Mount Everest [the boiling point is] 156°F.
>
> AB: 156? Wow, it must be tough to get a hard-boiled egg on Everest.
>
> MOUNTAIN CLIMBER: Yeah, but at that temperature you can reach right in and grab it.
>
> AB: Reach right in and grab it? Like Daryl Hannah did in *Blade Runner*?
>
> PHYSICIST: She was a replicant. It didn't count.
>
> AB: You got beat up a lot in school, didn't you?

Mile High Stadium

LOS ANGELES INTL. AIRPORT
Elevation: 125.5ft
Barometric Pressure: 30.14Hg
Boiling Point: 212.15°F

DENVER INTL. AIRPORT
Elevation: 5431ft
Barometric Pressure: 30.02Hg
Boiling Point: 201.7°F

Difference of: 11.33°F

FURNACE CREEK AIRPORT, DEATH VALLEY
Elevation: -210ft
Barometric Pressure: 30.32Hg
Boiling Point: 213.03°F

In the episode we discussed the effect of elevation on the boiling point of water. Truth is, atmospheric pressure also plays a role.

For instance, on the day I checked, the western states were relatively stable. I checked three airports and got three pressures ranging from 30.02 to 30.32, so on that day the boiling points were as shown above.

APPLICATION

SPICED BLUEBERRY JAM[1]

6 HALF-PINT JARS

Could you use fresh blueberries here instead of frozen? Sure, but you might have to tinker with the recipe a bit to get the set right, because local blueberry crops differ in sugar and acid content. The blueberries grown for the frozen market are typically very consistent.

TIDBIT | *Sanitized* means that harmful microbes have been minimized. *Sterilized* means that everything is dead.

// SOFTWARE

2	12-ounce bags	frozen blueberries	
1	1¾-ounce packet	powdered pectin	
¼	teaspoon	nutmeg	freshly grated
¼	teaspoon	ground ginger	
⅛	teaspoon	ground star anise	
2	tablespoons	lemon juice	freshly squeezed
5	tablespoons	cider vinegar	
22½	ounces	sugar	
½	cup	H_2O	

// PROCEDURE

PREPARE THE JARS, LIDS, AND UTENSILS:

1. Thoroughly wash the **jars**, **rings**, **lids**, **tongs**, **ladle**, and **funnel** with hot soapy water. Rinse.
2. Pile everything except the **lids**[2] in the **12-quart kettle**. Cover with **hot water** by at least 1 inch (leave part of the tongs above the water to snatch) and bring to a boil.
3. Maintain a boil for 10 full minutes to sterilize.
4. Kill the heat, wait 5 minutes, then add the lids.
5. Leave everything in place until you're ready to can.

NOW MAKE THE JAM:

1. Put the blueberries in the **4-quart saucepan** over low heat.
2. Sprinkle with the pectin, followed by the nutmeg, ginger, anise, lemon juice, and vinegar.
3. Once liquid starts to gather in the bottom of the pan, get to **mashing**.
4. Boost the heat to high and bring to a boil.
5. **Stir** in the sugar and water. Return to a boil, stirring occasionally. Boil *hard* for 1 minute. The jam should reach 220°F.
6. Remove from the heat and cool for 15 to 20 minutes.

NOW THE FUN PART:

1 Remove the **tongs**, **ladle**, and **funnel** from the pot. Use the **tongs** to remove and drain the jars, which then should be set upright on **paper towels**.

2 Place the **funnel** in the first jar[3] and, using the ladle, fill just to the bottom of the funnel about ⅓ of an inch from the bottom of the jar threads.[4]

3 Repeat with the remaining jars.

4 Wipe the jar rims with a **moist paper towel**. Double check for cracks or any abnormalities that might prevent a seal.

5 Use the **magnetic wand** to extract the lids from the hot water and place them on the jars.

6 Extract the rings and apply finger tight.

7 Return the jars to the pot, being certain that they don't touch the bottom of the pot or each other.

8 If necessary, add more hot water to cover the jars by at least 1 inch.

9 Bring to a hard boil over high heat. Find your elevation on the chart below and boil for the appropriate length of time.

0 to 1,000 feet above sea level: 5 minutes

1,000 to 3,000 feet: 10 minutes

3,000 to 6,000 feet: 15 minutes

6,000 to 8,000 feet: 20 minutes

Above 8,000 feet: Wait to make jam until you're back down to base camp.

10 Use the **tongs** to remove the jars from the water to a **folded towel**. Let the jars cool at room temperature for 6 to 8 hours. You may hear popping or hissing noises as the vacuum seals take hold. Check the lids before storing in a cool dry place: The lid should not flex when touched. Canning lids have a sealing compound on them that helps to create a vacuum when the jam or preserves cool. The ring helps hold it in place, but it doesn't need to be tight. After the lids set I usually remove the ring. Don't try to reprocess jars that don't seal. Instead, stash these in the fridge and use the jam within a few weeks.

11 Label your preserves with recipe name, where the food came from, the date it was "put up," and so on. Most experts suggest using preserves within 1 year. Discard the contents of the jar if the lid comes off, you see any mold, or if anything looks or smells funny. Bubbles, for instance, are bad. What would happen to you if you ate bad preserves? Acidic foods aren't very prone to botulism, so maybe not much—but you should never play around with these things.

SOME HISTORICAL PRESERVATION NOTES

- The earliest form of fruit preservation (besides simply drying) was probably accomplished by submerging cut fruits in honey. The Greek term for this, *melimelon*, is where we get *marmalade*.
- Mason jars with two-piece lids haven't changed design since John Mason first patented them back in 1857.
- In 1897 Jerome T. Smucker began pressing John Chapman's[5] apples to make cider. A few years later, he and his wife began cooking down the pulp to make apple butter.
- In 1869 Thomas Welch began making Concord grape juice. In 1918, he introduced Grapelade jam, and the U.S. Army bought his entire inventory.

[1] Jelly is clear; jam is not. Jam is typically 50 percent fruit and 50 percent sugar by weight. Conserves contain nuts or dried fruit. Preserves contain chunks of fruit, and marmalades always contain citrus zest. The FDA established standards of identity for jam, jelly, preserves, and whatnot in 1940.

[2] If you include the lids in the boiling phase the sealing compound may melt off, and that would be bad.

[3] You can handle this with clean hands; just don't touch the interior.

[4] Without this "headspace" there won't be enough air to expand and purge out, and without that air there will be no vacuum, and without a vacuum there won't be a seal. Without a seal there will be no preservation.

[5] As in Johnny Appleseed.

PANTRY RAID II: SEEING RED

EPISODE 25 | SEASON 2 | GOOD EATS

The pantry's more than just a closet. It's a testament to your preparedness. Having been a scout, I believe in being prepared, whether it's having a change of clothes for when you turn over the canoe . . . again . . . or plenty of canned tomatoes, without which I could not produce tomato sauce at a moment's notice. Oh, I know, some of you are shocked that I would make tomato sauce with canned product, but riddle me this: If you had a nice fresh, ripe, tomato off the vine, full of summer goodness, rich with perfume—perfect—what's the last thing you would do to it? If your answer isn't "cook it," then you don't deserve that fat vermillion orb in the first place. Nope, whether they're whole, chopped, diced, "put up," or store bought, canned tomatoes define tomato sauce, not to mention . . . good eats.

TIDBIT The lever-style can opener was invented in 1865 by Ezra Warner, of Waterbury, CT. The rotary can opener we're all familiar with wasn't invented until 1925. The electric can opener soon followed, in 1931. I'm not a fan of such devices because they're nearly impossible to keep clean. The cutting wheels tend to get dirty and stay dirty. When hunting for an opener, make sure it's fully washable.

KNOWLEDGE CONCENTRATE

Despite the fact that the U.S. Supreme Court determined in 1893 that the tomato is a vegetable (due to its common usage and the fact that at the time imported vegetables brought in big tariff money while fruits did not), tomatoes (*Lycopersicon lycopersicum*) are in fact berries that grow on a vine of the nightshade family. Although it's often considered the defining ingredient of Italian cuisine, the tomato is indeed a New World food that, like the potato, met with considerable distrust upon its arrival in Europe.

Canned tomatoes come in many forms for our convenience: crushed, diced, pureed, whole peeled, whole stewed, diced in puree, ground, crushed, whole with herbs, and organic. Now, all canned goods must be cooked, to some degree, in order to kill any pathogens that might stir up trouble. But since tomato sauces are usually cooked further, you might wish to avoid pureed and stewed specimens, which are often cooked even longer than more traditional canned models. I also avoid crushed tomatoes, because it's very difficult to vet out all the seeds—and seeds do a bitter sauce make. That leaves us with whole and diced. I generally assume that the less a food is processed the more it will taste like itself, so I generally stick to whole canned tomatoes over diced.

Although our sauce will be built on the fruit of the can, aromatics must be dispatched as well, and that means blades must be wielded.

The very, very first rule of knife work is that you must stand comfortably. If you're hunched over like Quasimodo you're not going to be able to cut.

The second thing to focus on is your grip. It needs to be secure yet comfortable. When wielding a chef's knife I prefer to grip the blade between thumb and forefinger. This gives me maximum steerability while reducing fatigue.

Never steer the knife with the hand holding the knife. Steer it with the hand not holding the knife by sliding the flat part of the blade up and down the front of the knuckles. (This is one of the reasons the chef's knife has evolved to have a wide blade at the back.)

TIDBIT | Tomatoes are a New World food and did not appear in Italian cookery until the nineteenth century.

Good

Bad

Super bad (and I don't mean in a good way)

APPLICATION

ALL-PANTRY TOMATO SAUCE

1 QUART

The broiler is one of my favorite cooking devices because it delivers fairly uniform, high-intensity radiant heat. I use it to make a darned tasty tomato sauce, suitable for serving on pasta or braising a rolled roast, entirely from the pantry. Browning the vegetables—including the drained canned tomatoes—under the broiler brings a depth of flavor to the sauce that wet methods such as simmering or boiling cannot deliver because they just don't produce enough heat.

// SOFTWARE

2	28-ounce cans	whole peeled tomatoes	
¼	cup	sherry vinegar	
½	cup	white wine[1]	such as Pinot Grigio or Sauvignon Blanc
2	tablespoons	sugar	
1	teaspoon	red pepper flakes	
1	teaspoon	dried oregano	
1	teaspoon	dried basil	
1		carrot	peeled and diced
1	medium	onion	diced
1	rib	celery	diced
4	tablespoons	olive oil	*not* extra virgin
4	cloves	garlic	smashed
3	ounces	capers	rinsed and drained
	to taste	salt and freshly ground black pepper	

// PROCEDURE

1. Set a large **strainer** over a **4-quart saucepan** and pour in the tomatoes, letting the juice run into the saucepan. Set the tomatoes aside.
2. Add the vinegar, wine, sugar, pepper flakes, oregano, and basil to the juice, put over high heat, and bring just to a boil, stirring occasionally.
3. Reduce the heat and simmer until the liquid is reduced by half or until it has thickened to a loose syrup consistency, 14 to 20 minutes.
4. Heat the broiler to high and place an oven rack in the middle position. Toss the carrot, onion, and celery[2] with the oil and garlic in a **roasting pan**. Place under the broiler for 3 to 5 minutes, or until the onions have begun to soften.

5 Carefully slide out the oven rack holding roasting pan and toss in the tomatoes and capers.

6 Return to the oven and broil for another 15 to 20 minutes, stirring every 5 minutes, until the tomatoes are browned around the edges. Carefully transfer the broiled tomato mixture to the saucepan. Remove from heat.

7 If you'd like, use a hand **masher** or a **stick (immersion) blender** to blend mixture to desired consistency.[3]

8 Serve immediately or cool to room temperature, seal in an airtight container, and freeze for up to 1 year.[4]

[1] Tomatoes are, botanically, berries, and most berries contain alcohol-soluble flavors that can be brought out by adding a little alcohol to the party. I like white wines for lighter sauces like this one, and reds for hearty, wintry fare. Although most of the alcohol that is added to long-cooking sauces does "cook out," some small percentage always remains behind.

[2] Mirepoix ("meer PWAH"): A 2:1:1 mixture of chopped onion, carrot, and celery.

[3] I use this sauce unblended on mussels, mashed with a hand masher for pasta, blended but still chunky for meatballs, and blended smooth for pizza.

[4] I keep ice cube trays around for freezing this sauce (as well as stocks) so that I can dose it out as needed without thawing an entire batch.

A FEW WORDS ABOUT KNIFE EDGES

I don't believe in home knife-sharpening systems. I believe in knife sharpeners—that is, trained professionals who either come by your house with a little van full of sharpening gear or who set up booths and sharpen your knives at kitchenware stores. My knives see some pretty heavy use, but I still don't have to sharpen them more than once a year. And I always have it done by a pro.

Honing a knife is not the same as sharpening. When a blade has lost its edge, either through use or abuse, it looks like this:

To retake an edge, material must be ground off of both sides. It must be sharpened.

An edge that is out of alignment or "true" looks like this:

It still has an edge; it's just not pointing at the food. Honing means to push the edge back into alignment via a honing steel.

Old-school high-carbon steel knives are soft enough to require occasional honing, but newer, high-end blades formed from technically superior alloys don't really benefit from it.

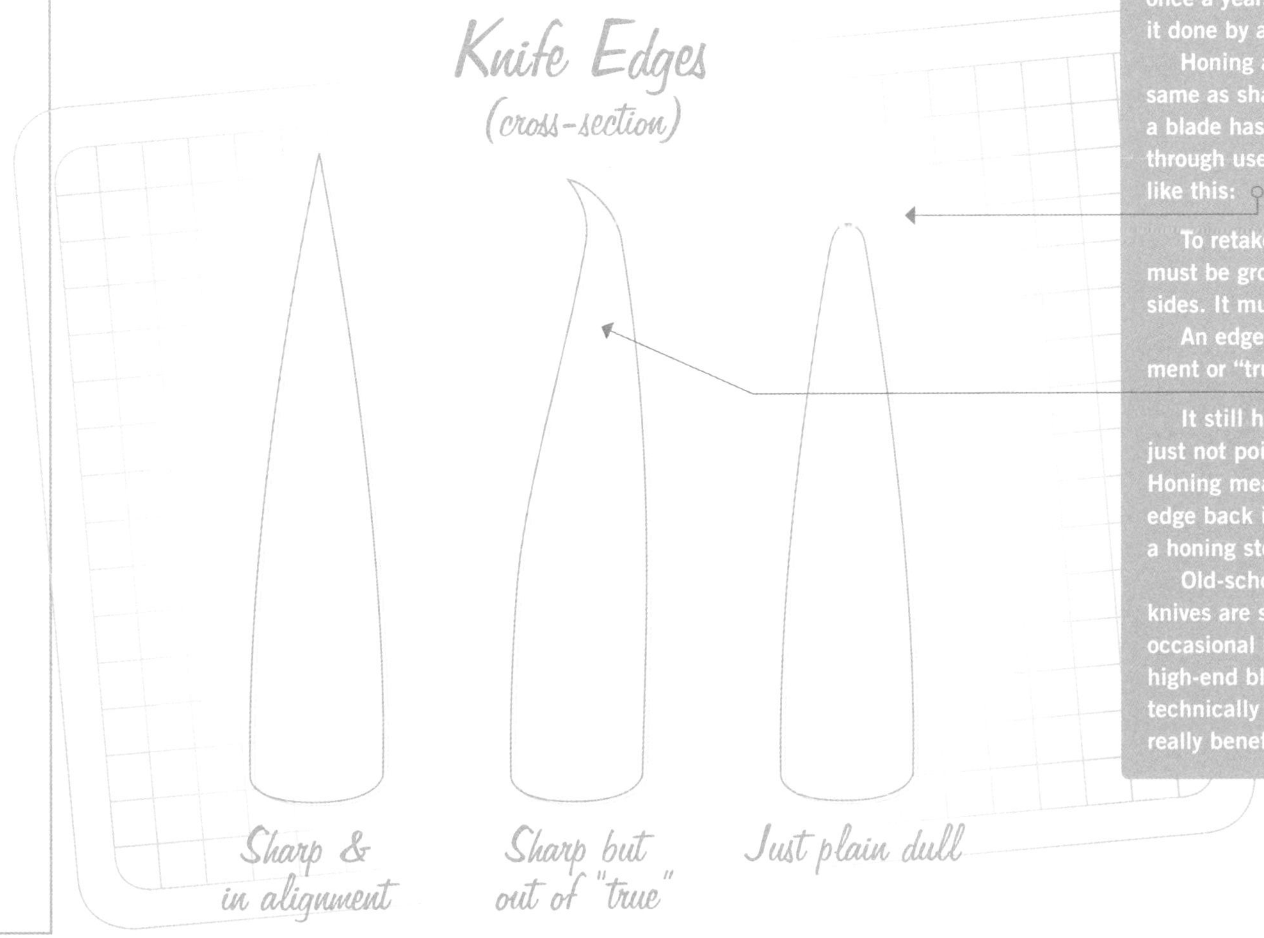

CITIZEN CANE

EPISODE 26 | SEASON 2 | GOOD EATS

At this point in the game we'd dabbled in sucrose, especially in "Churn, Baby, Churn" (page 36), but we hadn't given it full treatment as an ingredient. This show set out to do just that and give cooks a real feel for what those little crystals can do when you push them.

TRIVIA | This episode is probably not as enduring a classic as its namesake.

TRIVIA | The most uncomfortable afternoon of my life: In a big warehouse where raw sugar was piled sky high, we did a shot in which I fell back and made a snow angel in the white powder. Big mistake. The sugar got into everything—shirt, pants, boots, socks, underwear. Since it was hot and I was sweaty, it all dissolved. Then it cooled and recrystallized, setting every hair on my body in a solid candy matte so that every move I made pulled out hairs by the dozens. My boots were literally saturated with syrup and had to be thrown out.

SUGAR

Sugars are carbohydrates that come in many forms, but they are all composed of carbon, hydrogen, and oxygen. Simple sugars, or monosaccharides, are made up of just one molecule. Such sugars include:

GLUCOSE: Also called "blood sugar" because it is the sugar that our bodies use. In commercial applications glucose is called "dextrose." The simple glucose molecule is the basis for starches, which we'll get to later on. Glucose can be chemically converted into the sweeter-tasting fructose, which is how we get high-fructose corn syrup.

FRUCTOSE: Also known as levulose, fructose is found in fruits, vegetables, and honey. It's the sweetest of the common sugars.

MALTOSE: Mainly derived from grains, such as barley.

LACTOSE: The sugar commonly found in milk. It's mainly used in manufacturing processed foods, and it's not nearly as sweet as sucrose.

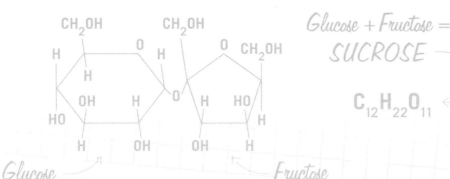

Glucose + Fructose = SUCROSE

$C_{12}H_{22}O_{11}$

Glucose

Fructose

Each molecule of table sugar, or sucrose, is composed of one glucose and one fructose molecule, making it a "double sugar," or disaccharide.

Sugars taste sweet, true, but they possess other qualities that make them valuable in preserving, baking, and candy making.

Sugar is hygroscopic, which means it attracts and binds to water. Because of that, baked goods containing high amounts of sugar tend to remain moister longer. Sugar acts as a preservative by binding to water and preventing it from becoming available for microbial consumption.

Unlike many simple sugars, sucrose dissolves easily in water. When boiled, some of the sucrose splits or "inverts," resulting in a stable "simple syrup" that will not recrystallize. This type of syrup is the basis for all nongranular or amorphous (smooth and clear) candies, including brittles and ice creams.

TIDBIT The average American consumes 142 pounds of sugar a year.

Sucrose takes dozens of forms. A few of the most common are:

GRANULATED SUGAR: Also called "table" or "white" sugar. It is processed so that the grains are uniform squares about .5mm across. Table sugar is almost pure sucrose.

SANDING SUGAR: Large sucrose crystals designed to add sparkle (via light refraction) and crunch to baked goods.

POWDERED OR CONFECTIONERS' SUGAR: granulated sugar that has been ground into a fine powder. Anticaking agents such as tri-calcium phosphate or cornstarch are added.

CASTER OR SUPERFINE SUGAR: Fine granulated sugar with a crystal size of about .35mm. Often called for in British recipes instead of confectioners' sugar. Also used in many cocktail applications because it dissolves quickly but contains no cornstarch.

MOLASSES: This thick syrup is a byproduct of cane sugar processing. (Although molasses can technically be produced from sugar beets it's generally held to be inedible.) It is essentially a slurry of sugars that are left over after all the available sucrose is crystallized.

BROWN SUGAR: Most commercial light and dark brown sugars are simply white granulated sugars to which varying amounts of molasses are added.

RAW SUGARS: Sugars that, unlike processed brown sugars, are not fully refined. This group includes demerara, muscovado, and turbinado. Raw sugars range in color from light tan to nearly black and are the most flavorful of all sugars. However, since they contain other ingredients, including acids, vitamins, and minerals, the cook must be careful when substituting such products for other sugars called for in recipes.

HOW CANE SUGAR IS PRODUCED:

1. A massive grinder called a "tandem" chomps the grass into cane juice.

2. Lime and other natural chemicals are used to clean the cane juice.

3. The juice is cooked down and filtered repeatedly until raw sucrose crystals form.

4. Raw crystals are sent to a refinery, where they are further purified.

5. A centrifuge separates pure crystals from the liquid (molasses) and is purified further.

6. The crystals are thoroughly dried and then packaged.

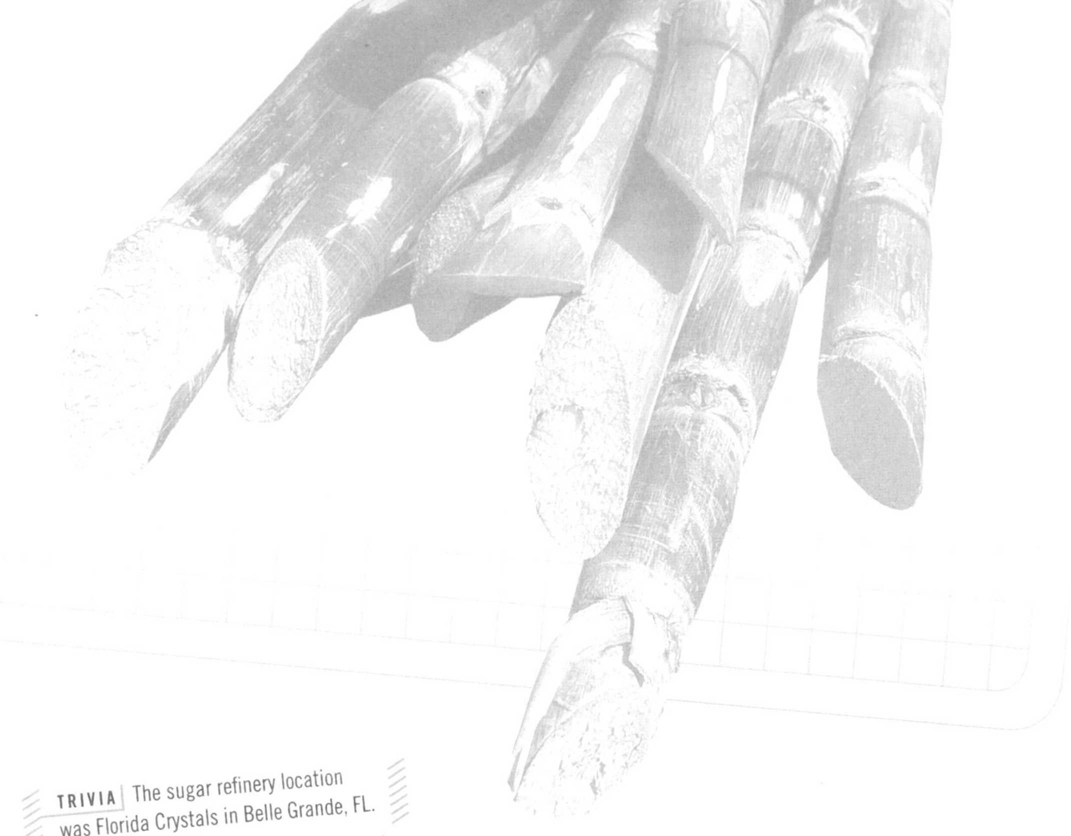

TRIVIA | The sugar refinery location was Florida Crystals in Belle Grande, FL.

KNOWLEDGE CONCENTRATE

CANDY MAKING

At its most basic, candy making is all about controlling the crystallization of sugar and the concentration of the sugar syrup the candy is being made from. Candies can be granular, like fudge, or smooth and chewy, like caramels, both of which contain a fair amount of water. Brittle is amorphous candy, like caramel, but it has had most of the moisture cooked out of it so it's very hard. The type of candy a cook produces is almost entirely a factor of moisture content, and that can be calculated by the temperature to which the syrup is cooked. That's because the less water that's present, the higher the temperature can rise above the boiling point of water.

Back before confectioners had reliable thermometers, they calculated the doneness of a syrup by dropping a bit in cold water and observing how it behaved once cool. This is where we get what are called the "ball" or "candy" stages:

Stage	Temperature	Use
Thread	230°–235°F	syrup, preserves
Soft ball	235°–240°F	fudge, pralines
Firm ball	245°–250°F	chewy candies
Hard ball	250°–265°F	nougat, marshmallow
Soft crack	270°–290°F	taffy, butterscotch
Hard crack	300°–310°F	brittle, lollipops
Caramel	320°–360°F	caramel sauce

Most of the applications in this show concentrate on the high end of the temperature scale, from 340°F up. At these temperatures, sugar has not only dissolved but is beginning to break down molecularly. This process is called, oddly enough, caramelization, and it involves, among other things, our old friend oxidation (more on that later). A lot of flavor can be created during caramelization, including smoky, bitter flavors that are quite desirable. But beware, because the door that separates caramelized from burnt is thin and flimsy. And remember that sugar syrups have a fair amount of mass so carryover cooking is an issue.

A SPOONFUL OF HISTORY

- The word *sugar* comes from the Sanskrit *sharkara*, which means "small bits" or "gravel." Candy comes from an Arabic derivation of the same term, *khandakah*.

- Almost all green plants manufacture sucrose via photosynthesis, but only two plants, sugar beets and the giant grass *Saccharum officinarum* (sugar cane) produce it in harvestable amounts. Although the process of making sugar from cane was probably developed in India, the popularization of sugar happened at the hands of Arab merchants, who perfected production and then moved the product across the northern rim of Africa and into Spain, which they invaded in 711 B.C.

- At various times in history, a spoonful of sugar cost upward of $100.[1]

- Christopher Columbus took sugar cane clippings to the Caribbean in 1493, and they immediately took hold. European colonial powers hoping to fuel sugar demand back home set up massive cane plantations and sugar refineries worked entirely by African slaves. Although much of the sugar was sent back to Europe, the molasses went to the American colonies, where it was made into rum. In many ways, the geopolitical structure of the Americas was shaped by the sugar industry.

APPLICATION

DOODADS AND CARAMEL SAUCE

APPROXIMATELY 30 DOODADS
AND 1 PINT OF CARAMEL SAUCE

Here we utilize high heat to create flavor in sugar and create a solid candy and a creamy sauce at the same time.

Before you get started, please note that in culinary schools caramel has a nickname: "napalm." It's just that hot and just that sticky, and you, my dear reader, should take care when handling it.[2]

TIP | So what do you do with a doodad? Shove one into the top of some vanilla ice cream and serve. Your guests will be flabbergasted by your sheer artistry. As for storing the little creatures, remember that sugar is hygroscopic, and doodads will quickly go gooey on you if they're left in a humid environment. I typically stash them in a Tupperware or other sealable containment with sheets of parchment paper between the layers. If you really want to make sure they keep, take a hint from sugar artists and stash a couple broken pieces of limestone in the vessel to soak up water from the air.

SOFTWARE

14½	ounces	sugar	
1	cup	H_2O	
1	tablespoon	light corn syrup	
¼	teaspoon	cream of tartar	(optional)
1	cup	heavy cream	

PROCEDURE

1. Combine all the ingredients except the cream in a **heavy 2-quart saucepan** and place over high heat. Stir occasionally until the sugar has dissolved.
2. Heat a **candy thermometer** under warm water and attach it to the side of the pan, making sure that the bulb tip is completely submerged. Oh, and no stirring for a while.
3. Meanwhile: For doodads, invert **two half sheet pans** and cover with **parchment paper**. For caramel sauce: have the cream standing by.
4. When the sugar mixture reaches 230°F (after 3 to 5 minutes), reduce the heat to medium and cook, without stirring, for 7 to 9 minutes, until the syrup is amber colored and is approaching 300°F. At this point there is less likelihood of crystallization (especially with the cream of tartar and corn syrup), so gently swirl the pan to help break up any hot pockets.
5. When the temperature starts edging toward 340°F, it will become deep amber. Remove the pan from the heat and slowly stir, this time with a **metal spoon**, until the caramel falls off the spoon in a solid, stringlike stream when the spoon is lifted. It's doodad time.

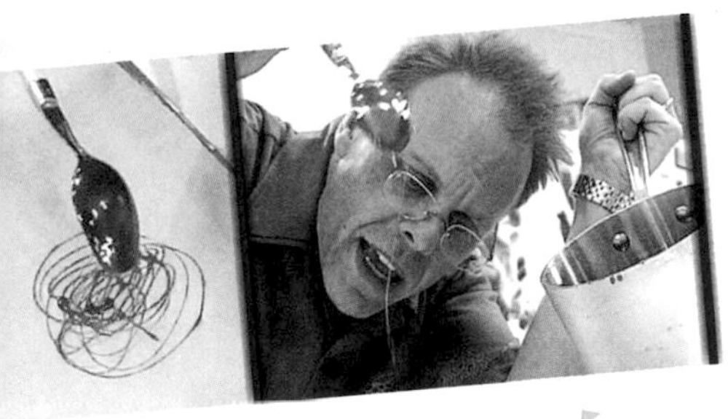

6. Dip the spoon into the caramel. Retract the spoon and let the caramel drain for a few seconds, then drizzle in whatever pattern you like onto the parchment. I usually go with spirals because they're more structurally sound when cool and dry. As you work your way across the pans you'll probably want to keep the pan in your opposite hand so you don't have to reach over your work and risk accidental dribbles.[3] Cover the two pans with doodads.

7 Return the remaining caramel to medium-high heat and continue cooking. When you detect the first wisps of smoke,[4] immediately remove from the heat, stand back,[5] and add the cream all at once. Return to medium heat and boil for 3 more minutes, stirring occasionally.

8 Cool to room temperature, then transfer the sauce to a squirt bottle and refrigerate for up to 1 month.

[1] In modern currency, that is.

[2] Whenever I handle molten sugar I wear a big red mitt that looks like this:

I'm scarred enough, thanks.

[3] Your first few doodads will look beady and, frankly, pathetic. But once you get your wrist movements worked out things'll shape up.

[4] Don't worry, it's not going to blow up. But if you don't act promptly the caramel will move from flavorful to sooty very quickly.

[5] What happens when a water-based liquid hits molten lava at over 300°F? Steam and hissing and foam, oh my. So, yes, stand back a bit.

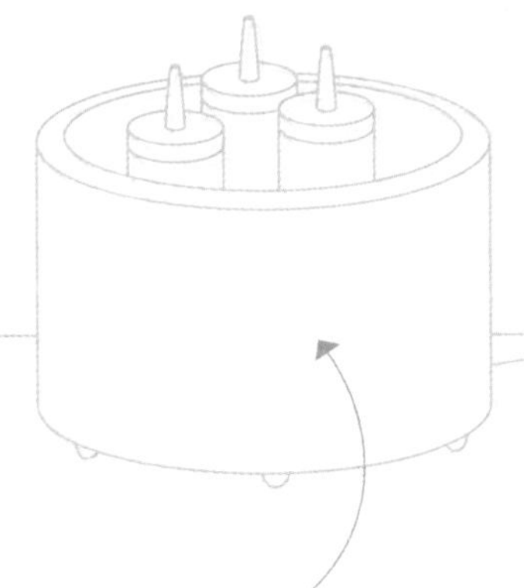

TIP Caramel sauce refrigerated in a squeeze bottle is like concrete. So, about an hour before you plan to squeeze, place the bottle in a vessel of hot but not scalding water and keep it there. If I'm tossing a big fête where several squeeze sauces will be involved, I fold a small kitchen towel and place it in the bottom of my slow cooker, fill it with water, set to low, and load up.

WHAT THESE INGREDIENTS DO

SUGAR

Provides the necessary molecular material: sucrose, which will be broken down into fructose and glucose and, if enough heat is applied, a mess of other compounds as well.

WATER

Although most of it will cook out, water plays a crucial role in candy making for two reasons. First, water is a solvent, which means the sugar can dissolve in it. Since it heats slowly and evenly, even when high heat is applied, water makes temperature control very easy, albeit a little slow.

CREAM OF TARTAR AND LIGHT CORN SYRUP

As the water evaporates and the temperature increases, the syrup becomes concentrated, which means that the sugars are so cramped together that it would be very easy for them to "fall out of solution" and recrystallize. This can be a good thing if it's initiated when and where we want (usually by stirring after the syrup has cooled for a while, as with fudge and fondant). In smooth or amorphous applications, this is a bad thing, and we can prevent it by doing three things:

1. Avoid stirring, which can smack sugars into each other, prompting crystallization. This is especially a factor when you use a metal spoon, which, being a conductor, can sap just enough heat out of the saturated solution immediately surrounding it to kick-start crystallization, which is why confectioners only use wooden spoons when they use spoons at all.

2. Now back to the chemicals: Cream of tartar is an acid, and a small amount can "invert" the sucrose—that is, split some of it into fructose and glucose, which can physically get in the way of the other sucroses and then keep them from hooking up. It doesn't take much.

3. Corn syrup is almost 100 percent glucose. Add enough of this stuff and the odds of sucroses getting together are next to nil.

EPISODE 27 | SEASON 2 | GOOD EATS

TRIVIA | Be cool, Honey Bunny.

Here in America we are fond of saying, "We use everything but the oink." . . . or is that the "squeal." All this versatility is great, of course, but it can lead to some confusion for the home cook. Consider the cuts. There are hams at both ends. The shoulder is called the butt. And what's with all those ribs? Funny I should ask, because we chose the loin ribs, or baby backs, as base camp for exploring the endless possibilities of pork.

Today's pork has 15 percent less fat than it did just fifteen years ago. The fat content of some cuts are, in fact, on par with skinless chicken. And guess what? Some cuts taste just like skinless chicken.

"No one stirred in the farm house before noon the following day. And the word went round that from some where or other the pigs had acquired the money to buy themselves another case of whisky."

GEORGE ORWELL, *ANIMAL FARM*

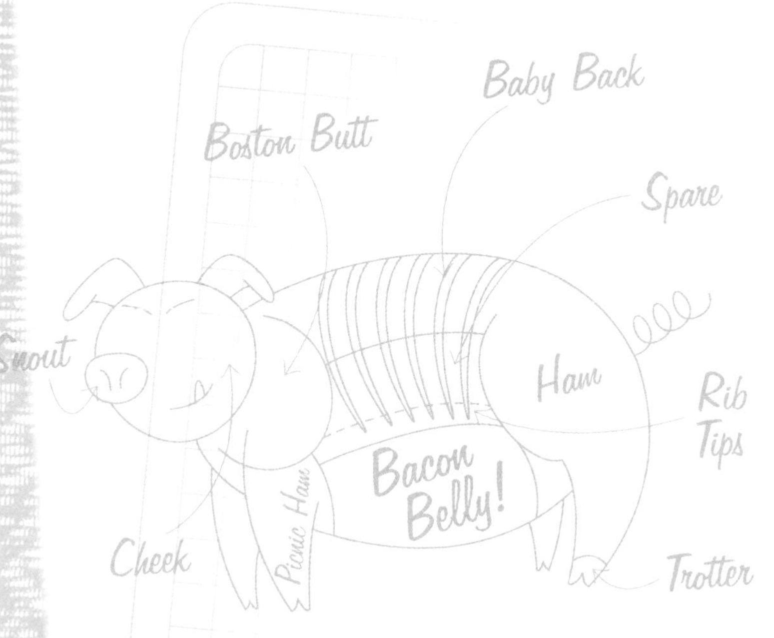

KNOWLEDGE CONCENTRATE

While big meat packers and processors have been busy designing and breeding pigs—descendants of Eurasian wild boars, *Sus scrofa*—that can grow fast and lean and make it to market with as low a price as possible, some farmers are working to bring back classic breeds such as Tamworth, Gloucestershire Old Spots, Duroc, and Six Spot Berkshire (which actually do have six spots). These pigs cost more, and they taste like it.[1]

So how do you make standard megamart or butchershop pork palatable? Once upon a time you had to cook pork to cinders (okay, 170°F, but that's well-well-done, if you ask me) to avoid having your body invaded by trichinella worms, which can do some very nasty things, like ball up inside muscle tissue. Although you can still easily confront this fate when eating cougar, fox, horse, seal, or walrus, the truth is that modern feed programs have pretty much taken trichinella out of modern pork. In fact, as of this writing the only recorded cases I could trace in the last decade involved wild game. In other words, you should feel free to eat your pork chops cooked to medium.

Following, a pork rib primer:

BABY BACK RIBS: Cut from right up near the spine, where the ribs are thinnest. Since they're next to the loin, the meat here is relatively tender and, I would argue, relatively tasteless. The only reason I used this cut on the show is that baby back ribs are easy to find and handle.

SPARE RIBS: Start where the baby backs leave off and continue all the way to the breast bone. These are meaty ribs, at least one and a half times the width of the rack ribs. These are also more work because more connective tissue is involved.

ST. LOUIS RIBS: Basically spare ribs from which the "skirt" flap and excess meat (including the rib tips) have been removed. Typically St. Louis ribs are served by establishments that also serve rib tips, since you wouldn't want to cut them off just to trash them.[2]

A FEW FUN FACTS REGARDING PIGS

- Pigs were probably first domesticated in China around 4900 B.C.
- Christopher Columbus brought eight pigs to Cuba in 1493. Hernando de Soto brought thirteen pigs to Florida in 1525. Today only China has a greater swine population than the United States.
- The world record for big pig still goes to Big Bill, a Poland China hog from Tennessee who, in 1933, weighed in at 2,552 pounds. At the time of his death (he had to be put down due to a broken leg) he was more than nine feet long.
- How come pork is lighter in color than beef? Grazing animals like cattle and sheep eat grass. Grass contains iron. Iron produces myoglobin, and myoglobin is responsible for making meat red. Although they do eat just about everything else (mostly corn), pigs don't do grass.
- In eighteenth-century Paris, pigs were allowed to roam the streets eating garbage.[4]

"The pig is but a giant dish which walks while waiting to be served."

GRIMOD DE LA REYNIERE[3]

TIDBIT | Although "Memphis in May" gets all the media attention, for my money, Vienna, GA's Big Pig Jig is *the* premiere porcine event in the United States.

APPLICATION

WHO LOVES YA BABY BACK RIBS

4 TO 6 SERVINGS

The rub amounts were originally given as a ratio so that folks could make up as much as they wanted and keep it in the pantry. I thought this was pretty clever, but that's because I'm light-handed with the rub. A lot of viewers shook it on hard and heavy and were rewarded with big, tender mouthfuls of succulent . . . salt. Still, I wanted the rub to be self-contained, the kind of mix you could always keep in a jar in the pantry.

Also, in the show I used something called Jalapeño Shake, which turns out to be really hard to find if not impossible in some parts of the country. People got mighty steamed at me about that, and I don't blame them. So we went back to the drawing board. Now the ratio is more like this: 6 parts firmly packed light brown sugar, 1 part kosher salt, 1 part chili powder,[5] 1 part free-form (which may or may not include jalapeño seasoning; it's your choice).

The rub that follows is how that ratio translates in my kitchen. Keep in mind that 1 tablespoon is 3 teaspoons.

TIDBIT In my own kitchen this application has morphed a bit. The rub remains the same, but I've replaced the braising liquid with frozen orange juice concentrate, straight from the can, mixed with twice as much margarita mix. I'm not sure what brand the mix is, but it's got a picture of a saucy señorita on it and that's good eats enough for me.

SOFTWARE

FOR THE RUB

6	tablespoons	light brown sugar	firmly packed
1	tablespoon	kosher salt	
1	tablespoon	chili powder	
½	teaspoon	black pepper	freshly ground
½	teaspoon	ground cayenne	
½	teaspoon	jalapeño shake	or other jalapeño-based seasoning
½	teaspoon	Old Bay seasoning	
½	teaspoon	dried thyme	
½	teaspoon	onion powder	
¼ to ½	teaspoon	canola or safflower oil	(optional)

FOR THE RIBS

2	2-pound slabs	baby back ribs	

FOR THE BRAISING LIQUID

1	cup	white wine	(cheap!)
2	tablespoons	white wine vinegar	
2	tablespoons	Worcestershire sauce	
1	tablespoon	honey	
2	cloves	garlic	minced

// **PROCEDURE**

MAKE THE RUB:

1 You can just put the sugar, all the spices, and herbs in a **jar**[6] and shake it up. But unless you shake it really well each time you use it, the larger grains tend to separate out from the smaller ones. Better to take everything for a spin in the **food processor** to homogenize it a bit. Also, if you know you're going to be storing it for a while, go ahead and work in a bit of oil to coat the spices and prevent them from losing all their volatile essential oils.

RUB THE RIBS:

2 Lay each slab out, bone side up (concave), on a piece of **heavy-duty aluminum foil** that's big enough to easily wrap around the ribs like this:

3 Sprinkle each side liberally with the rub, wrap as shown, and refrigerate overnight.

4 Combine all the braising liquid ingredients in a **mixing cup** with a spout for easy pouring.

5 Heat the oven to 250°F—no hotter.

6 Place the 2 pork pouches, seam up, on a **half sheet pan**. Unroll one end and pour in half the braising liquid.

7 Re-roll the end of the foil. If your pouch be true, nary a drop will leak. Put the pan on the center rack of the oven and bake for 2½ to 3 hours.[7]

8 Remove from the oven and using **insulated gloves** or **tongs** gently move pouch number 1 to a vertical position in a **medium saucepan** or **saucier**. Snip the end of the pack so that the braising liquid drains into the pan. Repeat with pouch 2.

9 Put the pan over high heat.

10 Place the wrapped pouches back on the half sheet pan. Open one and carefully take hold of a bone near the center of the rack and give it a twist. It should let go of the meat but not without a bit of a struggle. If they don't feel done, immediately re-wrap and return to the oven while you finish the sauce. (Don't worry, there's still enough moisture in the packs to get the job done.)

11 Once the braising liquid comes to a boil, decrease the heat to medium and cook until it has reduced to half its original volume and has thickened to a syrupy consistency. (At this point you can let the ribs and sauce cool to room temperature, then refrigerate. Bring the ribs to room temperature and spoon off the solidified fat from the surface of the sauce before broiling and reheating.)

12 Heat the broiler and move the oven rack to the second position from the top.

13 Unwrap the racks and turn them meat side up, leaving them on the foil. If you'd like, cut them into 2-rib portions with **kitchen shears**.

14 Use a **basting brush** to paint on a liberal coating of the sauce and broil just a couple of minutes to caramelize the sauce.

15 While the ribs broil, use a **gravy separator** to de-fat the remaining liquid if it hasn't been refrigerated.

16 Carefully remove the ribs from the oven and serve outside with a **hose** and **bath towel** on the side.

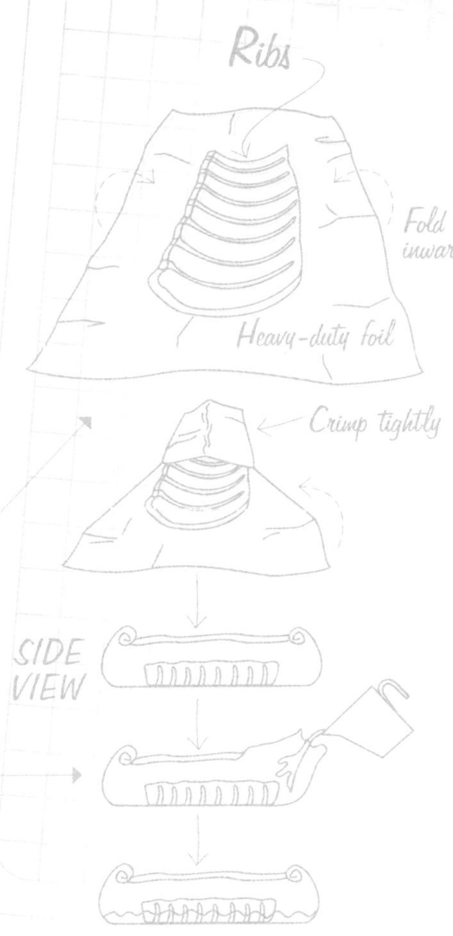

[1] When it comes to food, cheaper is very rarely better, unless you're talking tomatoes in August.

[2] Oddly, St. Louis–style ribs are common in the state of Missouri, though I can't say why.

[3] An eighteenth-century gastronome and lawyer who was about as close to a human pig as anyone in history. He supposedly blew the fortune he inherited from his father on food and parties.

[4] Several tales exist in the annals of that city that tell of such pigs occasionally wandering into houses and eating human babies.

[5] As opposed to chile powder, which would simply be powdered chiles.

[6] Why a jar? If you store this mixture for more than a few days it'll stain a plastic container.

[7] This low-heat, minimum-moisture cooking method is known as "braising." The purpose is to break down the connective tissue surrounding the ribs (mostly collagen) into lip-smacking-good gelatin. In the process the ribs will become toothy-tender. But wait, that's not all: Long, low, moist cooking also encourages flavor transfer between the liquid and the food.

EAR APPARENT

EPISODE 28 | SEASON 2 | GOOD EATS

"Though we have tried and tried, sex is not as good as sweet corn." Or so famed Lake Wobegoner Garrison Keillor once wrote. As far as I know, no one has made such claims on behalf of other corn varieties, though I suspect many a young American has thrilled to the sight of Jiffy Pop swelling enthusiastically on the stove.

Besides being the New World's greatest contribution to nutrition, corn as we know it has the distinction of being one of man's earliest inventions. Like the wheel, corn has rolled itself down the countless avenues of our lives, lending its ear to everything from plastics to pharmaceuticals. Creations can turn on their masters, and corn has caused its share of pain and suffering, but in the laboratory that is the kitchen, corn is our friend. If we'll just take the time to listen to it, to understand it, learn what it needs, well, I might not go as far as Garrison Keillor, but I'll admit corn is darned good eats.

KNOWLEDGE CONCENTRATE

Although corn—I mean maize—can be categorized in a number of ways, here's how we break things down:

FLINT CORN: This is very hard stuff, which is why it's named after a rock. The colored "Indian Corn" we hang on our doors at Thanksgiving is flint corn. These days it's used for animal feed and by industry.

POPCORN: A specialized version of flint corn that has just enough moisture inside to explode or "pop" when cooked.

FIELD/DENT CORN: Waxy starch and thick protein coat. Named after the dent that forms in each kernel. Used mostly as animal fodder but also in processed foods, dent corn figures in the production of corn syrup, ethanol, adhesives, dyes, batteries, book bindings, fireworks, surgical dressings, crayons, plastics, baby food, chewing gum, beer!, pet foods, salad dressings, mustard, aspirin, lipstick, body lotion, soda, ketchup, jam, jelly, and a wide range of insecticides.

FLOUR CORN: Has a soft, starchy kernel, which grinds easily. Native Americans used this variety extensively and still do.

POD CORN: Each kernel has its own husk, so it's pretty much useless for everything but scientific research.

SWEET CORN: Contains far more natural sugar than other types of corn. Although it's the corn we think of when we think of corn, it accounts for a relatively small percentage of the U.S. crop.

Though these days most corn research has turned toward developing hybrids that produce the chemicals necessary for ethanol production, our focus here will be on sweet corn. I cannot stress the importance of purchasing fresh corn from a local source. The second an ear is picked, its sugar begins converting to starch. In Iowa they actually say you don't pick the corn until the water's boiling.

Things to look for:

EAR: Plump and firm

HUSK: Bright and moist

CUT END: Bright and moist with no dark spots

THE TASSEL: Sticky and golden brown (black is bad)

KERNELS: Tight, plump, and rowed all the way up to the top[1]

If you must store fresh corn: Scientists at the University of Maryland figured out that you can hold corn at its peak flavor for up to 2 weeks if you shuck it and then give it a 15-minute soak in a gallon of iced water laced with a drop of lemon juice and 2 drops of household bleach. After the bath, seal in plastic (bags or wrap) and stash in the coldest part of the fridge. Skip the dip, and the best you can expect is a day or two.

EAR OPTIONS

HOW TO BOIL CORN

Dunk ears (husk on) into boiling water for 1 minute. If you fear that the ears may be past their prime, add 2 tablespoons of sugar to the water but no salt.

HOW TO STEAM CORN

If you have a large steamer basket, load it wih fresh ears and steam 10 minutes—peel and eat. (Preserves sweetness better than boiling.)

HOW TO ROAST CORN

In my kitchen we roast corn by lining up the ears, husk and tassel intact, in a 350°F oven. No foil, no nothing. The husk keeps the kernels moist, and I believe also injects them with flavor. Pull them in an hour, cool briefly, peel, and eat with obscene amounts of butter, salt, and pepper—or, if you grow your own, nothing at all.

APPLICATION

BETTER-THAN-GRANNY'S CREAMED CORN

4 TO 6 SERVINGS

Although many of their staple dishes were built on dried corn, the Native Americans of the colonies did eat fresh corn, and more often than not it was prepared by scraping off the kernels with an oyster or clamshell, which was then used to "milk" the cob. In fact this juicy goodness was about as close to milk as the original Americans had. And so creamed corn is about as American a dish as you can assemble from the most American ingredient.

SOFTWARE

1	tablespoon	unsalted butter	
½	medium (about 4 ounces)	onion	diced
2	pinches	kosher salt	
1	sprig	rosemary	bruised (that is, crushed roughly between your hands)
8	ears	fresh corn	(3 pounds total)
1	tablespoon	sugar	
¼	teaspoon	ground turmeric	(to up the yellow a bit)
2	tablespoons	stone-ground cornmeal	
1	cup	heavy cream	(it *is* called "creamed corn," ya know)
1	pinch	black pepper	freshly ground

PROCEDURE

1. Put the butter in a **3-quart saucier** and melt over medium heat. Add the onion, salt, and rosemary and sweat until the onion is translucent, about 5 minutes.
2. Meanwhile, place a **paper bowl** upside down in the middle of a **large mixing bowl**.
3. If you have an old-fashioned **corn on the cob holder**, insert one in the skinny end and place the ear vertically on—oh, just look at the picture.

MY FAVORITE CORN ON THE COB BUTTER MIX

Beat 1 stick of butter with 2 tablespoons olive oil, ½ teaspoon salt, ½ teaspoon cumin, and a pinch of cayenne until soft. Refrigerate and spread at will.

1 - Old-fashioned cobb holder
2 - Inverted paper bowl
3 - Metal mixing bowl
4 - Corn collection zone

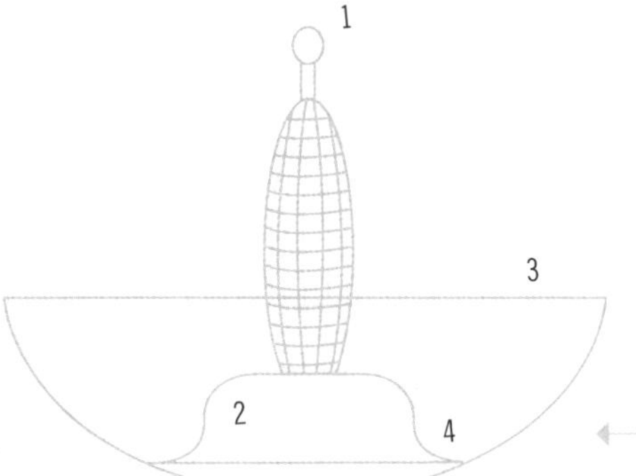

4 Use a **chef's knife** to cut off the kernels.[2]

5 After the kernels are off, turn the knife around and use the spine of the blade to scrape out any remaining pulp.

6 Add the corn, sugar, and turmeric to the saucier and continue cooking over medium-high heat until the liquid from the corn thickens a bit, about 2 minutes. Sprinkle the cornmeal onto the corn mixture and stir to combine. Add the cream, reduce the heat to medium, and cook until the corn is very soft, 2 to 3 minutes.

7 Fish out the rosemary, season with pepper, and serve as a side to just about anything.

FUN CORN FACTS TO KNOW AND TELL

- *Corn* is an Old English word meaning "a small hard thing," such as the small chunks of salt one uses to "corn" beef. The American cereal crop known to us as corn is actually maize, whose name comes from *zea mays*.

- Maize is a mutation of two types of cereal grasses that the Aztecs, some seven thousand years ago, discovered grew better when planted side by side. Over time the two cross-pollinated and gave birth to a plant that yielded eensy-beensy ears that looked and tasted like . . . nothing we have today.

- Cortez took maize back to Europe in 1528, and it quickly took hold as a staple grain. And here is where Montezuma's real revenge began to unfold. See, the Aztecs and other Native Americans were soaking dried maize in water mixed with wood ash, which was extremely alkaline. The process, called nixtamalization, changed the structure of the maize, specifically its amino acid structures. The result was not only easier to hull, but substantially more nutritious. The Spaniards paid not a lick of attention, and in their arrogance unleashed a plague on Europe called "pellagra," which is a nasty disorder caused by a lack of vitamin B3 (niacin). Pellagra, which can cause everything from gnarly skin lesions to death, reached epidemic proportions in parts of Spain, Italy, and, later, once maize spread back to America, in the southern United States, where it remained a problem well into the twentieth century. Nixtamalization unlocks the B3 in corn—sorry, maize—so that it's available for human absorption. Today we call corn that has gone through this process hominy. Most grits are now ground from hominy corn. But that's another show.

- Maize is the world's third largest food crop.

- Maize is a grass, like wheat or rye, and each kernel is an individual seed composed of a seed coat, an embryo, and an endosperm. The particular composition of this starchy endosperm is what sets most maize varieties apart from one another.

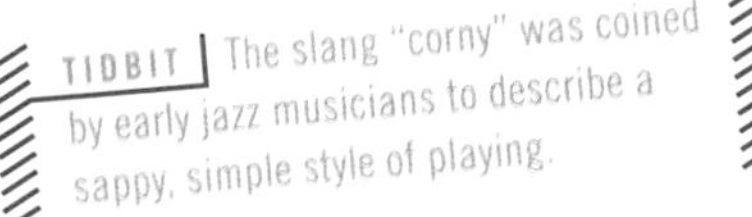

TIDBIT The slang "corny" was coined by early jazz musicians to describe a sappy, simple style of playing.

APPLICATION

CREAM OF THE CROP CORNBREAD

8 SERVINGS

So after you've gone to all the trouble to make creamed corn, what if you decide you just don't want to sit down and eat all that creamed corn? You make cornbread, of course.

The world of cornbread is mind-numbing in scope. Near as I can tell, every single culture that has ever grown or consumed corn in any fashion or form has ground it up and baked with it, whether it be the pattylike hoecakes cooked over fires on hoe blades, or corn pone baked in front of a fire, or light and sweet Texas cornbread as refined as a wedding cake. Heck, even hushpuppies are cornbread, as are true Johnnycakes, which in the Caribbean are as common as bagels. There are corn sticks, corn muffins, and various other corn cakes, but to me it's only cornbread if an iron skillet is involved.

SOFTWARE

12	ounces	stone-ground cornmeal	
1	teaspoon	kosher salt	
1	tablespoon	sugar	
2	teaspoons	baking powder	
½	teaspoon	baking soda	
1	cup	low-fat buttermilk[3]	(or more if needed)
2	large	eggs	
8	ounces	creamed corn	(look back a page or two, or use canned if you must)
2	tablespoons	vegetable oil	

PROCEDURE

1. Heat the oven to 425°F and place a **10-inch cast-iron skillet** in the middle of the box to heat.
2. In a **small mixing bowl**, whisk the dry stuff together.
3. In a **larger bowl**, **whisk** the wet stuff together—and no, the oil doesn't count because although it's a liquid it isn't wet.
4. Add the dry to the wet and whisk to combine. If the batter seems a little dry, add a touch more buttermilk.

TIDBIT The "ears" on early American corn were tiny, even smaller than the cocktail corn Tom Hanks tried to eat in *Big*.

5 Pour the oil into the hot skillet and swirl (carefully) to coat. Pour in the batter and jiggle the pan to evenly distribute. Bake for 20 minutes, or until the bread is golden brown and springs back when touched (it will read 200° to 205°F on a probe thermometer), about 20 minutes.

6 Remove from the oven and let cool for several minutes. Place an inverted dinner plate on top of the bread and flip it out of the skillet.

7 Serve with butter.

[1] Just reading this list makes me drool a little.

[2] Why bother with all this rigmarole? Because it's really difficult to cut corn off a cob without making a mess. A bowl gets rid of the mess but puts the corn at an awkward position. The inverted paper bowl takes care of it. I guess if you have a wooden salad bowl that would work too.

[3] If you're thinking of substituting low-fat milk for the buttermilk, beware. Not only do we need the thickness of the buttermilk, we need the acidity to react with the baking soda.

TRIVIA The Outtake: Just to set the record straight, there was no snake. That was acting! (Brilliant.) Thank you!

An African corn grinder (for field corn, not sweet)

TRIVIA Yes, we also made microwave popcorn in this show using an application that riled a lot of folks because the rig called for several metal staples, which several engineers assured me wouldn't be a problem due to the wavelength of microwaves. But since there's an entire popcorn show coming on down the line, I'm going to hold off on all this until then.

AMERICAN PICKLE

EPISODE 29 | SEASON 3 | GOOD EATS

TRIVIA | This title is a reference, of course, to *American Beauty,* which won a bunch of Oscars the year this was shot. The opening scene featuring my neighbor Chuck with a video camera in the produce department was a goof on a scene from the film.

You know, many of the mamas and the papas of this fine nation shared our third president's pickle passion: George Washington, John Adams, Dolly Madison, Elvis Presley—all major pickle heads. The King, in fact, liked his dills deep-fried. And, lest we forget, those peerless pickle pilgrims, the Pennsylvania Dutch, didn't come up with their concept of the Seven Sweets and Sours until after they settled on these shores. So pickles are in our nation's blood. Aunt Bea though it may be, we need pickling more than ever because it's one of the best ways to take advantage of the flavorful local produce that becomes available to us for such a short time each year.

If that weren't reason enough, consider this: The United States of America is named for Amerigo Vespucci, a cartographer from Seville known for his early maps of the North American coast. Amerigo began his career as a pickle merchant.

"On a hot day in Virginia I can think of nothing more comforting than a fine spiced pickle brought up trout-like from the sparkling depths of the aromatic jar kept below the stairs of Aunt Sally's cellar."

THOMAS JEFFERSON

TRIVIA | Here's my brother making his second *Good Eats* showing ("Use Your Noodle" was the first, on page 62.) His appearance was made possible by a generous grant by the Nevada board of corrections.

KNOWLEDGE CONCENTRATE

Pickle: (1) a solution or bath for preserving or cleaning, a brine or vinegar solution in which foods are preserved; (2) any food item preserved via definition 1; (3) a nasty bit of luck, a bad situation, as in "in a pickle."

The goal of pickling is to stop the march of time by shutting down enzymatic action in the target food and by rendering it either inhospitable to or unavailable to microbes, germs, little meanies, and so on.

There are three types of pickles:

FERMENTED PICKLES: The oldest and many would argue the best. In this process naturally occurring bacteria create lactic acid, which preserves the food. A brine is used as a control agent to keep all but the desired bacteria at bay. Also known as "processed" pickles, they can take up to 6 weeks to cure, though the fermentation can continue on to some degree for up to 2 years. Sauerkraut is a classic fermented pickle.

FRESH-PACK/QUICK-PROCESS: The most common method for commercial pickles. Fresh fruits and/or vegetables are bottled with a flavorful liquid, then pasteurized to at least 160°F. They last about 18 months but must be refrigerated after opening.

REFRIGERATOR PICKLES: In this method a combination of refrigeration and acid (or in some cases alcohol) are used to control bacteria. These are the easiest to make but also have the shortest shelf life . . . or should I say refrigerator life. These are not "keeping" pickles. But they are a good introduction to the art of pickling. As you'll see, this kind of pickling is pretty simple stuff, so there's really no excuse for not doing it.

And now a few words about vinegar, our favorite source of pickling acid.

vin = wine

aigre = sour

Vinegar is what happens when aceto bacteria go on a drinking binge. The bacteria construct a lumpy, gray, rubbery float called a "mother", which acts as a biological refinery converting alcohol (usually from wine) to acetic acid. Once the conversion is complete, the mother can be physically moved to a new alcohol source to continue its work.[1]

Although vinegar can technically be produced from any wine or spirit, I consistently turn to apple cider vinegar (made from hard cider, of course, because alcohol is required for vinegar), which has a crisp flavor and about 5 percent acidity, and rice wine vinegar, which has a distinct sweetness and lower acidity, around 4 percent. White distilled vinegar has a harsh flavor, so for pickling I usually avoid it along with more costly vinegars like sherry and balsamic, which would just get lost in the fray.

A FEW RANDOM PICKLE FACTS

- The Middle English word *pikel* meant "a spicy sauce or gravy served with meat or fowl." The Middle Dutch *pekel* referred to a solution such as a spiced brine used in preserving. The Dutch also give us the phrase *in de pekel zitten*, which means "sitting in the pickle," the obvious source of the concept of being "in a pickle."
- Anthropologists believe that pickling was common in Mesopotamia.
- Cleopatra attributed her good looks to a healthy diet of pickles.
- The word *kosher* used in reference to a pickle means simply that garlic has been added to the brine.
- During World War II, U.S. forces consumed 40 percent of the nation's pickle output.
- Today, the average American consumes 9 pounds of pickles a year.

TIP | Leftover pickle brine can be added to marinades, salad dressings, or mayonnaise. Oh, and pickle juice in beer really is quite refreshing.

APPLICATION

AB'S B&BS[2]

1 QUART

Behold: Give acid and spice a little time and some relatively bland produce is transformed.

SOFTWARE

½	medium	onion	thinly sliced
2	medium	cucumbers	thinly sliced
1	cup	H_2O	filtered if possible
1	cup	cider vinegar	
1½	cups	sugar	
1	pinch	kosher salt	
½	teaspoon	yellow mustard seeds	(not brown)
½	teaspoon	ground turmeric[3]	
½	teaspoon	celery seeds	
½	teaspoon	pickling spice[4]	

PROCEDURE

1. Combine the onion and cucumber slices in a clean, **1-quart spring-top jar.**[5]
2. Combine everything else in a **2-quart saucepan** and bring to a boil. Drop the heat and simmer for 4 full minutes.
3. Slowly pour the hot pickling liquid over the onion and cucumber slices, completely filling the jar. (A **large ladle** is a good tool for the job.)
4. Cool to room temperature before topping off with any remaining pickle (that is, the liquid) and sealing the jar.
5. Refrigerate for 1 week before serving and finish them within 2 months. Remember that these pickles are not actually preserved, so they need to be kept refrigerated.

TIDBIT | By the mid-seventeenth century, Dutch farmers were growing cucumbers all over what is now Brooklyn. The crop was converted to pickles and sold up and down Fulton and Canal Streets.

TRIVIA | The falling-over-dead soldier sequence was shamelessly "sampled" from *Forrest Gump.*

APPLICATION

SUMMER IN A JAR

1 QUART

We've worked this application out using Bartlett pears because those are the ones people know best. But personally I prefer Anjous for their more tender texture.

SOFTWARE

2		pears	not quite ripe; thinly sliced
2		red plums	not quite ripe, pitted and quartered
½		lemon	thinly sliced
1	sprig	fresh mint[6]	
1	tablespoon	fresh ginger	ultra-thinly sliced
1	cup	H_2O	filtered if possible
1	cup	sugar	
1	cup	rice wine vinegar	

PROCEDURE

1. Combine all the fresh stuff in a **1-quart spring-top jar**.
2. Bring everything else to a simmer in a **small saucepan** and cook until the sugar completely dissolves.
3. Carefully pour the pickle (that is, the liquid) over the fruit, being sure to fill jar to the top. (Again, look to your **ladle** for assistance.)
4. Cool to room temperature, then refrigerate for 1 week before serving. The pickle will keep, refrigerated, for 2 months. And don't forget to eat the lemon pieces.

[1] Mothers always remind me of jellyfish.

[2] Bread-and-butter pickles are called such because they were originally served alongside . . . you guessed it. B&Bs are characterized by crisp sweetness and the presence of onions.

[3] Turmeric, like its cousin ginger, is a rhizome. If you can find it fresh, feel free to grind your own—just use double the amount called for here.

[4] Although recipes vary, most mixtures contain allspice, bay leaves, cardamom, cloves, coriander, ginger, and mustard seeds.

[5] A Mason or Ball jar would be fine, but a spring-top jar is more convenient.

[6] Mint is the easiest herb to grow yourself, be it in yard or pot, so do the right thing.

TRIVIA The giant pickle that descended from the ceiling is actually a pool float.

TRIVIA The Cleopatra tomb set was nothing but play sand, a piece of Styrofoam, and some blue light.

"Oh, Hamlet, how camest thou in such a pickle?"
HAMLET, ACT 5, SCENE 1

MUSSEL BOUND

EPISODE 30 | SEASON 3 | GOOD EATS

Here my goal was to get American cooks to embrace a versatile bivalve that's packed with protein and flavor, is in bountiful supply, and is just about fat free.

Opening scene: The Dawn of Man, Thursday

Action: Having consumed the last mastodon, early man contemplates his next culinary move . . . a pile of suspicious-looking critters that would become known as mussels.

POGNIZ: Huh, huh, murrg? Hurgum. Ahhg hrrmg. (We have eaten the last of the big furries. Now we must dine on these small rocks that smell refreshingly of the sea.)

RIMSHOT: Hang bop. (I'm not going to eat it. You eat it.)

POGNIZ: Hang bop knobby. (No way!)

RIMSHOT: Ha! Wogg goey. Nat flap ba Mikog. (I know, let's give it to Mikog. He'll eat anything!)

Action: The mussels are presented to Mikog, who appears not to be as "bright" as the others. He sniffs, he dines with gusto.

RIMSHOT: Polly woggly! Flay Mikog! (He likes it. Hey Mikog!)[1]

TRIVIA | No *Good Eats* wardrobe has ever been less comfortable than those caveman suits.

TIDBIT | Judging by mussel shells found at coastal archeological digs in North America and Europe, it seems safe to say that the common mussel has been on the dinner table for at least eight thousand years, so this scene's not as farfetched as it might seem.

TIP | Mussels typically spawn from May to July. During this time they convert some of their stored glycogen (a type of sugar that makes their flesh taste sweet) into gametes, which taste bitter. Spawning also stresses the animal, reducing size and even shelf life. This explains why mussel supplies often reach their ebb in summer.

KNOWLEDGE CONCENTRATE

Some 6.5 billion pounds of mollusks are harvested from the world's waters each year. Besides making up the animal kingdom's second largest phylum, they are the most popular seafood on the planet Earth. If you've never pondered their variety, just take a stroll down any American beach and look down. That sand you're crunching on is actually the crushed remains of zillions and zillions of mollusk shells. Now, in the case of a snail or a nautilus it's one shell, but in the case of clams, scallops, oysters, or mussels there are two shells that oppose each other, which is why they're called *bi*valves.

There are hundreds of varieties of mussels, ranging from miniscule freshwater varieties[2] to 15-inch-long marine mammoths. Almost all of these varieties are edible, but we only press a small handful into active culinary service:

GREEN-LIPPED MUSSELS: From New Zealand; in the United States, these are sold frozen.

MEDITERRANEAN MUSSELS: These are being cultivated now out in the Pacific Northwest.

COMMON OR BLUE MUSSELS: These mussels monopolize the mussel market in both the United States and Europe, and they're the ones we'll be concentrating on here because they're readily available.

TRIVIA This show heralded the first appearance of prop man Paul as Leverman. At the time, we couldn't see ever using the suit again, but man have we gotten our money's worth out of it. Paul also wore it as Lactose Man, and if I'm not mistaken Leavening Man. And of course Leverman has shown up a time or two over the years (in the oyster show, for instance).

SPECIAL HARDWARE NOTE

The mussels are going to steam over the cooking sauce. On the show I used a METAL COLANDER inside the POT because I don't have a pot with a steamer insert and didn't want to have to buy one. If you have a POT with a STEAMER INSERT (not a pasta insert, which wouldn't leave room for the sauce), then by all means use it.

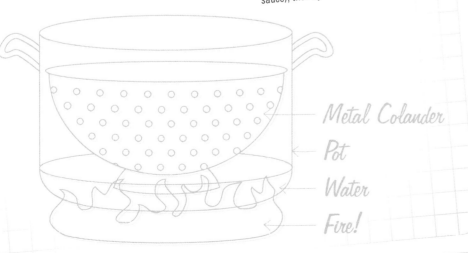

Metal Colander

Pot

Water

Fire!

TIDBIT Mussel meats range in color from white (males and immature females) to deep orange (mature female).

TIDBIT Some mussel varieties grow to up to fifteen inches long.

APPLICATION

MOJO MOULIES

4 APPETIZER OR 2 ENTRÉE SERVINGS

This is a riff on the bistro classic *moules marinière*. Steaming the mussels in a colander above the broth results in more tender meats.

SOFTWARE

3	tablespoons	olive oil	(not extra-virgin)
2	tablespoons	garlic	minced
1	large (about 7 ounces)	leek	washed, trimmed, chopped
1	pinch	kosher salt	
48		fresh mussels	Blue or Mediterranean
1		tomato	seeded and chopped
1½	cups	white wine	cheap but not totally undrinkable: Pinot Grigio or Sauvignon Blanc
	handful	fresh parsley	chopped

PROCEDURE

1. In a **large stockpot**, heat the oil over medium-low heat, add the garlic, leek, and salt, and sweat until softened, approximately 3 minutes.
2. Place the mussels in a **steamer insert or metal colander** and rinse them with cold water to remove any excess dirt or grit. Remove any beards with a pair of **needle-nose pliers**[4] (grab low and twist to remove).
3. Add the tomato and wine to the stockpot and boost the heat to medium-high to simmer. Insert the steamer insert or colander and cover. Cook for 3 minutes, then check to see if the mussels have opened. If some are still closed, replace the lid and cook for another 30 seconds to 1 minute.
4. Discard any unopened mussels at this point. (Whatever's in them, you don't want.)
5. Remove the pot from the heat.
6. Place the mussels in a **serving bowl**, reserving 8 proud specimens. Remove these from their shells and add their meat to the stockpot.
7. Tipping the pot so that the liquid pools on one side, use a **stick or immersion blender** to puree the mixture until it reaches a saucy consistency.
8. Pour the sauce over the mussels and garnish with parsley.
9. Serve with a loaf of crusty bread and chilled white wine (preferably a better one than you cooked with).

TIDBIT Every 2-pound bag of mussels sold in the United States bears a tag called a bed or lot tag, which clearly indicates where the mussels came from, who packed them, and when. Never, ever buy mussels unless their tag is clearly displayed. Although blue mussels can be sold in frozen or cooked states, I always buy live specimens. The best way to tell if they're still kicking is to take up one mussel in each hand and tap them together. You should be able to watch them close or at least start to in a few seconds.[3]

[1] If this reminds you somewhat of a certain cereal commercial from the '70s, you've been paying attention . . . or you're just old like me.

[2] Mussels harvested from the Mississippi River have never been utilized culinarily, but their shells were once the fodder of the world button industry.

[3] The reaction time depends on the temperature at which they're being stored.

[4] I have a pair of stainless-steel spring-loaded pliers that I use for removing fish bones. Mighty handy here.

[5] They're going to die anyway, of course, but you don't want them to expire until you're good and ready.

MUSSEL AQUICULTURE

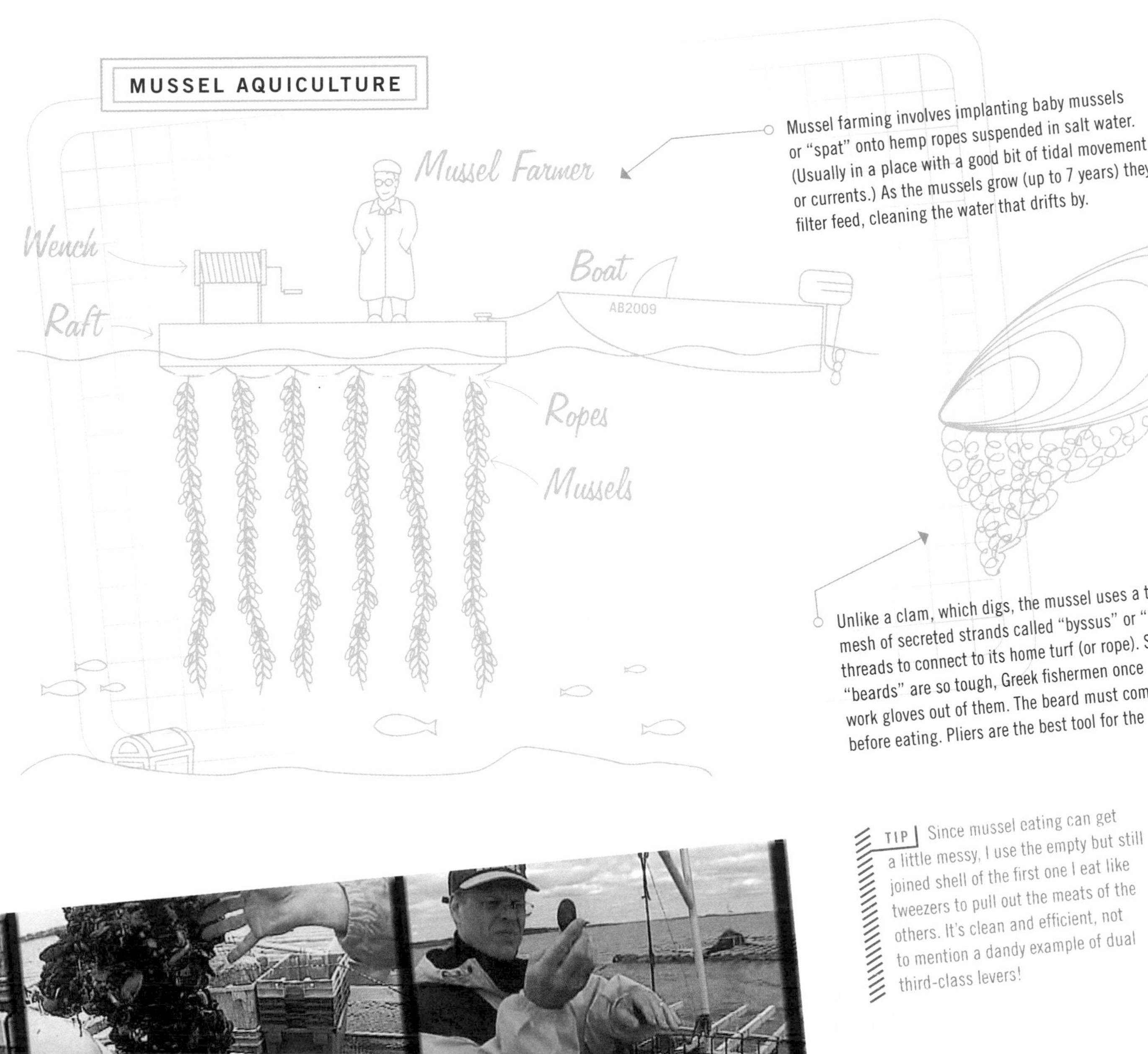

Mussel farming involves implanting baby mussels or "spat" onto hemp ropes suspended in salt water. (Usually in a place with a good bit of tidal movement or currents.) As the mussels grow (up to 7 years) they filter feed, cleaning the water that drifts by.

Unlike a clam, which digs, the mussel uses a tough mesh of secreted strands called "byssus" or "byssac" threads to connect to its home turf (or rope). Such "beards" are so tough, Greek fishermen once crafted work gloves out of them. The beard must come off before eating. Pliers are the best tool for the job.

TIP Since mussel eating can get a little messy, I use the empty but still joined shell of the first one I eat like tweezers to pull out the meats of the others. It's clean and efficient, not to mention a dandy example of dual third-class levers!

TRIVIA The mussel location we visited was Great Eastern Mussel Farms, Tenants Harbor, ME.

TIP Refrigerate mussels in a small bucket or bucket-like device topped with a few moist paper towels or even newspaper. Do not place them on ice or in fresh water, or die they will.[5]

TIDBIT Mussels are high in protein and are a good source of selenium, vitamin B12, and zinc.

THE EGG-FILES II: MAN WITH A FLAN

EPISODE 31 | SEASON 3 | GOOD EATS

When we first cracked the egg files we chose to concentrate on isolated applications, keeping the egg safely quarantined. But the time has come to unleash the most potent combination since nitro met glycerin: dairy and eggs. Once combined, this duo can be transformed by heat into a creamy quasi-solid possessing infinite versatility.

Bread pudding, pastry cream, crème anglaise, ice cream, crème brûlée, sabayon, quiche, and crème caramel—a.k.a. flan—are all born of this protean substance that we call "custard." This show concentrated on *baked* custards rather than *stirred* custards, which we'll get into soon enough, believe you me.

"Put all your eggs in one basket and watch that basket."

MARK TWAIN

"There are two things I know to be true: There's no difference between good flan and bad flan, and there's no war in Albania."

DAVID MAMET, *WAG THE DOG*

KNOWLEDGE CONCENTRATE

- **THE CUSTARD CODE: The higher the egg-to-dairy ratio, the firmer the custard will be; you must whisk; you must strain; you must cook low and slow; and you really should pull it just a little bit before you think it's ready.**
- **Whether sweet or savory, stirred or baked, all custards adhere to strict physical laws. Technically custard is any cooked combination of egg and a liquid.**

egg + liquid = custard

In Western cooking, the liquid is almost always dairy, usually milk, half-and-half, or heavy cream. If you whisk 2 eggs into 1 cup dairy, you'd have what the French call a *royale*.

In France, the *royale* is used to bind just about everything from dessert sauces to Renault engines to quiche, which is just a fancy-pants name for what I like to call Refrigerator Pie.

PROTEIN PARTY

Notice, please, that in the Refrigerator Pie on the next page, where once there was milky-eggy goo you now have a semisolid gel. How is this possible? I asked FSG[1] Shirley Corriher, and she put it this way:

"It all begins with egg proteins. Now, picture proteins as little pieces of ribbon, and they have little bonds holding them together, and then you heat them with custard and pow! These proteins pop open and then they're floating around, unwound, with their little bonds sticking out. And almost immediately they bump into another protein that's floating around with its bonds sticking out, and they join together, trapping all these wonderful ingredients in this mesh. And you have a wonderful custard."

If you really want to get a feeling for what makes a royale into a custard, do this:

1. Blow up about five hundred blue balloons and three hundred yellow balloons. Place in your living room.

2. Invite over a dozen or so friends.

3. Buy them all sweat suits and sew Velcro all over them.

4. Dress everyone in their suits, put them in the room with the balloons, and have them curl themselves into tight balls. At this point you and yourfriends are "natural" proteins floating among water droplets (blue) and fat globules (yellow).

5. You and your friends stretch out your arms, stand up, and run around the room. You are now "denatured" proteins.

6. Within minutes you should look like a Keith Haring painting gone wrong, arms and legs all stuck together with balloons stuck in between. You are now "coagulated" proteins holding captured liquid and fat. This condition is called "custard".

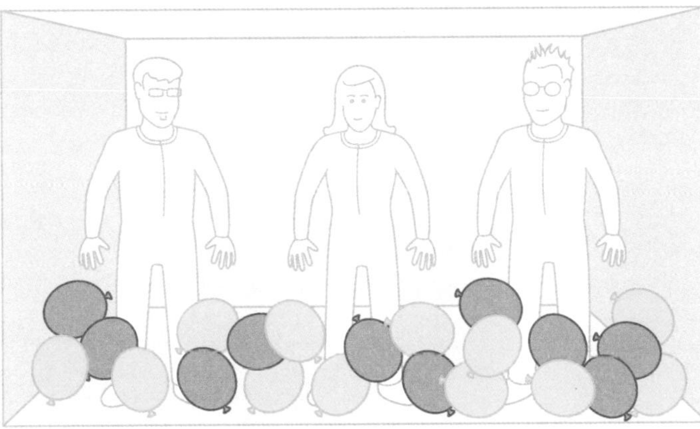

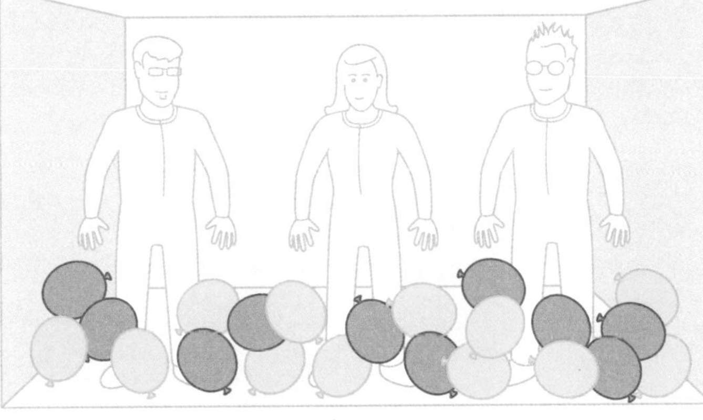

Room full of friends in velcro suits standing in blue and yellow balloons.

All balled up like we're natural proteins.

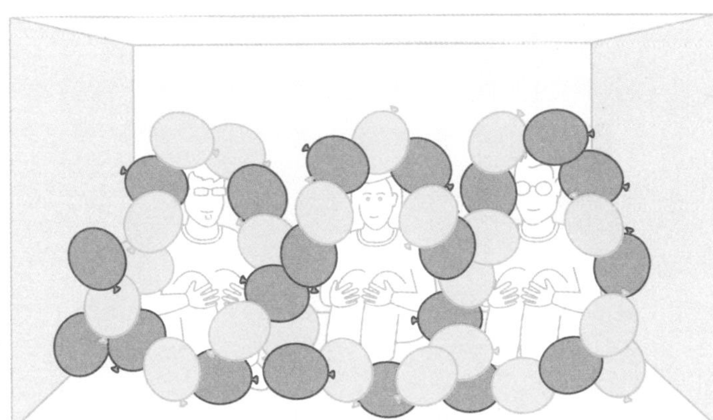

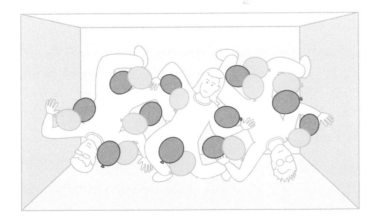

Tangled up like denatured proteins—fats and H_2O are captured.

APPLICATION

REFRIGERATOR PIE

8 SERVINGS

Here we use the coagulating power of the egg to create a delicious gel in which tasty remnants of other meals are captured and contained in a pastry crust.

You can put just about anything into Refrigerator Pie, but except for cheese and finely chopped herbs, the goods should be fully cooked first.

SOFTWARE

2	large	eggs	
1	cup	half-and-half	(or half heavy cream and half whole or low-fat milk)
1	pinch	nutmeg	freshly grated
1	9-inch	pie crust	fresh or frozen

SECONDARY SOFTWARE

The goods, or approximately 8 ounces (combined total) of anything you find hanging around. We humbly suggest:

Combo 1	diced city ham[2]	cooked or frozen chopped spinach	grated cheddar cheese
Combo 2	cooked bacon, crumbled	chopped sautéed leeks	grated Gruyère cheese
Combo 3	canned artichoke hearts, quartered	cooked or frozen chopped spinach	grated Parmesan cheese
Combo 4[3]	roasted chicken, shredded	chopped sun-dried tomatoes	crumbled goat cheese
Combo 5	smoked salmon	blanched asparagus, chopped	sautéed sliced mushrooms
Combo 6	sliced or diced pepperoni	pitted black olives	sautéed green peppers
Combo 7	diced Spam	roasted garlic	bits of Port Salut cheese

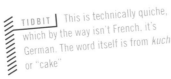

TIDBIT This is technically quiche, which by the way isn't French, it's German. The word itself is from *kuchen* or "cake"

PROCEDURE

1. Heat the oven to 350°F.
2. **Whisk** together the eggs, half-and-half, and nutmeg. If your eggs are very fresh, you may encounter one or more chalazae. Since these pieces of twisted egg white will not "cook out," you may want to strain them out. Personally, I never bother.
3. Place the unbaked crust (in its tin or pie pan) on a **half sheet pan** just in case the filling runneth over.
4. Evenly distribute the "goods" over the bottom of the crust and move the pan to the open door of the oven.
5. Carefully pour in the wet team until it comes to within ¼ inch of the top.
6. Move the pan into the oven and bake for 35 to 45 minutes. When finished, mixture will be set at the edges but jiggly in the middle.
7. Remove and cool for at least 30 minutes (I prefer to consume at room temperature, but it's good warm, too). Once cool, the pie can be wrapped in plastic, then aluminum foil, then frozen for up to 2 months. To reheat, uncover and stash in a 350°F oven for 20 to 25 minutes.

TRIVIA This scene remains one of my all-time favorite science bits because it visually illustrates the fine line between custard nirvana and over-coagulation. Plus, it was fun and I performed all of my own remote-control car stunts. Thank you . . . thank you very much.

APPLICATION

FLANDANGO

8 SERVINGS

Although I often bake with artificial (read: cheap) vanilla extract, when the flavors are this subtle I use the pure stuff, which I order off the Internet.

Flan is cooked in a water bath to avoid overcooking: As we've seen in earlier episodes, water can absorb a lot of energy before its temperature actually goes up. By baking in a bain marie or hot water bath, we can slow the march of heat into the flans. The slower the heat moves and the slower the temperature rises, the more evenly they'll cook.

// SOFTWARE

1½	cups	whole milk	
1	cup	half-and-half	
1	teaspoon	vanilla extract	
3½	ounces	sugar	
8	ounces	assorted jams, preserves, and sauces	such as caramel sauce (page 130), blueberry jam (page 120), apricot preserves, or chocolate sauce (page 301)
3	large	eggs	
3	large	egg yolks	

// PROCEDURE

1. Heat the oven to 350°F and put a **kettle**[4] of water on to boil.
2. Bring the dairy, vanilla, and sugar to a bare simmer in a **medium saucepan** over medium-low heat. Remove from the heat and set aside.[5]
3. Place a folded **kitchen towel** in the bottom of a **roasting pan** and place **eight 4-ounce glass or ceramic custard cups** on the towel, spaced evenly. Add a couple of tablespoons of jam, preserves, or sauce in the bottom of each custard cup. Don't be afraid to mix things up and use a different flavor in each cup.
4. **Whisk** the eggs and yolks together in a **large mixing bowl** until they thicken slightly. (I like to stabilize my bowl on a **moist side towel**—the white terry-cloth towels used in restaurants—or paper towels.)

FLAN VS. CRÈME

Although not all word-noodlers agree, it appears that the word *flan* stems ultimately from the Latin *flad*, meaning a flat cake. This may be because when they're turned out of the cups, flans often flatten and spread a bit.

So what's the difference between a flan and crème caramel? Near as I can tell, any flan that is small and round and when turned out displays caramel is a crème caramel. So, all crème caramels are flans but not all flans are crème caramels.

Although crème brûlée is often richer than flan, calling for eight to twelve eggs per batch, it would not be unreasonable to call a flan with a burnt sugar top a crème brûlée. Heck, I do it all the time.

5. Drizzle about one quarter of the hot dairy mixture into the eggs while briskly whisking. Then whisk this back into the remainder of the milk.[6]
6. Strain through a **fine-mesh strainer** into a **large measuring cup or pitcher**.
7. Fill the custard cups, going short on the first pass so that you don't run short at the end.
8. Move the roasting pan with the cups to the middle rack of the oven, and when you're sure it's secure, slowly pour in enough **hot water** to come just below the level of the custard (not the top of the cups).
9. Cook the flans for 40 minutes, or until they wobble slightly when the pan is jiggled.
10. Using **tongs with rubber bands wrapped around the ends**, remove the cups from the hot water and cool to room temperature. (Cool the roasting pan fully in the oven before discarding the water.) Chill the flans completely and serve.

NOTE: Although I usually eat them out of the custard cup, pudding style, flans are traditionally turned out so that the sauce that cooked on the bottom becomes sauce on the top. To accomplish this, place the tip of your sharpest paring knife flat against the inside of the custard cup and then rotate the cup while holding the knife still. Place a serving plate on top of the bowl and quickly invert. Remove the custard cup, and *voilà*.

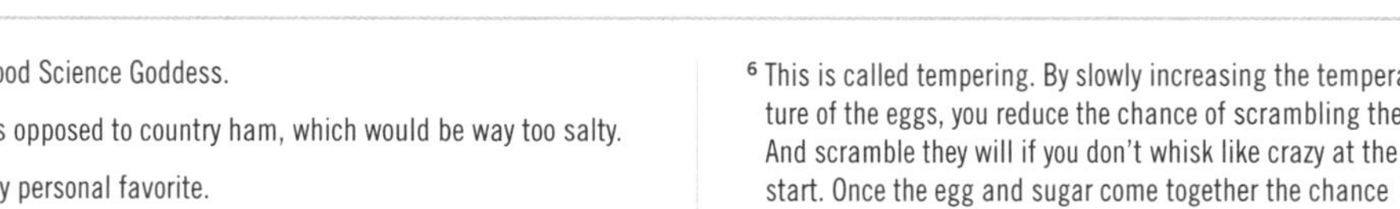
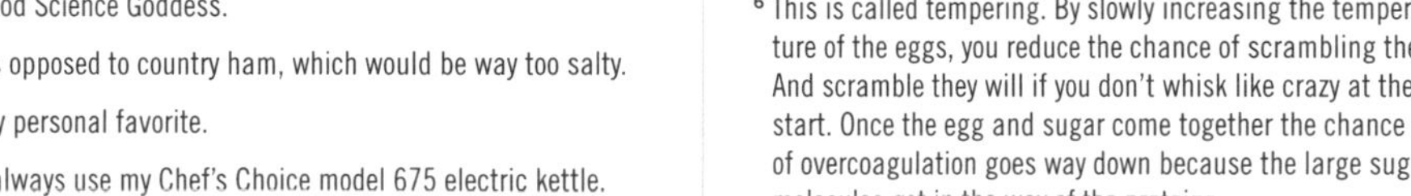

[1] Food Science Goddess.

[2] As opposed to country ham, which would be way too salty.

[3] My personal favorite.

[4] I always use my Chef's Choice model 675 electric kettle.

[5] Once upon a time this process, called "scalding", was a necessary step to shut down enzymes that could affect the custard. Pasteurization does this work for us now. But here it is simply used to dissolve the solids and raise the temperature of the mixture, thus reducing the baking time and in turn reducing the chances of overcooking.

[6] This is called tempering. By slowly increasing the temperature of the eggs, you reduce the chance of scrambling them. And scramble they will if you don't whisk like crazy at the start. Once the egg and sugar come together the chance of overcoagulation goes way down because the large sugar molecules get in the way of the proteins.

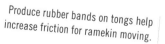

Produce rubber bands on tongs help increase friction for ramekin moving.

WHAT'S UP, DUCK?

EPISODE 32 | SEASON 3 | GOOD EATS

This may be my favorite *Good Eats* opening scene. Yes, it is a direct, flagrant, shameless rip-off of a scene from *Monty Python and the Holy Grail*, which is very good indeed, if you like that sort of thing. So my liking it isn't so much a statement of my cleverness as it is of the cleverness of others, though I do think it was clever of me to nick it in such a manner.

The Scene: an average American megamart meat department.

MOM: How about chicken?

POP: Had chicken last night.

MOM: Game hen?

POP: Yeah, last Thursday.

MOM: Turkey breast?

POP: A week ago, Friday.

MOM: That was fish.

POP: Tasted like turkey.

MOM: Fine.

POP: How about a . . .

AB: A duck.

POP: Heh! She'll only burn it.

MOM: Will not.

POP: Joan of Arc had less char than the last duck you cooked.

AB: Heh, heh, heh.

MOM: Why, I oughta . . .

AB: Alright, alright, kids. Come on. It doesn't have to be this way.

MOM: It doesn't?

AB: Nah, of course not. Look. What do ducks do?

MOM: Quack.

AB: Besides that.

CUSTOMER 1: Tastes gamy.

AB: Well, if you go out and shot one out of the . . .

CUSTOMER 2: Fly?

AB: Fly. Very good. That's why ducks have very high percentage of "slow-twitch" dark musculature, which is to say that they taste like dark meat. Okay, what else do they do?

MOM: Float.

AB: Float. Ah. What else floats?

CUSTOMER 1: Apples?

CUSTOMER 2: Empty beer cans?

CUSTOMER 3: Very small rocks?

AB: Small rocks. This isn't going exactly where I thought. Come on. Something else that floats.

MOM: Fat.

AB: Fat. Ah. Sooo?

CUSTOMER 2: Ducks are made of fat?

POP: That's why they burn.

AB: (sigh)

MOM: And make a mess of the oven.

CUSTOMER 1: And take six hours to roast.

AB: Okay. Yes. Ducks do contain some fat. But that doesn't mean that we have to eat it. In fact, if we just apply some good, thoughtful cooking methodology we can make this into a flavorful, crispy-on-the-outside, juicy-on-the-inside meal. We don't have to make a mess. We don't have to make six hours go by. We don't have to make the smoke alarm go off. In the end, we'll just make some good eats.

POP: Not going to burn it, are you?

MOM: See what I've got to live with?

KNOWLEDGE CONCENTRATE

When it comes to real flesh-and-feather ducks, there are dozens of varieties to choose from but odds are good you won't actually ever taste a black duck or a mallard or an American Canvass Back unless you've got a couple of Retrievers, a 12-gauge, and a wardrobe like Elmer Fudd's. A few ducks you might find on your plate someday:

MUSCOVY DUCKS: Very lean, very gamy, and usually only available in specialty stores or through mail order.

MOULARDS: These are generally raised for their livers for foie gras.

WHITE PEKIN OR LONG ISLAND DUCKS: These make up almost all of the American duck market.

An American businessman touring China in 1873 mistook "Peking" ducks for a rare breed of miniature goose. He bought twenty-five and shipped them home to New England. Only nine survived the trip, but when they reached their final destination—a farm on Long Island—they liked what they saw. They ate greedily, bred lustily, and grew very quickly, creating in just a few years an industry that thrives to this day.

Actually *thrive* might not be the best word.

Ducks are slaughtered between seven and twelve weeks of age, at which time they weigh between four and seven pounds. When shopping, look for a bird with a long, flat, wide breast. They're usually sold frozen. As for fresh ducks, all I can say is: I've never purchased one.

Which brings us to thawing, and the famous *Good Eats* scene in which we proved without a doubt that a hunk of duck-shaped ice will melt faster in cold running water than it will in still hot water. This is due to the power of convection, which also explains why a turkey roasted in a 300°F convection oven will cook faster than one placed in a 450°F still oven. The motion of molecules (be they water or air) can move heat away from or into a food very quickly.

Raw duck should be handled like any other poultry, which can contain salmonella, and though I have yet to find record of a case of someone being made sick by an American commercial duck,[1] you should never thaw it on the counter or in hot water. You have two options:

1. REFRIGERATOR METHOD: Place the duck in a drip-proof container in the lower portion of the refrigerator (I usually use the bottom drawer) and wait a few days. It'll take forever, but the method is safe and it generates a little less drip loss than speedier methods, like . . .

2. SINK THAW: Place the duck in a bucket or large pot in the sink and barely run cold water over it. If it floats, weigh it down with something. (I keep a three-foot length of plastic-coated marine chain for just such occasions). Depending on the size of your duck, it should be thawed in about an hour.

TRIVIA The plumber isn't my dad, and Paul isn't my apprentice. He's a prop guy who got stuck with playing the part as punishment for letting his house burn down with a bunch of our props in it. Bad Paul!

APPLICATION

DUCK!

2 SERVINGS

There are three goals here: Enhance flavor, render out excess fat, and then crisp the skin.

TIDBIT The word *duck* (the noun) stems from the word *duck* (the verb) because of the way ducks duck when fishing for food.

// SOFTWARE

½	cup	kosher salt	
1	pint	pineapple orange juice	
15	whole	black peppercorns	
1	sprig	fresh thyme	
4	medium cloves	garlic	smashed[2]
1	5½- to 6-pound	Long Island (White Pekin) duck	thawed
2	handfuls (about 2 ounces)	kale or chard	shredded
2		shallots	minced
1	dash	sherry or balsamic vinegar	

// PROCEDURE

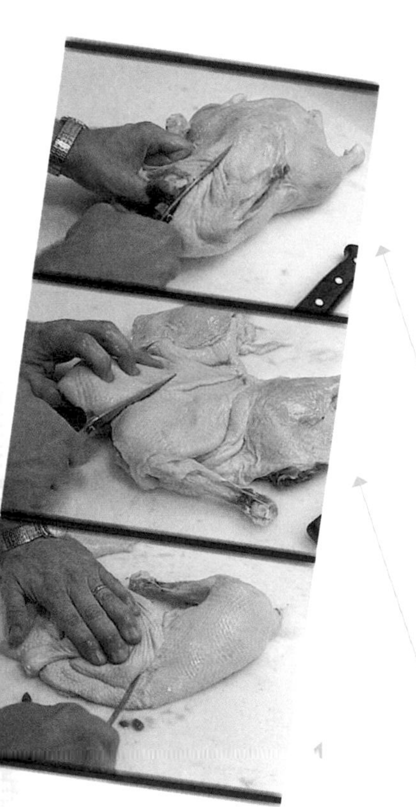

1. Combine the salt, juice, peppercorns, thyme, and garlic in a **sealable plastic container**. Seal and shake until the salt is dissolved. Set the brine aside.
2. Line the inside of **another container or pot** with a **gallon-size zip-top bag.**[3]
3. Remove the pop-up timer (if installed), liver, gizzard, heart, and anything else from inside the duck. Cut off the wings at the elbow with a **knife or shears.**[4]
4. Place the bird breast side down and find the spine at the base of the neck. Use **shears** to cut down one side of the backbone to the tail. Turn and make a return cut up the other side. Remove the backbone.
5. Turn the duck over and cut straight down the middle of the breastbone, thus splitting the bird in half.
6. To separate the legs, use a **boning knife** to make a crescent-shaped cut around the leg.
7. Lift the duck half in the air using the leg as a handle so that the thigh joint opens up. Cut straight through from front to back.
8. Lay your knife flat against the breast and gently push straight down. Then draw the knife toward you to slit the skin without cutting through the subcutaneous fat (under the skin) to the meat below.

9. Place the duck quarters inside the gallon bag and pour in the brine. Seal the bag, removing as much of the air as possible. Refrigerate for 2 to 2½ hours.
10. When you're ready to cook, bring a couple of inches of water to a boil in a **large (say, 8-quart) pot**.
11. Place a **metal colander or a steamer insert** into the pot and line it with the duck pieces, cut sides down.
12. Cover the pot. Reduce the heat to maintain a simmer. Steam the duck gently for 45 minutes to render some of the fat; the duck won't be completely cooked through at this point.
13. Place a **12-inch cast-iron skillet** in the oven and heat the oven to 475°F.
14. Remove the duck pieces from the colander (don't dare throw out the water—see below) and carefully place them skin side down in the hot skillet.
15. Return the skillet to the oven and roast for 10 minutes.
16. Carefully flip the pieces and cook for another 12 to 15 minutes, or until the skin is deep mahogany and very crisp.
17. Remove the duck from the skillet and set aside to rest, loosely covered with **aluminum foil**.
18. Add the chard and shallots to the hot skillet and toss in the fat remaining in the pan until the chard just barely wilts. Season with the vinegar and serve with the duck.

10 MINUTES MORE

Remember that steaming water: It's full of delicious, fragrant duck fat, quite possibly the finest cooking fat in the world. So, toss in several halved or quartered red potatoes and cook over high heat until the water evaporates out. Then allow the partially cooked potatoes to fry in the fat (*shiver of excitement*). Toss on some rosemary and serve alongside the duck. Ridiculously delicious. If you don't have time for this, refrigerate the pot until the fat solidifies into a disk. Remove, wrap with plastic, and freeze for another day. If that doesn't interest you, send via air mail directly to my home.

[1] That makes duck the Qantas of the meat world.

[2] The side of a bench knife/board scraper/dough blade is ideal for this.

[3] Although we avoid brand names on *Good Eats*, I'll tell ya right now that freezer Ziplocs are where it's at. And no, they don't pay me to say that.

[4] I keep a bag of wingtips and backs in the freezer. When I have a couple of pounds I make stock—just cover with water in a large pot, toss in some carrots and onions, and simmer for 6 hours, adding water as needed.

BEHIND THE BIRD

EPISODE 33 | SEASON 3 | GOOD EATS

So this is not your average, run-of-the-mill episode. It's set up as a faux documentary produced by an earnest young filmmaker named Blair McGuffin concerning the events that take place in the *Good Eats* house (house 1) when a blizzard blows in right after the completion of the "Romancing the Bird" episode (page 74). "Blair," by the way, comes from *The Blair Witch Project*, a clever if not exactly scary mockumentary. "McGuffin" is a term that Hitchcock and his cronies used to describe a plot device that propels a story but had no actual meaning or importance in and of itself. The letters of transit in *Casablanca*, the metal case in *Ronin*, and the statue in *The Maltese Falcon*—all classic examples. In this case, the entire show is pretty much a McGuffin. The character of my sister tortures everyone with craft projects, we discover W is an android, my DNA-challenged cousin Ray stalks Ms. McGuffin. In the end, my mom comes and rescues us using a V22 Osprey owned by none other than Emeril Lagasse. It's fun, and there are some tasty Thanksgiving leftovers, but otherwise this episode's waters ain't too deep.

TIP | One nice thing about brining a turkey is that the leftovers are so juicy—you barely need any mayo on your sandwich.

KNOWLEDGE CONCENTRATE

In 1905 Albert Marsh invented a nickel-chromium alloy capable of repeated heating via electrical current. It took four years for General Electric to produce a toaster for home use. The first pop-up toaster was marketed by Toastmaster in the 1920s.

When shopping for a toaster, keep in mind that you don't necessarily get what you pay for. Top drawer, mac-daddy models often look spectacular on the counter but make lousy toast. My own toaster has two slots, an on/off switch, a seven-setting browning selector, and a manual lift. No warmer, no "bagel" setting, no defrost, no automatic \pop-up, which would only serve to cool off the bread. It also has a crumb tray that falls out every time I try to put the toaster away. The dogs love this. I do not.

Toaster ovens rock, but when it comes to actually making toast you'd be better off using a wire coat hanger on a hot plate (like Elwood Blues). They really should rename those things.

Sandwich tips:

1. Fat repels liquids, so a thin coating of butter or mayo on sandwich bread is your best defense against sogginess. Toasting doesn't hurt either, of course.

2. Fillings are a lot less likely to fall out if the sandwich is halved corner to corner as opposed to side to side.

3. Although layering on things like slices of leftover turkey seems a matter of Dagwoodian simplicity, truth is, I usually chop my turkey and toss it with some mayo before building sandwiches. This proto-salad approach gives me better coverage and a more stable construction.

4. Think of an acidic or sweet ingredient to complement the rest of the sandwich fillings: Nothing's better on a turkey sandwich than a schmear of cranberry sauce.

5. Lest we forget, the quesadilla is a sandwich too, and the turkey did come from Mexico (sorta); try that turkey in a folded tortilla with some cheese.

Things to keep in mind when leftovering:

Air is not your friend. Package leftovers in the smallest sealable containers that will hold them, or in bags so you can remove as much air as possible.

If you're going to freeze meat, cut it small, chill it thoroughly, spread it out on a metal pan to freeze, then move it to airtight containment. All of these steps will lead to faster freezing, and that means smaller ice crystals, and that means better quality.

If you throw a bunch of Turkey Day leftovers into the fridge before the fridge has a chance to suck away the heat, all your other groceries will be kindasorta warm for hours. Avoid this by chilling your leftovers in a cooler with ice first.

Although I'm pretty cavalier with leftover cooked turkey, foods like leftover stuffing can be treacherous, so always reheat to at least 165°F.

As for the turkey carcass, it goes right into the soup pot the second it clears the table. Speaking of . . .

TRIVIA In this episode (as well as one other to come) we perpetuated the myth that the "sandwich" was born in 1762 when John Montagu, the fourth earl of Sandwich, placed roast beef between two slices of bread so that he could eat without leaving his card game. Although the handheld classic may very well be named for the earl, odds are it was not invented by him, as he was a rather sober sort with no reputation for gambling. Could he have consumed the device at his desk? I doubt we'll ever know.

APPLICATION

BIRD TO THE LAST DROP

6 SERVINGS

This soup extracts every last bit of goodness from the poultry remains. Resist the urge to pick the bones clean before using this application. A little meat in the soup, especially dark meat, will up the flavor ante considerably.

SOFTWARE

2	quarts	vegetable broth[1]	
1		turkey carcass	
1	10-ounce box	frozen vegetable medley	
½	cup	long-grain white rice	uncooked
2	cups	turkey meat	cubed or torn into small pieces
1	teaspoon	Old Bay seasoning	
2	teaspoons	dried thyme	
	to taste	kosher salt	
	to taste (lots)	black pepper	freshly ground

PROCEDURE

1. Put the broth and carcass in an **8-quart pot** over low heat and bring to a simmer. Cover and cook for 1 hour.
2. Remove the carcass.
3. Add the vegetables, rice, turkey meat, Old Bay, and thyme to the pot and simmer for another 20 minutes.
4. Season with salt and serve along with the pepper grinder. I don't know why it is turkey seems to be able to take so much pepper, but by the time I'm through with it the bowl is teeming with wee black bits. And I'm not a huge black pepper fan.

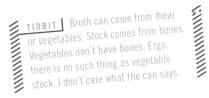

TIDBIT Broth can come from meat or vegetables. Stock comes from bones. Vegetables don't have bones. Ergo, there is no such thing as vegetable stock. I don't care what the can says.

APPLICATION

TURKEY SALAD

4 SERVINGS

I actually like this better than roast bird.

SOFTWARE

1	pound	roasted turkey meat	cubed
½	cup	mayonnaise	
½	small	lemon	freshly squeezed
2	stalks	celery	thinly sliced
½	small	red onion	finely chopped
½	cup	pecans	toasted and roughly chopped
¼	cup	dried cranberries	roughly chopped
2	tablespoons	fresh sage	chiffonade
½	teaspoon	kosher salt	
	to taste	black pepper	freshly ground

PROCEDURE

Combine everything in a **large airtight container**. Refrigerate for 1 hour before serving. Store in the fridge for up to 3 days.

[1] You can certainly use storebought, but if you have a bunch of just-past-prime vegetables—carrots, turnips, onions, celery (including the greens), leeks, green peppers—you can simmer them long and low in, say, 2¼ quarts of water and make your own

THREE CHIPS FOR SISTER MARSHA

EPISODE 34 | SEASON 3 | GOOD EATS

TRIVIA | In real life I do not wear piggy slippers—or bunny slippers, for that matter.

TRIVIA | This title is a goof on *Two Mules for Sister Sarah*, of course.

My goal in this episode

was to show how subtle changes to a proven recipe can have pronounced effects on the outcome. In this case the recipe in question came from the back of a rather famous bag of chocolate morsels. Please note that I'm not suggesting for one nanosecond that this recipe is better than that one. Just different. I believe cooks should have the power and the knowledge to adjust such documents, thus customizing the results to their liking.

MARSHA: I'm at the corner of Crocker and Hines. Make them fast and make them good.

TRIVIA | Most of the "Marsha" episodes follow the same format. I am pressed into service to prepare something I don't want to make, then coerced into further versions in an effort to get it just the way Marsha wants.

TIDBIT | The word *cookie* comes from the Dutch *koekje*, which means "small cake."

KNOWLEDGE CONCENTRATE

- Most food historians agree that the chocolate chip cookie as we know it was concocted by one Ruth Wakefield of the Toll House Inn in Whitman, Massachusetts, in 1933. Although one can find myths aplenty about the actual birth of the cookie, no one really knows how or why Mrs. Wakefield decided to do what she did. We do know that she gave her recipe to Nestlé in exchange for a lifetime's supply of the company's chocolate morsels.

- Chocolate chip cookies are generally born via the "creaming method," no doubt one of the most misunderstood of all culinary maneuvers. The goal is to punch a zillion tiny holes in soft but still solid fat. Later in the oven, chemical leavening blows these bubbles up, thus creating the cookie's final form and texture. A thousand things can go wrong during creaming, but the most common errors concern the temperature of the fat (too cold and the sugar can't beat its way in, too hot and the holes collapse) and the length of time the fat and sugar are actually beat together (most bakers stop well shy of success). Shortening is the most popular cookie fat, in part because of its relatively high melting temperature. Butter is harder to work with, but the flavor is vastly superior.

TRIVIA Whenever W appeared in this season she did so on a screen or some other device. This was because we had to shoot her parts well in advance so that she could journey to Vietnam to adopt a baby. I didn't want to write her out, so we stuck her on monitors, projection screens—anything we could think of.

General cookie tips:

- Great bakers weigh their ingredients. End of story.
- When assembling cookie dough, keep in mind that sugar is generally considered a "wet" ingredient.
- Cream using your mixer's paddle attachment.
- Think of a creamed cookie batter as an emulsion that needs to be brought together slowly. That's why eggs should be added one at a time and fully integrated before other ingredients are added.
- Always sift the dry ingredients together. Always. (A food processor can "sift" too.)
- High-protein bread flour produces more gluten than all-purpose flour and therefore can give you a chewier cookie.
- Low-protein cake flour ties up less moisture, thus making it available for steam production. Ergo, cake flour cookies have better lift and deliver a lighter crumb.
- If you like cookies that stay flat and spread out on the pan, up the baking soda a bit. Reducing acidity will slightly increase the setting temperature of the dough, allowing for more spread.
- A higher ratio of white to brown sugar will give you a crisper cookie.
- A higher ratio of brown to white sugar will give you a more tender cookie.
- Egg whites act as drying agents. Using more yolks than whites will make for a moister cookie.
- Replacing egg with milk can make a chewier cookie with more spread.
- Cold batter spreads in the oven more slowly than warm. I always chill my batters before baking if I can.

When it comes to dosing out the cookie batter, take a cue from the pros and use a "disher," the very device your lunch lady used to deliver mashed potatoes to your school tray. The trigger actuates a curved blade that sweeps out the food. A #20[1] will scoop 1½ ounces of dough, and that's just right in my book.

TIDBIT Chocolate chips contain less cocoa solids than bar chocolate, 27 to 30 percent, on average, and considerably more sugar. They're designed to melt more readily and to stay melted longer than other chocolates. For standard family and kid cookies I'm a fan of plain ole Nestlé semisweets. But if you want something more sophisticated, try Guittard Classic Dark Chips.

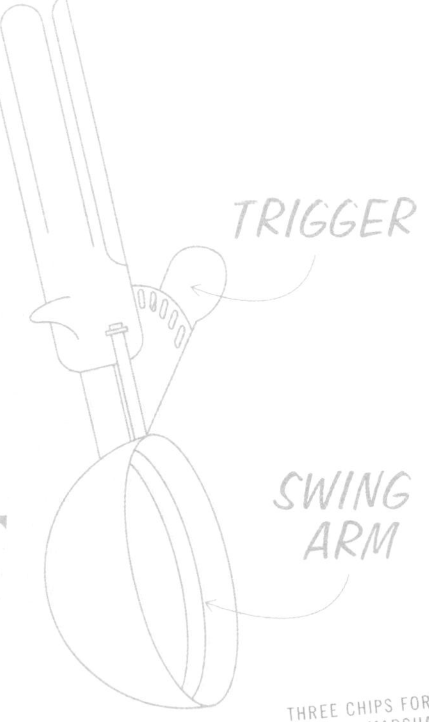

APPLICATION

THE CHEWY

APPROXIMATELY 2 DOZEN COOKIES

Here we hack the original Nestlé Toll House cookie recipe and make it chewy by substituting bread flour for regular, replacing one egg white with milk, and changing the ratio of brown to white sugar.

SOFTWARE

8	ounces	unsalted butter	
12	ounces	bread flour	
1	teaspoon	kosher salt	
1	teaspoon	baking soda	
2	ounces	granulated sugar	
8	ounces	light brown sugar	
1	large	egg	
1	large	egg yolk	
2	tablespoons	whole milk	
1½	teaspoons	vanilla extract	
12	ounces	chocolate morsels	

PROCEDURE

1. Melt the butter in a **2-quart saucepan** over low heat, then set aside to cool slightly.
2. Sift together the flour, salt, and baking soda onto a **paper plate**.
3. Pour the butter into your **stand mixer's work bowl**.[2] Add the sugars and beat with the paddle attachment on medium speed for 2 minutes.
4. Meanwhile, **whisk** together the whole egg, the egg yolk, milk, and vanilla extract in a **measuring cup**.
5. Reduce the mixer speed and slowly add the egg mixture. Mix until thoroughly combined, about 30 seconds.

TIP | We don't recommend half or double batches—but if you want 1½ batches, make a whole batch, bake what you want, portion, and freeze the rest.

TRIVIA | Puppets ain't easy. In the end our Stedicam operator Ramon had to operate Colonel Cookie—his timing was just right!

I dig the goatee.

6 Using the paper plate as a slide, gradually integrate the dry team, stopping a couple of times to scrape down the side of the bowl.[3]

7 Once the flour is worked in, drop the speed to "stir" and add the chocolate chips.

8 Chill the dough for 1 hour.

9 Heat the oven to 375°F and place racks in the top third and bottom third of the oven.

10 **Scoop** the dough into 1½-ounce portions onto **parchment paper-lined half sheet pans**, 6 cookies per sheet.

11 Bake two sheets at a time for 15 minutes, rotating the pans halfway through.

12 Remove from the oven, slide the parchment with the cookies onto a **cooling rack**, and wait at least 5 minutes before devouring.[4]

[1] The number on the blade represents the number of scoops required to produce a quart.

[2] If you need to use a hand mixer, just use another medium metal mixing bowl stabilized with a moist paper towel.

[3] At least one mixer manufacturer is making a mixer paddle with a built-in bowl scraper, but as of this writing I've yet to get my hands on one.

[4] Although I can certainly understand the allure of hot chocolate chip cookies, I prefer mine bagged and frozen rock hard. I like Girl Scout Thin Mints the same way.

TRIVIA | The Girl Scout is our key grip's daughter.

TIDBIT | Unlike wax paper, which is, well . . . paper and wax, parchment is infused with silicone, which has two amazingly useful properties: Nothing sticks to it, and it has a very high tolerance to heat. This makes it the ultimate cookie pan liner. Newborn cookies fresh from the oven are amazingly vulnerable to physical mishandling. By lining your pans with parchment you can simply pull the paper off, cookies and all, allowing them to cool on racks or the counter unmarred by spoon or spatula.

FLAP JACK DO IT AGAIN

EPISODE 35 | SEASON 3 | GOOD EATS

TRIVIA The title, of course, is a goof on the Steely Dan classic "Do It Again."

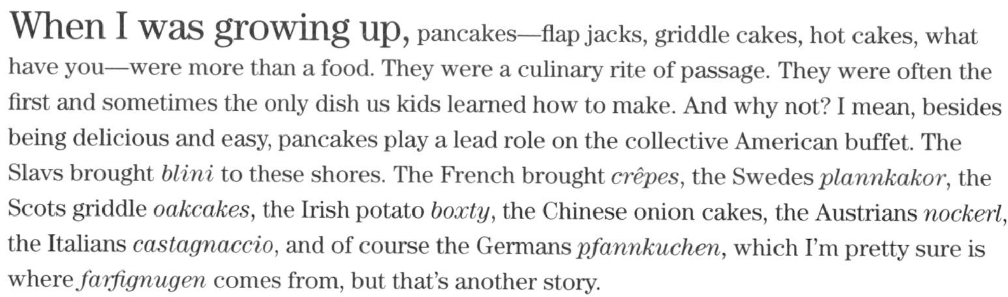

When I was growing up, pancakes—flap jacks, griddle cakes, hot cakes, what have you—were more than a food. They were a culinary rite of passage. They were often the first and sometimes the only dish us kids learned how to make. And why not? I mean, besides being delicious and easy, pancakes play a lead role on the collective American buffet. The Slavs brought *blini* to these shores. The French brought *crêpes*, the Swedes *plannkakor*, the Scots griddle *oakcakes*, the Irish potato *boxty*, the Chinese onion cakes, the Austrians *nockerl*, the Italians *castagnaccio*, and of course the Germans *pfannkuchen*, which I'm pretty sure is where *farfignugen* comes from, but that's another story.

And long before Columbus bumbled onto these shores, Native Americans had been making a kind of cornmeal pancake called *nokechick* for eons. In fact, a lot of anthropologists believe that primitive pancakes made of nothing but ground grains and water cooked on hot rocks by the fire may have been the first real cooked foods. And regrettably, many of us haven't improved on our executions much.

TRIVIA I measured the flour in the show volumetrically just so we could do a scene about dry measuring cups, which I almost never use for flour because I weigh it instead. But I knew that a lot of people measure their dry ingredients with cups and I wanted to arm them with better tools for the job.

KNOWLEDGE CONCENTRATE

- Pancakes fall into the baked goods category known as "quickbreads," which rise quickly because they contain considerable moisture and chemical leavening. Although it may sound confusing, pancakes are typically assembled via the "muffin method"; that is, the dry ingredients are mixed together, the wet ingredients are mixed together, then the batter is stirred together very quickly so that the starches don't get gummy and very little gluten is created.

- Flour: Cake flour makes extremely light and fluffy pancakes, which tend to fall apart during the critical flipping stage. Bread flour makes for very chewy pancakes. All-purpose flour is just right.

- Buttermilk: Four things I will not make without buttermilk: cornbread, biscuits, waffles, pancakes. Once upon a time, buttermilk was indeed the watery milk that was left over after butter was churned. This unpasteurized liquid fermented naturally through the action of lactic acid, which gives the milk a pleasant twang. When chilled it is an extremely refreshing drink. In the old South, buttermilk, kept cool in well houses, was used as a kind of antebellum Gatorade. Today buttermilk is made by adding lactic bacteria to pasteurized milk. As the acid lowers the pH of the milk, the proteins (casein) coagulate (a process that used to be called "clabbering"), thickening the milk. Since it's acidic, buttermilk lasts much longer in the refrigerator than regular milk.

- In pancake batter, the acidic nature of buttermilk helps to prevent gluten formation, and since it's thick we can make a batter with less flour.

- Leavening: I use a combination of double-acting baking powder and baking soda. The powder creates lift twice (hence "double-acting"): once upon mixing and then again when the batter heats. The soda, on the other hand, immediately reacts with the acid in the buttermilk, creating insta-bubbles, which thicken the batter so that it stands up nicely on the griddle. Folding in whipped egg whites doesn't hurt either.

- When it comes to cooking pancakes, it's tough to beat a nonstick electric griddle. There's plenty of surface area and low sides so you don't have to fight to get your turner under the cooking cake. If you don't want to go that route, try a heavy, square stovetop unit of either thick aluminum or cast iron. Speaking of turners: you want one that looks like this:

- I'm sure you're hip to my jive about weighing ingredients, but you still may need a set of scoop-style dry measure cups one day. When that day comes, make sure that they're made from either 18/8 or 18/10 stainless steel. (The numbers refer to the percentage of chromium and nickel, respectively.) Also make sure that the handles are long, attached with multiple welds (each weld will leave a dark spot; there should be at least two), and that they easily come off or away from whatever ring, chain, bar, or whatnot they're held together with.

TIP Baking powder loses its punch over time, so keep an eye on the expiration date and use within six months of opening.

Nice and Round

Pancake Turner

APPLICATION — SEMI-INSTANT PANCAKE MIX

1 QUART OF MIX, ROUGHLY ENOUGH FOR 3 BATCHES

By taking a note from the instant food industry, pancakes become "anytime" good eats.

// SOFTWARE

28	ounces	all-purpose flour	
1	tablespoon	baking powder	
1½	teaspoons	baking soda	
1	tablespoon	kosher salt	
1	ounce	sugar	

// PROCEDURE

Sift all ingredients together and store in an **airtight container** in the pantry for up to 3 months. Shake vigorously before each use.

SUB-APPLICATION — SEMI-INSTANT PANCAKES

12 PANCAKES

// SOFTWARE

10	ounces	Semi-instant Pancake Mix	(see above)
2	large	eggs	separated
2	cups	low-fat buttermilk	
2	ounces	unsalted butter	melted in a small saucepan and cooled
1	ounce	unsalted butter, shortening, or non-stick spray	for the pan
8	ounces	fresh fruit such as blueberries	optional; for serving

TIDBIT One cup of buttermilk will neutralize 1 teaspoon of baking soda and in doing so produce enough CO_2 to lift 1 cup's worth of flour.

// PROCEDURE

1. Heat an **electric griddle** to 350°F or set a **heavy skillet or griddle** over medium heat.
2. Heat the oven to the lowest possible temperature (not more than 200°F).
3. Place the pancake mix in a **large mixing bowl**.
4. **Whisk** the egg whites and the buttermilk in a second **bowl**.
5. Whisk the egg yolks into the cooled melted butter (right in the pan is fine).
6. Whisk the butter mixture completely into the buttermilk mixture.

7 Dump the wet team onto the dry team and quickly bring together with a large whisk. I allow myself only 10 stirs, then I walk away. . . just walk away. Yes, there will be some lumps in the batter. Yes, this is fine. Necessary, in fact.

8 Check on the griddle. When a drop of water skittles across the surface, it's ready. Lightly lube the griddle with the butter, shortening, or nonstick spray and wipe off the excess with a **paper towel**.

9 Ladle 1 ounce (by volume) of batter onto the griddle. (How will you know how much batter is 1 ounce? Because you're going to use either a **#20 disher or a 1-ounce ladle**.) Cook for 3 minutes, or until the bubbles around the upside edge set. If you wish to integrate the fruit into the pancake itself, add it after the batter has been on the griddle for about 1 minute.

10 Carefully flip and cook for another 2 to 3 minutes, until golden brown on the bottom.

11 Serve immediately or keep warm in the oven by placing cakes on a **half sheet pan** and covering them with a **tea towel** for up to 20 minutes. To freeze cooked pancakes, cool completely, then place them in **zip-top freezer bags**. Seal the bags, removing as much air as possible. The frozen pancakes can easily be heated up in a toaster or toaster oven.

TRIVIA The maple scenes were shot at Bragg Farm in Montpelier, VT. My wife and I used to go there for freshly bottled syrup while I was attending the New England Culinary Institute. That's where I first had sugar on snow, heavily reduced maple syrup served on fresh snow, with . . . pickles. Yes, it's good. Oh, and when they brew coffee with sap instead of water, that's pretty good too.

MAPLE SYRUP PRIMER

Maple syrup is one of the oldest agricultural commodities produced in the United States and Canada, mostly in Vermont, Maine, New York, and Quebec. Native Americans taught sugaring to the settlers.

Maple sap looks, feels, and tastes a lot like water, and in fact straight from the tree it's only 2 to 3 percent sugar. To get it, you drill a hole with a 7⁄16-inch bit into a maple tree that's at least 10 inches in diameter. You drive an iron spigot called a spile into the hole, then either hang a bucket on it or attach a tube system. You do this in the early spring when the temperatures drop well below freezing at night but rise above freezing in the daytime.

Syrup is graded according to flavor, color, and intensity. The grades do not have anything to do with quality or purity, as they all have the same sugar content.

GRADE A: LIGHT AMBER

Light, mild, delicate maple flavor. Usually boiled from sap gathered at the beginning of the season. Good for use in cakes and pastries, but way too weak for pancakes, in my opinion.

GRADE A: MEDIUM AMBER

This is the most popular grade in the United States. It's a bit darker than light amber and delivers a more distinct maple flavor. It's produced during the middle of the season.

GRADE A: DARK AMBER

Just like medium amber only more so. Usually produced a little later in the season. This is my personal choice for pancakes and waffles.

GRADE B

Very dark and very strong. Made from the very last sap of the season and used mostly for baking. I use it in baked beans and for glazing hams.

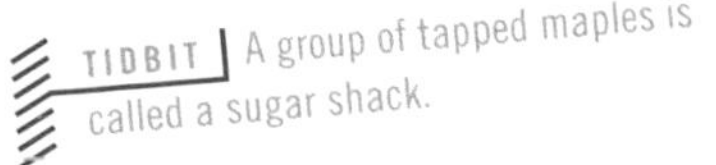

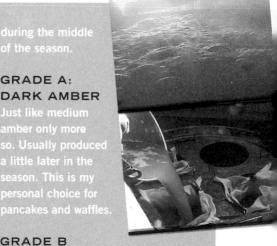

TIDBIT A group of tapped maples is called a sugar shack.

10 MINUTES MORE

PANCAKE FROSTING

1 POUND OF FROSTING

Believe it or not, cooled pancakes can be layered with frosting and stacked to produce a darned tasty cake. Maple frosting is of course *de rigueur*.

// SOFTWARE

6	ounces	unsalted butter	room temperature
2	tablespoons	mayonnaise	
¼	cup	maple syrup	
1	pound	confectioners' sugar	
1	teaspoon	vanilla extract	
	pinch	kosher salt	

// PROCEDURE

1. Combine the butter, mayonnaise, and syrup into the **bowl of a stand mixer with the paddle attachment**, and beat on high until light and fluffy, approximately 3 to 4 minutes.
2. Turn off the mixer and add ½ cup of the sugar. Mix on low until combined. Stop to **scrape** down the side of the bowl. Repeat until all of the sugar has been incorporated.
3. Add the vanilla and salt and continue to beat until the frosting is smooth and light, approximately 2 to 3 minutes. Use immediately or store in an **airtight container** at room temperature for up to 4 hours or refrigerate for up to a week. Bring to room temperature before using.

NOTE: The mayonnaise? A lot of American-style butter cream recipes (i.e., butter and confectioners' sugar) call for a raw egg, because the lecithin in the yolk creates an emulsion thereby creating a luxuriously smooth frosting. Well, mayonnaise is already an emulsion, which will create and stabilize the emulsion between the butter, syrup, and confectioners' sugar.

THE CASE FOR BUTTER

EPISODE 36 | SEASON 3 | GOOD EATS

During the '80s and '90s, butter was blamed for everything short of the Flock of Seagulls hairdos. By 2001, I'd had it. I was tired of seeing this stalwart ally suffer in silence. Vindication was due—and so the World Food Court convened.

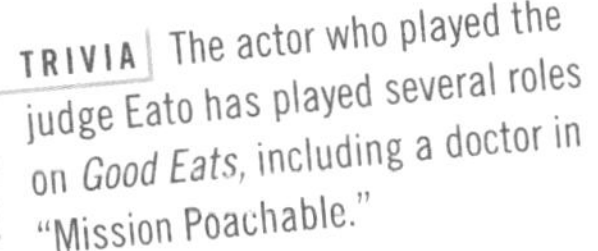

TRIVIA The actor who played the judge Eato has played several roles on *Good Eats*, including a doctor in "Mission Poachable."

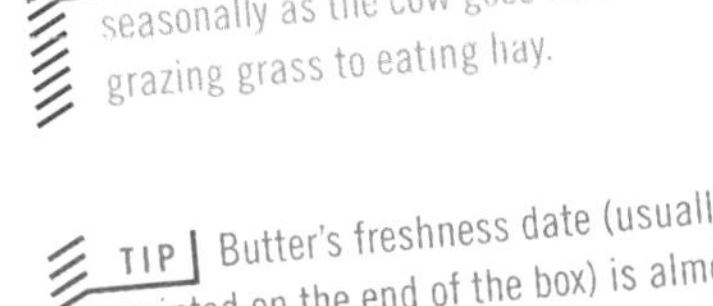

TIDBIT The color of butter changes seasonally as the cow goes from grazing grass to eating hay.

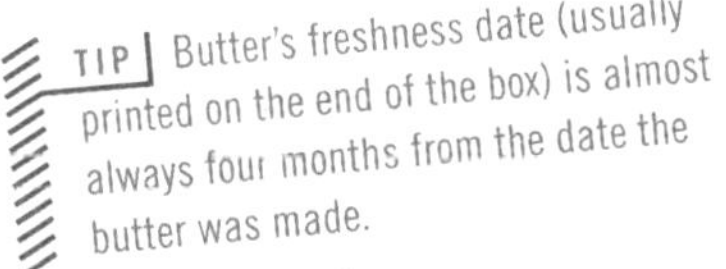

TIP Butter's freshness date (usually printed on the end of the box) is almost always four months from the date the butter was made.

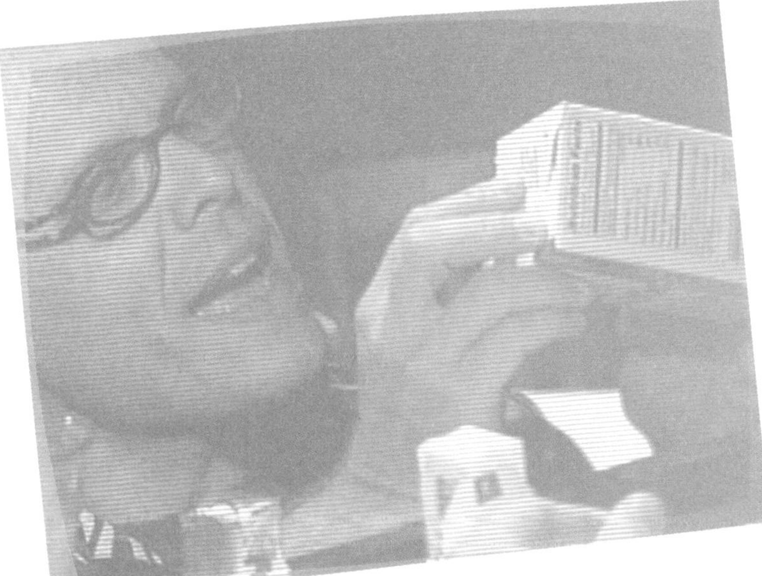

TRIVIA | The butter operation I visited in the episode was a Land O'Lakes factory in Carlisle, PA. They were very nice and helpful folks but were a little taken aback when I showed up by myself for the shoot. The producer at the time didn't want to shell out for crew, so I'd set up the camera and the audio, then hop in front of the camera and talk. I don't think the Land O'Lakes folks had seen that before.

TRIVIA | The doctor was played by our Steadicam operator, Ramon.

KNOWLEDGE CONCENTRATE

Butter is cream (fresh or sometimes slightly fermented) that has been agitated (churned) until the fat globules suspended in the liquid collide and coalesce, creating a semisolid mass that is then washed and packaged.

Here's how butter is made these days:

1. Fresh milk gets spun in a centrifuge, which separates out the cream, which is around 42 percent fat.

2. The cream is pasteurized at 190°F for about 30 seconds.

3. The cream is cooled so that fat crystals will form (this is important). This stage is called "tempering" the cream.

4. The cream then goes into the churn, where it's repeatedly smacked against an abrasive surface so that the fat crystals stick together. At this point, the butter and buttermilk appear.

5. The young butter is then "worked" or kneaded to drive out more moisture and develop better texture. At this point salt may be added, as well as annatto seed, which enhances the natural yellow color.

Butter is at least 80 percent butterfat. High-end "gourmet" butters often go as high as 88 percent. Besides water and butterfat, butter also contains milk solids, which contain phosphorus, protein, and calcium.

The USDA may grant the butter a grade of AA, A, or B depending on flavor, body, color, spreadability, and sometimes salt content. AA butters are amazingly smooth and creamy, while Bs tend to crack and deliver a rather acidic flavor. It should be noted, however, that B butters are highly desired by some pastry bakers. Lower grades aren't sold in most megamarts.

Butter boxes or wrappers bearing the USDA shield have been inspected for wholesomeness but not necessarily graded. Margarine, by the way, is a manufactured product and as such is not inspected.

Market varieties of butter:

UNSALTED BUTTER is generally wrapped in foil so that it doesn't go rancid as quickly as if it were wrapped in paper.

SALTED (sometimes sold as "sweet") BUTTER contains 1.2 to 1.4 percent salt. Although it tastes darned good on bread, you can't exactly take the salt out when you don't want it.

EUROPEAN-STYLE BUTTER is inoculated with a bacteria (like buttermilk), which gives it a pleasant tang. Many of the best are now made in America.

SPECIALTY BUTTERS include ghee, a clarified and cooked butter used in Indian cuisine, and whipped butter, which has had air added for easy spreading. Since so much of its volume (up to 50 percent) is air, it cannot be substituted for other butters in recipes unless it's melted and then measured.

APPLICATION

RAYMOND BEURRE BLANC[1]

4 SERVINGS

Because it's essentially an emulsion of water in fat, butter is a sauce waiting to happen. This classic sauce is great with fish, salmon, chicken, or asparagus.

SOFTWARE

2	tablespoons	shallot	finely chopped
¾	cup	dry white wine	such as Pinot Grigio
2	tablespoons	fresh lemon juice	
1	tablespoon	heavy cream	
6	ounces	unsalted butter	cut into 12 pieces and chilled
	to taste	kosher salt	
	to taste	white pepper	freshly ground

PROCEDURE

1. Combine the shallot, wine, and lemon juice in a **small saucepan, or better yet a 3-quart saucier**, and put over high heat.
2. Cook, **whisking** occasionally, until reduced to about 3 tablespoons, 8 to 10 minutes.
3. Whisk in the cream,[2] then reduce the heat to a bare simmer; do not boil.
4. Work in the butter a piece at a time, whisking constantly. If the sauce begins to boil, immediately remove the pan from the heat. When you're sure the last piece has melted, add another.[3]
5. By the time the butter is all in, the sauce should be thick and, well . . . *luxurious* is the only word for it. Since further heating would be counterproductive, I suggest moving the sauce straight to a clean Thermos, where it will stay warm for hours. If you don't have a **Thermos**, pour the sauce into a glass measuring cup set inside a bowl or pan of hot water.

TIDBIT Two cups of cold heavy cream will produce about 6 ounces of butter.

TRIVIA I wrote this script in a single day, a feat I've never been able to repeat with any other *Good Fats* episode. This show also has my favorite application name, Raymond Beurre Blanc. That just kills me.

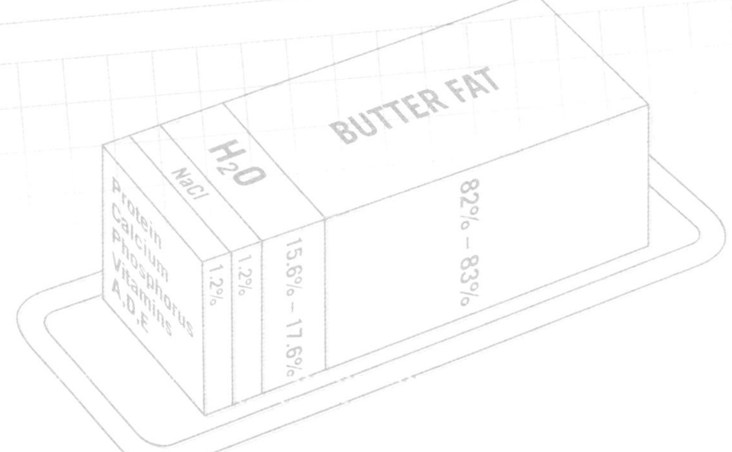

TIDBIT An ounce (2 tablespoons) of butter contains 201 calories and 23 grams of fat, 14 of which are saturated. It also contains a fair amount of vitamin A. Since it's a natural product butter contains no trans-fatty acids.

APPLICATION

COMPOUND BUTTER

ABOUT 1 POUND

Compound butter, in which you work a flavor enhancer (herb, spice, sugar, honey, vinegar) into softened butter, can be a very useful thing to have on hand in the kitchen. Although we tackled two specific applications in the show, you really just need some general guidelines to get going.

SOFTWARE

1	pound	unsalted butter	cold, chopped into small chunks

SECONDARY SOFTWARE

Try tinkering with the below suggestions or create your own, but use no more than 2 ounces of addition per pound of butter.

honey and cinnamon	(this butter is great on pancakes)
chopped olives and garlic	(if the olives are packed in oil, toss some of that in as well)
finely chopped fresh herbs and extra-virgin olive oil	
chopped jalapeño and grated lime zest	
chopped cooked bacon	
roasted garlic	
minced truffle	(the fungus, not the candy)
chopped capers and fresh parsley	
maple syrup and grated orange zest	
minced shallot and grated lemon zest	

PROCEDURE

1. Place cold butter in the **bowl of your stand mixer fitted with the whisk attachment**. Beat on low until the butter softens and lightens in color, 5 to 7 minutes.
2. Add 2 ounces of any of the suggestions above.
3. Whip for 2 minutes longer.
4. Remove the butter from the bowl and **spoon** onto a **sheet of parchment paper or plastic wrap**. Form into a log.
5. Twist the ends of the paper then wrap in **plastic** to seal your butter log as airtightly (is that a word?) as possible, then store in the freezer.
6. When you're ready to use, just cut off a thick medallion of goodness. Dropping a lozenge of compound herb butter onto a steak or a baked potato elevates humble victuals into seriously good eats.

[1] *Beurre blanc* is French for white butter sauce. This is, by the way, my favorite sauce because it can be built on almost any aromatic and flavored with a wide variety of seasonings.

[2] The cream will help to ensure that as the butter melts, the emulsion remains a stable water-in-fat emulsion rather than inverting to a fat-in-water emulsion. In other words, it's an insurance policy against sauce breakage.

[3] When I make beurre blanc I get into a rhythm of working on and off the heat. Add the butter when it's off the heat, then return to the heat to whisk. As the emulsion builds it will become thicker and creamier. The key is to not let it boil, or it will become basically an oil slick on water—not good eats.

FLAT IS BEAUTIFUL

EPISODE 37 | SEASON 3 | GOOD EATS

This was the first show I wrote that I had serious doubts about, simply because I didn't know how to possibly get it all into a half hour. Flour, gluten, yeast, rising, punching, tossing. This is one of those cases where something that seems simple isn't. But being forced into such a small envelope was actually a good thing because it focused us on the essence of pizza and that, of course, is crust.

TRIVIA | The pizza guy in the back seat is my brother-in-law, Christian. Pressing crew, family, and friends into supporting roles on the show is a proud *Good Eats* tradition.

NECESSITY IS THE MOTHER OF ALL PIZZA

Since they could be cooked on hot rocks at fireside, flatbreads are probably some of our earliest cooked foods. A thousand years ago or so, the Italians devised focaccia, flattened yeast bread covered with oil and herbs. They followed this up with the housewife standard *casa de nanza*, or "take out before." To make it, you simply pounded a piece of dough flat, stuck some leftovers on top, and chucked it in the oven. This bit of practical leger-demain is to my mind the heart of the pizza matter, but most of us can't get our heads (or mouths) around pizza without tomato sauce. The blessed day on which tomato sauce first met pizza dough took place sometime in the nineteenth century in Naples, a city whose name has become practically synonymous with "pizza."

Supposedly in 1889 Queen Margherita Teresa Giovanni, the consort of Umberto I, visited Naples, and a pizza tosser named Esposito concocted in her honor a pie composed of crust, tomatoes, mozzarella cheese, and basil, a juxtaposition that may have been made for no other reason than it mimicked the colors of the Italian flag.[1] The rest is history.

WHEN YEAST ATTACKS!

KNOWLEDGE CONCENTRATE

Putting pizza on sound footing requires a dough that is both plastic (can be shaped) and elastic (returns to original shape when deformed). Since these characteristics are diametrically opposed, the key word here is *balance*. If you want a good idea of what a pizza dough needs to be like, load up your mouth with about three pieces of bubble gum and chew for five minutes. Blow a bubble. That's what you need your dough to do. And that takes . . .

Gluten. A microscopic protein matrix, gluten acts like bungee cord nets stretched out and layered one upon the other, like a mesh of bungee cords. This makes it possible for doughs to expand as the yeasts do their thing, and for doughs to be stretched out very thin.

Factors that influence gluten formation are myriad, but the big three are:

1. PROTEIN: The higher the protein content of the flour the better, so reach for bread flour, which usually has a few percentage points on all-purpose. (I use Sir Lancelot bread flour from King Arthur Flour, which rings in at 14.2 percent.)

2. MOISTURE: Although doughs (as opposed to batters) contain more flour by weight than water, H_2O is still a critical element, as it hydrates the flour and makes gluten possible. The trick is to invite enough to the party so that the dough is soft and smooth but not so much that it's sticky and hard to work. Also, since chlorine can interfere with yeast's life cycle, it's important to use filtered water in all yeast doughs.[2]

3. AGITATION: In order to be "fully developed," (kneaded) dough needs to be vigorously agitated until enough gluten forms for the dough to "windowpane"—that is, when stretched thin the dough becomes an almost translucent membrane without tearing. Most home bakers don't knead nearly enough.

Yeast forms you're likely to encounter:

CAKE: A soft, crumbly mass full of wide-awake yeast happily housed in a moist support medium. This is my absolute favorite form of yeast to use, but since it's tough to find and only has a two-week life span in the fridge, we decided against using it in the show.

TOPPINGS
DO NOT
GREAT
PIZZA
MAKE!

ACTIVE DRY: Completely dried out and in a dormant state. Comes in packets (2¼ teaspoons is standard) and jars. This is the consumer yeast standard used for formulation of almost every modern bread recipe in print. Although active dry will remain viable for years if left unopened, it takes a lot of time to wake up and even longer to colonize. Since so many of the beasties inside are actually not sleeping but dead, most procedures call for soaking the yeast in warm water (often with sugar) to "proof" before mixing it with the rest of the ingredients.

INSTANT: Like active dry, only the pieces have been milled smaller and more of the beasties are actually alive. They're also packed with a dose of vitamin C that rouses them quickly when called to service. Instant yeast does not need to be proofed and can be added with the rest of the dry ingredients, which is nice. The only downside I can see is that instant yeasts tend to be more perishable than active dry, so you have to be mindful of expiration dates. This is my go-to yeast, especially for pizza.

RAPID-RISE: Like instant yeast, but the strains have been bred for maximum gas output. Since I feel that fast rises equal minimum flavor, I'm not a fan.

PIZZA-SPECIFIC HARDWARE

Tiles cut to fit bottom floor of oven

If you've got electric coils down there you're out of luck

AB ♥ EMMA

STONE: Pizzas like high heat, the hotter the better. Problem is, unless you want to grind the lock off your oven door that prevents you from opening the oven during the self-clean cycle, which can reach 800°F, thus invalidating your warranty, you're going to have to either grill your pizzas or settle for the wimpy 500°F your home box allows you. You can make the most of this situation by cooking on a stone, which will move what heat you do have into the crust as quickly as possible while wicking away excess moisture. Although limestone is the best material for the job, I use 6-by-6-inch unglazed quarry tiles.[3]

PEEL: A peel is essentially a long-handled wooden paddle used to deliver pizzas to and from the stone. Average handle length is 1 to 3 feet, and the size you need depends on how deep into the oven you need to reach.[4] I've seen a lot of folks head to the store for a peel and return with a cutting board that looks like a peel except for the fact that the forward edge of a peel is planed down so that it forms a spade that can shoot under a finished pie.

Some pizza places use metal peels. Don't. With wood, you can actually stretch and build the pizza right on the peel. You can't do that with metal, as the dough is more likely to stick.

FUN YEAST FACTS TO KNOW AND TELL

- Yeasts are single-cell organisms, which possess characteristics of both plants and animals.
- The strain of yeast used by bakers (typically) is *Saccharomyces cerevisiae*, which is a long-drawn-out-Latin way to say "beer sugar."
- Yeasts consume sugars and the glucose from starch and produce carbon oxide and alcohol. Not only does this provide the gas required for lift; it has a considerable effect on the quality of the gluten in the dough. The life cycle of yeast in food is referred to as "fermentation."
- Up until a couple of centuries ago, bakers got their yeast from breweries. Now, specific strains are available for baking.

TRIVIA Taking a cue from the episode, a fan a few years back presented me with a pizza peel intricately engraved with the word "Emma." For those of you who don't get it (probably those born post-1962), Google "Emma Peel" sometime.

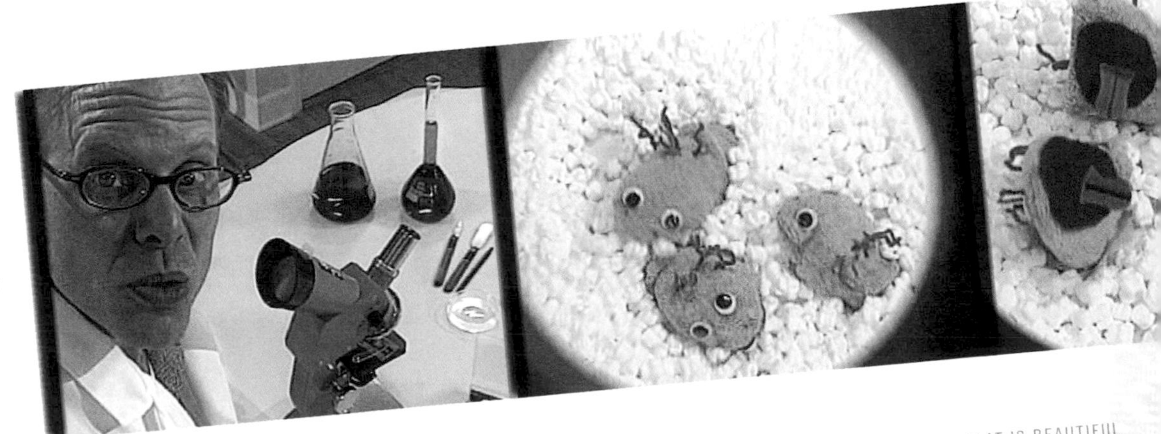

APPLICATION

PIZZA PIZZA

TWO 10-INCH PIZZAS

Instead of hard work, this application depends on patience to develop a pizza dough with flavor and body. I was dragged across the coals for the amount of salt called for in this recipe. After much analysis, I've come to the conclusion that I just like salt. We've amended it slightly. Other than that, we haven't messed with much.

SOFTWARE

9½	ounces	bread flour	plus ½ cup or so for rolling
1	teaspoon	instant yeast	(not rapid rise)
2	tablespoons	sugar	
2	teaspoons	kosher salt	
5	teaspoons	olive oil	(not extra-virgin) divided
¾	cup	filtered H_2O	warm (100°–105°F)
		sauce and pizza fixins as desired	

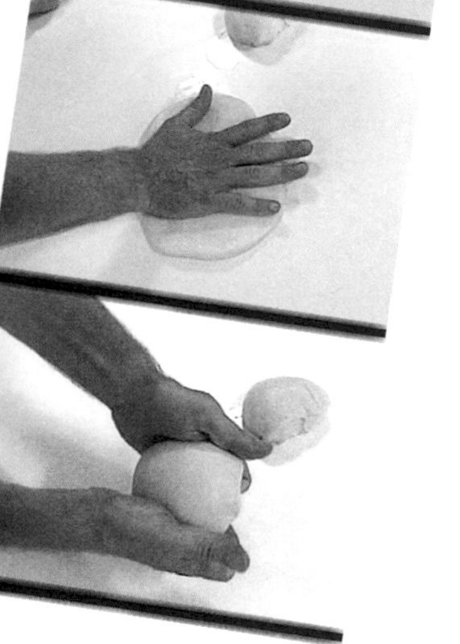

PROCEDURE

1. Place your **mixer's work bowl** on a **scale** and use the tare function to zero out its weight. Then weigh in the flour.
2. Install the bowl on the **mixer** and attach the **dough hook**. Add the yeast and turn the mixer to "stir," then add the sugar, salt, 2 teaspoons of the oil, and the water.
3. Mix until the dough just comes together, forming a ball and pulling away from the sides of the bowl. Increase the mixer speed to medium and knead for 10 minutes.
4. Tear off a small piece of the dough (about the size of the gum wad we discussed earlier) and flatten it into a disk with your fingers. Carefully stretch and rotate it, stretching the center with your middle fingers from behind until you have a thin membrane. If the dough tears without becoming thin enough to see through, knead for another 5 minutes on medium speed.[5]
5. Remove the dough to a lightly floured countertop and smooth it into a ball. Move to a clean **mixing bowl** (or the mixer work bowl if you're lazy like me) and coat it with the rest of the oil.
6. Cover with **plastic wrap** and refrigerate for 18 to 24 hours.
7. Split the dough into 2 equal parts using either a **large serrated knife or a dough scraper**. Flatten each into a disk, then shape it into a ball by folding the edges of the round in toward the center several times and rolling it between your hands on the counter. You may want to moisten the counter with water to up the surface tension a bit so that the ball tightens up instead of sliding across the counter.

8 Cover both balls with a **clean tea towel** and let rest for 30 minutes.

9 Heat your oven (**pizza stone** inside) to 500°F, or hotter if you've got it.[6]

10 When you're ready to build the pizzas, sprinkle a couple teaspoons of flour on a **peel** and place the dough right in the middle. Pound the dough into a disk with your hands, then pick it up and pull it through your fingers to create the outer lip, a critical feature that cannot be created with a rolling pin. (In fact, rolling rather than stretching will just ruin the whole gosh-darned thing.)

11 At this point you need to start stretching the dough. The most efficient way to do this is to spin the dough so that the weight of the outer lip stretches the dough via centrifugal force. You can also stretch the dough on the board by turning and pulling it, and turning and pulling. Shake the peel from time to time to make sure the dough doesn't stick. Sticking would be bad.

12 **Brush** the lip with oil, then dress the pizza with olive oil or tomato sauce (see page 124). Even distribution is tricky, so you may want to **ladle** an ounce or two into the middle and then spread it out with the back of the ladle. Top with fresh herbs (oregano and basil) and a good melting cheese. I usually go with a mixture of mozzarella, Monterey Jack, and provolone, but that's me.

13 Slide the pizza onto the hot **pizza stone**. To do this, position the front edge of the peel about 1 inch from the back of the stone. Lift the handle and jiggle gently until the pizza slides forward. As soon as the dough touches the stone, start pulling the peel back toward you while still jiggling. When a couple of inches of dough are on the stone, quickly snap the peel straight back. As long as the dough isn't stuck to the peel, it will park itself nicely on the stone.

14 Keep an eye on the dough for the first 3 to 4 minutes. If there are any big bubbles left in the dough, they may balloon up. If that happens, you can reach in and pop them with a **fork or paring knife**. Bake for 7 minutes total, or until the top is bubbly and golden brown.

15 Slide the peel under the pizza and remove to the counter or a **cutting board**. Let it rest for at least 3 minutes before slicing with a **chef's knife or pizza cutter** (one of my favorite multitaskers).

TIP | Pizza dough makes great rolls and even better breadsticks. Just roll (yes, roll) into a big rectangle, cut into strips with the pizza wheel, twist a few times, line up on a sheet pan, brush with olive oil, sprinkle with coarse salt, and bake till golden.

TIDBIT | Why in the world would you let dough rise for the better part of a day in the refrigerator when it will double in volume in just a couple of hours at room temp? Because when fermentation happens at room temp, the dough cannot possibly absorb the flavors being created, nor can the gluten structures become pliable but strong. All you get with a warm rise is gas, which is almost completely lost during the shaping. A long, cool rise is crucial to a tasty, chewy yet crisp dough. Yes, it takes time, but your patience will be rewarded.

[1] If I've learned anything through years of food research it's that stories like these, which hinge the creation of a dish on one particular moment or event, are almost always false or at the very least greatly exaggerated.

[2] Ten years ago I would have said "filtered or bottled," but then ten years ago I actually thought we'd be recycling water bottles rather than throwing them in landfills. Silly me.

[3] Italian terra cotta is best, but Mexican specimens will do as long as they're unglazed. Of course, there is always a chance of an impurity rising up to ruin your day, but I've been cooking on the same tiles for years without any issues other than this eye that showed up on the bottom of my foot.

[4] A lot of my fascination with pizza came from a pizza barn in Waitsfield, Vermont, called American Flatbread. In the middle of the restaurant (a barn) sits a massive adobe stove. To work pizzas around the interior requires peels with greenwood saplings attached that are anywhere from 8 to 12 feet in length.

[5] When your dough can form a "windowpane" (as it's called), it's fully developed. Although it is possible to overknead the dough with a home mixer, you'd probably have to leave the mixer on and go to a movie to come close.

[6] Make sure you heat the stone/tile with the oven. Don't insert it into a hot oven unless you want to hear it shatter into pieces.

PANTRY RAID III: COOL BEANS

EPISODE 38 | SEASON 3 | GOOD EATS

Each day we must ask ourselves the same old question, "What to eat?" Now, back when websites were places where spiders lived, our pantries and common sense told us what to eat. But common food-sense has been drowned out by the banter of nutritional bodhisattva who hail one food this week and condemn it the next. As for our pantries, well, what chance do they stand against the kaleidoscope of cornucopia that is the modern megamart? We need a hero to pierce the dark spell of media hype and rescue us from the tower of perplexing plenty.

Anyone who has read their Brothers Grimm knows the answer: magic beans. Whether canned or dried, baked or boiled, pulverized or solidified, beans deliver meatless yet meaty satisfaction along with high-octane nutrition and the shelf life of carbon 14. Magic? Maybe. Good eats? Definitely.

TRIVIA | So how do you make a working model of intestines on a shoestring-and-duct-tape budget? Well, you get yourself a big green fabric collapsible play tube from Toys-R-Us. Then you pop the trucks off a skateboard, strap a handicam to the deck (facing backward), and pull it through the tube with a crank-style fifty-foot tape measure. Then in editing you reverse the footage and composite in a shot of a moving conveyor belt with Legos and cheesy puppets holding hammers. It's easy and cheap, but not as much fun as it sounds.

TIDBIT | Beans are a fabulous source for soluble fiber, which is great for your heart and can help to lower your blood sugar and keep it more normal. They're a great protein substitute, rich in folic acid and calcium.

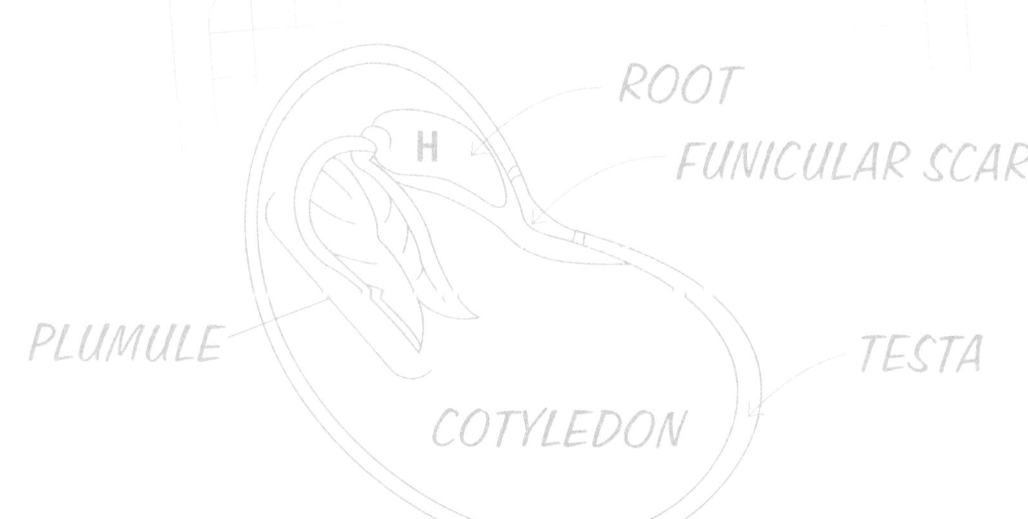

KNOWLEDGE CONCENTRATE

Here's how I see the canned versus dry issue: Canned beans are fully cooked, and their starches and proteins have taken all they can take and can't take no more. This makes them perfect for pureed dips, hummus, and salsas. However, further cooking can only deliver a diminishing return. For all applications in which heat must be applied, I go with either dry or fresh, the latter being, of course, another show. Following are standard operating procedures for dealing with dried beans.

SORT: Most of the dry beans available in American megamarts are harvested by machines, and machines have a hard time telling the difference between a mature bean and a small rock. Growers and packers do a fine job at sorting out such detritus, but due diligence is still recommended. I scatter beans out on a sheet pan and push them from one end to the other while scanning for mineral deposits. I probably find one rock for every five bags, but it only takes one to render a molar into shards.

Actual stones found in a bag of beans

RINSE: Beans, dirt, dust, mysterious powdery coatings of unknown origin . . . just rinse them in cold water, even if they look clean.

SOAK: Back when we produced this episode, I was a firm proponent of giving beans an overnight presoak. But in the years since, I've come to believe that whatever cooking time soaking saves comes at a price to flavor and texture. About the only good thing I can say about the soak is that it does seem to preserve the shape of some beans; but a burst bean here and there only helps to create a nice intrabean gravy, which I have come to thoroughly appreciate.

On "music": I'm proud to say that *Good Eats* was and remains the only cooking program to ever deal with the issue of bean-related flatulence by sending a camera through the GI tract of the host. Okay, I didn't really swallow a camera, and my guts don't actually house a conveyor belt, oven mitt puppets, or Legos, but we didn't flinch from the subject. The cause of the curse is oligosaccharides, gigantic carbo-constructs that human biology simply cannot disassemble.[1] And so, these über-molecules float on down, down, down to the nether regions of the colon, where they are set upon by voracious bacteria that make quick work of breaking them down. Problems ensue for the host (that's us) because these dusky denizens of our deep percolate gases, creating bloating and painful pressure that can only be relieved by . . . well, you know. Over-the-counter cures work by providing an enzyme that can process the troublesome sugars before they feed the bears. But truthfully, the more beans you eat the more your body becomes conditioned to the condition. So eat your beans.

Oh, speaking of bloating, the best way to blow your beans to bits during cooking is to cook them in too much liquid. Beans aren't pasta; they won't stop when they've drunk enough, so just use enough moisture to cover them and use a lid so it won't evaporate away.

Three substances slow the softening of beans and make slow cookery possible: acid, sugar, and calcium. Together, these substances keep the glue between the cells from dissolving. Ordinarily when you heat fruits or vegetables, this glue dissolves and the cells fall apart. But if you've got enough sugar or calcium[3] there, it won't dissolve.

BEANS, BEANS . . .

- Beans are members of the third most important flower family and the second most important plant family in human consumption: legumes.
- The word *legume* stems from the Latin *lego*, meaning "to gather, collect."[2]
- A legume is basically any plant that bears a pod containing edible seeds. Some young legumes are tender enough to eat pod and all. As they age, the pods toughen, and that's when we harvest the inner seeds. Great Northern beans, for instance, are simply the matured seeds of what we call green beans.
- Legumes are mostly starch and protein (stored in the cotyledon), surrounded by a seed coat (this can be up to 30 percent of the seed), which is mostly carbohydrates and fiber.

APPLICATION

THE ONCE AND FUTURE BEANS

10 TO 12 SERVINGS

This application riffs on pork-and-beans and classic Boston baked beans. The molasses helps to keep the cooked beans whole and distinct.

SOFTWARE

1	pound	bacon	chopped
1	medium	yellow onion	chopped
2	small	jalapeños	chopped
¼	cup	tomato paste	
¼	cup	dark brown sugar	
¼	cup	molasses	
1	pound	dry Great Northern beans	sorted and rinsed
1	quart	vegetable broth	
¼	teaspoon	cayenne pepper	
1	teaspoon	black pepper	freshly ground
2	teaspoons	kosher salt	

PROCEDURE

1. Heat the oven to 250°F.
2. Place a **cast-iron Dutch oven** over medium heat and add the bacon, onion, and jalapeños, stirring until the fat has rendered from the bacon and the onion is softened, about 5 minutes. Stir in the tomato paste, brown sugar, and molasses.
3. Add the beans to the Dutch oven, along with the broth, and bring to a boil over high heat. Add the cayenne, black pepper, and salt.[4]
4. Give them a stir and cover the pot. Place the pot in the oven and bake for 5 to 7 hours,[5] or until the beans are tender.

FUN BEAN FACTS TO KNOW AND TELL

- The Egyptians actually called their version of purgatory the Bean Field. The Romans believed that beans held the souls of the dead. The Greeks had a bean god named Keonetese.
- Due to their genetic diversity, there are more than fourteen thousand varieties of legumes. Only twenty-two are grown for human consumption.
- Beans contain iron, magnesium, and zinc.
- Boston baked beans were popularized by Puritan settlers, who cooked them on Saturday afternoon and ate them all through the Sabbath, when cooking was not allowed.
- Though it may not amount to a hill of beans, beans appear in more slang expressions than any other food.
- Beans contain protease inhibitors, which can neutralize cancer-causing free radicals.

TRIVIA | If there's ever been an underdeveloped contrivance in a *Good Eats* episode it's the bean board game in this show. I loved the idea and the board itself, but it never really came together conceptually. I still want to develop a food-based board game, so if you're a bigwig with Milton-Bradley, I await your call.

APPLICATION

BLACK BEAN SALAD

4 SERVINGS

I like these beans as a cold side or as a hot burrito filling.

//SOFTWARE

1	stalk	celery	halved
1	large	carrot	halved
	a few sprigs	fresh thyme	
	a few sprigs	fresh parsley	
1		dried arbol chile	
1	pound	dry black beans	sorted and rinsed
½	medium	onion	halved
2	teaspoons	kosher salt	
⅓	cup	olive oil	
⅓	cup	lime juice	freshly squeezed
1	small	red onion	minced
	a handful	fresh cilantro	chopped
1	teaspoon	ground cumin	
1	teaspoon	chili powder	
	to taste	salt	
	to taste	black pepper	freshly ground

//PROCEDURE

1. Tie the celery, carrot, thyme, parsley, and dried chile into a bundle using **cotton butcher's twine**. Place the black beans, bundle, and onion into a **4-quart pot**. Add just enough water to barely cover the beans. Bring to a simmer and partially cover. After 30 minutes, add the salt to the beans. Occasionally check on the beans and add water to cover the beans, if needed. Cook until just tender, 1–2 hours.

2. Combine the olive oil, lime juice, red onion, cilantro, cumin, and chili powder in a **medium mixing bowl**. When beans are just tender, drain them, remove the carrot bundle and onion and toss the beans while still hot with dressing. Chill thoroughly, about 1 hour, season with salt and pepper, and toss again before serving.

[1] Typically, nutrients are broken down by enzymes designed to take them apart nutrient by nutrient.

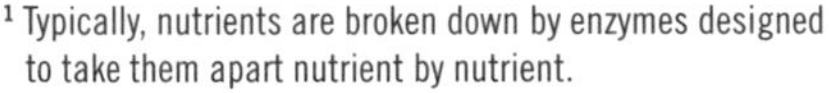

[2] So, yes, the toys we know as Legos are named after beans.

[3] Many classic bean recipes call for dark molasses, which, it just so happens, is loaded with calcium.

[4] More than a few chefs insist that adding salt from the get-go will toughen the skin of the beans—something about calcium. Well, I'm all for scientific explanations, but I've never experienced any troubles. I have, however, run into plenty of pots of miserably underseasoned beans.

[5] So why the oven, when the image of the bean pot on the back burner is so homey and comforting? Even, controllable heat is key to successful beanery, and short of burying them in a hole lined with hot rocks, lumberjack style, the oven's the best place for the job.

MISSION: POACHABLE

EPISODE 39 | SEASON 3 | GOOD EATS

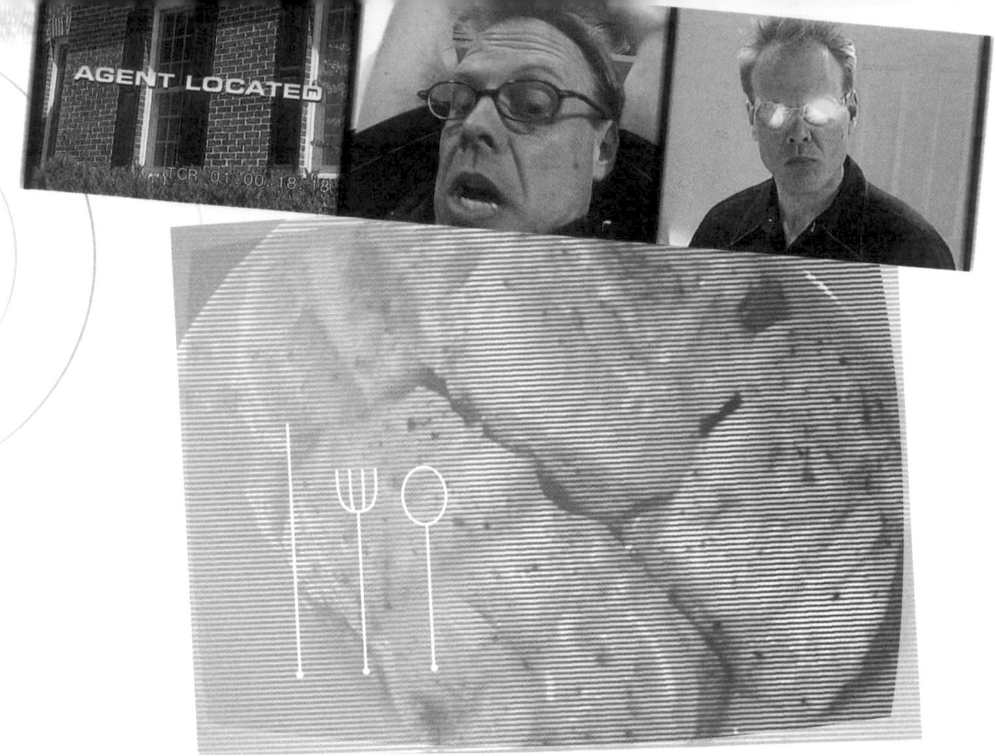

This was our first real "concept" show, in which the storyline almost ran the cooking out of town. The movie trailer for *Mission Impossible 2* was in heavy rotation at the time, and I wanted to goof it something terrible. And so we unfurled a rather wacky tale in which I play a government agent hunting down the Mad French Chef, a psychotic master criminal who's escaped from a high-security whatever. What does this have to do with poaching? I have no idea, but it seemed like a fun idea at the time.

KNOWLEDGE CONCENTRATE

- Traditionally, *poaching* refers to cooking by submersion in a flavorful liquid held just under the simmer (185°F) and is ideal for delicate foods (fish, some fruit, eggs) that are high in protein, especially those that will be served cold later (in chicken salad, as luncheon salmon, and so on). I would argue that liquids at temperatures as low as 145°F are suitable for poaching. The problem is that such temperatures are very difficult to maintain on the modern American cooktop.

- Controlling the poach comes down to two factors: how much liquid is used, and how much heat energy is poured into it. A common poaching mistake is to pour too much energy (heat) into the cooking liquid once the food has gone in. Due to the hydrogen bonds that hold it together (or not . . . depending on how you look at it), water is capable of holding on to a considerable amount of heat energy without actually changing temperature. This means that water has a high "specific heat" and is a much easier environment to manage than, say, oil, which must be constantly fiddled with, thermally speaking. Since you can count on water to store up a lot of heat, you don't have to put the spurs to it when the food goes in. My general MO is to bring the liquid to a simmer, add the food, and drop the heat to the lowest setting.

- Poaching is about equilibrium—that is, bringing the food and the liquid to a point where they share a common temperature. This means that if you can really control the heat so that the liquid never exceeds the desired target temperature of the food (say, 130°F for fish), you should be able to ensure that the food doesn't overcook. When poaching chicken, I typically shoot for liquid that's 165°F, which is also the final target temperature of the meat.

APPLICATION

POACHED EGGS

4 EGGS

When poaching a single serving (a single egg or two eggs that you want to cook together), trade the wide pan for one that's narrower and deeper, such as a 2-quart saucier. Use the handle of a wooden spoon to quickly stir the water in one direction until it's all smoothly spinning around, then carefully drop the egg into the center of the whirlpool and proceed with step 4 below. The swirling water will help prevent the whites from "feathering," or spreading out in the pan. Acid in the vinegar partially coagulates or "sets" the egg whites so that the resulting eggs are compact and smooth rather than ragged.

TIDBIT | *Poach* is French for "pouch" and refers to the shape an egg takes once it has been perfectly poached.

SOFTWARE

1	teaspoon	kosher salt	
2	teaspoons	white vinegar	
4	large	very fresh eggs[1]	

PROCEDURE

1. Add enough water to a deep **12-inch nonstick skillet** to come 1 inch up the side.[2]
2. Add the salt and vinegar and bring to a simmer over medium heat.
3. Crack each egg into a **small ramekin or custard cup**, then add the eggs to the poaching water one at a time, spacing them as evenly as possible around the edge of the pan.[3]
4. Turn off the heat, cover the pan, and set your timer for 5 minutes. Don't peek, poke, stir, or accost the eggs in any way.
5. Remove the eggs with a **slotted spoon** and serve immediately. Alternatively, move the eggs to an **ice bath** and refrigerate for up to 8 hours. Reheat in warm water just before serving.

THE WAY I POACH

THINGS I SERVE POACHED EGGS ON:

- Toast (of course)
- Tossed salad
- Spaghetti
- Sauteéd spinach
- Pulled pork barbecue (really)

OTHER LIQUIDS YOU CAN POACH EGGS IN:

- Tomato juice
- Clamato juice
- White wine
- Salsa (huevos rancheros)
- Beer . . . yes I'm serious—great with sausage

APPLICATION

CATFISH AU LAIT

4 SERVINGS

Use evaporated milk, spices, and aromatics to infuse a very mild fish with considerable flavor. Use the poaching liquid as a sauce.

SOFTWARE

1	12-ounce can	evaporated milk[4]	
1	teaspoon	Old Bay seasoning	
½	teaspoon	black pepper	freshly ground
1½	teaspoons	kosher salt	
½	medium	onion	thinly sliced
4	5-ounce	catfish fillets	also works well with shrimp, halibut, monkfish, or bluefish. I've even used this with lesser cuts of tuna.

PROCEDURE

1. Combine the evaporated milk, Old Bay, pepper, salt, and onion in an **electric skillet**,[5] cover, and bring to a boil.
2. Add the catfish to the liquid, **spooning** some of the liquid over the fillets.
3. Reduce the heat to low, 140° to 145°F, cover the skillet, and poach the fish for 7 to 9 minutes, until the fish is firm and cooked through.
4. Use a **large slotted spoon** to remove the fish to a serving dish. Top with some of the poaching liquid and serve immediately.

ON THE USE OF PARCHMENT

Most of the chefs I trained under topped poaching fish with parchment paper placed right on the surface of the liquid. This is done not to prevent evaporation but to prevent the surface of the food floating on the water (usually fish) from drying out. Although the method works, so does a properly fitted lid.

TIP | Poached fish tends to fall apart easily upon exiting the pan, so use either a wide, slotted turner or try poaching in a steamer basket, which can easily be retrieved from the liquid.

SUB-APPLICATION

A VERY FRENCH POACHING LIQUID: COURT BOUILLON[6]

1 PINT

Use this classic poaching liquid for salmon, halibut, sole, sea bass, or even shrimp.

// SOFTWARE

1½	cups	filtered H_2O	
½	cup	white wine	cheap
1		lemon	juiced
1	medium	onion	chopped
½	rib	celery	chopped
1	clove	garlic	minced
1	teaspoon	black peppercorns	
4 to 5	sprigs	fresh thyme	
1		bay leaf	

// PROCEDURE

1. Bring all the ingredients to a boil in a **saucepan**.
2. Reduce the heat and simmer for 8 minutes.
3. Poach away.
4. After use, boil for 1 minute, strain, cool, and refrigerate for use within 3 days or freeze for up to 2 months.

[1] Since the membrane surrounding the yolk dissolves with time, fresh eggs are best for poaching.

[2] Why such a big pan for such a relatively small payload? One quart of water is needed to deliver proper heat, and shallower water simplifies egg retrieval.

[3] Okay, this piling up of dirty dishes seems extreme to me, too, but unless you can keep up with which egg is which for timing purposes, this is the best way to go.

[4] Not to be confused with sweetened condensed milk, evaporated milk has had 60 percent of its original moisture removed. It does taste slightly sweet, as some of the natural sugars caramelize during the reduction process.

[5] I like electric skillets because they're efficient and easy to use. Although heat control used to be a real problem, modern units are far more precise than those our moms ruined liver and onions in. If you don't have one, you're officially cleared to use a heavy, lidded pan or casserole over medium-low heat, but you'll have to use a thermometer, which you should probably do anyway.

[6] That's French for "short boil."

TIP | Wine, stock, and lemon juice all make fine additions to a poaching liquid. Herbs smell nice, but since poaching is a relatively short cooking procedure, they won't impart much flavor. I also like to poach in dairy, and there is a long tradition of that in various European cultures. Almond milk is nice too. By the way, poaching in fat produces confit, but that will have to wait for another show.

TOFUWORLD

EPISODE 40 | SEASON 3 | GOOD EATS

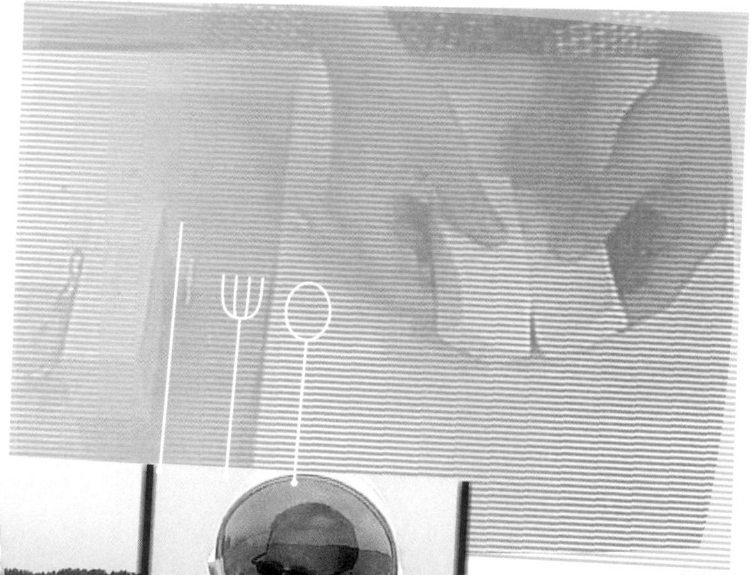

Maybe it was all the Tang I drank or those pop science films I gobbled up (the ones where the narrator always made big promises of the marvels of tomorrow), but when I was a kid, the future was where it was at! Of course, what I was really hot for was one of those food synthesizers, like the one on the *Enterprise*. I used to wonder what you would feed such a device. What foodstuff could possibly be that versatile? Then it hit me: Tofu! It's not very high-tech, but besides a 95 percent digestibility rate, eight essential amino acids, and all those trendy phytochemicals, tofu is a profoundly plastic proto-staple as flexible as any old Spacely Sprocket.

TIDBIT | Tofu was created in China nearly two thousand years ago, but it wasn't until the last century that tofu became popular in the West.

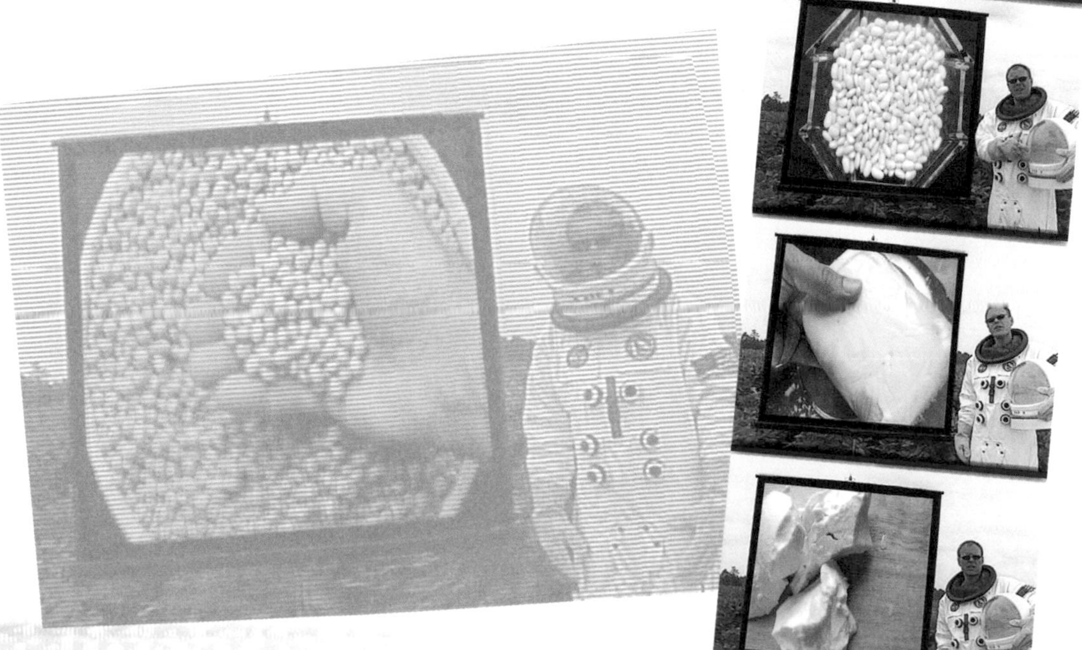

KNOWLEDGE CONCENTRATE

Tofu, also called bean curd, begins with dried, shelled soybeans, which are soaked overnight. The next day, the beans are boiled, crushed, and then separated into a solid called *okara* and soymilk. (This soymilk is significantly thicker than the soymilk we drink.) The soymilk is coagulated (like cheese) with the addition of calcium or magnesium salts (traditionally, *nigari*, a byproduct of salt production, was used). The soymilk is then poured into molds, where the carbohydrate-rich whey is allowed to drain off.

If tofu is cut as-is without pressing, a fine protein network is formed, trapping liquid in a creamy soft block of "silken"-style tofu. Silken tofu is a lot like Jell-O in texture and is not nearly as porous as regular tofu. It has a creamy quality that makes it a popular summer dessert. The biggest thing that separates silken tofu from regular tofu is this: The hot soymilk and coagulants are poured into an aseptic container and sealed, so it will keep in the pantry for three months. Silken tofu is great in smoothies and salad dressing. We use it as the base for a nutritious (yet delicious) pie filling.

If the tofu is cut and pressed immediately (much like cheddar cheese is pressed), "firm"-style tofu is created. Firm or regular tofu comes in two varieties, firm and soft. The main difference is the amount of moisture (whey) that is drained off. It's sort of like a sponge: If we wring out extra moisture, it can suck up lots of other flavors. Firm is great for grilling, sautéing, and frying. Soft nicely crumbles for salads and can be scrambled as an egg replacement or used for sandwiches.

Although artisanal tofu in China and Japan can convey an endless variety of flavors and textures, most megamart brands are on the bland side—which isn't necessarily a bad thing, as tofu's chameleon-like qualities are partly what make it so appealing.

These days, most megamarts carry tofu in vacuum-sealed packages, which may be sold fresh or frozen. In this containment, unopened, the tofu can last for three months (in the fridge for firm and in the pantry for silken). Always follow the manufacturer's best-by date. Some health food stores carry tofu in bulk bins: Be sure that normal sanitization practices are in play. The water surrounding the tofu should look fresh and clean. Utensils should be clean as well.

Once opened, tofu will keep for five days if its water is changed daily. Frozen, it will keep for up to three months. Freezing tofu will enhance tofu's meaty texture, and change it to a caramel color.

TOFU'S SUPERPOWERS

- Tofu is an excellent source of iron and magnesium and a good source of potassium, niacin, calcium, and zinc. It also contains lots of folic acid, thiamine, and B6.
- The fats in tofu are 78 percent unsaturated and contain no cholesterol.
- Tofu is rich in phytochemicals called isoflavones, specifically genistein and daidzein, which may help to protect the body from everything from osteoporosis to prostate cancer.
- Tofu is considered one of the most digestible foods on Earth. The many nutrients are easily broken down and absorbed by the body.

TIDBIT The first soy food manufactured in the United States was Baco-Bits.

TRIVIA The sponge puppet at left is supposed to be reminiscent of a 1950s Japanese movie monster. We didn't have much of a budget in those days.

APPLICATION — MOO-LESS CHOCOLATE PIE

8 SERVINGS[1]

This is my favorite tofu magic trick. I've served this pie to dozens of unsuspecting dessert lovers and not one has ever suspected the curd within.

TIDBIT | Although vanilla extract is often added at the very end of cooking, the melting chocolate will never get hot enough to damage its delicate sensibilities.

// SOFTWARE

13	ounces	semisweet chocolate chips	
⅓	cup	coffee liqueur	
1	teaspoon	vanilla extract	
1	pound	silken tofu	drained
1	tablespoon	honey	
1	9-inch	prepared chocolate wafer crust	(store bought or see below)

// PROCEDURE

1. Place enough water in the bottom of a **4-quart saucepan** to come 1 inch up the sides. Bring to a simmer over medium heat.
2. Melt the chocolate chips with the liqueur and vanilla in a **medium metal bowl** set over the simmering water, stirring often with a **rubber or silicone spatula**.
3. Combine the tofu, honey, and chocolate mixture in a **blender or food processor** and spin until smooth (about 1 minute).
4. Pour the filling into the crust and refrigerate for 2 hours, or until the filling sets firm.

SUB-APPLICATION — CHOCOLATE WAFER CRUST

ONE 9-INCH PIE CRUST

// SOFTWARE

6½	ounces	chocolate wafer cookies	
1	tablespoon	sugar	
3	ounces	unsalted butter	melted and slightly cooled

// PROCEDURE

1. Heat the oven to 350°F. Spin cookies and sugar in a **food processor** until fine crumbs. Then drizzle in the butter, pulsing to combine. Press this mixture firmly and evenly into the bottom, up the sides, and just over the lip of a **9-inch metal pie pan**.
2. Bake on the middle rack of the oven for 18 to 20 minutes, or until crust is set and appears dry.
3. Remove from the oven and cool completely, approximately 1 hour.

APPLICATION

FILET O'FU

2 SERVINGS

This dish takes advantage of tofu's surprisingly porous nature to produce a meaty yet meat-free delight.

SOFTWARE

1	pound	firm tofu	
2	tablespoons	sherry vinegar	
2	tablespoons	Worcestershire sauce	
	a few dashes	hot pepper sauce	
½	cup	all-purpose flour	
2	large	eggs	lightly beaten
½	cup	Japanese breadcrumbs	a.k.a. panko[2]
		canola oil	

PROCEDURE

1. Drain and cut the tofu into 4 equal portions.
2. Lay slices on 5 layers of **paper towels** and fold over to cover.
3. Sandwich this packet between 2 **half sheet pans** and weigh the top with approximately 2 pounds of weight. (Actually, a **28-ounce can of tomatoes** is perfect.)
4. Replace the paper towels after 1 hour and press another hour.
5. Place tofu in a **zip-top bag** and add vinegar, Worcestershire, and hot pepper sauce and marinate 1 to 2 hours.
6. Place flour, eggs, and breadcrumbs in 3 separate **shallow dishes** (disposable pie pans perhaps) arranged side by side.
7. Remove tofu from bag, and blot on paper towels. **Dredge** in flour. Tap off excess then repeat with eggs and breadcrumbs. Make sure all pieces are evenly coated. Set on **wire rack** to set.
8. Heat ⅛ inch of oil in a **12-inch nonstick skillet** over medium-high heat. When oil begins to shimmer, slide tofu pieces into pan and fry each side to golden brown—about 2 minutes per side.
9. Cool briefly on wire rack and serve hot.

NOTE: I like mine drizzled with sriracha—that's a hot sauce that comes in a squeeze bottle with a picture of a rooster on it.

[1] Actually, I've eaten an entire pie in one sitting. Is that wrong?

[2] Unlike traditional, Western breadcrumbs, which tend to be grainy, Japanese breadcrumbs are jagged with a more open, porous structure, which, when fried, produce a very crisp crust.

TRIVIA This episode also presents a tofu-based version of a Caesar salad dressing. I've never liked it much.

TIP To prevent "club hand" when battering, use one hand for dipping in the dry ingredients and the other for the wet.

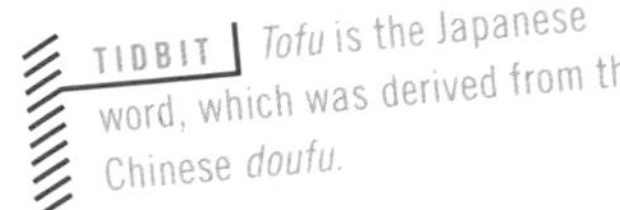

TIDBIT *Tofu* is the Japanese word, which was derived from the Chinese *doufu*.

HEAD GAMES

EPISODE 41 | SEASON 3 | GOOD EATS

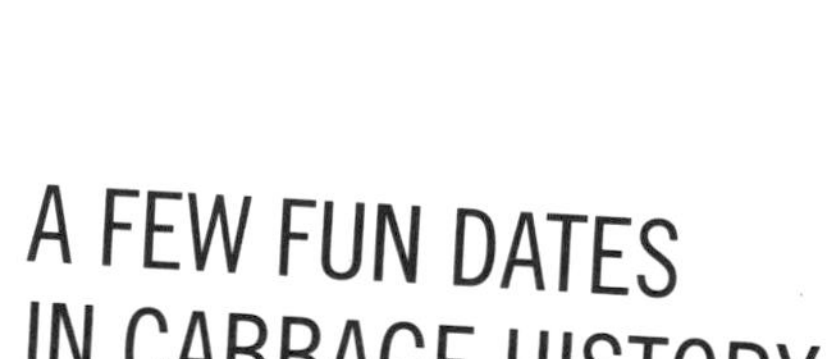

I grew up scared of cabbage. In my eyes it was a stinky, flavorless weed used to punish kids for being kids. Now I love the stuff. Ah, the mysteries of life. Anyway, I've always been a huge Rod Serling fan and had long hoped to goof his *Night Gallery* series somewhere along the line. Given its creepy nature, cabbage seemed the perfect food to use it on. We've continued to use the "Food Gallery" scenario through the years to handle foods with mixed reputations.

A FEW FUN DATES IN CABBAGE HISTORY

479 B.C.
In his blockbuster known today as the *I Ching*, Confucius goes on for pages about the health benefits of cabbage.

200 B.C.
Roman orator and poet Cato the Elder credits the existence of his twenty-eight sons to a high-cabbage diet. Ancient Romans also held that cabbage munching allows one to imbibe unlimited volumes of alcohol without suffering intoxication.

1558
Flemish refugees fleeing religious persecution at the hands of the king of Spain bring cabbage to the shores of England, a country later accused of having but three vegetables, two of which are cabbage.

1769
Forty of Captain Cook's crew are injured by a storm upon his ship *Courageous*. The ship's surgeon dresses the many wounds with cabbage leaves, thus staving off a boatload of gangrene.

KNOWLEDGE CONCENTRATE

- Cabbage is a member of the *Cruciferea* family, which also includes broccoli, collards, kale, and Brussels sprouts. A "head" of cabbage consists of layers of strong leaves that may form a head; the leaves may be smooth or curly, and vary in color from white to green to red.
- Cabbage began as a weed growing along the rocky coastlines of Europe and Asia. As people collected the seeds and cultivated it, the seeds of ideal specimens were saved and replanted. Different cultures coaxed different characteristics from the plants, giving rise to different varieties of cabbage. Southern Europeans developed tense, dense clusters of leaves and call it *caboche* (Old French for "head"; hence *cabbage*).
- Smaller heads that are fresh are best for raw applications (such as coleslaw) or for lightly cooked applications (such as ours, next page). Larger heads are best for preserving, and several cultures have their own versions: sauerkraut, chow-chow, and kimchi.
- When shopping, look for tight, bright heads that are heavy for their size.
- Green cabbage is the most grown of the varieties and contains the most sulfuric compounds, which can cause considerable stinkiness when cooking is prolonged.
- The best cabbage storage device comes preinstalled: the outer leaves. Leave them in place and stash the head in your refrigerator's crisper drawer. No need for plastic wrap or bag. A fresh head will keep for 2 weeks, easy.
- Cabbage is almost 90 percent water, but does contain a fair amount of fiber and nutrients such as vitamin C, calcium, and folate. Due to the sulfur content, a cabbage leaf does make a pretty decent wound dressing.
- Green vegetables contain two types of chlorophyll: chlorophyll A, which is bright blue-green, and chlorophyll B, which is bright yellow-green. Together they balance to form a green vegetable's color the way red, blue, and green go together to make a TV picture. If the two are in balance, the cabbage looks healthy and normal. But chlorophyll A is fragile, and if it gets too warm it breaks down and fades, leaving chlorophyll B all on its yellow own. And that's why old cabbages develop yellow spots.
- And now, a few words from cabbage's good buddy, caraway:
  - Caraway is an ancient cousin of anise and cumin.
  - The "seeds" are actually dried fruits, not just the plant's seeds.
  - Caraway is said to possess many powers, including the ability to limit cabbage's production of hydrogen sulfide.
  - The very best caraway comes from Holland.
  - Buy it whole and grind it within 6 months.

TIDBIT Alaska, where the sun doesn't set all summer long, is known for the size of its cabbage: heads weighing seventy-five pounds aren't uncommon there. A typical head of cabbage ranges in size from two to seven pounds.

TRIVIA The baby in the Rome scene is my daughter making her *Good Eats* debut. She's appeared in about ten episodes since my last count.

APPLICATION

SHRED, HEAD, BUTTER, AND BREAD

4 SERVINGS

By quickly blanching the cabbage leaves we can partially set the color so that further cooking won't turn them gray.

// SOFTWARE

2	ounces	unsalted butter	
1½	ounces	seasoned croutons	pulverized
¼	teaspoon	dry mustard	
1	teaspoon	caraway seeds	
1	tablespoon	kosher salt	
1	tablespoon	sugar	
1	small (2-pound) head	green cabbage	shredded

// PROCEDURE

1. Fill your **largest pot** three quarters full with water and bring to a boil over high heat.
2. Melt the butter in a **skillet** and add the croutons. Add the mustard and caraway seeds and stir over medium heat until the butter browns and smells nutty. Remove the skillet from the heat, but leave the dressing in the pan.
3. Add the salt and sugar to the boiling water and cook until dissolved. Add the cabbage to the boiling water and cook for exactly 2 minutes.
4. Drain the cabbage in the **bowl of a salad spinner**. Spin the cabbage to remove any excess water. Add the cabbage to the butter-crumb dressing and toss to coat thoroughly.
5. Serve immediately.

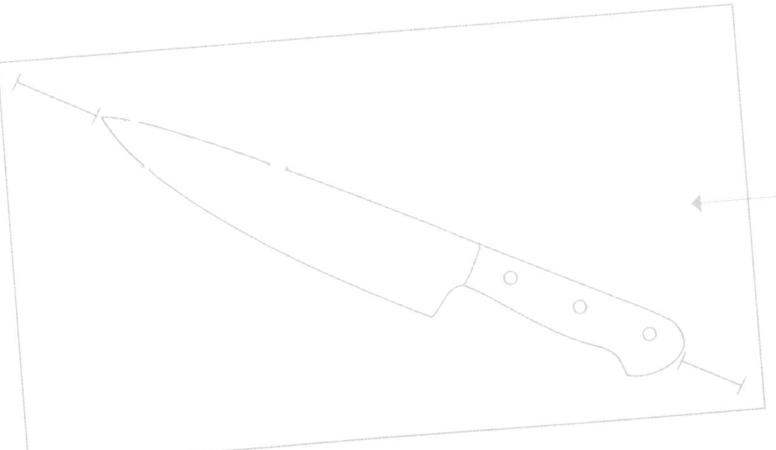

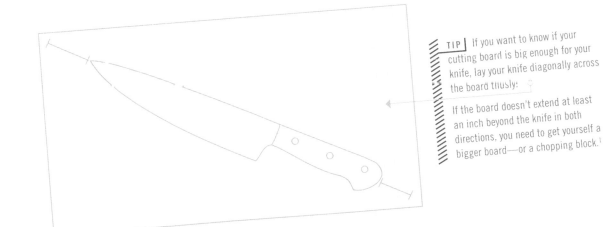

TIP | If you want to know if your cutting board is big enough for your knife, lay your knife diagonally across the board thusly:

If the board doesn't extend at least an inch beyond the knife in both directions, you need to get yourself a bigger board—or a chopping block.[1]

APPLICATION

HOME OF THE BRAISE

4 SERVINGS

By introducing acidic ingredients, red cabbage can cook long and low without losing any of its chromatic intensity.

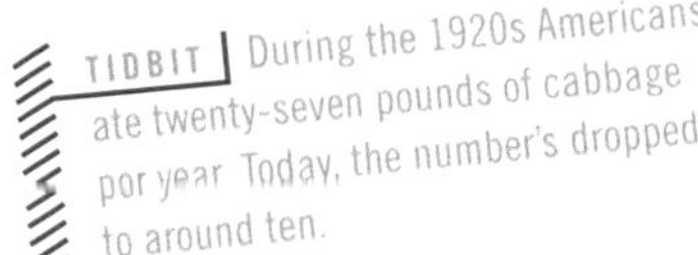
TIDBIT During the 1920s Americans ate twenty-seven pounds of cabbage per year. Today, the number's dropped to around ten.

SOFTWARE

2	tablespoons	canola oil	
1	large (8-ounce)	Granny Smith apple	peeled, cored, and cubed
1	cup	unfiltered apple juice	
¼	teaspoon	caraway seeds	
1½	teaspoons	kosher salt	
	to taste	black pepper	freshly ground
1	pound (about 1 small head)	red cabbage	shredded
½	small	lemon	juiced
1	tablespoon	unsalted butter	

PROCEDURE

1. Heat the oil in a **10-inch straight-sided sauté pan** over medium heat. Add the apple to the pan and cook until lightly browned, approximately 1 minute.
2. Increase the heat to high and add the apple juice, caraway seeds, salt, pepper, and cabbage to the pan. Cover the pan and shake to toss the cabbage to coat.
3. Reduce the heat to low and cook for 10 minutes. Remove the lid and cook for 5 minutes longer.
4. Add the lemon juice and butter just before serving. Serve immediately.

[1] I really do use a homemade chopping block.

TIDBIT Knowing how to manipulate the pigment in red cabbage, anthocyanins, is the secret behind the old red wine/white wine bar trick. First, bet a friend that you can change his Merlot into Chardonnay using only the power of your brain. Once he's laid down his Jackson, misdirect his attention momentarily, add a few drops of ammonia—which is a powerful alkaline—and then voilà! Red has become white. Spill it first so he doesn't drink it, take the money, and run.

GRILL SEEKERS

EPISODE 42 | SEASON 3 | GOOD EATS

Food + fire = dinner.

This is the primeval equation responsible for allowing man to rise, for better or worse, to a position of dominance on planet Earth. The most common modern expression involves a device called a grill, which uses metal bars to suspend the food in question (usually a tasty hunk of critter) over a heat source such as flames or, better yet, a glowing bed of coals. Simple, yes, but not always easy. In this episode, we concentrate on charcoal.

TRIVIA Eighty-three percent of American families own a grill, which they use an average of five times per month.

TIP I have found in recent years that meat with a good coating of coarse or kosher salt doesn't stick to the grill as much as unsalted meats do. I have yet to properly account for this phenomenon, but the results are irrefutable.

KNOWLEDGE CONCENTRATE

Heat wood hot enough and long enough in an oxygen-free environment, and you drive off all the water and volatile substances (and in wood that's a lot of stuff) until you're left with mostly carbon, which burns hotter and cleaner than any wood possibly could in its natural form. So, you can think of charcoal as wood that's been refined to its most energy-concentrated state. Once upon a time, small communities got together and built conical mounds of wood that would be covered with sod or mud and lit to smolder for weeks or even months before being disassembled for charcoal. Modern methods are far more efficient.

When shopping for charcoal, you've got choices.

STANDARD BRIQUETTES: Cheap amalgams of some charcoal and lots of filler. The only advantage is uniformity.

NATURAL BRIQUETTES: Charcoal and a natural binder like cornstarch. Far superior to standard stuff but often hard to find.

NATURAL CHUNK/LUMP CHARCOAL: Nothing but wood (or rather the remains thereof). The only drawback is lack of uniformity. Top brands contain more whole chunks and fewer shards.

When buying a charcoal grill, look for:

Solid construction (thick metal).

Air-flow control (preferably on the bottom as well as the lid).

A thermometer (and make sure you can get replacements for it, as it'll probably give out after a couple of seasons).

Grate material: The wider the better, and steel is best. Avoid anything enameled. (Although on the show I used a grill with iron grates I've all but given up on trying to maintain them because they rust so darned easily. If you don't mind washing and oiling them after every use, they're the best way to go. For me, it's just too much dang work.)

Ash removal system: This is crucial because ashes are full of alkaloids and if they get wet, or even moist, they become very caustic and will corrode right through the bottom of the grill. Remember, wood ash is what soap makers used to make lye out of. (Remember the "this is a chemical burn" scene from *Fight Club*? I thought so.)

A good cover: Nothing wears down a quality rig like Mother Nature. I roll my grills into the garage whenever possible, but if you don't have room for that, buy a good cover and use it every single time.

About lamb:

Culinarily speaking, lamb is the meat from sheep that are less than a year old. Although the meat is tender due to the fact that the connective tissue has not fully developed, the flavor is strong enough to stand up to the grill.

Lamb is generally available in five different cuts: shoulder (whole or steaks), rack, shank or breast, loin, and leg. Some megamarts sell ground lamb, too, which is great for burgers, meatballs, and meatloaf. The leg comes in three versions: whole, shank cut, and sirloin cut, which still has a good-sized hunk of sirloin connected to it. This is the cut you want for the grill. Save the shank end for the braising pot.

As with other meat we've covered thus far, USDA inspection of lamb is mandatory, but grading is voluntary. Prime and Choice are the most tender and flavorful, but also have the higher fat content.

Purchase lamb whose flesh is firm and fine textured and pink in color. Any fat surrounding or marbled throughout the lamb should be white, not yellow. Vacuumed-sealed cuts are fine, but remember that you're likely paying for a lot of the surrounding liquid.

LITTLE LAMB KNOWLEDGE

- The most abundant livestock in the world, sheep were probably domesticated in the Middle East and Asia more than ten thousand years ago.
- The Romans brought sheep to Great Britain, where lamb is very popular, more than two thousand years ago.
- Lamb was not introduced into the West until the sixteenth century, when Cortez's armies brought sheep with them on explorations.
- Since ancient times, lamb has been regarded as a religious symbol. It was commonly used as a sacrifice, and a symbol of sacrifice. (I think this is a prime reason for grilling it.)
- Lamb is a traditional dish at Easter in honor of the Last Supper, at which lamb may have been served.
- Lamb is a staple in Turkey, Greece, New Zealand, Australia, and countries of the Middle East.
- New Zealand leads the world in lamb production.

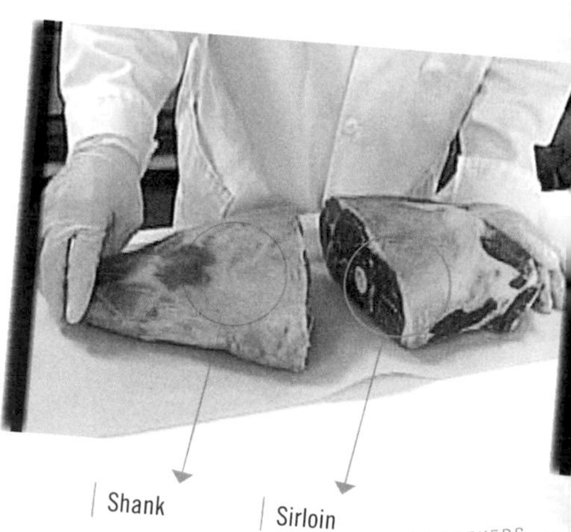

Shank Sirloin

APPLICATION

SILENCE OF THE LEG O' LAMB

8 SERVINGS

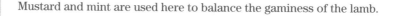

Mustard and mint are used here to balance the gaminess of the lamb.

SOFTWARE

4	cloves	garlic	
8	leaves	fresh mint	
1	tablespoon	light brown sugar	
1	tablespoon	kosher salt	
2	teaspoons	black pepper	freshly ground
5	tablespoons	strong mustard	such as Dijon
2	tablespoons	canola oil	plus additional for the grill
1	3½-pound	leg of lamb	sirloin end, boned[1] and trimmed
2	sprigs	fresh rosemary	

TRIVIA The grill that I used in this episode rotted away from use some time ago, but the red Weber kettle I've been using since "Hook, Line, and Dinner" (page 54) is still going strong. That's not a product endorsement, mind you, but it is a testament to solid technology.

PROCEDURE

1. Roughly chop the garlic cloves in a **mini food processor**. Add the mint and repeat. Follow with the brown sugar, salt, pepper, mustard, and oil. Blend to a paste.
2. Spread the paste evenly on the meat side of the roast (as opposed to the fat side). Roll the leg into a tube shape. Now start trussing by tying one piece of **cotton twine** right around the middle of the roast, bone side down, and close with a surgeon's knot.

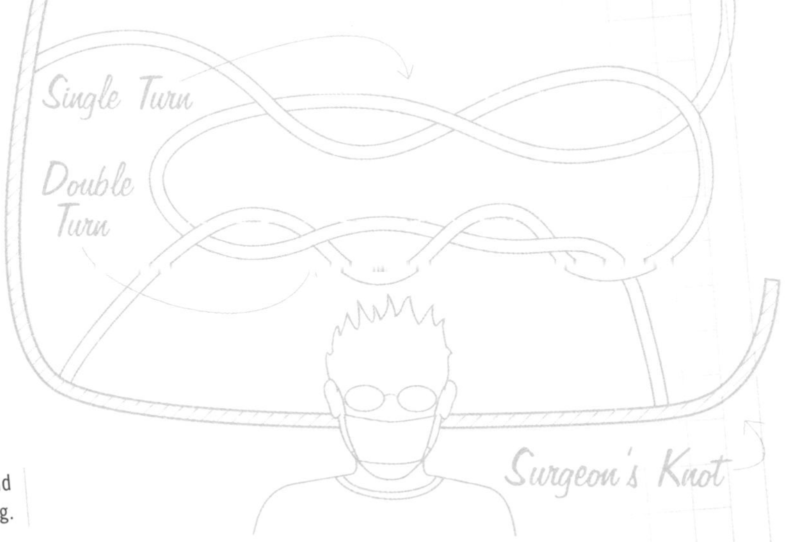

Best for trussing and culinary binding.

3 Repeat as many times as necessary to secure a tube shape. Take a long piece of twine and place it underneath the center piece. Hold up the ends until it is of even length in both directions. Take one end of the twine and just loop it underneath the middle twine so it is captured in a loop. Now, you're going to repeat that around every twine across the roast, trying not to get anything too tight. Once it is trussed all the way from one end to the other, gently roll the roast over and repeat the same process, moving from the fat end down to the pointy end. Make sure it's secure and perform the exact same surgeon's knot. Trim off all the loose ends.

4 Fire up the **charcoal** in the **chimney**. When the charcoal is lightly covered with gray ash, split the coals into 2 piles and move them to the far sides of the cooker. Close the lid and allow the grate to heat.

5 When the grill is nice and hot, coat the grate using the oil and a **kitchen towel** (see sidebar). Place the lamb, skin side up, in the middle of the hot grate. Add the rosemary sprigs[2] to the charcoal briquettes and close the grill.[3]

6 After 20 minutes, flip the roast and rotate it 180 degrees. Insert a **probe thermometer** into the roast and continue to grill until it reaches an internal temperature of 135°F, 25 to 30 minutes. Remove the roast to a **cutting board**. Remove the string from the roast. Cover with **foil** and let it rest for 15 minutes before carving[4] and serving.

[1] Sometimes a "boneless" leg of lamb is only *mostly* boned; this is okay.

[2] Thyme, oregano, and basil can also be used as smoking agents.

[3] Every time you flip your lid, you add 5 minutes to the cooking time, so keep it closed.

[4] In the episode I carve with a round-end, wide-blade grant-on-style carving knife that has little indentations ground out of the side of the blade, which are intended to reduce friction between the meat and the blade for smoother cutting. Although I do prefer this knife for disassembling trussed joints composed of several muscles that might fall apart, you can use any carver or large chef's knife.

TIDBIT | The word *truss* comes from the Latin *torsus*, or "twist." "To secure food (meat or poultry) using string, pins, or skewers in order to maintain a compact shape during cooking" (*Food Lover's Companion*). We truss to make the roast as even in thickness throughout as possible, which ensures even cooking and doneness. It makes the roast easier to handle, too, with no flaps of meat flopping about.

NEVER FACE YOUR GRILL WITHOUT THE FOLLOWING

- Table
- Spring-loaded tongs (long are best)
- Spritz bottle or water gun for calming flare-ups
- Grill cleaner (I prefer heavy steel wool models over brushes)
- Old hand towel with a little oil (hold this with the tongs and rub down the grate right before you bring the meat to the party)
- Probe thermometer
- Heavy-duty aluminum foil (for wrapping and transporting results)
- Clean platter/tray/pan (never place cooked foods back on the platter you carried them out on unless you wash it first)

TIP | To light natural charcoal, you'll need a chimney.

Although I didn't have time to explain it on the show, if you lightly oil the newspaper pre-ignition, it will burn up to 10 minutes longer, giving your carbonaceous load time to get good and cranked up.

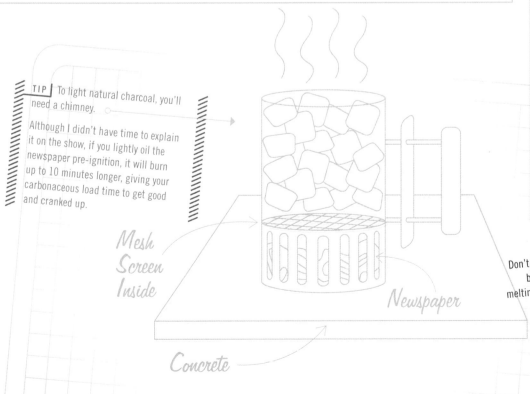

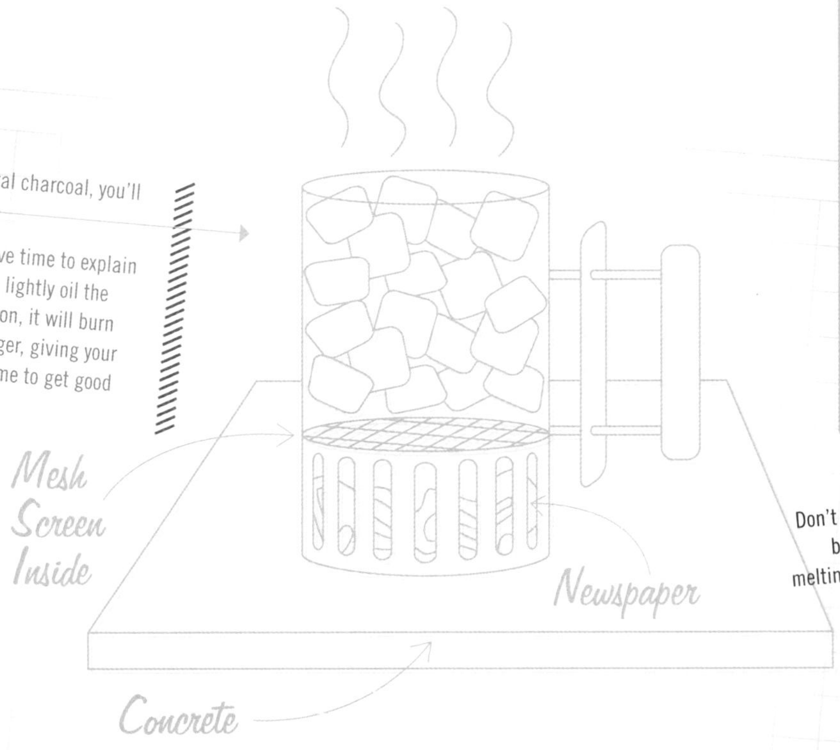

Mesh Screen Inside

Newspaper

Concrete

Don't use a charcoal chimney on gravel because heat can travel through it, melting nearby items, and don't forget a fire extinguisher, just in case.

WHERE THERE'S SMOKE, THERE'S FISH

EPISODE 43 | SEASON 4 | GOOD EATS

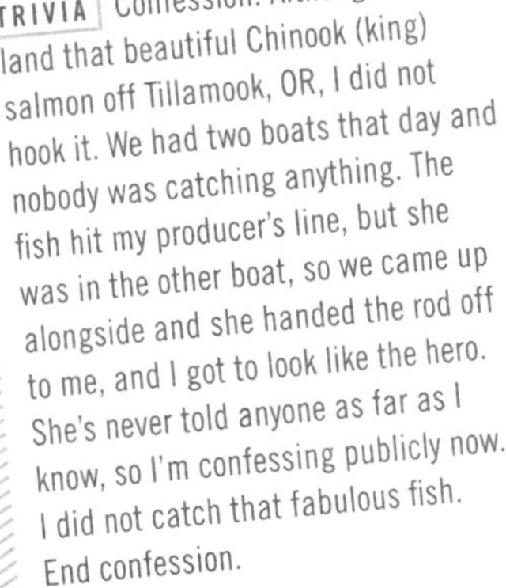

TRIVIA | Confession: Although I did land that beautiful Chinook (king) salmon off Tillamook, OR, I did not hook it. We had two boats that day and nobody was catching anything. The fish hit my producer's line, but she was in the other boat, so we came up alongside and she handed the rod off to me, and I got to look like the hero. She's never told anyone as far as I know, so I'm confessing publicly now. I did not catch that fabulous fish. End confession.

In this episode I wanted to present a way for regular folks who don't own or operate complicated smoking apparatuses to reliably produce hot-smoked salmon with tasty results for minimum investment of cash.

KNOWLEDGE CONCENTRATE

There is only one variety of Atlantic salmon, and it is almost nonexistent in the wild. A great majority of the salmon available in American megamarts is Atlantic salmon raised in aquiculture facilities known as fish farms. I don't like this fish one bit.

There are seven varieties of Pacific salmon in the wild, including Chinook (king), Coho (silver), Sockeye (red),[1] Chum (dog), and Pink salmon.

Most wild fish are caught as they return to fresh water. At this point they are full of fat (healthy omega-3 fats) and flavor. Wild salmon has a depth of flavor that can't be matched. Since farm-raised salmon do not live in anything close to their natural cycle, they taste flat and fatty. It's better than no salmon at all, but not by much. I'd rather have frozen Alaska salmon than fresh Atlantic farmed salmon. But that's just me.

The smoking of fish probably began when early fisherman dried their fish over fires to preserve them. Early smoked fish likely originated in northern fishing communities in Germany, Holland, Norway, and Nova Scotia.

To make serving easier, remove the pin bones, which are actually a second set of heavy ribs, before you smoke the salmon: Rub your fingers up the flesh, moving from the tail to the head, and you'll feel them just barely poking up. Grab hold of each one with a clean pair of pliers (needlenose is best) and gently extract, being sure to pull it out at the angle at which it's embedded in the flesh to avoid unsightly tears in the fillet.

Curing is a critical first step to smoking. A cure is nothing but a mixture of salt and sugar that is applied to the fish to add flavor and pull out excess moisture, which firms the fish. The moisture that's pulled out includes water-soluble proteins. Rinsing then air-drying the fish allows these proteins to set into what is called a "pellicle", which bonds with various chemicals in the smoke. No pellicle, no bonding, no smoky flavor. Do not skimp on or rush the curing and drying process lest disappointment be your aim.[2]

Never smoke with anything but pure hardwood, as chunks, chips, or sawdust. Never use any kind of treated wood: You cannot smoke with leftover two-by-fours from your deck. Either buy smoking wood or get sawdust and scraps from a quality cabinetmaker working with pure wood.[3]

When working with an electric heat source, I really believe that shavings or sawdust gives the best results. A pile of hardwood shavings has relatively little surface area, and that means less contact with air and so less combustion resulting in flames. Flames, of course, mean soot, and soot is never good eats. If you can't get hold of hardwood sawdust, then go with the smallest, most uniform chips you can get. Although I do soak the wood when smoking over charcoal, I don't bother when using a hotplate.

I use hotplates made by Toastmaster that are available at my local hardware store. I prefer the exposed-coil models over those that provide a solid metal disk for the pan to rest on. They heat quickly and efficiently.

TRIVIA You'd be surprised at how many emails and letters we've received through the years regarding the pig T-shirt I wore in the hotel room scenes. For those of you who aren't Southerners, this is the logo of the Piggly Wiggly grocery store chain, America's original supermarket. As I type this, I'm actually wearing the very same shirt. It's starting to look a little faded, so if you're an executive for Piggly Wiggly how about sending me another one?

APPLICATION

BOX-SMOKED SALMON

20 TO 30 SERVINGS

There's no hot-smoked salmon like home-hot-smoked salmon.

SOFTWARE

1	cup	kosher salt	
½	cup	granulated sugar	
½	cup	dark brown sugar	
1	tablespoon	black peppercorns	crushed
2	1½-pound sides (fillets)	salmon	pin bones removed

TIP Trout, mackerel, and bluefish also smoke well. Non-fishy possibilities also abound. I use this very same rig to smoke various cuts of pork and beef ribs. I've smoked many a chicken (which I don't generally cure beforehand) in it, and various vegetation including onions, tomatoes (for soup), and eggplant, which you need to heavily salt anyway for purging (but that's another show).

PROCEDURE

1. In a **bowl**, mix together the salt, sugars, and peppercorns. Set the cure aside.
2. Spread **extra-wide aluminum foil** a little longer than the length of the fish and top with an equally long layer of **plastic wrap**.
3. Sprinkle one third of the cure onto the plastic. Lay 1 fillet, skin side down, on the cure. Sprinkle one third of the cure onto the flesh of the salmon. Place the second fillet, flesh down, on top of the first. Use the remaining cure to cover the skin on the top piece.
4. Fold the plastic over to cover, then close the edges of the foil together and crimp tightly around the fish. Place the wrapped fish on a **half sheet pan** and top with **another half sheet pan**. Weight with a **heavy phone book or a brick or two** and refrigerate for 12 hours. Flip the fish over and refrigerate for another 12 hours. Some juice will leak out during the process, so make sure there's a place for the runoff to gather.
5. Unwrap the fish and rinse off the cure with cold water. Pat the salmon with **paper towels**, then place in a cool, dry place (not the refrigerator) until the surface of the fish is dry and matte-like, 1 to 3 hours depending on humidity. A **fan** may be used to speed the process.
6. Heat the **smoking rig** (see opposite page) to 150°F.
7. Place the sides of fish on **the rack** in **the smoker** over the smoldering hardwood chips. Place a **probe thermometer** into the thickest part of one of the fillets and set the alarm to sound when it reaches 150°F.
8. Maintain a temperature of 150° to 160°F inside the smoker. Smoke until the fish reaches its temperature, replacing the chips as needed. Serve immediately or cool to room temperature, wrap tightly, and refrigerate for up to 3 days.

NOTE: A properly cared for box can be re-smoked several times. My current box, a heavy moving box from U-Haul, has been with me for nearly a year.

[1] My personal favorite.

[2] Add herbs like tarragon and dill to the cure and you can make gravlax, which of course is cured but not smoked. But remember, it is still raw fish.

[3] At my culinary school we smoked with scrap from a clothespin factory that used nothing but maple.

[4] Yes, corrugated cardboard is indeed flammable. But I've been smoking this way for a decade and have never once experienced a fire.

[5] I've started putting a pan under the hotplate in recent years simply to keep drippings off the bottom of the box.

[6] I wouldn't run a cord from an indoor outlet unless I was very, very sure no water could come in contact with anything.

The Smoking Rig

If possible use a Dual-Probe Digital Thermometer

Cardboard Box

Fish

Metal Cooling Rack

Wooden Dowels

Electric Plate

Concrete Surface

Fire Extinguisher

COLD VS. HOT SMOKE

When fish is exposed to long periods of smoke at low temperatures the result is a "cold-smoked" Nova Lox–style fish . . . like you'd put on a bagel. Such fish is cured (like bacon) but not actually cooked. Due to the long time and constant heat management required, cold smoking is not an easy undertaking for most home cooks, myself included. The salmon we're smoking here is hot-smoked and thus fully cooked.

CARDBOARD BOX SMOKING RIG

- Large cardboard box (at least 16 by 22 by 26 inches)[4]
- 3 (3⅝-inch) wooden dowels
- Metal cooling rack
- Electric hot plate
- Heavy-duty outdoor extension cord
- Small cast-iron skillet
- 2 probe-style thermometers
- Aluminum pie plate with multiple holes punched in bottom (optional)
- Half sheet pan[5]
- Outdoor space with level, nonflammable surface (concrete driveway)
- Fire extinguisher (I've never had to fire mine)
- Properly installed and grounded outdoor electrical outlet[6]

PRESSURE

EPISODE 44 | SEASON 4 | GOOD EATS

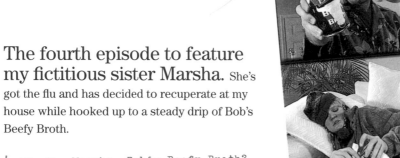

The fourth episode to feature my fictitious sister Marsha. She's got the flu and has decided to recuperate at my house while hooked up to a steady drip of Bob's Beefy Broth.

> AB: Oh. Marsha. Bob's Beefy Broth?
>
> M: Yeah.
>
> AB: Say it ain't so.
>
> M: Okay. It ain't so. Now give it back.
>
> AB: Oh. It appears that my poor, sick, addle-minded sister has gotten herself addicted to over-the-counter broths.

Real, home-made broth is of course the answer, and the pressure cooker, that much-maligned marvel of the modern kitchen, is going to make it for us.

Pressure Stems Often Clog and That's Bad!

15

Old "jigger" pressure cooker with psi 15 weight in place on pressure stem.

Spring Plunger

Steam Release

Rings Display Pressure

Second-generation pressure cookers use a spring-loaded plunger rather than a weight. My personal favorite is made by WMF. Its plunger rises up as pressure builds. Colored bands ring the plunger that correspond to a given pressure. The lid locks in place and cannot be opened as long as pressure is higher than outside.

COOKING UNDER PRESSURE

A boiling point is simply the state at which a liquid becomes energized to the point that its molecules can break out of the liquid state to the gaseous state. For water, this is 212°F at sea level. This happens because the pressure the atmosphere applies to any liquid at this altitude (variances for barometric changes notwithstanding) is 14.7 psi. In a pressure cooker this pressure is elevated (usually by 15 psi), and that means the boiling point increases. This is powerful medicine, because in this environment, food tissues, especially connective tissues like collagen, break down and soften very quickly. This also means that pressure cooking is the ultimate method for extracting flavor compounds from foods, making it ideal for broth, stock, and soup.

KNOWLEDGE CONCENTRATE

Soup derives from the old German word *sup*, and it's the only food I know of to inspire such devotion as to have a meal named after it, supper.

Since soups in general and broths and bouillons[1] in particular were thought to contain the vitality or life essence of the animals that went into them, they used to occupy a shadowy territory between food and medicine. In fact, many old broth recipes are named for the ailment they were meant to cure: goiter broth, colicky baby broth, and, of course, the ever-popular plague broth.

To make a stock you need three things: a pot, some water, and bones . . . any type of bones. The word *stock* actually refers to the trunk of tree without any branches or leaves attached. And it's a pretty fair culinary analogy, because once bones and joints have given up their connective tissue you're left with a liquid that's got a lot of body but not much flavor. That's why most classic sauces have stocks at their base, but you would never order up a bowl of stock as an appetizer.

Broth is medieval-speak for "brew," and that's exactly what it is. It's basically water that's had meat and or vegetables cooked or brewed in it. If you leave all the bits and pieces in, you've got soup. Most good broths are hybrids of stocks and broths, because most soup meat has bones attached. But such liquids are still considered broths, not stocks.

When it comes to broth-able critters, chicken used to be king. But modern chickens are usually slaughtered long before they develop truly broth-able flavor. Pork broths are, well . . . piggy, so that leaves us with beef, which, despite the popularity of chicken soup as a cure-all, is my preference for medicinal applications.

Oddly enough, the best beef pieces for broth come from radically different ends of the animal. First we have the shanks, or the cross-cut pieces of the forearm. They look kind of like meaty donuts, and they've always got a kind of round bone just off center. On the other end of the animal is the tail, which is marketed as "oxtail" despite the fact that no oxen are involved. These are also crosscut and they look like little bitty versions of the shank.

Credit for the invention of what is now called the pressure cooker goes to French mathematician and physicist Denis Papin (1647–1712), who in 1679 devised a cast-iron vessel with a locking, airtight lid that he called a "digester." Since early models lacked valves to vent excess pressure, there were many explosive mishaps.

Modern pressure cookers use spring-loaded pressure regulators, pressure-actuated locks, and emergency valves. When shopping for a pressure cooker, remember that first and foremost, it's a pot and needs to properly do all the things a pot does. That means it needs to have a heavy-duty bottom, useful handles, appropriate volume, and so on. They're pricey but should last you a lifetime—at least.

"I live on good soup not fine words."
MOLIÈRE

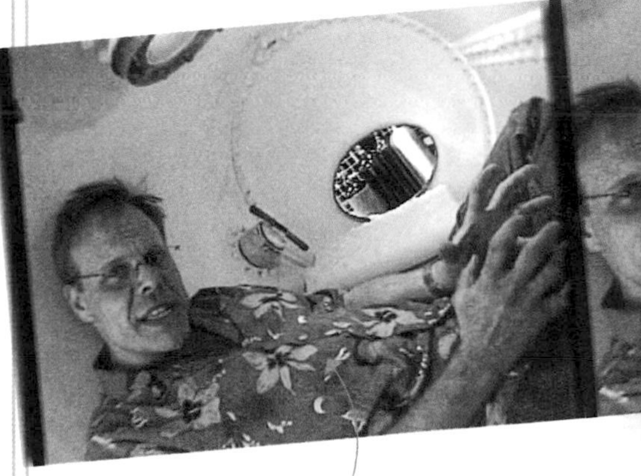

TRIVIA I'm not claustrophobic, but shooting a scene in a decompression chamber was not a comfortable experience.

Chunks of Oxtail—with Bone Hunks Intact

"Only the pure of heart can make a good soup."
BEETHOVEN

APPLICATION

AB'S BEEFY BROTH

2 QUARTS

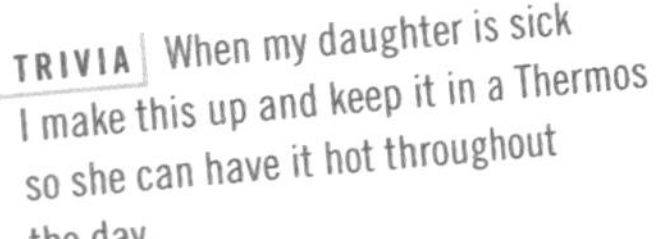

Pressure cooking tends to knock down brighter flavors, so I usually add a squeeze of lemon or splash of sherry just before serving. You can use this broth as the base for French Onion soup (page 52).

SOFTWARE

3	pounds	combined shank and oxtail pieces	
1	tablespoon	canola oil	
1	teaspoon	kosher salt	
2	medium	yellow onions	quartered
2	ribs	celery	rinsed and halved
2	large	carrots	peeled and halved
3	cloves	garlic	smashed
1	small bunch	parsley stems	
1	teaspoon	black peppercorns	
2	quarts	filtered H_2O	

TRIVIA When my daughter is sick I make this up and keep it in a Thermos so she can have it hot throughout the day.

PROCEDURE

1. Place your **pressure cooker** over high heat.
2. Toss the beef pieces in the oil and salt.
3. When the cooker is hot, transfer half of the pieces to the cooker and sear on both sides until very brown.[2] Remove the pieces and repeat with the second half.
4. Wipe out any excess fat from the bottom of the pot with a **paper towel** held with **tongs**.
5. Return all of the meat to the pressure cooker and add the remaining ingredients. Be careful not to fill above your cooker's "maximum fill" line, or two thirds full.
6. Bring to a boil, skimming off any foam that gathers at the surface. Cover and lock the lid. Once pressure builds up inside the cooker, reduce the heat to low, so that you barely hear hissing from the pot.[3] Cook for 50 minutes.
7. Release the pressure using your cooker's release device (read the manual!) or cool the cooker by running cold water over the lid for 5 minutes. Open carefully.
8. Set a **cheesecloth-lined colander** in a **large pot** and pour in the broth, discarding the solids. Taste and season the broth with additional salt, if desired.

APPLICATION

BEEF AND BARLEY STEW

10 SERVINGS

This is just about my favorite beef broth application. Now that I think about it, it's my favorite barley dish, too.

SOFTWARE

1	pound	stew beef	
1	28-ounce can	crushed tomatoes	
3	cups	AB's Beefy Broth	(see opposite page)
½	cup	pearl barley	
3	large	carrots	peeled, halved, and cut into ½-inch slices
2	stalks	celery	cut into ½-inch slices
1	large	russet potato	peeled and diced
1	medium	onion	diced
½	teaspoon	dried thyme	
½	teaspoon	dried rosemary	
½	teaspoon	dried marjoram	
1	teaspoon	kosher salt	
½	teaspoon	black pepper	freshly ground
	for serving	malt vinegar	balsamic or sherry will do too

PROCEDURE

1. Brown the beef in a **pressure cooker** over high heat, 5 to 7 minutes. Drain off fat. Add the tomatoes, broth, and barley and return to high heat. Close pressure cooker and bring up to full pressure. Reduce heat until cooker barely hisses, and cook for 10 minutes.
2. After 10 minutes, release the pressure. When lock can be opened, carefully remove the lid and add the vegetables, herbs, salt, and pepper.
3. Relid the pressure cooker and heat to full pressure over high heat. Reduce the heat to maintain pressure and cook another 10 minutes. Release the pressure. Remove the lid, cool for 5 minutes, and serve with vinegar.

[1] *Bouillon* is simply French for "cooking liquid."

[2] I always sear meat over high heat before putting the pressure to it. The flavor it creates is crucial.

[3] During cooking, you want your cooker to maintain a low, even hiss. A loud hiss or visible steam means you're wasting energy and liquid.

TIP | You can't open the cooker until the pressure has been released, and if you use the valve on the top of the lid this could take several minutes. If you're in a rush, simply set the cooker in the sink and let cold water run over the lid. The water will quickly suck heat away from the vessel, allowing quicker access to the interior.

TIP | Freeze broth in ice cube trays, then move to zip-top bags and keep frozen so you can dose up dishes as needed.

FRY HARD II: THE CHICKEN

EPISODE 45 | SEASON 4 | GOOD EATS

This episode opens with

what must be the worst poem ever written for a food show:

Once upon a mid-morn dreary, as I pondered with eyes quite bleary
Over many a curious volume of culinary lore,
On a latte I was sucking, when suddenly there came a clucking
As if some salesman were a-mucking, mucking 'bout my kitchen door.
'Tis some salesman, said I. Only this, and nothing more.
Yet presently the noise repeated, so I hollered, no longer seated,
Beat it, pesky husker mucking about my kitchen door.
At my business I'm now working, so my chain you'd best stop jerking.
Then throwing wide the kitchen door, I found there a chicken and nothing more.
Leapt I back then with a stutter, as the phantom bird did with a flutter
Mount the folk-art bust of Julia Child there upon my kitchen floor.
Perched and sat and nothing more.
Then the pallid poultry, most perplexing, did set my meager mind to guessing,
From whence did you come to perch upon the bust of Julia on my kitchen floor?
Quoth the chicken: Fry some more.
As certain as my heart is ticking, I am sure no living chicken
Has ever so clearly commanded a living cook before
With an utterance so clear and shocking that even I could not ignore.
Quoth the chicken: Fry some more.
Then thought I, Perhaps she's onto something.
For too long now I have been supping
On feed incapable of nourishing my anguished soul.
Perhaps some truly good eats my hungry soul could restore.
*Quoth the chicken: Fry some more.**

* Edgar Allen Poe, please forgive me.

TIDBIT Gainesville, GA, is often called the Chicken Capital of the World, because Jesse Jewell, the man who revolutionized the poultry industry by utilizing assembly line techniques, started there. There is a giant column in the middle of town with a bronze (or maybe it's iron) chicken on it.

TIDBIT Fried chicken probably came to America with the Scottish immigrants, who had a strong tradition of frying chicken in fat. The English preferred boiled or baked chicken.

KNOWLEDGE CONCENTRATE

Buy a broiler/fryer (about 3½ pounds; see "Bird in the Pan," page 30) and dissect at home. Why cut your own?

It's cheaper than buying parts.

Some of the better birds on the market only come whole.

You can portion better.

Whole birds stay fresher longer.

Soak overnight in buttermilk. Low-fat buttermilk has a greater viscosity than nonfat, which will help to form a sort of batter overnight. The buttermilk's acid and sugars will invade the chicken's meat, which helps to tenderize it and lends a delicious tang.

Avoid cross-contamination by setting up a three-zone method: raw, hot, and recovery. Only move the food in one direction and *never* use the same tools to touch both raw and cooked foods.

Season liberally, then dredge. I prefer to season the chicken, as opposed to simply adding salt and pepper to the dredge. Seasoning is just too critical to leave to chance. Although nearly any wheat flour will do the trick, all-purpose seems to work just fine. When dredging, take care to shake away any and all excess flour.[1] Take time for a short rest post-dredge, to allow the acid in the buttermilk to slightly gelatinize the starch in the flour, thus enabling the resulting crust to have better adhesion (i.e., it will stick to the meat).

Pan-fry in shallow shortening, and turn once. Although lard works just fine I still reach for shortening when frying chicken. Shortening does have a relatively low smoke point, but it is very, very refined, which will give us a nice color and won't fill the house with fried-chicken stink (is that a good thing?). You only need to fill the pan one third full at most.

When we pan-fry, both the oil and pan are heat conductors, which is great. It creates a temperature near 350°F, which is ideal for achieving the Maillard reaction, especially where the food touches the pan. When you deep-fry, the fat surrounds the food, so no moisture can escape, creating a hard shell; however, it doesn't adhere well. As soon as you bite into deep-fried chicken the crust comes off in your hand. Pan-frying allows moisture to escape on one side, which makes a crisp crust that adheres well. As long as the water in the meat is kept above a boil, outward pressure will prevent oil from soaking in.

Drain. A cooling rack is the best way to ensure that every bite is crisp, because it allows even air flow. And don't put your chicken in a warm oven, unless, of course, you like soggy skin.

Eat. A two-bit paper paint bucket is the perfect service and storage device because it wicks away extra moisture and oil. (Consider the Colonel's chicken.)

TRIVIA | After shooting at Lodge I sneezed black for three days.

CAST IRON

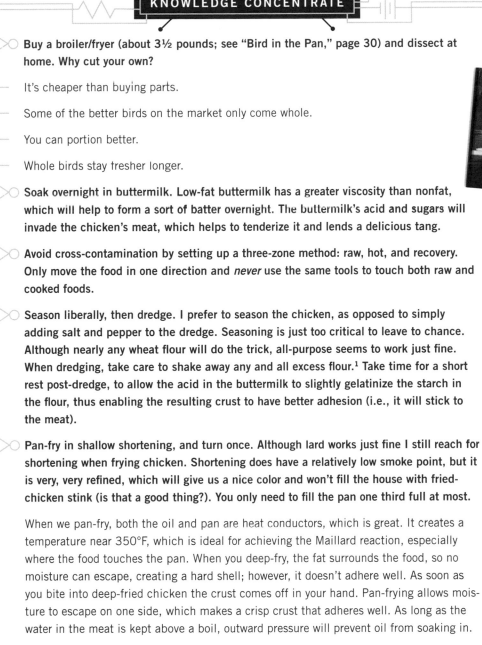

Joseph Lodge founded Lodge more than a century ago. Today, his descendents oversee the production of the only cast-iron cookware made in the United States.

It all starts with pig iron, scrap steel, and Lodge's own left-overs, weighed. It's dropped into an electromagnetic field furnace, where it simmers and any impurities cook off or are skimmed off. The iron is then hauled into an automated casting machine, a premeasured dose of iron is poured into the cakes (molds) and run through a cooling tunnel. When they tumble out the other end, the cakes break open, revealing the rocket-hot but now solid cookware within. What sand isn't dislodged by the shaking troughs is blasted off by steel buckshot and recycled.

Each piece is then inspected, hand ground, washed with soap, water, and river rocks, dipped in a rust-retarding food-grade wax, packaged, and shipped.

APPLICATION

FRIED CHICKEN

4 SERVINGS

Buttermilk is the ultimate chicken marinade because it changes the way the fatty skin responds to the hot fat, producing a crispy crust. Oh, and it tastes good, too.

TIDBIT The Etruscans started making wishes and breaking wishbones more than 2,500 years ago.

TIDBIT Colonel Sanders was the second most recognized public figure in the world in 1979. President Jimmy Carter was, of course, the first.

// SOFTWARE

1	3½-pound	broiler/fryer chicken	cut into 8 pieces (see sidebar)
2	cups	low-fat buttermilk	
		vegetable shortening	for frying
2	tablespoons	kosher salt	
2	tablespoons	Hungarian paprika[2]	
2	teaspoons	garlic powder	
1	teaspoon	cayenne pepper	
1	cup	all-purpose flour	for dredging

// PROCEDURE

1. Put the chicken pieces in a **plastic container** and pour the buttermilk over them. Cover and refrigerate for 12 to 24 hours, turning the meat at least once.
2. Place enough shortening to come ¼ inch up the sides of a **12-inch cast-iron skillet**. Set over low heat. Once the shortening liquefies, raise the heat until it reaches 325°F on a **fat or candy thermometer**. Do not allow the oil to exceed 325°F.
3. Drain the chicken in a **colander**.
4. Combine the salt, paprika, garlic powder, and cayenne pepper in a **shaker or small bowl**. Liberally season the chicken with this mixture.
5. Put the flour in a **bag or container with a lid** and dredge the chicken in the flour. Shake off the excess and set aside for 2 minutes before frying.
6. Place the chicken skin side down in the pan, thighs in the center, and breast, legs, and wings around the edge of the pan. The oil should come halfway up the sides of the pan.
7. Cook until golden brown on each side, 10 to 12 minutes per side. More importantly, the internal temperature should be right around 165°F. (Be careful to monitor the shortening temperature every few minutes.)
8. Transfer the chicken to a **draining rig**. Let rest 15 to 20 minutes before serving.

NOTE 1: Due to the paprika the fried chicken will be very dark, even appearing burned, but do not dismay: It's still finger-licking satisfying!

NOTE 2: What sets true southern-fried chicken apart from deep-fried chicken is that the southern variety is cooked in fat that's shallow enough for the pieces to actually touch the bottom of the pan, thus enhancing browning.

[1] Excess flour will only result in the dredge floating away in the pan.

[2] If you've got smoked paprika, this would be a fine time to use it.

[3] That is, to split into eight pieces. I'm pretty sure I made that word up.

HOW TO OCTO-SECT[3] A CHICKEN

Set up your largest cutting board (if you only use one for raw meat, then this should be it). Once you've got your board set up, approach the bird with the breast facing up and neck facing towards you.

1. Grab a wing and lift the bird off the board. Let gravity do some work for you here. Just open up between the wing and the body, cutting from back to front, and the knife will slide through what used to be the joint. Repeat on the other side. Remember, gravity is the butcher's best friend.

2. Next we've got to get the wishbone out. Place the knife, blade up, inside the neck cavity. Moving the blade in one direction along the cavity, scrape the little bit of meat off of the wishbone. You'll see it almost immediately. Now repeat in the other direction. Don't worry. It won't hurt your knife.

3. Now reach in with two fingers—just wiggle them in—and work your way up to dislocate the wishbone at the top. Now you can make a wish with yourself.

4. Next the legs. Make an incision just through the skin on either side where the little depression forms between the breast and the drumstick. And make sure you've got good separation there.

5. Then roll the bird over and feel for where the thigh bone meets the back. Just feel around for it. It'll be just underneath the skin, right off the spine. Simply grab the leg quarter and bend it backward. Again, the thing is to pop the socket. You literally want to dislocate that joint; there's going to be absolutely nothing to cut through. Slice far enough ahead to get the oyster, that little piece of meat that poultry lovers everywhere give their eyeteeth for. Repeat on the other side.

6. Now, to separate the thigh from the drumstick, again we're going to let the joint tell us where to go. So just squeeze the two pieces together, and you'll feel the joint start to open up, kind of like a little depression. Place the knife there and very carefully cut down no more than about half an inch. Remember, you're cutting toward your hand, so be careful. Once the joint opens you'll see how to finish the job. There. Now repeat on the other side.

7. To remove the breast halves from the bone, cut right down one side of the keel bone—the breast bone—to the ribs. It doesn't matter which side you start with. You see that you have to literally peel the breast meat off the ribs. This is a skill that takes a little bit of practice. Use very, very shallow cuts and literally peel it away. Think of it like an orange peel. With the wishbone gone it is a piece of cake. We've got a nice clean breast with skin intact. Now repeat on the other side and just keep opening it up and looking at what you're doing, and off it comes. Very rarely do you see a chicken breast that nice in a grocery store.

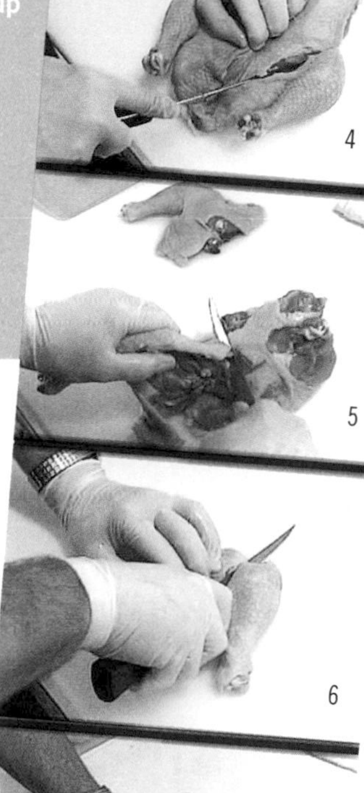

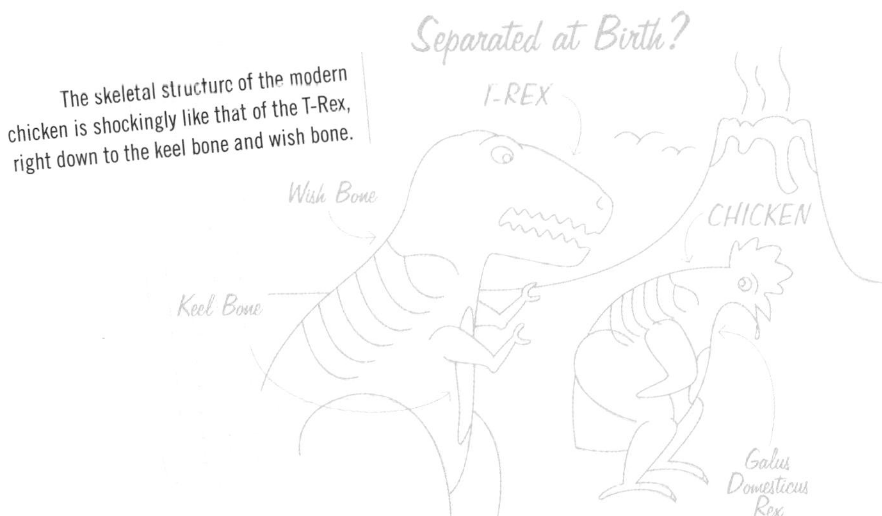

The skeletal structure of the modern chicken is shockingly like that of the T-Rex, right down to the keel bone and wish bone.

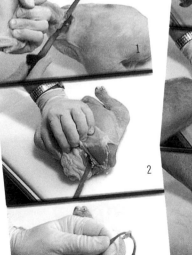

The chicken, never flitting, still is sitting, still is sitting
On the folk-art bust of Julia on my kitchen floor.
In her thighs I see the quiver of a future pan-fried dinner
Whose crunchy, golden goodness does my appetite implore
To go ahead and fry some more.

CRUSTACEAN NATION II: CLAWS

EPISODE 46 | SEASON 4 | GOOD EATS

Ask ten people to make a list of their top five favorite foods, and I'm willing to bet that nine out of ten of those lists will include the word "lobster." Ask the same ten people to make a list of the top five foods they're afraid to cook and I'm betting eight out of ten of them will say "lobster."

I suspect that this is the result of an evil scheme hatched by restaurateurs to convince us regular folks that we cannot prepare our own lobster.

And when I say our own lobster, I mean our *own* lobster. America, *behold Homarus americanus*, or American lobster, a.k.a. the Maine lobster.

It is a clawed lobster, a citizen of cold waters and cousin to the European lobster. Warm-water lobsters, such as the clawless spiny lobster, have their own virtues, to be sure, but their meat cannot equal the sweetness of that of *Homarus americanus*.

TIDBIT | Three ounces of lobster meat contains 60 mg of cholesterol. The same amount of skinless chicken breast contains almost 75 mg. Lobster is also high in B12.

KNOWLEDGE CONCENTRATE

- **Handling *Homarus*: Buy only live lobsters. As soon as a lobster dies, its digestive system allows gastric juices to seep into the meat, turning it to mush. Check the lobster by grabbing hold of either side of the thorax just above the walking legs and move him around. The more he moves, the better. Lively is good. Give the thorax a gentle squeeze; you want a hard thorax with little to no give. Boy lobster or girl lobster: easy to tell. Just flip it over and check the first set of swimmerets, the small appendages just behind the last set of walking legs. If they're hard the specimen is a male; if feathery, a female.**

- **Purchase lobster the day you plan to eat it. If necessary you can store live lobster for about a day, wrapped in moist towels in the fridge. To bring live lobsters home, line a cooler with cold packs and cover with damp newspaper. Put the lobsters on top of this and cover with more paper. Store not your bugs on ice lest they perish before you have the chance to dispatch them yourself.**

Consuming lobsters comes with a bit of moral baggage. Aside from faceless shellfish like mussels or maybe the occasional crab, lobsters are probably the only critters you'll ever actually kill in the comfort of you kitchen. If this troubles you, please consider the animal kingdom.

If you feel at all guilty about eating lobster, I humbly suggest you consult this food chain. Notice proximity of succulent meal to stompable pest.

Down at the bottom, of course, we have germs. Higher up, flatworms, and then way up in phylum *chordata* subphylum *mammalia*, just above the wombats and the lemurs, us: man.

Now, way over on the other branch, we find phylum *anthropoid* subphylum *crustacean* and the lobster. What's interesting is that just next door in subphylum *uniramia*, we've got the cockroach. Actually, a lobster brain's more like a grasshopper's, but then in this case we really do have to use the term *brain* very, very loosely. The point is that a lobster is a bug. And if you can stomp a roach or smush a spider just for crossing your path, you shouldn't get too teary-eyed about sending a lobster to sleep with the fishes, especially if you're going to eat it. But that doesn't mean you shouldn't opt for a humane method. And morbid or not, it does seem to be a subject that a lot of people have strong opinions on.

There are only two methods recognized by the Geneva Convention. The first one is instantaneous, and if I were a lobster and somebody gave me a choice this is the method I would choose.

1. Take a chef's knife, a big heavy one, and place the point right in the crack that runs down the head, about an inch behind the eyes. [Ominous music.] Hmm. Okay. Uh, if you think you're up to it, push that knife straight down to the board and chop forward, thus bifurcating the head. The bug will be dead instantaneously. No fuss, but a little muss.

2. If you don't feel you're up to it, go with the big chill. After 15 to 20 minutes in the freezer, they won't feel a thing when the time comes as long as the time comes quickly.

As for cooking, the traditional boil is actually my least favorite method. First, it takes a lot of energy to bring a gallon of water to a boil. Second, it dilutes the flavor of the lobster. I prefer steaming, which, although a bit slower than boiling, produces far better flavor and is also more forgiving of overcooking.

Harvesting the meat: Since the shell can harbor considerable (hot) moisture, and broken shards of it are sharp, I usually keep a side towel in my hand the entire time I'm working.

Turn the tail over in your hand so that the underside is up and snip the thin under-shell down the middle with kitchen shears. Then pop the meat out.

Twist off the hard knuckle end of each claw, snip an opening at the base of the knuckle, then fold the towel over it and give it a few whacks with your fist. Twist out the small, hinged section of the claw and use a chopstick to push out the large section of meat.

Don't miss the goodness lodged in the walking legs. Twist off the legs and cut off the joints with your shears. Lay the leg facing away from you on the towel and use a rolling pin to squeeze the meat right out.

TIDBIT | Lobsters were known to Greeks and Romans, and while they were loved by the British, they were not so by American colonists. During colonial times, Massachusetts servants went on strike insisting they not be forced to eat lobster more than three times a week. In the 1880s the wholesale price of lobster was less than ten cents per pound.

APPLICATION

STUFFED LOBSTER

4 SERVINGS

The goal here is to maximize every morsel this tasty bug has to give.

// SOFTWARE

2	1½-pound	lobsters	
1	small bunch	combo of parsley, rosemary, and thyme	
2	tablespoons	unsalted butter	
½	cup	onion	finely chopped
1	small	lemon	zest only
10		Ritz crackers	crushed
		extra-virgin olive oil	for brushing and drizzling

TIP | If you prefer plain steamed lobster, steam it as follows:

Lobster weight	Total steaming time
1 pound	7 minutes
1¼ pounds	9 minutes
1½ pounds	12 minutes
1¾ pounds	14 minutes
2 pounds	17 minutes

// PROCEDURE

1. Heat the oven to 450°F.
2. Place the lobsters in a **roasting pan** and chill in the freezer for 15 to 20 minutes.
3. Meanwhile, place a layer of **river rocks**[1] in the bottom of a **wide 12-quart pot** and fill with 1 inch of water. Bring to a boil over high heat. Spread the herbs across the rocks, then quickly place the lobsters on top. Cover and cook for 2 to 3 minutes. Remove and place in an **ice bath** to halt the cooking.
4. Lay **paper towels** across a **cutting board**. Bring one lobster to the board and, using your **chef's knife**, cut the lobster straight down the center, from head to tail. Remove tomalley and discard. Remove legs and claws. Snip off the joint of each leg with **kitchen shears**. Using a **rolling pin**, roll over the legs to extract the meat. Roughly chop the meat. Repeat with the second lobster.
5. Move the claws to a **half sheet pan** and roast for 4 minutes.
6. Meanwhile, melt the butter in a **10-inch sauté pan** over medium heat. Add the onion and stir to coat. Once the onion is translucent, add the lemon zest and leg meat and stir to combine. Remove the pan from the heat, add the crackers, and toss until all the liquid has been absorbed.
7. Make a dish out of **aluminum foil**, shaping it so the lobster bodies can lay flat in it. **Spoon** the filling into the open body cavities. **Brush** tail meat with olive oil and place the foil dish with bodies on the pan along with the claws. Roast for 12 to 16 minutes, until the filling browns and the tail meat becomes opaque.
8. Crack the claws and remove the meat. Serve on top of stuffed lobster with extra-virgin olive oil on the side for dipping.

10 MINUTES MORE

EXTREMELY EASY YET AMAZINGLY VERSATILE LOBSTER BUTTER

8 OUNCES BUTTER

This clever (and economical) creation can be used to finish soups, risottos, eggs (page 22), sauces, or be spread on hot biscuits (page 42), mashed potatoes (page 18) or just about anything except ice cream. And since the butter is clarified, it can stand the high heat of sautés, such as the mushroom one on page 96—shiitakes or lobster mushrooms are highly recommended.

TIDBIT Lobsters have been known to live one hundred years and weigh more than forty pounds.

// SOFTWARE

1	6- to 8-ounce	shell of 1 medium to large cooked lobster	body, tail, claws, and whole legs
8	ounces	unsalted butter	cut into hunks

// PROCEDURE

TIDBIT The pigment responsible for the red color that appears in cooked lobster, astaxanthin, was always in the crustacean, but it is connected to a series of proteins that produces the original dark look. The heat cooks the proteins, which let go of the astaxanthin, making the shell red.

1. Break or tear the body, legs, and tail shells into small pieces. Crush the harder claws with a **hammer, meat tenderizer, heavy skillet, or bowling ball** and set aside.[2]
2. Process the non-claw shell in a **food processor** for 3 to 5 quick pulses. Add the butter and pulse until the butter is soft, approximately 30 seconds.
3. Transfer the butter mixture to a **2-quart saucepan** and add the claw pieces. Bring to a simmer over low heat. Simmer for 15 to 20 minutes, until the bubbling has stopped and tiny white lumps have settled away from the now red liquid.
4. Cool slightly and strain through a **fine-mesh sieve**. Store in an airtight container for up to 1 month or wrap in parchment, then plastic wrap, and freeze for up to 3 months.

[1] Available at nurseries and wherever landscape materials are sold. Although river rocks are best from a heat-conduction and herbal-infusion standpoint (and gee, aren't they pretty), if you have a canning kettle, which is really the best vessel for this anyway, then it probably came with a can rack. You can certainly use that instead.

[2] Seriously, these shells can mangle even the stoutest food processor blade.

A FEW FUN LOBSTER FACTS

- Lobsters are crustaceans and therefore kin to spiders and insects. Big bugs, that's what they are.
- Most edible crustaceans are decopods, which means they have five pairs of legs, one of which is often very large claws.
- Like insects, lobsters have a hard outer exoskeleton, which is broken up into several large segments, and many rigid appendages. The only way a lobster can grow is to shed its exoskeleton.
- After a lobster sheds its exoskeleton it is called a soft-shell lobster; while edible, I don't recommend buying them, as you usually end up paying for more water than meat. That being said, many softy fans find the meat to be sweeter than that of hard shells.

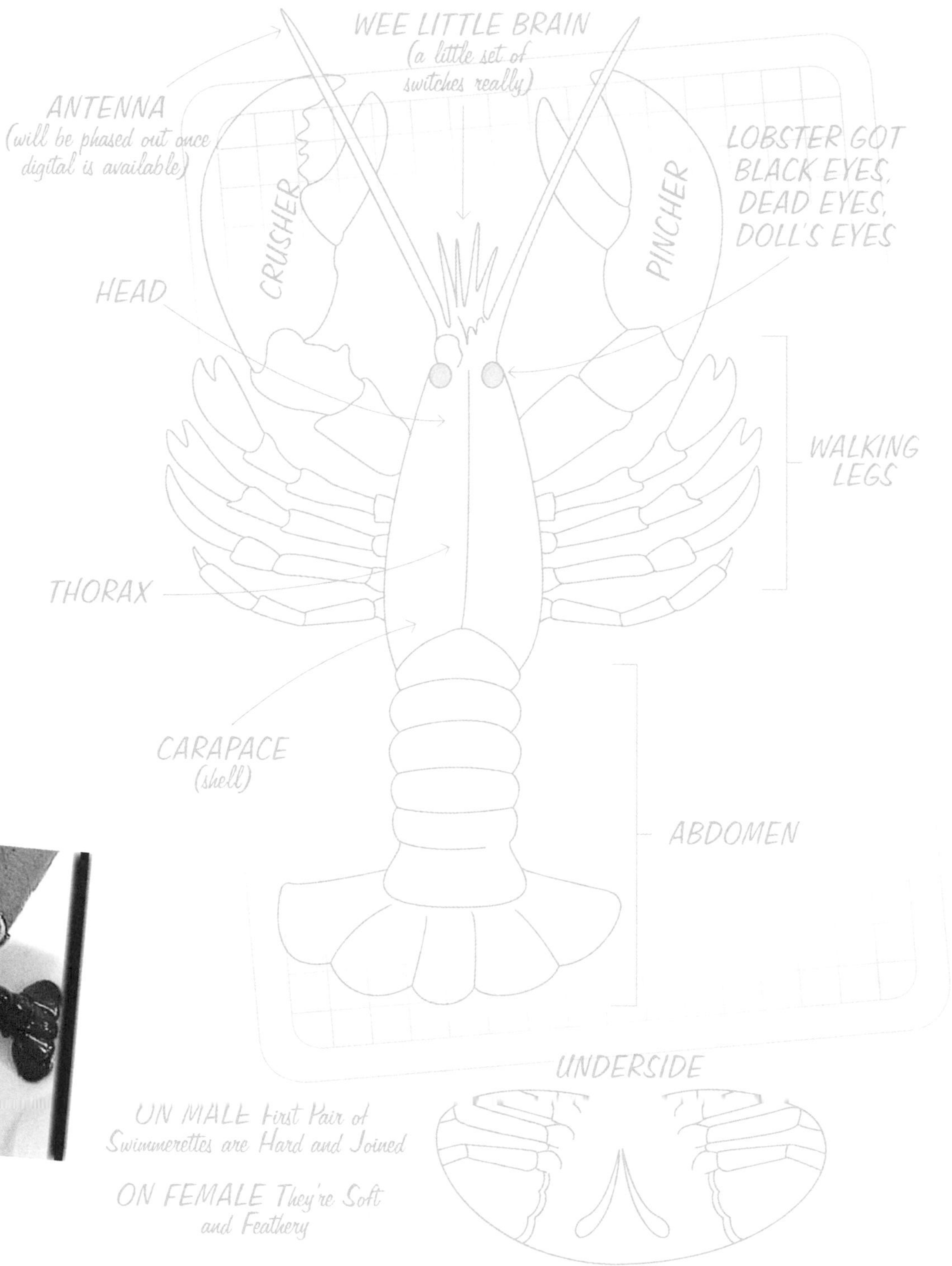

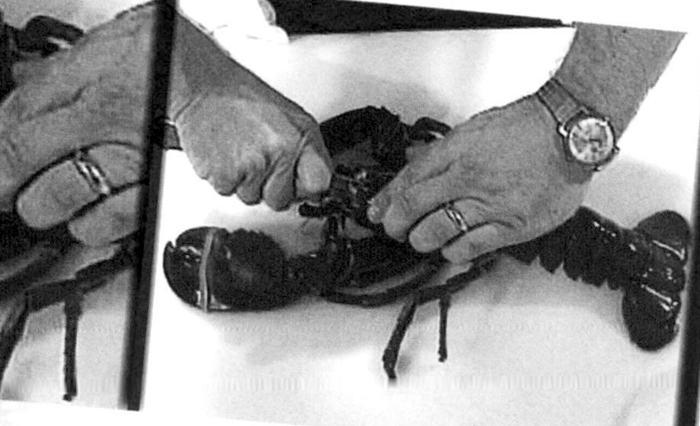

TRIVIA Actual lobsters were harmed during production. And we ate them.

ANATOMY OF A LOBSTER

WEE LITTLE BRAIN
(a little set of switches really)

ANTENNA
(will be phased out once digital is available)

CRUSHER

PINCHER

LOBSTER GOT BLACK EYES, DEAD EYES, DOLL'S EYES

HEAD

WALKING LEGS

THORAX

CARAPACE
(shell)

ABDOMEN

UNDERSIDE

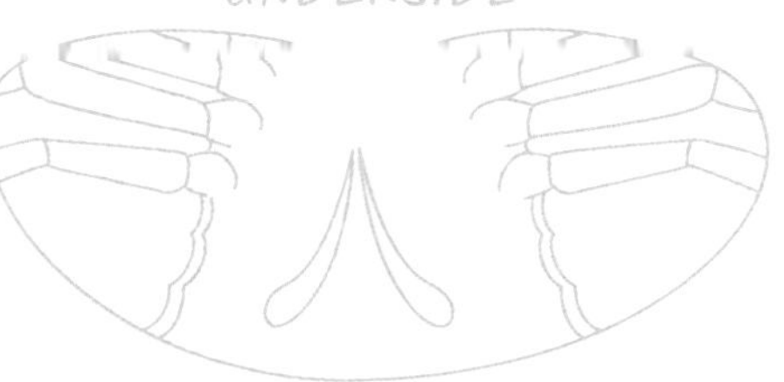

ON MALE First Pair of Swimmerettes are Hard and Joined

ON FEMALE They're Soft and Feathery

HAM I AM

EPISODE 47 | SEASON 4 | GOOD EATS

How else but by magic could a common, lowly, everyday leg of pig be transformed into a rich, luscious, delicious, fragrant, wonderful, beautiful—did I mention ridiculously delicious—ham? All right. So there's some osmosis, chemistry, smoke, and time involved. But, hey, any time you can feed twenty people for a buck a head, I say that's magic. Besides, if you're willing to try out a few spells of your own, you'll find that ham is not only magic, it's good eats.

Note: Preserving or curing hams follows many traditions in many cultures, and the results are always delicious. Although I'm a huge fan of both prosciutto and serrano hams, here we decided to focus on American varieties.

I know what you're thinking. You're thinking hey, the shoulder's called the butt . . . how can the, well . . . butt be the butt? Because they both used to be packaged in barrells called butts!

Country hams are usually shank end while city hams are often butt end.

KNOWLEDGE CONCENTRATE

Ham is a pig's hind leg . . . simple as that. Said appendage may be used fresh, but more often than not it is cured and/or smoked for preservation and flavor. And of course, as is true with most meats, texture is radically improved by curing as well.

A whole ham is immense, weighing as much as fifteen pounds. For practicality, hams are often cut in half and sold in two pieces, the butt and the shank. I like the shank end because it has less connective tissue.

Hams can be sold with the bone left in. There are also semiboned hams, in which the aitchbone (pronounced "H-bone") and the knuckle are removed for easier carving, leaving only the round leg bone. For even easier carving, ham manufacturers came up with boneless hams, which are sold in cylindrical loaf shapes of various sizes. Make Ma Mae proud and buy bone-in, then save the bone for collards or baked beans.

The U.S. Department of Agriculture recognizes four classifications of processed ham, each defined by its water-to-protein ratio. A ham containing at least 20.5 percent protein and no added water may bear the label "ham." A ham containing no less than 18.5 percent protein may be labeled "ham in natural juice." Such hams are usually sold on the bone and may be fully or partially cooked for your convenience. If a ham contains up to 10 percent added water while maintaining at least 17 percent protein, it must be labeled as "ham, water added." Many ready-to-serve spiral-sliced hams fall into this category. Hams labeled "ham and water product" can legally contain more water than meat and are usually boned, reconstituted, and molded or tumbled into a hamlike shape. If after curing, smoking, and cooking a ham's weight exceeds its original green weight, it must be labeled according to the amount of water that has been added.

There are two basic types of cured ham: city ham and country ham.

CITY HAMS, also known as wet-cured hams, are by far the most common hams sold in supermarkets. This is the ham most people think of when they think of ham. Many city hams are also smoked over hardwoods, such as hickory or maple. City hams are cured in a solution of salt, water, preservatives (including nitrites and nitrates), and various sweet or savory flavorings.

COUNTRY HAMS, or dry-cured hams, date to the days before refrigeration, when salting was a method of preservation. Country hams are rubbed with a layer of salt and other ingredients and hung to cure for several months. The process is similar to that used for prosciutto. American country hams are usually smoked as well, to add flavor. Country hams can be eaten raw, like prosciutto, but Americans typically prefer them cooked.

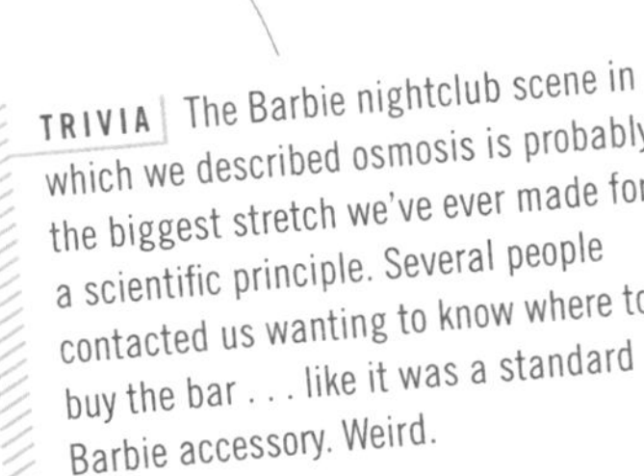

TRIVIA | The Barbie nightclub scene in which we described osmosis is probably the biggest stretch we've ever made for a scientific principle. Several people contacted us wanting to know where to buy the bar . . . like it was a standard Barbie accessory. Weird.

APPLICATION — CITY HAM

15 TO 20 SERVINGS

Breathe new life into a fully cooked city ham by installing a crispy crust of contrasting flavors.

Some viewers had some trouble with this crust, so we went back and reworked it for increased stability.

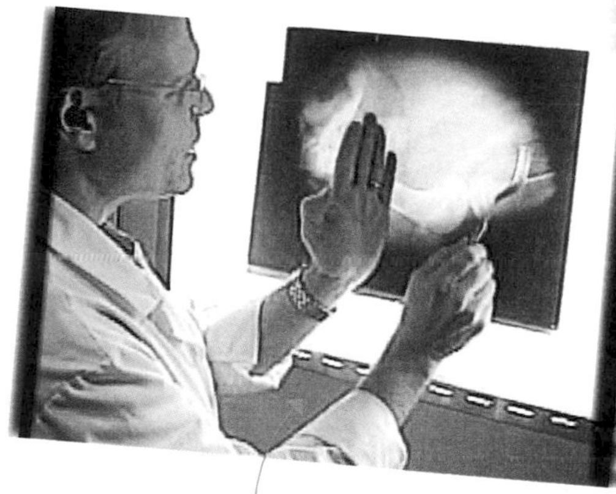

TRIVIA This was the first time we talked an X-ray technician into shooting film of food. I'm seriously thinking about doing an exhibit of food X-rays.

SOFTWARE

1	6- to 8-pound	ham	city style,[1] preferably shank end
2	tablespoons	brown mustard	
½	cup	dark brown sugar	
2	tablespoons	bourbon	in a spritz bottle
1	cup	ginger snap cookies	crushed

PROCEDURE

1. Heat the oven to 250°F.
2. Remove the ham from its packaging, rinse, and drain thoroughly. Place the ham, cut side down, in a **roasting pan lined with a clean kitchen towel**.
3. Using a **small paring knife or clean utility knife** set to the smallest blade setting, score the ham from bottom to top, spiraling clockwise as you cut. (If you're using a paring knife, be careful to cut only through the skin and first few layers of fat.) Rotate the ham after each cut so that the scores are no more than 2 inches apart. Once you've made it all the way around, move the knife to the other hand and repeat, spiraling counter clockwise. The aim is to create a diamond pattern all over the ham. (Don't worry too much about precision here.)
4. Remove the towel and tent the ham with **heavy-duty aluminum foil**, insert a **probe thermometer**, and cook for 3 to 4 hours, until the internal temperature at the deepest part of the meat registers 130°F. Remove from the oven and use **tongs** to pull away the diamonds of skin and any sheets of fat that come off with them.
5. Increase the oven temperature to 350°F.
6. Pat the ham dry with **paper towels** (otherwise the coating is going to slide right off), then **brush** on a liberal coat of mustard. Sprinkle on brown sugar, packing loosely as you go, until the ham is coated. Spritz this layer lightly with bourbon, and tightly pack on as much of the crushed cookies as you can. You may not use all the mustard, brown sugar, bourbon, or cookies, depending on the size of your ham.
7. Insert the thermometer (don't use the old hole) and return the ham to the oven, uncovered. Cook for about 1 hour, until the internal temperature reaches 140°F. Let the ham rest for 30 minutes before carving.

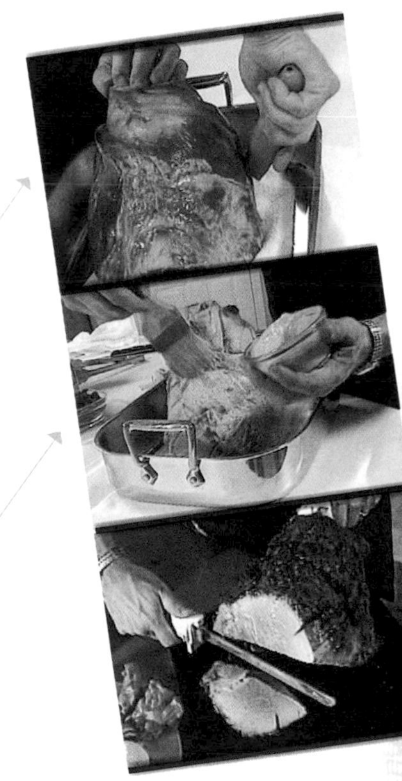

APPLICATION

COUNTRY HAM RESURRECTED

30 TO 40 SERVINGS

By soaking in water and braising in soda, a rock hard, salty pig leg loosens up and finds its balance. Originally this was to be executed outdoors, but I've now shifted to the tub, which I never really use for bathing anyway. If you do, it's back outdoors.

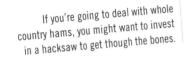

If you're going to deal with whole country hams, you might want to invest in a hacksaw to get though the bones.

SOFTWARE

1	15- to 17-pound	country ham[2]	
1	2-liter bottle	Dr. Pepper	(not diet)
1	cup	pickle juice	(sweet or hot)

PROCEDURE

1. Unwrap the ham and scrub off any surface mold (if you hung in a sack for 6 months you'd have mold too).
2. Carefully remove the hock with a **handsaw**. (You can ask your butcher to do this, but really, it's easier than it sounds.)
3. Place the ham in a **large cooler** (Styrofoam or plastic are fine as long as it has a drain with a plug) in your bathtub. Cover with cold water. Soak the ham for 2 days, changing the water twice a day and rotating the ham when you do.
4. Heat the oven to 400°F.
5. Place the ham in a **large roasting pan** and add enough Dr. Pepper to come about halfway up the side of the ham. Add the pickle juice. Tent the ham with **heavy-duty aluminium foil** and bake for 30 minutes. Reduce the oven temperature to 325°F and cook for another 1½ hours.
6. Carefully turn the ham over, insert an **oven-safe thermometer**, and cook for another 1½ hours, or until the deepest part of the meat hits 140°F (15 to 20 minutes per pound total).
7. Removing the ham can be tricky. Use **insulated gloves** to transfer the ham to a **half sheet pan**, cover with foil, and let rest for 30 minutes. Slice paper-thin and serve with biscuits (page 42) or soft yeast rolls.

10 MINUTES MORE — HAM AND RED-EYE GRAVY

If you want a breakfast Johnny Cash would be proud of, cut a thin steak (about ¼ inch) of ham, dredge lightly in flour, and fry in some of the fat from the side of the ham. Remove the steak when brown, then deglaze the pan with black coffee. Look down at the way the red juices from the ham mingle with the fat and coffee. That's red-eye gravy, my friend. Pour atop the ham and enjoy to the music of your arteries hardening.

[1] Any brined ham that's packed in a plastic bag, held in a refrigerated case, and marked "ready to cook," "partially cooked," or "ready to serve." Better city hams are also labeled "ham in natural juices."

[2] That is, dry-cured.

A FEW FAMOUS "COUNTRY" HAMS FROM AROUND THE WORLD

SMITHFIELD HAM

This is an aged, dry-cured ham made exclusively in Smithfield, Virginia. Originally made only from hogs fattened up on Virginia peanuts, the ham must come from animals raised, cured, and smoked in Smithfield. There are several quality processors in the area producing hams that are so darned salty you must soak them in several changes of clean water before cooking and consuming. But, properly hung, one of these babies will keep for a decade.

PROSCIUTTO

An Italian-style dry-cured, unsmoked raw ham often coated with pepper. Prosciutto is generally sliced paper-thin and consumed raw. Parma ham is prosciutto from the area around the city of Parma in Italy. These hams tend to be larger than the U.S.-produced product, as Italian hogs are larger at slaughter.

SERRANO

Spain's version of prosciutto but wonderfully different. It is typically leaner and less gamey than prosciutto. It's my favorite raw ham by far. Until a few years ago it was pretty much impossible to find in America. That's changing now, and the change is good.

BLACK FOREST HAM

Probably the most famed of the German smoked hams, and stand out because they are by definition boneless. Pepper, coriander, and juniper are usually rubbed on prior to smoking over pine.

IRISH HAM

Usually brined rather than cured and smoked over juniper.

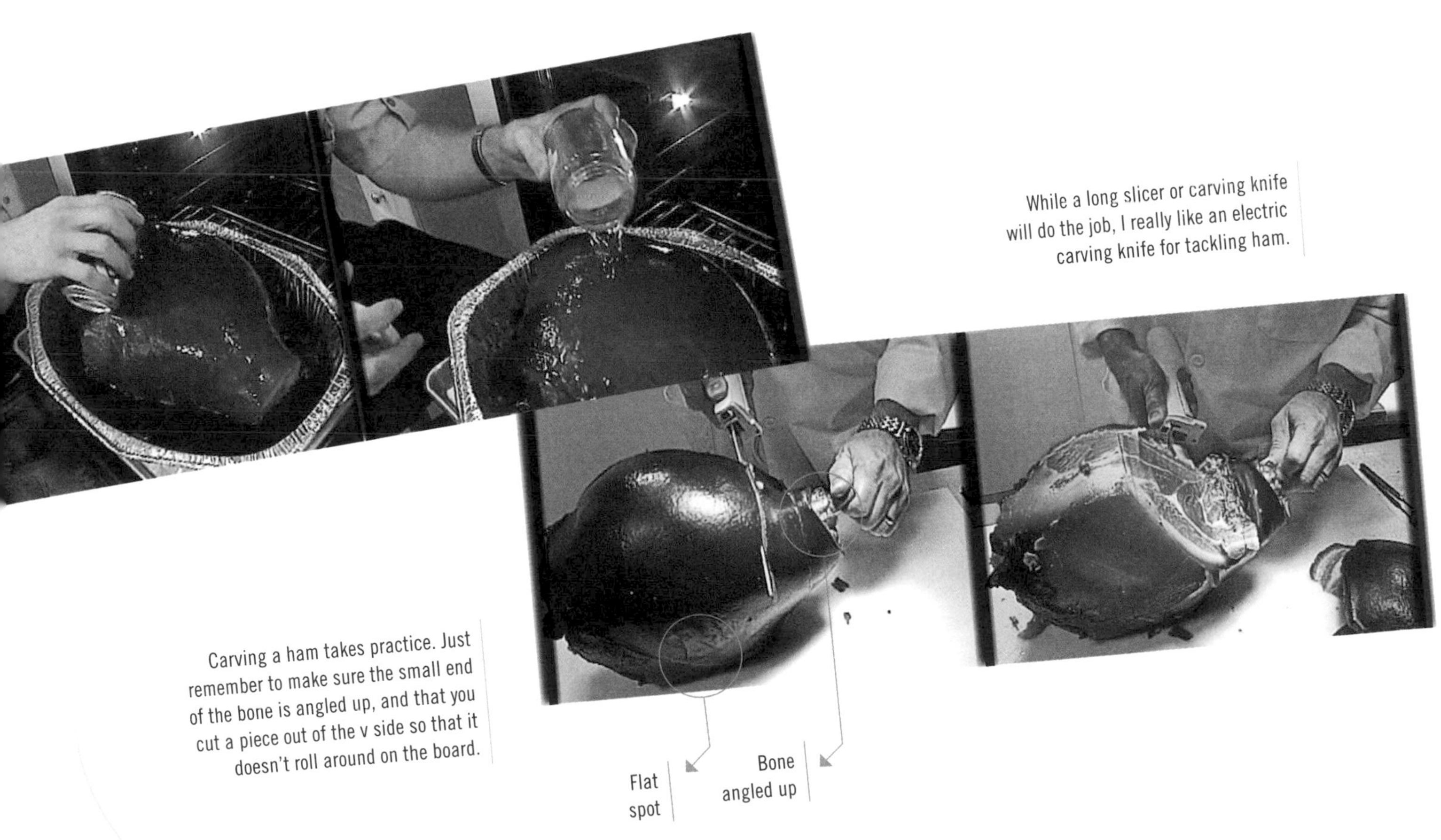

While a long slicer or carving knife will do the job, I really like an electric carving knife for tackling ham.

Carving a ham takes practice. Just remember to make sure the small end of the bone is angled up, and that you cut a piece out of the v side so that it doesn't roll around on the board.

Flat spot

Bone angled up

THE EGG-FILES III: LET THEM EAT FOAM

EPISODE 48 | SEASON 4 | GOOD EATS

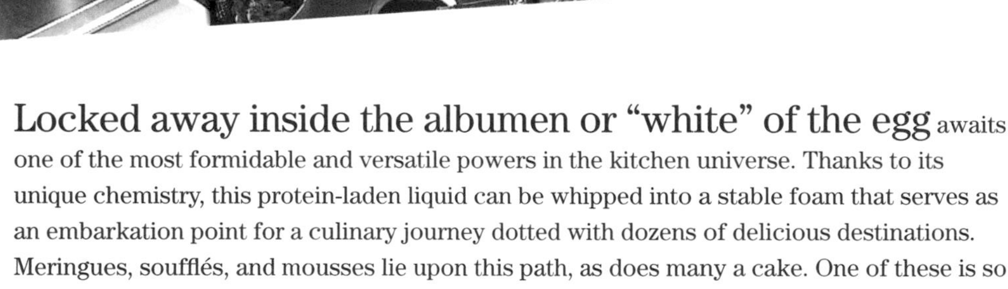

Locked away inside the albumen or "white" of the egg awaits one of the most formidable and versatile powers in the kitchen universe. Thanks to its unique chemistry, this protein-laden liquid can be whipped into a stable foam that serves as an embarkation point for a culinary journey dotted with dozens of delicious destinations. Meringues, soufflés, and mousses lie upon this path, as does many a cake. One of these is so impossibly light, so ethereally delicious, so amazingly versatile, so ridiculously easy to make (not to mention completely fat-free) that it is referred to as "angel food." Having never dined with angels, I just call it good eats.

TIDBIT | Cake recipes with the name "angel food" began showing up in American cookbooks sometime in the late nineteenth century, about the same time as mass-produced bakeware hit the market. Some food historians speculate that the Pennsylvania Dutch invented angel food, though this connection has not been fully documented.

KNOWLEDGE CONCENTRATE

Whether it's floating on your beer, topping your pie, or cleaning your car, a foam is simply a collection of tiny bubbles. And a bubble is nothing but a pocket of gas surrounded by a thin layer of liquid. But blowing a bubble, much less an edible one, isn't as easy as you might think. Pure water, or any pure liquid for that matter, cannot bubble. The reason is surface tension. Water molecules are so attracted to each other that when faced with an alien environment, like air, any body of water will attempt to shape itself to expose as few of its molecules as possible to that environment. Now, the shape that exposes the fewest molecules just so happens to be a sphere, which is why water "beads" on a freshly waxed car.

To turn water into foam we must break the surface tension, and that means adding molecules that can get it to loosen up a little. In the case of egg whites, protein does the job. There's so much protein in egg whites that you can add water to them and still whip up a healthy foam. All you have to do is break up the proteins with physical agitation. If you really want to make your foam sturdy you'll also add sugar to the mix, because dissolved sucrose is a wonderful bubble enhancer, which is why sweet egg foam applications are easier to manage than savory (e.g., those created when making soufflés).

As egg whites are agitated, the proteins that make up the walls of the bubbles come together, or coagulate, tighter and tighter. The term "medium peaks" refers to a state in which the walls of the bubbles are flexible enough to stand up to heat expansion. "Stiff peaks" are more structurally sound but not very flexible. If the beating continues, the whites will "break," resulting in a nasty, dry, useless clump floating on a pool of water. So, what are these "peaks" we speak of? Stick your beaters (mixer off) into the middle of the foam and pull it out. Turn the beaters upright . . .

If you see this, then you have medium peaks:

If you see this, you have stiff peaks:

If you see this, I hope you have more eggs:

Classic egg foam applications call for the use of a copper bowl. Does it really make a difference? Yes. During the whipping process, copper ions bond with the proteins in egg whites, thus preventing them from overcoagulating and creating a big, dry useless clump. Does this make enough of a difference to warrant dropping a C-note for a single bowl? No. Just stick with a good stainless-steel bowl and use proper technique.

The tube in a tube pan provides support for the batter. Without this structure to cling to, the middle of the cake would sink disastrously. The tube also provides even heat contact to ensure even baking. Unlike Bundt pans, which also have center openings, true tube pans are smooth-sided and usually break down into two pieces, which certainly makes depanning easier. Oh, and since the foam needs to be able to climb up the pan, a nonstick surface wouldn't make a lick of sense. For that reason, too, never, ever grease an angel food pan; lubrication will also cause it to fall out of the inverted pan before it has a chance to set.

APPLICATION

ANGEL FOOD CAKE

10 TO 12 SERVINGS

An egg white foam can be whipped to maximum lightness with carefully timed additions of sugar and flour.

// SOFTWARE

12½	ounces	sugar	
5	ounces	cake flour	
¼	teaspoon	fine salt	
12	large	egg whites	fresh or previously frozen, at room temperature
2½	fluid ounces	warm H_2O	approximately 90°F
1½	teaspoons	cream of tartar[1]	
1	teaspoon	vanilla, orange, or lemon extract	

// PROCEDURE

1. Heat the oven to 350°F.
2. Take the sugar for a 2-minute spin in a **food processor**, then transfer half of it to a **small mixing bowl** and set aside. Add the flour and salt to the remaining sugar in the processor. Pulse several times to combine (and aerate). Set aside.
3. **Whisk** the egg whites and water in a **large metal mixing bowl** until the mixture just starts to foam.[2] Add the cream of tartar and begin whipping with a hand mixer on medium speed for 1 minute. Add the extract of your choice and keep whipping on medium speed while very slowly adding the reserved sugar. Whip until all the sugar is in and you're looking at medium peaks. Play your cards right, and 3 minutes will do the trick.
4. Add enough of the flour mixture to just dust the top of the foam. Fold it in using a **rubber or silicone spatula** and repeat until almost all of the flour mixture is incorporated.[3]
5. Gently spoon the batter into an ungreased tube pan and bake for 35 minutes. Use a long wooden skewer to check for doneness, inserting it halfway between the inner and outer walls of the pan. If the skewer doesn't come out dry, bake for 5 minutes longer.
6. Cool the cake in the pan, upside down,[4] for 2 to 3 hours before removing it from the pan and serving.

TIDBIT | Some Pennsylvania Dutch bakers keep a clean fly swatter in the kitchen just for folding batters.

10 MINUTES MORE — SPICED ANGEL FOOD CAKE

If we'd had time I would have liked to have cranked out a flavored version. Although chocolate angel food is an option, I'd rather preserve the fat-free characteristic that makes this cake special—and chocolate just doesn't work without fat, if you ask me. Freshly ground spices can add considerable flavor, and since they're extremely aromatic, and angel food is full of air, they make for a darned fine-smelling cake. At home I typically add ¼ teaspoon each of ground allspice and mace and ⅛ teaspoon ground cloves to the flour mixture. It's not worth doing with preground spices, so grind fresh or don't bother.

TIP For efficient egg separation, crack the egg into one hand and allow the white to run through your fingers while gently jiggling. Fresh eggs separate much easier than old because the membrane around the yolk is strong and almost never breaks during the procedure. Always separate over a "quarantine" bowl so that any yolk that sneaks through won't ruin the batch.

[1] Cream of tartar is not freeze-dried tartar sauce but partially neutralized and finely ground tartaric acid crystals harvested from the inside of barrels in which wine has fermented. You often see them on the underside of wine bottle corks. As a mild acid, it adds just enough hydrogen atoms to the whites to stabilize the foam.

[2] I used to begin my foams with a hand whisk because I really thought it built a better foam. However, I've come to believe that egg whites are far more flexible than I perceived. It's certainly possible to undertake this operation armed only with a hand whisk, but you'll need forearms like Popeye.

[3] The key here is to find a balance between homogenization of the batter and maintenance of the foam. If you completely work in the flour, odds are the foam will be seriously deflated, so shoot for about 95 percent integration and leave it at that.

[4] Many tube pans have little feet on the rim to hold it off the work surface when inverted. Others have a center tube that's taller than the rest of the pan on which the whole can be balanced. If your pan has neither, try sticking the tube down on the neck of a wine bottle.

As you start to whip, a foam of big bubbles forms. As you continue to beat, and add sugar, these bubbles subdivide and rapidly increase in number. The sugar helps hold water inside the bubble walls.

A CHUCK FOR CHUCK

EPISODE 49 | SEASON 4 | GOOD EATS

Pot roast is one of those dishes that seems to have been dropped in the generational handoff of culinary know-how from the "greatest" generation to the present one. Pot roast was an evolutionary technique born out of the simple necessity to make tough, cheap cuts of cow palatable. Many modern incarnations fail because they attempt to gussy up the dish with fancy victuals and in doing so lose sight of the basic goal of the dish: the conversion of collagen to gelatin.

The setup: My neighbor, Chuck, has a problem. He lives with his mom (in a trailer, no less . . . long story[1]), but she's run off to Branson, Missouri, leaving him kibbleless—on pot roast night no less. He hasn't a clue of what to buy or what to do, so AB takes pity and dives in to teach him. (This was Chuck's fourth appearance on the show.)

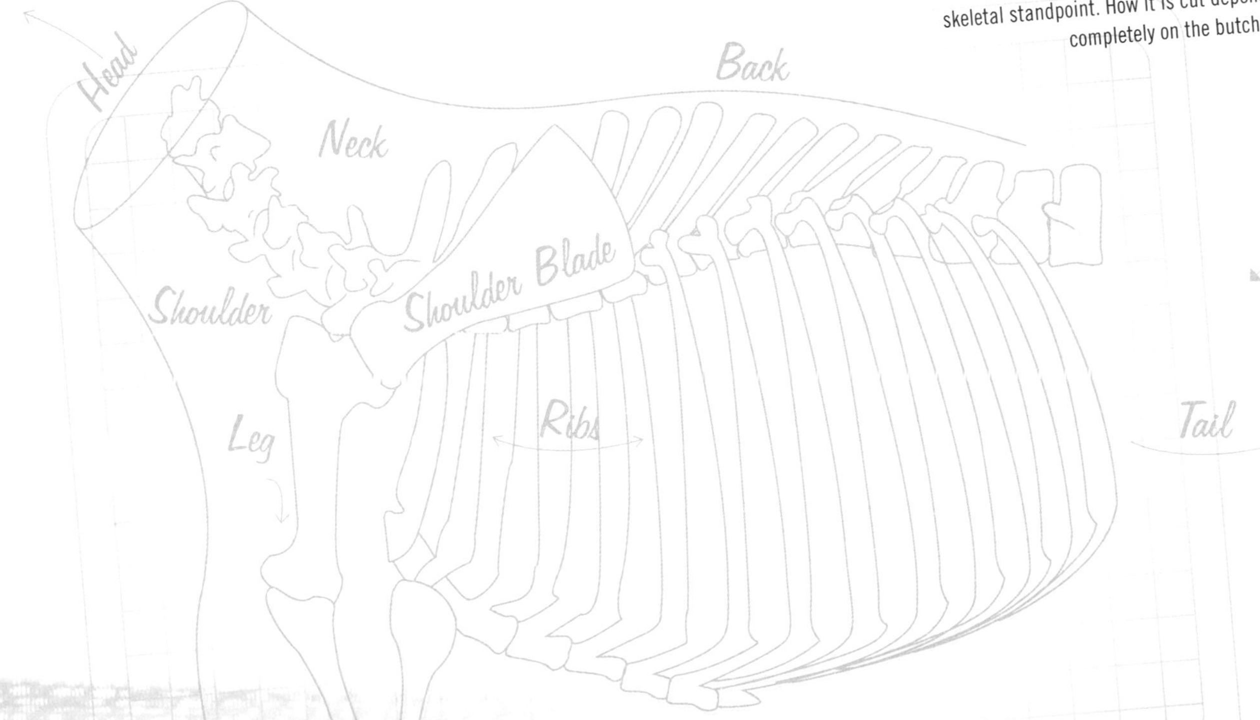

The chuck primal is complex from a skeletal standpoint. How it is cut depends completely on the butcher.

KNOWLEDGE CONCENTRATE

Generally speaking, a "roast" is any hunk of critter that is roasted or braised, then sliced into individual portions. Roasts destined for the pot need to contain a fair amount of connective tissue, which when broken down through long, moist cooking converts into gelatin. Such cuts reside close to the "hoof or the horn," and for my money the best pot roasts hail from the chuck.

The chuck primal takes up a lot of territory, nearly 23 percent of the carcass, in fact, and the meat at one end is very different from the meat at the other. The area right around the shoulder blade is where the best pot roast meat can be found, and although it's sometimes butchered by muscle group, more often than not it's cut in the form of gigantor steaks, meaning flat hunks cut across the grain. Actually I should say "sawed," because they use a big band saw to produce these cuts and because of that the shape of the blade bone is different in each piece.

The first roast (closest to the head) has a very small piece of shoulder blade. This is a perfectly good pot roast. If we keep cutting, we move into the middle of the shoulder/chuck blade. The piece of bone here is longer, and it looks something like a seven, which is why this entire class of roast is called a "seven-bone roast." You cannot go wrong with a seven-bone roast for pot roast, but it does get a little bit better than this if you go all the way to the back of the blade, where the roast will have a very long piece of shoulder blade and tons of connective tissue. That is the crème de la crème.

Most braising recipes call for searing the meat—that is, browning all sides in a very hot pan—before braising. Contrary to long-held belief, searing does not seal in juices. But searing does bring real flavor to the party via a series of complex processes known as the Maillard reaction.[2]

Pot roast is made possible by braising, a wet cooking method characterized by a small amount of flavorful liquid, an enclosed vessel, and relatively low heat. (At home I often braise in a 250°F oven.) The goal is to keep the liquid at just a bare simmer. This method is useful for slow cooking a wide range of meats and vegetables but especially meat cuts containing a lot of connective tissue. Does the meat overcook? Technically, yes. But the moisture that's lost from the muscle tissue is made up for by the gelatin that's created, fat that melts, and by the cooking liquid that is drawn into the meat as its structure gradually unravels.

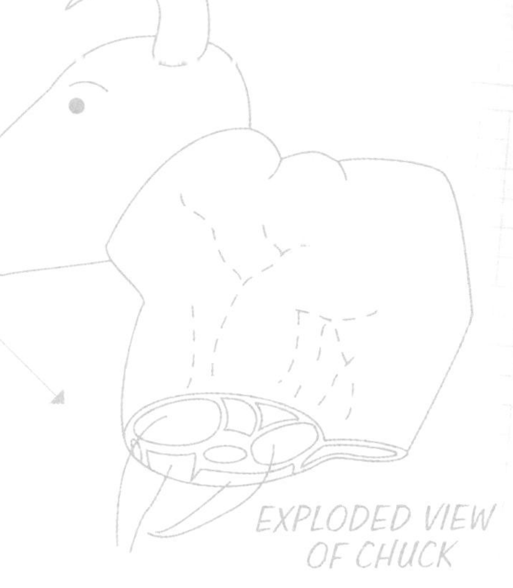

Because so many muscles connect into the shoulder, the chuck is like a switchboard of fibers, and there's a lot of connective tissue.

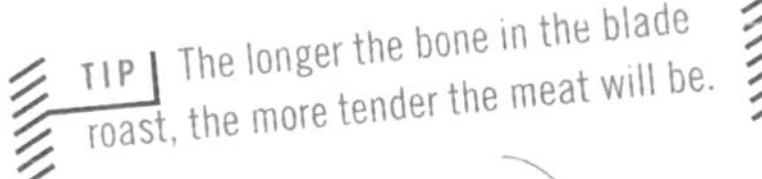

TIP | The longer the bone in the blade roast, the more tender the meat will be.

Tender

Not So Much

APPLICATION

TRADITIONAL BUT BY NO MEANS BLAND POT ROAST

4 TO 6 SERVINGS

Okay, a lot of you sent cards, letters, emails, faxes, etc. complaining that the version of this dish we prepared in the show was—is—weird. So it has olives and raisins in it. Is that so strange? Fine, America, you want traditional, here's as traditional as I get.

I would have loved to have taken some time in this episode to dig into why it is that pot roast is so much better the second day. The reason has to do with the fact that as it cools, gelatin forms a new type of gel with the moisture that's still inside the meat, just as Jell-O sets up when it chills. When reheated, this new gel creates a succulent mouthfeel that wasn't present when the meat was first cooked.

TIDBIT Yankee pot roast, a.k.a. "pot roast with potatoes and other vegetables," grew out of the tradition of the New England boiled dinner, a colonial-era one-pot meal generally composed of whatever was laying around that could fit in the pot, including tough meat cuts and root vegetables.

SOFTWARE

1	2-pound	blade-cut chuck roast	
2	teaspoons	kosher salt	
½	teaspoon	black pepper	freshly ground
2	teaspoons	vegetable oil	
9	ounces	frozen pearl onions[3]	cooked according to package instructions and drained
2	large	carrots	peeled and chopped into 1-inch hunks
6	cloves	garlic	sliced
1	cup	tomato juice	
⅓	cup	red wine vinegar	
2	large	russet potatoes	rinsed, scrubbed, and cut into 1-inch hunks
2	teaspoons	fresh thyme	finely chopped

PROCEDURE

1. Heat the oven to 250°F.
2. Place a **12-inch cast-iron skillet** over high heat for 2 minutes.
3. Meanwhile, make a **big ol' pouch with a double layer of heavy-duty aluminum foil**[4] and set aside.
4. Rub both sides of the meat with the salt and pepper and brown on both sides until golden brown, 2 to 3 minutes. (Flip with **tongs**, not a fork. You don't want to punch any holes in the meat.) Transfer the roast to the foil pouch.

5 Lower the heat to medium and add the oil, followed by the onions, carrots, and garlic. Stir constantly until the garlic is browned slightly, 2 to 3 minutes.

6 Add the tomato juice and vinegar and bring to a boil; cook until the liquid is reduced by half, 3 to 5 minutes. Lift the roast with tongs and place half of the potatoes and half of the reduced mixture under the roast, then top with the remaining mixture and potatoes. Close the pouch, and wrap tightly in another complete layer of foil. Triple-fold your seams so that the package is water-tight.

7 Place on the middle rack of the oven and cook for 3½ hours, or until a fork pushes easily into the meat. (Just in case the pouch does spring a leak, place a **half sheet pan** on the lower rack.) Remove from the oven and set the pouch aside, unopened, for at least 30 minutes. Serve with the vegetables, braising liquid, and a sprinkling of thyme.[5]

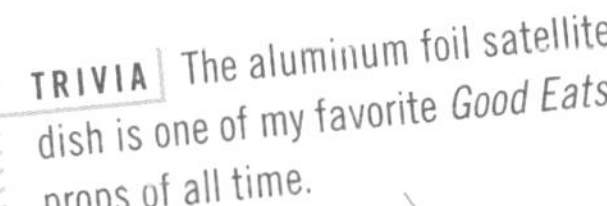

TIP | Many ovens have a tough time maintaining a low temperature, so always monitor your heat with an oven thermometer.

TRIVIA | The aluminum foil satellite dish is one of my favorite *Good Eats* props of all time.

[1] I honestly can't remember why we shot in a trailer, but it wouldn't be the last time. I think I may have some RV issues I need to work out.

[2] Named after Louis-Camille Maillard, the French chemist who investigated the phenomenon in the early twentieth century.

[3] If pearl onions are just too daring, go with a regular old onion, chopped.

[4] Why aluminum foil? Making your own braising vessel from foil works because it enables you to use a very small amount of liquid because the pan essentially conforms to the food. Also, aluminum is a great conductor of heat. But always use heavy-duty foil. Heck, I don't even own any regular foil. It's too scrawny to be much good.

[5] I always make fresh herbal additions to pot roasts because the long cooking tends to turn down the brighter flavors of the meat.

WHERE FOIL COMES FROM

Aluminum, by the way, is amazing stuff. Although it's the most common substance in the Earth's crust aside from oxygen and silicon, it never appears in its metallic form in nature. In fact, it's almost always locked inside a rock such as bauxite. However, unleashing the aluminum in bauxite is no easy trick. The ore must first be pulverized and refined into a powder called alumina, which is dissolved in molten sodium aluminum fluoride, known to schoolchildren everywhere as cryolite. An electric current is then zipped through the mix, and the aluminum sinks to the bottom of the vat, where it's siphoned off. It's then flushed with gases to remove any lingering impurities and mixed with recycled aluminum as well as other metals to customize the character of the final mix. The aluminum is cast into ingots and shipped to and fro for fabrication.

Rolling these ingots into foil is a lot like rolling pie dough, only the rolling pins are a good deal heavier. If the final thickness is ¼ inch or more, the aluminum is referred to as "plate" and can be used as armor on fun things like tanks. If it's rolled ¼ and 1/6000 inch, it's called sheet aluminum and can used for things like baking pans. Roll it thinner, and you've got foil. At this point the foil tears so easily that two sheets have to be rolled together, each supporting the other through the final rollers. That's why there's a dull side and a shiny side.

PANTRY RAID IV: COMB ALONE

EPISODE 50 | SEASON 4 | GOOD EATS

Even if it wasn't the most mentioned food in literature, hadn't been pondered by the likes of Aristotle, didn't posses preternatural preservative powers, and couldn't claim to be the only food manufactured by animals, well, honey's culinary chameleonic nature would still ensure it a spot here on the pantry shelf of fame. So, if you haven't given honey much thought you may want to stick around, because this elixir, celebrated by John the Baptist and Winnie the Pooh alike, is definitely good eats.

TRIVIA | The bee puppets used in the episode were modified golf club covers.

TIDBIT | The honeybee was brought to America from Europe around 1625. Native Americans called it the "white man's fly."

TRIVIA | I like honeybees so much, I got a tattoo of one. It looks like this:

KNOWLEDGE CONCENTRATE

What exactly is honey? Processed flower nectar and honeydew. All flowering plants have glands called nectaries, which produce a sticky, sweet liquid that's secreted through a tube on the flower. Besides helping to regulate the fluid content in the plant, it attracts hummingbirds and insects such as *Apis mellifera*, the honeybee, which collects both nectar and pollen, which provide carbohydrates and protein, respectively. Honeydew is the liquid that oozes out of a plant stem where aphids have been drilling.

Inside the hive, a whole team of worker bees (and all workers are female) set to work repeatedly sucking up and expelling the nectar through their proboscises until their body chemistry breaks down the sucrose—the disaccharide, or double sugar—into simple sugars or monosaccharides, fructose and glucose. Why bother with this? Because simple sugars are more soluble in water than double sugars, which means that a drop of water can hold more energy if the sugar is simple. And that means a more efficient food source. Once the new honey is loaded into a newly constructed wax cell (honeycomb), it will be constantly fanned by the beating of tiny wings until evaporation reduces the moisture level to the point that the honey is essentially microbe-proof. The cell is then capped with wax for long-term storage. So on the one hand honey is an amazingly sophisticated and efficient food source. On the other hand it's bee backwash.

TRIVIA | Our production company logo is a bee with a "2" over it.

There are four common market varieties of honey:

COMB HONEY is the original version, and it's still the one preferred by most connoisseurs. Chunks of the comb are simply cut out and packaged, and the honey remains sealed in its original containment—that is, wax.[1]

CUT COMB HONEY is honey with a big hunk of comb floating in it. Like ice in a soda drink, the comb just takes up space, if you ask me. If I want comb honey, I'll buy comb honey.

LIQUID HONEY is the most common form and doesn't include any of the comb. The degree of filtration that the honey has been run through depends on the processor. Honey can also be pasteurized. Although bacteria aren't fond of the stuff, there are varieties of yeast that do like it, and pasteurization keeps them out. I find the flavor of pasteurized honeys to be bland, so I steer clear of them.

CREAM HONEY has been seeded with microscopic honey crystals, which gives the product a creamy mouthfeel and spreadability. Since it's not drippy, it makes for a nice breakfast spread.

Buying locally: Honey is one of the easiest foods to find on a local level because there are very few areas of the country that don't support bees. I live in Georgia, and every time I stop at a farmers' market or roadside stand someone's selling honey made within twenty-five miles. Eating locally made honey is said to ease hay fever and other allergies, but as you might suspect, that's nonsense.

Honeybees practice flower fidelity, which means they'll harvest one type of plant until the bloom is over. If at least 80 percent of a honey's nectar comes from a single botanical source, that honey can claim to be a varietal. Some three hundred varietal honeys are produced in the United States, including alfalfa, clover, basswood, eucalyptus, orange blossom, sourwood, fireweed, lavender, palmetto, gallberry, tupelo (which is very rare and very expensive), tulip poplar, and buckwheat. Honeys that lack a predominant botanical pedigree but are still taken straight from the hive without further blending can be called "wildflower" honeys.

Darker honeys are more distinctive and stronger than light honeys. Pine honey, for instance, is much stronger than wildflower honey, which is a little bit stronger than sourwood honey, which is indeed a little bit darker and stronger than orange blossom honey, which is stronger than alfalfa honey.

Since it is a supersaturated solution, honey will crystallize under the right conditions. Some varieties, like orange blossom honey, will actually begin to crystallize the minute they're put inside a jar. A good tight lid and warm storage will help guard against this. Although it has a shelf life that can reach to decades, if a honey begins to crystallize it can eventually spoil because as the crystals grow the sugar content of the remaining liquid will eventually go down to the point that bacteria will come to call.

HONEY, BABY

Honey is hygroscopic, so it can pull moisture out of wounds. It contains hydrogen peroxide, so it's an antiseptic, and it's sticky, so it stays put. The next time your toddler takes a header, maybe you should slather on a little honey instead of an expensive medical cream.[2]

Note, however, that babies under one year of age should never be fed honey because, like most agricultural products that are raw, honey carries a small number of botulism spores, which are impervious to many of the conditions that kill active bacteria. This is no problem for adults or even toddlers. But an infant system is not acidic enough, so the spores can grow and produce their paralyzing toxin. In other words, until a kid turns one, of honey there will be none.

TRIVIA | The "teletubby" kid with the botulism-ridden guts is my daughter making her second *Good Eats* appearance (after the young Roman in "Head Games" on page 194). She's all big now and loves honey . . . and bees.

APPLICATION — HONEY PLUMS

4 TO 6 SERVINGS

This simple application takes advantage of honey's hygroscopic nature to perfectly poach my favorite stone fruit.

SOFTWARE

½	cup	wildflower honey	
8	about 1¾ pounds	under-ripe common plums[3]	stones removed and quartered

PROCEDURE

1. Put the honey in a **10-inch straight-sided sauté pan** and place over medium heat for 2 minutes, or until the honey thins.
2. Add the plums, cut side down. Cook for 5 to 6 minutes, until the cut sides are slightly browned. Increase the heat to high, toss the plums, and cook for another 1 to 2 minutes, until the fruit is soft but not mushy.
3. Serve with ice cream or eat as is.

APPLICATION — HONEY MUSTARD DRESSING

5 OUNCES

If you have a kid, this dipping sauce for chicken fingers will save you hundreds of dollars a year.

SOFTWARE

5	tablespoons	medium-bodied honey	(sourwood works well)
3	tablespoons	Dijon mustard	
2	tablespoons	rice wine vinegar	

PROCEDURE

1. Measure all of the ingredients in a **plunger cup**, moving the inner part of the cup down as you go.
2. Press all of ingredients into a **small bowl** and **whisk** until smooth. Serve as a dressing or a dip.

10 MINUTES MORE

LEMONY LOVE LOZENGES

200 CANDIES

Here we use basic candy-making methodologies to convert honey and its known associate lemon into a golden, translucent disk, which is quite nice when dissolved in a shot of whisky.

SOFTWARE

1	pound	sugar	
12	ounces	honey	
½	cup	H_2O	
1	large	lemon	zest only

PROCEDURE

1. Combine the sugar, honey, and water in a **4-quart saucepan**. Bring to a boil over medium heat, cover and boil for 5 minutes. Line **4 half sheet pans** with **silicone baking mats or parchment paper** and set aside.
2. Remove the lid and clip a **candy thermometer** to the side of the saucepan. When the mixture reaches 295°F remove from the heat. Cool 5 minutes (the mixture should thicken slightly) and add the lemon zest. Then use a clean **teaspoon** to dose the mixture out onto the prepared pan. Allow 1 inch on either of the candies, as some spreading will occur. Cool for 30 minutes then store in an **airtight container** between pieces of parchment for up to a week.

[1] The wax is edible, but since it doesn't melt until it reaches around 140°F, don't expect it to melt in your mouth.

[2] I'm not a doctor, nor do I play one on TV, but it's worked for me.

[3] Common plums, or European plums, are also known as purple plums.

TRIVIA | Honeybees in North America and the U.K. are in trouble. Large numbers are dying due to what is being called colony collapse disorder, which doesn't have any clear causes. Pollution? Virus? Climate change? No one really knows. One thing's for sure: We need to get on it, because without a healthy bee population healthy agriculture is impossible.

TRIVIA | The rig we used to get the camera into the real beehive was made out of a self-wringing sponge mop.

COOL FACTS ABOUT BEES

- In summer, a queen can lay a thousand eggs a day.
- A normal bee colony can survive a hard winter on just 35 pounds of honey.
- All worker bees are females. The male drones don't do anything but mate with the queen once every few years. Drones can't sting.
- 6 weeks is a long life for a worker bee. A queen however can live for years.
- The average bee will only make ½ teaspoon of honey in its life.
- Bees must consume 8 pounds of honey to produce 1 pound of beeswax.

THE BULB OF THE NIGHT

EPISODE 51 | SEASON 4 | GOOD EATS

For years this was my favorite *Good Eats* episode. I grew up on a steady diet of monster movies, and the whole vampire-garlic paradigm lent itself perfectly to the lessons I wanted to get across. From a technique standpoint it was kinda tricky because the entire show is seen through Vlad's eyes and the only way to get it right was to have the cameraman do Vlad's hands while shooting at the same time. Not an easy task.

V: Good evening.

AB: Oh. Mr. Vladimir. Right on time. Oh, please. Come on in. Come on. That's a very dashing cape you have there.

V: Thank you. And please call me Vlad.

AB: Okay, Vlad. Have a seat. I have to tell you, I don't take many food phobia cases, okay? But I've looked over your chart and I have to say I am intrigued.

V: I never cook...garlic.

AB: And how long have you had this problem?

V: Centuries, it seems.

AB: Why seek help now?

V: Modern vimen all vant chefs. I tried to cook, but today's recipes call for heaping piles of that cursed Italian veed.

AB: Vlad, garlic is not cursed. It's not a weed, and it's not even Italian. In fact, it's from your neck of the woods, Budapest? No, no. The Carpathians, right?

V: In the neighborhood.

AB: And yet you don't eat garlic. Fascinating. Um, it says here that you're only available nights?

V: Is this problem?

AB: Oh, I shouldn't think so. We'll see how it goes. Vlad, trust me. Garlic is a healthful, delicious, unique food. And you're gonna love it, okay? I just want you to keep saying to yourself, "Garlic is good eats." Say it with me now, okay?

AB & V: Garlic is good eats. Garlic is good eats.

KNOWLEDGE CONCENTRATE

Known as the "stinking rose" in ancient Rome, this edible bulb is actually a member of the lily family. There are dozens of different varieties of garlic grown around the world. Most megamart specimens are American garlic, grown in California.[1] It has a solid garlic flavor and a bit of heat to it. The outer paper of Mexican or Italian garlic is white with faint purple stripes, though the cloves are white. It's generally milder than American garlic. I usually use two cloves of Mexican or Italian garlic for one clove of white garlic. The white-skinned, mild-flavored elephant garlic is not a true garlic, but rather a first cousin of the leek. Green garlic is young garlic harvested before the cloves form. They resemble baby leeks, with long green tops and white bulbs. They're typically available in the spring. When I can get them, I can't get enough of them.

When shopping for garlic, go for the loose heads, not the ones sold packaged in little cellophane-wrapped boxes that don't allow for close inspection. Look for heads with no spots of mold or signs of sprouting. Choose firm, plump heads with dry skins. Avoid any with soft or shriveled cloves, and any garlic stored in a refrigerated case. Take a whiff. It should smell like nothing at all. Give it a squeeze. If you feel hollow skins where cloves used to reside or if the head feels at all spongy or rubbery, pass. Store in an open container in a cool, dark place. Unbroken heads can be stored for up to two months. Once the head is breached, individual cloves will keep for seven to ten days.

Good Eats's three rules of garlic:

1. Small mince = Strong / Big mince = Mild
2. Longer cooking = Milder and sweeter / Short cooking = Pungent
3. Burned = One of the worst flavors on Earth

TIDBIT The word *garlic* comes from the two Anglo Saxon words *gar* ("spear") and *leac* ("leek").

TIDBIT China produces more than 60 percent of the world's garlic.

TIP To remove the outer paper, place the clove on a counter or cutting board, cover with a bench scraper, and lightly strike with the heel of your hand. Then simply roll it between the plams of your hand (hard) until paper comes off.

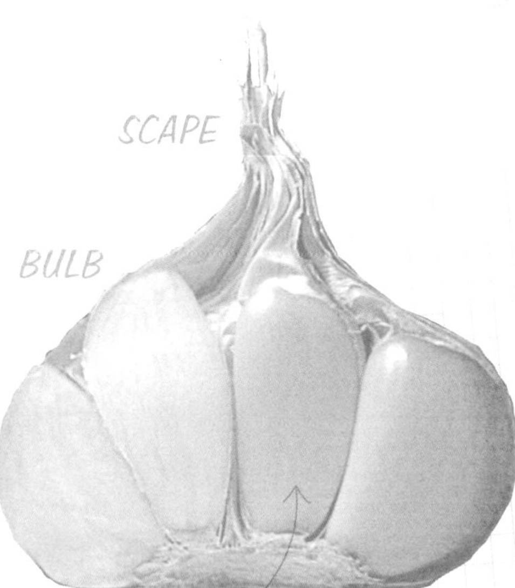

A FEW FUN GARLIC FACTS

- In ancient Rome, the priestesses of Cybele would not allow anyone smelling of garlic into any of their temples.
- King Alfonso of Spain forbade his knights to ever consume garlic.
- Aristotle, by 35 B.C., had written an entire book about the medicinal qualities of garlic. Marco Polo, during his travels, wrote of seeing the Tartars consume all kinds of nasty, raw meat and suffer no ill effects as long as it was eaten with chopped-up raw garlic.
- Romanian lore holds that garlic is a crucial tool in the ongoing battle with supernatural evil and especially against the undead. But why? The answer may simply be that garlic is very healthy stuff and people who keep it around tend to stick around longer themselves. (Garlic eaters suffer fewer incidents of stomach cancer, stroke, and cardiovascular disease.) But there may be a more scientific reason. Certain elements from garlic do transfer to the blood, changing the essential odor of a person's body. Mosquitoes are repelled by this, as are ticks. And what is a vampire but a tick in evening clothes?
- In 1875, Doctor Albert Schweitzer successfully fought an outbreak of dysentery in Africa using only garlic.

TIDBIT That whole bit about stainless steel removing garlic odors? Haven't seen it work, ever. But I like the smell of garlic on my hands. Beats any perfume I know.

APPLICATION

40 CLOVES AND A CHICKEN

6 SERVINGS

This is a classic European peasant dish, but people rarely eat it today because forty just seems like a crazy number. I've talked to gobs of people who have tried this dish and been shocked and surprised by the smooth, sweet, earthy flavor. That's due to the long cooking time at relatively low heat. Although I can't prove it (yet), I also feel that the infusion of chicken juice, especially fat, into the cloves has far-reaching effects. This dish is certainly a case of kitchen alchemy. It may not be my all-time favorite *Good Eats* dish, but it's close.

TIDBIT | In 2006, Americans consumed a record-breaking 2½ pounds of garlic per person.

SOFTWARE

1	3- to 4-pound	broiler/fryer chicken	cut into eight pieces (page 213)[2]
	to taste	kosher salt	
	to taste	black pepper	freshly ground
2	tablespoons, plus ½ cup	olive oil	(not extra-virgin)
5	sprigs	fresh thyme	
40	cloves	garlic	peeled

PROCEDURE

1. Heat the oven to 350°F.
2. Season the chicken all over with salt and pepper. Coat the chicken pieces on all sides with 2 tablespoons of the oil.
3. In a **12-inch straight-sided oven-safe sauté pan** over high heat, cook the chicken for 5 to 7 minutes per side, until nicely browned. Remove the pan from the heat; add the remaining ½ cup oil, the thyme, and garlic cloves. Cover and bake for 1½ hours.
4. Remove the pan from the oven and set aside for 15 minutes with the lid on. Serve family style with plenty of toasted bread to spread the softened, fragrant garlic on.

TIP | Pull all the leftover meat from the bones and chop it with the garlic and fresh herbs to make a chicken salad for a darn fine lunch. Use some of the leftover garlic to make garlic toast sprinkled with Parmesan and fresh parsley.

TIDBIT | Garlic breath is tough to beat because certain oils in garlic are absorbed into the blood and then the lungs. So a mint isn't going to help unless you inhale it, and I wouldn't advise that.

GARLIC VARIETIES

Although there are some six hundred subtypes of garlic grown around the world, there are only two subspecies—hardneck and softneck. In each case, "neck" refers to the stalk or scape.

Hardnecks are the older variety; they grow larger cloves but fewer in number than softneck varieties. They also tend to be more perishable because they have less outer wrapper to protect them.

Although hardneck garlics rarely appear at American megamarts, they often show themselves at farmers' markets.

Softneck garlics were bred from hardnecks and are popular with growers and producers because their scape is pliable, even braidable. Unlike most hardnecks, softneck garlics typically have two layers of cloves, with the larger on the outside and the smaller on the inside.

APPLICATION

VLAD'S VERY GARLICKY GREENS

4 SERVINGS

Although garlic can be quite strong, when quickly cooked it can turn down the volume on the bitterness in dark greens.

// SOFTWARE

3	tablespoons	olive oil	
5–7	cloves	garlic	peeled and lightly crushed
1	pound	greens, like baby mustard or chard	picked, rinsed, and roughly chopped
2	cloves	garlic	one sliced and one minced
	to taste	kosher salt	
	to taste	black pepper	freshly ground

// PROCEDURE

1. Place a **12-inch sauté pan** over medium heat. When the pan is hot, add the olive oil to cover the bottom of the pan and add the crushed garlic. Cook, stirring frequently until the garlic is golden brown, 3 to 5 minutes. Remove the cloves from the oil. At this point, the greens can be quickly sautéed for a mild garlic flavor.
2. If you're looking for something a little stronger, add the thinly sliced clove to the pan, stirring constantly. Once the slices turn golden, approximately 1 minute, remove the pan from the heat, add the greens, and toss to coat with the hot oil. Season with salt and pepper as soon as the greens start to wilt, and plate immediately.
3. If you're looking for even more garlic flavor, finely mince a clove of garlic and toss it into the greens during the last 30 seconds of cooking and toss the greens to distribute. Keep the pan and the greens moving constantly, if you can.
4. To up the garlic further, reincorporate the crushed garlic into the finished greens.
5. Serve as a side dish or toss with pasta and serve as a main course.

ALLIIN + ALLIINASE = ALLICIN

Garlic is what I call a binary, meaning that two substances stored within its cells must first be brought together to "arm" the device. In the case of garlic, the agents in question are a sulfur-based compound, alliin, and an enzyme, alliinase. When the garlic is cut, the enzyme comes into contact with the alliin and converts it to allicin, a new and very pungent compound that gives raw garlic its typical aroma. This compound also gives garlic its bite.

When you slice garlic, only a small amount of enzyme and sulfur compound come into contact, so just a small amount of allicin is produced. The result is a milder garlic flavor. When you mince it or crush it, however, a much higher percentage of cells are breached, and more allicin is produced. More allicin means more aroma and flavor. So, for the strongest garlic flavor, mince cloves into a smooth paste or simply crush with the side of a chef's knife. For milder flavor, slice. Since heat breaks down the harsh-tasting allicin, roasting or toasting garlic cloves before adding them to a dish will eliminate any harsh garlic flavor. The longer you cook it, the sweeter garlic becomes.[3]

[1] Garlic imported from South America is almost as common now.

[2] In my own kitchen I use only thighs, and occasionally I toss a few dark olives into the mix as well.

[3] Some of the compounds in cooked garlic are fifty times sweeter than sugar.

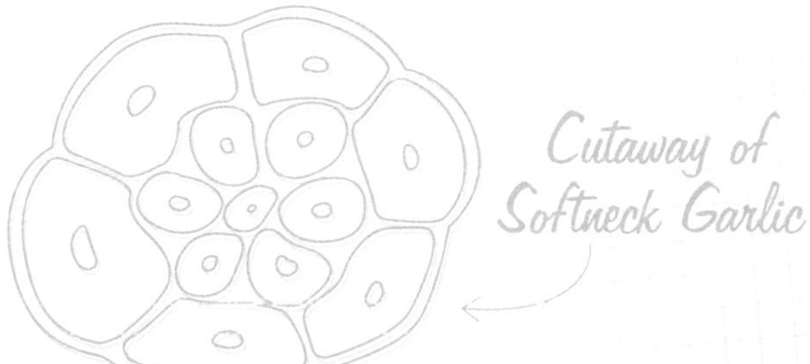

Cutaway of Softneck Garlic

TIDBIT More than forty clinical trials have proven that allicin can lower LDL or "bad" cholesterol.

THE EGG-FILES IV: MAYO CLINIC

EPISODE 52 | SEASON 4 | GOOD EATS

In the beginning were the mother sauces: espagnole, velouté, béchamel, tomato, and the ethereal emulsions, miraculous marriages of fat and water bound by the supernatural properties of the egg. Of these, none was mightier than the sauce created by the Duc de Richelieu chef in commemoration of his boss's 1756 conquest of Menorca and its capital, Port Mahon.

Dubbed *mayonnaise*, this versatile sauce reigned on high until those twin specters of the modern age, speed and convenience, came to town, dancing to the jangle of a jillion jars. Those who resisted would eventually be frightened away by the third specter, salmonella.

As a result, an entire generation would grow up without having tasted the delicious difference homemade mayo makes. Luckily, a new sauce day is dawning. Armed with the right tools, a few basic ingredients, and some honest science, what was recently taboo is once again . . . well, you know.

Phospholipids (always happy), one end loves oil, the other water.

KNOWLEDGE CONCENTRATE

Mayonnaise is a colloidal emulsion a lot like a vinaigrette. Oil droplets are still suspended in water (lemon juice usually), but they're so compact that the resulting substance is spreadable. Why doesn't it separate in a few hours? Lecithin, a powerful emulsifier found in mustard, and especially egg yolks.

Lecithin is a phospholipid, which means that one end of the molecule is attracted to oil and the other end, a mild acid, grabs hold of water, thus holding the two together. By including these molecules in the liquid phase before beating in the oil and breaking it into droplets, we get a scenario that I like to think looks like this:

The phospholipids also carry an electrical charge, so once in place they prevent the oil droplets from coming back together (think of how two magnets repel each other when like poles come together)—and that is crucial if the emulsion is going to be stable.

The average egg yolk is 50 percent water, 16 percent protein, 33 percent fat, and 1 percent, well, other stuff. Phospholipids, including lecithin, make up about a quarter of that total fat, which doesn't sound like much but is more than enough. Lecithin content goes down as an egg gets older, so make your mayo with the freshest eggs that you can get your hands on.

Another essential ingredient here is mustard. Besides bringing some flavor to the party, mustard also contains a small amount of lecithin. The word *mustard* is derived from the Latin *mustum ardens*, meaning "burning grape juice," and refers to early concoctions that were made from grinding up the seeds along with vinegar.

There are three varieties of mustard seeds:

WHITE (ACTUALLY YELLOW) MUSTARD SEEDS: The smallest and mildest mustard seed, this is what's used in most American mustard preparations.

BROWN MUSTARD SEEDS: Much more pungent brown mustard give Asian foods heat.

RARE BLACK MUSTARD SEEDS: The plants are so finicky to grow that the seeds are rarely cultivated or used in cooking.

To make a paste or prepared mustard, take one part mustard seeds and soak in 6 to 7 parts of the liquid of your choice: wine, vinegar, water, even beer. Let it sit overnight, then grind it up into a paste. The English use a lot of dry or powdered mustard, and I do, too. You don't have to calculate its moisture in the recipe, so it's easy.

Three of the most common paste (prepared) mustards are:

DIJON MUSTARD: The liquid is a very specific kind of verjus, made from unripe grapes from the wine region. It gives the mustard a very distinctive flavor.

AMERICAN MUSTARD: Big Yellow. Made from white mustard seeds with the addition of turmeric.

ENGLISH MUSTARD: They leave out the turmeric and add a bit of brown mustard, so it's a little hotter. I like it.

MAYONNAISE-MAKING HARDWARE NOTES

Avoid aluminum or iron mixing bowls, which will turn your mayo gray—which I'm pretty sure isn't good eats. A balloon whisk is an ideal implement, because its wide tines allow for more violent emulsification, and its shape conforms to the sides of the bowl. A nonskid pad will save your arms and your sanity, plus you need a free hand for dosing oil (a wet towel works too). A ladle or cup with a spout can be used to drizzle in the oil, but a squeeze bottle gives you complete control. This is especially important during the first few additions of oil.

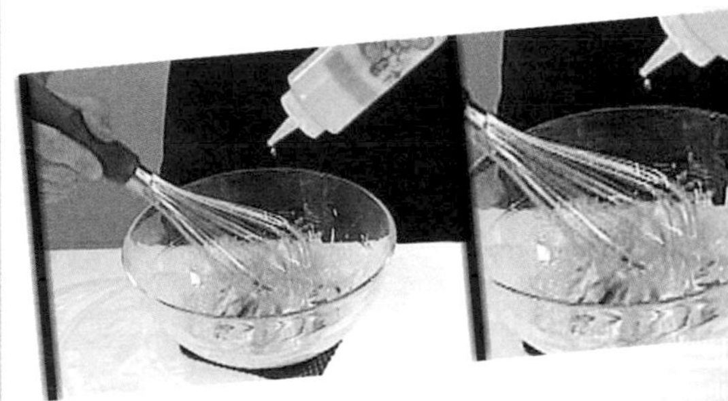

TIDBIT When choosing a fat for your mayo, any neutral oil will do fine. Avoid using extra-virgin olive oil if you plan on prepping your mayo in a food processor, as its delicate flavor gets knocked down by the machine's speed. Also think about the application: nut or herb oils may work well in a mayonnaise destined for dressing a salad, but can overpower a simple sandwich.

APPLICATION

MAYONNAISE

1¼ CUPS

Aside from being the finest mayonnaise you're ever likely to eat, this miraculous concoction works and plays remarkably well with others. For instance, mayonnaise plus chopped gherkin pickles plus dill plus capers equals tartar sauce. Mayonnaise plus tomato sauce or ketchup plus diced red bell peppers equals what the French call *sauce andalouse*. Here in America we would replace the peppers with pickle relish and call it Thousand Island, which is still good eats in my book. Now beyond this there is a world of other flavors that you can add. Curry powder makes for a wonderful mayonnaise. So does citrus zest and, of course, just about every dry or fresh herb under the sun.

*RAW EGG WARNING

Per the American Egg Board, "Use only properly refrigerated, clean, sound-shelled, fresh, grade AA or A eggs. Avoid mixing yolks and whites with the shell."

If you don't want to worry about the whole raw egg thing, buy pasteurized eggs which are gently heat-treated in the shell to be bug free. Use pasteurized eggs if very young children, pregnant women, or anyone with a compromised immune system will be consuming the mayonnaise.

In the days before pasteurized eggs were so easy to find, I used to leave my freshly made mayo (tightly sealed) at room temperature for a few hours before refrigerating. Why? Cold can slow salmonella down and prevent a few bad bugs from breeding, but it won't actually kill them. The acid from the lemon juice and vineger can, but only at relatively warm temperatures. If you're using pasteurized eggs and have followed good sanitation practices, this step isn't necessary.

SOFTWARE

1	large	egg yolk*	
½	teaspoon	fine salt	
½	teaspoon	ground mustard	
⅛	teaspoon	sugar	
2	teaspoons	lemon juice	freshly squeezed
1	tablespoon	white wine or champagne vinegar	
1	cup	safflower or corn oil	

PROCEDURE

1. In a **glass bowl**, **whisk** together the egg yolk, salt, mustard, and sugar.
2. Combine the lemon juice and vinegar in a **separate bowl**. Put the oil in a **plastic squeeze bottle**.
3. **Whisk** half of the lemon juice mixture into the yolk mixture.
4. On a **nonskid pad**, whisk briskly, adding the oil a few drops at a time until the liquid seems to thicken and lighten a bit, which means you've got an emulsion on your hands. Once you reach that point you can relax your arm a little and increase the oil flow to a constant, but thin, stream. Once half of the oil is in, add the remaining lemon juice mixture.
5. Continue whisking until all of the oil is incorporated. Store in a **large container** with a lid. Leave at room temperature for 1 hour, then refrigerate for up to 1 week (see sidebar).

TIDBIT | Mayonnaise was one of the first prepared foods to be commercially packaged in the United States.

APPLICATION — PARTY MAYONNAISE

2½ CUPS

Need a lot of mayo, fast? Here it is..

SOFTWARE

2	cups	safflower or corn oil	
2	tablespoons	chile oil	or other flavored oil
2	tablespoons	champagne vinegar	
2	tablespoons	lime juice	freshly squeezed
1	large	egg yolk*	
1	large	egg*	
1	teaspoon	fine salt	
1	teaspoon	ground mustard	
¼	teaspoon	sugar	

PROCEDURE

1. Put the safflower or corn oil and the chile oil into a **squeeze bottle** or **measuring cup with a spout**.
2. Combine the vinegar, lime juice, egg yolk, egg, salt, ground mustard, and sugar in the bowl of a **food processor**. Pulse 5 times. Turn the processor on and add the oils in a steady stream until incorporated, approximately 2 minutes. Store the mayonnaise in a **large container** with a lid. Refrigerate for up to a week.

TIDBIT In 1905, a German immigrant named Richard Hellmann opened a deli in New York City. Sandwiches prepared there featured a mayonnaise made by Hellmann's wife. The gooey goodness became so popular the couple decided to bottle and sell two different versions, one of which carried a blue ribbon on the bottle. A picture of that ribbon still appears on every jar of Hellmann's. Personal note: I admit that as much as I love homemade mayo, I do still buy it in jars and will continue to as long as Duke's Mayonnaise is made. This Carolina classic has plenty of vinegar in it, and that gives it the zing I crave.

TIP You can rescue a broken mayonnaise by creating a new emulsion: Whisk another egg yolk thoroughly in a clean bowl until it's frothy. Slowly add the broken sauce, a little bit at a time, continuing to whisk thoroughly.

TIDBIT Mayonnaise is easier to rescue than other egg-based sauces because the egg proteins remain uncooked.

PUFF THE MAGIC PASTRY

EPISODE 53 | SEASON 4 | GOOD EATS

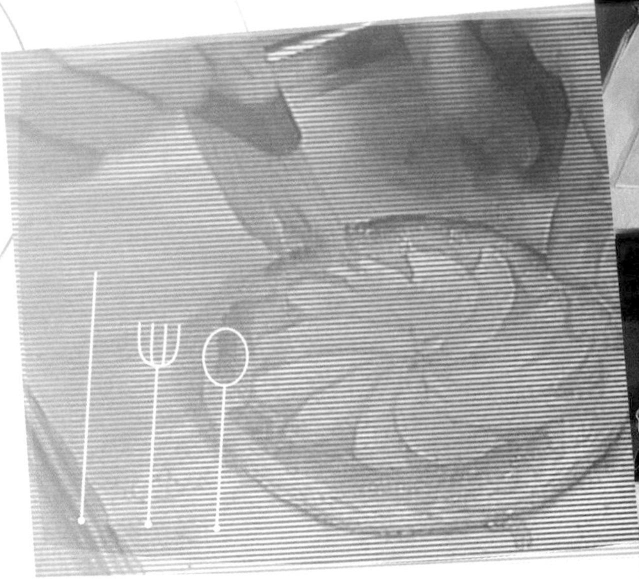

```
   Who's the laminated pastry
   That's always fast, always tasty?
Puff.
   And who's standing by
   when you need your appetizer on the fly?
   Could it be . . .
Puff.
   What do you call those thousand layers
   That can wipe away all your edible cares?
Puff.
   Dang right.
   And what's the name of that flaky sheet
   That can wrap around veggies, fruit, cheese, and meat?
Puff.
   Can you dig it?
   And who is there for the common cook?
   Well, pop your freezer lid and take a look.
   You know who it's got to be.
Puff.
   Pastry, that is.
   But if you're going to taste that flake
   There are precautions you'll have to take.
   So tune in and together we'll . . . good eats make?
```

Lyrically, things really went downhill after that, and my little homage to Isaac Hayes came to a hasty and well-deserved end.

What's so special about puff pastry? What other dough starts cardboard thin and, with little more than a blast of heat, balloons, jumps, and erupts into a tall, light stack of golden goodness? What's the secret? Layers, lots and lots of layers, which are pushed apart in the oven as the water phase of the butter turns to steam. The golden brown comes from the fat of the butter essentially frying each layer. Learning to work with puff is all about managing all these layers.

TIDBIT How many layers, exactly? Well, if your initial "packet" of dough gives you four layers of dough and two of butter, and you turn, fold into thirds, and roll six times . . .

First turn: $4 \times 3 = 12$
Second turn: $12 \times 3 = 36$
Third turn: $36 \times 3 = 108$
Fourth turn: $108 \times 3 = 324$
Fifth turn: $324 \times 3 = 972$
Sixth turn: $972 \times 3 = 2,916$

And that is a lot of layers.

Well-made puff pastry is composed of thousands of alternating layers of dough and butter.

KNOWLEDGE CONCENTRATE

Puff pastry's layers are actually alternating strata of dough and butter, which is why it's called a "laminated" dough—like strudel dough and croissant dough. It's kind of the samurai sword of the pastry world. Although it can be made by hand, it's a lot easier with a power-rolling device called a "sheeter."

To make puff, you make a kind of envelope out of an elastic dough that has a sizeable hunk of butter in the middle of it. By folding into thirds and then rolling, turning, folding, and rolling some more, you end up with an impressive array of layers, all separated by the butter.

Since I don't have a sheeter, I settle for frozen store-bought stuff, which, it turns out, works just fine. Although some markets carry puff pastry in flat sheets, trifolds are more common and generally come two sheets to a box. To thaw, move to the refrigerator for 12 hours or lay it out on the counter, covered in paper towels (to absorb condensation), for 30 minutes.

RULES OF PUFFAGE:

KEEP IT COOL: Put a half sheet pan in the freezer while you thaw your puff, then any time your dough starts to get limp, place a piece of parchment over the dough (to protect against condensation) and park the cold pan on top. In thirty seconds the dough will be good as new.

CUT IT CLEAN: Mashing the edges will seal the dough layers to each other, resulting in very uneven lift in the oven. So cut your puff with either a very sharp knife or, better yet, a sharp pizza cutter. If you must use a cookie cutter to produce specific shapes, make sure the dough is very cold and make sure you push straight down through it. If you don't want puff to puff, "dock" it by poking it all over with a fork.

This will give steam a way out, thus preventing lift. I dock any piece of puff that's going to serve as bottom crust for a filling.

VENT THE TOP: Steam is good, but too much can rip the lid right off your piece. This is especially true of stuffed pieces like the Salmon Turnovers, next page. Venting also prevents seams from splitting. Unlike docking, venting should be done by creating short, clean gashes with a paring knife, a razor blade, or even a utility knife.

REST BEFORE BAKING: Agitation from shaping and filling can cause some gluten development, which leads to shrinkage in the oven. Letting the puff rest in the fridge for 10 to 15 minutes before baking not only prevents this, but chills the butter, which helps achieve a loftier puff.

BAKE IT HOT: A hot oven creates more steam, and more steam means a better puff and more even browning. Filled pastries can be started in a hot oven (400°F) and finished in a lower oven (about 350°F).

TIDBIT | Puff pastry probably evolved in the kitchens of Tuscan dukes during the Renaissance. Like just about every other edible on Earth, puff pastry was perfected in France, where it's called *pâte feuilletée* or *feuilletage*. Puff pastry became famous during the eighteenth century, when famed chef Marie Antoine Carême created the dessert *mille-feuille*, or Napoleon.

TIDBIT | Quality puff pastry will boast nearly fifteen hundred layers of butter and flour.

TIP | Stretching is bad for puff pastry, so when cutting, err on the large side.

APPLICATION

FRUIT TART

2 SERVINGS

This is the best easy dessert I know. The fact that it looks hard makes it taste even better.

// SOFTWARE

1	8½-ounce sheet	frozen puff pastry	
2	teaspoons	sugar	divided
1	cup	H_2O	
1	tablespoon	lemon juice	freshly squeezed
1		Granny Smith apple[1]	peeled, cored, and quartered
1	tablespoon	apricot jam	

TIP | No rolling pin? Pick up a wide wooden dowel at the hardware store or use a clean empty wine bottle.

// PROCEDURE

1. Place the folded frozen sheet of puff pastry on a **clean towel** and cover. Thaw at room temperature for 30 to 40 minutes. Place a **half sheet pan** in the freezer to chill.
2. Heat the oven to 400°F.
3. Gently unfold the thawed puff pastry sheet and crimp the seams together with your fingertips.

   Dust each side of the pastry with ½ teaspoon of the sugar. Using a **rolling pin**, roll the pastry in each direction to smooth out the seams. With a **sharp pizza cutter**, cut out two 6-inch circles of pastry. Place the pastry circles on the chilled sheet pan and chill in the refrigerator for 2 to 3 minutes.
4. Combine the water and lemon juice in a **small mixing bowl**. Using a **vegetable peeler**, cut wafer-thin apple slices. Put the apple slices in the lemon-juice-spiked water.
5. Flip the pastry circles over on the half sheet pan and dock them with a **fork** to provide an outlet for steam. Put a piece of **parchment paper** on the pan underneath the pastry circles. Sprinkle the pastry with the remaining teaspoon of sugar and arrange the apple slices on top in an overlapping spiral.
6. Bake in the middle of the oven for 15 to 20 minutes, until golden brown and crisp. Poke the crust; if it feels soft, it needs more time in the oven.
7. Place the apricot jam in a **small bowl** and microwave for 30 seconds. Dab (don't brush) the jam on the tops of the tarts. Cool the tarts for at least 4 hours, then store in a zip-top plastic bag. Serve at room temperature or heat in the microwave and top with Serious Vanilla Ice Cream (page 38).

APPLICATION

SALMON TURNOVERS

4 TURNOVERS

Consider this procedure a guideline, as you can fill these turnovers with whatever ingredients you have on hand. The Russians make a classic puff dish called *koulebyaka*, which does, indeed, contain all of these elements, especially the salmon.

TRIVIA My favorite puff filling? Manwich mix and cheddar cheese.

// SOFTWARE

1	8½-ounce sheet	frozen puff pastry	
		all-purpose flour	for dusting
6	ounces	canned or smoked[2] salmon fillet	skin removed
½	cup	cooked rice[3]	
¼	cup	sautéed mushrooms[4]	
1½	teaspoons	sour pickle relish	
1	tablespoon	chopped scallion	
1½	teaspoons	chopped parsley	
	to taste	kosher salt	
	to taste	black pepper	freshly ground
1	large	egg	beaten with 2 tablespoons H_2O

// PROCEDURE

1. Place the folded frozen sheet of puff pastry on a **clean towel** and cover. Thaw at room temperature for 30 to 40 minutes.
2. Heat the oven to 400°F.
3. Gently unfold the thawed puff pastry sheet and crimp the seams together with your fingertips. Lightly dust the counter with flour. Using a **rolling pin**, roll the pastry in each direction to smooth out the seams. Cut into 4 equal squares.
4. In a **bowl**, combine the salmon, rice, mushrooms, pickle relish, scallion, and parsley. Taste and season with salt and pepper as desired.
5. Place 2 tablespoons of filling in the center of each square. **Brush** the inside edges of the puff pastry with egg wash and fold over to make a triangle. Using a **fork**, seal the edges. **Poke** a slit or two in the top of each turnover. Brush the tops with egg wash. Bake for 30 minutes, or until golden brown.
6. Cool for 10 minutes before serving.

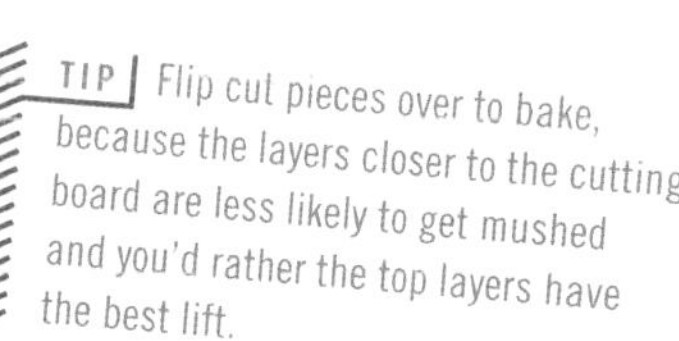

TIP Flip cut pieces over to bake, because the layers closer to the cutting board are less likely to get mushed and you'd rather the top layers have the best lift.

[1] Other tart-friendly fruits: pear, mango, strawberry, nectarine. Frozen berries can also be used if thawed and tossed liberally with sugar.

[2] See page 204 for hot-smoked salmon.

[3] White and brown rice work equally well, as does the rice pilaf on page 66.

[4] See the fungal sauté on page 96.

TRUE BREW II: MR. TEA

EPISODE 54 | SEASON 4 | GOOD EATS

For some reason

Americans have never gotten hip to the fact that tea is the most popular beverage in the world, second only to water. Maybe it's the mind-numbing nomenclature, the complex paraphernalia, or tedious terminology. Either way, it's a shame because with a few basic truths, some decent tools, and a few good leaves, tea—either hot or cold—is definitely good eats.

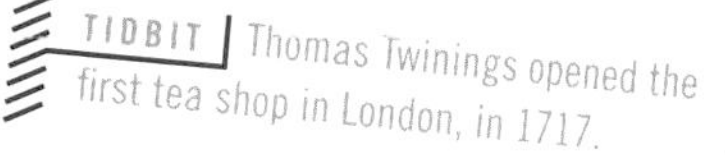

TIDBIT
Thomas Twinings opened the first tea shop in London, in 1717.

- **Meet *Camellia sinensis*, a cousin of garden-variety camellia that grows primarily in China, India, and Sri Lanka. The trees, which left to their own devices would grow to sixty feet, are pruned into a short flat shape called a "plucking table". This makes it possible to pick the two top leaves and the tip-top leaf bud of each twig, which are the only leaves the processor is concerned with. Properly maintained, a tea garden can be harvested, or "flushed," many times a year, though no leaves are as desirable as those from the first flush.**

- **Although all true teas come from the same plant variety, how those leaves are processed defines the different styles.**

BLACK TEA: When most people in the U.K. and America think of tea, the tea we're thinking of is black tea, which is picked then withered or dried for twelve to twenty-four hours. The withering process reduces moisture so that the leaves can be rolled. Rolling is done either by hand or by machine, and it lightly crushes the leaves, exposing compounds inside to oxygen, thus setting off a series of chemical reactions. When the desired level of oxidation is reached, the process is halted with a blast of hot air. The leaves are then sorted and packed.

OOLONG TEA: Very popular in Formosa, parts of China, and my house, oolong tea leaves are lighter than black teas because they are only partially oxidized. Oolongs don't create as pungent a brew as black tea, but they more than make up for this with a kind of a smoky complexity. In fact, the best ones remind me a little of good Scotch whisky.

GREEN TEA: Green teas are different because they are either pan-fried or steamed immediately after withering so that there is no oxidation at all. No oxidation means no color change (think of blanching broccoli), which is why they're still green. The fresh leaves are either crushed, flattened, or rolled into different shapes before they are finally dried and shipped off. Green tea creates a very aromatic brew much loved for its medicinal properties.

WHITE TEA: Just like green teas only the leaves are quickly dried rather than cooked, white teas result in a very mild brew. Although they smell great, I think they taste like water. But that's just me.

After processing, black, oolong, and some green teas are graded by size by passing the leaves through progressively smaller mesh screens (see sidebar).

Until you get your tea legs, take a cue from the wine world and stick with big, reliable names. Black teas from Darjeeling and Assam in India will never let you down. Neither will those from Sri Lanka, which is still called Ceylon in the tea trade and Keemun in China. When it comes to oolongs, always look to Taiwan. And for green teas, well, just about anywhere in China. Japan also makes excellent green teas, although they're a bit more subtle than the Chinese versions.

Blends such as Irish and English breakfast teas and Earl Grey (which is composed of black India tea leaves that have been tumbled with a peel of a bitter Mediterranean fruit called bergamot) are formulated according to house recipes and differ from brand to brand.

Storing: Like coffee, tea doesn't appreciate the company of heat, light, air, or moisture until its brewing time. That's why fine teas have traditionally been sold and stored in little airtight tins like this:

In fact, a lot of American merchants sell tea in generic tins so that you can buy in bulk and still keep it properly stored.

Measuring: I've consulted many an expert on this, and they all argue that since volumetric measuring devices can't compensate for leaf size or shape, tea lovers would be better served by weighing their leaves on a gram scale. Now, I am all for weights and measures but I want to make tea, not TNT. So I stick with the spoon that's actually named after tea. I use one rounded teaspoon per cup. I just scoop and whatever, uh, hangs on the spoon, hangs on the spoon.

Black teas including Ceylon and blends like Earl Grey, Irish breakfast tea, and English breakfast tea prefer to bloom in water at a full, whistling boil, thus the adage "bring the pot to the kettle."

DEMYSTIFYING THE LEAF

- **DUST:** Just like it sounds. These pieces of leaves are so small that they're basically dust. Some tea companies will put dust in their tea bags, but the good ones avoid the practice.
- **Fannings:** These pieces are larger than dust. Because of their large surface area, fannings are ideal tea-bag fodder because they infuse very quickly. And this is okay as long as the tea is of high quality to begin with.
- **Broken Orange Pekoe:** Next up we have a grade that's called B.O.P.—basically just larger pieces of broken leaves.
- **Orange Pekoe:** O.P. are completely whole leaves. In this case, "Orange" does not refer to color. It doesn't refer to flavor or aroma. What it refers to is the Dutch royal house of Orange. Although we most often think of the British when it comes to the European tea trade, the Dutch East India company was deep in the biz long before the Brits caught their first whiff of the stuff.

Now, there are a plenty of other grades you could toss on top of these (Tippy Orange Pekoe, Special Golden Tippy Orange Pekoe, Finest Tippy Golden Flowery Orange Pekoe, and so on), but unless you intend to blend tea or become an importer, you really don't have to understand them. Just know that the more words in the grade the more expensive the tea will be. Purchase Orange Pekoe, and all will be well.

APPLICATION

A VERY NICE CUP OF TEA INDEED

4 (6-OUNCE) SERVINGS

The goal here is to extract the good stuff and leave the bad stuff in the leaves.

// SOFTWARE

4	cups	fresh H_2O	preferably filtered
4	heaping teaspoons	high-quality loose tea	about ¼ ounce for teas like chamomile, ¾ ounce for black and green teas

// PROCEDURE

1. Bring the water to a boil in a **stove-top or electric kettle**.[1]
2. Heat a **teapot** by pouring about 4 ounces of the water inside and carefully sloshing it around. Discard this water. (If using a **French press**, don't bother with this step.)
3. **Measure** (using a teaspoon) the loose tea leaves into the warmed teapot. Pour the heated water over the tea leaves. Let steep according to the chart below.

Tea Type	Water Temperature	Steeping Time
Green	180°F	2 to 3 minutes
Oolong	200°F	4 to 7 minutes
Black, Irish, or English	212°F	3 to 5 minutes

4. **Strain** the tea into individual cups and serve. (If you're using a French press, plunge, then pump up and down a couple of times before pouring, just to make sure the more concentrated brew at the bottom is thoroughly mixed in).

CLOUDING

If I'd had more time in the episode I would have spent it contemplating the problem of iced-tea clouding. Clouding typically happens when tannins that dissolve during brewing precipitate out—that is, resolidify—when said brew is quickly cooled. Slowly cooling the tea to room temperature before chilling can take care of the issue, as can using tea blends or bags formulated specifically for iced tea. Alternatively, you can use the "cold water" brewing method in which the tea is given 12 hours to infuse in water in the fridge. This method doesn't extract as many of the troublesome tannins as boiling, but neither does it extract as much flavor. Another popular way to avoid clouding is to make sun tea, in which tea bags are left to steep in a jar of water in direct sunlight. Since many bacteria find tea irresistible (cases of salmonella have been linked to tea dispensers), sun tea is a risky, if tasty, tradition.

TIP | Although a teapot with a strainer makes leaf separation simple, it just doesn't provide the leaves the room they need to bloom. That's what's nice about a French press. When you're ready to pour, you just push the leaves to the bottom. If I'm making tea to get me through an afternoon, I press then pour into a Thermos that I've rinsed with hot water.

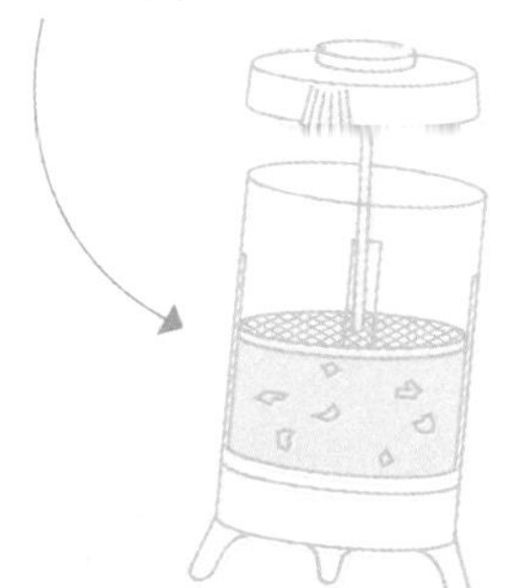

APPLICATION

SWEET TEA

8 TO 10 SERVINGS

The year was 1904. The place the St. Louis World's Fair. Among the many booths was that of Richard Blechynden, an English promoter who had been hired by a group of Indian tea growers to get the fairgoers tea-ed up. Problem was, there were no takers. It was just too darn hot that summer. Finally, in an act of inspired desperation, Blechynden poured his tea over ice. America would never be the same again.[2]

TIDBIT In the years since the show, I've taken to drinking iced green tea via cold extraction. I pour 3 pints cold, filtered water into a pitcher, pitch in 4 green teabags, and refrigerate for 2 hours. I don't take the bags out until the tea is gone.

SOFTWARE

FOR THE SIMPLE SYRUP

5	cups	sugar	
3	cups	H_2O	
6	medium	lemons	sliced (optional)
5	sprigs	fresh mint	(optional)

FOR THE TEA

1	quart	fresh H_2O	preferably filtered
1	ounce	loose black tea	
1	quart	room-temperature H_2O	

PROCEDURE

MAKE THE SIMPLE SYRUP:

1. In a **3-quart saucier**, combine the sugar and water. Slowly bring to a boil over medium heat, stirring occasionally. At this point, the simple syrup can be cooled and stored in an **airtight container** in the refrigerator for 1 month. For infused syrup, remove the pan from the heat and add the sliced lemons and sprigs of fresh mint. Cover, infuse for 10 minutes, strain, and store as you would simple syrup.

MAKE THE TEA:

2. Bring the quart of cold water to a boil over medium-high heat in a **kettle or small saucepan**.[3]
3. In a **large, heat-resistant container**, pour the boiling water over the loose tea and steep for 4 to 5 minutes. **Strain** the tea into the room-temperature water in a **large pitcher**. Serve over ice, sweetened with simple syrup if desired.

TIDBIT Tea doesn't contain as much caffeine as coffee, but it does contain polyphenols. And polyphenols help what caffeine is in tea to absorb slowly into the system, which is why tea drinkers get a longer-lasting but gentler lift.

TIDBIT Who drinks the most tea? The average Irishman, who consumes four cups a day.

[1] The electric kettle is indeed one of my favorite multitaskers. I boil eggs in it, keep broth warm for risotto in it, and use it any time I need boiling water.

[2] Actually, the above, as reported by me, is hooey. Although iced tea was served at the fair, and many may have been first exposed to it there, iced tea had long been a southern tradition. The true inventor or inventress has yet to be revealed.

[3] Besides a kettle to boil water, you also need a teapot in which to steep your leaves. Although I really dig Japanese cast-iron tea pots, in the years since this show was made I've pretty much ditched them in favor of a French coffee press because it's so much easier to separate the leaves from the brew.

CHILE'S ANGELS

EPISODE 55 | SEASON 4 | GOOD EATS

1966. North Hollywood. Gelson's Market. Produce department. Wednesday. I'm in the bottom of a grocery cart. Having failed in my third attempt to spring Cap'n Crunch from the clink, my finely tuned candy radar detects a bogey at three o'clock.

```
MOM: I'll be right back, Dear.
```

Mom turns her back on me, opening a window of opportunity I don't plan to waste. Scanning the verdant landscape of icky vegetables, I spy one hope. Some errant produceman has accidentally filled a nearby bin with a stack of jewel-like fruit candies, bright and shimmering. But which one to try? I'd never finish the big lime one before mom busted me. And cherry wasn't my favorite. But orange . . . orange never failed to satisfy.

I grab and, fearing imminent capture, shove the whole thing into my mouth and bite down.

After spitting out the remains of the habañero I flee to the bottom of the cart, gasping for breath and clawing at my throat in a futile attempt to put out the fire that threatened to consume my head. As my mother cries for help, I realize that there is something about this fruity Sterno sear that I dig. Sure, there is pain aplenty, but there was gain, too. Now, white-bread Wonder boy that I was, I hadn't a clue as to what to do with this new-found infatuation, so for years I left chiles in the hands of the professional practitioners of Mexican, Tex-Mex, and Asian cuisines.

Then came the day in 1991 when a chunky chile concoction called "salsa" beat out ketchup as the top-selling condiment in the country. Unwilling to shell out five bucks for what I knew could be made for one, I started cranking out my own salsas, and in doing so took charge of my own addiction.

In this episode I aimed to give people the intel they need to buy, handle, and cook fresh (and dry) chiles.

TIDBIT Capsaicin is not water soluble, so beer, tea, soda, or what have you are not effective at washing it away. Like most hydrophobic substances, capsaicin will hook up to fat, which is why milk, sour cream, and guacamole will each help to ease the pain. And, as Mr. Scoville displayed, sugar can also ease the misery. Curiously, combining sugar with chiles allows their true fruit flavors to emerge, which is why I like chiles in desserts.

TRIVIA The super-cool metal, sliding lab door rig was made from backsplash material from the hardware store and a stick-on garage door opener. Total cost: 50 bucks.

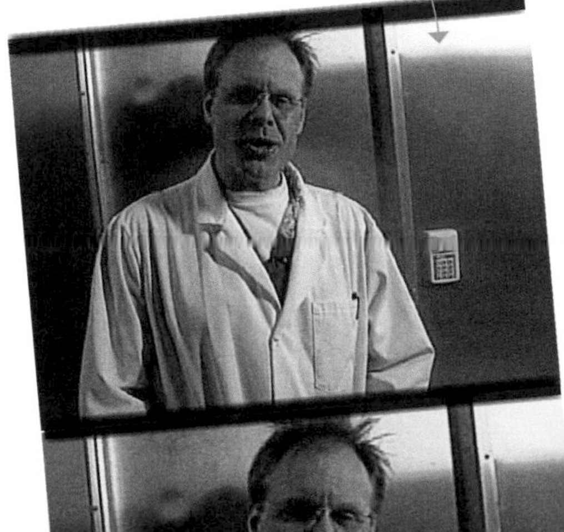

KNOWLEDGE CONCENTRATE

Chiles range in size from one to six inches. Immature specimens are usually green, while most mature models are red, yellow, or orange. They grow most abundantly in warm climates and can reach five feet in height.

When shopping, choose peppers that are bright in color and free of soft spots or blemishes. The skin of fresh peppers should be glossy and wrinkle free. Fresh peppers should be stashed in a paper bag in the refrigerator and used within a week. Dry peppers, which can last virtually forever, should be stored inside an airtight container in a cool, dry place.

The heat we mammals feel when we consume chiles is due to the chemical 8-methyl-N-vanillyl-6-nonenamide, which is molecularly related to vanilla. But what's important is how this unique molecule affects your tongue.

The human tongue sports a pretty impressive array of sensation centers called taste buds, each of which contains anywhere between fifty and a hundred taste cells capable of grappling with each of the five primary flavors: salty, sweet, sour, bitter, and umami.[1]

Each of these taste cells contains receptor cells along its tip.[2] And this receptor is keyed to fit a particular kind of molecule in food. When that molecule comes by—say, from a piece of asparagus, maybe some chocolate cake—the various components dock into the appropriate receptors, thus completing a series of chemical circuits that send a collective message to the brain, which we then perceive as asparagus, or maybe chocolate cake.

Now, the thing about capsaicin is that it doesn't care about chemical locks. In fact, there hasn't been a taste bud invented that capsaicin can't pick. It just wiggles its way down into that taste bud and locks into place. And when it does, it sends a unique message to the brain: "Hot!" How hot depends on how many taste buds are affected and how much capsaicin's in your capsicum.

Back in 1912, a researcher at Parke-Davis Pharmaceutical named Wilbur Scoville became interested in the neurological effects of capsaicin.[3] The problem is, when he tried to do controlled experiments with chiles, he was stymied by the fact that there was no scale, no way for him to know how hot one chile was compared to another. So he decided to get his lab together and devise his own capsicum heat scale.

Here was his method. He would take a chile—say, a bell pepper, which, despite the moniker, really is a chile—and he would cut off a little piece of it and grind it into a paste, which he would then feed to each of a number of volunteers. Then he would stand by with a container of sugar syrup and he would see how many squirts it took of that syrup to cool the fire in their mouths. Based on that data, he would assign that chile a certain rating based on scales of 100. And that scale became known as the Scoville Heat Scale. Here's how some popular chile models rate.

TIP When it comes to chiles, size matters. Smaller chiles are always hotter than larger chiles. Ditto green over red chiles, though there are always exceptions to all the rules, at least when it comes to chiles.

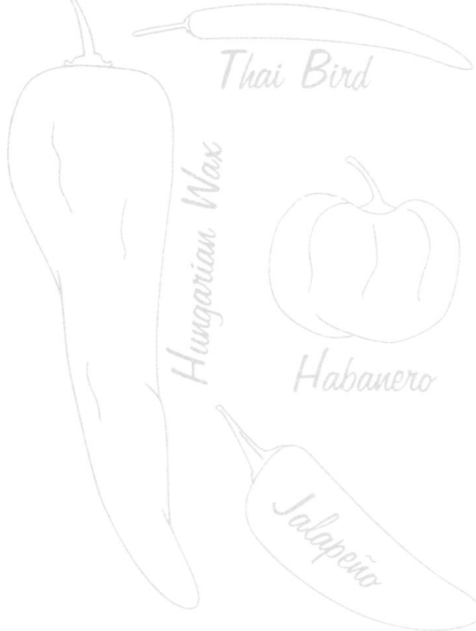

Type of pepper	Scoville rating
New Mexico	500–2,500
Poblano	1,000–1,500
Jalapeño	2,500–10,000
Serrano	10,000–20,000
Cayenne	30,000–50,000
Tabasco	30,000–50,000
Thai	50,000–100,000
Jamaican	100,000–200,000
Scotch Bonnet	100,000–250,000
Pepper Spray[4]	2,000,000–5,000,000
Pure capsaicin	15,000,000

APPLICATION

SALSA[5]

4 TO 6 SERVINGS

This salsa is better than the stuff in jars because it's fresh. The stuff in jars is, of course, cooked.

SOFTWARE

2	medium	jalapeño chiles	1 seeded and minced
6	(about 1 pound)	Roma tomatoes	chopped
4	cloves	garlic	minced
1	small	red bell pepper	chopped
½	small	red onion	finely chopped
1		dried ancho chile	snipped with scissors into strips and then into pieces
1	tablespoon	olive oil	
1	small	lime	juiced
1	teaspoon	kosher salt	
½	teaspoon	black pepper	freshly ground
	to taste	chili powder	
	to taste	cilantro, scallions, or parsley	finely chopped

PROCEDURE

1. Heat the broiler to high and move an oven rack to approximately 6 inches underneath it. Place the whole jalapeño on a **pie plate** and set it under the broiler. Using **tongs**, turn the chile every 2 to 3 minutes until the skin is black and crisp. Let the jalapeño cool slightly, then rub away the skin, remove the seeds, and mince.
2. In a **small mixing bowl**, combine the roasted jalapeño with the seeded and minced jalapeño, tomatoes, garlic, bell pepper, onion, ancho chile, olive oil, lime juice, salt, black pepper, chili powder, and herbs. Place in the refrigerator for at least 1 hour for flavor infusion.
3. Serve with tortilla chips.

TAKING SOME HEAT

Capsicum is sticky stuff, molecularly speaking, and once it's on your tools, your cutting board, or your hands it can hang around for days. It can even resist soap and water. Your best protection is to wear either latex or vinyl surgical gloves while handling your pods. You can buy them at any decent drugstore; just make sure you go for the vinyl if you have even a touch of latex allergy.

Capsaicin concentrates in the inner membrane and seeds of chiles, which is why I almost always remove them before use. This is especially true of jalapeños, whose sharp heat can render them completely inedible.

The seed cluster is almost always attached to the sides of the fruit with ribs. So we remove them. That's going to leave you with nothing but the fruit, which you can then fabricate however you choose: dice, mince, julienne, and so on.

TIDBIT Capsaicin is registered with the FDA as a repellent for everything from voles to humans. By the way, you macho types should know that capsaicin overload can result in contact dermatitis of the tongue, which can be fatal to your taste buds. Of course, they'll grow back in a couple of weeks, so, uh, it's up to you.

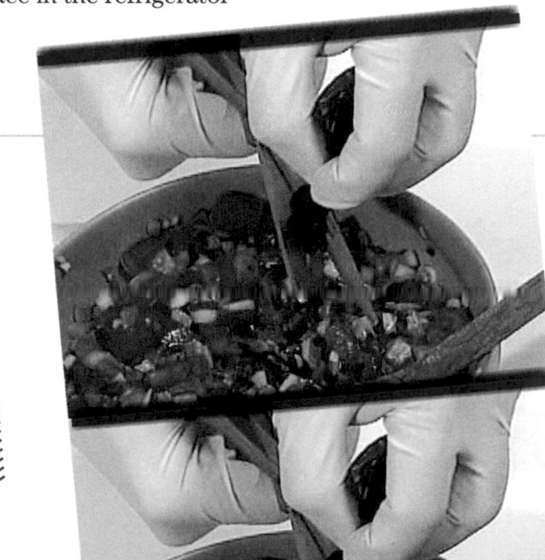

APPLICATION

HABAÑERO SALSA AND FIXINS

4 TO 6 SERVINGS

Heighten and illuminate the fruit flavor of habañeros by using sugar to counteract their considerable heat.

SOFTWARE

1	12-ounce can	crushed pineapple bits	
1	small	habañero chile	seeded and minced
4	leaves	fresh mint	bruise[6] three and cut the rest into thin strips
1	cup	corn or canola oil	
2	10-inch	corn tortillas	cut into 8 wedges each
¼	cup	sugar	
1	teaspoon	ground cinnamon	
		vanilla ice cream[7]	for serving

PROCEDURE

1. In a **2-quart saucepan**, combine the pineapple bits and habañero chile and simmer for 5 minutes. Transfer to a **small mixing bowl**, add the mint leaves, and place in the refrigerator to cool.
2. In a **2-quart saucepan** with a **deep-fry thermometer**, bring the oil to 325°F. Carefully add the tortilla wedges and cook until golden brown on each side, approximately 3 minutes total. Drain on paper towels.
3. In a **small bowl**, combine the sugar and cinnamon with a **fork**. Liberally dust the warm tortillas with the sugar-and-cinnamon mixture.
4. Remove the mint leaves from the chilled pineapple sauce and serve the sauce over vanilla ice cream with the tortillas and sliced mint.

[1] Back when this show was produced, umami was still an issue for debate. It's a meaty, "glutamic" flavor found in certain mushrooms, MSG, and other ingredients. It's a Japanese thing, and I for one am not a hundred percent sure that it exists.

[2] By the way, this means that the elementary-school map of the tongue they shoved down our collective throats was completely, utterly wrong.

[3] Because of its curious effect on nerve endings, capsaicin is used to treat postsurgical pain and one day, perhaps, certain types of cancer. At the time Scoville was working, the subject was arthritis.

[4] Not for culinary use.

[5] *Salsa* is Spanish for "sauce."

[6] To bruise the mint, simply wad it up and rub it between your palms. This will break enough of the cell structure to release essential oils.

[7] See page 38 for a great version.

A FEW WORDS ABOUT A FEW WORDS

CHILLI
A Nahuatl word that refers to the edible fruits of the Capsicans, a genus of plants in the nightshade family. Native Americans in Central America have been cultivating them for at least seven thousand years.

CAPSICUM
Another New World word that roughly translates to "the bite that bites."

CHILE
What the Spaniards did to the above term.

PEPPER
The stuff that Christopher Columbus promised to bring back. Although there wasn't any *Piper nigrum* in the New World, there were plenty of hot pods, so he decided to call them "peppers." Problem solved.

CHILI
Strictly a North American term for a meaty stew (often with beans) seasoned with chiles or, in most cases . . .

CHILI POWDER
A mixture of dried chiles, cumin, black pepper, various herbs, and sometimes cinnamon.

CHILE POWDER
Contains nothing but ground dried chiles.

DEEP SPACE SLIME

EPISODE 56 | SEASON 5 | GOOD EATS

The beginning of season 5 marked our move to a new kitchen location

which was good news because the old white one was small and pitiously appointed. Problem was, our new digs wouldn't be ready to roll until after our scheduled start date. So we needed a show that could shoot entirely on location. I'd wanted to do a gelatin show for a while and liked the whole special effects movie angle and so "Deep Space Slime" was born—completely out of necessity.

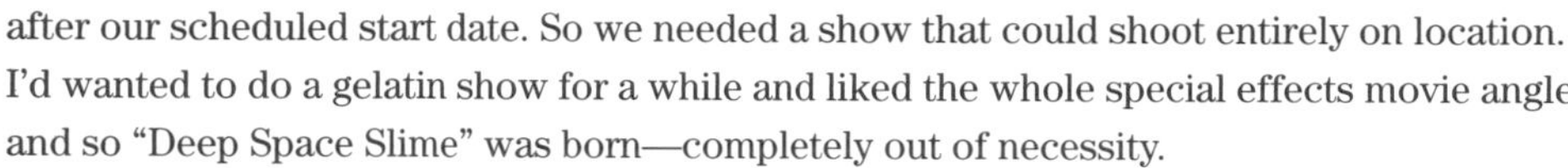

This episode also marked my first as director of the series. A job I'm happy to say I've had ever since—mostly because I'm cheap. Hey, that's show biz.

TIDBIT | Gelatin is used in many prepared foods, from marshmallows and gummy bears to ice cream and medicine capsules—though I'll admit one of those is not really food. Also, the emulsions that make photographic film possible are composed of gelatin. Oh, and let's not forget paint-ball capsules, which are also made up of gelatin.

TIDBIT | Although most of us consider gelatin a dessert, historically it's been a savory ingredient used to set vinegar, wine, and vegetable juices, the classic example being aspic, which if you ask me is about the worst name for a food you could ever concoct.

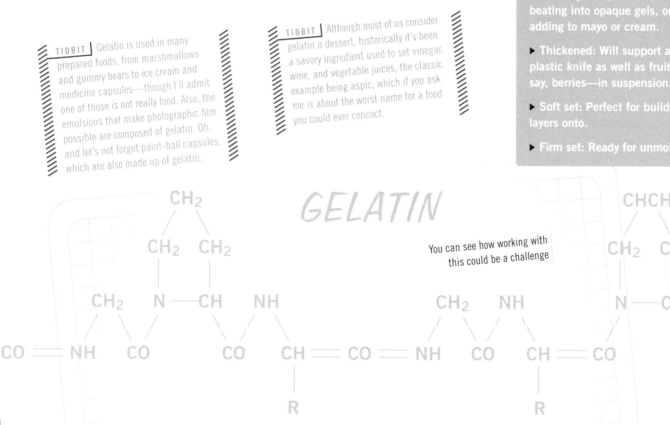

GOOD EATS'S FOUR DEGREES OF GEL SET

- **Egg-white consistency:** Good for adding to layered molds, beating into opaque gels, or adding to mayo or cream.
- **Thickened:** Will support a plastic knife as well as fruit—say, berries—in suspension.
- **Soft set:** Perfect for building layers onto.
- **Firm set:** Ready for unmolding.

GELATIN

You can see how working with this could be a challenge

KNOWLEDGE CONCENTRATE

Gelatin is a flavorless, colorless matter derived from the collagen in animals' connective tissue and bones.[1] It's a pure protein containing specific amounts of eighteen different amino acids joined together in sequences to form polypeptide chains scientifically known as the primary structure.

Three of these polypeptide chains form this way, joined together as a left-handed spiral to create the secondary structure. In the tertiary structure, the spiral winds and folds itself into a right-handed spiral, which results in a rod-shaped molecule, the so-called protofibril.

All you really need to know is that gelatin strands are long and very thin. And they move around a lot. That is, until they drop below about, umm, 50°F. Then they slow down and start to tangle up. The result? A microscopic mesh capable of holding a flavorful liquid—say, a margarita—in a firm gel. What's really cool is that the electrostatic bonds responsible for holding this together are relatively weak. In fact, as long as the gelatin isn't very acidic and isn't exposed to heat in excess of 150°F, it can be melted and reset again and again and again and again.

Gelatin is sold in two forms:

SHEET GELATIN: Preferred by four out of five pastry professionals because it's easy to measure. A sheet's a sheet. Typically, sheet gelatins (especially those from Europe) are of a higher grade than . . .

POWDERED GELATIN: Powdered gelatin is readily available, easy to use, and always comes in ¼-ounce packets. When properly handled it produces a jewel-clear gel, but that gel tends to melt at a lower temperature than gels set with sheet gelatin.

Always bloom gelatin in cold water. Adding gelatin directly to hot liquid can cause the exterior of the gelatin granules or sheets to hydrate quickly, developing a coating that keeps the center of the granules from absorbing water. Direct contact with hot liquid may also cause the granules to clump, which may cause the gelatin to lose some of its ability to absorb water and set properly.

Almost any water-based fluid will do, from soda-pop to wine to fruit juices, with the exception of fresh pineapple, mango, papaya, and kiwi juices, which contain a protein-munching enzyme that destroys gelatin. Heat deactivates this enzyme, so canned and pasteurized versions of these are okay.

Also keep in mind that salt and acid will weaken gel strength, but dairy, sugar, and alcohol will strengthen it.

MOLDS

- A mold used for gelatins can be any clean, nonporous, watertight form. Most molds are made from spun or extruded aluminum, so they can double as cake pans. Newer, less traditional molds are vacuum formed from food-grade plastic.
- Every time you get a new mold, fill it right up to the top with water, then pour it off into a measuring cup to determine its exact volume. Write the volume on the side of the mold so you never forget.
- Spritz your landing zone with water to prevent sticking.
- When it comes to unmolding, metal molds need a little coercing. Skip the traditional hot water routine and turn your mold over, place it on the target platter, and hit it with a hair dryer.

TIDBIT *Gelatin* comes from the Latin *gelatus*, meaning "stiff."

HOW IT'S MADE

These days, most commercial gelatin is produced by treating cattle and pig skins with various chemicals and then boiling them in water, which converts the connective tissue collagen (via hydrolyzation) into gelatin, creating a solution. The resulting solution is cooled, then cut into thin strips and dried. This dried product is either ground into powder or redissolved and set into commercial sheets.

AB (VO): In days of old, the Gelatin Maker's task took him to the barn, where he had to find a pig or, better yet, a calf. After dispatching the creature, the collagen-rich legs and hooves had to be "harvested."

The appendages were scraped and split and boiled for up to twelve hours so that the collagen would dissolve into gelatin. After defatting and straining, the brew had to be boiled yet again, this time clarified with the whites and shells of a dozen eggs.

Once the liquid was strained and flavored, it had to be poured into molds and refrigerated overnight. A tough task, considering there were no refrigerators at the time. The next day, if nothing had gone wrong, the Gelatin Maker was rewarded with a quivering tower of jewel-like jelly. Wha-ha-ha-ha-ha!

TRIVIA The "Igor harvesting hooves" sequence remains one of my all-time favorite *Good Eats* scenes. The sets were made out of cardboard . . . literally.

APPLICATION

PANNA COTTA BRAIN WITH CRANBERRY GLAZE

6 TO 8 SERVINGS

Panna cotta is Italian for "cooked cream," which is funny since it is barely cooked at all. It's a classic relative of the Spanish flan but made with gelatin.

SOFTWARE

FOR THE PANNA COTTA

3	12-ounce cans	evaporated milk	
1	ounce	unflavored powdered gelatin	
1½	cups	heavy cream	
5	ounces	sugar	
1		vanilla bean	split and scraped
1	teaspoon	fine salt	
¼	cup	bourbon	(optional)
		food coloring	as desired

FOR THE GLAZE

¼	ounce	unflavored powdered gelatin	
2	cups	cranberry juice	divided

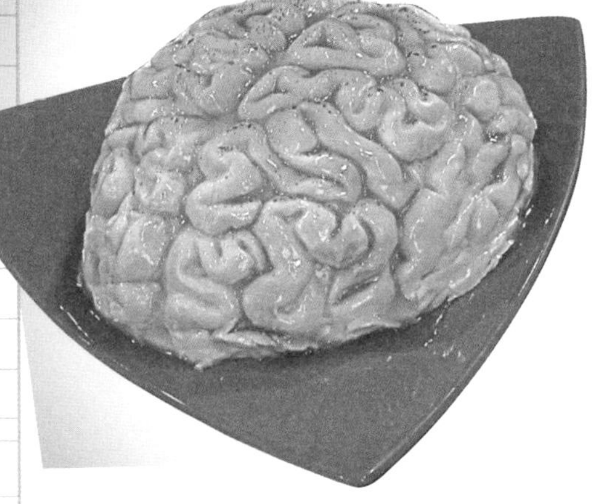

TIDBIT Inspired by his wife's laborious preparation of a calves' foot jelly in 1890, one Charles B. Knox, of Jamestown, New York, set out to manufacture a dry, prepackaged and easy-to-use form of gelatin. The Knox brand of plain powdered gelatin is the market standard to this day. Not long after, another New Yorker named May Wait added sugar and artificial flavoring to the equation and called it . . . Jell-O. The product didn't catch on until after refrigerators became commonplace.

PROCEDURE

MAKE THE PANNA COTTA:

1. Combine 1 can of the evaporated milk with the gelatin in a **medium mixing bowl** and bloom for 5 minutes.
2. Put the remaining evaporated milk, the cream, sugar, vanilla bean, salt, and bourbon in a **3-quart saucier** and bring to a bare simmer over medium heat. As soon as you see bubbles in the mixture, pour it into the gelatin mixture and stir until all the solids have dissolved. Add food coloring if using.
3. Cool at room temperature for 1 hour. Pour through a **strainer** to remove the vanilla bean, into a **6-cup brain mold.** Refrigerate overnight to fully set.

MAKE THE GLAZE:

4. Combine the gelatin with ½ cup of the cranberry juice in a **small bowl** and let bloom for 10 minutes.
5. Put the remaining cranberry juice in a **2-quart saucepan** and bring to a boil. Remove from the heat and pour it into the gelatin mixture, stirring to dissolve the solids. Transfer to a **squeeze bottle** and leave at room temperature until the panna cotta brain is set.
6. Unmold the panna cotta and drizzle the glaze over it. The glaze will set up immediately.

APPLICATION

SPARKLING GINGERED FACE

10 TO 12 SERVINGS

Although the recipe we presented on the show works just fine, we like this one better.

SOFTWARE

1	750ml bottle	sparkling white wine	cold; such as Champagne or prosecco[2]
2¼	ounces	unflavored powdered gelatin	
5	cups	ginger beer	
3	tablespoons	sugar	

TIP | For a firm gel, use 2 teaspoons powdered gelatin per cup of flavorful liquid. For a softer set, go with 1 teaspoon per cup.

PROCEDURE

1. Put the Champagne and gelatin in a **mixing bowl** and stir to combine. Let bloom for 5 minutes.
2. Combine the ginger beer and sugar in a **3-quart saucepan** and bring to a boil over high heat. Remove from the heat and add to the gelatin mixture, stirring to dissolve the solids. Pour into a **9-cup face mold.**[3] Refrigerate overnight to set.

[1] If you've ever made a homemade chicken stock that has set up in the fridge, that's gelatin.

[2] Prosecco is an effervescent white wine from Italy; it's a lot like Champagne.

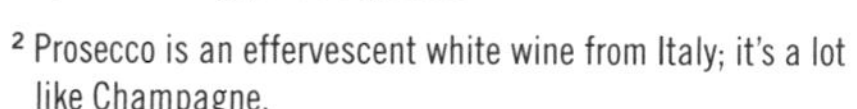

[3] Check the internet for unusual molds.

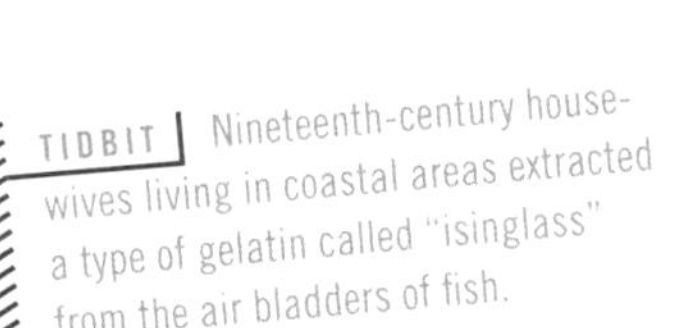

TIDBIT | Nineteenth-century housewives living in coastal areas extracted a type of gelatin called "isinglass" from the air bladders of fish.

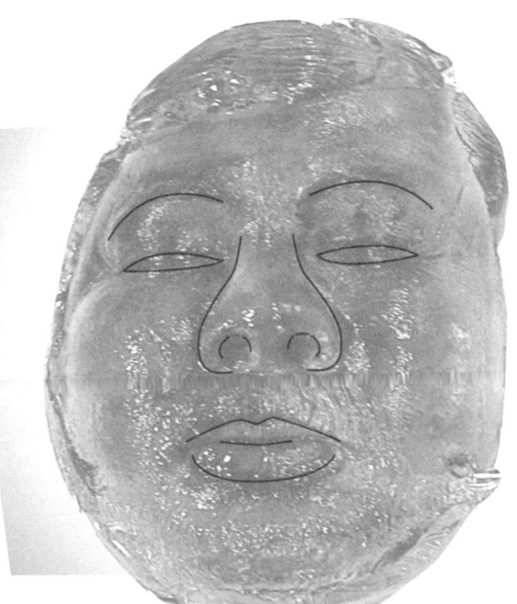

I have no idea who this is supposed to be. These days you can buy kits and make a reusable silicone mold of your own face. Sweet!

OAT CUISINE

EPISODE 57 | SEASON 5 | GOOD EATS

The eighteenth-century English essayist Samuel Johnson described oats in his *Dictionary of the English Language* as "a grain, which in England is generally given to horses, but in Scotland supports the people." A few years later, his own biographer, the equally venerable James Boswell, himself a Scot, wrote back, "Aye, which is why in England you'll raise fine horses, while in Scotland we'll raise fine peepul." Bad accents and cultural differences notwithstanding, it turns out that oats are, well, pretty much a wonder food, and this episode set out to prove it.

This remains one of my top five favorite episodes. It's a cool subject, and there were some pretty nifty scenes in here—for example, the grocery track pull, the Barbie doll love triangle, and, of course, the infamous haggis fiasco.

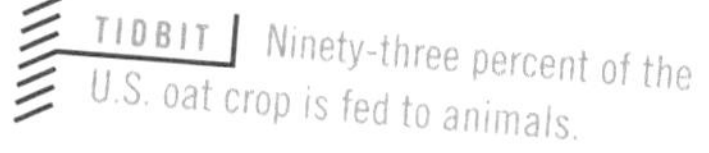

TIDBIT | Ninety-three percent of the U.S. oat crop is fed to animals.

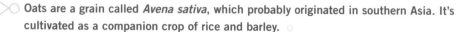

KNOWLEDGE CONCENTRATE

Oats are a grain called *Avena sativa*, which probably originated in southern Asia. It's cultivated as a companion crop of rice and barley.

Oats are available in a variety of forms, and it does make a difference which one you use for each application:

WHOLE OATS (GROATS): Oats with only the outer hull removed. They still have their entire bran coat on, a lot like brown rice—and also taste kind of like brown rice. Even if you soak them overnight and cook them for hours, they're chewy as Gumby.

STEEL-CUT OATS (SCOTCH OATS, IRISH OATS, PINHEAD OATS): The groats are run through steel cutters into two or four pieces. They take a little while to cook, but produce a very creamy porridge. Easily found among the other grains in the megamart, usually sold in an airtight tin can.

ROLLED OATS (OLD-FASHIONED OATS, OATMEAL): Steel-cut oats that are steamed, pressed out in rollers, and then dried. These are the oats we usually think of when if we think of oats. The idea of mashing them flat? That was an American thing. The thinner they are, the faster they cook. The problem is, faster is not always better. In fact, compared to steel-cut, they tend to produce a rather insipid mush.

QUICK-COOKING OATS: Like rolled oats, but made with groats that have been cut into very small pieces.

INSTANT OATS: Rolled oats mashed even thinner, then par-cooked and dried. I wouldn't feed them to my horse.

OAT BRAN: The outer layer of the grain, just under the hull. Bran is included in most cut and rolled oats but can also be purchased by itself. (Why you'd want to, I have no clue.)

OAT FLOUR: Can be used in various breads and cookies, but since it contains no gluten it's not a substitute for wheat flour.

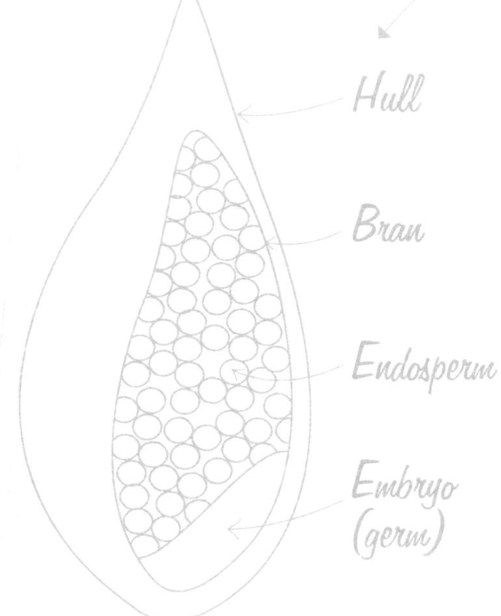

TRIVIA Paul and I were "real" Scotsmen for that scene. Even if my accent (as always) tends more to Australia than Aberdeen.

And now, the infamous haggis scene:

Sew, yew want tu make a Hah-gis. Well, step one is you're gonna have to find a stoomick, a ship's (sheep's) stoomick, and sook it overrrnight in salty water, right?

Step tew, you're gonna have to find yourself soom bits and pieces like a ship's tongue, a ship's long, a ship's liver or bladder, and the like.

Step three, is yew put 'em in the salty water and bring 'em to a burrl for at least two 'owers. Excellent.

Nowew, when they're done, take outs your parrts and put 'em out on the cuttin' board. Ew, be careful about the burlin' water, would yuu? Now, hack at them until they're little eentzy, beentzy bits, bein' extra careful to look out for any skin or grilse or you'll get the back of me hand!

Next, hack inta maybe three or even four u'nions while you're at it. Now that that's duun, gew ahead and add half a pound of suet chopped fine . . .

APPLICATION

OVERNIGHT OATMEAL

4 SERVINGS

Start the oatmeal right before you go to bed, and your oatmeal will be finished by morning. Remember, though, that we are leaving an appliance on overnight, and that can be kind of dangerous. So make sure you've got it on a nice stable platform without any flammables around. Sweet dreams.

TIDBIT | Muesli, or Swiss oatmeal, is usually cooked or soaked overnight.

// SOFTWARE

1	cup	steel-cut oats	
1	cup	dried cranberries	
½	cup	dried figs	chopped
1	quart	H_2O	
½	cup	heavy cream	
1	large pinch	kosher salt	

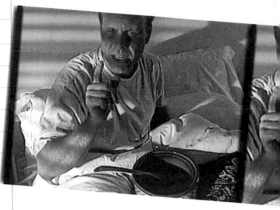

// PROCEDURE

1. Combine the oats, cranberries, figs, water, and cream in a **slow cooker**[1] and set to low heat. Cover and cook for 8 to 9 hours.
2. Stir, season with salt,[2] and remove to **serving bowls**.

TRIVIA | The haggis Paul and I prepared in full *Braveheart* regalia was in no way meant to be taken seriously. If any of you purchased sheep's stomachs with the express purpose of preparing this dish . . . sorry.

Once you've hacked it all into wee bits, add half a bag of Scotch oats. Right. Nowew, time to stoof the stoomick. Don't be shy. (Camera hangs back) Don't be shy! (Camera approaches)

Nowyer, stoof you're soppin' stoomick full of the mixture thusly. Right! Get yourself a wee bit of string and tie it up into a lovely, knotily portion and boil it fer three hours to three days but not a minute longer . . . or you'll get the back of me hand!

APPLICATION

GRANOLA

APPROXIMATELY 1½ POUNDS; 12 SERVINGS

The original recipe was written with volumetric measures. We've converted to weight because it's a lot easier in this case to weigh the ingredients. The dry team can be measured all in one bowl as long as your scale has a tare function, and the liquids can be weighed in a plunger cup. Also, we've done away with the parchment-paper pan lining, as it tends to stick to the granola in a most unappealing way.

// SOFTWARE

10	ounces	rolled oats	
4½	ounces	slivered almonds	
5	ounces	raw cashews	
1½	ounces	unsweetened shredded coconut	
3	ounces	dark brown sugar	
¾	teaspoon	kosher salt	
3	ounces	maple syrup	
2	ounces	vegetable oil	
4	ounces	raisins	or other dried fruit

// PROCEDURE

1. Heat the oven to 250°F.
2. Combine the oats, nuts, coconut, brown sugar, and salt in a **large bowl**.
3. Measure the syrup and oil into a **plunger cup**. Add to the dry mixture and stir to combine.
4. Transfer the mixture to a **half sheet pan** and bake on the middle rack of the oven for 1 hour and 15 minutes, stirring every 15 minutes to achieve an even color.
5. Remove from the oven and transfer to a **large bowl** and cool for 30 minutes. Add the raisins and mix until evenly distributed. Store in an airtight container and enjoy for up to 2 weeks.

Can also be used in self defense!

TIDBIT In Scotland, oatmeal is stirred with a special stick called a "spurtle."

APPLICATION

REFRESCO DE AVENA

4 8-OUNCE SERVINGS

Although most of us don't think of oatmeal as a drink, in the Caribbean they do. I enjoyed a version of the following while visiting St. Martin. Good and good for you.

SOFTWARE

½	cup	demerara sugar	
1	quart	H_2O	slightly warmer than body temperature
½	cup	rolled oats	
1	small	lime	peeled, body reserved for squeezing
¼	teaspoon	cardamom seeds	(optional)

PROCEDURE

Dissolve the sugar in the water. Steep the oatmeal in the sugar water with the lime peel, and cardamom, if using, for an hour. **Strain** and serve with a squeeze of the lime juice.

[1] There are a lot of electric cookers on the market, and most have metal inserts. And since metal is such a fast conductor, as the thermostat cycles on and off the food goes through the highs and lows. At Good Eats Industries we recommend a cooker with a ceramic interior and a thermostat that goes from a simmer all the way up to 425°F. This dish can also be accomplished overnight in a heavy Dutch oven in a 250°F oven.

[2] Oats are loaded with polysaccharides called pentosans, which must fully hydrolize before the oat they're in can soften. Salt can hinder this process, which is why it's better not to add salt until cooking is well under way.

A FEW WORDS ON FIBER

You can't talk about oats without talking about fiber, 'cause you've gotta have fiber if you're going to be regular and you gotta be regular if you're going to be happy, right? What is fiber? It's usually defined as the portion of a plant that we eat but can't easily digest.

There are two kinds of dietary fiber, soluble and insoluble, and they act very differently inside the ol' gastrointestinal tract. Insoluble fiber won't dissolve in water, so it tends to move through the body very quickly, taking whatever groceries are around with it. Hence its nickname, "nature's broom."

Soluble fiber does dissolve in water. In fact, in the body it turns into a kind of thick, viscous gel, which moves very slowly toward, well . . . where it's going. And that's good, because if you eat a food that's really high in soluble fiber, your stomach stays fuller longer—so, odds are, you'll eat less. Soluble fiber also slows the absorption of glucose into the body, which means you're going to avoid those nasty sugar peaks and dips. What's more, it inhibits the reabsorption of bile into the system, which means your liver is going to have to get its cholesterol fix from your blood, which means your blood-serum cholesterol's going to go down. Oats contain more soluble fiber than any other grain. I pity the poor fool who don't eat his oatmeal.

CRÊPE EXPECTATIONS

EPISODE 58 | SEASON 5 | GOOD EATS

In making this episode I had to get over my fear of crêpes, which up to this point was unilateral and nonnegotiable. My crêpe skills were so bad that in culinary school they called me "crêpe killer." Truth is, crêpes are simple (if not easy) critters to conjure if you have the right batter, the right pan, and some patience.

SHIRLEY CORRIHER: (Answering phone) Suicidal Chef's Hotline. This is Shirley.

AB: (On phone) Shirley. Shirley. It's Alton Brown calling.

SC: Alton, what did they do? Cancel the program?

AB: No. It's worse than that. It's my crepes. They're fat and lumpy.

SC: Fat crepes. Sounds like leavening to me, Alton. Did you add any baking powder to them?

AB: No. No. No, I would never do that.

SC: Did you let the batter rest for a full hour?

AB: Should I have?

SC: Yeah. Absolutely. You need time for the bubbles to escape and you need to hydrate your starch so they'll be nice and tender. Lumpy. How'd you mix these together?

AB: Well, a whisk, of course.

SC: Go with a blender, Alton. It's much, much smoother and much, much faster. Try that and give me a call later, okay?

AB: Okay. I will. Thanks. Thanks, Shirley. (Sighs)

KNOWLEDGE CONCENTRATE

- Crêpes are nothing more than wafer-thin, unleavened pancakes. More often than not, they are served filled, folded into quarters, and sauced.
- The word *crêpe* (pronounced "crep" not "craip") is French for "pancake" and comes from *crispus*, which is Latin for "wavy" or "curly." The original models hail from Brittany, where they are traditionally constructed of buckwheat flour, which, since it doesn't contain gluten, makes for a very tender crêpe indeed.
- Traditionally, crêpes are prepared in a "black" steel pan with very low, sloped edges. Such pans can still be found, but they're very tricky to deal with. I strongly prefer a nonstick skillet with sloping sides, preferably one with a distinct bottom.
- And you don't really need one of those "neat little wooden spreaders"; just use a smooth circular motion to swirl the batter in the pan.
- No matter how many crêpes you make, you'll mess up at least one per batch. But so what? Sprinkle some sugar on it and enjoy it as a snack. Or feed it to the family dog.

Note: bubbles at edges means crêpe is ready to flip.

Teflon Polymer

F = FLUORINE
C = CARBON

$$\cdots \mathrm{-}\underset{\substack{|\\F}}{\overset{\substack{F\\|}}{C}}\mathrm{-}\underset{\substack{|\\F}}{\overset{\substack{F\\|}}{C}}\mathrm{-}\underset{\substack{|\\F}}{\overset{\substack{F\\|}}{C}}\mathrm{-}\underset{\substack{|\\F}}{\overset{\substack{F\\|}}{C}}\mathrm{-}\underset{\substack{|\\F}}{\overset{\substack{F\\|}}{C}}\mathrm{-}\underset{\substack{|\\F}}{\overset{\substack{F\\|}}{C}}\mathrm{-}\underset{\substack{|\\F}}{\overset{\substack{F\\|}}{C}}\mathrm{-}\underset{\substack{|\\F}}{\overset{\substack{F\\|}}{C}}\mathrm{-}\underset{\substack{|\\F}}{\overset{\substack{F\\|}}{C}}\mathrm{-}\underset{\substack{|\\F}}{\overset{\substack{F\\|}}{C}}\mathrm{-}\underset{\substack{|\\F}}{\overset{\substack{F\\|}}{C}}\mathrm{-}\underset{\substack{|\\F}}{\overset{\substack{F\\|}}{C}}\mathrm{-}\underset{\substack{|\\F}}{\overset{\substack{F\\|}}{C}} \cdots$$

ON NONSTICK SURFACES

One day in 1938 a Dupont scientist named Doctor Roy Plunkett was playing around with a gas called tetrafluoroethylene. He was trying to make a coolant like Freon, but he made a mistake and polymerized the gas into this kind of nasty, waxy solid, which was chemically inert and extremely slippery. He didn't know what to do with it, but he went ahead and named it polytetrafluoroethylene, or Teflon for short. The military used it for a while, as a coating for atom bomb parts and missile nose cones. But it took a French fisherman to put it to culinary use. He started by putting it on fishing tackle so that it wouldn't tangle up, and then his wife asked him to put it inside one of her pots. The rest is nonstick history. The pans made the couple a mint, and to this day Teflon is considered the slipperiest substance on Earth.

Addendum: Since this episode first aired, a lot has been written about the fact that at high temperatures Teflon can give off toxic fumes. Since this fretful event does not commence until the vessel reaches a temperature of 550°F, it is of no concern to the crêpe maker.

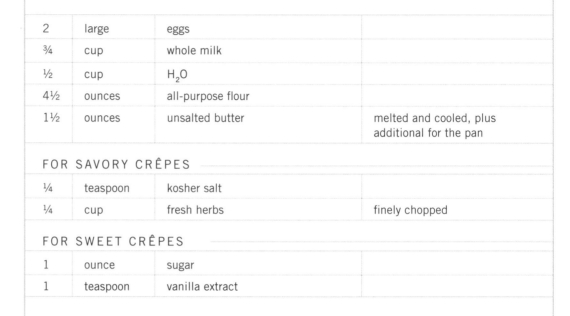

APPLICATION — **CRÊPES**

12 TO 16 CRÊPES

What we're after here are flat, uniform disks that are pliant, pliable and tasty.

SOFTWARE

2	large	eggs	
¾	cup	whole milk	
½	cup	H_2O	
4½	ounces	all-purpose flour	
1½	ounces	unsalted butter	melted and cooled, plus additional for the pan

FOR SAVORY CRÊPES

¼	teaspoon	kosher salt	
¼	cup	fresh herbs	finely chopped

FOR SWEET CRÊPES

1	ounce	sugar	
1	teaspoon	vanilla extract	

PROCEDURE

1. Place the eggs, milk, water, flour, melted butter, and additional ingredients for savory or sweet crêpes in a **blender**[1] and blend for 7 to 10 seconds. Rest the crêpe batter in the refrigerator for 1 hour.[2]
2. If you plan to serve the crêpes soon, heat the oven to 200°F or its lowest setting.
3. Place a **10-inch nonstick pan** over medium heat and coat it with butter. Heat the butter until it begins to sizzle. Pour 1 ounce of the batter into the center of the pan and swirl the pan to spread it around evenly. Cook for 30 seconds, or until the edges of the crêpe begin to turn up. **Flip** and cook for another 10 seconds.
4. Place the crêpes in the oven on a **cooling rack set in a half sheet pan** and cover with a **tea towel** until all of the crêpes are ready. If you plan to serve them later, remove them to a **cutting board** and lay them out flat so they can cool. After they have cooled, stack them, separated with **sheets of parchment paper**, and store in **zip-top plastic bags** in the refrigerator for a week or in the freezer for up to a month. When using frozen crêpes, thaw the stack on a cooling rack, then gently peel them apart.

TIP | If you prefer darker, crisper crêpes, use a little more butter.

APPLICATION

MUSHROOM CRÊPE CAKE[3]

6 SERVINGS

This is what I do with all my leftover crêpes.

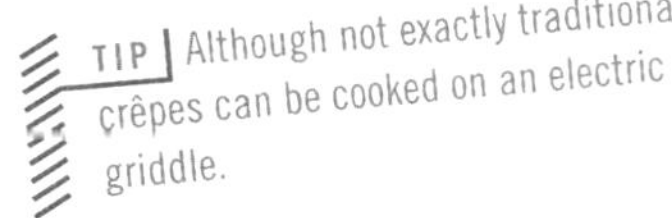

TIP Although not exactly traditional, crêpes can be cooked on an electric griddle.

// SOFTWARE

8	ounces	shiitake mushrooms	thinly sliced
8	ounces	cremini mushrooms	thinly sliced
2	tablespoons	unsalted butter	plus additional for the pan
1	medium	onion	diced
1	teaspoon	kosher salt	
¼	teaspoon	black pepper	freshly ground
½	cup	whole milk	
2	ounces	provolone cheese	shredded
6 to 8		savory crêpes	
2	tablespoons	chives	chopped
1½	ounces	Parmesan cheese	shredded

// PROCEDURE

1. Finely chop half of the shiitake and cremini mushrooms. Set aside.
2. Heat the broiler to high.
3. Place a **12-inch sauté pan** over medium-low heat and add the 2 tablespoons butter. When it has melted, add the onion and cook until translucent, about 5 minutes. Add all the mushrooms, the salt, and pepper and cook, stirring occasionally, until the mushrooms are soft and the entire mixture has reduced to about one third of its original volume, 4 to 5 minutes.
4. Add the milk and cook until the mixture becomes a loose paste,[4] about 2 minutes. Add the provolone and cook for another minute.
5. Lay two crêpes in the center of a **buttered half sheet pan**. (This way if the bottom one sticks you can still remove your "cake" from the pan.)
6. Spread a thin layer of the mushroom mixture on the crêpes. Sprinkle a few chives on top. Top with another crêpe, more mushroom filling, and chives. Repeat until you are out of filling. Top with one last crêpe and sprinkle on the Parmesan.
7. Place under the broiler until the Parmesan is melted and golden brown, about 4 minutes. Transfer to a **cutting board** and cool for 5 minutes before slicing into 6 wedges. Serve immediately.

APPLICATION

CRÊPES SUZETTE

4 SERVINGS

Through much of the twentieth century, no dessert could top this one—crêpes filled with an orange sauce, rolled, and flambéed with orange liqueur—for elegance and sophistication. Although several myths claim to tell the tale of Suzette's origin (as is true of every dish bearing a woman's name), no one really knows the who, where, why, or how on this one.

TIDBIT | Use a sharp knife to cut off the top and bottom of the orange, then peel it (using the knife) from top to bottom, the way you might a melon, removing all the pith. Carefully cradle the fruit in one hand and cut inward with the other, going right down either side of the membrane to liberate each segment. That's a supreme, a perfect wedge of orangy goodness. The color orange, by the way, stems from a group of nutrients called carotenoids, not unlike those found in carrots.

SOFTWARE

¼	cup	orange juice	freshly squeezed
2	tablespoons	Grand Marnier	
¼	ounce	sugar	
¼	ounce	light brown sugar	
1½	ounces	unsalted butter	
1		orange	zest finely grated, flesh cut into supremes (see tidbit, left)
4		sweet crêpes	
		vanilla ice cream	optional

PROCEDURE

1. Place an **8-inch sauté pan** over medium heat and add the orange juice, liqueur, and sugars. **Whisk** until the liquid reduces slightly, about 1 minute.
2. Add the butter,[5] and when the sauce "tightens," after about 1 minute, use **tongs** to gently lay a crêpe in the pan. Turn it to coat it with sauce. Lay it out on a **serving plate** and fold it into quarters. Repeat with the remaining crêpes.
3. Add the orange zest and supremes to the remaining sauce, then pour it over the crêpes and serve immediately—as is or with ice cream.

[1] No blender? Build a batter in your food processor using 5 to 10 quick pulses.

[2] The batter will keep for up to 24 hours in the fridge; just be sure to stir it thoroughly before using.

[3] This is one of my favorite *Good Eats* applications.

[4] This paste of mushrooms and onions cooked together is called "duxelles." You can use it as a soup base, a sauce base, or you can stuff it into crêpes.

[5] *Monter au beurre:* To incorporate, with a whisk or rotating movements, butter into a sauce. It is applied during the final phases of sauce making.

TIDBIT | The most popular crêpe filling in France is jam. Personally I go for Nutella

CELEBRITY ROAST

EPISODE 59 | SEASON 5 | GOOD EATS

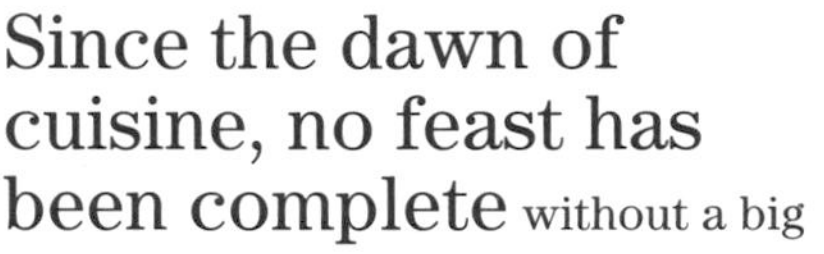

Since the dawn of cuisine, no feast has been complete without a big ol' hunk of roast beast. The trouble is that every time a modern cook reaches for one of those skimpy little single-serving cuts at the megamart, the roast and its marvelous mound of leftovers inches closer to extinction—and that is a real shame. Because if history has taught us anything it's that no matter how lame the toast, a good roast is always good eats.

TIDBIT If your oven walls are all scummed up, the energy meant for your roast is being either deflected or absorbed by the grunge on your oven walls. While your roast is still going to cook, in the end it's going to end up being done on one side and underdone on the other.

TRIVIA The scene with the papier-mâché chicken in the racquetball court is one of my favorite *Good Eats* science skits. But I'll tell you this, my friends, tennis balls fired by a machine can put a hurtin' on you.

RIB EYE

CHUCK
RIB
SHORT LOIN
SIRLOIN
ROUND

USDA CHOICE

TIDBIT The term "prime rib" is almost always a misnomer, as very little of what is served as prime rib is actually Prime-grade beef. The correct term is "standing rib roast." Now, if you have a standing rib roast that is Prime grade you would have a Prime standing rib roast. I've cooked a couple such hunks and thought they were way too fatty. To my taste, Choice-grade meat makes for the best standing rib roast.

KNOWLEDGE CONCENTRATE

Like *barbecue*, *toast*, and *cream*, the word *roast* suffers from multiple meaning disorder. Among its many connotations, *roast* can refer to the exposure of food to dry heat, as in "chestnuts roasting on an open fire." *Roast* can also mean any cut of meat that can be or has been prepared by such action. (Technically, this means that pot roast isn't a roast at all because it's braised.) On the other hand, would you call a roasted turkey a "roast"? Of course not. So, for our purposes, a roast is a big hunk of mammal cooked in dry heat and carved at table.

All true roasts share certain common physical characteristics. For one thing, they've got a low surface-to-mass ratio, meaning they're shaped more like *Sputnik* than, say, a dictionary. They also work and play well with dry heat, and that means they should come from relatively tender regions of the body.

Like balsamic vinegar and hard cheese, beef improves with age. That's because like vinegar and cheese, beef is mostly water. In fact, about eight and a half pounds of a ten-and-a-half-pound roast is water, a substance not famous for flavor. However, in just a few days you can eliminate enough of that water to seriously intensify the flavor of the meat. This takes time, but that's okay, because meanwhile, enzymes inside the meat will be hard at work breaking down connective tissue, and that means a more tender piece of meat.

Here's the catch: The line between aging and rotting is a skinny line indeed. So we must observe some guidelines. The proper drying environment is 36° to 38°F, has a humidity level right at 50 percent, and has plenty of air circulation. Sounds like a job for your friendly neighborhood chill chest. Now, you could leave the roast in the fridge just hanging around on a platter, but we are talking about raw meat here. I cover mine with a prolifically perforated plastic bin (see page 274). The holes promote air flow, while the meat's juices are safely sequestered. Place this as far back and down in your fridge as possible. How long should you age a roast? Well, as little as 24 hours would make a difference, but for a 10-pounder 72 would be a lot better.[1]

Most reliable roast recipes suggest a two-tiered cooking approach. First you sear the meat over high heat in order to create a golden brown and delicious crust. Then you drop the temperature so that the roast can finish low and slow. This is a fine philosophy and yet fatally flawed, because the higher the heat involved the more proteins in the meat are damaged, therefore the more juices lost. If we give it all this high heat at the very beginning, we're going to have more juice lost through the cooking process. So flip it: Start the roast at a balmy 200°F and bake until it reaches a certain internal temp, then jack the heat up high to get a nice crust.

As far as I'm concerned, there's only one temperature for a rib roast, that narrow range of joy between 127° and 132°F called medium-rare. I'm going to count on about 10 to 12 degrees of carry-over, so I'm going to set the alarm on my thermometer for 118°F.

Once upon a time, doneness was believed to be a factor of weight, time, and oven temperature. This led to many a discouraged cook and disappointed diner, because this formula cannot factor in the most critical piece of information in meat cookery: the shape of the meat. And since that's a rather fuzzy piece of logic, I think it's best to skip the time thing altogether.

The only way to know what's going on in your meat is to take its temperature. There are a lot of different meat thermometers to choose from, but I like the probe style that can stay inside the meat throughout the cooking process. I like knowing what's going on. Positioning the probe is crucial: Set the probe dead center and drive it down into the middle of the mass of meat, making sure you don't hit any bones.

KNOW YOUR GRADES

Here in our fifty-ninth episode it may be time for a review of beef grades.

PRIME

The solid-gold watch of the beef world. Personally, I'm more than happy to cook and consume a piece of Prime beef as long as somebody else is paying for it.

CHOICE

The watch you wear to work and to the occasional wedding. When I'm buying, I usually buy Choice.

SELECT

You know, that watch you keep in your desk at work for when you leave your real watch at home. Select beef makes great stew because it has a lot of connective tissue.

Beef doneness cheat sheet
Rare: 120° to 127°F
Medium-rare: 128° to 135°F
Medium: 136° to 145°F
Toast: 146°F and up

APPLICATION

DRY AGED STANDING RIB ROAST WITH SAGE AU JUS

10 SERVINGS

This roast procedure is unorthodox, to be sure, but having experimented with standing rib roasts for a decade or so I've really come to believe that the approach herein is the way to go, as long as you don't skip any steps. For instance, I think the dry aging is as important as proper cooking. That said, if you don't have time to age, the twice-roasted flowerpot maneuver will still grant you excellent results.

Although I stand by the original procedure, I think we have perfected it here by resting the roast in the terra-cotta pot, which reduces the time needed to reach the desired internal temp and also reduces the risk of burns. Also, we changed the procedure for the jus, as some oven-safe glassware is not rated for stove-top use.

AGING RIG

1. Perforate the body of a large, hard plastic storage container, place the meat on the lid of said container, and use the body as the lid.

2. Place the standing rib roast upright on a half sheet pan fitted with a cooling rack. The rack is essential for drainage.

3. Place in the refrigerator, where the humidity is 50 to 60 percent and the temperature is 34° to 38°F. (You can measure both with a weather thermometer.[2]) The lowest, deepest part of you fridge is ideal.

SOFTWARE

1	4 bone-in (approx. 10 lb)	Choice standing rib roast	
		canola oil	to coat
2	teaspoons	kosher salt	
	plenty, to coat the roast	black pepper	freshly ground
1	cup	red wine	
1	cup	H_2O	
4	leaves	fresh sage	

PROCEDURE

1. Place the roast inside the **aging rig** and set in the refrigerator for 3 days.

2. When ready to cook, remove the roast from the refrigerator and bring to room temperature for 1 hour.

3. Place a **16-inch round azalea terra cotta planter** into a cold oven. Invert the planter to become a lid over the bottom of the planter. The oven should be cold to start, to avoid any cracking in the terra cotta pieces. Turn the oven to 200°F.

4. Rub the roast with canola oil. Remember to rub the bones with oil, as well. Once the roast is completely coated with oil, sprinkle with the kosher salt and enough freshly ground pepper to coat the surface. Place the roast over a **glass bake-ware dish slightly shorter than the roast is long**. This will catch the drippings needed for the sauce. Finally, place a **probe thermometer** into the center of the roast and set for 118°F. Put the roast and the glass dish onto the planter dish, cover with the terra cotta pot, and return to the oven. Roast for approximately 4 to 6 hours, until it reaches an internal temperature of 120°F.

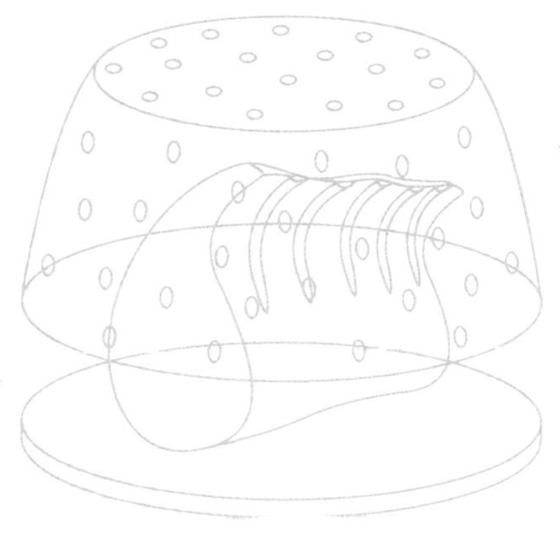

Old Cake Carrier
(with perforated lid)

5 Remove the planter with the roast and turn the oven up to 500°F. Allow the roast to rest until an internal temperature of 130°F is reached. Return the roast (terra cotta pot and all) to the hot oven for 10 to 15 minutes or until you've achieved your desired crust. Remove the roast from the oven, then from the planter and transfer to a **cutting board**. Rest at least 15 minutes before carving.

6 Drain off the fat from the glass dish and scrape the drippings to a **2-quart saucepan**. Place the pan over low heat, add the wine and water, and reduce by half, stirring with a **wooden spatula**. Roll the sage leaves in between your fingers to release the flavors and aroma. Add to the sauce and cook for 1 minute. **Strain** and serve with the roast.

7 Carve the roast with **an electric knife**. Start by separating the bones from the meat by placing the roast with the bone ends facing with the meat side up. Cut, following the curve of the bone, toward the meat. Save the ribs for yourself, and you've basically got a big, boneless roast. Remove any large layers of fat. Then start slicing from the end and make sure you don't go less than a half inch.

ALTERNATIVE CONVECTIVE METHOD:

Although I love the roast that comes out of the flower pot, I bought my first convection oven just a couple of years ago and it's a great tool for large roasts. Here's how.

1 Set oven rack to lower third and place a **roasting pan containing a half inch of water** on the floor of the oven.[3] Set the oven to convection (convection roast if you have it) and the heat to 200°F.

2 Rub the roast with oil, salt, and pepper just as above. **Insert the remote thermometer probe** and set the roast directly on the oven rack over the pan. Cook for 2 hours then rotate the roast to ensure even air flow. Continue cooking until the interior temp reaches 120°F.[4]

3 Remove the roast to a **half sheet pan**, cover with **foil,** and rest 10 minutes. Crank the oven to 500°F (still on convection).

4 Replace the roast and cook until the internal temperature hits 130°F.[5] Remove and rest for half an hour before slicing.

5 Meanwhile, move the contents of the roasting pan to a **small saucepan**. Add the wine and reduce by half. Add the fresh herbs or thicken with a flour slurry if a thicker gravy is desired.

6 Slice off the ribs, then carve the meat as desired. Before serving, pour any and all drippings from the cutting board into the sauce.

[1] Always keep an eye (and nose) out for signs of meat gone bad, such as mold or a funky aroma. If you open and close your refrigerator a great deal you may want to consider skipping the aging process. I have a small fridge out in the garage where I age uncovered cuts in a controlled environment.

[2] I bought a cheap digital weather center (made by Oregon Scientific, I think) that has a sensor that goes inside the dry-aging fridge and a readout that sticks to the outside. This device tells me the temp and the humidity, which is very useful for this kind of work.

[3] The water will prevent the drippings from burning and generating a lot of smoke. The water will also greatly ease sauce making later.

[4] I usually go with a 4-rib roast, which takes 4 to 5 hours to reach temperature.

[5] There will be smoke, so open a window or crank up your hood.

SCRAP IRON CHEF: BACON CHALLENGE

EPISODE 60 | SEASON 5 | GOOD EATS

Although I did make bacon on the show, in no way, fashion, or form do I expect anyone out there to actually do what I did. Because it involves long curing and cold smoking, bacon making is neither easy nor fast and should be left to serious smokers. That said, I hope this show made folks appreciate real bacon enough to seek out high-end artisan brands rather than cheap megamart rashers, which are truly the lowest expression of the craft. Look at it this way: If you're going to consume a product that's more than half fat, shouldn't it be the best you can get?

On the goof: Long before there was *Iron Chef America*, there was plain old *Iron Chef*, a Godzilla-movie of a cooking competition I always got a hoot out of. At the time, there was also a show out of the U.K. called *Junk Yard Wars*, which I found equally compelling though for different reasons. In my head, the idea of putting the two together was completely and utterly natural.

"Life expectancy would grow by leaps and bounds if green vegetables smelled as good as bacon."

DOUG LARSON

TIDBIT | Certain breeds of pigs are raised for their bacon-makin' capabilities, notably the Yorkshire and Tamworth.

FLIP SPICERACK: Which of these magnificent Scrap Iron Chefs do you challenge?

CHEF BIJOU: I'll whomp your butt, boy. I guar-aon-tee.

CHEF SOUTHWEST: I'm commin'. And the hat's commin' with me.[1]

CHEF PRAIRIE: (All sweet) Hi.

AB: I...I challenge her.

LOIN
Canadian / Irish Bacon
BELLY
American Bacon / Pancetta
The Good Stuff

KNOWLEDGE CONCENTRATE

The word *bacon* actually comes from the Old German word *bah*, or "back."

CANADIAN BACON AND IRISH BACON both come from the back—the loin, to be exact. They're a heck of a lot leaner than the bacon that comes from the belly, and they don't taste anything like what we think of as bacon, so don't try to use them in these applications.

FATBACK also comes from the back. It's actually a solid layer of fat that lays just on top of the meat. You would not eat it like bacon . . . at least I hope not. You'd usually render it into lard or wrap it around leaner pieces of meat to keep them moist during cooking.

SALT PORK comes from parts of the belly that are too fat to be used for bacon. It's cured, but never smoked.

ITALIAN BACON, PANCETTA, is also taken from the belly. It's cured, not smoked. And it comes all rolled up and kind of funny-looking. It's really hard to cut; the secret is to partially freeze it first.

One of the reasons American-style bacon keeps so long is that it's usually been both cured and smoked. The curing process uses salt to pull moisture out of the meat. And the less moisture that's in the meat, the more inhospitable it is to the bacteria that cause spoilage. Curing also prepares the meat for its date with smoke by coaxing water-soluble proteins to the surface of the meat. When the surface of the meat is dried, this creates a layer called the pellicle, which holds on to smoke like Velcro.

TRIVIA Riding a bike in a grocery store is harder than it looks.

TIDBIT The BLT became popular during the rapid expansion of supermarkets after WWII, when lettuce and tomatoes became available year round.

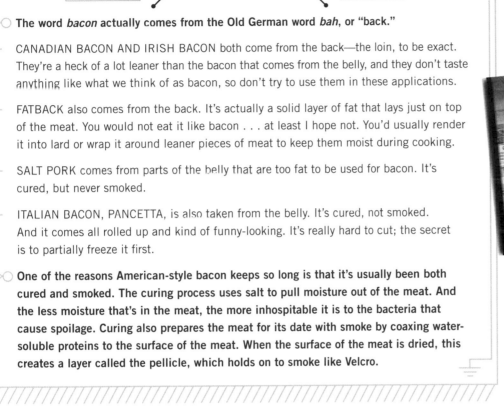

Cold smoker I've actually used

TRIVIA My set guys built the stadium completely from stuff they found in the scrap yard.

APPLICATION

ROAST BACON

8 SERVINGS

Although bacon frying in a pan is iconic, there is a better way . . . much better.

SOFTWARE

1	pound	thick-cut bacon	
1	tablespoon	black pepper	coarsely ground
2	tablespoons	dark brown sugar	

PROCEDURE

1. Lay the bacon in a single layer on a **cooling rack** set in a **parchment paper–lined half sheet pan**.
2. Liberally sprinkle each side of the bacon slices with 1 teaspoon of the pepper, pressing the pepper firmly onto the bacon before flipping. Repeat with the brown sugar.
3. Set the sheet pan in the hotbox and set the temperature to 400°F. Bake for 30 minutes, then rotate the pan and continue to cook until desired doneness, about 15 minutes for chewy and 18 for crisp.
4. Cool for 5 minutes on the pan before devouring.

BRINGING HOME THE SLAB BACON

Buy slab bacon instead of presliced: You can slice it thin and fry it, slice it thick and roast it, you can cut it into lardons and render the fat for sautéing greens, or slice it paper-thin and eat it raw. Slab bacon also stays fresher longer and gives you more bang for your buck.

Look for bacon with thin streaks of rosy, pink meat and evenly distributed strips of snowy white fat. The fat-to-meat ratio can vary greatly. Choose accordingly: Leaner is better for eating straight, fattier better for mixed applications.

"Slicing a warm slab of bacon is a lot like giving a ferret a shave. No matter how careful you are, somebody's going to get hurt." Freeze it partway first and use a long, thin blade with a granton edge.

Packed sealed bacon can survive in the fridge for a week past its fresh date (though I've rarely seen it last that long in my house). Frozen bacon will keep for a month.

APPLICATION

BACON VINAIGRETTE WITH GRILLED RADICCHIO

8 SERVINGS

The salty, fatty sweetness of this dressing perfectly balances the bite of the radicchio.

SOFTWARE

¼	cup	extra-virgin olive oil	
¼	cup	cider vinegar	
3	tablespoons	bacon drippings[2]	divided
1	tablespoon	dark brown sugar	
1	tablespoon	coarse-grain mustard	
1	teaspoon	kosher salt	
1	teaspoon	black pepper	freshly ground
2	heads	radicchio (about 12 ounces each)	quartered

PROCEDURE

1. Fire up a charcoal **grill** or heat a **cast-iron grill pan** over medium-high heat.
2. Combine the oil, vinegar, 2 tablespoons of the bacon drippings, the brown sugar, mustard, salt, and pepper in a **small nonreactive bowl**. **Whisk** until an emulsion is formed and set the vinaigrette aside at room temperature.
3. Coat the quartered radicchio in the remaining tablespoon bacon drippings. Put the radicchio onto the hot grill or grill pan and cook for about 2 minutes on each side, until the edges are slightly wilted.
4. Transfer to a plate and cover with a **stainless-steel bowl**; steam the radicchio for 5 minutes.
5. Drizzle the vinaigrette over the radicchio and serve immediately.

[1] The line's a goof on one from *Tombstone*, one of my favorite movies.

[2] Six slices of bacon will provide enough drippings for the salad dressing—and why not crumble the bacon over the radicchio before serving?

TRIVIA | The guy who played Chef Bayou is the show's lead electrician. In real life, the guy who played Flip Spicerack (the chairman) is married to the woman who plays W.

FLIP SPICERACK: So, judges, what say ye?

JUDGE #1: (With a dub-over à la Iron Chef) Mmm. This bacon is exquisite. I'm very surprised by the flavor of this leafy red stuff. On the other hand, Chef Midwestern's belly stew is disgusting.

JUDGE #2: Yes. I am very vegetarian, but this bacon is delectable. The dish prepared by Chef Midwestern is wretched.

JUDGE #3: This sandwich is sublime. The balance of salty, smoky, sweet, and crunchy reminds me of a haiku. This other dish is crap.

DEEP PURPLE: BERRY FROM ANOTHER PLANET

EPISODE 61 | SEASON 5 | GOOD EATS

Like most American mutts, I grew up wary of eggplant. Without an ethnic culinary heritage to fall back on (other than boiling stuff), I had no point of eggplant reference other than suspicious experiments my mother undertook in the fun-filled '60s. Luckily, while in college I lived next to some hippies who tended a garden that brought forth a bumper crop of eggplant every summer, most of which they magically converted into a strange, garlicky paste they called baba ghanouj, often referred to as "poor man's caviar." In the years since, I've come to believe that eggplant is the plastic of the culinary world, capable of taking on any edible guise with the possible exception of dessert. It has little if any flavor of its own but can unify almost any combination tossed into its midst. Of course, the other reason we should appreciate the eggplant is that everybody else but us does. What does the rest of the planet know that we don't? That eggplant is good eats.

TRIVIA I'm a huge fan of old sitcoms, and the Mr. McGregor character was based on the tradition of the meddling older neighbor. As a comic device it allows for some relatively outrageous hijinx.

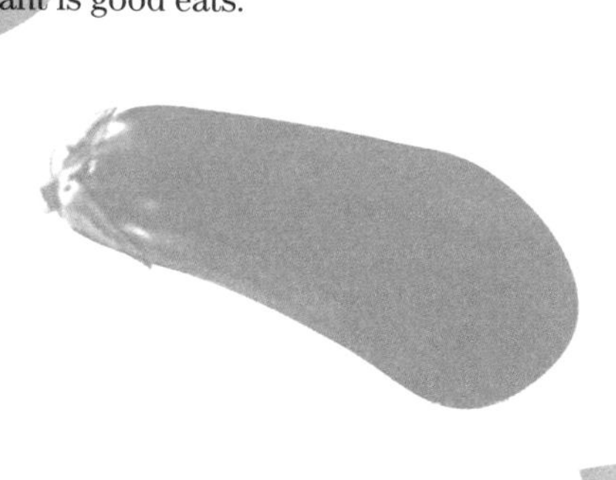

TRIVIA When I threw the eggplant at Mr. McGregor, it hit a passing car. Luckily no one was injured. Oops.

KNOWLEDGE CONCENTRATE

***Solanum melongena* has been cultivated in India since at least the fifteenth century. It then spread to Africa and the Middle East but got stuck in Europe, where eggplant was recognized as belonging to the notorious nightshade family, whose members were all thought to be, if not downright poisonous, then seriously anti-nutritious. The Spanish brought this large berry to the New World, where it continues to languish despite the fact that Pixar made a film named for its most famous application.[1]**

A field guide to common megamart eggplant:

AMERICAN EGGPLANT is often labeled as "Globe eggplant." This is the ubiquitous, dark-purple, pear-shaped variety. A one-pound American eggplant can yield up to 4 cups of peeled and cubed flesh. Italian eggplant can be substituted equally.

ASIAN OR "ORIENTAL" EGGPLANTS include Japanese, Chinese, and Filipino varieties. These eggplants usually have thin skins and a sweeter flavor than American eggplants. These slender and colorful eggplants contain fewer seeds, which are the source of the eggplant's bitterness.

BABY EGGPLANTS are small versions of American eggplants, but tend to have thin skins and sweeter flesh, like Asian eggplants. Larger eggplants should be peeled and purged (see below) if substituted for baby eggplants.

Purging: Eggplants are 95 percent water, and that water is laden with rather bitter-tasting alkaloids. This is why most of the eggplant served in America feels like Styrofoam and tastes like old coffee. By "curing" the eggplant with salt, much of this troublesome fluid can be drawn out. The result: better flavor and a meaty, toothsome texture that won't remind you a bit of biting off a chunk of cooler.

Shopping and storage:

Choose an eggplant with tight skin, no wrinkles or blemishes, with a bright green calyx that has a nice clean cut. It should be kind of heavy for its size, and when pressed with a finger the flesh will give slightly but bounce back all the way.

The bigger the pod gets, the seedier it becomes and the more bitter it's going to taste. That's because the seeds contain alkaloids, which are related to nicotine and morphine. Sex is also a factor. Females—recognized by the oval navel they have on the blossom end—contain more seeds than males, which have a round bellybutton. More seeds, more bitterness. The difference isn't really noticeable in young specimens, but when faced with larger, older pods, always go with the boy veggies.

Eggplants keep best between 45° and 50°F. If you're going to cook your eggplants within a day or two, just set them in the coolest spot you can find in your kitchen. If you need to hold them longer than that, wrap in a couple layers of plastic wrap and keep them on the top shelf of your fridge. Under perfect conditions an eggplant is only going to keep for 2 weeks, and there's no real way to know how long it's been on the run, so eat quick. Go ahead and slice, purge, and dry your pods and seal them in heavy freezer bags. Refrigerate this way for up to 1 week or freeze for up to 3 months.

TIDBIT | Eggplant Aliases of Other Lands

England: aubergine
India: brinjal
Australia: egg fruit
West Africa: garden egg
West Indies: brown jolly

APPLICATION

BABA GHANOUJ

2 CUPS

Baba Ghanouj is *the* Middle Eastern eggplant application. The key to getting it right? The plastic wrap.

SOFTWARE

2	large	eggplants	about 2½ pounds total; enough to produce 2 cups of roasted flesh
5	cloves	garlic	sliced
¼	cup	lemon juice	freshly squeezed
4	tablespoons	tahini[2]	
¾	teaspoon	kosher salt	
½	bunch	fresh parsley	rinsed, leaves only
	to taste	black pepper	freshly ground

PROCEDURE

1. Heat a **grill** to medium-high or crank your hot box to 375°F.[3]
2. Pierce the skin of the eggplants several times with a **fork** and grill over indirect heat (or roast in the oven[4]), turning every 5 minutes or so, for about 30 minutes, until the skin is blackened and the flesh soft. Immediately wrap the eggplant in **plastic wrap** and cool for 1 hour.
3. **Cut** off the stem end off the plastic-wrapped fruit, and squeeze the interior flesh out (just like toothpaste) into a **strainer** and drain for 30 minutes.
4. Process the eggplant, garlic, lemon juice, tahini, and salt in a **food processor** for 10 to 15 seconds, until smooth but not quite pureed. Add the parsley and pulse 2 or 3 times. Taste and add pepper as desired.
5. Serve with toasted pita bread (hey, the grill's already hot, right?).

NOTE: The eggplant's bitterness can be countered with a tablespoon of honey.

TIDBIT Thomas Jefferson is often credited with planting the first eggplants in America at Monticello, but then Thomas Jefferson is credited with just about everything that has to do with food in the United States, and I don't believe the half of it.

APPLICATION

EGGPLANT PASTA

2 SERVINGS

I love Eggplant Parmesan but don't care for the time it takes. So as we were sitting around trying to think of applications for this show, I thought: noodles. Can you make noodles out of eggplant? Turns out you can. Best thing about this dish is that you get all the flavor of eggplant parmesean in just 60 seconds.

// SOFTWARE

1	large	eggplant	about 1 pound
		kosher salt	
1	tablespoon	olive oil	
¼	teaspoon	garlic	minced
¼	teaspoon	red pepper flakes	
1	small	tomato	seeded and chopped
3	tablespoons	heavy cream	
1	tablespoon	basil	chiffonade
2	tablespoons	Parmesan cheese	grated
1	tablespoon	breadcrumbs	

// PROCEDURE

1. Peel the eggplant, leaving 1 inch of skin at the top and bottom. Slice the eggplant lengthwise into ¼-inch-thick slices. (I would use a **mandolin** for this.)
2. Place the eggplant slices on a **cooling rack** set over the sink and sprinkle generously with kosher salt. Wait 15 minutes, flip, sprinkle again, and wait another 15 minutes. Rinse thoroughly under cool water and gently squeeze out excess water. Place on **paper towels** and pat dry, then cut the slices into ¼-inch-wide strips so that they resemble linguine.
3. Heat a **10-inch sauté pan** over medium-high heat and add the oil. When it shimmers, add the garlic and red pepper flakes and toss for 10 seconds. Add the eggplant and toss to coat. Add the tomato and toss for 15 to 20 seconds. Add the cream and toss for another 10 seconds. Finish with the basil and Parmesan. Transfer to a **serving dish**, top with breadcrumbs, toss, and serve immediately.

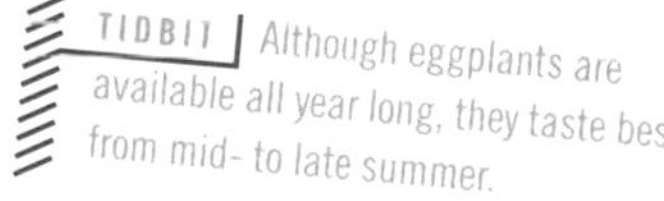
TIDBIT | Although eggplants are available all year long, they taste best from mid- to late summer.

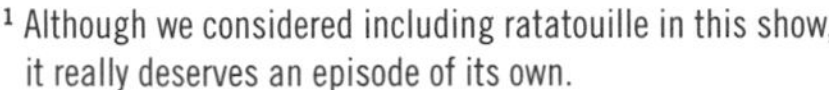

[1] Although we considered including ratatouille in this show, it really deserves an episode of its own.

[2] A paste made from sesame seeds.

[3] The oven will do, but only the grill, preferably fired by charcoal, can produce the smoky sweetness that puts this dip over the edge. I usually cook the eggplants right in the coals and ashes of a dying fire, but then I'm a romantic. In a pinch, you can roast them right on a gas burner.

[4] You'll get your ghanouj, but you'll sure miss that smoky goodness.

PEELERS

I learned while testing dishes for this episode that proper peeler evaluation is critical to your health and happiness. There are many factors for you to consider. First: the handle. Let's face it. If your hand cramps after two minutes, you're in possession of a bad tool. So all flimsy, measly, and uncomfortable-looking handles have got to go. Next: blade configuration. What's good for shaving is good for peeling, so all non-swivel blade models are out. Of course, a swivel is a moving part, so you need to check the connection. If it's flimsy, if the blade just pops right out, imagine what a few bags of carrots will do. So cheap connections are out.

As far as the blades go, you've got two choices. Ceramic models never need sharpening, but they're expensive, and what's more they are breakable. I don't care for them. That leaves us with stainless, but even there we've got some choices: smooth or serrated. I find that serrated blades stay sharper a lot longer, and those little teeth really grab hold of thick skin like on an eggplant or, say, a rutabaga. So smooth blades are out.

Finally we have to consider style. Straight models are nice for taking a very thin layer off of a relatively uniform object, like a carrot or potato. Some even have a little digger tool on the end for getting eyes out of a potato. Yeah, I like that. That's nice. Then there are harp or "Y" peelers. They usually have a deeper, wider bite, so they're really adept at handling heavy peels and large surface areas like a really big eggplant. I also like these for shaving chocolate.

The answer seems clear. Every kitchen needs two peelers, a straight and a "Y" peeler with a comfortable grip and swiveling, microserrated blades heartily attached to the rest of the device. Oh, you don't want to spend money for two? Well, fine. The next tragedy will be on your head.

TIDBIT | According to a fifth-century Chinese scroll, fashionable Chinese women used to make a dye out of the skin of purple eggplants and polish their teeth with it until they were a shiny gray.

SWIVEL BLADE STANDARD PEELER

Wide Arch Support

Micro Serrations

HARP/"Y" STYLE PEELER

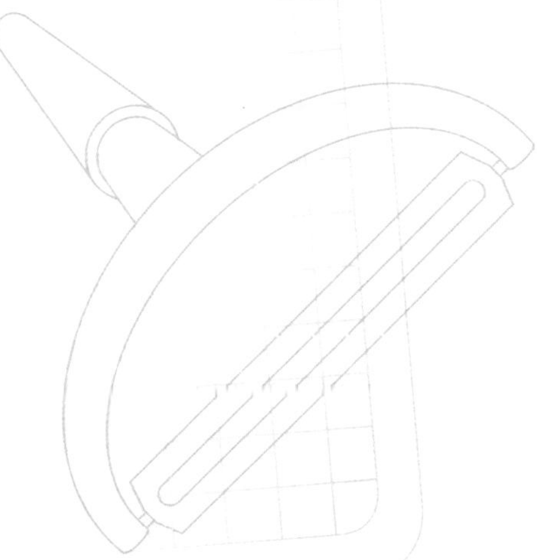

THE TROUBLE WITH CHEESECAKE

EPISODE 62 | SEASON 5 | GOOD EATS

Cheesecake is tricky. Take the name: cheesecake . . . cheese + cake. Would it be safe to assume that the product referred to by this moniker might be a cake made with cheese? Of course it would. But it isn't. In fact, I'd bet that nine out of ten cheesecake failures stem from the fact that cooks expect cheesecake to act like cake. But cheesecake isn't a cake.

Cheesecake is pie.

Think about it. Aside from the crust, a cheesecake contains only sugar, vanilla, eggs, and dairy. It is in fact custard, plain and simple, and that means that cooking it properly is all about temperature control.

TRIVIA | If I'd been thinking straight at the time I would have made this episode one of the Egg-Files set.

KNOWLEDGE CONCENTRATE

The "cheese" in cheesecake is cream cheese—a soft, smooth, tangy cow's milk cheese containing no less than 33 percent milk fat and no more than 55 percent moisture. It was created in 1872 by a New York dairyman named William Lawrence, who was attempting to whip up a batch of Neufchâtel, a soft, unripened cheese. Something went deliciously wrong, and Lawrence named his accidental invention after the big, fancy, food town of the day: Philadelphia.

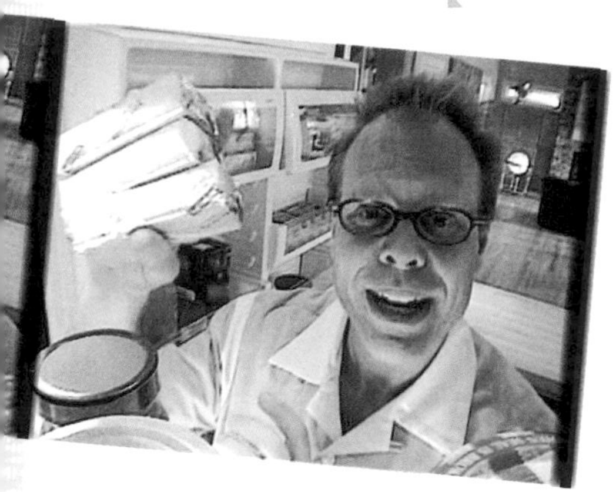

Choosing a pan: A cheesecake needs a springform like a fish needs a bicycle. Most recipes designed for use by civilians call for a springform pan, which isn't really a pan at all but a collar/clamp doohicky that locks (sometimes) around a disk that forms the bottom of the "pan." The idea is that it's easier to undress a dense, sticky cheesecake wearing such a device than it is to turn one out of a solid, 9-inch round aluminum cake pan with 3-inch sides. Perhaps. But I should point out that I've never, ever seen one in a professional bake-shop, where constant use would warp, bend, and mangle such flimsy folly into useless scrap metal. What's worse, cheesecakes are usually cooked in a water bath, and two-piece pans leak no matter how much foil you wrap them in. And here's the death knell: Springforms are unitaskers, and I have neither the space nor the patience to deal with unitaskers.

What's with water baths? Since they're actually custards, it's not surprising that cheese-cakes are almost always baked in a water bath—that is, the primary vessel sits inside a second pan that is filled with water and placed in the oven. Water has a very high "specific heat" and can absorb a considerable amount of energy without undergoing a change in temperature, and I used to think this thermal impediment would slow the march of heat into the custard thus preventing overcoagulation of the egg proteins and creating a dense, grainy texture. But here's the thing: The water used is usually boiled just before it's added to the pan! Now granted, 212°F water is cooler than a 350°F oven, but the water conducts its heat much faster than hot air or even radiation can, so this step doesn't protect the product any more than pouring boiling oil on your face would protect you from a sunburn. I suspect that the water's real purpose does not become clear until the end of the cooking. Remember, most cheesecake procedures call for finishing the pie for an hour or so in a dead oven—one that has been turned off. Since water cools much more slowly than the air or even walls of the oven, this aqueous heat sink can actually finish the cooking by slowly, gently giving its energy up to the custard. Can a cheesecake be cooked without a water bath? Certainly. But the texture will never be as light, creamy, or moist as a bathed specimen, and deep cracks will likely appear on top as the overcoagulated custard cools and contracts.

TIP | Storing pans (flat, springform, or otherwise) is a pain. Stacking them in drawers and cabinets means that the one you need is always, inevitably, unfailingly, on the bottom. I get around this with magnets. Just hot glue a few to the back of your pantry door, hold a pan up to the magnet, and then slap another magnet on top like this:

ON PARCHMENT PAPER

Although it's nothing more than paper dipped in sulfuric acid (which renders it all but impermeable to grease and heat) and coated in silicone (which makes Teflon look sticky), parchment paper is something I just can't bake without. It does everything waxed paper can and much, much more. By placing a strip around the inner wall of the pan and a round in the bottom, even cheesecake can be easily de-panned. Here's how to cut it:

First measure and cut the bottom: Cut a piece of roll parchment 9 inches long. Fold it over into a triangle six times, as in the illustration below, then align the tip with the center of the pan. Snip off the excess and bingo, you've got a nonstick bottom for your pan. Measuring for the side piece (or pieces) is even easier because we have π—which is funny considering we're making a pie. Multiply the diameter of the pan (9 inches) by π (which we'll round to 3.141592653590793 for simplicity's sake) for a circumference of 28.27433882308139, which I'm more than happy to round up to 28½ inches. Since roll parchment is usually 15 inches across and I'm stingy, I just cut two 3-inch-wide pieces across the roll and call it a day.

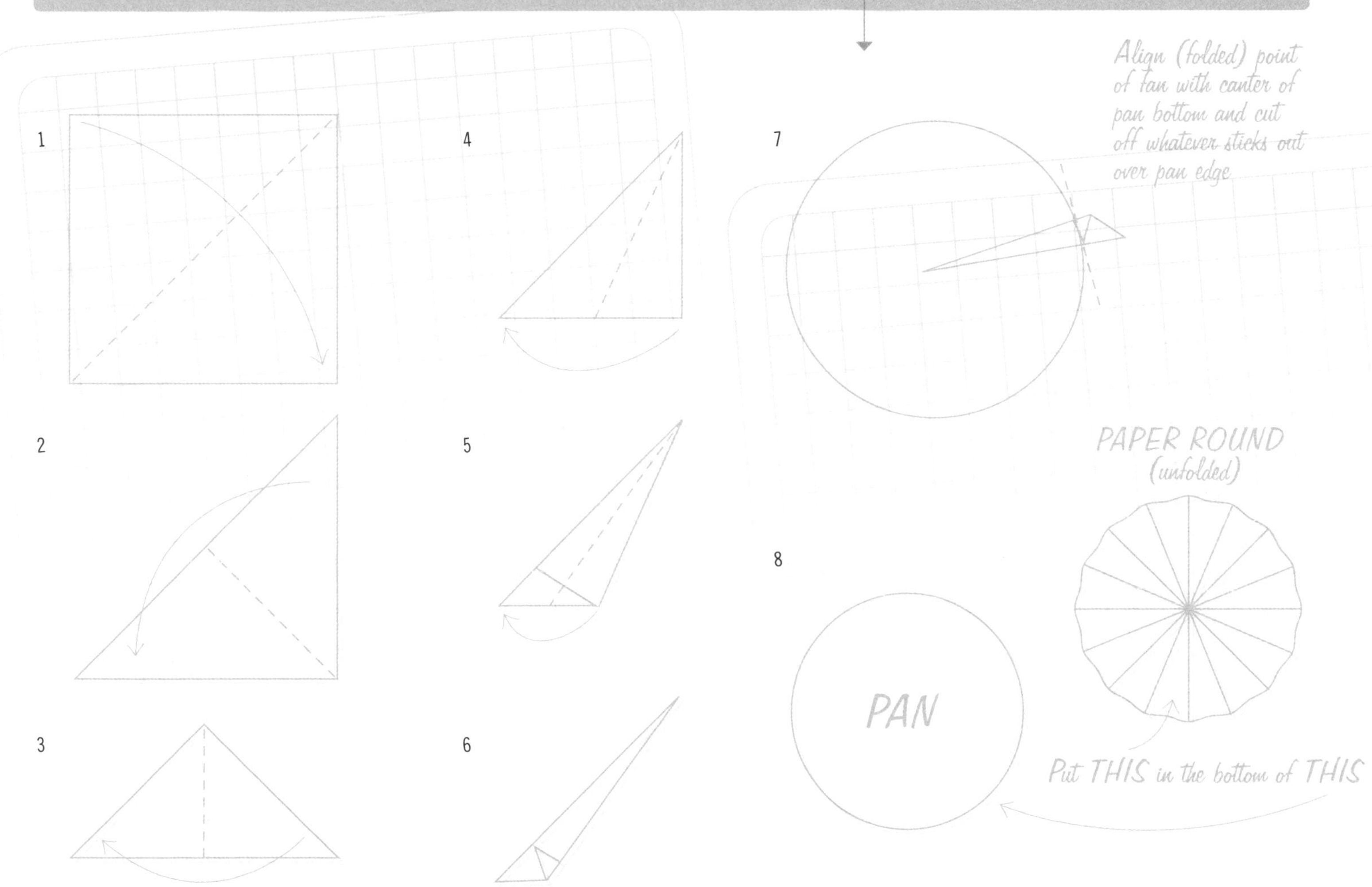

1
4
7
Align (folded) point of fan with center of pan bottom and cut off whatever sticks out over pan edge
2
5
PAPER ROUND
(unfolded)
8
3
6
PAN
Put THIS in the bottom of THIS

π helps with pie: $9 \times \pi = 9 \times 3.141592653589793 = 28.274333882308139 = 28.5$

APPLICATION

SOUR CREAM CHEESECAKE

12 SERVINGS

This is a very creamy "cake" rather than the dryer, tighter New York-style cheesecake . . . not that there's anything wrong with it.

SOFTWARE

FOR THE CRUST

4	ounces	unsalted butter	
10¼	ounces	graham crackers	that's about 18 whole crackers
1	tablespoon	sugar	

FOR THE FILLING

1	tablespoon	vanilla extract	
2	large	eggs	
3	large	egg yolks	
⅓	cup	heavy cream	
24	ounces	cream cheese	at room temperature
8	ounces	sugar	
10½	ounces	sour cream	at room temperature

Push crumbs up the sides

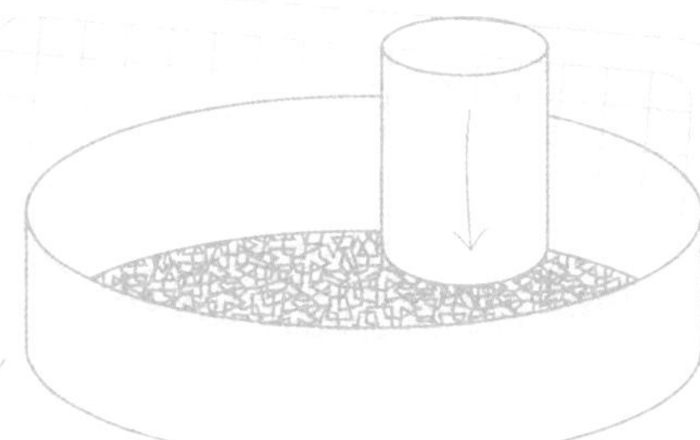

TOP VIEW

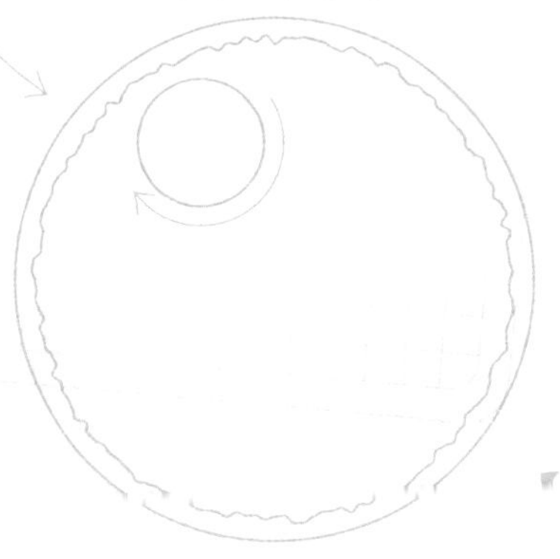

PROCEDURE

MAKE THE CRUST:

1. Heat the oven to 300°F.
2. Melt the butter in a **3-quart saucier** over medium-low heat. **Brush**[1] a **9-inch round cake pan with 3-inch sides** with some of the melted butter. Cut and insert parchment paper into the pan as described on the previous page.
3. In a **food processor**, process the graham crackers with the sugar, being sure to leave some larger hunks. Drizzle in the rest of the melted butter and pulse to combine.
4. Dump two thirds of the crumb mixture into the bottom of the parchment-lined cake pan and tamp into place with the bottom of a **water glass**. When your floor of crumbs is well packed, add the last third of the crumbs to the pan then move the glass in a circular motion to push the crumbs up the side of the pan, forming a wall 1½ inches high. As the wall forms, begin rolling the glass around the inside of the pan to pack the wall in place. (This sounds complicated, but it isn't.)
5. Bake for 15 minutes, then cool for 10 minutes before filling. Reduce the oven temperature to 250°F.

MAKE THE FILLING:

6 Bring 2 quarts of water to a boil in an **electric kettle**.[2]

7 Combine the vanilla, eggs, egg yolks, and cream in a **small bowl** and set aside.

8 Using a **stand mixer with the paddle attachment**, beat the cream cheese with the sugar for 1 minute on low speed. Scrape down the bowl, add the sour cream, and mix on low for another 30 seconds. Scrape the bowl again, boost the speed to medium, and beat until lump free, 2 to 3 minutes.

9 With the mixer running, slowly pour in the egg mixture, stopping every now and then to scrape down the bowl. When the mixture is homogenous, pour the filling into the cooled crust.

10 Center a **roasting pan** in the oven and line it with a **kitchen towel**.[3] Place the cheesecake in the middle of the pan and add boiling water to 1½ inches up the side of the pan.

11 Bake for 2 hours, then kill the heat. Open the door for 1 minute, then close it and leave it closed for 1½ hours.

12 Remove the cheesecake from the water bath and refrigerate for 6 hours before serving. Let the water bath cool completely before removing it from the oven.

13 To serve, set the cake pan in 1 inch of hot water for 15 seconds to loosen the butter at the bottom of the pan. Gently pull out the side parchment pieces. Cut another parchment round and place on top of cake. Top that with a **paper plate** or **cardboard cake round** (easily cut from a corrugated shipping box) and finally a **coffee can** or **Tupperware container**—anything that will provide a stable base that isn't as wide as the cake pan. Invert the whole rig and gently remove the pan. Invert again, then slice with the **longest, thinnest blade** you have, wiping it with a hot, wet paper towel between slices.

1

Canned Something

Cardboard

Parchment Round

Cake

FOOD

2

Turn over on can and slowly remove pan then place platter or cake round on (cake) bottom and flip upright.

3

Platter or Cake Round

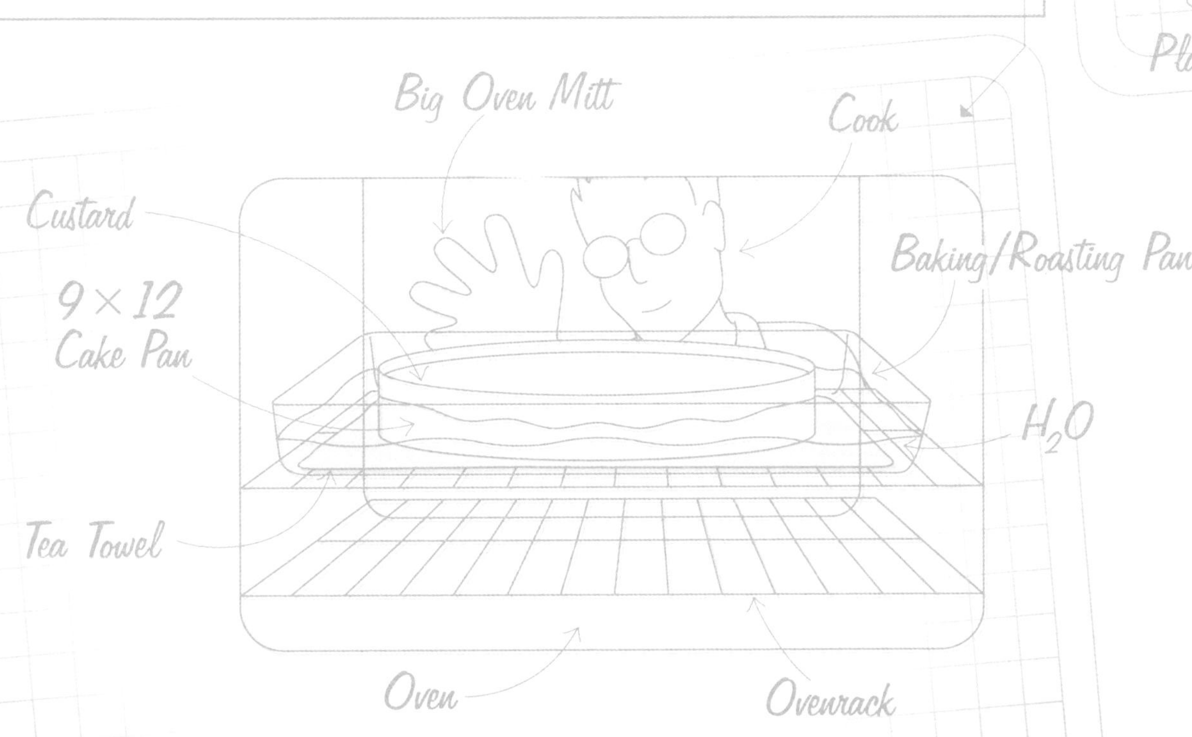

Many modern Silicone pastry brushes have reservoirs in the middle that hold butter and oil in little holes.

10 MINUTES MORE — SAVORY CHEESECAKE

8 TO 10 SERVINGS

I actually prefer savory cheesecakes to sweet, and this is one of my favorites. I had planned to run this in act 4 but ran slap out of time. I think the tub scene pushed us over.

SOFTWARE

FOR THE CRUST

3	ounces	unsalted butter	melted
1	large	egg white	
5	ounces	bagel chips	crushed

FOR THE FILLING

24	ounces	cream cheese	at room temperature
3	tablespoons	cornstarch	
1	teaspoon	kosher salt	
4	ounces	sour cream	
2	large	eggs	at room temperature
6	ounces	smoked trout	diced
⅓	cup	chives	chopped

PROCEDURE

MAKE THE CRUST:

1. Heat the oven to 350°F.
2. Combine the melted butter, egg white, and bagel chips in a **small bowl**. Press them into the bottom of a **10-inch pan** using procedure on previous page. Bake for 8 minutes to crisp up. Cool. Reduce the oven temperature to 250°F.

MAKE THE FILLING:

3. Using a **stand mixer fitted with the paddle attachment**, blend the cream cheese, cornstarch, salt, and sour cream for 1 minute, or until smooth. Add the eggs and beat until smooth, occasionally stopping the mixer and scraping down the sides of the bowl. Fold in the trout and chives.
4. Pour the batter into the cooled crust. Bake for 1 hour. Turn the oven off and leave the cake in the oven for 1 hour without opening the door. Cool in the chill chest for at least 2 hours. Carefully unmold. Keep refrigerated until ready to serve.

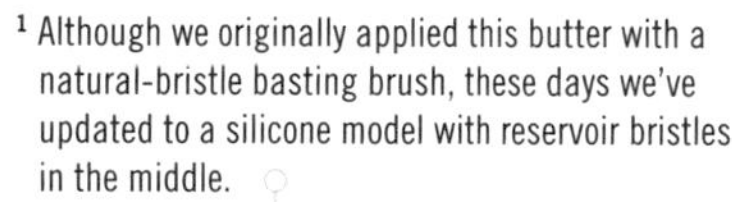

[1] Although we originally applied this butter with a natural-bristle basting brush, these days we've updated to a silicone model with reservoir bristles in the middle.

[2] You can heat the water in a saucepan on the cook top, but an electric kettle is a lot faster.

[3] The towel will slow the march of heat into the bottom of the pan.

SQUID PRO QUO

EPISODE 63 | SEASON 5 | GOOD EATS

In this episode I sought to bring one of the cleanest and most plentiful protein sources on the planet to the front of the plate, where it belongs . . . and to illuminate the myriad possibilities presented by the wok . . . and to avoid shooting a show in the kitchen . . . and to build a huge and fully articulated giant squid tentacle . . . and of course to tell the honest and true tale of Squidman. He's close . . . real close.

This episode was really an experiment to find out if we could pull off an exterior setting on a soundstage on a cable TV budget. I'm still not sure if the answer is yes or no, but what we learned was put to use later in the year, when we shot the epic "Down and Out in Paradise" (page 334).

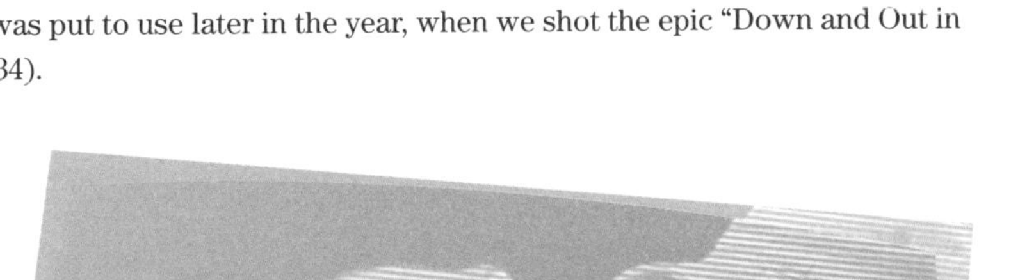

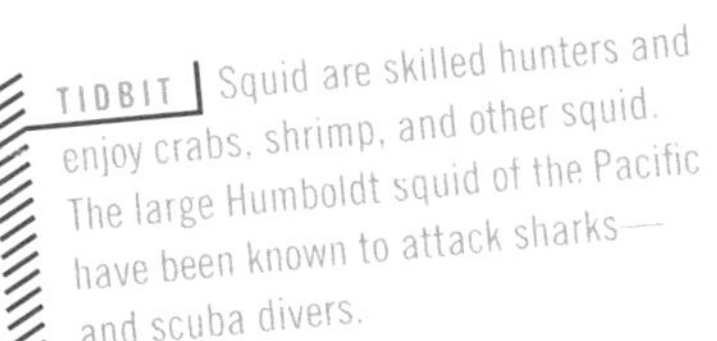

TIDBIT | Squid are skilled hunters and enjoy crabs, shrimp, and other squid. The large Humboldt squid of the Pacific have been known to attack sharks—and scuba divers.

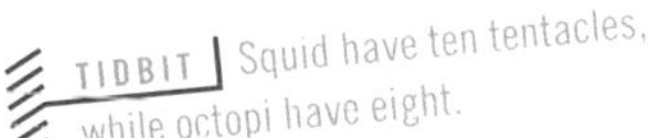

TIDBIT | Squid have ten tentacles, while octopi have eight.

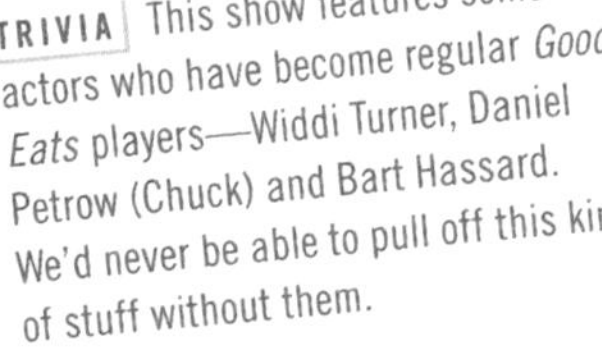

TRIVIA | This show features some actors who have become regular *Good Eats* players—Widdi Turner, Daniel Petrow (Chuck) and Bart Hassard. We'd never be able to pull off this kind of stuff without them.

KNOWLEDGE CONCENTRATE

Squid are mollusks just like snails and clams, only the shells have been internalized in the form of sharp beaks. Their subgroup or class is *cephalopoda*, which means "head footed" and includes the cuttlefish and the octopus. Many cephalopods produce ink, which they can shoot out of a jetlike opening in their head. The resulting cloud confuses predators, thus allowing time for escape. Cuttlefish ink itself is used in Mediterranean dishes.

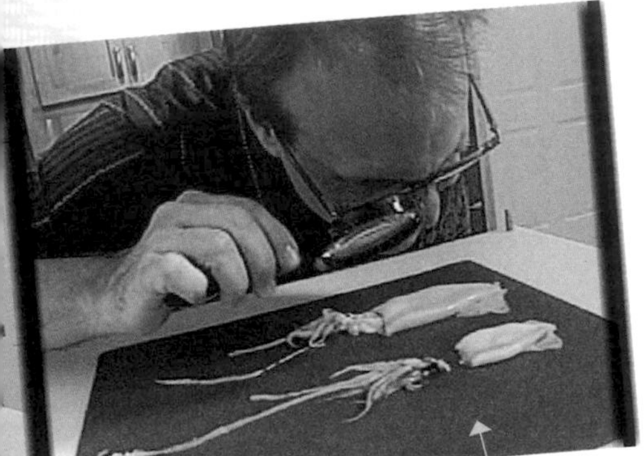

Most of the squid consumed in the United States are *Loligo opalescens*, which are named for the cornea that grows over their eyes. Also known as California Market Squid, these plentiful critters range in shallow waters from southern Alaska to Baja California, with the greatest concentration in southern California. Squid are available year round. The southern California season runs from November to February, while Monterey rakes in the calamari from May to October.

If you're looking for sustainable seafood options, the squid may be for you. Market squid have a very short life span, usually no more than a year, and the entire California population replaces itself annually. So, unlike consuming fish like tuna, which are often captured before they've had a chance to mature and breed, eating squid is really taking advantage of nature.

Squid come in two common culinary sizes: small calamari and 10/20 calamari, named such because you generally get ten to twenty pieces per pound. I prefer the 10/20s, because although the head and tentacle size is the same as that of the smaller models, the tube is much larger. Since most recipes call for more tube than head pieces, this seems the smart way to buy.

Although fresh squid can be found in seafood markets on the West Coast and some ethnic markets on the East, since they are quite perishable most of what you're going to find at your local megamart will be frozen—and, frankly, that's okay with me because that way I can keep them on hand at all times. Unlike shrimp, which often come IQF (individually quick-frozen), squid come in solid blocks. There are two acceptable thawing methods:

1. If you want to thaw the entire container, just place the unopened package inside a watertight vessel (to prevent any cross contamination) in the bottom of your refrigerator for a day.

2. If speed is of the essence, or if you want to harvest only a handful, unwrap the block and place it in watertight containment deep enough to allow for full submersion. Place said vessel in the sink and top the block with a pot lid or other weight (ice floats, ya know). Fill with cold water, then leave the water barely trickling. This will create just enough convection in the water to speed thawing.[1] As they thaw, simply remove what you want and seal the rest in a zip-top freezer bag and reintroduce the still frozen block to the deep freeze.

TIP Remember that squid start off tough, as they cook they get tender, then they get tough again, then they get tender again. When using a fast cooking method your goal is to hit the first window of tenderness. When braising, you're after the second window. But that's another show.

TIDBIT Fisherman often place high-wattage lights over the water to lure squid to the surface.

BREAKING IT DOWN

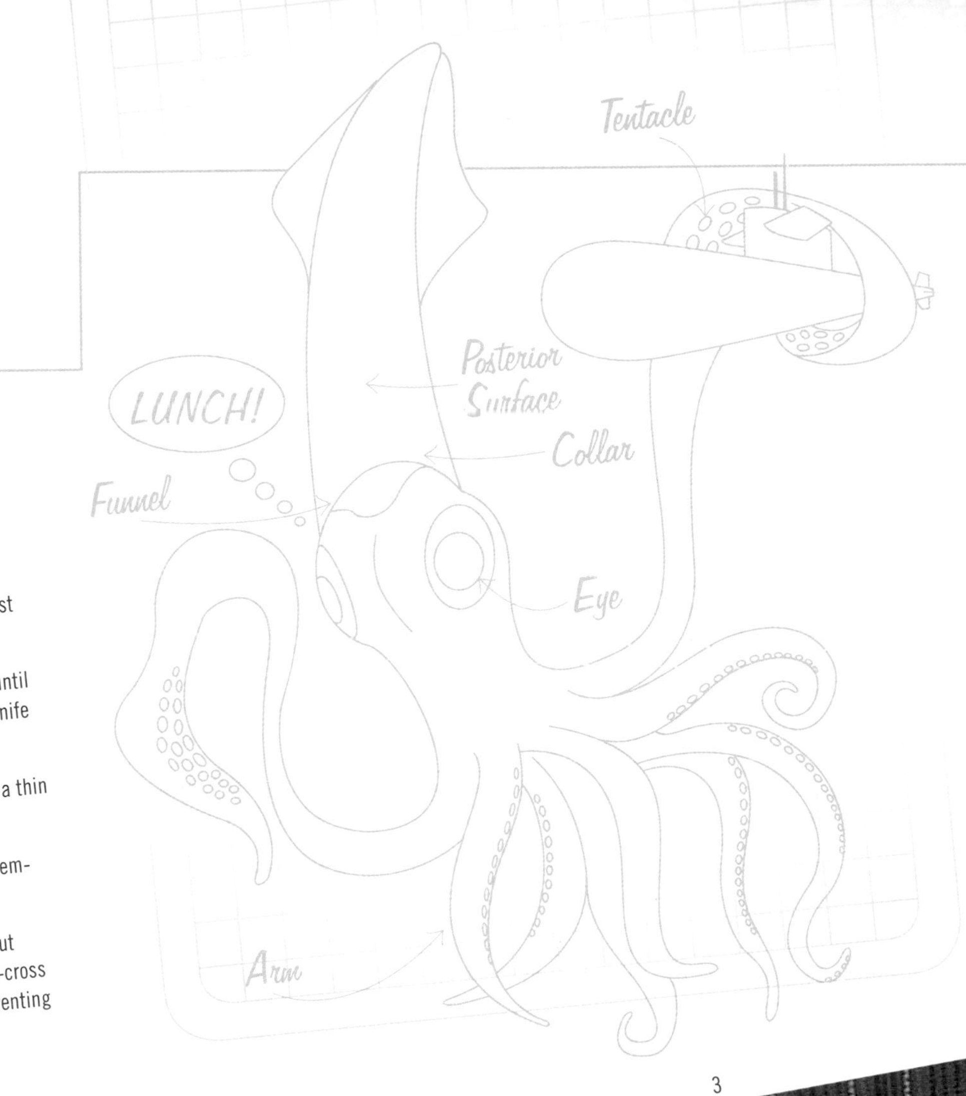

1 - Generally, the head is still attached to the tubes. Just reach up and pull gently, and it'll come right out.

2 - Reach your hand up from where the tentacles are until you feel something kind of hard. Then just grab your knife and slice. Discard the head and keep the tentacles.

3 - Pull off the way-too-chewy rudder fins, then slide a thin knife up inside the tube and slice outward.

4 - Spread the tube open and scrape off the inner membrane.

5 - Use a clean utility knife set for the shallowest cut possible and score the inside of the tube in a criss-cross pattern. This breaks up the connective tissue, preventing curling during cooking.

6 - Cut into quarters.

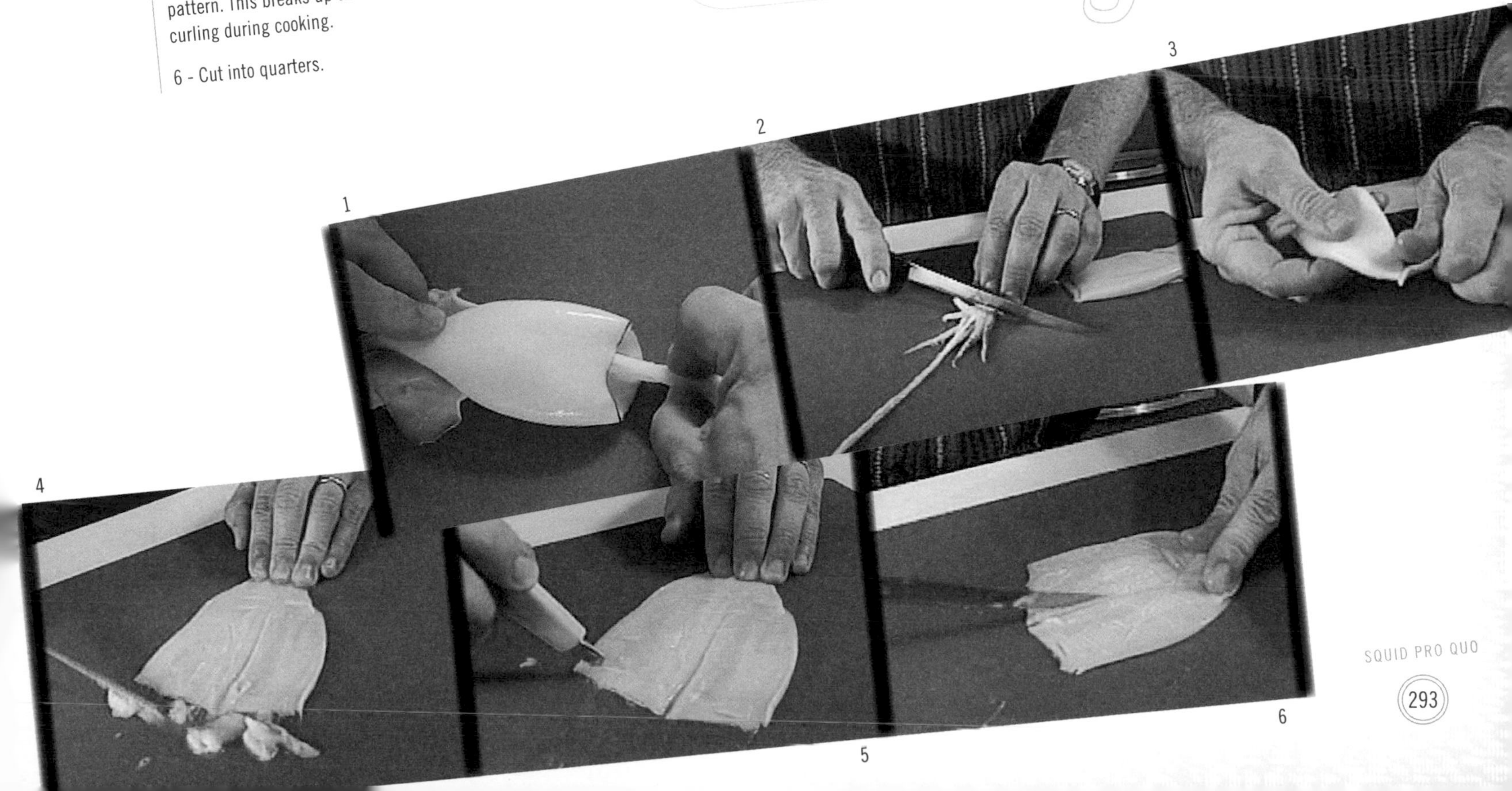

APPLICATION

SQUID VICIOUS

2 SERVINGS

Lightening-fast cooking keeps squid tender.

SOFTWARE

1	pound	whole 10/20 squid	
1	tablespoon	soy sauce	or more to taste
2	teaspoons	cornstarch	divided
½	cup	miso broth	½ cup warm H_2O combined with 1 tablespoon miso paste
1	teaspoon	balsamic vinegar	
2	teaspoons	sesame oil	
1	clove	garlic	thinly sliced
¼	teaspoon	fresh ginger	minced
2	medium	dried arbol chiles	
⅓	cup	sweet onion	diced
¼	cup	oyster mushrooms	torn into strips
⅓	cup	red bell pepper	diced
	to taste	white pepper	freshly ground
		cooked rice	for serving

PROCEDURE

1. On a **clean cutting board**, remove the tentacles from the bodies of the squid and set them aside. Make sure the tubes are cleaned, then split them open lengthwise so they look like flat triangles. Using a **utility knife**, lightly score the tubes in a crosshatch pattern. Cut each tube into four pieces of roughly equal size.

WOK THIS WAY

Since it's meant for fast, high-heat cooking, a wok is the perfect squid-cooking vessel. And although it's not classic tailgating hardware, its sturdy construction and versatility certainly lend themselves well to last-minute outdoor cookery.

The very best woks, which are also some of the cheapest, are made of high-carbon steel, which is an excellent heat conductor. But the real secret's the shape. The bowl configuration means that anything you have in it pools down in the bottom, close to the fire, so you can cook large volumes of food or small.

Wok hey: It's not a greeting but rather the traditional flavor of the wok, which comes courtesy of very high heat. How high? I often stir-fry in mine outdoors at night, and it's not unusual for the bottom of my wok to glow just before the food goes in. Try that with your cast-iron fry pan!

That said, my kitchen cook top doesn't generate the level of heat I need to produce wok hey. My outdoor propane pot burner does, which is why I only make the following dish al fresco. If you do use an outside burner, of course, you must adhere to any and all manufacturer's instructions.

TIDBIT | A squid is 80 percent edible.

2 Combine the soy sauce with 1 teaspoon of the cornstarch and toss the squid in it to coat in a **small bowl**. Set aside to marinate while you prepare the rest of the dish. In **another bowl**, combine the miso broth and balsamic vinegar with the remaining cornstarch.

3 In a **hot pan or wok**, heat the sesame oil and swirl to coat the pan. Working quickly, add the garlic, ginger, and chiles. Fry for 10 to 15 seconds. Add the squid and cook for 30 to 40 seconds (it's going to curl up—that's okay). Add the onion, mushrooms, and bell pepper and sauté for 1 minute. Pour in the miso mixture and simmer until the sauce begins to thicken, 1 to 2 minutes. Season with the white pepper and additional soy sauce, if desired. Serve over rice.

[1] Restaurant cooks thaw just about everything this way.

COOLER PACKING

A crucial skill for tailgating. Here's a break-away view of a cooler packed for successful chilling.

Most folks don't realize that you can turn a cooler into a food warmer. Get yourself a couple of bricks, wrap them in heavy-duty aluminum foil, and park them in a 500°F oven for half an hour. Place them on top of a towel—a thick, old one, preferably—in the bottom of the cooler. Moisten another towel with hot water and spread it over the bricks.

Heat rises, right? That's why we've got the hot bricks in the bottom. But then every time you open the lid you let the hot air out. So, place another towel on top to act as insulation. That way when you open the lid and go around hunting for something, you're not going to let all the heat out.

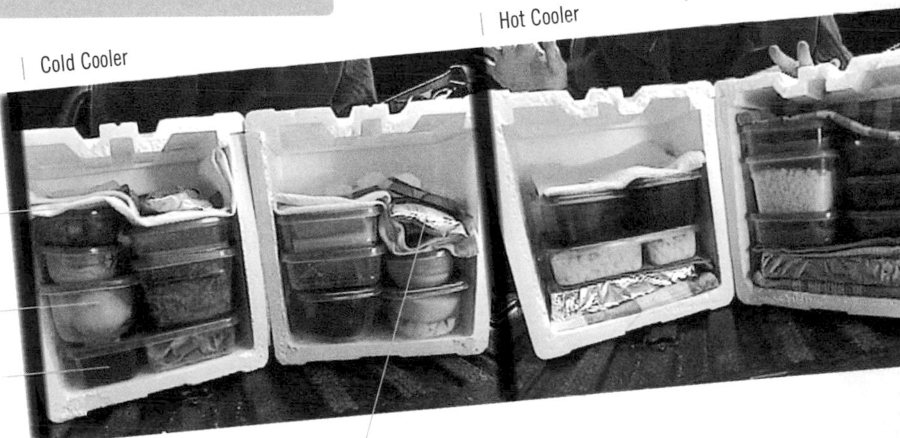

Cold Cooler

Hot Cooler

Kitchen towel on top with frozen cold packs (ice melts, and the resulting water can saturate everything).

The goods. Everything separately sealed (no cross contamination here).

Raw ingredients on bottom.

Cold packs

Make sure all items are thoroughly chilled before they go into the cooler. After all, it's not a refrigerator.

THE ART OF DARKNESS II: COCOA

EPISODE 64 | SEASON 5 | GOOD EATS

Cocoa powder doesn't get a lot of respect. I suspect the problem is the word *powder*, which connotes convenience products that don't necessarily reflect the full potential of the original ingredients: garlic powder, onion powder, curry powder. Cocoa powder, on the contrary, is the pure essence of chocolate, its truest expression, and, if forced to choose, I'd rather have a good-quality cocoa powder in my pantry than chocolate itself.

After the fall of the Mad French Chef came the rise of Coco Carl (later Koko Karl), my new nemesis. Representing greed, corner-cutting, and general unwholesomeness, he is Slugg-worth to my Willy Wonka and is stunningly portrayed by Bart Hansard, a charter member of the *Good Eats* Players. Like every good nemesis, I just can't keep Coco down, and he'll return in many a guise, including Auntie Pudding.

KNOWLEDGE CONCENTRATE

In 1828 a Dutch chocolatier named Coenraad Johannes van Houten devised a hydraulic press capable of squeezing chocolate liquor—not an alcohol but cacao nibs that have been crushed to a paste—so that the fat or cocoa butter separated from the cocoa solids, or "cake." Finely crushing the cake gave birth to natural cocoa powder, which is easily recognized by its brick-red color and bitter flavor. Van Houten continued tinkering and found that by treating the cocoa with an alkali the flavor of the powder mellowed and the color darkened quite a bit. To this day, this type of cocoa powder is referred to as Dutch process or "Dutched" cocoa. Since they don't taste or look anything alike, the well-stocked pantry will be home to both natural and Dutch process powders: In baked goods[1] they are not interchangeable, as the difference in acidity can really throw things off.

COCOA POWDER PRODUCTION

Pick the Pod

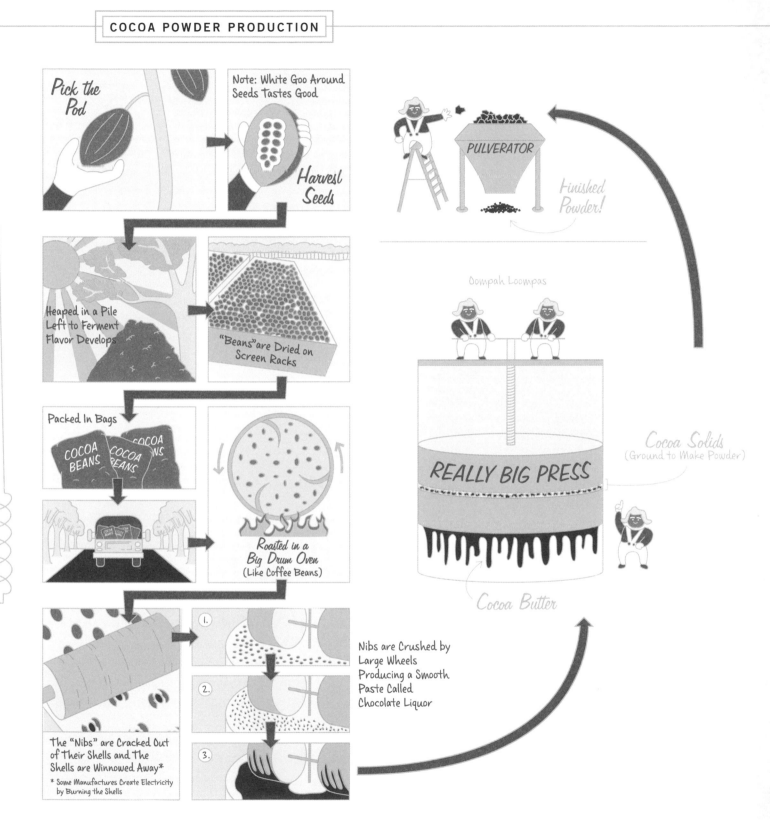

Note: White Goo Around Seeds Tastes Good

Harvest Seeds

Heaped in a Pile
Left to Ferment
Flavor Develops

"Beans" are Dried on Screen Racks

Packed In Bags

COCOA BEANS

Roasted in a Big Drum Oven (Like Coffee Beans)

The "Nibs" are Cracked Out of Their Shells and The Shells are Winnowed Away*

* Some Manufactures Create Electricity by Burning the Shells

1.

2.

3.

Nibs are Crushed by Large Wheels Producing a Smooth Paste Called Chocolate Liquor

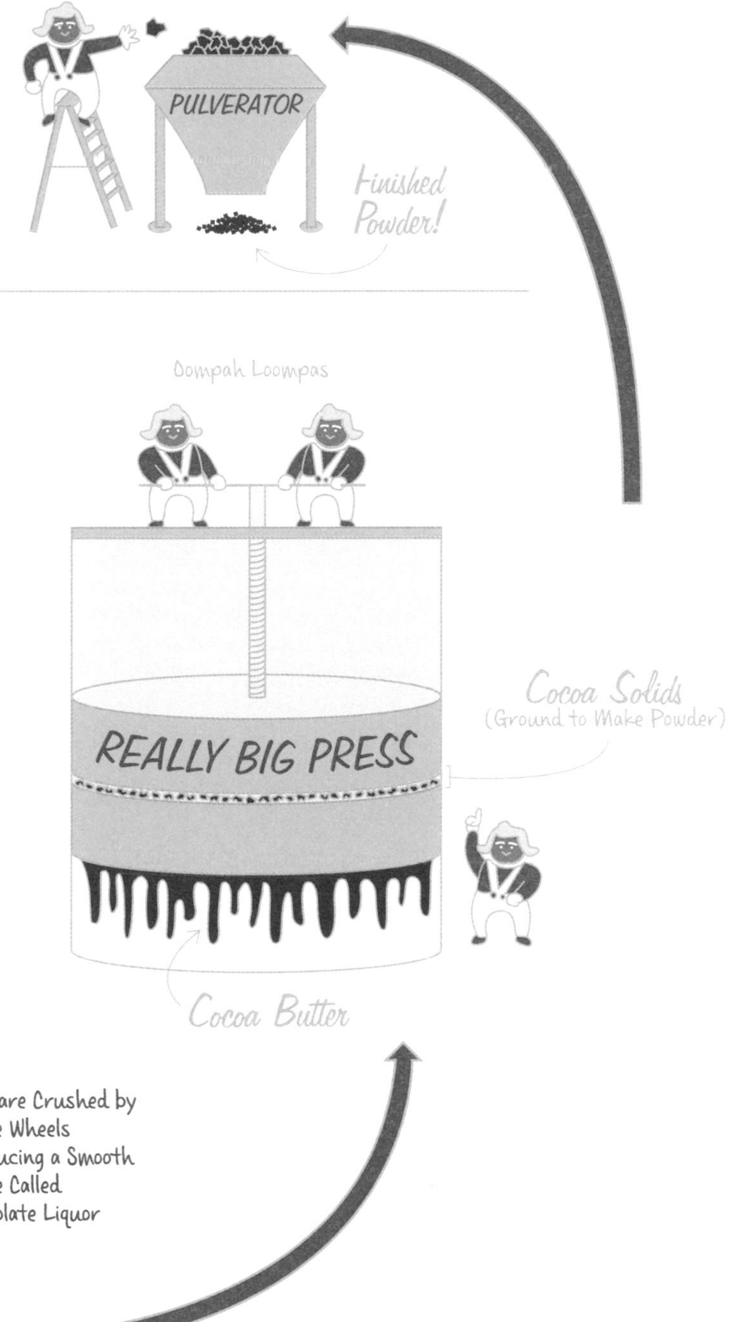

APPLICATION

COCOA BROWNIES

9 BROWNIES[2]

In the annals of food mythology, few figures are as revered as one "Brownie" Schrumpf, the late-nineteenth-century baker-librarian who left the baking powder out of a chocolate cake one day and was brave enough to serve the results, which became this country's favorite dessert. Now, uh, I have no idea whether Mrs. Schrumpf actually existed. But I am willing to bet that the brownie was born of just such a bungle.

SOFTWARE

4	large	eggs	
7	ounces	granulated sugar	
6	ounces	light brown sugar	
5¾	ounces	natural cocoa powder	(not Dutch process)
2½	ounces	all-purpose flour	
½	teaspoon	kosher salt	
8	ounces	unsalted butter	melted
2	teaspoons	vanilla extract	

PROCEDURE

1. Crank the oven to 300°F.
2. Lube an **8-inch square baking pan** with non-stick spray. Trim a piece of **parchment paper** so that it fits just inside the baking dish with overhang on two sides and place it inside the pan.
3. Beat the eggs with a **stand mixer fitted with the paddle attachment** at medium speed until fluffy and light yellow, 2 to 3 minutes.
4. In a **separate bowl**, combine the granulated sugar, brown sugar, cocoa powder, flour, and salt. Drop the mixer speed to low and slowly introduce the sugar mixture. Follow with the butter and vanilla. Continue mixing until you've got a nice, smooth goo.[3]
5. Pour the batter into the prepared pan and bake for 45 to 50 minutes.
6. Check for doneness by inserting the tip of an **instant-read thermometer** into the middle of the brownie, being careful not to touch the bottom of the pan; 195°F is the target. Cool in the pan for 3 minutes, then lift the brownie out using the parchment paper as a sling.
7. Cut the brownies into 9 pieces using a **pizza wheel** and move to a **rack** to cool completely.

Pizza wheel: best for cutting brownies

SIFTING

Because of cocoa powder's bad habit of clumping as it ages, most cocoa powder–based applications call for sifting—and sifting, more times than not, means the use of a sifter.

I'll be honest. I hate sifters. If a recipe tells me to sift, I generally just take whatever it is for a spin in the food processor. That said, if you don't have a food processor or simply feel you must have a sifter, read on.

A spring-trigger sifter works by actuating a second screen disk over a primary stationary screen. As it shifts back and forth, the flour passes through.

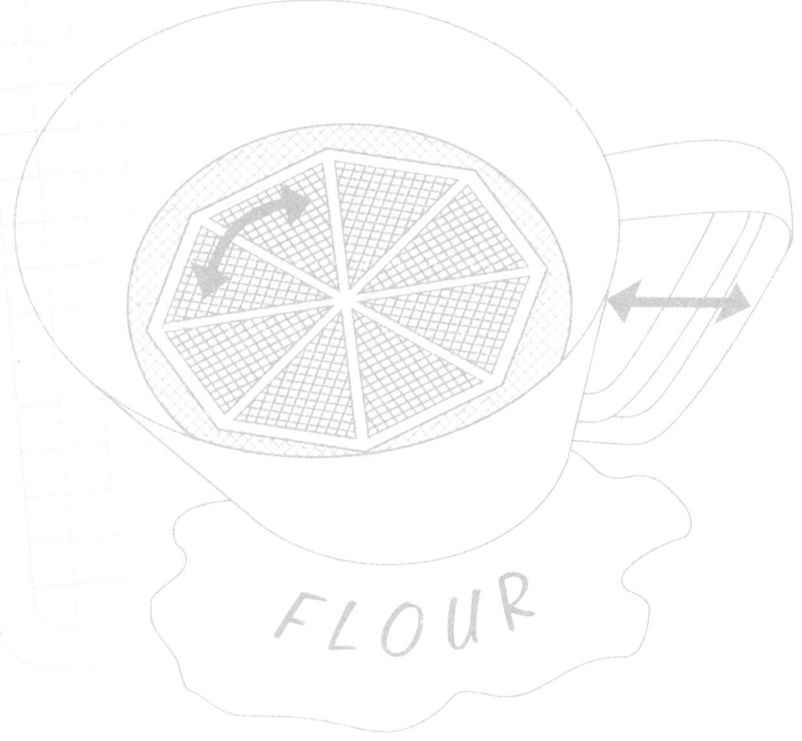

Location: Kitchenware Store

AB: Sifting accomplishes three things: It breaks up the small clods that form in things like cocoa powder, it aerates compressed powders like flour, and if used properly it can integrate small amounts of powders like baking soda and baking powder.

W: Mixing.

AB: What?

W: Why say "integrating" when you can say "mixing"? Why do you always have to go for the words with the most syllables?

ROTARY SIFTERS (like Grandma's) make a mess and are notorious for falling apart.

SHAKER SIFTERS make a mess and tire out your wrist.

SPRING-LOADED SIFTERS possessing trigger handles that actuate multiple screen oscillation are the way to go. Or, as W says . . .

W: They're fast and a lot less messy than other models but the problem is that the spring can wear some people's hands out before the sifting is done.

AB: Wow. Look at that tight pattern. That's really beautiful. You know, being ambisinister I think I'll opt for the more neoteric of the, uh, quintuplet (*sic*). And although I delectate in discommoding you, I will tarry here no longer. As always, you have been supernumerary.

W: And as always you've been super-numbing.

APPLICATION

HOT COCOA MIX

4½ CUPS DRY MIX, ENOUGH FOR APPROXIMATELY 36 CUPS COCOA

Instant cocoa is a fine concept, but most commercial mixes aren't exactly packed with quality ingredients or flavor. No matter—this is fast, easy, and will keep for a year if kept in an airtight container in a cool place.

SOFTWARE

2	cups	confectioners' sugar	
1	cup	unsweetened cocoa powder	preferably Dutch process
2½	cups	nonfat dry milk powder	
1	teaspoon	fine-grain salt	
2	teaspoons	cornstarch	
1	pinch (or more to taste)	ground cayenne pepper[4]	
		hot milk or H_2O to serve	

PROCEDURE

1. Combine the confectioners' sugar, cocoa powder, milk powder, salt, cornstarch, and cayenne in a **large airtight container**. Secure the lid and shake vigorously to combine, and remember to shake prior to every extraction.
2. To serve: Place 2 tablespoons of the mix in a mug and add about 2 fluid ounces hot water or milk. Stir to combine. Fill the mug with more hot water or milk and enjoy.

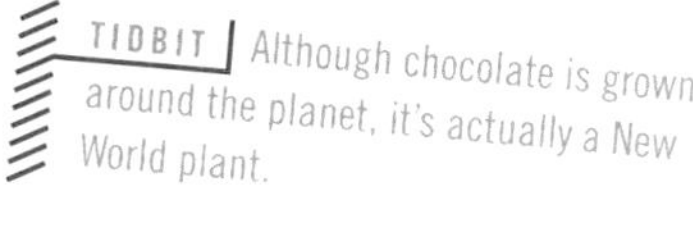

TIDBIT | Although chocolate is grown around the planet, it's actually a New World plant.

APPLICATION

BIG BROWN SQUEEZE

5 CUPS

I find most chocolate syrups too sweet. This version has a nice bitter balance like Bosco did 30 years ago.

SOFTWARE

1½	cups	H_2O	
3	cups	sugar	
2	tablespoons	corn syrup	
1½	cups	cocoa powder	Dutch process
1	tablespoon	vanilla extract	
¼	teaspoon	kosher salt	

PROCEDURE

1. Bring the water, the sugar, and corn syrup to a boil over medium heat in a **3-quart saucier**. Decrease the heat to low and gradually **whisk** in the cocoa powder. Continue to whisk until all the cocoa has been incorporated. Cook until slightly thickened, about 5 minutes. Remove from the heat and add the vanilla and salt. Let cool for 15 minutes, then pour into **squeeze bottles** using a **funnel**. Store in the refrigerator.
2. To use, place the squeeze bottle in hot water for 10 minutes. Squeeze into cold milk and stir for delicious chocolate milk or serve on your favorite ice cream. And, hey, it's fat free!

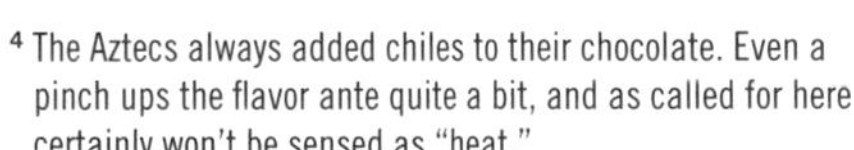

[1] Many experts still claim that Dutch process cocoa powder is more soluble in water-type liquids and therefore easier to work with in lean applications. Personally, I don't think there's any difference whatsoever.

[2] Or three, depending on how you portion.

[3] Could you add nuts? Sure, you could add nuts—walnuts, to be precise—but as far as I'm concerned brownies are about chocolatey goodness, and that's that.

[4] The Aztecs always added chiles to their chocolate. Even a pinch ups the flavor ante quite a bit, and as called for here certainly won't be sensed as "heat."

SQUASH COURT

EPISODE 65 | SEASON 5 | GOOD EATS

I like most *Good Eats* episodes. After all, each one is my child and as beautiful and unique as a snowflake. This one, not so much. I had big hopes for it, but the applications just got in the way. We shot this big scene reviewing all the varieties of squash, and it had to go. There was a doctor scene . . . nixed. Funny to think that sometimes the cooking gets in the way of the food show. Oh, bother.

KNOWLEDGE CONCENTRATE

Some "hard" facts: Squash are fruits, edible members of the gourd family, and fall roughly into two categories. Soft-skinned or "summer" squash are harvested young, and can be consumed skin and all. Hard-skinned squash ripen in late summer. They're referred to as "winter" squash because their tough skin keeps them viable for months. In the days before deep freezes and global agriculture, hard squash in the root cellar meant high-quality nutrition on the plate throughout winter.

I think one of the reasons Americans aren't exactly gobbling up hard squash is that by and large they are, well, hard. What's worse is that they are rounded, so going after one with a knife is like trying to stab a bowling ball. Here are a couple of methods for breaching the castle walls.

THE PEELER APPROACH: Some hard squashes are only mostly hard and can be skinned like a carrot or potato. Delicata and butternut often yield to a heavy-duty vegetable peeler, and that's usually the first thing I try.

THE MALLET ENTRY: Place the squash on a heavy cutting board in whatever position it's most stable. For short squash this will usually be standing upright on the blossom end (the dimple on the bottom). For long, smooth squash such as butternuts, use a peeler to whittle a flat spot on one side that you can use as a base. Place a heavy chef's knife or cleaver at the angle you want to split the gourd. While holding the knife securely, tap the back of the blade with a wooden or rubber mallet. Use of a metal mallet (otherwise known as a hammer) will damage the knife no matter how gentle you are. When tackling a larger specimen, the spine of the knife may disappear within before bifurcation is achieved. In this case the blade is usually lodged in the fruit in such a manner that it is possible to lift the squash off the board by the knife handle and gently rap it down on the board until it splits.

THE JACK-O'-LANTERN ENTRY: Recipes focusing on pumpkin-shaped squashes (I don't actually cook pumpkins themselves, as they're usually close to flavorless) often call for topping the gourd the way you would a jack-o'-lantern. This is especially true of acorn squash, which can be very hard indeed. For these, I use the very same hand saw I use on the big orange things at Halloween. I got it at the hardware store, and it looks like this:

A quick guide to a few of my favorite squash:

ACORN: This common small squash does indeed resemble an acorn. Its size makes it a reasonable single serving. Slice off the bottom tip, lid the top, remove the seeds, stuff with just about anything from rice to dried fruit, and bake whole (I usually go for an hour at 350°F, just like a big potato). Acorns are often two-tone, with orange splotches on green. Look for specimens with as much green and as little orange as possible.

BUTTERNUT: Very common in American markets. Shaped something like a vase married to a lightbulb. Seeds are only in the big end, so the longer the squash the more flesh you'll have. Although the flavor is a little on the insipid side, the butternut's easy handling characteristics make it worth having around. The texture is like a sweet potato and lends itself well to soups. I usually cut it into chunks and steam it.

DELICATA: Also called the Bohemia squash. This heirloom variety is long and variegated and has a relatively thin, easy-to-manage skin. This is one of the sweetest of the hard squashes, and I often peel it, slice it into rounds, and fry it like tempura. You can also bake it whole and mash it.

KABOCHA: When we made this episode I'd never even tasted one of these large, striated Japanese squashes. The kobacha has a sweet, nearly fiberless orange flesh that's a good deal drier than, say, butternut squash. I like to dice it and sauté it. It's also good in pies.

SPAGHETTI: Many a weeknight meal at my house has been rescued by this strange gourd. Cut it in half lengthwise and scoop out the seeds. Wrap in plastic and microwave on high for 10 to 13 minutes, depending on the size. Cool for a few minutes, then, using a fork, scrape the flesh from end to end. Behold the golden strands of goodness the size and shape of spaghetti! Toss in a bowl with butter, salt, pepper, and grated Parm. Toss on an herb if you like. Eat. That's the only way I cook the stuff, and I cook it a lot.

Stick it in the top at an angle and gently saw while rotating the gourd, like this.

APPLICATION

BUTTERNUT DUMPLINGS WITH BROWN BUTTER AND SAGE

10 TO 12 SERVINGS; ABOUT 12 DOZEN DUMPLINGS

This is my favorite recipe from the episode but sadly not a favorite with viewers, some of whom had a tough time getting the dough to come together. To address the problem we've included cooked weights for both the potato and squash.

SOFTWARE

FOR THE DUMPLINGS

4	medium	russet potatoes	about 1½ pounds total, scrubbed and rinsed, and skins pierced
1	small	butternut squash	about 2½ pounds total, halved and seeded
1	large	egg	lightly beaten
1½	tablespoons	kosher salt	plus additional for cooking water
½	teaspoon	freshly grated nutmeg	
1½	cups	all-purpose flour	plus an additional ½ cup for dusting
		oil	to coat

FOR SERVING

1	bunch	sage leaves	chiffonade
8	tablespoons	unsalted butter	at room temperature
1½	ounces	Parmesan cheese	freshly grated

PROCEDURE

1. Heat the oven to 375°F.
2. Bake the potatoes directly on the middle rack of the oven for 1 hour, or until very tender. At the same time, place the squash flesh side down on a **half sheet pan** and roast until very tender, about 45 minutes.
3. Split the potatoes and cool just until they can be handled safely. Don't let them cool completely. Scoop the flesh of the potatoes into a **large mixing bowl** and smash with a **potato masher**.

TIP | Store ripe hard squash in a cool, dry, dark place for up to 3 months.

4 **Scoop** the squash from its skin and add to the potatoes. You should have about 10 ounces of potato and 20 ounces of squash. Mash them together with a **potato masher**, until mostly smooth. There may be some small lumps.

5 Mix in the egg, salt, and nutmeg. Then add the flour and mix with a **large wooden** spoon until a soft dough forms. Do not do this in a mixer; it will overwork the dough. Add more flour by the spoonful if it's still too moist.

6 Turn out onto a clean, floured counter and divide into 8 portions. Roll each portion out into ropes about 2 feet long, and cut into 1-inch pieces. Line the pieces up on a floured **half sheet pan** as you work. At this point you could freeze them on the sheet pan until solid, then transfer to zip-top bags and store in the freezer for up to 1 month.

7 Bring a **large pot** of salted water to a boil and gently drop in about 2 dozen of the dumplings. Don't overcrowd the pot. As they begin to float, after 3 to 4 minutes, remove them with a **slotted spoon** and toss them into an **ice bath** for 1 minute.

8 Drain the dumplings, pat dry with a **clean kitchen towel**, and toss with a little oil. Store loosely in a large container until ready to use. The dumplings can be cooked and stored in the refrigerator this way for up to 3 days.

9 To serve, melt 1 tablespoon of soft butter in a **large sauté pan** over high heat. Cook until the butter begins to foam and turn brown. Add 2 teaspoons sage leaves and 1 cup of dumplings. Cook for 1 minute, or until the dumplings are heated through. Repeat until you have the desired number of servings. Plate and top with Parmesan.

APPLICATION

PUMPKIN BREAD

1 (9-INCH) LOAF OR A DOZEN MUFFINS

Pumpkin bread has a bad rap and that's a shame. Fresh pumpkin and fresh cinnamon are key.

SOFTWARE

10	ounces	all-purpose flour	
2	teaspoons	ground cinnamon	
1	teaspoon	baking soda	
¼	teaspoon	baking powder	
½	teaspoon	kosher salt	
12	ounces	sugar	
¾	cup	vegetable oil	
3	large	eggs	
1	teaspoon	vanilla extract	
1	pound	fresh pumpkin	peeled and seeded, cut into chunks
4	ounces	hulled[1] pumpkin seeds	toasted

PROCEDURE

1. Crank the oven to 325°F.
2. Take the flour, cinnamon, baking soda, baking powder, and salt for a spin in your **food processor**, then move them to a **large mixing bowl**.
3. Spin the sugar, oil, eggs, and vanilla in the processor, pulsing just a few times to bring everything together. Dump the goo right on top of the dry team and stir to combine. (Don't worry if there are a few lumps.)
4. Install the processor's shredding blade[2] and shred the pumpkin in the food processor. Dump onto a **kitchen towel** and twist into a ball to wring out as much water as possible (within reason)—oh, and do this over the sink. Fold the pumpkin and the pumpkin seeds into the batter using a large **rubber spatula**, or, better yet, your **hand**.
5. Pour into a **nonstick 9-by-5-by-3-inch loaf pan or a standard nonstick muffin pan**, filling the latter two thirds full. (If your only loaf pan is not nonstick—i.e., it's a "stick" pan—lightly butter it and dust with flour.)
6. Bake the loaf for 1 hour and 15 minutes to 1½ hours, or until an internal temperature of 200° to 210°F is reached. Cool for 15 minutes in the pan, then turn out onto a **cooling rack**. Cool completely. If making muffins, bake them for 30 minutes, and remove from the muffin tin to a cooling rack immediately.

[1] Also known as *pepitas*, Mexican pumpkin seeds have had their hulls removed. Do not use the unhulled seeds that come out of a standard jack-o'-lantern.

[2] A shredding blade came with your food processor; you may have put it in the bottom drawer over by the bread box.

FOR WHOM THE CHEESE MELTS II

EPISODE 66 | SEASON 5 | GOOD EATS

This was the first episode to feature my nephew Elton, and let me be the first to confess that I don't have a nephew. Nor do I have a sister, which means Elton's mother, Marsha, is equally fraudulent. The young man who played Elton in this and two other episodes is now taller than me, plays varsity football, and has applied to West Point.

I can't remember why I came up with Elton other than I thought it would be fun. And it was. He was a good kid and a good listener. Learned his lines, too, which is more than I can say for myself most days.

Although Jeffersonian mythologists hold that mac & cheese was invented in the kitchen at Monticello, I've never encountered a shred of evidence supporting the claim. The fact that I perpetuated this culinary . . . fib . . . is evidence of how desperate I was for a good storyline.

ELTON: Jefferson didn't visit Italy until 1807, so macaroni and cheese couldn't be a comfort food for the fathers at the time they were founding.

AB: Boy, you're getting bogged down in details. You've got to keep your eye on the—on the bigger, more marketable picture, okay? You know what? For your presentation we ought to dress you up like Thomas Jefferson.

ELTON: You want me to go to school wearing stockings and a bow in my hair? Think of the emotional scarring.

A FEW CHEDDAR FACTS

- The European Union recognizes the term "West County Farmhouse Cheddar" as a legal protected designation of origin.
- A Wisconsin cheddar weighing 34,951 pounds was produced for the 1964 New York's World Fair.
- That cheddar flavor and aroma come from naturally occuring esters, ketones, acids, and aldehydes.

KNOWLEDGE CONCENTRATE

The pasta: The word *macaroni* refers to any semolina and water pasta that doesn't contain eggs. There are hundreds if not thousands of shapes and sizes to choose from, and many chefs are expressing their creativity by inviting rigatoni, penne, and fusilli, and even shapes like farfalle and radiatore, to the mac & cheese party, which is just crazy. Not me. When it comes to macaroni and cheese, I stick with the traditional elbow noodle, which, with its discreet angle and petite opening, is just right for binding the casserole and taking a bit of cheesy goodness on board. Speaking of . . .

Elbow macaroni: the perfect size and shape for cheesy casserole

The cheese: Cheddar is a semi-firm cow's milk cheese originally produced in and around the village of Cheddar in southwestern England since the twelfth century. After coagulation, the cheese curd is cut and stacked so that the collective weight wrings out a considerable amount of moisture resulting in a firmness that, with time, becomes crumbly. Whether used in England, Ireland, Wisconsin, or Vermont, this process is known as "cheddaring."

The flavor and texture of cheddar depends on its age. Qualifiers such as mild, medium, sharp, and extra sharp describe cheeses anywhere from 3 to 30 months old. New York and Vermont cheddars are typically quite sharp.

Although most of us think of cheddar as pale yellow, its natural hue is creamy white. The yellow comes from annatto seed.

TIDBIT Annatto is a spice and coloring agent derived from the seeds of the achiote tree. Although it does lend a slight bitterness to Hispanic and Indian cuisine, annatto is used more often as a natural food dye to give cheddar its golden glow.

The vessel: Since it is an amalgam of ingredients, mixed, baked, and served in a single vessel, macaroni and cheese qualifies as a casserole and as such can be baked in almost anything that's wide and low. But I do have preferences. I'm not a fan of metal roasting pans for casseroles because metal is too good a conductor. Mac & cheese has a lot of mass, so it takes a long time to cook, and metal tends to burn the sides and bottom long before the bulk is done. This may explain why the traditional cooking vessel for a casserole is—get this—a casserole. In Europe casseroles are almost always made out of earthenware, terra cotta, and the like, which being insulators are slow to heat. I'm proud to say my favorite casserole materials were born right here in the good ol' U. S. of A.

PYREX. This heat-resistant glass was originally developed for use in railroad lanterns. It was converted into bakeware in about 1915. But its proudest moment came in the '60s, when it was chosen as the window material for the Apollo spacecraft. It's heavy, it's heatproof, and it's inexpensive. The only problem is that it can be a beast to keep clean, and it's not the prettiest thing to bring to the table (casseroles aren't known for their attractive undersides).

CORNINGWARE was developed in the 1950s by scientists who figured out that if you take a certain type of photosensitive glass and put it in a very, very hot furnace, it converts into an opaque, heat-resistant, and extremely durable ceramic. When it comes to baked goods, Corningware has an advantage over Pyrex: It's opaque, and with its polished surface it looks more refined if you go for that kind of thing.

Whatever you do, I suggest you steer clear of rectangles and squares, unless of course you like burned, dry, chewy corners—and I know some people do. If you're not one of them, stick with round vessels. I usually bake my mac & cheese in the same dish I bake soufflés in.

APPLICATION — **MAC & CHEESE**

6 TO 8 SERVINGS

Mac & cheese: Enough said. Originally this application called for a bay leaf, which I've decided is pretty much useless.

SOFTWARE

8	ounces	elbow macaroni	
3	tablespoons	unsalted butter	
3	tablespoons	all-purpose flour	
1	tablespoon	ground (powdered) mustard[1]	
½	teaspoon	paprika[2]	
½	cup	onion	diced
3	cups	whole milk	
1	large	egg	
9	ounces	sharp cheddar cheese	grated
1	teaspoon	kosher salt	
½	teaspoon	black pepper	freshly ground

FOR THE TOPPING

3	ounces	sharp cheddar cheese	grated
3	tablespoons	unsalted butter	melted
1	cup	Japanese bread crumbs	(a.k.a. panko)

TIDBIT Although President Jefferson did enjoy a type of mac & cheese in the White House, most Americans didn't discover the dish until 1937, the year Kraft introduced their instant version, which became even more popular during World War II. Why? It only cost 1 ration coupon.

PROCEDURE

1. Heat the oven to 350°F.
2. Bring 2 quarts water and 1 tablespoon kosher salt to a rolling boil in a **4-quart pot**. Add the macaroni and cook until firm al dente (chewy), about 6 minutes. Drain in a **colander** and rinse with cold water to stop the cooking.
3. Meanwhile, melt the butter in a **3-quart saucier or saucepan** over medium heat. **Whisk** in the flour and cook until the mixture is pale blond, stirring occasionally, about 3 minutes. Whisk in the mustard, paprika, and onion. Whisk in the milk and cook, whisking constantly, for 7 to 8 minutes, until slightly thickened. Remove from the heat.[3]
4. Lightly beat the egg in a **small bowl**. Add a few ounces of the milk mixture and whisk to combine.[4] Whisk the egg mixture back to the milk mixture. Stir in the cheese, 1 teaspoon salt, and the pepper. Fold in the macaroni and pour into a **4-quart casserole dish**.
5. Top the casserole: Sprinkle with the remaining cheese, then toss the bread crumbs with the melted butter and sprinkle them over the cheese.
6. Bake for 30 minutes, cool for 5 minutes, then serve to a grateful world.

APPLICATION

NEXT-DAY MAC & CHEESE "TOAST"

DEPENDS UPON THE AMOUNT OF LEFTOVERS. THE BREADING IS ENOUGH FOR 1 DISH OF MAC & CHEESE, OR ABOUT 12 (1½-INCH) SQUARES.

There's only one thing you can do to make mac & cheese even better . . . fry it.

// SOFTWARE

2	quarts	peanut oil	for frying
		leftover mac & cheese (page 309)	refrigerated overnight
½	cup	all-purpose flour	
½	teaspoon	kosher salt	
½	teaspoon	black pepper	freshly ground
½	teaspoon	ground cayenne	
1	large	egg	
¼	cup	H_2O	
1	cup	Japanese breadcrumbs	(a.k.a. panko)

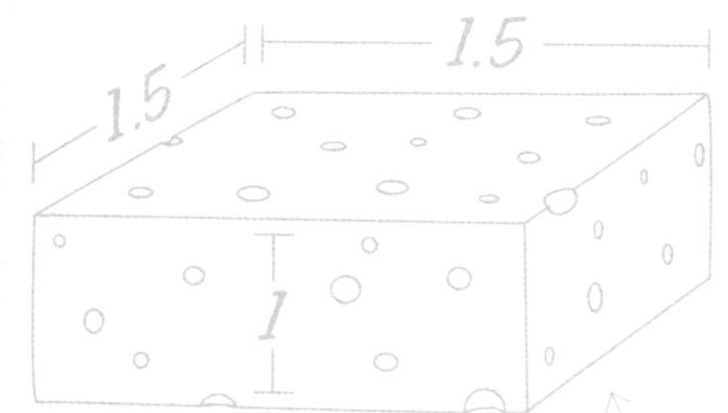

The perfect size for fried mac & cheese

// PROCEDURE

1. Heat the oil in a **5-quart Dutch oven** (fitted with a **deep-fry thermometer**, of course), to 375°F.
2. Cut the refrigerated mac & cheese into slabs roughly the size and shape of a deck of cards, or into 1½-inch squares.
3. Combine the flour, salt, pepper, and cayenne in a **pie plate**.[5] **Whisk** the egg and the water together in a **second pie plate**. Breadcrumbs go in a **third pie plate**.
4. **Dredge** each slab of mac in the flour and tap off the excess. Dip in the egg wash, then coat with the breadcrumbs. Set aside on a **cooling rack** for 5 minutes.[6]
5. Ease 3 or 4 pieces into the oil and fry until golden brown, 3 to 4 minutes. Remove to the cooling rack set over newspaper (to catch the drips). Repeat until there's nothing left to fry. Serve hot.

[1] This fine powder is nothing more than pulverized mustard seeds. Colman's, the leading brand, is a special blend of white and brown mustards first concocted by Englishman Jeremiah Colman in 1814.

[2] Smoked paprika is a nice touch . . . if you dare.

[3] Butter cooked with flour makes a roux. Adding milk maketh a classic béchamel sauce, and adding cheese to that makes a Mornay sauce. So, mac & cheese is nothing more than elbow noodles baked with a souped-up French cheese sauce.

[4] This odd maneuver is called "tempering," and it's meant to slowly heat the eggs to prevent curdling.

[5] I keep disposable aluminum models around for this.

[6] Skip this step and your breading will probably fall off into the oil.

SEND IN THE CLAMS

EPISODE 67 | SEASON 5 | GOOD EATS

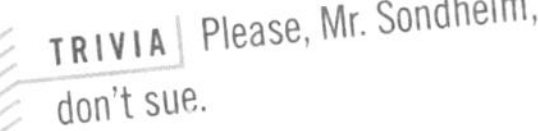

TRIVIA | Please, Mr. Sondheim, don't sue.

Although it may seem tacky to poke fun at Steve "Crocodile Hunter" Irwin now, back when we concocted this episode his wide-eyed "crikeys" and goofball enthusiasm made him a clear and present spoof target. This is actually one of my favorite show openers because I really don't think anyone took this for a set in the middle of a parking lot until we pulled back the curtain. Our lead electrician, David Traylor, once again played the required law-dog.

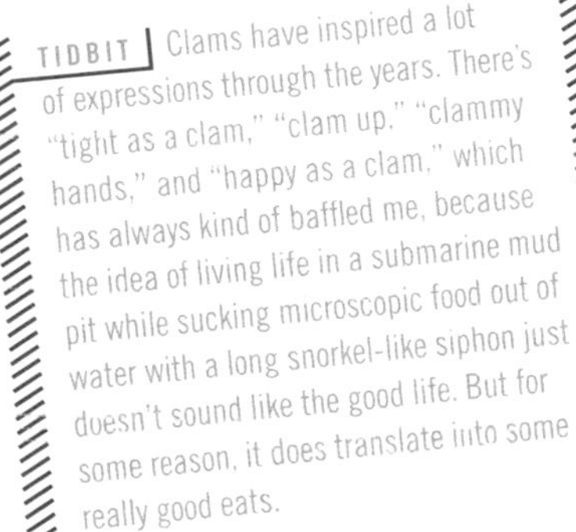

TIDBIT | Clams have inspired a lot of expressions through the years. There's "tight as a clam," "clam up," "clammy hands," and "happy as a clam," which has always kind of baffled me, because the idea of living life in a submarine mud pit while sucking microscopic food out of water with a long snorkel-like siphon just doesn't sound like the good life. But for some reason, it does translate into some really good eats.

KNOWLEDGE CONCENTRATE

Clams are bivalve mollusks, which feed by siphoning water through their tightly closed shells. Unlike oysters, clams have symmetrical shells. There are dozens of edible varieties, but most fall within two broad categories: soft- and hard-shell clams. In this episode we concentrated on the most common hard-shell variety in the American marketplace: the quahog.

***Quahog* ("KO-hog") is short for the Narragansett word *poquauhock*. Native Americans of the Northeast made money called "wampum" from quahog shells. This explains the clam's scientific name, *Mercenaria mercenaria*, which has its root in the Latin word for "money." It may also explain why "clams" has long been American slang for cash.**

Depending on their size, quahogs are given the following market names:

LITTLENECKS, named after Littleneck Bay, Long Island, are the smallest of the quahogs, usually measuring no more than 2 inches across. They're delicious raw.

MIDDLENECKS are a little bigger and can be cooked or served raw.

TOP NECKS are a little bigger still and are rarely served raw.

CHERRYSTONES are up to 3 inches in diameter and are often used in chowders.

If the above classifications sound completely wrong to you I wouldn't be surprised. That's because market names for clams aren't controlled or regulated, and in different parts of the country these terms can have very different meanings. In fact, different processors in the same region may use different terms.

Buying: When buying clams, make sure your fishmonger can present the tags or "bed" tags that show where and when the clams were harvested. When you tap them together the clams should sound like rocks with no "hollow" sound. Hard clams should be, well, all clammed up tight.

Storing: Stash your clams in your refrigerator in a leakproof container topped with a wet towel, paper towels, or newspaper. Do not expose them directly to fresh water and don't put them on ice. (They may have been on ice at the store, but odds are as it melted the water drained away. That's a tough trick to pull off in a residential refrigerator.)

As far as I'm concerned, there's no better way to serve a littleneck or middleneck than raw on the half shell. You really don't need more than a squeeze of lemon and a shucked clam . . . ah, the plot thickens.

A clam's shell is his fortress, and if you want to breach a fortress it helps to know its weaknesses: faulty drawbridge, weak rampart, shallow moat. Now consider the clam. He has a hinge, and on the inside it's flanked by two adductor muscles, which hold the shells shut. Physics would suggest that we attempt to enter at the farthest point from the hinge, at the far lip. Ah, but the shell there is so thin and brittle, it crumbles at the mere sight of approaching weaponry. But on the edge of the tightest curve, just down from the hinge, the shell is strong enough to support a lever of some type, and there's even a bit of a slot in which said tool can find purchase. But what tool? There are many models of shucking knives on the market, but I find an ordinary butter knife beats them all.[1]

TIDBIT Clams are very nutritious, containing 11 percent protein and only around 1.7 percent fat.

TIP Canned clam juice makes a nice addition to Bloody Marys.

THE ART OF OPENING CLAMS

First, stash the clams in your freezer for 30 minutes. This will relax them and make shucking much easier.

Hold the clam thusly in your open hand. Place the blade against the curve and close the fingers of the holding hand to push the blade inward. Work the blade up and across the width of the opening to the hinge and lever it open. Use the end of the blade (which is rounded on most butter knives) to gently scrape the critter off of the shell at the point where the adductor meats the shell. Scrape underneath to disconnect the muscle holding the bottom piece of shell and serve ice cold.

1

2

HINGE

If you shuck with anything sharper than a butter knife, I suggest you wear a Kevlar glove in the other hand. They're easily found in good kitchen stores and online.

BRING IN MORE CLAMS

A few types to keep your eyes and mouths open for that we didn't deal with in this episode:

GEODUCK CLAMS
Gigantic ocean clams with long siphons or "feet" that make them look like something one might find lodged on a deep space probe. Geoduck feet are especially popular in China. They're considered soft-shell clams.

COCKLES
Include any of about two hundred species of very small hard-shell clams.

MAHOGANY CLAMS
(a.k.a. golden neck) from Maine.

MANILA CLAMS
From the West Coast.

STEAMER CLAMS
From the mid-Atlantic to New England: They never close all the way and so must be cleaned thoroughly before eating.

RAZOR CLAMS
Long and narrow with thin brittle shells.

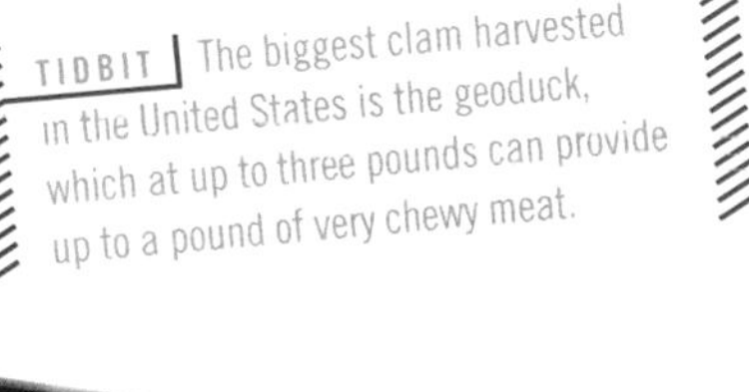
TIDBIT The biggest clam harvested in the United States is the geoduck, which at up to three pounds can provide up to a pound of very chewy meat.

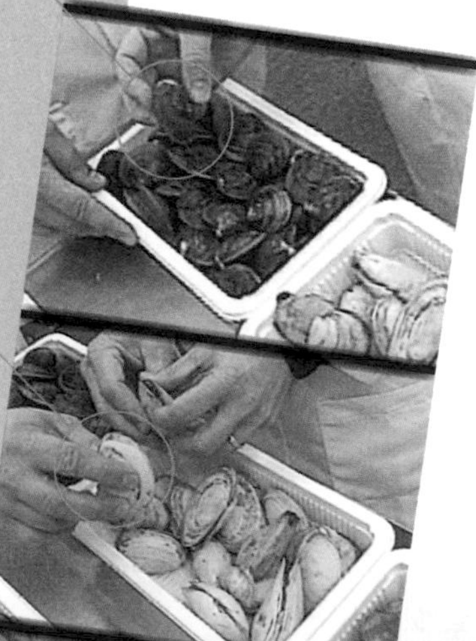

APPLICATION

CLAM CHOWDA

2 QUARTS; ABOUT 4 LARGE SERVINGS

I'm amazed at how much salt goes into canned versions of this classic. Our goal: play to the clams.

SOFTWARE

3	ounces	salt pork[2]	finely diced
1½	cups	onion	finely diced
6	cups	russet potatoes (about 3)	not peeled and finely diced
3	cups	whole milk	
1	14-ounce can	clams[3]	drained, juices reserved
12		fresh littleneck clams	
	to taste	kosher salt	
	to taste	black pepper	freshly ground
		fresh parsley	chopped, for garnish
		sour cream	for garnish
		grape tomatoes	halved, for garnish

PROCEDURE

1. Render the salt pork in a **heavy-bottomed saucepan** over medium heat until the pork is just crisp, 5 to 7 minutes. Remove with a **slotted spoon** and set aside. Sweat the onion in the pork fat until tender, 4 to 5 minutes. Add the potatoes, cover with milk, and bring to a boil. Decrease the heat and simmer until the potatoes are soft, 10 to 12 minutes.
2. Bring the reserved clam juice to a boil in a **3-quart saucier fitted with a steamer basket** over medium heat. Add the fresh clams, cover, and steam for 3 minutes, or until the clams open. Transfer to a bowl and add the steaming liquid to the chowder.
3. Puree to desired consistency with an **immersion or "stick" blender**. Season with salt and pepper.
4. Finely chop the drained canned clams and fold them into the chowder. Serve with the steamed clams, salt pork, parsley, sour cream, and grape tomatoes as garnish.

[1] This is true when small batches are concerned. If you're shucking twenty pounds of clams, I'd suggest a shucking knife for the comfy, ergonomic handle alone.

[2] Salt pork is the fattiest part of the pork belly that's been cured with salt, and you can't make chowder without it. That said, if your megamart doesn't carry it, go with slab bacon.

[3] There is no shame in using canned clams here. When shopping you'll probably have two choices: minced clams and whole baby clams. I go with the minced here but if you're making this dish when you can't get any fresh clams at all, finish with drained canned baby clams.

CHOWDA

It's tough to talk about clams without talking about chowder. The word's actually from the French *chaudière*, or "cauldron." But as a culinary tradition it refers to the pot of seafood stuff that fishermen used to keep going on board while they were out to sea. Although it's European in origin, this tradition made it across the North Atlantic to Nova Scotia and eventually to New England, where *chowder* came to mean any chunky fish or clam stew that had potatoes in it and was enriched with milk or cream. Of course, a whole other tradition evolved on the island of Manhattan, where the milk was replaced with tomatoes. (Actually, Portuguese immigrants in Rhode Island are responsible for the shift from milk to tomatoes. It seems that folks in New England, especially those from Maine, like to blame things on New Yorkers, so they made the switch in the name, calling it Manhattan-style clam chowder, which in my opinion is not chowder at all but soup.)

THIS SPUD'S FOR YOU TOO

EPISODE 68 | SEASON 5 | GOOD EATS

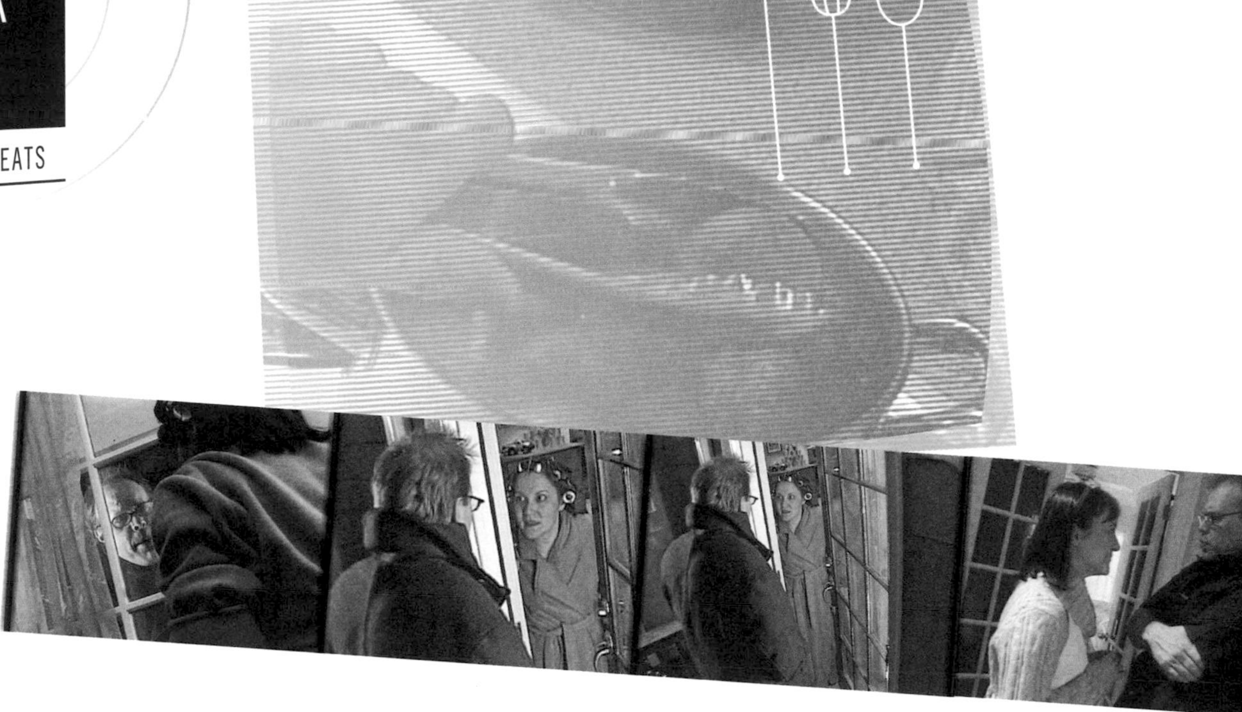

The challenge: You really want to do another potato show

because you haven't made one in sixty-something episodes and you've got some applications you'd like to get off your chest. Problem is you put just about everything you know about potatoes in that first episode, so you're a little lacking for material. Solution: Why not try a take-off on *Misery*, wherein a lot of air time is taken up with dialogue and character stuff and story and whatnot? Hey, it could work!

Another reason for doing this show was the fact that our new kitchen wasn't ready yet and I had to shoot something . . . anything.

The part of Francis Andersen was written for Widdi Turner, who up to that point had played only bit rolls on *Good Eats*. But once she dished out this tour de force, she was box-office gold and has since appeared in at least four other episodes that I can think of, including a reprisal of the role that first made her infamous.

TIDBIT | Marie Antoinette was known to decorate her hair with potato blossoms.

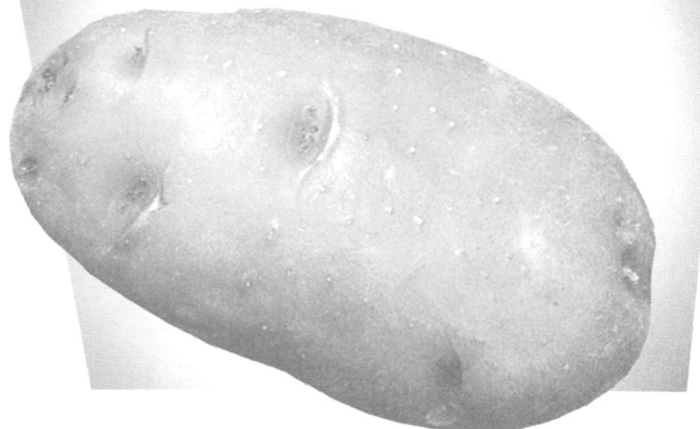

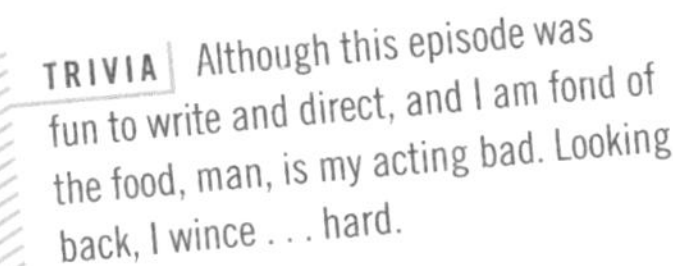
TRIVIA | Although this episode was fun to write and direct, and I am fond of the food, man, is my acting bad. Looking back, I wince . . . hard.

KNOWLEDGE CONCENTRATE

- A vast majority of the potatoes consumed in the United States are Russet Burbank potatoes, a variety developed by horticulturalist Luther Burbank in the late 1870s. Burbank developed many other edibles including several varieties of blackberries, peaches, and plums. He also developed the Shasta daisy.
- If kept in a dry, dark environment at 40°F, Russet potatoes can keep for up to two hundred days. (Never keep potatoes in a plastic bag.)
- Several multinational food companies are working on converting potato peels to biofuel.
- Spuds are a fine source of vitamins C and B6 as well as copper and manganese. The peel is very high in fiber.

SOME POTATO STATS

- Potatoes are the fourth most important food crop in the world, after maize, wheat, and rice.
- The UN proclaimed 2008 the international year of the potato.
- The largest recorded potato weighed in at 18 lbs 4 oz.
- The potato became a critical food in northern Europe during the nineteenth century because it delivered more calories per acre than any other plant.
- The average American eats potatoes twice a week, about a third as much as the modern Irishman.

TRIVIA If you're a really well-studied fan of *Good Eats* you'll be able to name the episodes that each of Francis's purloined props came from.

APPLICATION

POTATO SOUP

8 SERVINGS

I'm not going to say that a well-made potato soup is actually better than baked potatoes, but I will tell you that I rarely bake potatoes without throwing in a couple extra for soup the next day. In fact, leftover potatoes make better soup because the starch has had time to restabilize. Still, gumminess is a distinct possibility, especially if you employ a food processor, immersion blender, mixer, or other electrical engine of destruction. The best device for the job is a ricer, which, if you haven't used one, is a lot like something we used to squeeze Play-Doh through back in the '60s.

SOFTWARE

4	large	leftover baked potatoes (about 10 ounces each)	halved width-wise
3	tablespoons	unsalted butter	
1½	cups	leeks	finely chopped
1½	tablespoons	garlic	minced
1	quart	chicken stock	hot
1½	cups	low-fat buttermilk	
½	cup	sour cream	
6	ounces	Parmesan cheese	freshly grated
2½	teaspoons	kosher salt	
1	teaspoon	black pepper	freshly ground
1	tablespoon	sherry vinegar	
¼	cup	chives	minced

PROCEDURE

1. Place the potatoes, cut side down, through a **ricer** with its smallest die into a **medium mixing bowl**.
2. Melt the butter in a **large saucepan** over medium heat. Add the leeks and garlic and cook until soft, about 5 minutes. Stir in the hot stock.
3. **Whisk** together the riced potatoes, buttermilk, sour cream, and cheese. Add this mixture to the soup, stirring constantly. Season with the salt and pepper. Remove from the heat and add the vinegar.
4. **Ladle** into **bowls** and finish with chives.

TIDBIT A good ricer will come with a range of dies—that is, plates with different-size holes for mashing things through. The small dies force the potatoes into small ricelike shapes, which is why it's called a "ricer."

APPLICATION | **ROESTI**

4 SERVINGS

Think of roesti as a hash brown, only Swiss. I suppose you could make a hash brown that's not a roesti or a roesti that isn't a hash brown, but I wouldn't be able to tell the difference. Since, when making a roesti, or hash browns, you want the individual pieces to soften but not to mush, and you want them to adhere without becoming gummy, medium-starch potatoes such as Yukon Golds are ideal, especially if you park them in the fridge overnight before you grate them. The cold tells the potato to start converting starch into sugar. Sugar browns quicker and deeper than starch does, and when it comes to hash browns (roesti), brown is good.

TIDBIT | Thomas Jefferson introduced French fries to the White House during his presidency in the first decade of the nineteenth century.

SOFTWARE

1	pound	Yukon Gold potatoes	chilled and shredded
4	teaspoons	onions	shredded
4	teaspoons	vegetable oil	
4	tablespoons	unsalted butter	
	to taste	kosher salt	
	to taste	black pepper	freshly ground

PROCEDURE

1. Combine the potatoes and onions in a **salad spinner**. Spin for 1 to 2 minutes to remove as much liquid as possible from the mixture.
2. In a **large mixing bowl**, combine this mixture with the oil and divide into 4 equal parts.
3. Heat the oven to 200°F.
4. Melt ½ tablespoon of the butter in a **10-inch nonstick skillet** over medium heat.
5. Season one part of the potato mixture with salt and pepper, then spread it into a thin layer in the pan. Using a **spatula**, form the potatoes into a round and press down gently; cook for 5 to 7 minutes, until browned on the bottom.
6. Top the roesti with another ½ tablespoon butter and slide it onto a pan lid. Carefully invert the pan over the lid and flip the pan and lid back over (the raw side of the roesti should now be down in the pan). Return the pan to the heat and cook the roesti for 5 to 7 minutes, until browned.
7. Remove to a **cooling rack** and hold in the oven. Repeat with the remaining potato mixture.

SUB-APPLICATION — WAFFLED ROESTI

In tinkering with this application over the years we've discovered that roesti cook very nicely in a waffle iron, which is good because that blessed device needed something to keep it from becoming a unitasker.

// PROCEDURE

1. Combine the potatoes and onions in a **salad spinner**. Spin for 1 to 2 minutes to remove as much liquid as possible from the mixture.
2. In a **large mixing bowl**, combine this mixture with the oil and divide into 4 equal parts.
3. Heat a **waffle iron** on its highest setting.
4. Melt the butter. **Brush** each side of the preheated waffle iron with about ½ tablespoon of the melted butter.
5. Season one part of the potato mixture with salt and pepper, then add it to the iron and spread into an even layer. Close the iron and cook for 8 to 10 minutes. Remove the roesti to a **cooling rack** and hold in the warm oven. Repeat with remaining portions.

TIDBIT | Potatoes have been cultivated in South America for seven thousand years. The Inca measured time according to how long it took potatoes to cook. The Quacho Indians have more than a thousand words for *potato*.

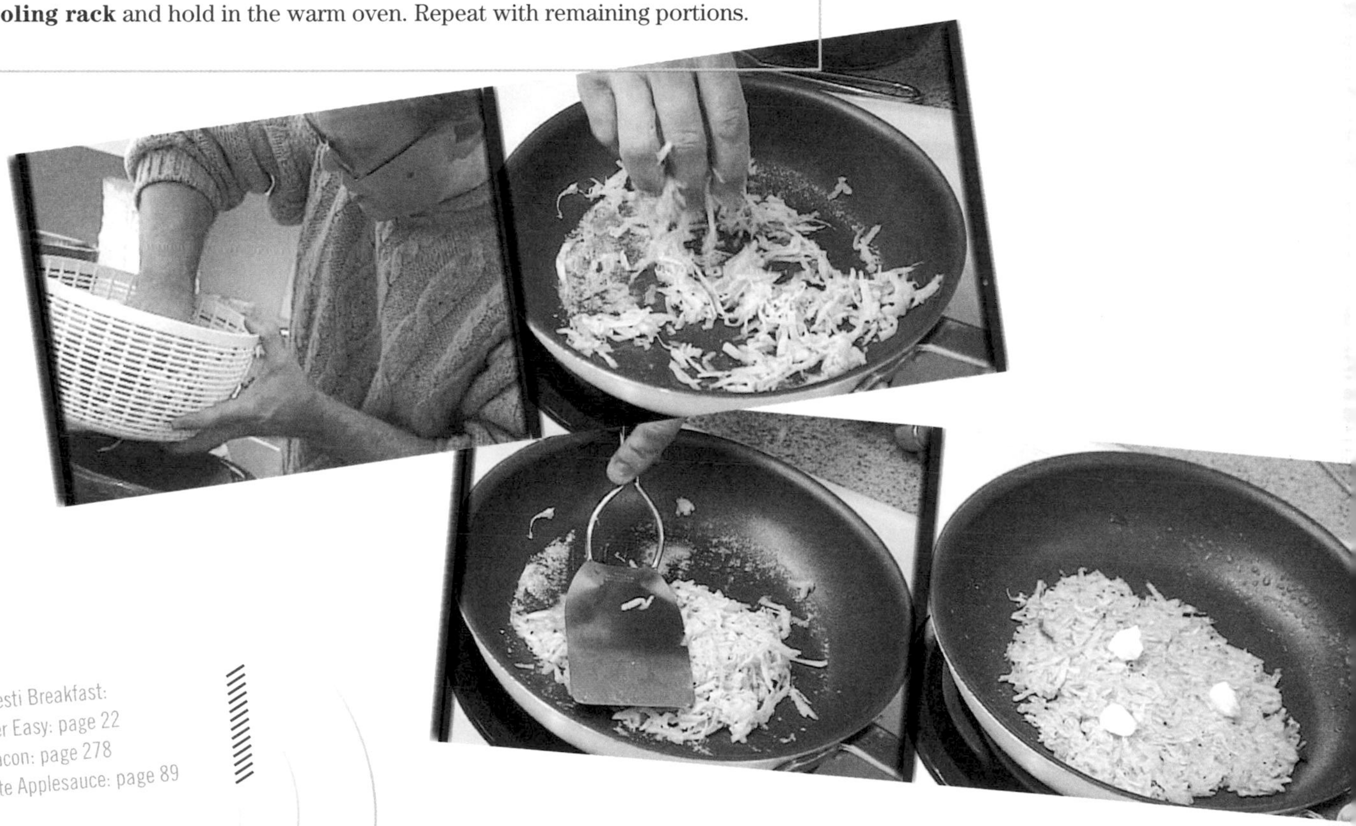

TIDBIT | Roesti Breakfast:
Eggs Over Easy: page 22
Roast Bacon: page 278
10 Minute Applesauce: page 89

APPLICATION

COLD-FASHIONED POTATO SALAD

4 TO 6 SERVINGS

Although this application does call for a fair amount of fat (mayo), it's balanced by the cider vinegar and mustard. The tarragon is a French (but unfussy) touch. This is as good warm as cold.

SOFTWARE

2½	pounds	small red potatoes	
3	tablespoons	cider vinegar	
¾	cup	mayonnaise	preferably homemade, page 242
1	teaspoon	ground mustard	
¼	cup	fresh parsley	chopped
1	tablespoon	fresh tarragon	chopped
2	teaspoons	garlic	minced
¼	cup	cornichons	diced
½	cup	red onion	diced
½	cup	celery	diced
½	teaspoon	kosher salt	
½	teaspoon	black pepper	freshly ground

PROCEDURE

1. Place the potatoes in an **8-quart pot**. Cover with **cold water** and place over medium heat. Cover the pot and bring to a boil. Immediately reduce the heat and remove the lid. Gently simmer until the potatoes are fork tender, 10 to 15 minutes. Drain in a **colander** and place in an **ice bath** to cool for 2 to 3 minutes. Remove the skin by rubbing with a clean **tea towel**. Slice the potatoes into rounds using an **egg slicer or a chef's knife**. Place the potatoes in a **zip-top bag**, add the vinegar, and toss to coat. Place the bag in the refrigerator overnight.
2. Combine the mayonnaise, mustard, parsley, tarragon, garlic, cornichons, onion, and celery in a **large mixing bowl**. Add the potatoes and season with the salt and pepper. Let the salad chill in the refrigerator for at least 1 hour before serving.

TIDBIT | In October 1995 the potato became the first vegetable grown in space.

TUNA: THE OTHER RED MEAT

EPISODE 69 | SEASON 6 | GOOD EATS

TRIVIA | I'm pretty sure this is the only food show ever made where the host dies in the opening scene.

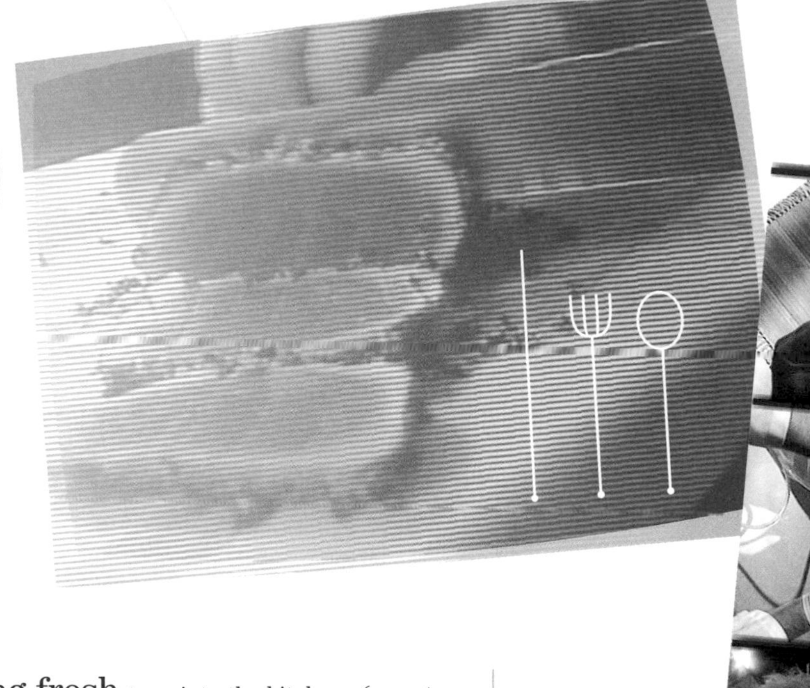

In this episode I sought to bring fresh tuna into the kitchens (or onto the grills) of the average American, one who might previously have only encountered the fish in a can or in a restaurant.

Setting: Fancy restaurant, AB prepares to dig in to a steak.

AB: I was getting ready to dive into my third Delmonico of the week when the pain struck. It was just pressure at first, and then God made a fist . . . with me in it.

Of course, the doctors did all they could, but medical science was no match for my neglected vascular system. Game over. Or was it?

Suddenly AB is transported to an empty megamart seafood department.

AB: (looking around) Hello?

TUNA: Guess you really did it this time, boy.

AB: (looks around at a huge turtle hanging from the ceiling)

TUNA: No. Over here, dummy.

AB: (to Tuna) You talking to me?

TUNA: See anybody else here, smart guy?

AB: I guess not. How'd I get here?

TUNA: Your diet. You know how much cow meat you've been puttin' away each week?

AB: Well, no.

TUNA: Four pounds.

AB: Gee is, uh, that a lot? (laughs)

TUNA: Hey! Don't crack wise with me. Or you'll find yourself working the grill station permanently.

AB: (winces at intense red light emanating from below, à la Hades) All right. All right. All right. Sorry . . . Charlie.

TUNA: Forget about it. Okay. What do you know about Tuna?

AB: About Tuna? Well . . . uh . . . you're, you're a very good-looking fish and you're very versatile, flavorful, and you're packed with nutrition, like omega-3 fatty acids. And because of your unique physiognomy you can be cooked to temperature, you know, like red meat. In fact, I'd even say you could be called the other red meat. Well, one time, I . . .

TUNA: All right. All right. I'll let you go this time.

AB: Thank you. Thank you.

TUNA: But you'd better start walkin' that talk or you'll be back here quicker than you can say . . .

Retractable fin drops into dorsal slot when hypermode kicks in

KNOWLEDGE CONCENTRATE

The word *tuna* refers to a relatively small group of sea-dwelling fish in the Scombridae family, most of which are also members of the *Thunnus genus*. By and large they look like bullets, which is essentially what they are:

Before you can understand the real difference between tuna and other fish on the plate, it helps to appreciate the difference between tuna and other fish in the water. You see, like sharks, tuna never stops swimming, ever. But unlike sharks, which can attain real speed only in short bursts, tuna are built for speed and distance.

Take, for instance, the increasingly rare Atlantic bluefin. This thing can grow to fifteen hundred pounds and nine feet in length, and still maintain cruising speeds of up to fifty miles an hour. Imagine what that would look like passing you in the water.

How do they do it? Well, tuna are a lot like sports cars. Their bodies are bullet-shaped—thus low-drag. They've got specialized drive trains and high-performance parts all around. At low speeds their fins stay up for agility in the turns, but then when they lay on the speed in the straight-aways, the fins retract into recessed grooves along the body. Nice, huh? No wonder the U.S. Navy studies these guys when they build submarines. Oh, and inside? A specialized metabolism allows them to raise and lower their blood temperature as they dive.

Some tuna can actually control their body temperatures, allowing for deeper dives.

Major edible varieties:

ALBACORE TUNA is light and flaky when cooked. It's usually canned.

BIGEYE TUNA are quite large and live long lives (when we let them) in deep water. Like yellowfin tuna, they are often caught off the coast of Hawaii, where they are also called "ahi" . . . which can cause some confusion. Bigeye maintains its bright red color longer than any other tuna.

BLUEFIN TUNA is very rare and almost never seen in a consumer/retail outlet. Most bluefin goes straight to sushi bars or to Japan.

YELLOWFIN TUNA is also called by its Hawaiian name "ahi." Most of the fresh tuna that comes to American megamarts is yellowfin.

SKIPJACK TUNA are small and fatty and are often marketed as "bonito." In the United States most skipjack is canned, while in Japan most is dried.

TIDBIT | Wild bluefin tuna have been overfished nearly to extinction.

Tuna Internal Architecture: Unlike, say, a salmon or grouper, tuna and many of its cousins are basically skin wrapped around four huge muscles, or loins, which run the length of the body and deliver the propulsion for which the tuna is famed. They also provide considerable flavor. The meat ranges from tawny to ruby red. Since they never stop moving, tuna muscles require a lot of oxygen. To burn oxygen you've got to have myoglobin in the muscle. And myoglobin is red.

Shopping: Some tuna are redder than others. That's why color along with firmness and fat content are the deciding factors in whether a tuna receives a quality grade of 3, 2, or 1, which is sushi grade and the most expensive. Good markets carry 2-grade tuna.

Unfortunately for the retail customer, color is a tricky thing. You see, myoglobin turns brown when it's frozen, but processors have figured out that they can set the red by exposing the meat to carbon monoxide before freezing it. In itself, this isn't a bad thing. I mean, the meat comes out looking great. But it means that unscrupulous fishmongers might be tempted to sell that meat as fresh and you'd never know the difference because it looks the same. Just another in a long line of reasons to know your fishmonger.

Like any red meat, tuna looks better the longer it's left intact. So, if I'm planning on cooking several steaks, I'll try to purchase one "block" of loin and then cut my own steaks at the very last minute. If you're lucky enough to get a thick center-cut loin, plan on an inch per diner. With a narrower loin, go an inch and a half per.

Storage: In a perfect world, tuna is consumed the day it is purchased. But, hey, this isn't a perfect world, is it? That's why we have the homemade fish rig, which keeps the fish in contact with crushed ice but away from the water as the ice melts. See page 55 for how to set one up. In the back of your refrigerator, you should be able to hold your tuna for three or four days without a discernable loss of quality.

Cooking: Unlike most fish, whose muscles are downright nasty when undercooked, tuna's more like beef tenderloin. Its flavor and texture reaches peak when it's seared on the outside but left rare on the inside. In fact, when beyond medium rare even the best tuna starts to taste and feel like canned.

So what does this mean to the home cook? High heat. And unless you've got a fusion reactor in the basement, odds are good there's nothing around the house that'll generate more heat than the carbonous remains of natural hardwood chunks.

It's called natural because it is. It's just chunks of wood that have been partially burned in a low-O_2 environment: no additives, no fillers, no binders. Natural chunk charcoal burns very hot and it burns fast, which means you're going to need more of it than you might think. So even though we're not cooking a lot of tuna, you'll want to fill a two-quart charcoal chimney all the way to the brim.

Nutrition: Omega-3 fatty acids are great for your heart. They act as an arterial lubricant, which decreases your risk for heart attack and stroke. They increase your levels of HDL cholesterol, which is the good cholesterol, and they decrease your triglycerides, or the bad cholesterols. And they also help with your memory, your learning ability, and your vision. Some studies suggest that omega-3s may help with depression, not to mention dry eye syndrome, which I didn't even know existed.

APPLICATION

CHIMNEY TUNA LOIN

4 SERVINGS

Despite close family ties to the mackerel, tuna's flavor is actually complex and subtle. In fact, really great tuna's kind of like listening to Debussy with the volume turned way down. What's a cook to do? Well, we need to apply flavors that turn the tuna back up without drowning it out. Now, I can't think of anything that supports a melody better than a chord. So I like to back up tuna with three flavors: sweet, pungent, and salty—in this case, honey, wasabi power, and soy sauce.

SOFTWARE

½	cup	dark soy sauce	
½	cup	honey	
¼	cup	wasabi powder	
2	pounds	tuna loin	cut into 4 (2-by-4-by-2-inch) rectangles
½	cup	sesame seeds	white or black or both
1	tablespoon	peanut oil	

PROCEDURE

1. **Whisk** the soy sauce, honey, and wasabi powder together in a **glass container**. Transfer ⅓ cup of the liquid to a **small bowl** and reserve for dipping. Place tuna in the remaining marinade, turn to coat, and refrigerate for at least 1 hour and up to 4 hours, turning once halfway through that time.
2. Fill a **chimney starter** with natural chunk charcoal and light (see tips, right).

SOMEWHERE OVER THE FISHBOW

You ever notice the rainbow effect that sometimes appears on the surface of freshly cut tuna? It's not from age and it's not fat. It's birefringence. Here's the deal. The surface is pretty smooth, but if you look closely you'll see that it's actually a vast landscape of parallel fibers. When cut, the reduced surface pressure coaxes microscopic beads of moisture to the surface, each one of which acts as an independent prism. When viewed in concert, they look like a rainbow.

TIDBIT Wasabi is a form of horseradish grown in Japan and, now, Oregon state. The ripe radishes are dried and ground into powder, which is then mixed with water or sake and plopped on the side of sushi plates. Unfortunately much of the wasabi powder sold in the United States is mixed with much more pungent Chinese mustards. If you want the real thing, look to an Internet/catalog-based spice company.

3. Remove the tuna from the marinade and pat dry. Sprinkle the sesame seeds onto a **dinner plate** and roll the tuna pieces in the seeds, pressing down lightly to evenly coat.

4. Place a **grill grate**[1] on the top of the chimney starter to heat for at least 1 minute. The charcoal should have burned down to one fourth of its original size and be at least 8 inches from the grill on top.

5. Once it's hot, carefully move the grate off the heat and **brush** with the oil. Return to the chimney, place the tuna pieces on the grill, and cook for 30 seconds per side for a total of 2 minutes cooking time for rare. Add an additional 15 seconds per side for medium. Remove the pieces to a **clean dinner plate**, cover with **plastic wrap**, and rest for 3 minutes. Thinly slice the tuna and serve warm with the dipping sauce, or chill and serve cold.[2]

[1] I keep a very small grill grate around for this. Weber makes a replacement grate for their Lilliputian Smokey Joe that costs about fifteen bucks and is easily found at hardware stores.

[2] When chilled, thin slices of this tuna can be served on a green salad tossed with a ginger dressing.

TIP If you're really grill crazy, you may also have a gas grill with a side burner for pots and pans. You can set your chimney starter right on top of this and just fire the burner to high. It works very quickly but, um . . . may void your warrantee so forget I mentioned it.

TIP Before you wad your paper up, drizzle on just a capful of vegetable or canola oil. Then wad it up, shove it under the chimney, and light. Basically what we've made here is an oil lantern, which will burn for several extra minutes.

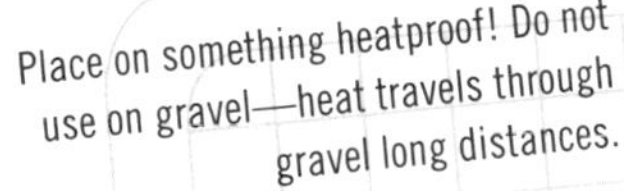

Place on something heatproof! Do not use on gravel—heat travels through gravel long distances.

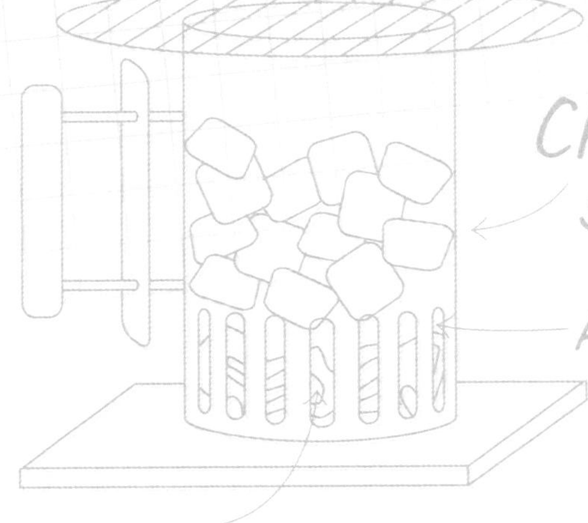

STRAWBERRY SKY

EPISODE 70 | SEASON 6 | GOOD EATS

"Doubtless God could have made a better berry, but doubtless God never did."
//////////////////////////////////
WILLIAM BUTLER

Somehow, "strawberry" has become a flavor without a fruit. We enjoy strawberry-flavored gum and ice cream and all manner of processed goods, but when it comes to actual strawberries we'd just as soon buy imported berries in October because they look pretty. This half hour was all about bringing it back to the fruit, which as far as I'm concerned should be purchased in late spring and early summer or not at all.

TIDBIT | Strawberries grow on runners, little vines right along the ground. When they sit in the dirt they rot very quickly. So growers put a lot of straw in the fields for the berries to rest on. That's why they call them "straw" berries.

TIDBIT | In France strawberries are usually eaten with wine, while Italians prefer a splash of balsamic vinegar.

KNOWLEDGE CONCENTRATE

Technically speaking, strawberries are "false" fruits or "accessory" fruits, because the fleshy part is not the plant ovary but a swollen hypanthium (trust me). When you gobble a strawberry, you're actually consuming about two hundred fruits—the average strawberry has about two hundred seeds, or achenes, on its exterior, and these are the real fruit of the strawberry. The rest of the strawberry is called the receptacle, and it's little more than a swollen stem.

Buying: When buying strawberries, use your nose. If the aroma is strong and sweet, the berries will be good regardless of what they look like. The best strawberries you'll ever taste will have been bought from a roadside stand or out of the back of a truck next to a strawberry field with a hand-painted "Strawberries for sale" sign on a sunny afternoon in spring. It's as simple as that.

Freezing strawberries: Come the Ides of March, great strawberries become very affordable. I always earmark a few quarts for suspended animation so that they may provide comfort in the winter of my discontent. Suspended animation, of course, means freezing, which is a bit of a challenge because home freezers don't get that cold. Sure, they freeze, but when they do the water in things like berries freezes very slowly, and that creates big, long, jagged ice crystals, which can break through cell walls, which can make a mess upon thawing. Smaller crystals do less damage. Here's how to freeze quickly:

1. Wash the berries, then chill them in the refrigerator for at least 4 hours. This will mean a shorter thermal trip to the ice age, and the quicker the trip, the better.

2. Get hold of a 2- to 5-pound block of dry ice (carried by many megamarts). They call it dry ice because it's made from carbon dioxide, which sublimates or turns from a solid to a gas at about -109°F. That means that this block will give you frostbite quicker than sticking your tongue to a flag-pole on top of K2 on New Year's Eve. So use heavy-duty insulated kitchen or welding gloves. If you do not have any, go break out your ski gloves.

3. Pulverize the dry ice while it's still in its bag and dispense into a 60-quart cooler (Styrofoam is best). Gently toss the chilled berries in with the dry ice and put the lid on loosely. As the dry ice sublimates the gas is going to expand exponentially, so if your cooler has a tight-fitting lid or latch make sure you leave it ajar. And don't stick your head inside the cooler because the CO_2 will replace all the air and you'll pass out and freeze your face off.

4. In thirty minutes your berries will be rock hard. Immediately move to freezer bags, suck out all the air possible, label, and stash in the bottom of your freezer for up to a year.

TRIVIA | While shooting the scene where the camera was inside the cooler, I almost did pass out and freeze my face off. So be careful.

TIP | Dry ice is useful stuff, but remember that -109.3°F is not a temperature bare skin tolerates well. Dress accordingly.

TIDBIT | Strawberries, members of the rose family, are native to both the Old and New Worlds. Ancient Romans used strawberries to whiten their teeth.

APPLICATION

MACERATED STRAWBERRIES

4 SERVINGS

This is what I serve on the Shortcake from "The Dough Also Rises," page 42.

SOFTWARE

1	pint	medium strawberries	rinsed, hulled, and sliced
½	bottle (325ml)	red wine	Pinot Noir or Merlot will do nicely
2	tablespoons	orange blossom honey	
½	teaspoon	lemon zest	
½	teaspoon	black pepper	freshly ground
½	cup	sugar	

PROCEDURE

1. Combine all the ingredients in a **large airtight container** and stir gently. Cover and chill in the refrigerator for 2 hours. To freeze, simply assemble the ingredients in heavy-duty zip-top bags and freeze for up to 1 year.
2. Enjoy in Strawberry Pudding (opposite page) or spooned over shortcake.

FREE RADICALS V. ANTIOXIDANTS

Besides being delicious, strawberries pack a wallop of antioxidants, which make them frontline fighters in the battle against free radicals. Now what exactly are free radicals? Think of them as molecules that have lost electrons through exposure to toxins, oxidation, etc. This makes them unstable, so they look around and steal electrons from neighboring molecules, thus rendering those molecules free radicals. A vicious cycle ensues, and if the process takes place in, say, your lungs or your DNA or some other vital location over a long enough period of time, you might just wake up one day with a nice ripe tumor. Luckily, antioxidants can donate electrons without becoming free radicals themselves. So the more antioxidants in your body, the better off you're going to be.

TIP Strawberry leaves can be brewed like tea. The resulting liquid isn't very tasty, but it is a fine laxative.

TIDBIT The average American eats 4.85 pounds of strawberries a year. The United States is the world leader in strawberry production.

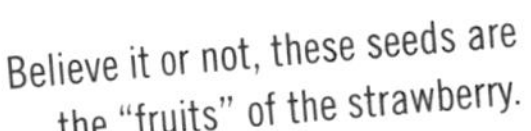

Believe it or not, these seeds are the "fruits" of the strawberry.

APPLICATION — STRAWBERRY PUDDING

4 SERVINGS

This is an update on an English classic that's often a lot fussier than it's worth. I like it because it's got great textures and a strawberry flavor without being too sweet.

SOFTWARE

		Macerated Strawberries (opposite page)	
16	slices	stale potato bread	or brioche or challah
1	tablespoon	unsalted butter	at room temperature
		whipped or clotted cream	for serving

PROCEDURE

1. Remove both ends from **4 empty 15-ounce soup cans**. Save **4 of the ends**. Using one of the soup cans with the ends removed, cut the potato bread into 16 rounds. To avoid torn bread press straight down, and do not twist.
2. Butter one side of 4 of the bread rounds.
3. Place the soup cans on a **half sheet pan** lined with **parchment paper.** Place a buttered bread round, buttered side up, in each can. Spoon 1 tablespoon of the strawberries and liquid over each round. Repeat layering strawberries and bread rounds until you have 3 layers of strawberries and 4 layers of bread. Top each can with an additional tablespoon of strawberries.
4. Place the reserved ends of the soup cans on top and weigh with cans of soda. Refrigerate for 8 hours. Remove the cans and serve with whipped or clotted cream.

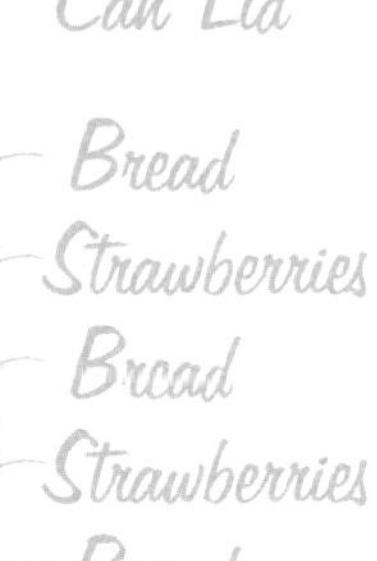

ARTICHOKES: THE CHOKE IS ON YOU

EPISODE 71 | SEASON 6 | GOOD EATS

The artichoke is nothing more than the immature blossom of a giant, mutant thistle. Doesn't sound like good eats, but trust me: It is. And besides, we eat lots of flower buds. You like capers, don't you? Flower buds. Cabbage? Flower bud. Cauliflower? Flower bud. Granted, it takes a bit of work to coax the goodness out of an artichoke, but with a little practice, some sound technique, and a touch of science, artichokes most certainly rank as . . .

TIP | Before digging in, make sure you have a sauce on hand. If the artichoke's hot, I usually go with something simple like lemon butter. If the choke's chilly, I'll go with either garlicky vinaigrette or a thin mayonnaise (see page 242).

ANATOMY OF AN ARTICHOKE

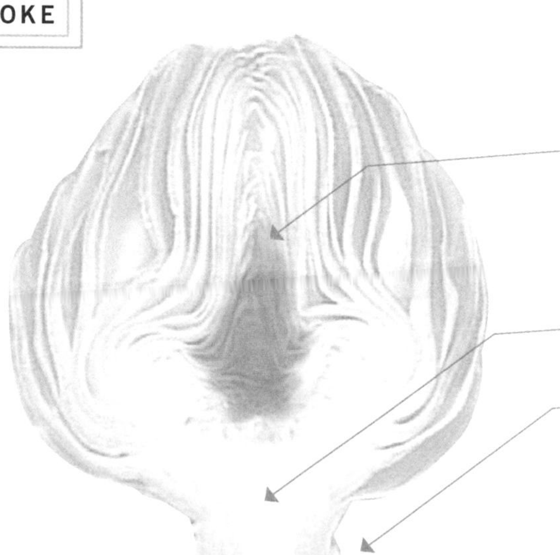

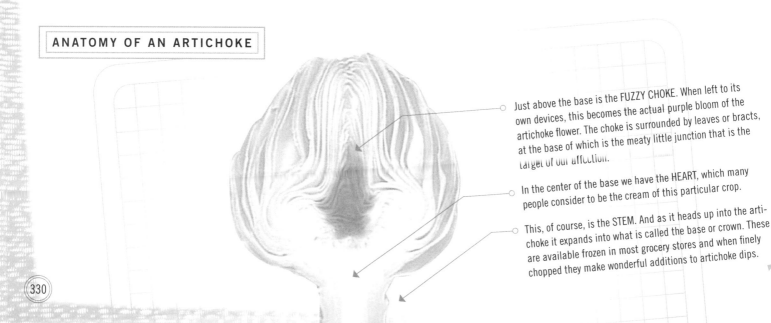

Just above the base is the FUZZY CHOKE. When left to its own devices, this becomes the actual purple bloom of the artichoke flower. The choke is surrounded by leaves or bracts, at the base of which is the meaty little junction that is the target of our affection.

In the center of the base we have the HEART, which many people consider to be the cream of this particular crop.

This, of course, is the STEM. And as it heads up into the artichoke it expands into what is called the base or crown. These are available frozen in most grocery stores and when finely chopped they make wonderful additions to artichoke dips.

KNOWLEDGE CONCENTRATE

Shopping: When it comes to hunting globe artichokes, which are the only form found in American megamarts, look for specimens the size of a large navel orange. These possess enough flesh to make them worth your while without being so large that they're fibrous. And like a good orange, an artichoke should feel heavy for its size.

Color is kind of a tricky quality in this species because artichokes grown during different parts of the season ripen to different colors. They might be bright green or green and purple, or, if they're harvested in summer, olive drab. Early spring crops are actually tinged with bronze from frost. All are delicious.

If the leaves have started to spread out, the globe is probably past its prime. Now the real quality test is this: Just take a leaf and break it. If it snaps, it's still fresh. But if it just bends over, it's lost too much of its moisture. Also, if the artichokes are sold by the piece rather than the pound, pick those with the longest stems possible. The stems are almost as tasty as the heart.

Storage: As with all green goods, the shorter the trip from field to face, the better. And that can be a challenge with artichokes because 9.5 out of 10 are grown in and around Castroville, California.[1] So you can assume the further you are from California, the longer the artichoke has been on a truck. And that's a problem because it is going to lose a lot of moisture in the process and that cuts down on your storage options.

My favorite artichoke holding chamber is a two-liter soda bottle cut in half. Here's how to set it up:

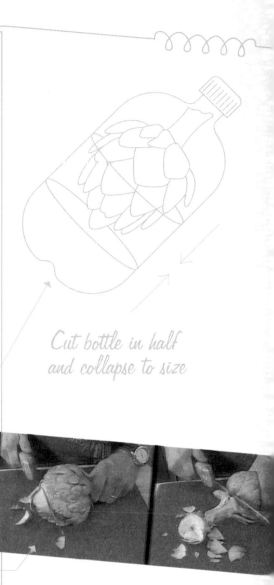

Cut bottle in half and collapse to size

This system keeps moisture in but not too much, and it holds three or four globes, no problem. And, of course, there's nothing better than recycling.

Prepping: Start with a bath. Fill a deep bowl, pot, or sink with water and dunk them upside down. Work them up and down for a few seconds to dislodge any dirt, dust, or critters.

Artichokes need to be trimmed before cooking, but they don't need to undergo the butchery often suggested by classic culinary tomes. In fact it only takes two cuts to prep an artichoke for cooking.

Do not throw away the stems. Peel them as you would a broccoli stem and cook them along with the rest of the artichoke.

Cooking vessels: Artichokes contain compounds that react with aluminum and iron, creating some pretty nasty flavors and stains on food and vessel alike. So stick with nonreactive pans such as stainless steel or anodized aluminum, which is gray rather than dull silver in color.

For a simply cooked artichoke, place 2 teaspoons kosher salt in your widest pot and cover 4 prepped artichokes with at least ½ inch of water. Use a steamer basket and a small weight to submerge the chokes.

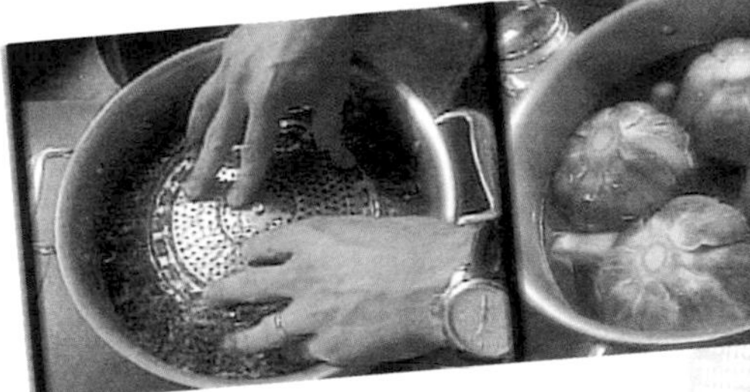

Bring to a boil, uncovered, over high heat, then reduce the heat to medium. Cook for 10 minutes, then start testing for doneness by inserting a paring knife into the stem end. It should enter smoothly, with only slight resistance. Drain in a colander and cool for 5 minutes before consuming. Of course, that means taking it apart, and for that a bit of structural familiarity would be helpful.

APPLICATION — HERB OIL

3 CUPS

// SOFTWARE

½	bunch	fresh parsley	
½	cup	fresh basil	tightly packed
½	bunch	fresh thyme	
½	cup	fresh oregano	tightly packed
2	teaspoons	orange zest	
1	whole	dried arbol chile	
1	teaspoon	whole black peppercorns	
2	cups	canola oil	
1	cup	extra-virgin olive oil	

// PROCEDURE

1. In a **1-quart mason jar**, place all of the herbs, the orange zest, chile, and peppercorns. Pour both oils into a saucepan and heat to 200°F. Pour into the jar and cover with a **kitchen towel**. Let stand overnight.
2. Place **cheesecloth** over the top of the jar and replace the outer ring of the lid. Invert and strain the oil into another Mason jar filled with the broiled artichokes. Cover and let sit for 2 days. Refrigerate and enjoy within 2 weeks.

APPLICATION — MARINATED BROILED CHOKES

4 SERVINGS

TIDBIT Artichokes are very low in calories, yet high in vitamin C, iron, and potassium.

TIDBIT Artichokes contain an acid that makes almost any liquid taste sweet, so pair them with a wine that won't mind, like a Riesling.

// SOFTWARE

6	cups	cool, fresh H_2O	
¼	cup	lemon juice	freshly squeezed
8	whole	artichokes	
¼	cup	olive oil	
2	teaspoons	kosher salt	
1	teaspoon	black pepper	freshly ground
		Herb Oil	(above, optional)

PROCEDURE

1. Combine the water with the lemon juice in a **large plastic container**. Keep the acidulated water standing by while working with the artichokes.
2. Heat the broiler to high and set a **broiler pan or half sheet pan fitted with a roasting rack** about 6 inches beneath it.
3. Cut the top quarter off an artichoke and snap off the outer leaves until you reach pale green, soft leaves. Dunk a **vegetable peeler** in the acidulated water and peel the fibrous exterior from the stem.
4. Cut the artichoke in half and, using a **grapefruit spoon**, remove and discard the hairy choke from the center. Immediately plunge the artichoke in the acidulated water to prevent discoloration. Repeat with remaining artichokes. Drain the artichokes and pat dry with paper towels.
5. Toss the artichokes in a **large bowl** with the oil, then season with salt and pepper. Lay them out on a **half sheet pan** lined with **aluminum foil** and place on the lower rack of the oven; broil for 5 to 6 minutes, until lightly browned. Flip the artichokes and return to the oven for 6 minutes. Eat as they are, as part of a salad, or marinate them in Herb Oil.

10 MINUTES MORE

ARTICHOKE PASTA SALAD

4 SERVINGS

We allude to this application at the end of the show but don't get around to making it.

TIDBIT The artichoke came to Europe from North Africa when the Moors invaded Spain.

SOFTWARE

1	pound	penne or bow-tie pasta	cooked, still warm
2	tablespoons	red wine vinegar	
3	tablespoons	Herb Oil	(left)
5	ounces	grape tomatoes	halved
2	tablespoons	fresh basil	chiffonade
1	tablespoon	fresh oregano	finely chopped
8	ounces	roasted chicken	roughly chopped
5	ounces	Marinated Artichokes	chopped
½	teaspoon	kosher salt	
¼	teaspoon	black pepper	freshly ground

PROCEDURE

1. Toss all of the ingredients together in the **vessel** of your choice and refrigerate for 2 hours before serving.

[1] Marilyn Monroe was crowned Castroville Artichoke Queen in 1948.

DOWN AND OUT IN PARADISE

EPISODE 72 | SEASON 6 | GOOD EATS

Here my goal was to make the most of an almost-abandoned trip to Hawaii and goof on the movie *Castaway* while dealing with some tropical ingredients we hadn't dealt with before.

Our second hour special wouldn't have happened if it weren't for an accident. I was booked to appear at a Food Network live show in Honolulu back in 2001. The tickets were bought, housing set, then the show was canceled, for what reason I never knew. We couldn't get our money back for the tickets, so we decided to take a few more people (what the heck) and shoot part of a one-hour special.

The idea was that I was shipwrecked on what I thought was a deserted island. I lose my glasses during the storm so I can't see that I'm on the north shore of Oahu. Luckily I trip over a World War II–era army survival kit, which happens to have grenades in it, which I later use to blow a pig to smithereens (a Food Network first) for Sweet and Sour Pork (page 342). After living on the beach for some time, I'm finally discovered by a surfer, who tells me I'm just a couple of miles from downtown Honolulu. The fun part is that during my seclusion, I go a little wacky, talking nonstop to an inflatable sea monster named Wilbur (a riff on Wilson the soccer ball from *Castaway*) and falling under the spell of an increasingly evil coconut named, appropriately, Coco.

The beach scenes were filmed in a small cove called Smugglers Cove on the north shore of Oahu. The mango grove was supplied by the fine folks at the University of Hawaii, while Dole graciously allowed us onto their pineapple plantation and cacao fields. Papaya trees were made possible by the University of Hawaii. Everyone—and I do mean everyone—on the island was as helpful as can be and nicer than humanly normal, which was good because at the time we didn't have a script. We were making it up as we went along and were completely at the mercy of strangers.

The interior scenes on the boat and all the "hovel" scenes were shot on a soundstage in Atlanta. Todd Dailey and my prop department did such a jam-up job of putting that set together it looked like I'd lived in it for years. The only down side is that I had sand coming out of my ears for weeks after the shoot.

Here follow my favorite culinary highlights from the most epic *Good Eats* to date.

Having abandoned any hope of rescue, I have decided to write down my story on the off chance that one day my fate might be known. I also want to leave a record of the foods that have kept my body sound and my mind sharp as a . . . a . . .

KNOWLEDGE CONCENTRATE

COCONUTS

The coconut palm, one of the world's most commercially important trees, happens to produce the most commercially important nut on earth, not to mention a darned tasty beverage. But before you can get to the liquid inside, you have to make it through a very thick and very tough fibrous husk, which itself can be fabricated into just about anything from floor mats to rope to army helmets (it's usually removed before coconuts make it to the local megamart).

Once the outer husk is removed, gaining access to the liquid inner goodness is a snap. Just look for the three dots that look kind of like a monkey face and drill into two of them. Then you've got yourself up to two cups of a cool, refreshing sucrose-and-invert-sugar solution.

Getting to the flesh takes a bit more effort. Baking the coconuts makes them easier to deal with. On the island, I didn't have an oven, so I filled a shallow hole with rocks from my fire and topped it with an old ammo box. You might think about using an oven at 350°F for half an hour. The flesh will pull away from the shell and removal will be a breeze.

In the shell, a coconut will keep for 2 to 4 months depending on how long it's been off the tree. Just be sure that you buy specimens that feel heavy for their size. And although some sloshing should be audible upon shaking, a lot of sloshing means that the coconut is drying up. Also, avoid coconuts with cracks and softer, moldy eyes, either of which can be a sign of trouble inside.

Coconuts, like almonds and pecans, are actually the inner seed of a nonedible fruit called a drupe. When very, very young, there's really nothing in there but water. But as it matures, the flesh develops and it's like jelly. You can eat it with a spoon. It's delicious.

By the time the coconut is ten months old, the mature flesh is hard and white and can be grated or dried into something called copra, which is pressed for coconut oil, which is used in everything from baked goods to margarine to soap.

APPLICATION

COCONUT SHRIMP WITH PEANUT SAUCE

4 TO 6 SERVINGS

This is one of the most popular restaurant dishes of the last twenty years, yet no one makes it at home. Well I've made it a few dozen times and I love it. But you really do want to use fresh coconut.

SOFTWARE

FOR THE PEANUT SAUCE

¼	cup	chicken stock	
⅓	cup	unsweetened coconut milk	
2	tablespoons	lime juice	freshly squeezed
2	tablespoons	soy sauce	
1	tablespoon	fish sauce	or 2 to 3 anchovies, ground
1	tablespoon	hot sauce	
2	tablespoons	garlic	chopped
1	tablespoon	fresh ginger	chopped
¼	cup	fresh cilantro	chopped
1½	cups	creamy peanut butter	

FOR THE COCONUT SHRIMP

		peanut oil	for frying
25	15–20 count	shrimp	peeled and deveined
½	cup	cornstarch	
¼	teaspoon	kosher salt	
¼	teaspoon	white pepper	freshly ground
¼	teaspoon	ground cayenne pepper	
4	large	egg whites	
2½	cups	fresh coconut	shredded

PROCEDURE

MAKE THE PEANUT SAUCE:

1 In a **food processor**, puree the stock, coconut milk, lime juice, soy sauce, fish sauce, hot sauce, garlic, ginger, and cilantro. Add the peanut butter and pulse to combine. Refrigerate if preparing in advance, then bring to room temperature while prepping the shrimp.

MAKE THE COCONUT SHRIMP:

2 Heat an **electric skillet** to 350°F and add enough peanut oil to come 1½ inches up the side.[1]

3 Pat the shrimp dry with a **paper towel**. In a **small bowl**, combine the cornstarch, salt, pepper, and cayenne. In **another small bowl**, **whisk** the egg whites until foamy. Place the coconut in a **pie plate**. Coat the shrimp with the cornstarch and shake off any excess. Dip them into the egg whites and then press them into the coconut to get full coverage.

4 When the oil reaches 350°F, gently add half of the shrimp. Fry for 3 to 5 minutes, until golden brown, then cool for 3 to 5 minutes on a **cooling rack**. Repeat with the remaining shrimp. Serve with the peanut sauce.

Coco
(Look into the face of evil!)

KNOWLEDGE CONCENTRATE

PAPAYAS

Although some varieties produce fruits in excess of fifteen pounds, the more common in the market, the smaller solo varieties, are perfect for one diner. Papaya's flavor—a little bit melon, a little bit vanilla, a little bit, well, turpentine—is best when the fruit has turned 80 percent yellow. But since ripe specimens can't survive shipping, papayas bound for the mainland markets are picked when they just begin to show yellow. They're then chilled to halt their metabolism, crated up, and shipped. When they get to America they're warmed to 68°F, and the ripening miraculously continues.

Always shop for specimens showing as much yellow as possible. Small dark spots or even little patches of mold are okay, but large discolorations or bruises are bad news. Oh, and when you get your fruit home, set it stem side down for faster and more even ripening.

Papaya are loaded with black seeds that are covered in a kind of a slippery membrane. They actually look like caviar. To get them out, cut the papaya in half longitudinally and scoop them out; real papaya lovers usually leave a few seeds behind to enjoy the contrast of their peppery crunch. They are so peppery, in fact, that in parts of India they're dried and used as filler in black pepper—an effective, albeit dirty, trick.

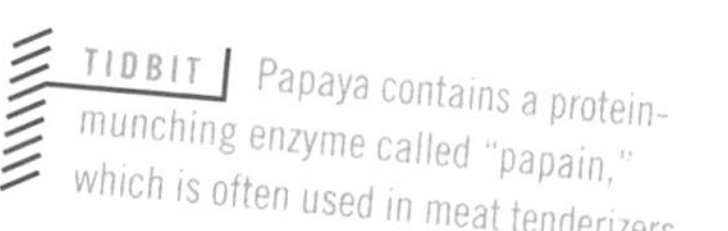

TIDBIT | Papaya contains a protein-munching enzyme called "papain," which is often used in meat tenderizers.

APPLICATION

ISLAND CEVICHE

8 SERVINGS

When selecting the fish for this dish, be sure to tell your fishmonger what you're up to so that he or she can guide you to the freshest selection.

// SOFTWARE

8	ounces	pompano fillets	or other firm white fish
8	ounces	bay scallops	
¾	cup	lime juice	freshly squeezed, from about 7 medium limes
		kosher salt	
		black pepper	freshly ground
2	medium	Solo papayas	about 1 pound each, halved and seeded
1	cup	Vidalia onions	finely diced
4	small	serrano chiles	seeded and diced
1	small	jalapeño chile	seeded and diced
2	medium	plum tomatoes	seeded and diced
½	cup	fresh cilantro	chopped
¼	cup	tomato juice	
1	tablespoon	white wine	
2	teaspoons	Worcestershire sauce	
1	tablespoon	Mexican-style hot sauce	
		Pink Pickled Onions	(next page)

// PROCEDURE

1. Cut the fish into pieces about the size of the scallops. Place the fish and scallops in a **glass or other nonreactive dish** and coat with the lime juice. Cover and marinate in the refrigerator overnight.
2. Next day, pour off the lime juice and season the fish and scallops with salt and pepper. Scoop the flesh from the papaya halves, leaving the skins whole, and finely dice it. Fold the diced papaya, onions, chiles, plum tomatoes, cilantro, tomato juice, wine, Worcestershire sauce, and hot sauce into the fish. Serve the ceviche inside the papaya skins topped with Pink Pickled Onions.

10 MINUTES MORE

PINK PICKLED ONIONS

1 QUART

Although we did reference this dish on the show, we never got around to making it. It's not exactly tropical, but it's easy and versatile.

SOFTWARE

1	cup	champagne vinegar	
½	cup	sugar	
2	small	serrano chiles	seeded
2	medium	red onions	julienned

PROCEDURE

1. In a **2-quart saucepan**, bring the vinegar, sugar, and chiles to a boil over medium heat. Stir until the sugar is dissolved. Remove from the heat.
2. In a **heat-resistant plastic container or glass jar**, place the sliced onions and pour the liquid over them. Place the container in an **ice bath** to cool. Serve chilled with meats and seafood. These are also great on sandwiches.

KNOWLEDGE CONCENTRATE

PINEAPPLE

By the time Columbus made it to the New World, the pineapple or *ananas* (meaning excellent fruit) had migrated up from Brazil to Mexico and many of the West Indies. Confused by its appearance, the Spanish decided to name it after the pine cone. In their infinite botanical wisdom, the English added "apple."

Produce men often say that if you can easily pluck a leaf from the crown of a pineapple, it's ripe. But I quickly found that all but the greenest specimens will abdicate their crowns. Color can also be a fair indicator, but only if you know what species you're dealing with—and I definitely didn't.

In the end, I found that the best flavor comes from large specimens that are half green, half gold in color and that have relatively small crowns for their size and a sweet aroma. Big crowns mean that most of the fruit sugars have been used up. No aroma means that the fruit is waterlogged. Of course, in the end there is no substitute for a taste test . . . but I wouldn't try this down at the megamart.

After fighting my way through several jungles and a nasty piece of quicksand, I found myself on a massive plain, surrounded by miles of what appeared to be a terrestrial herb. It was about two and a half feet high, with a spread of maybe three feet. Each had at its center a rosette of waxy pointed leaves, atop of which sat what appeared to be a large compound fruit, like a blackberry, only bigger, heavier, and golden...

APPLICATION

SWEET AND SOUR PORK

4 TO 6 SERVINGS

I wanted to include this application in the show for two reasons: 1) It's a great dish with a bad reputation; 2) I wanted to blow up a pig with a hand grenade.

SOFTWARE

⅔	cup	soy sauce	
2	teaspoons	garlic	minced
1	tablespoon	fresh ginger	minced
½	cup	all-purpose flour	divided
¼	cup	cornstarch	
1	pound	pork butt	cut into 1-inch cubes
		kosher salt	
		black pepper	freshly ground
3	tablespoons	vegetable oil	divided
1	tablespoon	sesame oil	
⅓	cup	Vidalia onion	diced
⅓	cup	celery	diced
⅓	cup	carrots	sliced ¼ inch thick on the bias
⅓	cup	red bell pepper	chopped
⅓	cup	green bell pepper	chopped
1	cup	fresh pineapple	cut into 1-inch cubes
1	cup	ketchup	
¼	cup	sugar	
½	cup	red wine vinegar	
1½	fluid ounces	honey	
		steamed white rice	to serve

TIDBIT | Since they were highly desirable and rare, pineapples became symbols of high-end hospitality. Pineapple motifs are common decorative arts to this day.

PROCEDURE

1. Combine the soy sauce, garlic, ginger, ¼ cup of the flour, and the cornstarch in a **large non-reactive bowl**. Season the pork generously with salt and pepper, then place it in the bowl and toss to coat. Refrigerator overnight.
2. Place the remaining ¼ cup flour in a **pie plate** and season with salt and pepper. Drain off any excess marinade and dredge the pork in the seasoned flour.
3. Heat 1 tablespoon of the vegetable oil in an **electric skillet** set to 375°F. Add the pork and sauté until golden brown on all sides, about 10 minutes. Remove the pork to a **warm plate** lined with **paper towels**.
4. Reduce the electric skillet temperature to 350°F and add the remaining 2 tablespoons of vegetable oil and the sesame oil. Add the onion, celery, and carrots and sweat until the onion is translucent, 3 to 4 minutes. Add the red and green peppers, pineapple, and pork and stir to combine.
5. In a **small bowl**, combine the ketchup, sugar, vinegar, and honey. **Whisk** to blend. Add this sauce to the skillet. Cook until the pork is tender, 4 to 5 minutes, then serve over rice.[2]

[1] You can certainly do this in a pot or pan on the cook-top but I like the wide-open space the electric skillet has to offer.

[2] If an explosive device was utilized, be careful to pick out the shrapnel before serving.

Mr. Brown was picked up by the Hawaii State Patrol and taken to a local hospital for "observation." Officials determined that he had been living in his hovel for only seven days. Meanwhile, his crew, having been rescued by local fishermen, had been staying in a luxury hotel. Brown is recovering from his ordeal and writing *Marooned: The Cookbook*.

He walks Wilbur twice a day.

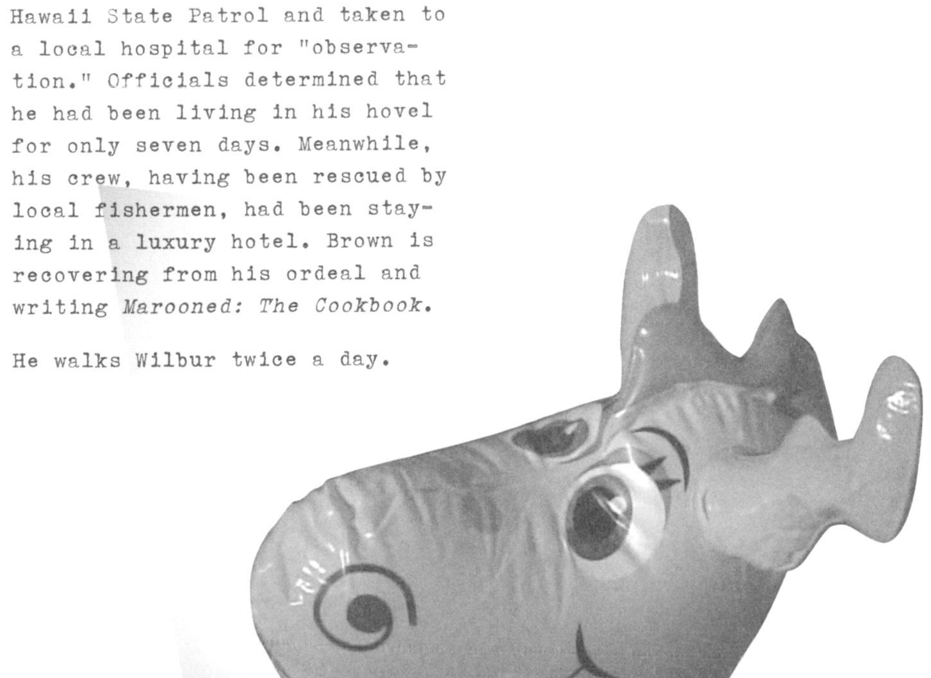

YOGURT: GOOD MILK GONE BAD

EPISODE 73 | SEASON 6 | GOOD EATS

I love this open so much I just have to relive it.

AB: (sitting on deck) I . . . love . . . milk. I love the stuff. I can't get enough of it. The problem is, I'm lactose intolerant.

Enter Lactose Man

LACTOSE MAN: I'm Lactose Man!

AB: Hi, Lactose Man.

LM: Hi.

AB: You see, lactose or milk sugar is a disaccharide, okay, composed of two simple sugars: one molecule of glucose and one molecule of galactose. Now, you can't digest this stuff without dissolving the bond that holds these two things together. And that requires an enzyme called lactase.

When we're babies we make plenty of this stuff because we've got to digest our mother's milk. But when solid food comes into the picture later on, 20 percent of European descendents, 80 percent of African descendents, and almost 100 percent of Asian descendents just stop making lactase. So when any of us drink dairy or eat dairy we consume a lot of these molecules that move unhindered through our systems. That is, of course, until they get to the colon. And there, armies of hungry bacteria latch onto the lactose and consume it. And in doing so they produce a lot of gas—hydrogen, methane, things like that—and that feels a lot like this.

Lactose Man punches AB in the gut. AB doubles over.

LM: I'm not a doctor, but that has to hurt.

AB: Urrggghmmhhggh.

LM: What's that you say? You can never have milk products again, eh?

AB: Urrggghmmhhggh.

LM: You say that yogurt contains bacterial cultures that love nothing more than snacking on lactose?

Two large men enter. One wears a shirt that says LACTOBACILLUS BULGARICUS, the other STREPTOCOCCUS THERMOPHILUS. They grab Lactose Man.

LM: Wait. Wait. Guys. Guys. I'll give you five dollars if you beat him . . .

(we hear a beating in the background)

AB: Those cultures, by the way, produce lactic acid, which is responsible for yogurt's creamy texture and wonderfully tangy flavor. They also happen to be really good for you . . .

Lactose Man continues getting whomped.

AB: Unless, of course, you're Lactose Man. So stick around, won't you? Because when you strip away its commune-livin', VW-bus-drivin', earth-shoe-wearin', hippy image, yogurt isn't just good for you, it's good eats.

KNOWLEDGE CONCENTRATE

The best thing about making your own yogurt is that you get to pick the milk that goes into the yogurt. Any milk will do. You could use goat's milk, yak's milk—it doesn't matter. But if you're a suburbanite like myself, odds are good that you're going to stick with good old cow juice. I prefer organic brands because organic dairy cattle are generally fed a better class of feed than their mainstream sisters, and I can taste the difference. (Or at least I think I can, which is the same thing.) You can use whole milk, but I think the fat kind of gets in the way of the protein coagulation. Makes for a loose yogurt. Skim goes the other way and you end up with a grainy texture. Two percent milk seems just right.

For those of you who are lactose intolerant, yogurt is a great source of calcium. The live cultures in yogurt have been shown to stimulate the immune system and to police the many flora that thrive in the lower G.I. tract. And that means less "tummy trouble." But remember that cooking and freezing yogurt will wipe out the live cultures, so you need to eat your yogurt straight up every now and then to receive the full benefits.

Homemade yogurt does not contain gelatin or other stabilizers, so the more you stir it, the more the gel matrix is going to break down. If you want to add granola or fruit, think fold, not stir. Of course, if you like your yogurt kind of runny and loose, well, stir away. This also means that anytime you cut into this big curd, whey is going to puddle up inside. Do not try to stir this back in. Just drain it, or drink it. It's loaded with protein.

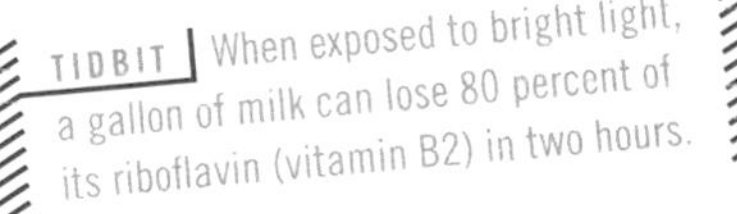
TIDBIT When exposed to bright light, a gallon of milk can lose 80 percent of its riboflavin (vitamin B2) in two hours.

APPLICATION — FRESH YOGURT

1 QUART

If there is a trick to making yogurt (and I'm not saying there is), it's in managing the temperature during inoculation. Although a closely watched water bath will do the trick, I've found a standard heating pad is even better.

SOFTWARE

1	quart	2% milk	
½	cup	nonfat dry milk powder	
2	tablespoons	honey	
½	cup	plain low-fat yogurt	must contain live cultures, at room temperature

PROCEDURE

1. Pour the milk into a **2-quart saucepan** and **whisk** in the milk powder and honey. Place over medium heat and bring to 180°F on an **instant-read digital probe thermometer**, then immediately remove from the heat and allow to cool to 110°F, 5 to 7 minutes.
2. Pour into a **clean cylindrical plastic container**, reserving 1 cup. **Whisk** the reserved cup into the yogurt.
3. Place the plastic container in a **narrow wine bucket lined with a heating pad**. Add the yogurt mixture and set the heating pad to medium. Let the mixture ferment for 12 hours *without stirring*, being sure to maintain the temperature as close to 110°F as possible.
4. After fermentation is complete, place the plastic container in the refrigerator overnight. Pour off any whey that may separate from the yogurt as it sits. Store in an airtight container for up to 2 weeks.

TIDBIT | Yogurt may be the oldest processed milk product, predating cheese by several millennia.

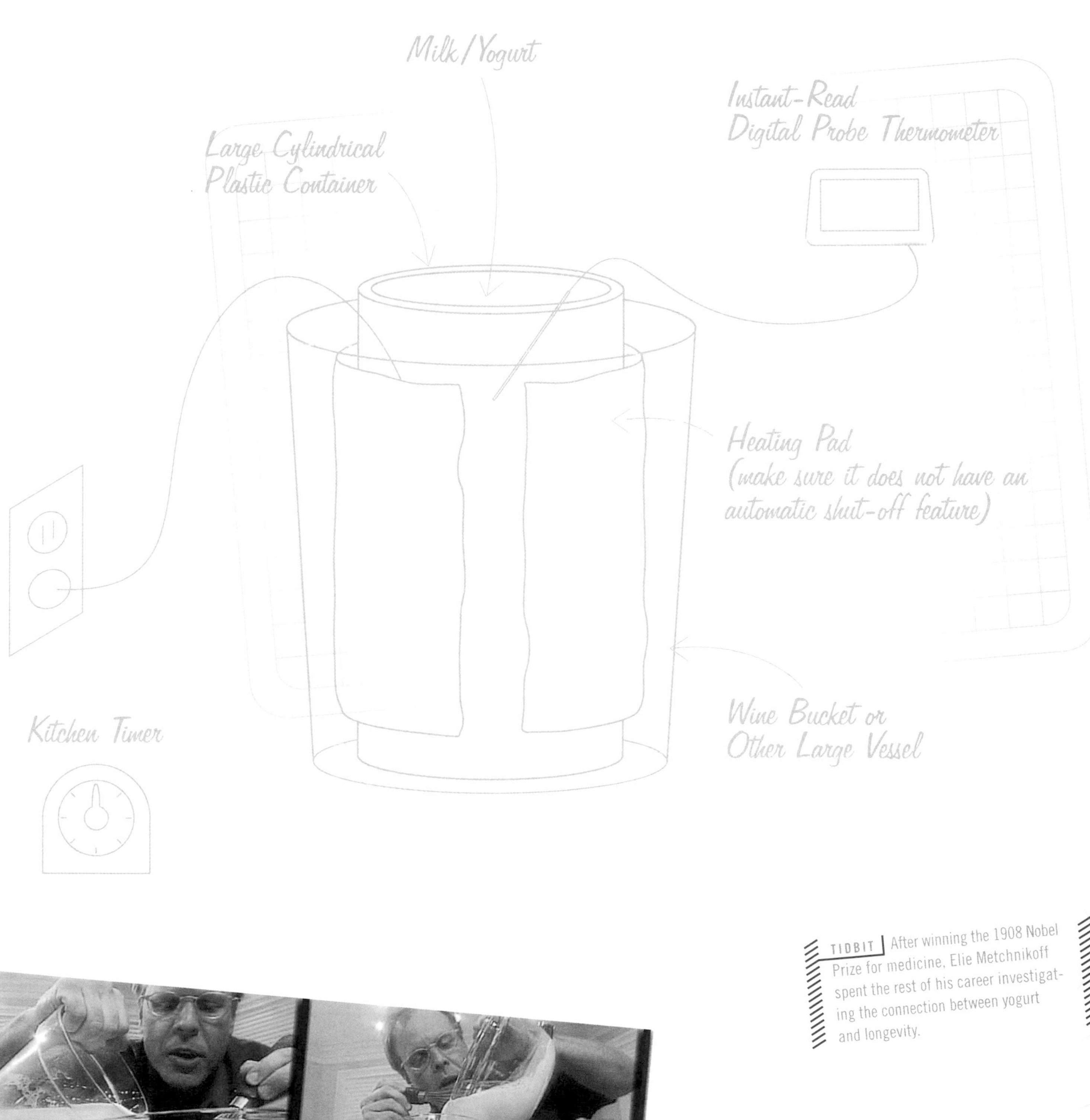

TIDBIT After winning the 1908 Nobel Prize for medicine, Elie Metchnikoff spent the rest of his career investigating the connection between yogurt and longevity.

APPLICATION

YOGURT HERB CHEESE

1 CUP

Fundamentally speaking, there's really only one big difference between yogurt and cheese: the whey. The cheese has had the whey removed before the fermentation process. Of course, in yogurt it's still there. Remember, whey is the liquid—the very protein-laden liquid—that won't coagulate no matter what you do to it. So it makes sense that if we could find a way to get the whey out of our yogurt, we'd have cheese. Very basic cheese, but cheese nonetheless.

// SOFTWARE

1	quart	plain yogurt	preferably homemade
1½	teaspoons	ground cumin	
2	tablespoons	fresh parsley	finely chopped
1	teaspoon	kosher salt	
½	teaspoon	black pepper	freshly ground

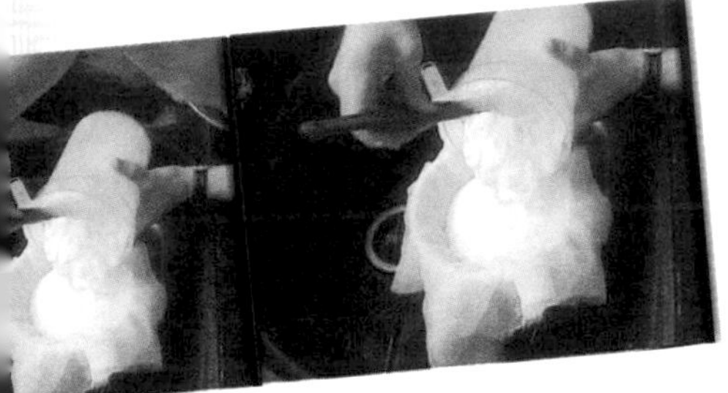

// PROCEDURE

1. Combine all the ingredients in a **medium mixing bowl**.
2. Place 4 layers of cheesecloth in a **fine-mesh strainer** set over a **large plastic container**. Add the yogurt and cover with the cheesecloth overhang. Place a **plate or pot lid** about the size of the strainer on top of the cheesecloth and secure with a **weight** (a 16-ounce can from the pantry should do).
3. Park the whole thing in the fridge for at least 4 hours, or up to overnight. The desired consistency is that of soft cream cheese. Store in an airtight container for up to 10 days.

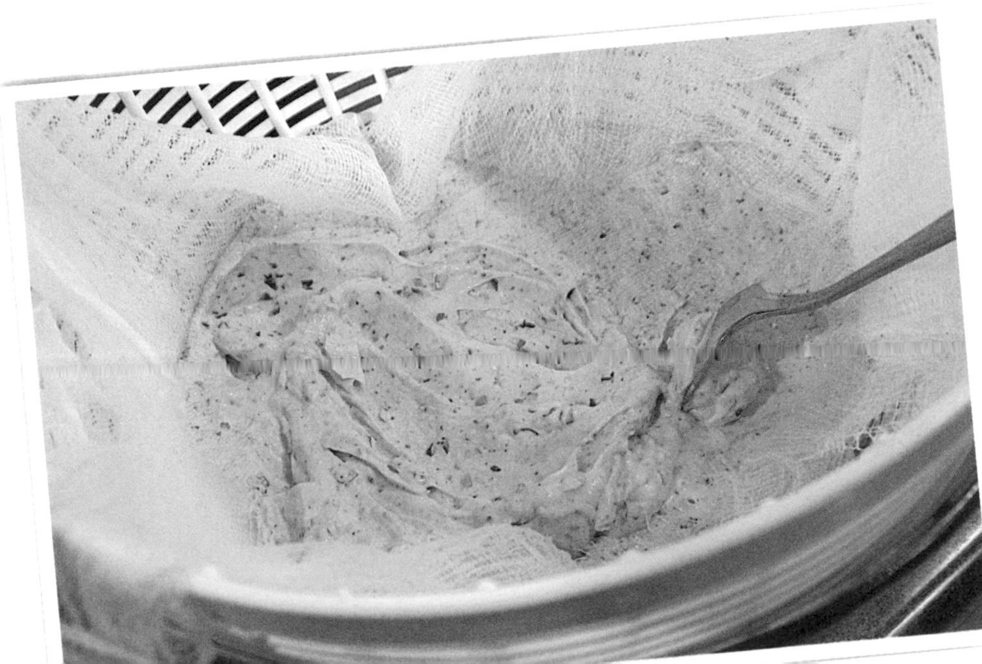

APPLICATION

LEMON-GINGER FROZEN YOGURT

1 QUART

This one should make the lactose-intolerant ice cream lover very happy indeed.

SOFTWARE

2	quarts	plain yogurt	preferably homemade
½	cup	light corn syrup	
¾	cup	sugar	
2	teaspoons	lemon zest	
3	tablespoons	lemon juice	freshly squeezed
1	tablespoon	fresh ginger	minced
¼	cup	candied ginger	diced

PROCEDURE

1. Place 4 layers of **cheesecloth** in a **fine-mesh strainer** set over a **large plastic container**. Add the yogurt and cover with the cheesecloth overhang. Place a **plate or pot lid** about the size of the sieve on top of the cheesecloth and secure with a **weight** (a 16-ounce can from the pantry should do.)
2. Park the whole thing in the fridge for at least 4 hours, or overnight. The desired consistency is that of soft cream cheese.
3. Combine the drained yogurt, corn syrup, sugar, lemon juice, lemon zest, and fresh ginger in a **large bowl**.
4. Transfer the mixture to an **ice cream maker** and freeze according to the manufacturer's instructions. The consistency should be similar to soft-serve ice cream. During the last minute of mixing, add the crystallized ginger. Transfer the frozen yogurt to an **airtight container** and freeze for 2 hours before serving.

TIDBIT | Yogurt is to the Balkans what rice is to Asia: a staple served at almost every meal.

THE EGG-FILES V: SOUFFLÉ—QUANTUM FOAM

EPISODE 74 | SEASON 6 | GOOD EATS

Here's where we sought to demystify a dish that scares the bejeebers out of most home cooks and gives the French an undeserved sense of superiority.

Making a soufflé is easier than learning to pilot a radio-control blimp.

TIDBIT | Sixteenth-century European cooks often whipped egg whites using birch twigs.

"Love and eggs are best when they are fresh."
////////////////////////////////////
RUSSIAN PROVERB

KNOWLEDGE CONCENTRATE

Souffle means "blow" in French, but the dish really should be named "balance" because a successful soufflé is in Zen-like balance. The lightness comes from protein-laden egg whites whipped into a bubbly battalion, while richness hails from a yolk-enforced base or sauce. If there is a trick to making a soufflé (and I'm not saying that there is), it's in bringing these two contrary components into concert.

The vessel: Any tall-sided ceramic vessel will work for a soufflé, but a true soufflé dish does have some special characteristics that are worth noticing. For instance, the fluted exterior: pretty, yes, but functional, too. It actually increases the surface area of the outside of the dish, and that means faster heat absorption. Also, the bottom is unglazed. There are a lot of guys out there with funny accents and tall hats who will tell you that an unglazed surface—because it is porous—also absorbs heat faster.

Making the base: Traditional savory soufflés depend on a modified white sauce as a base. All white sauces, of course, have two things in common: milk and a roux. We've spoken roux-fully before, I know, but some things deserve repeating.

A roux is a cooked paste in which flour granules are suspended in melted butter. A roux has two purposes:

1. Encase the flour granules in fat so that they won't clump when they come in contact with a hot liquid.

2. Cook the flour so that it no longer possesses a raw cereal flavor.

Remember, butter is 6 to 8 percent water, so if you just dump in the flour before the water's cooked out—that is, before it stops bubbling—you're going to get clumps. And once you've got them it's very hard to get rid of them.

Temper, temper: Like so many egg-based applications, this procedure calls for slowly adding some of the hot liquid to the egg mixture, then adding that back to the remainder of the hot liquid. The point of this exercise is to heat the eggs gradually, because the slower they heat the less likely they are to curdle. Since the liquid contains a fair amount of fat, huge molecules that can block protein coagulation, once about a third has been beaten into the eggs you can just dump it all back into the rest of the milk. No reason to dribble or drizzle at this point.

Bring on the bubbles: The worst mistake that novice soufflé-ers make is over-beating their egg whites, stretching the protein so much that the resulting foam isn't flexible enough to stand up to the expansion that should happen in the oven. Increasing the acidity of the whites will help, because it keeps the proteins from binding to one another too tightly. Any acid will do the trick, but I like cream of tartar, an acidic salt derived from wine grapes. (I never leave foam without it.)

"The egg is to cuisine what the article is to speech."

ANONYMOUS

APPLICATION

CHEESE SOUFFLÉ

5 SERVINGS

The secret to a soufflé is to strike a balance between the airy foam and the heavy, starchy sauce. Although ingredients do matter, technique is key.

SOFTWARE

1	tablespoon	ground Parmesan cheese	not grated
1½	ounces	unsalted butter	plus additional, chilled, for the soufflé dish
1	ounce	all-purpose flour	
1	teaspoon	ground mustard	
½	teaspoon	garlic powder	
⅛	teaspoon	kosher salt	
1⅓	cups	whole milk	hot (180 to 185°F)
4	large	egg yolks	2½ ounces by weight
6	ounces	sharp cheddar cheese	grated
5	large	egg whites	5½ ounces by weight
1	tablespoon	H_2O	
¼	teaspoon	cream of tartar	

TIP | When greasing a soufflé dish, never use margarine, shortening, or, for that matter, grease.

PROCEDURE

1. Use the cold butter to grease a **2-quart round soufflé mold**. Add the ground Parmesan, tightly cover the mold with **plastic wrap**, and shake to cover the sides with the cheese.[1] Place in the freezer for 5 minutes. Heat the oven to 375°F.

2. Melt the butter over medium heat in a **3-quart saucier**. Simmer until all the water has cooked out of the butter and it stops bubbling, about 2 minutes. Combine the flour, mustard, garlic powder, and salt in a **small bowl**. **Whisk** this mixture into the melted butter. Cook for 2 minutes, or until the roux appears dry.

3. Whisk in the hot milk and turn the heat to high. As soon as the mixture boils—this should happen almost immediately—remove from the heat.

4. Beat the egg yolks in a **medium mixing bowl** until creamy, about 1 minute. Temper the yolks by adding a few ounces of the milk mixture to the yolks and whisking constantly. Add another few ounces of the milk mixture to the yolks and then pour the yolk mixture back into the saucier, whisking vigorously. Remove the pan from the heat and whisk in the cheese. Transfer this mixture back to the **medium mixing bowl**. This base mixture can be covered with **plastic wrap** and refrigerated for up to 1 week; bring it to room temperature before using.

5 Using an **electric mixer** and a **clean metal bowl**, whip the egg whites, water, and cream of tartar until medium peaks form.

6 Time to fold. The goal: Bring the light foam and the heavy base together in such a way as to avoid bursting all the bubbles. For this you'll need a **really big rubber or silicone spatula**.

Start by quickly stirring a quarter of the foam into the base. This will lighten the viscosity of the base enough to ease continued integration. Fold in the remaining foam in thirds. The spatula goes down right in the middle, then sweeps up the side and turns its load over. Turn the bowl a quarter and repeat the exact same action.

7 When about half of the foam has been folded in, add half of the remainder. Lay it right on top and gently fold, turning the bowl as you go. Let the bowl work for you. Digging down, sweeping up and over, making no more than two rotations of the bowl for any one dose of egg whites; don't worry if there is still a lot of egg white visible. Fold in the remaining foam.

8 Immediately pour the mixture into the chilled mold, filling the soufflé to ½ inch from the top. Place on an **aluminum pie pan** and bake for 30 to 35 minutes. Do not open the oven door during the first 30 minutes of baking. When done, a paring knife inserted in the middle of the soufflé should come out mostly clean. The internal temperature should be between 180° and 185°F.

9 Serve immediately by plunging a **wide spoon or ice cream spade** right down into the middle of the soufflé and scooping out portions so that everyone gets some of the creamy middle and some of the brown cheesy side. Odds are, it won't be pretty. But it will be delicious.

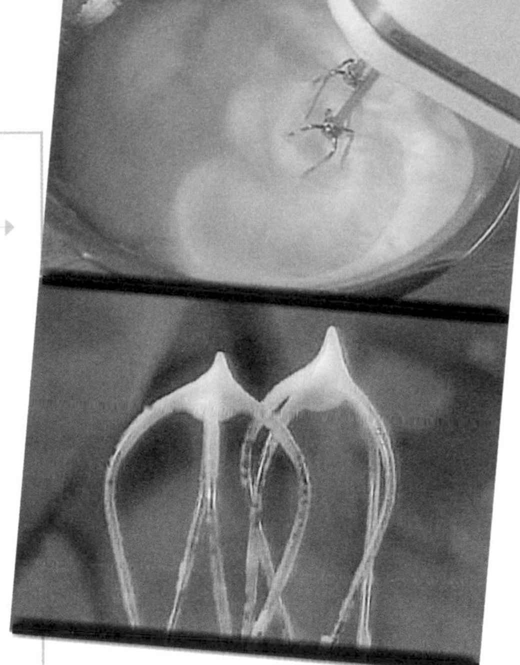

[1] Soufflés grow best when they can get hold of the side of the vessel. So here we're creating a bit of traction by applying a layer of ground Parmesan cheese.

TRIVIA | The writing-on-the-window bit was a riff on a scene from *A Beautiful Mind*.

TIP | Always separate eggs when cold, but whip whites at room temperature.

TOMATO ENVY

EPISODE 75 | SEASON 6 | GOOD EATS

The average American eats seventeen pounds of tomatoes each year. After the potato, these fruits are America's favorite vegetables. That's right, fruits. They are, in fact, berries. And like all berries, they are amazingly wonderful when they're in season and miserably mediocre when they're not. The problem with tomatoes is that the season is really, really short and tomatoes don't like to travel. That is why many Americans will go to their graves having never munched a truly magnificent tomato. But not me. Oh, no. When the big red orbs rise, I am all about *carpe Lycopersicum*. Why the 'mater mania? Maybe it's because they're packed with nutrition, antioxidants, lycopene, vitamin A, and vitamin C. Maybe it's because they work and play so well with other ingredients. Or maybe it's because they're just plain old . . . good eats.

TRIVIA | The opening scene set in my neighbor McGregor's garden was actually filmed at the Atlanta History Center. And I'm proud to say that most of those tomatoes were attached with florist wire.

TIDBIT | In the 1830s, tomato ketchup became known as America's national condiment.

TIDBIT | *Lycopersicum* translates to "wolf peach" in Latin.

TIDBIT | Although tomatoes are technically fruits, the U.S. supreme court decided in 1887 that they are legally vegetables because they are generally served as a side course, rather than a dessert. (Nix *v.* Hedder)

KNOWLEDGE CONCENTRATE

Because they are so easy to hybridize—cross-pollinate—there are hundreds if not thousands of tomato models to choose from. In just the last few years home growers have been rediscovering old heirloom varieties like little zebra tomatoes, big purple tomatoes, and old strains of classic plum tomatoes.

Commercially speaking, there are six major types of tomato: globe, plum, cherry, pear, grape, and little bitty currant tomatoes. A beefsteak tomato is any extra-large red globe tomato. And although there are varieties of tomato that remain green when completely ripe, "green tomato" usually refers to a red globe tomato that has reached full size but has not turned red yet.

Each one of these unique styles has unique characteristics. And when you understand those and learn how to take advantage of them, that's when you can find true tomato happiness. Of course, it helps to have a nonstop supply of fresh garden-grown tomatoes at your fingertips.

Why is it that garden-grown are so much better than grocery-store tomatoes? Well, maybe it would help to understand the government's point of view. The U.S. Department of Agriculture standards for fresh tomatoes recognizes six official color designations:

Color	Description
Green	Green
Breaker	Some red, tan, or pink visible
Turning	10 to 30 percent tan, pink, or red
Pink	30 to 60 percent pink or red
Light red	60 to 90 percent pink or red
Red	More than 90 percent red

Most commercial tomatoes are picked at the breaker stage when they have reached full size and weight. After washing, sorting, sizing, and packing, tomatoes are moved to an airtight room where they are exposed to a "ripening" agent—ethylene gas. Ethylene gas is a hydrocarbon that occurs naturally as a growth hormone in many fruits and vegetables. A lot of connoisseurs, however, claim that the process reddens the tomatoes but doesn't really ripen them (hence "'ripening'" above)—that is, it doesn't advance the cellular maturation of the fruit.[1]

Shopping and storage: The key is to shop as seasonally and as locally as you can. And for me, that means farmers' markets and roadside stands. Choose firm, fragrant tomatoes. They should be heavy for their size and yield to gentle pressure without ever being mushy. Listen, as long as they don't have any big open splits or, you know, bugs crawling in and out, don't get too carried away with aesthetics, okay? Some of the tastiest tomatoes you will ever eat will also be the ugliest you'll ever look at. And those heirlooms? You'll never find those at the megamart.

When you get them home, don't keep them in direct sunlight, no matter how pretty they look. Oh, and never put them in the refrigerator. If they drop below 50°F, a flavor compound called (Z)-3-dexenal is just going to flip itself off like a chemical switch . . . permanently.

Another scene with the feds. Notice that the girl changes every season. What's up with that?

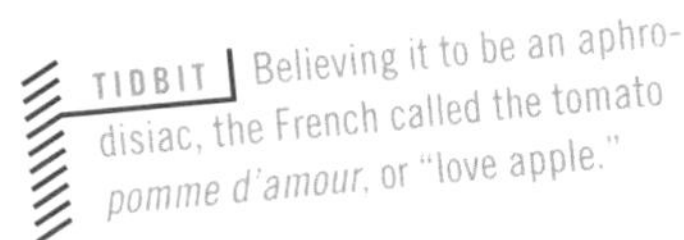

TIDBIT Believing it to be an aphrodisiac, the French called the tomato *pomme d'amour*, or "love apple."

APPLICATION

TBL PANZANELLA[2]

6 SERVINGS

I've morphed my favorite sandwich into my favorite salad. Originally we called for letting the bread get stale overnight, but, truth is, stale bread can pick up a lot of funky flavors and, depending on humidity, it may not dry enough. So now we bake it.

SOFTWARE

12	ounces	French bread	cut into 1-inch cubes (about ¾ of a standard loaf)
8	slices	bacon	chopped and cooked, fat reserved
12	ounces	grape tomatoes	halved
¼	cup	red wine vinegar	
¼	teaspoon	kosher salt	
¼	teaspoon	black pepper	freshly ground
3	tablespoons	extra-virgin olive oil	
12	ounces	yellow pear or other heirloom tomato	halved or roughly chopped, if using heirlooms
4	ounces	romaine lettuce	chopped (1 small head)
1	tablespoon	fresh mint	chiffonade
1	tablespoon	fresh basil	chiffonade

PROCEDURE

1. Heat the oven to 350°F.
2. Spread the bread cubes on a **half sheet pan** and bake until dry but not browned, 10 to 12 minutes. Cool for 5 minutes. Place the bread cubes and half of the bacon drippings in a **large bowl** and toss to combine.
3. Place the rest of the bacon drippings in a **10-inch sauté pan** set over high heat. When the fat is nice and hot, add the grape tomatoes, cut side down, and cook until brown, about 5 minutes. Remove from the heat.
4. Whisk the vinegar, salt, pepper, and oil in a **large metal bowl** to emulsify.
5. Invite the bacon, all the tomatoes, and the lettuce to the vinaigrette and toss to combine. Add the bread cubes and toss again.
6. Garnish with the mint and basil and serve.

APPLICATION

ROASTED TOMATO SOUP

1 QUART; 8 SERVINGS

Originally this application was formulated as a sauce. But with a little tinkering we've decided it makes a much better summer soup, which can be served warm or chilled, and it freezes very well for up to 6 months. It's best when accompanied by a Big Cheese Squeeze (page 84).

// SOFTWARE

40	medium	Roma tomatoes	halved
½	cup	olive oil	divided
2	tablespoons	fresh oregano leaves	finely chopped, divided
2	tablespoons	fresh thyme leaves	finely chopped, divided
1	teaspoon	kosher salt	divided
1	teaspoon	black pepper	freshly ground, divided
1	tablespoon	garlic	minced, divided
1	cup	onion	finely diced, divided
½	cup	white wine	such as cheap Chardonnay

// PROCEDURE

1. Heat the oven to 325°F.
2. Place a single layer of the tomato halves, cut side up, in **two 9-by-13-inch glass baking dishes**. Drizzle with ¼ cup of the oil and sprinkle with half of the herbs, salt, pepper, garlic, and onion, in that order. Top with a second layer of the remaining tomatoes and drizzle with the remaining oil and sprinkle with the remaining herbs, salt, pepper, garlic, and onion. Bake on the middle rack of the oven for 1 hour.
3. Boost the oven temperature to 400°F and bake for another 30 minutes, or until the tomatoes are very tender and starting to brown on top. Some liquid will have accumulated in the bottom of the baking dishes. Remove from the oven and transfer the tomatoes and liquid to a **food mill fitted with the medium die** set over a **4-quart pot**. Pass the tomato mixture through the mill and discard the skins. Add the wine to the pot and bring to a boil, then reduce the heat to low and cook for 10 minutes.
4. Serve warm or chilled.

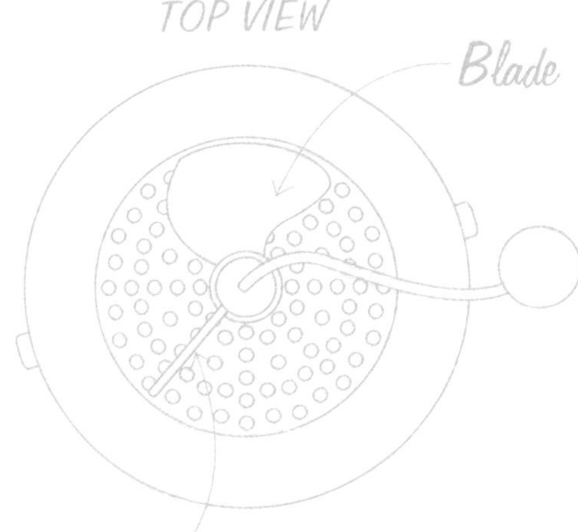

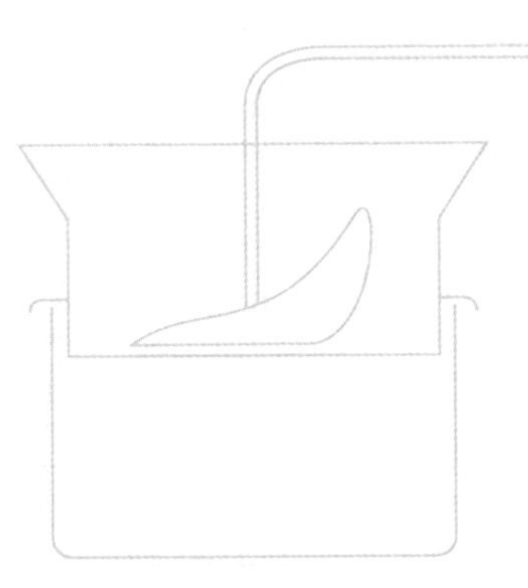

[1] The term "vine-ripened" is commonly applied to any tomato that shows red coloration prior to harvest. Currently there are no federal regulations regarding its use.

[2] A Tuscan summer salad containing dried bread.

AMBER WAVES

EPISODE 76 | SEASON 6 | GOOD EATS

Mission: Convince every beer lover within the sound of my voice that beer-making isn't just a fantasy. Sure, home brewing takes a little bit of work. It requires some specialized tools and some rather exotic ingredients, but they're not hard to find, nor are they difficult to implement. In a way, it's like setting up an aquarium because it's all about creating an environment where unicellular critters called yeasts can grow and eat and raise little baby yeasts and live out their amazingly short little lives . . . lives we can press into service creating . . . mmm . . . beer.

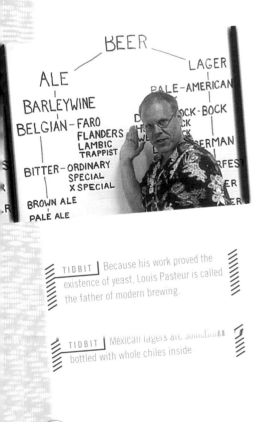

TIDBIT | Because his work proved the existence of yeast, Louis Pasteur is called the father of modern brewing.

TIDBIT | Mexican lagers are sometimes bottled with whole chiles inside.

There are two major branches in the beer family tree: lagers and ales.

ALES are the product of top fermenting yeast, which stay on top of the beer in contact with the air while they do their work. They prefer warm temperatures, and they ferment quickly. Ales are typically robust and full bodied with complex flavors.

LAGERS are produced by bottom fermenting yeast, which prefer to work over a long period of time at relatively cold temperatures. *Lager* comes from the German *logern* meaning "to store". Lagers are typically light and crisp and mellow. Since Germans invented the North American beer industry, it only makes sense that most of our suds are generated in that vein.

Yeast: Unicellular creatures that aren't quite animals yet not exactly plants either. They convert sugars into alcohol, carbon dioxide, and various flavor compounds. Any yeast that will ferment a wort (a grainy brew that needs fermenting in order to become beer) can be called brewer's yeast, and your local brew supply has oodles of them, including vials of liquid-bound "pitchable" yeasts that are ready to be tossed right in to the equation.

Barley: Like its cereal cousins wheat and rye, barley stores energy as starch in its kernels. Yeast can't eat this starch until it's been broken down into simple sugars through the process of malting. To malt barley, the harvested kernels are kept warm and moist until they germinate. The germ produces enzymes, which break the starches down into simple sugars. The kernels are then roasted, producing malted barley. Malting also shuts down the enzymes.

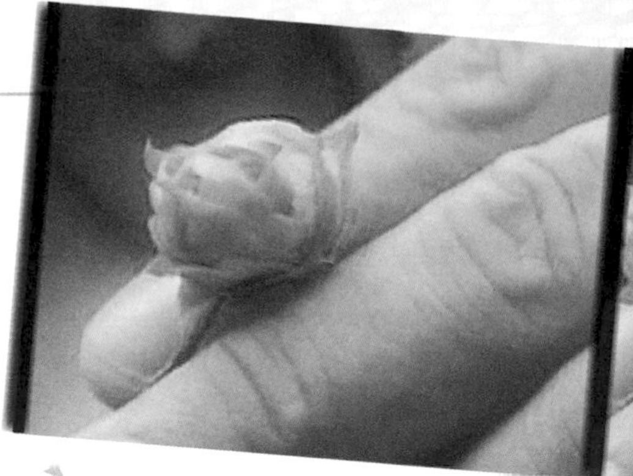

Hops: A pinecone-like flower that grows on a vine of the cannabis family. Each one of these little flowers contains glands that secrete a witch's brew of essential oils, acids, and resins that, when added to brewing beer, provide a perfect counterpoint to barley's simple sweetness. Hops also help to preserve beer, and in the days before refrigeration, this was a big deal. I mean, imagine you were a brewer in Dresden in, say, 1125. If you wanted your beer to have any shelf life at all, you had to make it very, very high in alcohol. This is no problem until you consider the fact that most European cities didn't have a decent water supply, so people drank beer morning, noon and night. No wonder they called it the dark ages. Nobody remembered anything.

TIP | While a quick internet search will yield you plenty of sources for the hardware and software required to brew your own beer, you're better off hunting for your local brewer's supply. Keep two things in mind about a brewer's supply shop. One, it should be completely lacking in decor. Never trust a well-decorated brewer's supply shop. Number two, the shop is only as good as the brain that's running it, so ask questions!

Hops are typically added two times during brewing: once for flavor early on and then at the end for aroma. I use Cascade hops, which come from the Cascade region of the United States and, also, Kent Goldings hops, which come from the Kent region of England.

Water: Since the stuff that comes out of most kitchen faucets tastes and smells like a public pool, brew with bottled. It always tastes the same, it's relatively cheap, it's sterile, and it's pre-measured. But never ever use mineral water. Never ever use distilled water because its lack of mineral content makes it a lousy solvent.

Hardware: At this point in your brewing career, your hardware needs are relatively few—some stuff you may even have laying around the house already. Other stuff you will need to procure from a brewer's supply store. Most of it can be found bundled in brewing kits.

A pot that can hold three gallons of H_2O with room to spare

A colander that will fit inside the fermenters

One probe thermometer

A fine-mesh strainer with a handle long enough to securely rest on the lid of the fermenting bucket

Two 7-gallon fermenters. (Note the air-tight lid with a small hole that can receive an air lock or bubbler, which allows CO_2 to escape without letting germ-laden air back in. Also note the spigot.)

6 feet of plastic tubing that can fit onto the spigot

A bottling tube with a filling valve

Muslin or grain bag

Long metal spoon

Whisk

5 gallons of H_2O mixed with 2 ounces unscented household bleach

Latex or vinyl gloves

If you're going to use bottles, you'll need a bottle brush for cleaning.

Bottles—I use 20-ounce bottles with a little bound-up stopper that can be used over and over again. They're a little more expensive, but they're very convenient. Oh, make sure you'll have enough bottles by dividing 640 ounces by the number of ounces in the bottle of your choice.

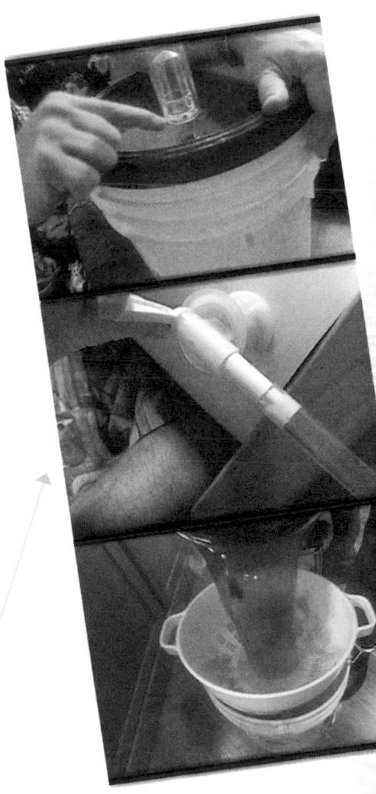

APPLICATION — GOOD BREW

5 GALLONS

We've expanded this procedure quite a bit to enhance your chances for success.

TIDBIT | An enzyme is like a chemical crowbar that breaks down other chemical compounds.

TIDBIT | Finely ground malt is mixed with dry milk to make malted milk, the stuff in malted milk balls.

SOFTWARE

FOR FERMENTING

½	pound	crystal grain	milled
4	gallons + plus 1 pint	bottled H_2O[1]	(filtered is fine, too, but not distilled or mineral) divided
7	pounds	pale or light liquid malt extract	
1	1½-ounce vial	liquid British yeast	
1	fluid ounce	Cascade hops	
1¾	fluid ounces	Kent Golding hops	divided
½	teaspoon	Irish moss	
1	7-pound bag	ice	

FOR BOTTLING

6	ounces	priming sugar	
16	fluid ounces	H_2O	

Ale drinker

Lager drinker

PROCEDURE

FERMENTING:

1. Thoroughly clean all equipment.
2. Sanitize all equipment in 5 gallons of water and bleach mixture: fill one **fermenting bucket** with the solution and place the remaining equipment in it. Be sure to wipe the outside of the bucket with the solution as well. Only the probe of the thermometer should be sanitized. Let sit for 30 minutes and then thoroughly rinse everything in hot water and air dry.
3. Place the crystal grain in a **muslin** or **grain bag**, and situate it along with two gallons of the water in a **large pot** over medium-high heat. Attach the **probe thermometer** to the side of the pan (a **binder clip** works well for this) and set to 155°F. Steep the grains at 155°F for 30 minutes.
4. Meanwhile loosen the container of malt extract by placing it in warm water. This will aid in removing it from the container.
5. After 30 minutes, remove the grain bag. Allow the bag to drain, but do not squeeze it. Add another gallon of water and bring to a boil,. The liquid will foam at the top, and some proteins should coagulate and look like clumps. This will take 10 to 20 minutes, stirring occasionally.

6 Remove the yeast from the fridge and bring to room temperature.

7 Add the malt extract and stir constantly to dissolve and return the water to a boil. Add the Cascade hops and 1 ounce of the Kent Golding hops, carefully, and continue boiling for 45 minutes. Add the Irish moss and continue to boil for 15 minutes. Turn off the heat, add the remaining Kent Golding hops, and steep for 5 minutes.

8 Meanwhile, combine the remaining gallon and pint of water with the ice in the fermenting bucket. Set the **colander** inside the **strainer** on top of the bucket.

9 Strain the mixture into the bucket and cool to at least 80°F. Thoroughly **whisk** this wort for approximately 1 minute. You want to aerate the wort, but avoid creating a whirlpool or splashing. Give the vial of yeast a hardy shake, let settle for 30 seconds, and open away from you. Add the yeast to the wort and give the mixture one good stir.

10 Lid the fermenter and secure the airlock (make sure there is about an ounce of water in your airlock for it to operate). Place the fermenter in a cool place (68° to 72°F is optimal) for 10 to 14 days. The airlock should bubble within 24 hours and continue bubbling on and off during fermentation. Fermentation is complete when bubbling from the airlock stops for at least 24 hours.

BOTTLING:

11 Thoroughly clean all equipment. Sanitize the fermenting bucket, spigot, bottles, bottling tube, plastic tube and metal spoon using the bleach-spiked water. Rinse with hot water and allow to air dry.

12 Bring the priming sugar and water to a boil in a **2-quart saucepan**. Boil for 2 minutes. Remove from the heat and cool.

13 Place the full fermenter of beer on an elevated surface such as a countertop and place the empty fermenter on the floor below. Attach the plastic tubing to the spigot and lead into the empty fermenter. Remove the airlock from the fermenter. Add the cooled priming sugar to the empty fermenter and slowly add the beer through the plastic tubing. When all the beer is removed to the second fermenter, stir the mixture once.

14 Elevate the now full fermenter as before and attach the bottling tube to the spigot. Use the bottling tube to fill the sanitized bottles. Remember to only fill the bottles to within 2 inches of the top. Close or cap the bottles. Place the bottles in a cool, dry place for another 10 to 14 days. Refrigerate and enjoy within 2 months.

TIDBIT Belgian wheat beer spontaneously fermented by wild yeast is referred to as "lambic" beer.

[1] Although this is the sure and easy way to go, in the years since making this show I've come to believe that bottled water is, at the very least: stupid. Now, I boil filtered water. It's an extra step but one I feel good about.

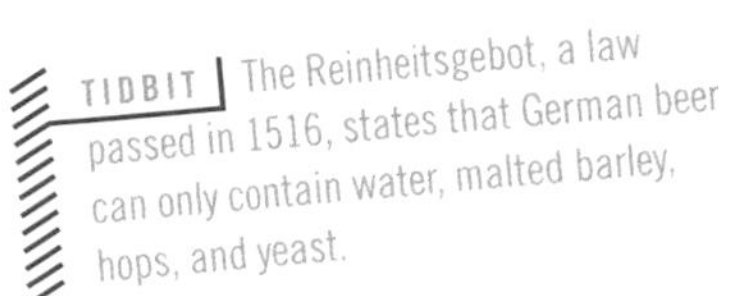

TIDBIT The Reinheitsgebot, a law passed in 1516, states that German beer can only contain water, malted barley, hops, and yeast.

As much as we Americans love to dip things, it's sheer madness not to make our own.

This episode is set sometime in the future. I've gone insane attempting to devise a Unified Dip Theory and as a result now reside (apparently against my will) at the Beard Home for the Culinarily Confused. As the show opens, my old apprentice Paul is paying me a visit. In the time since my breakdown, he's become a big food star himself.

TRIVIA The solarium scenes were filmed in the conservatory at the famed Callanwolde Arts Center in Atlanta. By noon, it was around 100°F in there, and most of us were wearing heavy robes. The temperature rose throughout the afternoon. It looked great but was a great deal like I envision hell. Insanity and heat with floppy slippers.

TRIVIA The crazy lady stumbling around in a chef's hat also played Chef Midwest in episode 60.

KNOWLEDGE CONCENTRATE

- You can make an American dip out of just about anything, as long as you stick to a basic formula: creamy base, plus one or two main ingredients—usually the ones the dip is named for—and then no more than three supporting seasonings, excluding salt, of course.
- After countless hours of experimentation, we have come to the conclusion that the best all-purpose sour cream dip base is in fact a combination of two parts sour cream and one part mayonnaise. It's not exactly a dairy product, but it is white and creamy and a little can do a lot for a dip's flavor and texture. Also, the emulsifying power of the egg in mayonnaise can help hold dips together.
- History: Dipping has long been a way of life in cultures where flat breads, like pita, are often used as eating impliments. (When's the last time you saw a fork in a Moroccan restaurant?) But Americans didn't really catch on until after World War II. The foods of the '50s were all about fun and convenience, and dips fit the bill. I've got a pile of community cookbooks from that period, and some of them are half dips. There are dips for every phase of life, except, oddly, breakfast. There are no breakfast dips. But that's another show.
- The fall of dips: America has but one dip now—salsa. We've abandoned the rich and creamy dips because we just can't face the guilt of serving up all that mayo and sour cream. Get over it, I say.

AB'S DIP DIARY:

In order to formulate a Unified Dip Theory, one must first establish a system for classifying all dips. This is predicated on devising a working definition of what a dip actually is. To this end, we employ the three foot rule, which states that in order to qualify as a dip, the candidate substance must be able to maintain constant contact with its transport mechanism over three feet of white carpet. (Salsa fails this test soundly, but then the word *salsa* means "sauce," not "dip.") From this we can extrapolate that a successful dip is creamy. Of course, there are a lot of different ways to get creamy into a dip.

APPLICATION

ONION DIP FROM SCRATCH

1 QUART

SOFTWARE

3	tablespoons	olive oil	
1	pound	onions	diced
1	teaspoon	kosher salt	divided
1½	cups	sour cream	
¾	cup	mayonnaise	
¼	teaspoon	garlic powder	
¼	teaspoon	white pepper	freshly ground

PROCEDURE

Place the oil, onions, and ½ teaspoon salt in a **10-inch sauté pan** over medium heat. Cook, stirring occasionally, until the onions are golden brown, about 20 minutes. Remove from the heat and set aside to cool for 15 minutes. Place the remaining ingredients and the remaining ½ teaspoon salt in a **medium mixing bowl**, add the cooled onions, and stir to combine. Refrigerate for 1 hour and stir again before serving.

TIDBIT During its heyday in the 1960s, onion dip was better known as California dip.

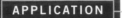

APPLICATION

GUACAMOLE

1 PINT; 8 SERVINGS WITH TORTILLA CHIPS

// SOFTWARE

3	medium (about 8 ounces each)	ripe Hass avocados	halved and pitted, peel removed
1	medium	lime	juiced
½	teaspoon	kosher salt	
½	teaspoon	ground cumin	
¼	teaspoon	ground cayenne pepper	
½	medium	onion	diced
2	small	Roma tomatoes	seeded and diced
1	large clove	garlic	minced
1	tablespoon	fresh cilantro	chopped
1	tablespoon	jalapeño	minced

// PROCEDURE

Place the avocado pulp and lime juice in a **large mixing bowl** and toss to combine. Add the salt, cumin, and cayenne and mash using a **potato masher**, leaving some larger chunks for texture. Add the onion, tomatoes, garlic, cilantro, and jalapeño and stir to combine. Lay **plastic wrap** directly on the surface of the guacamole and allow to sit at room temperature for 2 hours before serving.

CUTTING AVOCADOS

When cutting avocados, get in the habit of moving the knife as little as possible. Instead, move the fruit across the blade. Just make an incision right at the stem end, straight down the middle, and then rotate the fruit around the knife. Give the two halves a little bit of a twist and open them up.

As for the pit: First make yourself a little catcher's mitt out of a kitchen towel. Place the avocado right in the middle of the mitt. Then take your heaviest chef's knife, hold it a few inches from the pit, and thwack it right into the center of the seed. All you need is ½ inch of penetration.

Gently twist, and the pit will pop right out. To remove the slippery pit from the blade reach around the back of the blade, and gently pinch the pit off. No drama and no stitches.

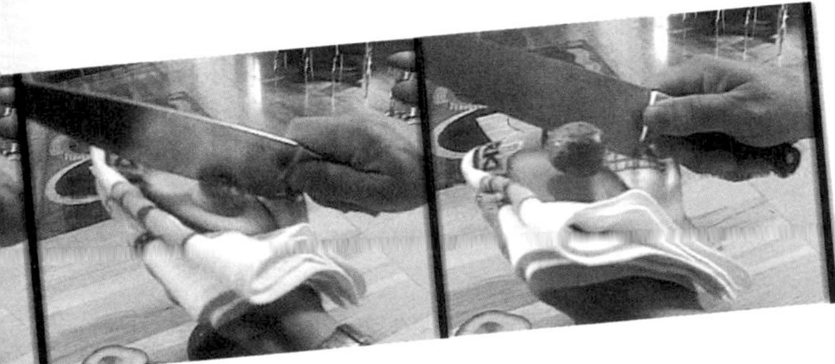

Sure, these guys *look* like peasants, but in reality we've got a gaffer (David) on the left, and a prop master (Todd) on the right.

APPLICATION

HOT SPINACH AND ARTICHOKE DIP

1 QUART

SOFTWARE

1	5-ounce box	frozen spinach	
1	9-ounce box	frozen artichoke hearts	
1	cup	H_2O	
8	ounces	cream cheese	
¼	cup	sour cream	
¼	cup	mayonnaise	
1	ounce	Parmesan cheese	grated
½	teaspoon	red pepper flakes	
¼	teaspoon	kosher salt	
¼	teaspoon	garlic powder	

PROCEDURE

1. Place the spinach, artichokes, and water in a **2-quart saucepan** over high heat. Cook just until the vegetables are heated through. Drain and squeeze as much liquid out as possible.
2. Heat the cream cheese in a microwave oven for 1 minute, or until hot and soft. Add the drained spinach and artichokes as well as the remaining ingredients. Stir to combine and serve hot.

GARLIC POWDER V. GARLIC SALT

Garlic powder never delivers because people don't give it a chance to rehydrate. If you're in a hurry you ought to use HBI garlic powder. No, I am not making that up: high bulk index is a special kind of garlic powder that's dried and ground in such a way as to provide each grain with twice the surface area of regular garlic powder. You can just put a little bit of this in water for two minutes and it's up to 100 percent flavor. It's like instant garlic. Amazing.

By the way, garlic powder is *not* too salty. Garlic *salt* is salty. The problem is that retailers either mix them up, or they put them together and put the same label on them. Which just goes to show that shopping for spices in a regular grocery store, well, that's what's crazy!

TIP | Chafing dishes are the ultimate unitaskers. Why not just grab hold of your old faithful slow cooker, put a couple of inches of hot water in it, turn it to low, and put your dip in a bowl that will fit over the top of it? That way your dip stays hot all night long. And, you know, if you don't like the way it looks, tie a scarf around it!

CHOPS AHOY!

EPISODE 78 | SEASON 6 | GOOD EATS

Nothin' like a pork chop. Back before the Civil War, pork was king of the meats in America, and the richer you were the higher off the animal you ate. And since the pork chop came from the loin or back, eating one meant you were dining "high on the hog." Of course, firing up a pork chop today is risky business, because the modern American hog is lean and clean and potentially dry as a martini. And as for flavor, well, although heritage versions of the pig are again being bred, most American megamart pork is far from . . .

TIDBIT | "Center cut" is often used to describe both rib and loin chops.

ANATOMY OF A PORK CHOP

SHOULDER CHOP: An economy cut that contains pieces of a lot of different muscles and a good bit of connective tissue, so it's good for braising, but not grilling or pan-frying.

SIRLOIN CHOP: From the other end comes the sirloin chop, which is just like a shoulder chop, only more so. Cheap, and definitely a wet-method cut.

RIB CHOP: My favorite chop for fast, dry-heat cooking. And since it's composed almost entirely of one muscle, it's ideal for stuffing.

LOIN CHOP: The T-bone or porterhouse of the pork world. But since the loin chop contains two muscles, the loin and the tenderloin, and each cooks so differently, I'm not a big fan.

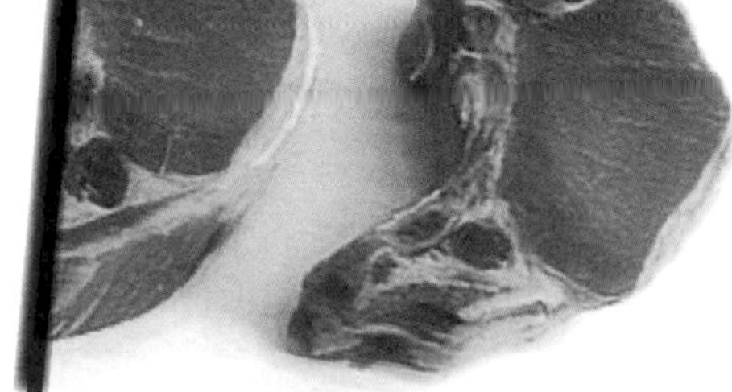

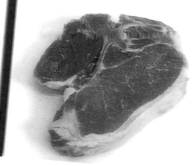

KNOWLEDGE CONCENTRATE

Unlike the beef critter, which has three primary cuts along the back, the hog has but one, the loin. And it is from this region that all pork chops are chopped. As you might expect, the chops cut from the front of the loin are very different from those cut from the back or middle.

Brining: With the possible exception of tenderloin, I brine every hunk of pork I cook. Why? Well, from the 1860s to the early 1960s, American hogs were fat. In fact, most American hogs were called "lard hogs," because they were raised as much for their fat as their meat, which was indeed juicy, succulent, and flavorful. But the advent of the fitness craze drove consumers away from pork to the relatively lean chicken. Undaunted, the pork industry set out to redesign the hog, cross-breeding American lard hogs with various strains of long-bodied bacon hogs. Then they put them on a special diet that promoted fast growth of lean meat. As a result, today's pork chop is about 60 percent leaner than the chop of yesteryear. And if you cook it just right, it actually tastes like chicken . . . whatever that means.

Now, since you are a loyal viewer (and reader), I'm not going to waste yet more ink on the intricacies of brining. But rest assured that when it comes to pork, osmosis is our friend.

On stuffing: Let me set the record straight: I never said "Stuffing is evil." Okay . . . actually I did, but what I really meant is that stuffing a turkey is evil. That's because turkeys have a lot of mass, so getting heat to the stuffing is tricky, and it's dangerous because the part of the turkey we stuff is where the guts once were, and so there's a good chance bacteria reside there and, if they're not heated to at least 165°F they could ruin several of our days. A pork chop is not a turkey. It has low mass, and the pocket we wish to stuff is to be cut by us right through the middle of the meat, about as far from guts as you can get. There's little danger involved.

Making the pocket: I prefer a boning knife for this because it has a very thin blade and a curve at the end, both desirable attributes when trying to cut a large pocket with a small hole. Start by putting the pork chop in a bagel slicer, bone side down. Point your knife straight down and push all the way through until you hit bone. Sweep the blade up one side while not making the hole any larger, then turn the knife around, go back in the same hole until you hit the bone, and move upward.

GAS FOR GRILLIN'

The clean-burning efficient fuel we know as propane is born of petroleum—oil, that is, black gold, Texas tea. Petroleum is composed of hydrogen and carbon atoms linked together to form chains of varying lengths and molecular weights, each possessing unique characteristics. Since they have different boiling points, these chains can be distilled at a refinery. The shortest of these chains is methane, next comes ethane, butane, and propane. When burned in the presence of oxygen, a mere cubic foot of propane, or LP-Gas, can generate a whopping 2,500 BTUs[1] compared to natural gas, which can only manage 1,000 BTUs.

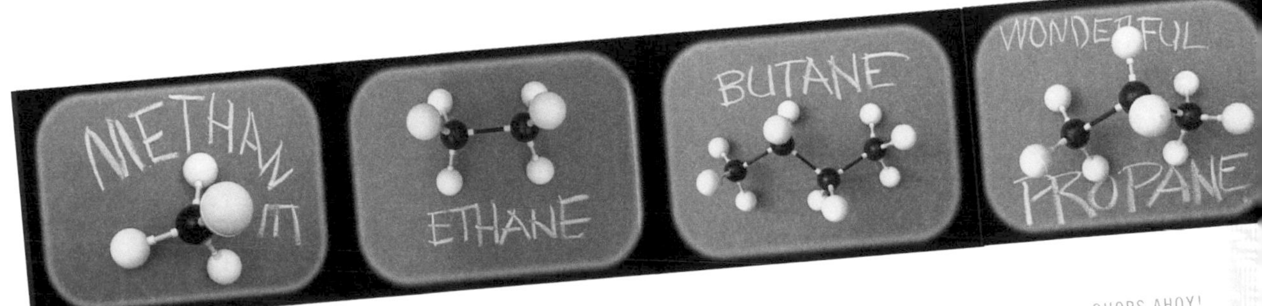

APPLICATION

STUFFED GRILLED PORK CHOPS

4 SERVINGS

Stuffing is not always evil.

SOFTWARE

1	cup plus ½ teaspoon	kosher salt	
1	cup	dark brown sugar	packed
1	tablespoon	whole black peppercorns	
1	tablespoon	ground mustard	
2	cups	apple cider vinegar	hot
1	pound	ice cubes	
4	about 12 ounces each	double-thick (1- to 1½-inch) bone-in, loin pork chops	
1½	cups	cornbread crumbs	
2	tablespoons	golden raisins	
¼	cup	walnuts	roughly chopped
¼	cup	dried cherries	coarsely chopped
½	teaspoon	black pepper	freshly ground
2	teaspoons	fresh sage	chiffonade
¼	cup	low-fat buttermilk	
1	tablespoon	vegetable oil	

PROCEDURE

1. Place the 1 cup salt, the brown sugar, peppercorns, mustard, and hot vinegar in a **6-quart container** and stir until the salt and sugar dissolve. Let the mixture sit for 5 to 10 minutes. Add the ice cubes and stir to melt most of the ice. Add the chops and make sure they are submerged in the brine. Cover and refrigerate for 2 hours.
2. Heat a **grill** to high.
3. Remove the chops from the brine, rinse, and pat dry.

TRICHINELLA SPIRALIS

Notice when cutting into your chop it is indeed juicy and pinkish. I know, your grandmother told you, "You'd better cook that pork 'til it's good and done, or you'll be good and done, you wretch." Well, back when she was young, much of America's porcine population was fed table scraps or were simply left to scrounge around. They often picked up *Trichinella spiralis* along the way.

Now, the eggs of this nasty little worm have the ugly habit of getting into your bloodstream and lodging into your muscle tissue. They just sit there for a while, then . . . well, it's ugly and painful, rest assured. But don't worry. Thanks to carefully formulated hog chows and better sanitation, America's pigs are as clean as they are lean. Even if you were to run into the rare *T-spiralis*, they can't survive beyond 137°F, which is way under medium. So relax and enjoy your chops. Just be sure you buy them thick, brine them, and stuff them conservatively.

4 Place one chop at a time in a **bagel slicer** on its side and cut a horizontal pocket in each for stuffing. If you don't have a bagel slicer, you might want to consider a kevlar glove like the one pictured on page 313.

5 Combine the cornbread, raisins, walnuts, dried cherries, pepper, sage, ½ teaspoon salt, and the buttermilk in a **mixing bowl**. Place about ¼ cup of the stuffing into the pocket of each chop. **Brush** both sides of each chop with the oil.

6 Place the chops on the grill and cook for 4 minutes with the lid closed. Rotate each chop 45° and cook for another 4 minutes. Flip the chops over and cook for another 4 minutes. Rotate each chop 45° and cook for a final 3 to 4 minutes, until they reach 140°F for medium. Be sure to temp the chops in the thickest part of the meat close to the bone, not in the stuffing. If you prefer your chops more well done, decrease the heat to low and continue cooking until desired doneness. Remove from the heat and allow to rest for at least 5 minutes before serving.

[1] That's British Thermal Units—the unit of heat required to raise the temperature of a pint of water by 1 degree at 1 atmosphere of pressure.

TIP | The worst thing that can happen in any grill session is for your grill to go cold in the middle of things, so check your fuel before you fire up. If your gas grill doesn't have a fuel gauge, no problem. Just pour about a cup of boiling water down the side of the tank, wait a few seconds, then feel it. Wherever the metal goes from warm to cold, that's where the gas line is.

TIDBIT | London chophouses were popular as early as the seventeenth century.

CHOUX SHINE

EPISODE 79 | SEASON 6 | GOOD EATS

If you were to ask a historian, an industrialist, and a physicist to vote on the most influential physical force on planet Earth, I bet they'd all say the same thing: steam. So how is it that steam's the stuff that gets stuff done? When water reaches the boiling point of 212°F at sea level, the volume of the water increases some sixteen hundred times. That means that a single ounce of water can grow to fill a twelve-gallon container. And if you don't give it room to grow, you get pressure. And if you harness that pressure you can convert it to work, be it pushing a locomotive, turning a generator, or lifting great pastry.

TRIVIA | The locomotive featured in the show open is the Great Smoky Mountain Railway: Dillsboro. Pay it a visit sometime.

SCALES

Most people's baking can be drastically improved simply by switching from volume measurements to weights. Practically speaking, there are three types of scales to choose from: balance, spring, and digital.

If you've ever stood on a scale in a doctor's office, you have firsthand knowledge of a balance scale, which works by sliding a counterweight up and down the arm on the opposite side of the fulcrum from the load until the load is counterbalanced. Quite a load, I might say. Since they rely on physics alone, balance scales are perfectly accurate and they never wear out, but they are notoriously hard to read. They are big. They are clunky. They are expensive. But they're always right.

Most culinary scales are spring-loaded. Such scales don't weigh items so much as they measure the pressure required to push the spring to a particular point. The problem is, springs are not accurate across a wide range. Uh, they bounce, so they're tough to read and calibrate and, in the end, springs wear out.

Digital scales are different animals because they don't have any moving parts that can get out of whack. The item to be weighed places downward pressure on the metal plate. This metal plate has an electrical current running through it. As the pressure changes, it creates minute fluctuations in this electrical current. The scale's circuitry interprets that and displays it as weight.

Not only are these scales amazingly accurate and reliable, they're cheap. Look for a model with these features:

- Easily switches from standard to metric.
- Can handle at least 10 pounds.
- Has a readability of at least ¼ ounce.
- Doesn't run on strange batteries you have to send off for.
- Has a "tare" function that allows the scale to be "zeroed out" so that additional items can be weighed. This is especially useful when weighing different ingredients into a bowl, as for a batter or bread.
- Easy to read from any angle.

KNOWLEDGE CONCENTRATE

The pastry batter best known for harnessing the power of steam is choux paste, or *pâte à choux* ("pah tuh SHOE"). When baked, choux balloons with steam to several times its original size and then it sets, leaving a cavernous emptiness inside. This space may be filled with a wide variety of delicious substances, both sweet and savory. I suspect American cooks avoid making pâte à choux for two reasons. One is the fussy name, which actually means "cabbage paste" in French, a reference to its appearance when cooked. The other is the fact that it is very technique driven, requiring the cook to understand what's going on and make adjustments accordingly.

Most doughs and batters are designed to capture lots and lots of little-bitty bubbles, and that's why muffins and loaves of breads have the kind of texture that they do; it's where they get their very soul. Not so with pâte à choux. No, sir. The stuff of chocolate éclairs and cream puffs is actually designed to capture one or two very, very large bubbles. How can that be? Well, it's part process and part software, although the ingredients are certainly very ordinary. Pâte à choux contains nothing but flour, a little butter, some water, and some eggs. 'Course, there's a *little* more to it than that.

There are no special requirements for the water or the butter or the eggs, as long as the eggs are grade A large. But the flour type matters. Besides being able to create that elastic network we're always talking about, gluten, the flour has got to be able to soak up a lot of liquid. A general rule is that the more protein there is in flour, the thirstier it is. So I use bread flour or, even better, flour formulated for bread machines, which generally has the highest protein content of anything on the megamart shelf.

TIDBIT | The French dessert *religieuse* consists of chocolate mousse surrounded by chocolate and coffee éclairs.

APPLICATION

PÂTE À CHOUX

2 DOZEN ÉCLAIRS, OR 4 DOZEN CREAM PUFFS

SOFTWARE

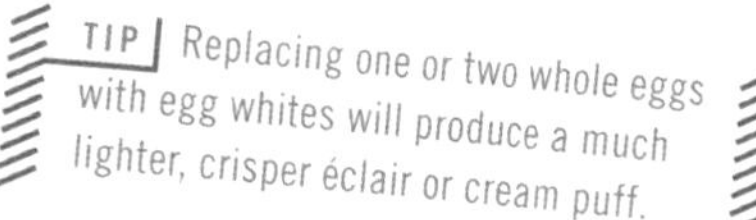

TIP | Replacing one or two whole eggs with egg whites will produce a much lighter, crisper éclair or cream puff.

FOR THE SHELLS

1	cup	H_2O	
3	ounces	unsalted butter	
1	tablespoon	sugar	
1	pinch	kosher salt	
5¾	ounces	bread flour	
4	large	eggs	
1 or 2	large	egg whites	

FOR ÉCLAIRS

		Pastry Cream (page 374)	
6	ounces	semisweet chocolate chips	
1	teaspoon	vegetable oil	

FOR CREAM PUFFS

Serious Vanilla Ice Cream (page 38), or Turkey Salad (page 163)

PROCEDURE

1. Heat the oven to 375°F.

2. Place 1 cup water, the butter, sugar, and salt in a **3-quart saucier**, set over high heat, and bring to a boil. As soon as it boils, add all of the flour at once and stir with a **wooden spoon** until the mixture starts to come together, about 1 minute. Decrease the heat to low and continue stirring until the mixture forms a ball and is no longer sticky, 3 to 4 minutes.

3. Transfer the mixture to the **bowl of a stand mixer** and mix on low speed for 5 minutes to cool, or until there is no more steam rising. With the mixer still on low speed, add the eggs and eggs whites, one at a time, making sure each is completely incorporated before adding another. You may need to stop the mixer occasionally and scrape down the sides of the bowl. Before adding the last egg white, check the mixture for consistency: It should tear slightly as it falls from the beater, creating a "V" shape. The mixture may need only 1 egg white.

   Transfer to a **1-gallon zip-top** bag fitted with a **plastic coupler and a round tip**. Pipe a little of the mixture into the four corners of a **half sheet pan** and lay **parchment paper** down. This will prevent the paper from slipping.

FOR ÉCLAIRS:

4 Pipe the mixture into 2½-inch-long strips on the parchment, 4 rows of 6. Use your clean dampened finger to smooth any tips left from piping. Pipe and bake one pan at a time: Increase the oven temperature to 425°F and bake on the middle rack for 15 minutes. Turn the oven temperature down to 350°F and bake for 10 to 12 more minutes, until golden brown. Remove from the oven and immediately pierce one end of each éclair with a **paring knife** to release steam.

5 Using another **gallon zip-top bag** fitted with a **small star tip**, fill the shells with Pastry Cream. Cool the filled shells completely.

6 In a **small mixing bowl** set over **a 4-quart pot of simmering water,** melt together the chocolate chips and oil. Remove the bowl from the heat and dip the top side of each cooled éclair in the chocolate to coat. Allow the chocolate to set slightly before devouring.

TIDBIT I know, I just told you to heat the oven to 375°F, but cranking the heat to 425°F gives the choux a burst of hot air that creates more steam. More steam means a bigger puff.

FOR CREAM PUFFS:

4 Pipe the mixture into concentric circles 1½ inches in diameter on the parchment, 4 rows of 6. Use your clean dampened finger to smooth the tip left from piping. Pipe and bake one pan at a time: Increase the oven temperature to 425°F and bake on the middle rack for 15 minutes. Turn the oven temperature down to 350°F and bake for 10 to 12 more minutes, until golden brown. Remove from the oven and immediately pierce the bottom of each puff with a **paring knife** to release steam. Fill sweet puffs with Serious Vanilla Ice Cream or, for savory puffs, Turkey Salad.

NOTE: Empty shells can be stored in zip-top bags and frozen for up to 1 month.

TIDBIT Profiteroles are miniature choux pastries used in the holiday classic *croquembouche*.

SUB-APPLICATION | PASTRY CREAM

1 QUART

Okay, the vanilla pudding filling we originally suggested to go inside the éclairs was a bit of a cop-out, but there was just no way to make the traditional éclair filling, pastry cream, in the time we had left. Besides, it really deserves a show of its own. When that show comes, the application will no doubt look something like this.

SOFTWARE

2	cups	whole milk	
4	ounces	sugar	divided
1	ounce	cornstarch	
1	pinch	kosher salt	
2	large	eggs	
1	large	egg yolk	
1	teaspoon	vanilla extract	
1	ounce	unsalted butter	at room temperature

PROCEDURE

1. Combine the milk and 2 ounces of the sugar in a **3-quart saucier**. Bring to a bare simmer over medium-low heat.
2. **Sift** together the remaining sugar, the cornstarch, and salt.
3. Place a **mixing bowl** on a **rubber pad** or a wet towel to prevent the bowl from spinning out of control. In the bowl, combine the whole eggs and the yolk. Add the cornstarch mixture and whip with a **whisk** until mostly smooth.
4. While whisking the eggs, drizzle in about a quarter of the hot milk. Whisk the tempered eggs back into the saucepan with the remaining milk mixture.
5. Return the pan to medium-low heat and immediately begin whisking. The cream will begin to thicken and boil. Continue whisking for about 6 minutes, or until the boiling pastry cream appears to pull away from the pan.
6. Place a **fine-mesh sieve** over a **glass** or **stainless-steel bowl**. Pour the cream through the sieve in order to catch any curdled egg bits or particles that may be in the mixture. **Whisk** in the vanilla and butter. Store the pastry cream with a **layer of plastic wrap** directly on the surface to prevent a film. Cool completely before piping into éclairs.

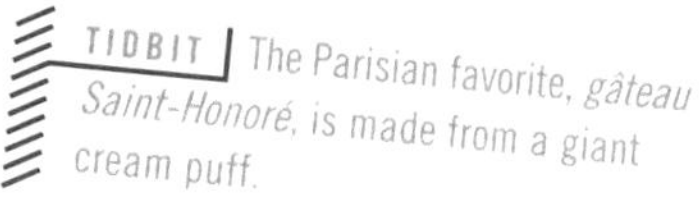
TIDBIT The Parisian favorite, *gâteau Saint-Honoré*, is made from a giant cream puff.

CASSEROLE OVER

EPISODE 80 | SEASON 6 | GOOD EATS

Here we valiantly bring the casserole out of the Middle Ages, where it's pretty much been since, well, the Middle Ages.

NARRATOR: Once upon a Sunday afternoon, a mild-mannered cook and his faithful cur were out for an afternoon drive, when suddenly an aroma tickled their noses. Feeling rather rumbly in his tummbly, the cook decided to investigate.

(AB drives by a small country church. Out front is a sign: "Covered Dish Dinner Tonight." There are several tables loaded with casseroles but not a soul is around.)

NARRATOR: Mmmm. Casseroles. If there was anything the cook could not resist...

DOG: Rrrrwaf!

NARRATOR: ...or his dog, for that matter...it was casseroles. He decided to take a closer look. Then he spied a fork. And seeing that no one was around, he thought he might give a casserole a try. The first he tried was a broccoli casserole. But he found it salty and insipid. Next, a chicken pot pie he decided to try. Mmm. Promising. Very promising. But alas, its mushy crust concealed canned vegetables and a greasy sauce. The cook then spied something called Peking Surprise... and what a surprise it was. Of course, it was nothing compared with the surprise that was coming.

(Church ladies exit church and sneak up behind him)

CHURCH LADY #1: (clears throat)

NARRATOR: Busted like Goldilocks by church ladies. Although the congregation voted for harsher measures, the weather was too dry for a bonfire. So a bargain was struck. The cook would be given until dinnertime to replace what he had so greedily taken. To make sure he wasn't distracted, they decided to keep his dog.

TRIVIA This is still a very hard show for me to watch because I really, really loved that dog. Matilda was the best pet ever, but she took her leave of us back in '07 at the ripe age of fourteen. I have two Cardigan Corgis now, but it would take an ark of dogs to replace that silly ol' hound. (Sound of tear hitting keyboard.)

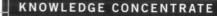

KNOWLEDGE CONCENTRATE

- Etymologically speaking, the word *casserole* is French for "saucepan," from the Middle French *casse* or "pan," from the Middle Latin *cattia*, and probably the Greek *kyathos*, meaning "bowl" or "cup." So technically, any wide, shallow cooking vessel with two handles and a lid can technically be called a casserole.
- Despite its French genealogy, the concept of the one-dish meal was actually perfected by American cooks who were seeking to make ends meet through two World Wars and a nasty bout of Depression. Then, during the 1950s and '60s, home magazines told housewives that the casserole would "set them free," especially if they relied on those space-age processed foods that were so heavily advertised in their pages.
- Typically, casseroles are either bound, like broccoli or tuna casserole; layered, like lasagna or moussaka; or scoop-able, like bean or pot pie. It is my belief that a casserole must contain one or two main ingredients, some kind of starch, aromatics, seasonings, and a binder such as eggs or mayonnaise.
- Vessels: Since they're typically slow cooking, casseroles are best built in insulative material (glass, ceramic) rather than metal. I often use terra cotta saucers that I steal from under my wife's potted plants. As long as they're unglazed (and Italian) I don't see a problem with it . . . unless my wife waters the plants while I'm cooking.

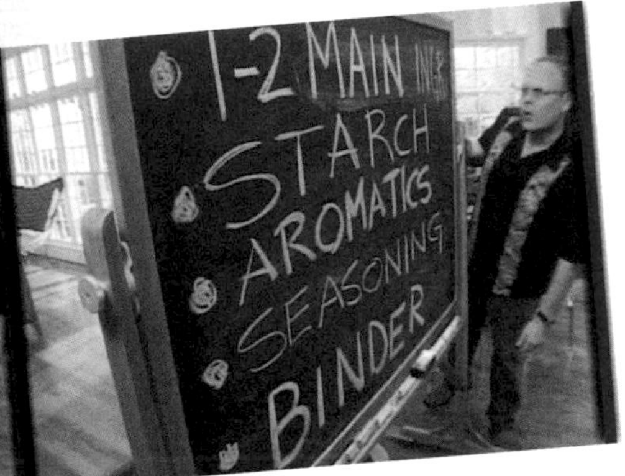

TIDBIT Texan's King Ranch Casserole: boiled chicken + cheese + tortilla chips + cream of mushroom soup + cream of chicken soup.

Widdi, Actress | Sarah, Coordinator | Mandy, Wardrobe | Stephanie, Script Supervisor

APPLICATION

BROCCOLI CASSEROLE

6 TO 8 SERVINGS

Here's a version of the classic that is nowhere near as heavy, salty, or fatty as the one your grandmother used to make . . . okay, *my* grandmother used to make.

TIP | If you're in a casserole-building mood (and who isn't from time to time) just build, wrap in plastic and foil, and freeze. To reheat, just take off the plastic, replace the foil, and bake at 300°F. No thaw necessary.

TIP | Casseroles are great for the Sabbath because they require only one pot and can be cooked ahead of time.

SOFTWARE

		kosher salt	
1	pound	broccoli	peeled stems and heads
1	tablespoon	unsalted butter	
12	ounces	mushrooms	sliced
1	3-ounce package	chicken-flavored ramen noodles	broken up, seasoning pack reserved
½	cup	mayonnaise	
½	cup	plain yogurt	
4	ounces	sharp cheddar cheese	grated, divided
⅓	cup	blue cheese dressing	
2	large	eggs	lightly beaten
½	teaspoon	kosher salt	
1	teaspoon	black pepper	freshly ground

PROCEDURE

1. Bring 3 quarts water to a boil in **an 8-quart pot** over high heat and add several heavy pinches of salt. Prepare an **ice bath** large enough to hold the broccoli. When the water boils, add the broccoli and blanch for 1 minute. Drain in a **colander** and immediately place in the ice bath to shock. Swirl around to cool completely, drain, and set aside.
2. Heat the oven to 350°F. Spray an **8-inch square glass baking dish** with nonstick spray.
3. Melt the butter in a **10-inch straight-sided sauté pan** and set over medium heat. Add the mushrooms and sauté until they are just beginning to brown, about 5 minutes. Add the broccoli and noodles and toss to combine. Turn off the heat. Add the mayonnaise, yogurt, half of the cheese, the blue cheese dressing, eggs, ½ teaspoon salt, and the ramen noodle seasoning pack and toss to combine well. Transfer the mixture to the prepared baking dish and smash down with a **spatula** to compact the casserole. Sprinkle the top with the pepper and the remaining cheese.
4. Cover with **heavy-duty aluminum foil** and bake on the middle rack of the oven for 45 minutes. Remove the foil and bake for an additional 15 minutes. Cool for 30 minutes before serving.

APPLICATION

GARLIC SHRIMP CASSEROLE

4 TO 6 SERVINGS

Ultimately, this casserole should be about utilizing leftovers, even if they're Chinese takeout.

SOFTWARE

2	tablespoons	cornstarch	
1	tablespoon	cold H_2O	
2	cups	chicken stock	
½	cup	heavy cream	
½	teaspoon	red pepper flakes	
2	cups	cooked rice	
2	cups	Garlic Shrimp (opposite page)	
2	cups	sautéed veggies	leftovers are fine
¾	cup	Japanese breadcrumbs	(a.k.a. panko)

PROCEDURE

1. Crank your hot box to 350°F.
2. Place the cornstarch and water in a **small jar**, seal, and shake to combine.
3. **Whisk** together the stock and the cornstarch slurry in a **3-quart saucier** and set over medium-high heat. Bring to a simmer and cook for 3 minutes. Add the cream and red pepper flakes and stir to combine. Remove from the heat.
4. Place the rice, the Garlic Shrimp, and vegetables in a **9-by-11-inch baking dish**. Pour the cream mixture over the leftovers and press down to evenly distribute the liquid. Sprinkle the breadcrumbs evenly over the top and bake for 25 minutes, or until the mixture is hot and bubbly. Turn the broiler to high and brown the topping for 2 to 3 minutes, until golden. Cool for 15 minutes before serving.

I always felt a little guilty about using the takeout garlic shrimp. So . . .

10 MINUTES MORE

GARLIC SHRIMP

1 PINT; 4 SERVINGS

Okay, what if you don't have leftover takeout shrimp? Fine. Make your own.

// SOFTWARE

1	pound	21/25 shrimp	peeled and deveined
¼	cup	olive oil	
4	medium cloves	garlic	minced
¾	teaspoon	kosher salt	
¼	teaspoon	black pepper	freshly ground

TIP For reheating casseroles, portion onto plate, cover with plastic, and microwave

TIDBIT French-fried onions have been a favorite casserole topper since 1955.

// PROCEDURE

1. Place all the ingredients in a **1-gallon zip-top bag**, seal, and toss to combine. Allow to sit at room temperature for 30 minutes.
2. Heat a **10-inch cast-iron skillet** over medium heat for 5 minutes. Add the shrimp along with the marinade to the pan. Sauté, tossing constantly, just until the shrimp begin to turn opaque in the center, 3 to 4 minutes. Serve immediately and save leftovers for Garlic Shrimp Casserole.

NOTE: It's perfectly fine to use frozen shrimp here, but please make sure they're American. Tiger shrimp farmed in Southeastern Asia are grown . . . disgustingly, and their impact on the environment is equally horrific.

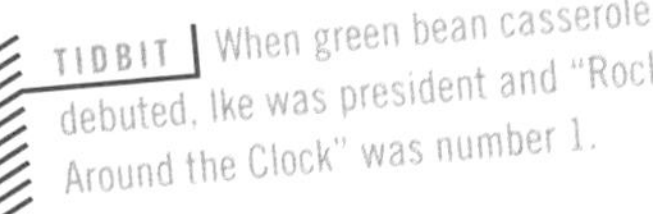

TIDBIT When green bean casserole debuted, Ike was president and "Rock Around the Clock" was number 1.

APPLICATION

CURRY CHICKEN POT PIE

6 TO 8 SERVINGS

A twist on the perennial classic that gets a bit of bite from curry powder.

SOFTWARE

1	8½-ounce sheet	frozen puff pastry	thawed
3	tablespoons	unsalted butter	divided
1	cup	onion	diced
1	cup	celery	diced
4	cups	frozen vegetable medley	
1½	cups	low-sodium chicken broth	
½	cup	whole milk	
3	tablespoons	all-purpose flour	
1	teaspoon	curry powder	
2	teaspoons	dried parsley	
1	teaspoon	kosher salt	
½	teaspoon	black pepper	freshly ground
12	ounces	cooked chicken	coarsely chopped

TIDBIT If you're not "the sharpest knife in the drawer," then you may also be "a few peas short of a casserole."

PROCEDURE

1. Unfold the thawed puff pastry and seal the seams using a **rolling pin**. Dock the sheet by piercing it several times with a **fork**. Cut into 12 (2-inch) rounds, place on a **half sheet pan**, and refrigerate while preparing the rest of the casserole. Heat the oven to 400°F.
2. Melt 1 tablespoon of the butter in a **12-inch straight-sided sauté pan** over medium heat. Add the onion and celery and sweat until the onion is translucent, about 5 minutes. Add the frozen vegetables and cook, stirring occasionally, until heated through, 7 to 8 minutes.
3. Meanwhile, combine the broth and milk in a **2-cup microwave-safe container** and heat in the microwave oven until almost boiling, about 2 minutes.
4. Add the remaining 2 tablespoons butter to the vegetables and melt. Add the flour and curry powder and **whisk** for 1 to 2 minutes. Whisk in the hot milk mixture and cook until thickened, 3 to 4 minutes. Add the parsley, salt, and pepper. Add the chicken and stir to combine. Pour into a **9-by-13-inch baking dish**. Mash down the mixture to compact the casserole. Top with the circles of puff pastry, spacing them so they do not touch. Bake on the middle rack of the oven for 45 minutes, or until the puff pastry has browned and the mixture is hot and bubbly. Cool for 30 minutes before serving.

FINAL THOUGHTS

In my opinion:

1. My motto as a cook is *primum non nocere*, “first, do no harm.”
2. When flight attendants serve me meals they always apologize. That’s funny.
3. I rarely spend more than $20 on a plate of food.
4. Kids should take Home Ec. No exceptions.
5. Chickens don’t have fingers.
6. I never criticize a meal unless it’s served to me with pretension. That really sets me off.
7. I meet a lot of people who tell me they’re “gourmet cooks.” I still have no idea what that means.
8. Boys are starting to have cooking birthday parties. That’s cool.
9. Girl Scout Thin Mints, frozen . . . ’nuff said.
10. I don’t understand why we need canned chili from China, or dog food, or toothpaste for that matter.
11. If we don’t diversify our seafood portfolio, I suspect in a hundred years there will be no seafood left but farmed shrimp and krill.
12. Americans need to worry as much about how things live as how they die.
13. There are two kinds of food: good food and bad food.
14. Kids’ menus are, by and large, a bad thing.
15. It wouldn’t hurt us all to be a little more grateful.

TO BE CONTINUED...

ACKNOWLEDGMENTS

The Author Wishes to Thank:

THE CREW:

Most of the people listed below have worked on *Good Eats* for years, some have even been around since the pilot shoot back in 1997. I'm not going to confuse you by describing each and every job they do. Just know that without their talent, skill, humor, and heart, this show would never have made it out of the blocks. It should also be noted that every single person on this list has appeared on the show and some play recurring roles.

(Asterisks denote "lifers" who have been there since the beginning)

Carmi Adams: *Culinarian*

Todd Bailey*: *Production Designer*

Patrick Belden*: *Music and Sound Design*

Walter Biscardi: *Animation and HD editor*

Stephanie Hammond-Caperton: *Script Supervisor*

Cole Cassell: *Production Assistant*

Ginger Cassell: *Editor*

Patty Catalano: *Culinarian/Research Coordinator*

Michael Clark: *Sound*

Tamie Cook: *Culinary Director*

Mike Cosky: *Grip*

Rick Crank: *Electric*

Ramon Engle*: *Camera/Steadicam Operator*

Meghan Foley: *Culinary Dept. 2nd*

Stan Fyfe: *Electric*

Amanda Kibler: *Wardrobe/Special Costumes*

Anna Krantz: *Production Assistant*

Brian "Bear" Lamar: *Production*

Marion Laney*: *Director of Photography*

Paul Merchant: *Art Department*

Marshall Millard*: *Key Grip*

Jim Pace: *Production Coordinator*

Vanessa Parker-McIntyre: *Executive Chef*

Dana Popoff: *Producer/Candidate for Sainthood*

Leigh Ann Reagan-Barnes: *Art Department*

Calvin Rouse III: *Culinarian*

Brett Soll: *Assistant Editor*

Katherine Steets: *Script Supervisor*

Troy Toebben: *Electric*

David Traylor*: *Gaffer*

Although most of the roles on the show are played by crew members, we also abuse the talents of a small group of actors and experts who have become known as the *Good Eats Players*. Here they are with a few of their most memorable roles:

Zoey Brown: *Teletubby, Little Miss Muffet, Fairy of Enzymatic Action, Marsha Jr.*

Shirley Corriher: *Biochemist and baking expert* (which she is)

Arch Corriher: *Alton's High School Teacher*

Merrilyn Crouch: *Sister Marsha*

Deb Duchon: *Culinary anthropologist* (which she is)

Vickie Eng: *W*

Bill Greely: *Mr. McGregor, Plumber*

Bart Hansard: *Coco Carl, Talent Agent Sid, Santa, Auntie Puddin'*, and many more

John Herina: *Nephew Elton*

Matilda: *Dog*

Carolyn O'Neil: *Registered Dietician, Lady in the Refrigerator*

Daniel Petrow: *Chuck, Rusty the Cowboy, Capt. Squint, Jack in the Beanstalk, Mr. Todd*, and many more

Widdi Turner: *Frances Anderson, Mother of Culinary Invention, Mrs. Lovett*, and many more . . . most of them disturbed

Lucky Yates: *Dungeon Master, Grim Reaper, Louis Pasteur, Reverend Sylvester Graham, Satan*

THE FOLKS AT BE SQUARE:

Getting this book made required all hands on deck, but Meghan Foley oversaw the project and in the process aged approximately 3.7 years . . . that's okay, she's still young. Our Culinary Director Tamie Cook was our first full-time employee and has worked to develop and test almost every recipe featured on *Good Eats* over the last five years. Patty Catalano handles culinary research and Jim Pace takes care of everything else, and darned well, too.

THE FOLKS AT STEWART, TABORI & CHANG:

Galen Smith at STC has designed every book I've ever written, and I hope he'll design every book I ever write in the future. I also want to thank Senior VP and publisher Leslie Stoker, my lead editor Luisa Weiss, designer Danielle Young, and illustrators Eric Cole and Michael Koelsch.

THE NETWORK FOLKS:

I've enjoyed a creative freedom at Food Network that's really, well, unheard of. For that, I offer humble thanks to President Brooke Johnson, and especially to Senior VP Bob Tuschman, who almost never tells me "no" (though I still think anchovies would make a great show).

THE HOME FOLKS:

My wife and business partner, DeAnna, has been the driving force of this project from day one. I would have quit over and over, time after time, had she not been there to back me up and in many cases pull me along kicking and screaming. What I don't owe to God I owe to her. Simple as that. And I especially want to thank Zoey for putting up with all the late nights and early mornings, and all the books she had to read alone. You're my pride and joy, kid.

CONVERSION CHARTS

// WEIGHT EQUIVALENTS

The metric weights given in this chart are not exact equivalents, but have been rounded up or down slightly to make measuring easier.

Avoirdupois	Metric
¼ ounce	7 grams
½ ounce	15 grams
1 ounce	30 grams
2 ounces	60 grams
3 ounces	90 grams
4 ounces	115 grams
5 ounces	150 grams
6 ounces	175 grams
7 ounces	200 grams
8 ounces (½ pound)	225 grams
9 ounces	250 grams
10 ounces	300 grams
11 ounces	325 grams
12 ounces	350 grams
13 ounces	375 grams
14 ounces	400 grams
15 ounces	425 grams
16 ounces (1 pound)	450 grams
1½ pounds	750 grams
2 pounds	900 grams
2¼ pounds	1 kilogram
3 pounds	1.4 kilograms
4 pounds	1.8 kilograms

// VOLUME EQUIVALENTS

These are not exact equivalents for American cups and spoons, but have been rounded up or down slightly to make measuring easier.

American	Metric	Imperial
¼ teaspoon	1.2 milliliters	—
½ teaspoon	2.5 milliliters	—
1 teaspoon	5.0 milliliters	—
½ tablespoon (1½ teaspoons)	7.5 milliliters	—
1 tablespoon (3 teaspoons)	15 milliliters	—
¼ cup (4 tablespoons)	60 milliliters	2 fluid ounces
⅓ cup (5 tablespoons)	75 milliliters	2½ fluid ounces
½ cup (8 tablespoons)	125 milliliters	4 fluid ounces
⅔ cup (10 tablespoons)	150 milliliters	5 fluid ounces
¾ cup (12 tablespoons)	175 milliliters	6 fluid ounces
1 cup (16 tablespoons)	250 milliliters	8 fluid ounces
1¼ cups	300 milliliters	10 fluid ounces (½ pint)
1½ cups	350 milliliters	12 fluid ounces
2 cups (1 pint)	500 milliliters	16 fluid ounces
2½ cups	625 milliliters	20 fluid ounces (1 pint)
1 quart	1 liter	32 fluid ounces

// OVEN TEMPERATURE EQUIVALENTS

Oven Mark	°F	°C	Gas
very cool	250–275	130–140	½–1
cool	300	150	2
warm	325	170	3
moderate	350	180	4
moderately hot	375–400	190–200	5–6
hot	425–450	220–230	7–8
very hot	475	250	9

INDEX

D

E

F

COPYRIGHT

Published in 2009 by Stewart, Tabori & Chang
An imprint of ABRAMS

Illustrations based on sketches by Alton Brown, rendered by Eric Cole.

Library of Congress Cataloging-in-Publication Data
Brown, Alton, 1962-
Good eats / Alton Brown.
p. cm.
Includes bibliographical references and index.
ISBN 978-1-58479-795-1 (alk. paper)
1. Cookery. 2. Good eats (Television program) I. Good eats (Television program) II. Title.
TX651.B727 2009
641.5–dc22
2009007148

Editor: Luisa Weiss
Designers: Galen Smith, Danielle Young, Liam Flanagan
Production Managers: Jacquie Poirier, Tina Cameron

The text of this book was composed in ITC Century, Trade Gothic, Vintage Typewriter, and Freehand 575
Printed and bound in the United States
10 9 8 7 6 5 4 3

115 West 18th Street
New York, NY 10011
www.abramsbooks.com